THE ROCK WHO'S WHO

THE ROCK WHO'S WHO

A Biographical Dictionary and Critical Discography
Including Rhythm-and-Blues, Soul, Rockabilly, Folk,
Country, Easy Listening, Punk, and New Wave

Brock Helander

SCHIRMER BOOKS
A Division of Macmillan Publishing Co., Inc.
NEW YORK

Collier Macmillan Publishers
LONDON

Schirmer Books
A Division of Macmillan Publishing Co., Inc.
866 Third Avenue, New York, N.Y. 10022

Collier Macmillan Canada, Inc.

Library of Congress Catalog Card Number: 82–80804

Printed in the United States of America

printing number
3   4   5   6   7   8   9   10

Library of Congress Cataloging in Publication Data

Helander, Brock.
    The rock who's who.

    1. Rock musicians—Dictionaries.   2. Rock music—
Discography. I. Title.
ML102.R6H5   1982   784.5'4'00922   82–80804
ISBN 0–02–871250–1   AACR2
ISBN 0–02–871920–4 (pbk.)

This book is dedicated to Elvis Presley and John Lennon

INTRODUCTION

This project began in 1974 as a personal and private attempt to identify the "best" songs by contemporary popular recording artists of the Sixties and Seventies. Following careful investigation of my own extensive album library and those of friends and acquaintances, I was forced to conclude that to attain my goal, I would need to examine and listen to as many albums by major acts as possible. To this end, I began compiling lists of album releases of the Sixties and Seventies. My interests became so pervasive that I began writing career synopses of groups and individual artists. Initially I restricted myself to the Sixties and Seventies, because prior to the successes of Bob Dylan and The Beatles and the rise of FM radio, popular recording artists were confined primarily to the singles arena: most albums comprised one or two hits, filler material such as rerecorded Tin Pan Alley standards, and "cover" versions of then-popular songs. I was convinced by pop music critic Joel Selvin to expand the discography into the Fifties, to include rhythm-and-blues, rock-and-roll, and folk artists of the era who had helped create the foundations for Sixties rock and soul musics and the various subgenres that evolved—folk-rock, jazz-rock, country-rock, hard rock, soft rock, progressive or art rock, glitter rock, and heavy-metal and psychedelic musics. This book is the product of my years of painstaking and sometimes frustrating research attempting to delineate the "best" songs, from rock-and-roll to rock.

The book is an annotated critical and historical discography of rock and soul musics, encompassing the major acts since the early mid-Fifties that have contributed significantly to the development of contemporary popular music. Recognizing the importance of individuals who are not recording artists, I have included several disc jockeys, music industry luminaries, and songwriting-production teams. In choosing the musical acts to be covered, I have attempted to focus on musicians and singers who were unique and innovative in their stylizations, musicianship, and/or songwriting, who were significant and influential in the evolution of rock and soul musics, who were in the forefront of developing musical trends, who accomplished unprecedented feats, who changed the look and sound of the music, and who had an enduring impact on the development of contemporary popular music, the music and recording industries, and popular culture. Mere popularity is not sufficient reason for inclusion in this text.

I have chosen to exclude white "cover" artists of the Fifties, most "bubblegum" acts, and virtually all artists of the "twist" and "disco" genres. White cover artists of the Fifties coopted the success and accomplishments of truly innovative and distinctive rhythm-and-blues acts in an exploitative and crassly commercial fashion. Bubblegum acts were specifically directed at pubescent and prepubescent audiences in a contrived and exploitative manner, with little regard to quality of music or lyrics. As to the exclusion of most twist and disco acts, although rock can be seen as essentially dance music, these developments served to distract from the evolution of rock and trivialize the music's significance, while seeking to legitimize clearly derivative and facile trends and expand audiences to include superficially affected middle-aged adults largely unfamiliar with rock. Ultimately, although the final decision as to inclusions and exclusions has been my own, I encourage readers who believe conscientiously that some excluded act requires inclusion to write to me regarding their justifications.

To elucidate and investigate the evolution of rock and soul musics and their various allied forms, I have chosen as the basis of analysis the 33⅓ RPM long-play (LP) records, certainly the primary unit of today's music consumption. I am concerned primarily with monophonic and stereophonic album releases, to the exclusion of recently instituted specialty processes such as quadraphonic, digital, and high-technology recordings, although I do occasionally include direct-to-disc recordings. I include only record albums (no tapes of any kind) that were regular releases in the United States. Therefore, no foreign releases are listed (although they may be discussed) and, furthermore, no so-called "bootleg" albums are listed. I have endeavored to be comprehensive in my discographies, yet certainly some albums have been omitted because of oversight or my inability to confirm an album's existence. This problem is especially significant for albums issued on small, independent record labels (particularly in the Fifties for rhythm-and-blues artists) that did not regularly report their releases to the compilers of the Schwann catalogs, one of my primary sources of information. Although the bulk of the research covered many years, the discography information was updated constantly, in order to provide as complete a recording history as possible. To the best of my ability, the discographies are complete through February 1982, just before this book went for composition. Again, if readers can confirm additional album releases (particularly if accompanied by an estimate of either their recording or release date) for included acts, I encourage them to contact me. I wish to make this work and succeeding editions as accurate and comprehensive as possible.

Recording artists are listed in alphabetical order, by group name for groups and by last name for individual artists. Where a group leader and group name coincide (e.g., Brinsley Schwarz), the listing is under the group leader's last name. A group name that is not the name of a member (e.g., The Marshall Tucker Band) is listed under the name of the group. Releases by former group members are generally listed with their former groups (e.g., Cher's albums are listed under Sonny and Cher). However, subsequent releases by the four members of The Beatles are each listed separately. If the reader experiences confusion, he or she need merely consult the index, which cross-references all included album releases to the heading under which they are listed. Finally, albums are listed in their recording order rather than by release date, where sufficient information for a determination exists, and anthology and compilation albums are usually listed separately if three or more such albums exist.

In the discussion of hit singles, the gradation from biggest to smallest success is indicated in the following order: top, smash, major, moderate, and minor.

I have sought to provide a comprehensive and definitive critical and historical discography of rock and soul musics. All conclusions herein are my own. I urge readers to contact me regarding errors, omissions, comments, and reasonable complaints. I hope the use of this book will provide as much pleasure to the reader as the writing of it provided to me.

Brock Helander

USE OF THE DISCOGRAPHIES

The organization of the album discographies appearing herein is illustrated by the examples below:

I	II	III	IV	V

THE BEATLES

| Meet The Beatles! * | Capitol/Apple | ST–2047 | January '64 | A |

THE KINKS

| Kink Kronikles | 2-Reprise | 2XS–6454 | April '72 | A |

CURTIS MAYFIELD

| Superfly (sound-track) * | Curtom | CRS–8014 | August '72 | |

ELVIS PRESLEY

Elvis *	RCA	LPM–1382(M)	October '56	
		reissued as LSP–1382(E)	January '62	A
Elvis (TV Special) *	RCA	AFM1–4088(M)	December '68	A

FRANK ZAPPA AND THE MOTHERS

| Over-Nite Sensation * | DiscReet/Reprise | MS–2149 | September '73 | |
| | reissued on DiscReet | 2288 | | A |

From left to right, the columns supply the following information: Column I lists the album title. Where sufficient information for a determination exists, I have endeavored to list albums in order of recording rather than in order of release. Following the album title, parenthetical indicators signify the occasional movie soundtrack album (soundtrack) or album from a television show (TV). Following the album title and any parenthetical indicator, single asterisks (*) and double asterisks (**) indicate gold-award and platinum-award albums, respectively. The Recording Industry Association of America, Inc., (RIAA) began certifying albums and singles as gold-award in 1958. Until 1975, certification of an album as gold-award meant that the album had achieved $1 million in sales at one-third manufacturer's list price, i.e., approximately 450,000 copies. In 1975 the level for album gold-award certification was raised to 500,000 copies. Beginning in 1976, the RIAA certified albums as platinum-award when 1,000,000 copies were sold. Presumably, albums issued prior to 1976 had to be sold in the requisite number after the beginning of 1976 in order to achieve platinum-award certification. Determinations for certification are made by the RIAA based on sales figures provided by the manufacturer. Readers should be aware that the Motown family of labels (Tamla, Motown, Gordy, and Soul) only recently submitted their sales figures to RIAA, thus precluding "official" certification of many gold- and platinum-award albums despite extensive sales.

Column II lists the name of the record label on which the album was released. When an album is a multiple-record set, the number of records in the set is indicated by a numerical prefix to the record label (*Kink Kronikles* is a two-record set on Reprise). Albums are often reissued on a label different from the original. In the case of *Meet The Beatles!*, the album was issued initially on Capitol, later reissued on The Beatles' Apple label, and eventually reissued on Capitol after the dissolution of Apple. Frank Zappa and The Mothers' *Over-Nite Sensation* was initially issued on Disc-Reet, reissued on Reprise, and finally reissued on DiscReet with a new designation number.

Column III contains the record label's designation number for the album, usually in the form of several letters followed by the numbers. However, not all album designation numbers include an alphabetical prefix—the essential information may be contained within the numerical listing. These numerical designations are sometimes followed by parenthetical indicators. All albums without parenthetical indicators are in stereo. Where an album was issued simultaneously in monophonic and stereophonic sound, only the stereophonic album is listed. Monophonic albums are indicated by (M). Early monophonic albums (stereophonic listings began in the June 1958 edition of *Schwann-1*) were often later reissued in electronically reprocessed stereo, indicated by (E). Thus Elvis Presley's *Elvis* was issued in monophonic in October 1956 and reissued in electronically reprocessed stereo in January 1962. One other parenthetical indicator is occasionally utilized—(DD) for direct-to-disc recordings, recordings manufactured without the use of recording tape, thus eliminating the possibility of editing or alteration.

Column IV shows the approximate release date of the album by month and year. Release date determinations are based on two sources: the

Schwann–1 catalogs issued monthly since October 1955, and Joel Whitburn's *Top LP's 1945–1972* and yearly supplements through 1980, which compile a variety of information based on *Billboard* magazine's "Top LP's" album charts, including chart entry date. Problems exist with both sources, however. The *Schwann* listings are based on information supplied by manufacturers, and not all manufacturers, particularly small, independent labels, report to Schwann. Moreover, some reports by manufacturers (e.g., the early albums on the Motown family of labels and recent albums on the Takoma label) were not timely. As to Whitburn's *Top LP's*, not all albums listed in the discographies made the *Billboard* charts. Therefore, no information exists concerning chart-entry dates. In an effort to resolve the dilemma posed by these problems, I have used supplemental information provided directly by various record labels, listings contained in Harry Castleman and Walter J. Podrazik's *All Together Now*, and information on record albums and jackets, as well as my personal recollections and those of my discographical consultant, Jeff Hughson of American Music Company. When determination of release date proved impossible, no listing appears in Column IV.

Column V notes the current availability of albums as indicated by the most recent editions of the *Schwann-1* (monthly) and *Schwann-2* (semi-annual) catalogs. This information, of course, is the most tentative of any listed. Record companies delete important albums from their catalogs on a regular basis. Moreover, the reader should be forewarned that the lack of the availability indicator (A) does not mean he or she will be unable to obtain a specific album. However, many albums, particularly those more than a few years old, are unavailable from commercial dealers and must be obtained from used-record dealers. Furthermore, some albums have been unavailable for so long that they have become valued collector's items and can be secured only through various individuals and businesses that deal in hard-to-find records, such as Mr. Hughson's American Music Company.

I have attempted to be as accurate and comprehensive in my album discographies as possible. Readers are urged to contact the author regarding any omissions and errors herein, and to provide any additonal information. Closing dates for the information supplied by sources discussed above are as follows: RIAA gold- and platinum-award certifications, November 3, 1981; Joel Whitburn's *Top LP's*, December 31, 1980; *Schwann-1* catalog, February 1982; *Schwann-2* catalogue, Fall and Winter 1981–1982.

ACKNOWLEDGMENTS

First, I would like to thank my parents, Ed and Helen, and all of my friends who have supported and encouraged me throughout this project, particularly Mark Staneart, Gerry Helland and Susan McGowan, David Hobss, and Neil Hyman. I would especially like to thank Susan Espey, who has lovingly and almost literally supported me through the last three years of this work and who has since become my wife. I wish to thank Sacramento FM radio station K–ZAP music directors Robert Williams, Bruce Meier, and Cynde Slater for providing their station's playlists through 1978. I would like to acknowledge the assistance of lecturer, critic, and author Frank Kofsky, who suggested I contact Joel Selvin and in whose class I met Jeff Hughson. I wish to thank *San Francisco Chronicle* pop music critic Joel Selvin, the first media-type to recognize my work, for his support and encouragement and his suggestion that I expand my investigations into the Fifties. I would like to thank record collector, music fanatic, and restaurateur Jeff Hughson for his expertise and his assistance with the album discographies. Additionally, I would like to thank Mr. Emerson from the Music Library at the University of California at Berkeley for helping me drag out from storage the boxes of Schwann catalogs that proved so crucial to my discographies. I would like to thank my editors at Schirmer Books, Ken Stuart and Abigail Sterne, for their support and encouragement. Finally, I thank the following record companies (and their subsidiary labels) for providing biographical and discographical information during the course of my research: CBS, Warner Brothers, Atlantic, Elektra/Asylum, Motown, MCA, Mercury/Phonogram, RCA, Polydor, and Amherst, A&M, ABC, Bearsville, Capricorn, Caribou, Casablanca, DJM, Epic, Fantasy, Flying Fish, Jet, Kicking Mule, Lifesong, Pacific Arts, Paradise, Philadelphia International, Pickwick, Rolling Stones, RSO, Shelter, Sire, Stax, Sunnyvale, Swan Song, Takoma, Texas Re-Cord, Twentieth Century, and Vanguard.

Grateful acknowledgment of the assistance and cooperation in compiling and confirming the album discographies included herein is hereby accorded the following sources.

The primary source of date information used in this compilation is as tabulated in Joel Whitburn's *Top LP's 1945–1972* book and yearly supplements to that book through 1980, as compiled from *Billboard's* album charts. This book is published independently. Write to: Record Research, P.O. Box 200, Menomonee Falls, Wisconsin 53051.

New listings information from the *Schwann Record and Tape Guides* used here with permission of the copyright owner, ABC Schwann Publications, Inc. © All rights reserved.

Release information on Beatles recordings taken from *All Together Now: The First Complete Beatles Discography* by Harry Castleman and Walter J. Podrazik. Used with permission.

In grateful acknowledgment of the assistance provided by Jeff Hughson in confirming the existence of many difficult-to-find albums and cross-checking other discographical data, I heartily recommend readers patronize his American Music Company, P.O. Box 19143, Sacramento, California 95819, when seeking rare and valuable recordings of both singles and albums of a wide variety of music.

Gold- and platinum-award certifications provided at no charge by the Recording Industry Association of America, Inc., 888 Seventh Avenue, New York, New York 10019.

ABBA. One of the few rock groups from a country other than the United States or Great Britain to achieve major stateside success, ABBA issued an uninterrupted and unprecedented series of international hits beginning in the mid-Seventies that established them as the number one pop musical group around the world by 1977. Producing bland, sterile, yet highly melodic and commercial songs, ABBA bills themselves as "the largest selling group in the history of recorded music."

ABBA

Waterloo	Atlantic	SD–18101	July '74	A
ABBA	Atlantic	SD–18146	August '75	A
Greatest Hits**	Atlantic	SD–18189	August '76	
		later 19114	June '78	A
Arrival*	Atlantic	18207	December '76	
		later 19115	June '78	A
The Album**	Atlantic	19164	February '78	A
Voulez-Vous*	Atlantic	SD–16000	July '79	A
Greatest Hits, Volume 2*	Atlantic	SD–16009	December '79	A
Super Trouper*	Atlantic	16023	December '80	A

THE ALLMAN BROTHERS BAND. The first and perhaps best of the many blues and country-oriented bands to emerge from the South in the Seventies, The Allman Brothers Band established themselves as one of the finest live bands in the country through performances and the best-selling double-record set, *At Fillmore East*. Propelled by twin lead guitarists "Dickey" Betts and Duane Allman, the latter already a respected and revered sessions guitarist whose greatest outside work included *Layla* with Eric Clapton's Derek and The Dominoes, The Allman Brothers Band persevered despite the death of Duane Allman in 1971 and the death of bassist Berry Oakley in 1972, only to disband for separate projects in 1974. Reunited in late 1978 following Gregg Allman's brief and equivocal involvement with Cher, The Allman Brothers achieved another major success with *Enlightened Rogues* and its hit single "Crazy Love."

Duane and Gregg Allman, born in Nashville, Tennessee, on November 20, 1946, and December 8, 1947, respectively, moved to Florida in 1958 and formed their first band there while in high school. In 1965 the brothers formed the regional band, The Allman Joys, which existed for two years and played briefly on the West Coast. After the breakup of The Allman Joys in 1967, Duane and Gregg formed Hourglass for two albums on Liberty, only to split up in the spring of 1968 as Duane pursued sessions work at Muscle Shoals, Alabama, with Wilson Pickett ("Hey Jude"), Aretha Franklin, and others. Duane Allman's sessions work was later compiled on two double-record sets following his death.

The Allman Brothers Band was formed in March 1969 after a jam session between Duane Allman and the members of The 31st of February, which included Butch Trucks, and The Second Coming, which included Richard "Dickey" Betts (born December 12, 1943, in West Palm Beach, Florida) and Berry Oakley (born April 4, 1948, in Jacksonville, Florida). The members: Duane Allman (first lead guitar, slide guitar, vocals), Gregg Allman (keyboards, guitar, vocals), Richard "Dickey" Betts (second lead guitar, slide guitar, dobro, vocals), Berry Oakley (bass), Butch Trucks (drums), and Johnny Lee Johnson—also known as Jai Johanny Johanson—(drums, percussion). Picked up by Phil Walden, who subsequently formed Capricorn Records in the band's adopted hometown of Macon, Georgia, The Allman Brothers Band recorded their debut album for Atco in 1969; Duane continued his sessions work with Boz Scaggs (the overlooked *Boz Scaggs*), Delaney and Bonnie *(To Bonnie from Delaney)* and, most notably, with Eric Clapton (Derek and The Dominoes' *Layla*). Duane declined Clapton's invitation to join his group and The Allman Brothers band recorded the moderately popular *Idlewild South*, which included Betts' "In Memory of Elizabeth Reed" and Gregg's "Midnight Rider." Having established themselves as exciting and dynamic live performers, the band switched to Walden's Capricorn label, where they broke through with the live double-record set *At Fillmore East*, which contained an outstanding 13-minute version of "Elizabeth Reed" and a side-long version of Gregg's "Whipping Post."

Then, on October 29, 1971, Duane was killed in a motorcycle accident in Macon. The band subsequently abandoned the double lead-guitar format in recording their second gold-award album, *Eat a Peach,* in 1972. Chuck Leavell was added on piano in October 1972, but on November 11, 1972, Berry Oakley was fatally injured in a motorcycle accident, also in Macon. Despite the double loss, The Allman Brothers Band persevered, recruiting Lamar Williams to take up the bass chores. *Brothers and Sisters,* released in 1973, was certified gold almost immediately and featured the band's only top-ten hit, Betts' "Ramblin' Man." Band members subsequently pursued solo projects. Gregg Allman retained Trucks, Leavell, and Johanson for *Laid Back,* its major hit single "Midnight Rider," and touring during 1974. That same year, Betts recorded his first solo album and completed his first solo tour. Reunited for 1975's *Win, Lose or Draw* album, The Allman Brothers Band fragmented in 1976 following Gregg's testimony against former road manager John "Scooter" Herring on drug charges. Betts formed Great Southern with guitarist Dan Toler; Leavell formed Sea Level with Williams, guitarist Jimmy Nalls, and Johanson, who eventually departed; Butch Trucks assembled the jazz-influenced Trucks; and Gregg formed his own band for *Playing Up a Storm*. After a single album, Great Southern experienced some personnel changes with the addition of bassist David Goldflies and keyboard player Michael Workman, among others. During 1977, songwriter–multi-instrumentalist Randall Bramblett and guitarist Davis Causey joined Sea Level; after the 1978 concert season, original drummer George Weaver left, to be replaced by former Wings drummer Joe English. In the meantime, Gregg had married Cher (of Sonny and Cher fame) in June 1975, and suffered through a stormy marriage, a poorly received duet album, and a dismal European tour.

In October 1978 The Allman Brothers Band re-assembled, with Gregg Allman, Dickey Betts, Johanny Johanson, Butch Trucks, Dan Toler, and David Goldflies from Betts' Great Southern band, and harmonica player Jim Essery. Having resumed the double lead-guitar format, the reconstituted Allman brothers scored a major hit with "Crazy Love" from *Enlightened Rogues* and subsequently switched to Arista for *Reach for the Sky* and *Brothers of the Road*, with its hit "Straight from the Heart." During 1981 Johanson departed the group and was replaced by David "Frankie" Toler.

THE ALLMAN JOYS

Early Allman	Dial	6005	October '73

HOURGLASS

Hourglass	Liberty	LST–7536	December '67
Power of Love	Liberty	LST–7555	May '68
Hourglass	2-United Artists	LA013	October '73

DUANE AND GREGG ALLMAN

Duane and Gregg Allman	Bold	33–301	May '72

31ST OF FEBRUARY (WITH BUTCH TRUCKS)

31st of February	Vanguard	6503	October '68

DUANE ALLMAN

An Anthology*	2-Capricorn	2CP–0108	November '72	
An Anthology, Volume 2	2-Capricorn	2CP–0139	August '74	
Best	Polydor	6338	November '81	A

THE ALLMAN BROTHERS BAND

The Allman Brothers Band	Atco	SD33–308	November '69

Idlewild South	Atco later Capricorn	SD33–342 0197	September '70	
Beginnings*	2-Atco later 2-Capricorn	2–805 2CX–0132	March '73	
At Fillmore East*	2-Capricorn	SD2–802 later 2CX–0131	July '71	
	reissued on Polydor	CPN–0131		A
Eat a Peach*	2-Capricorn	ZCP–0102	February '72	
	reissued on Polydor	CPN–0102		A
Brothers and Sisters*	Capricorn	CP–0111	August '73	
	reissued on Polydor	CPN–0111		A
Win, Lose or Draw	Capricorn	0156	September '75	
The Road Goes On Forever*	2-Capricorn	0164	November '75	
Wipe the Windows, Check the Oil, Dollar Gas	2-Capricorn	2CX–0177	November '76	
The Allman Brothers Band	2–Polydor	CPN–0196		A

GREGG ALLMAN

Laid Back*	Capricorn	CP–0116	November '73
The Gregg Allman Tour	2-Capricorn	2C–0141	October '74
Playin' Up a Storm	Capricorn	CP–0181	June '77

DICKEY BETTS

Highway Call	Capricorn	0123	August '74

SEA LEVEL

Sea Level	Capricorn	CP–0178	February '77	
Cats on the Coast	Capricorn	0198	January '78	
On the Edge	Capricorn	0212	September '78	
Ball Room	Arista	9531	August '80	A

DICKEY BETTS AND GREAT SOUTHERN

Dickey Betts and Great Southern	Arista	4123	April '77
Atlanta's Burning Down	Arista	AB–4168	April '78

GREGG ALLMAN AND CHER—ALLMAN AND WOMAN

Two the Hard Way	Warner Brothers	BSK–3120	December '77

THE ALLMAN BROTHERS BAND

Enlightened Rogues*	Capricorn	CPN–0218	March '79	
Reach for the Sky	Arista	9535	August '80	A
Brothers of the Road	Arista	9564	September '81	A
Best	Polydor	6339	November '81	A

AMERICA. One of the many so-called "soft rock" groups to achieve success in the Seventies with original songs featuring acoustic guitars and close harmonies, America has achieved no major hits since the departure of Dan Peek in 1977.

AMERICA

America*	Warner Brothers	BS–2576	February '72	A
Homecoming*	Warner Brothers	BS–2655	November '72	A
Hat Trick	Warner Brothers	2728	October '73	A
Holiday*	Warner Brothers	W–2808	June '74	
Hearts*	Warner Brothers	BS–2852	April '75	
History—America's. Greatest Hits*	Warner Brothers	2894 reissued as BSK–3110	November '75	A
Hideaway*	Warner Brothers	BS–2932	April '76	
Harbor	Warner Brothers	BSK–3017	February '77	
Live	Warner Brothers	K–3136	December '77	
Silent Letter	Capitol	SO–11950	June '79	A
Alibi	Capitol	SOO–12098	August '80	A

DAN PEEK

All Things Are Possible	Lamb and Lion	1040	October '79

THE ANIMALS. Often labeled the greatest blues band to emerge from England in the early mid-Sixties, The Animals for a time rivaled both The Beatles and The Rolling Stones in stature despite their lack of the songwriting talents that sustained the two longer-lived groups. Gaining their first widespread popularity on the basis of Eric Burdon's raw and often compelling vocals and Alan Price's subtle arrangements and inspired organ playing (as evidenced on their classic 1964 single "House of the Rising Sun"), The Animals faded within a year and a half of Price's departure. Burdon, considered by some to be the greatest singer produced by England (a claim later challenged by Rod Stewart), subsequently disbanded the group for a dismal solo career, eventually re-emerging in 1970 backed by War, an American soul outfit that soon went on to enormous success on their own. Animals' bassist Chas Chandler, in the meantime, had "discovered" Jimi Hendrix, whereas Price pursued a neglected career rooted in a distinctive blend of the British music hall tradition and the blues. Though the original Animals reunited for a poorly received album around 1976, only Alan Price continues to record to this day.

Originally formed in 1958 by Alan Price (born April 19, 1942, in Fairfield, County Durham, England) as The Alan Price Combo, the group came to be known as The Animals sometime after Eric Burdon (born May 11, 1941, in Newcastle-on-Tyne, England) joined in 1962. Originating in Newcastle, The Animals were lead vocalist Burdon, organist Price, lead guitarist Hilton Valentine (born on May 21, 1943, in North Shields, England), bassist Bryan "Chas" Chandler (born on December 18, 1938, in Newcastle-on-Tyne), and drummer John Steel (born on February 4, 1941, in Gateshead, England). Gaining local popularity, the group signed with manager–producer Mickie Most and moved to London in January 1964, initially scoring a top hit with an excellent remake of the blues classic "House of the Rising Sun" (note Price's outstanding arrangement and organ work). They followed up with the major hits "I'm Crying" (by Price and Burdon), "Don't Let Me Be Misunderstood" and "We Gotta Get Out of This Place" (by songwriters Barry Mann and Cynthia Weil), and moderate hit cover versions of John Lee Hooker's "Boom Boom" and Sam Cooke's "Bring It on Home to Me."

Following Alan Price's departure for a solo career in May 1965, and his replacement by Dave Rowberry, The Animals hit with "It's My Life," only to suffer the loss of John Steel, who was succeeded by Barry Jenkins. After major hits with Carole King and Gerry Goffin's "Don't Bring Me Down" and "See See Rider," Burdon disbanded the group in September 1966. Burdon retained the Animals' name and recorded *Eric Is Here* with New York studio musicians. With a reconstituted Animals, he recorded several second-rate psychedelic-style major hits, most notably "When I was Young," "San Franciscan Nights," "Monterey," and "Sky Pilot," before "retiring" in late 1968.

In the meantime, Alan Price had formed The Alan Price Set, hitting with a remake of Screamin' Jay Hawkins' "I Put a Spell on You" in 1966. The group recorded one album, *The Price Is Right*, which contained some of the first Randy Newman songs ever to be recorded, before disbanding in 1968. Price later toured and did television shows with Georgie Fame ("Yeh Yeh"), whereas Chas Chandler "discovered" Jimi Hendrix and became his first manager. Hilton Valentine surfaced briefly in 1969 to record one solo album.

Moving to California, Eric Burdon helped form the backup group War, with members of Los Angeles' all-black Night Shift and Danish harmonica player Lee Oskar. Recording two albums and the smash hit single "Spill the Wine" with Burdon, War later became a popular act in its own right. After recording an album with blues singer Jimmy Weatherspoon, Burdon formed yet another band, cutting two albums for Capitol.

Re-emerging with his band of three years in 1973 for the soundtrack recording of (and appearance in) Lindsay Anderson's *O Lucky Man*, Alan Price recorded one other album for Warner Brothers before again dropping out of sight, concentrating his activities in Great Britain, where three of his albums were released before 1977's *Alan Price*. In 1976–77, the original Animals reunited for *Before We Were So Rudely Interrupted;* Price subsequently toured and recorded on his own.

THE ANIMALS

In the Beginning	Wand	WDS–690	
Early Animals	Pickwick	SPC–3330	
The Animals (with Eric Burdon)	MGM	SE–4264	September '64
On Tour	MGM	SE–4281	February '65
Animal Tracks	MGM	SE–4305	August '65
Animalization	MGM	SE–4384	August '66
Animalism	MGM	SE–4414	November '66

ERIC BURDON

Eric Is Here	MGM	SE–4433	February '67

ERIC BURDON AND THE ANIMALS

Winds of Change	MGM	SE–4484	September '67
Twain Shall Meet	MGM	SE–4537	April '68
Every One of Us	MGM	SE–4553	July '68
Love Is	2-MGM	SE–4591	December '68

THE ANIMALS ANTHOLOGIES AND COMPILATIONS

The Best of The Animals*	MGM	SE–4324	January '66	
The Best of Eric Burdon and The Animals—Volume 2	MGM	SE–4454	May '67	
Greatest Hits	MGM	SE–4602	February '69	A
The Best of The Animals	2-ABKCO	AB–4226	September '73	A

ALAN PRICE

The Price Is Right	Parrot	PAS–71018	January '68
	later London	71018	October '73

HILTON VALENTINE

All in Your Head	Capitol	ST–330	January '70	

ERIC BURDON AND WAR

Eric Burdon De-clares "War"	MGM	SE–4663	April '70	
reissued as Spill the Wine	Lax	PW–37109	April '81	A
Black Man's Burdon	2–MGM	4710	December '70	
Love Is All Around	ABC	988	December '76	

ERIC BURDON AND JIMMY WITHERSPOON

Guilty!	MGM	SE–4791	November '71	

ERIC BURDON BAND

Sun Secrets	Capitol reissued on	ST–11359	November '74	
	Lax	PW–37110	April '81	A
Stop!	Capitol	SMAS–11426	August '75	

ALAN PRICE

O Lucky Man	Warner Brothers	2710	June '73	
Between Today and Yesterday	Warner Brothers	BS–2783	March '74	
Alan Price	United Artists	LA809	October '77	
Lucky Day	Jet	JZ–35710	August '79	
Rising Sun	Jet	JZ–36510	July '80	
House of the Rising Sun	Townhouse	SU–7126	November '81	A

THE ANIMALS

Before We Were So Rudely Inter-rupted	Jet	LA790	August '77	

PAUL ANKA. One of the more sophisticated performers to come out of the rock-and-roll Fifties, Paul Anka had a number of hits with his own compositions while still a teenager, beginning with "Diana." Established as a nightclub performer by 1960, Anka pursued a successful career as a songwriter until coming back with several hits since the mid-Seventies.

Born in Ottawa on July 30, 1941, and raised in Canada, Paul Anka first performed in public at the age of 12. Traveling to Hollywood in 1956, he recorded his first albeit unsuccessful single for Modern Records. In May of the following year at age 15, while in New York, Anka auditioned a song for Don Costa of ABC–Paramount that would become one of the biggest selling singles of the Fifties—"Diana." Over the next three years, he hit the charts consistently with songs he composed which often reflected the simple, even naive, but nonetheless poignant concerns of teenagers. His best remembered smash hits of the period include "You Are My Destiny," "Lonely Boy," "Put Your Head on My Shoulder," "Puppy Love," "My Home Town," and "Dance On, Little Girl."

No longer showing up on the charts after 1963, Paul Anka continued to perform his past hits on the nightclub circuit through 1966, when he became disillusioned with living in the past. Having written songs for other performers beginning with "It Doesn't Matter Anymore" for Buddy Holly in 1958, Anka concentrated on his songwriting. Subsequently, his "The Tonight Show Theme" became one of his most profitable compositions; but his rewrite of the French ballad "Comme d'Habitude" as "My Way" in 1968 became perhaps his best-known song and Frank Sinatra's theme song. Anka's "She's a Lady" was a smash hit for Tom Jones in 1971.

Penetrating the lower levels of the charts again in 1969, he reestablished himself as a recording artist in 1974 with "(You're) Having My Baby," recorded with Odia Coates, with whom he toured for several years. His *Anka* album went gold-award the year of its release, as did *Times of Your Life* in 1976. He continues to write, record, tour eight months of the year, and appear on an occasional television special. More recently, Paul Anka has formed his own movie production company, Paul Anka Films, in order to pursue yet another facet of his career.

PAUL ANKA

Paul Anka	ABC–Paramount	ABC–240 (M)	August '58
My Heart Sings	ABC–Paramount	ABCS–296	October '59
Swings for Young Lovers	ABC–Paramount	ABCS–347	July '60
Paul Anka at the Copa	ABC–Paramount	ABCS–353	November '60
It's Christmas Everywhere	ABC–Paramount	ABCS–360	
Instrumental Hits	ABC–Paramount	ABCS–371	February '61
Diana	ABC–Paramount	ABCS–420	March '62
Young, Alive and in Love	RCA	LSP–2502	March '62
Let's Sit This One Out	RCA	LSP–2575	August '62
Our Man Around the World	RCA	LSP–2614	January '63
Italiano	RCA–Italian	LPM–10130 (M)	July '63

Songs I Wish I'd Written	RCA	LSP–2744	November '63	
		reissued as ANLI–2482	November '77	
Excitement on Park Avenue	RCA	LSP–2966	October '64	
Strictly Nashville	RCA	LSP–3580	August '66	
Live!	RCA	LSP–3875	October '67	
Goodnight My Love	RCA	LSP–4142	March '69	
Sincerely	RCA	LSP–4203	September '69	
Life Goes On	RCA	LSP–4250	November '69	
70's	RCA	LSP–4309	May '70	
Paul Anka	Buddah	5093	January '72	
Jubilation	Buddah	5114	June '72	
Live	Barnaby	6013	August '75	
		later 4008	April '79	
Anka*	United Artists	LA314	August '74	
Feelings	United Artists	LA367	April '75	
Times of Your Life*	United Artists	LA569	December '75	
	reissued as	LN–10001		A
The Painter	United Artists	LA653	October '76	
The Music Man	United Artists	LA746	June '77	
Listen to Your Heart	RCA	AFL1–2892	August '78	
Headlines	RCA	AFL1–3382	July '79	
Both Sides of Love	RCA	AQL1–3926	April '81	A

PAUL ANKA ANTHOLOGIES, COMPILATIONS, AND REISSUES

Paul Anka Sings His Big 15	ABC–Paramount	ABC–323	June '60	
Paul Anka Sings His Big 15, Volume 2	ABC–Paramount	ABCS–390	August '61	
Paul Anka Sings His Big 15, Volume 3	ABC–Paramount	ABCS–409		
21 Golden Hits	RCA	LSP–2691	May '63	
		reissued as AYL1–3808		A
Remember Diana	RCA	ANL1–0896	July '75	
Lady	RCA	ANL1–1054		
She's a Lady	RCA	ANL1–1098	September '75	
	reissued on Accord	SN–7117	April '81	A
Paul Anka Sings His Favorites	RCA	ANL1–1584	August '76	
This Is Paul Anka	Buddah	5622	April '75	

The Essential Paul Anka	2-Buddah	5667	November '76	
Gold—28 Original Hit Recordings	2-Sire	3704	November '74	
Vintage Years (1957–1961)	Sire	K–6043	December '77	
My Way	Camden	ACL–0616	January '76	
Puppy Love	Pickwick	3508	May '76	
Lonely Boy	Pickwick	3523	May '76	A
Paul Anka	2-Pickwick	2087	May '76	A
His Best	United Artists	LA922 reissued as LN–10000	December '78	A
Very Best	Ranwood	8203	December '81	A

NICHOLAS ASHFORD AND VALERIE SIMPSON.

Achieving their first success as the co-authors of "Let's Go Get Stoned" as recorded by Ray Charles, Nicholas Ashford and Valerie Simpson wrote and produced major hits for Marvin Gaye and Tammi Terrell and for Diana Ross between 1967 and 1970 before launching a duo recording and performing career that established them as album artists in the late Seventies.

VALERIE SIMPSON

Exposed	Tamla	311	June '71	
Valerie Simpson	Tamla	317	August '72	
Keep It Comin'	Tamla	6–351	March '77	

NICHOLAS ASHFORD AND VALERIE SIMPSON

Gimme Something Real	Warner Brothers	BS–2739	September '73	A
I Wanna Be Selfish	Warner Brothers	BS–2789	May '74	A
Come as You Are	Warner Brothers	2858	April '76	A
So so Satisfied	Warner Brothers	BS–2992	January '77	A
Send It *	Warner Brothers	BS–3088	September '77	A
Is It Still Good to Ya*	Warner Brothers	3219	August '78	A
Stay Free*	Warner Brothers	HS–3357	August '79	A
A Musical Affair	Warner Brothers	HS–3458	August '80	A
Performance	2-Warner Brothers	2WB–3524	October '81	A

THE ASSOCIATION. Hitting in 1966 with the psychedelic classic "Along Comes Mary," The Association nonetheless achieved greater success with the softer and more urbane sound of pop hits such as "Cherish," "Windy," and "Never My Love" through 1968. Continuing to record through 1973, The Association suffered a crippling blow to their career with the death of group mentor Brian Cole in 1972.

THE ASSOCIATION

And Then . . . Along Comes The Association *	Valiant later Warner Brothers	5002 1702	August '66 July '69	
Renaissance	Valiant later Warner Brothers	5004 1704	January '67 July '69	
Insight Out *	Warner Brothers	1696	July '67	
Birthday	Warner Brothers	1733	April '68	
Greatest Hits *	Warner Brothers	1767	November '68	A
Goodbye Columbus (soundtrack)	Warner Brothers	1786	May '69	
The Association	Warner Brothers	1800	October '69	
"Live"	Warner Brothers	1868	July '70	
Stop Your Motor	Warner Brothers	1927	August '71	
Waterbeds in Trinidad	Columbia	KC–31348	May '72	

RUSS GIGUERE

Hexagram 16	Warner Brothers	WS–1910	April '71

THE ATLANTA RHYTHM SECTION/THE CLASSICS IV. One of the most successful "soft rock" groups of the late Sixties, scoring smash hits with "Spooky," "Stormy," and "Traces," The Classics IV included two members who subsequently became sessions stalwarts at Studio One in Doraville, Georgia. Joined by several former Candymen, Roy Orbison's backup group, the two formed The Atlanta Rhythm Section in the early Seventies, ultimately breaking through in the late Seventies with hits such as "So into You," "Imaginary Lover," and a remake of "Spooky."

THE CLASSICS IV

Spooky	Imperial	12371	March '68
Mamas and Papas/ Soul Train	Imperial	12407	December '68

Traces	Imperial	12429	April '69	
Very Best of The Classics IV	Liberty	LN–10109	April '81	A

DENNIS YOST AND THE CLASSICS IV

Golden Greats— Volume 1	Imperial	16000	December '69	
Song	Liberty	11003	September '70	
What Am I Crying For	MGM South	702	April '73	
Very Best of Dennis Yost and The Classics IV	United Artists	LA446	August '75	

DENNIS YOST

Stormy	Sunset reissued on	5323	March '71	
	Accord	SN–7107	April '81	A

THE CANDYMEN

The Candymen	ABC	616	November '67	
Bring You Candypower	ABC	633	April '68	

THE ATLANTA RHYTHM SECTION

The Atlanta Rhythm Section	Decca	DL75265		
Back up against the Wall	Decca	DL75390	April '73	
Atlanta Rhythm Section	2-MCA	4114	April '77	A
Third Annual Pipe Dream	Polydor	6027	July '74	A
Dog Days	Polydor	PD–6041	August '75	A
Red Tape	Polydor	6060	May '76	
A Rock and Roll Alternative*	Polydor	6080	December '76	A
Champagne Jam**	Polydor	6134	March '78	A
Underdog*	Polydor	PDl–6200	June '79	A
Are You Ready!*	2-Polydor	PD2–6236	November '79	A
The Boys from Doraville	Polydor	6285	August '80	A
Quinella	Columbia	FC–37550	September '81	A

BURT BACHARACH AND HAL DAVID. One of the most successful of the professional songwriting teams in rock music history, Burt Bacharach and Hal David have written literally dozens of hit songs. Their compositions feature David's Tin Pan Alley-style lyrics and Bacharach's distinctive melodies and bridges, uncommon rhythms, and key changes. In arranging horn and string parts for the Drifters in the early Sixties and for Dionne Warwick throughout the Sixties, Bacharach helped change the sound of contemporary rhythm-and-blues and soul music.

Having written lyrics as early as 1943, Hal David collaborated with a number of tunesmiths before joining Burt Bacharach regularly in the Sixties. After formal musical training which included studying with French composer Darius Milhaud, Bacharach became a much sought-after conductor and arranger in the Fifties and early Sixties. One of Bacharach and David's earliest collaborations was "Magic Moments," recorded by Perry Como in 1958. During these years, the two often worked separately and were associated with a number of hits, including Sarah Vaughn's 1959 near-smash "Broken-Hearted Melody" (by David and Sherman Edwards), Gene McDaniel's 1961 smash "Tower of Strength" (by Bacharach and Bob Hilliard), and The Shirelles' 1961–62 near-smash "Baby, It's You" (by Bacharach, Mack David, and Barney Williams).

In the early Sixties, the team collaborated on many smash hits, such as Gene Pitney's "Only Love Can Break a Heart" (1962), Dusty Springfield's "Wishin' and Hopin'" (1964), and Jackie DeShannon's "What the World Needs Now Is Love" (1965).

Since the mid-Sixties, the duo has provided Dionne Warwick with at least 39 chart records, among which are "Anyone Who Had a Heart," "Walk On By," "Message to Michael," "I Say a Little Prayer," and "Do You Know the Way to San José?"

Throughout the Sixties, Bacharach and David composed a number of hit movie themes and songs, including the title songs to *What's New, Pussycat?* (by Tom Jones in 1965) and *Alfie* (by Dionne Warwick in 1967), "The Look of Love" (by Dusty Springfield in 1967) from *Casino Royale*, and the top hit "Raindrops Keep Fallin' on My Head" (by B.J. Thomas in 1969) from *Butch Cassidy and The Sundance Kid*.

In the late Sixties, the two collaborated on the smash Broadway musical *Promises, Promises*, from which Dionne Warwick scored two hits, "Promises, Promises" and "I'll Never Fall in Love Again." Although Bacharach and David provided smash hits for the Carpenters ("Close to You") and The Fifth Dimension ("One Less Bell to Answer") in 1970, the team soon broke up. During the Seventies, Bacharach has performed in public to enthusiastic audiences, both live and on television. Having embarked on his own recording career years earlier, Burt Bacharach recorded his first symphonic suite with the Houston Symphony in 1979.

BURT BACHARACH

Man! His Songs	Kapp	3447	October '66	
Burt Bacharach Plays His Hits	Kapp later MCA	3577 65	July '69	A
Reach Out*	A&M	4131 reissued as 3102	October '67	A
Make It Easy on Yourself*	A&M	4188	June '69	A
Butch Cassidy and The Sundance Kid*	A&M	4227	November '69	
Burt Bacharach*	A&M	3501	June '71	A
Living Together	A&M	3527	January '74	A
Greatest Hits	A&M	3661	December '74	A
Futures	A&M	4622	April '77	A

BURT BACHARACH WITH THE HOUSTON SYMPHONY

Woman	A&M	3709	May '79	A

BAD COMPANY. A third-generation British "superstar" rock band whose antecedents lie with Free, Mott the Hoople, and King Crimson, Bad Company quickly rose to widespread popularity in 1974 with its loud, hard-driving music and Paul Rodgers' distinctive vocals.

BAD COMPANY

Bad Company*	Swan Song	SS–8410 later SS–8501	June '74	A
Straight Shooter*	Swan Song	SS–8413 later SS–8502	April '75	A
Run with the Pack**	Swan Song	SS–8415 later SS–8503	February '76	A
Burnin' Sky*	Swan Song	SS–8500	March '77	A
Desolation Angels**	Swan Song	SS–8506	March '79	A

JOAN BAEZ. One of the finest female singers to emerge from the early Sixties folk scene, Joan Baez was most likely the first folksinger to achieve massive international success. One of the first solo folksingers to record best-selling albums of traditional material, she helped introduce Bob Dylan to a wider audience as she became one of the first folksingers to be involved with the "protest" movement. Associated with the protest classic "We Shall Overcome," Baez later enjoyed popularity as a song interpreter before emerging as a singer–songwriter, particularly with the 1975 gold-award album *Diamonds and Rust.*

Born on Staten Island, New York, on January 9, 1941, Joan Baez started performing in public, accompanying herself on guitar, at small clubs around Cambridge and Boston in the late Fifties and soon graduated to Greenwich Village. Successful appearances at the 1959 and 1960 Newport Folk Festivals followed, with Baez moving to California in 1961. Her first three albums, consisting of standard folk fare, primarily traditional English and American ballads, were eventually certified gold in 1966. Her fourth album, *In Concert, Part 2*, featured "We Shall Overcome," a song that was to become the protest anthem of the Sixties. That and subsequent albums contained her versions of songs by then-unrecognized folk artists such as Phil Ochs ("There but for Fortune") and early Greenwich Village friend Bob Dylan ("Don't Think Twice," "It's All Over Now, Baby Blue," and others). After *Noël*, an album of traditional folk and religious songs, her albums again included songs by contemporary songwriters such as Lennon and McCartney ("Eleanor Rigby") and Tim Hardin ("If I Were a Carpenter"). *Any Day Now*, released in 1969, was a double-record set of Dylan songs, certified gold-award in 1972.

Continuing to cover material by songwriters such as Willie Nelson, Hoyt Axton, and John Prine, Joan Baez's first and only major hit came in 1971 with Robbie Robertson's "The Night They Drove Old Dixie Down." Having begun writing her own songs in the early Seventies, she put six of her songs on *Come from the Shadows* (her first album for A&M Records) including the undisguised "To Bobby," as well as sister Mimi Farina's "In the Quiet Morning (for Janis Joplin)." Her 1975 *Diamonds and Rust* album, a tremendous hit, was certified gold-award within seven months of its release and contained her own "Winds of the Old Days" and "Diamonds and Rust," as well as John Prine's "Hello in There" and Janis Ian's "Jesse." During late 1975 and 1976, Baez toured with Bob Dylan's curious Rolling Thunder Revue. After two final albums on A&M, one a live double-record set, Joan Baez switched to Portrait Records for *Blowin' Away* and *Honest Lullaby*. Having founded the Institute for the Study of Non-Violence in 1965, Joan Baez confirmed her commitment to humanitarian causes with the 1979 formation of the human rights organization, Humanitas International.

JOAN BAEZ

Joan Baez *	Vanguard	VSD–2077	October '60	A
Joan Baez, Volume 2 *	Vanguard	VSD–2097	September '61	A

| In Concert* | Vanguard | 2122 | September '62 | A |
| In Concert, Part 2 | Vanguard | 2123 | November '63 | A |

JOAN BAEZ WITH BILL WOOD AND TED ALEVIZOS

| The Best of Joan Baez | Squire | 33001 | November '63 | |

JOAN BAEZ

Five	Vanguard	VSD–79160	October '64	A
Farewell Angelina	Vanguard	VSD–79200	October '65	A
Noël	Vanguard	79230	October '66	
Joan	Vanguard	79240	August '67	A
Baptism—A Journey Through Our Time (Schickele)	Vanguard	VSD–79275	June '68	A
Any Day Now*	2-Vanguard	VSD–79306/7	December '68	A
David's Album	Vanguard	79308	May '69	A
One Day at a Time	Vanguard	VSD–79310	January '70	A
Blessed Are . . .*	2-Vanguard	VSD–6570/1	August '71	A
Carry It On (soundtrack)	Vanguard	79313	December '71	
Come from the Shadows	A&M	SP–4339 reissued as 3103	May '72	A
Where Are You Now, My Son	A&M	SP–4390	May '73	
Gracias a la Vida—Here's to Life	A&M	3614	March '74	A
Diamonds and Rust*	A&M	SP–4527	April '75	A
From Every Stage	2-A&M	SP–3704	January '76	A
Gulf Winds	A&M	SP–4603	November '76	
Blowin' Away	Portrait	PR–34697	June '77	A
Honest Lullaby	Portrait	JR–35766	July '79	

JOAN BAEZ ANTHOLOGIES

First Ten Years	2-Vanguard	VSD–6560/1	October '70	A
Hits/Greatest and Others	Vanguard	79332	July '73	A
Ballad Book	2-Vanguard	VSD–41/2	November '72	A
Contemporary Ballad Book	2-Vanguard	49/50	August '74	A
Love Song Album	2-Vanguard	79/80	May '76	A

The Best of Joan Baez	A&M	4668	December '77	A
The Country Music Album	2-Vanguard	105/6	August '79	A

HANK BALLARD AND THE MIDNIGHTERS.

The early rhythm-and-blues vocal group that helped open the developing field of rock-and-roll to overt eroticism with the 1954 smash "Work with Me Annie," Hank Ballard and The Midnighters endured the banishment from radio airplay of that and other similar songs and the co-optation and popularization of a bowdlerized version of Ballard's "Roll with Me Henry" by a white artist long before losing the rights to his "The Twist," the song that launched the dance craze in the early Sixties.

HANK BALLARD AND THE MIDNIGHTERS

Greatest Jukebox Hits	King/Federal	541(M)		
Hank Ballard and The Midnighters	King	581(M)	July '58	
Singing and Swinging	King	618(M)	May '59	
The One and Only	King	674(M)	December '60	
Mr. Rhythm and Blues	King	700(M)	October '60	
Spotlight on Hank Ballard	King	740(M)	May '61	
Let's Go Again	King	748(M)	May '61	
Sing Along	King	759(M)	November '61	
The Twistin' Fools	King	781(M)	April '62	
Jumpin'	King	793(M)	January '63	
1963 Sound	King	815(M)	March '63	
Greatest Hits	King	867(M)	June '64	
A Star in Your Eyes	King	896(M)		
Those Lazy, Lazy Days	King	913(M)		
Glad Songs, Sad Songs	King	927(M)		
24 Hit Tunes	King	950(M)		
Hank Ballard Sings 24 Great Songs	King	981(M)		
20 Hits (1953–1962)	King	5003(M)	December '77	A
Finger Poppin' Time	Power Pak	PO–276		

HANK BALLARD

You Can't Keep a Good Man Down	King	KSD–1052	October '69	

THE BAND. One of the United States' most popular bands between the late Sixties and mid-Seventies, The Band was ironically manned by four Canadians and only one American, Levon Helm. With only an underground reputation despite years of playing together, The Band achieved their first recognition as Bob Dylan's backing rock band, later breaking through into mass popularity with the landmark *Music from Big Pink* album, without benefit of the usual supporting tour. In refreshing contrast to the then-popular "psychedelic" music, The Band featured a country–gospel sound supplemented by electric instrumentation, loose yet precise musicianship combined with oblique vocal harmonies, and incisive original songs that frequently reflected an Americana of yore, as evidenced by the Robbie Robertson classic, "The Night They Drove Old Dixie Down." Following The Band's dissolution with 1976's "The Last Waltz," Robertson and Levon Helm initiated acting careers.

The Band began its evolution in the person of Levon Helm (born in Marvell, Arkansas, on May 26, 1943), when he and several other Arkansans moved to Canada in 1958 to back Ronnie Hawkins as The Hawks. Having pursued an unspectacular career as a country musician, Hawkins turned to rock-and-roll, hitting with "Forty Days" and "Mary Lou" in 1959. During 1961, "Robbie" Robertson (born in Toronto, Canada, on July 5, 1944) replaced Fred Carter, Jr. on guitar; within a few months, the Arkansans, except Helm, were replaced by Canadians Rick Danko (born in Simcoe, Ontario, on December 9, 1943), Richard Manuel (born in Stratford, Ontario, on April 3, 1944), and Garth Hudson (born in London, Ontario, on August 2, 1942). Parting company with Hawkins around 1963, the group toured East Coast clubs as Levon and The Hawks under Helm's leadership.

After the release of his first rock-oriented album, *Bringing It All Back Home*, Bob Dylan contacted the group while in New Jersey in the summer of 1965. Between the fall of 1965 and the summer of 1966, the group and Dylan toured and recorded together, however without the recalcitrant Helm. Following Dylan's much-publicized motorcycle accident, Helm was summoned from Arkansas and the group and Dylan retired to upstate New York to rehearse and record the so-called "Basement Tapes." Available for years only on bootleg albums of questionable legality, this material was eventually released officially in 1975.

The Band's members were: Jaime Robert "Robbie" Robertson (electric, acoustic, and bass guitars; piano, vocals), Richard Manuel (keyboards, drums, vocals), Rick Danko (bass, vocals), Garth Hudson (keyboards, brass, woodwinds), and Levon Helm (drums, mandolin, vocals). While in New York, the group, known simply as The Band, prepared their first album under the influence of Dylan. Released in mid-1968, *Music from Big Pink* contained one Dylan song, "I Shall Be Released," two Dylan collaborations, "Tears of Rage" (with Manuel) and "This Wheel's on Fire" (with Danko), and several excellent songs by chief–songwriter Robertson, including "The Weight" and "Caledonia Mission."

Making their solo debut performance at Bill Graham's Winterland in San Francisco in April 1969, The Band's second album was even more popular than their first and revealed a growing maturation of Robertson's songwriting abilities. *The Band* included his classic "The Night They Drove Old Dixie Down" as well as "Across the Great Divide" and "Up on Cripple Creek." Though it included only one minor hit, "Time to Kill," *Stage Fright* contained several memorable cuts, including the title song, "The Shape I'm In," and "Just Another Whistle Stop." During 1970, Robertson began his outside musical activities, producing Jesse Winchester's first album. The Band's *Cahoots* album included several interesting Robertson songs ("Smoke Signal," "Shootout in Chinatown"), the collaborative "Life Is a Carnival," and "4% Pantomime," co-authored by Van Morrison. After the live *Rock of Ages* album, the group recorded the entertaining and amusing *Moondog Matinee*, which consisted primarily of old rock-and-roll songs.

In 1974 The Band again backed their old mentor and friend Bob Dylan for his *Planet Waves* album and his first tour since 1965. From the tour came *Before the Flood*, an album combining both Dylan and Band favorites. Subsequently, The Band's first album of original material since 1971, *Northern Lights—Southern Cross*, was critically acclaimed as one of their best since *The Band*. Comprised entirely of Robertson songs, the album included "Acadian Driftwood," "Ophelia," and "Jupiter Hollow."

Again busy outside the group, Robertson produced Neil Diamond's *Beautiful Noise* album in early 1976. Later that year, The Band announced their retirement after more than 15 years on the road. Only days after recording their last album as a group, *Islands*, they made their final appearance at Bill Graham's Winterland on Thanksgiving Night, 1976. Billed as "The Last Waltz," this final show included performances by a number of stars and superstars of rock, from Bob Dylan to Joni Mitchell, Eric Clapton, Neil Diamond, and Van Morrison. Both a film and a triple-record album set from the show were released the following spring.

Subsequently, both Rick Danko and Levon Helm recorded solo albums, Helm first with the RCO All Stars (who included Paul Butterfield and Dr. John), later with his own group. During 1980 Levon Helm appeared in the highly successful film, *Coal Miner's Daughter*, as Loretta Lynn's father, whereas Robbie Robertson co-wrote, produced and co-starred in the equivocal *Carny* film with Gary Busey and Jodie Foster. In the meantime, Garth Hudson had become Los Angeles' premier sessions accordion player.

THE BAND

Music from Big Pink	Capitol	SKAO–2955	June '68	A
The Band *	Capitol	STAO–132	September '69	A
Stage Fright *	Capitol	SW–425	July '70	
		reissued as SN–16006		A
Cahoots	Capitol	SMAS–651	September '71	
		reissued as SN–1603		A
Rock of Ages *	2-Capitol	SAAB–11045	August '72	

		reissued as SN– 16008, 16009		A
Moondog Matinee	Capitol	SW–11214 reissued as SN– 16004	October '73	A

THE BAND AND BOB DYLAN

Planet Waves*	Asylum	7E–1003	January '74	
Before the Flood*	2-Asylum	AB–201	July '74	
The Basement Tapes	2-Columbia	C2–33682	July '75	A

THE BAND

Northern Lights— Southern Cross	Capitol	ST–11440 reissued as SN– 16005	November '75	A
The Best of The Band	Capitol	ST–11553	September '76	A
Islands	Capitol	SO–11602 reissued as SN– 16007	March '77	A
The Last Waltz	3-Warner Brothers	3WS–3146	March '78	A
Anthology	2-Capitol	SKBO– 11856	November '78	A

LEVON HELM AND THE RCO ALL STARS

Levon Helm and The RCO All Stars	ABC	AA–1017	November '77	

RICK DANKO

Rick Danko	Arista	AB–4141	November '77	

LEVON HELM

Levon Helm	ABC	AA–1089	September '78	A
American Son	MCA	5120	June '80	A

JEFF BARRY AND ELLIE GREENWICH. Barry and Greenwich made up one of several New York songwriting–production teams who composed a series of hits, primarily in 1963 and 1964, for the then-popular "girl groups" of Phil Spector and Jerry Leiber–Mike Stoller.

Originally intending a career as a recording artist, Jeff Barry became a songwriter for a music publishing company. Early hit compositions included "Tell Laura I Love Her" (with Ben Raleigh) by Ray Peterson in 1960 and "Chip Chip" (with Cliff Crawford and Arthur Resnick) by Gene McDaniels in 1962. In 1962, he met and married songwriter Ellie Greenwich. The two collaborated on a number of hit compositions in conjunction with producer Phil Spector for The Crystals and The Ronettes on Spector's Philles label in 1963: "Da Doo Ron Ron" and "Then He Kissed Me" by The Crystals, and "Be My Baby" and "Baby I Love You" by the Ronettes. Also in 1963, Barry and Greenwich recorded an album and several singles as The Raindrops, including their composition and major hit, "The Kind of Boy You Can't Forget."

Signed to write and produce for Jerry Leiber and Mike Stoller's Red Bird label in 1964, Jeff Barry and Ellie Greenwich wrote a number of hits for several different "girl groups": "Chapel of Love" (with Phil Spector) and "People Say" by The Dixie Cups, "I Wanna Love Him So Bad" by The Jelly Beans, and "Leader of the Pack" (with George "Shadow" Morton) by The Shangri-Las. Additionally, two other Barry–Greenwich compositions became hits in 1964: "Maybe I Know" by Lesley Gore and "Do Wah Diddy Diddy" by Manfred Mann.

When Red Bird was sold, Jeff Barry and Ellie Greenwich took fellow songwriter Neil Diamond to Bert Berns' Bang Records, producing his five albums with the label. During 1966, their composition "Hanky Panky" (an old Raindrops song) became a hit for Tommy James; "River Deep—Mountain High," co-written with Phil Spector and recorded by Ike and Tina Turner, was conspicuously unsuccessful and led to Spector's withdrawal from the music scene for several years. Subsequent production chores for Barry included The Monkees and the studio-formed Archies, who had a smash hit with Barry and Andy Kim's "Sugar, Sugar" in 1969. Earlier that year "I Can Hear Music," composed by Barry, Greenwich, and Spector, was a major hit for The Beach Boys.

Jeff Barry became a producer for A&M Records in 1971, with little success. Having recorded her first solo album in 1968, now ex-wife Ellie Greenwich recorded another for Verve Records in 1973. For Barry, recent songwriting ventures have included "I Honestly Love You" with Peter Allen, a minor hit for Olivia Newton-John in 1977. Recent productions by Jeff Barry include Tommy James' *Midnight Rider* album and John Travolta's second album.

THE RAINDROPS

The Raindrops	Jubilee	SJ–5023	

ELLIE GREENWICH

Composes, Produces, and Sings	United Artists	UAS–6648	May '68
Let It Be Written, Let It Be Sung	Verve	V–65091	May '73

THE BEACH BOYS. One of America's most popular groups in the Sixties, The Beach Boys were perhaps the first white vocal-and-instrumental rock group to employ complex vocal arrangements to create a distinctive, characteristic ensemble sound. The biggest popularizers of "surf" music, The Beach Boys established themselves with songs of their own creation at a time dominated by artists who recorded songs written by professional songwriters. With Brian Wilson writing, singing the falsetto parts, arranging the other voices, and producing the group's records, The Beach Boys were most likely the first self-produced rock group, using studios, musicians, and technicians of their own choosing. Furthermore, *Shut Down* is considered by some to be rock music's first concept album. Brian's increasing sophistication of production, beginning with the "California Girls" single of 1965 and culminating in "Good Vibrations" and the *Pet Sounds* album, revealed a unique use of a wide range of instrumentation, styles, and sound effects rivaled at the time only by The Beatles (under George Martin) and Phil Spector (independently). Finally, The Beach Boys' formation in 1967 of their own label, Brother Records, with distribution to be handled by Capitol, was one of the first artist's custom label deals. Experiencing a decline in popularity and influence with Brian's recession from the group following the 1971 *Surf's Up* album, The Beach Boys staged a remarkable comeback with Brian's return for the 1976 *15 Big Ones*, only to again endure his withdrawal and subsequent intra-group clashes and divergent outside projects. Making their debut in a Nevada casino showroom in 1980, The Beach Boys are now generally regarded as an "oldies" act.

Formed in 1961 as Kenny and The Cadets and Carl and The Passions, The Beach Boys consisted of the Wilson brothers Brian, Dennis, and Carl (born June 20, 1942, December 4, 1944, and December 21, 1946, respectively, all in Hawthorne, California), cousin Mike Love (born March 15, 1941, in Los Angeles), and friend Al Jardine (born September 3, 1942, in Los Angeles). With all members contributing vocals, Brian played bass and keyboards, Carl was lead guitarist and Al rhythm guitarist while Dennis drummed and Mike added saxophone. Recording the Southern California hit "Surfin'" for a small local label in 1961, The Beach Boys debuted in Long Beach on New Year's Eve, 1961–62. Replaced by David Marks for approximately six months, Al Jardine returned to the group by the spring of 1963. Between 1962 and 1965, The Beach Boys issued smash hits ad nauseum on the Southern California themes of surfing, cars and motorcycles, girls, and high school, virtually all written solely by or in collaboration with Brian. These hits included the title songs to *Surfin' Safari, Surfin' U.S.A., Shut Down* (an anthology album with only two Beach Boys songs), *Surfer Girl,* and *Little Deuce Coupe,* as well as "Be True to Your School" and "Fun, Fun, Fun" from *Shut Down, Volume 2.* Beginning with "Surfer Girl," the group's releases included ballads such as the underrated "In My Room," "Don't Worry Baby," and "The Warmth of the Sun." Subsequent rockers included "I Get Around," "Wendy," "Dance, Dance, Dance," and "Help Me Rhonda."

Suffering a nervous breakdown in December 1964, Brian Wilson ceased touring with The Beach Boys by the following April. With Carl becoming the onstage leader and Al taking over Brian's falsetto parts, the group was augmented by sessions guitarist Glen Campbell, soon to be replaced by Beach Boys' associate Bruce Johnston. Johnston had previously recorded surf albums and been a member of The Rip Chords, who scored a smash hit in 1963–64 with "Hey Little Cobra." Relieved of his arduous touring duties, Brian continued to write for the group and, with "California Girls," started using elaborate production techniques on the group's recordings. While the rest of The Beach Boys were on tour, Brian began working on his *Pet Sounds* epic, employing scores of studio musicians and utilizing advanced studio techniques. Though perplexed by Brian's work on the album in the absence of the group, the returning group persevered to complete their critically acclaimed masterpiece. However, despite the lush orchestral sound and the inclusion of songs such as "Wouldn't It Be Nice," "God Only Knows," "Caroline No," and the folk song "Sloop John B.," *Pet Sounds* sold poorly compared to their previous releases.

Severely disappointed, Brian Wilson nonetheless initiated work on the next album, tentatively called *Smile*, with lyricist Van Dyke Parks. While Brian was deeply immersed in the project, Capitol Records issued the monumental single, "Good Vibrations." Taking more than six months to record, using 90 hours of studio time, and costing $16,000, "Good Vibrations" became The Beach Boys's only million-selling single. Meanwhile the already troubled Brian, working against the perceived competition of Phil Spector and The Beatles, began behaving eccentrically as rumors of his heavy drug usage abounded. For whatever reason, *Smile* was never issued. *Smiley Smile* was issued in its place on the group's recently formed custom label, Brother Records, distributed by Capitol. The album, produced by "The Beach Boys," contained several songs from the abortive Parks–Wilson collaboration, including the hit "Heroes and Villains."

A fascination with Transcendental Meditation, particularly in the person of Mike Love, culminated in the near disastrous tour with the Maharishi Mahesh Yogi in 1968. *Friends* reflected the group's conversion to TM, with one of its songs naturally being entitled "Transcendental Meditation." *20/20*, The Beach Boys' final album of new material for Capitol, featured a remake of the Phil Spector–Jeff Barry–Ellie Greenwich song "I Can Hear Music," which became a minor hit. The group switched to Warner Brothers/Reprise Records in 1970, re-establishing Brother Records under that company's distributorship. The Beach Boys appeared to be emerging from their doldrums that year with their successful appearance at the Big Sur Folk Festival and the issuance of the underrated *Sunflower* album. However, Brian's recession from the group as songwriter and producer with the *Surf's Up* album and his traumatizing appearance at the Whisky A Go Go in 1971 left the group to its own devices. Bruce Johnston departed the group in 1972 to pursue his own career, and South Africans Ricky Fataar and Blondie Chaplin were added. The shallow *Carl and The Passions—So Tough*, issued alone and coupled with a reissue of *Pet Sounds*, was followed by *Holland*, recorded over the period of a year in Amsterdam. Despite the success of two old *Smile* songs, "Surf's Up" and the hastily completed "Sail On Sailor," The Beach Boys seemed to be fading out again. However, reissues of their early material by Capitol on *Endless Summer* and *Spirit of America* saw yet another revival, both albums being certified gold.

Chaplin and Fataar left the group during 1974, and The Beach Boys again toured successfully in 1975. During 1976 Brian Wilson rejoined the group for *15 Big Ones*, an hour-long television documentary aired by NBC in August, and a three-month concert tour of the United States and Canada. The album, comprised half of new original material and half of remade oldies, saw Brian once again producing though eschewing the production style pioneered on *Pet Sounds*. In late 1975 Barry Manilow scored a top hit with "I Write the Songs," written by Bruce Johnston, who recorded *Going Public* in 1977. That year the group issued *The Beach Boys Love You*, whereas Dennis Wilson recorded *Pacific Ocean Blue* and Mike Love recorded with both Waves and Celebration, the latter featuring jazz artist Charles Lloyd and scoring a major hit the following year with "Almost Summer," from the film of the same name. Yet another Beach Boys TM album, *M.I.U.*, fared poorly in 1978, as did 1979's *L.A. (Light Album)* on their new Caribou label, despite the singing and co-production of Johnston and the inclusion of the moderate hits "Here Comes the Night" and "Good Timin'." After a second solo set from Dennis Wilson, The Beach Boys issued *Keepin' the Summer Alive*, produced by Johnston. The album contained two songs co-written by Carl Wilson and Randy Bachman (including the title song) and Johnston's "Endless Harmony," yet fared little better than *L.A.* In 1981 Carl Wilson, in support of his Caribou debut, became the first Beach Boy to undertake a solo tour, and the group toured and appeared in a television special without him.

THE BEACH BOYS

Surfin' Safari	Capitol	DT–1808 reissued as N–16012 (M)	October '62 December '80	A
Surfin' U.S.A.*	Capitol	SM–1890 reissued as SN– 16015	March '63	A
Shut Down (2 songs)	Capitol	1918	June '63	
Surfer Girl*	Capitol	SM–1981 reissued as SN– 16014	September '63	A
Little Deuce Coupe*	Capitol	SM–1998 reissued as SN– 16013	October '63	A
Shut Down, Volume 2*	Capitol	ST–2027	March '64	

All Summer Long*	Capitol	ST–2110 reissued as SN–16016	July '64	A
Christmas Album	Capitol	ST–2164	October '64	
Concert	Capitol	SM–2198 reissued as SN–16154	October '64	A
Today!	Capitol	DT–2269	February '65	
Summer Days (and Summer Nights)*	Capitol	DT–2354	July '65	
Party!	Capitol	DMAS–2398	November '65	
Pet Sounds	Capitol	DT–2458 reissued as N–16156 (M)	May '66 September '81	A

BRUCE JOHNSTON

Surfin' Round the World	Columbia	CS–8857	October '63	
Surfers Pajama Party	Del Fi	DFST–1228		

THE BEACH BOYS

Smiley Smile	Brother later Capitol	DT–9001 ST–2891 reissued as N–16158 (M)	September '67 May '68	A
Wild Honey	Capitol	ST–2859 reissued as N–16159 (M)	December '67	A
Friends	Capitol	ST–2895 reissued as SN–16157	June '68	A
20/20	Capitol	SKAO–133 reissued as SN–16155	January '69	A
Live In London	Capitol	ST–11584 reissued as SN–12011 reissued as SN–16134	October '76 October '79	A A
Sunflower	Reprise	RS–6382	May '70	
Surf's Up	Reprise	RS–6453	June '71	

Pet Sounds/Carl and The Passions —So Tough	2-Reprise later 2-Brother later 2-Warner Brothers	2MS–2083 (M)	March '72 November '72	
Carl and The Passions—So Tough	Brother	2090	July '72	
Holland	Reprise	MS–2118	December '72	
In Concert *	2-Reprise	2RS–6484	November '73	
15 Big Ones *	Reprise	MS–2251	July '76	
The Beach Boys Love You	Reprise	MSK–2258	April '77	A
M.I.U.	Reprise	2268	September '78	
L.A. (Light Album)	Caribou	PZ–35752	March '79	A
Keepin' the Summer	Caribou	FZ–36283	March '80	

THE BEACH BOYS ANTHOLOGIES AND REISSUES

Best *	Capitol	DT–2545 (E)	July '66	A
Best, Volume 2 *	Capitol	DT–2706 (E)	July '67	A
Deluxe Set	3-Capitol	DTCL– 2813	October '67	
Best, Volume 3	Capitol	SKAO– 2945	July '68	
Stack-O-Tracks	Capitol	DKAO– 2893	June '68	
Close Up	Capitol	SWBB–253	July '69	
Good Vibrations	Capitol	ST–442	February '70	
All Summer Long/ California Girls	2-Capitol	STBB–500	July '70	
California Girls	Capitol	SN–16017		A
Fun, Fun, Fun/ Dance, Dance, Dance	2-Capitol	STBB–701	March '71	
Fun, Fun, Fun	Capitol	SN–16018		A
Dance, Dance, Dance	Capitol	SN–16019		A
Endless Summer *	2–Capitol	SVBB– 11307	June '74	A
Spirit of America *	2–Capitol	SVBB– 11384	April '75	A
Greatest Hits, 1961–1963	ERA	805	November '70	
Best of The Beach Boys	Scepter	CTN– 18004	'72	
Beach Boys	Pickwick	SPC–3221	August '70	
Good Vibrations	Pickwick	SPC–3269	March '71	
Wow! Great Concert	Pickwick	SPC–3309	August '72	
High Water	2-Pickwick	PTP–2059	May '73	
Surfer Girl	Pickwick	SPC–3351	July '73	
Little Deuce Coupe	Pickwick	SPC–3562	December '76	

Pet Sounds	Reprise	2197	May '74	
Wild Honey; 20/20	2-Reprise	2MS–2166	July '74	
Friends/Smiley Smile	2-Reprise	2MS–2167	September '74	
Good Vibrations	Reprise	2223 later 2280	July '75	
Ten Years of Harmony	2–Caribou	Z2X–37445	November '81	A

BRUCE JOHNSTON

| Going Public | Columbia | PC–34459 | May '77 | |

DENNIS WILSON

| Pacific Ocean | Caribou | PZ–34354 | August '77 | A |
| One of Those People | Elektra | 230 | December '79 | A |

WAVES (WITH MIKE LOVE)

| Waves | Polydor | 6107 | August '77 | |

CELEBRATION FEATURING MIKE LOVE

| Celebration | Pacific Arts | 122 | April '79 | |

CARL WILSON

| Carl Wilson | Caribou | JZ–37010 | March '81 | A |

THE BEATLES. The music group that made possible many of the changes within the music scene during the Sixties, The Beatles also helped foster a youth culture based, in large part, on long hair, music, and drugs. Musically, The Beatles will be known as the group that consolidated many of the advances achieved in popular music in the late Fifties. In encompassing so many diversified forms of music (pop love songs, ballads, novelty songs, folk, country-and-western, rhythm-and-blues) within the basic rock-and-roll format, The Beatles revitalized rock-and-roll. Their music exhibited a fresh, clean, exuberant sound, in contrast to the vapid pop ballads and dance songs pervading the music scene in the early Sixties. Initiating an eclecticism that was to become their trademark with *Something New*, The Beatles moreover went beyond the standard three-chord progression, often utilizing diminished, seventh, and ninth chords while devising intriguing melodies and developing interesting vocal harmonies.

Particularly after the *Help* album, songwriters John Lennon and Paul McCartney brought an unprecedented lyric sophistication to rock music, writing songs of a personal and emotionally evocative nature which often contained pointed social commentary. Their frequently philosophical concerns in lyrics widened the intellectual boundaries of rock in a manner rivaled only by Bob Dylan. Beginning with the *Revolver* album, perhaps the most innovative rock album ever made, The Beatles introduced novel instrumental combinations into rock, explored elaborate electronic production techniques under George Martin that were to be exploited by many contemporary and later musicians, and sparked the use of the East Indian sitar in rock music. The *Sgt. Pepper* album, regarded by some as the first fully realized "concept" album and certainly a remarkably unified work, may be the best known rock album of all time; its intricate jacket design also set new standards for the developing field of album artwork.

Within the music industry, The Beatles were the most commercially successful musical phenomenon, whether group or individual, to hit rock music, becoming even bigger than Elvis Presley, eventually selling well over 100 million singles and 100 million albums. Their success turned the industry away from its preoccupation with individual singers performing songs written by professional songwriters toward music groups performing original material. The consistency of The Beatles' musical performances switched the focus of the consuming public's attention from singles to albums and essentially united the hitherto separate concepts of composer and performer. The Beatles' rise enabled dozens of other English musicians to become popular and to express themselves musically, thereby breaking the American stranglehold on British popular music. Perhaps most significantly, the musical and songwriting advances pioneered by The Beatles led critics to view rock music in an unprecedented light, considering it as a valid art form in and of itself, and induced the public to perceive rock music as a total, internally coherent form of conscious experience.

In social terms, The Beatles brought public attention to drugs, Indian music, and Transcendental Meditation. Moreover, they helped promote a growing youth culture and inspired many young people to begin playing music by and for themselves, making music an essential part of their lifestyle.

The evolution of The Beatles began in 1955 when John Lennon (born in Woolton, Liverpool, England, on October 9, 1940) formed a "skiffle" group called The Quarrymen. Lennon met Paul McCartney (born in Allerton, Liverpool, on June 18, 1942) in June 1956, and McCartney subsequently joined the group. George Harrison (born in Wavertree, Liverpool, on February 25, 1943) joined in August 1958, and by 1959 they were down to a trio. The group's name changed several times during that year, eventually becoming The Silver Beatles. In 1960 The Silver Beatles, with Lennon, McCartney, Harrison, Peter Best on drums, and Stu Sutcliffe on guitar, backed singer Tony Sheridan in Hamburg, Germany. Later, recordings done with Sheridan were released as albums. In Hamburg the group completed their musical apprenticeship, playing rigorous nightlong shows to unappreciative audiences; live recordings made at the Star Club were eventually released in 1977. In 1961 Stu Sutcliffe left the group; he died of a brain hemorrhage in Hamburg on April 10, 1962.

The Silver Beatles returned to England and took up residence at The Cavern club in Liverpool starting in February 1961. In late 1961 record shop owner Brian Epstein discovered the group at The Cavern and attempted to secure them a recording contract; they were initially rejected by Decca and then picked up by EMI (British Capitol) in early 1962. In August 1962 Ringo Starr (born Richard Starkey in Dingle, Liverpool, on

July 7, 1940), whom they had met in Hamburg in 1960, quit Rory Storme's Hurricanes and replaced Pete Best on drums. Best later recorded an album for Savage Records and served as "technical advisor" for the 1979 Dick Clark production "The Birth of The Beatles," aired on ABC–TV. In September, with George Martin producing, The Beatles, as they were now known, had their first recording session. In October their first single, "Love Me Do," was issued in Great Britain. Their second single, "Please, Please Me," was released in January 1963, making number one in February. The Beatles' first British album, issued in April, remained number one on the charts for six months.

The members: John Lennon (rhythm guitar, harmonica, piano, vocals), Paul McCartney (bass, piano, banjo, trumpet, vocals), George Harrison (lead guitar, sitar, piano, vocals), and Ringo Starr (drums, vocals). In the United States, the next Beatles' single, "I Want to Hold Your Hand," backed with "I Saw Her Standing There," was released in January 1964, with heavy promotion by Capitol. The song became number one within two weeks, becoming one of the fastest selling singles of the Sixties. The group's first United States tour began in February 1964, with massive media coverage.

The dam burst. Nothing could stop The Beatles, and in their wake followed dozens of British groups. Indeed, Lennon and McCartney provided a number of hit songs to up-and-coming groups, including "Bad to Me" for Billy J. Kramer and The Dakotas and "I Don't Want to See You Again" and "World Without Love" for Peter and Gordon. Lennon and McCartney's "I Wanna Be Your Man" was one of The Rolling Stones' first hit singles.

For many weeks after the release of "I Want to Hold Your Hand," The Beatles dominated the top chart positions with "Can't Buy Me Love," "She Loves You," "Please, Please Me" and "Do You Want to Know a Secret" (both on VeeJay Records), and "Twist and Shout" and "Love Me Do" backed with "P.S. I Love You" (on Tollie Records). In March 1964 the group began work on their first film, *A Hard Day's Night*, and John Lennon published his first book, *In His Own Write*. The film premiered in July, and The Beatles' second U.S. tour began in August. The following February and March, they recorded and filmed their second movie, *Help*, which premiered in late July. In June, Lennon published his second book, *A Spaniard in the Works*. Through mid-1965, The Beatles continued their string of hit singles with " A Hard Day's Night," "And I Love Her," "I'll Cry Instead," Carl Perkins' "Matchbox" backed with "Slow Down," "I Feel Fine" backed with "She's a Woman," "Eight Days a Week," and "Ticket to Ride."

An increasing sophistication in the lyrics of Lennon and McCartney became evident after mid-1965. The words to single releases "Help," "Yesterday," "Nowhere Man," and "Eleanor Rigby," and songs such as "In My Life" (from *Rubber Soul*) possessed a profound emotional intensity not apparent in earlier work. Moreover, George Harrison's songwriting ability was being showcased, with *Revolver* containing three Harrison songs: "Taxman," "Love You To," and "I Want to Tell You." With the single "Rain" (the flip side of "Paperback Writer"), and songs such as "Tomorrow Never Knows" (from *Revolver*), The Beatles began utilizing involved studio production techniques in their recordings. The influence of producer–arranger George Martin became particularly strong between 1966 and 1968. Lyrically, the songs of Lennon and McCartney began a tendency toward the bizarre and surreal, often defying logical explanation. This penchant for the surreal, first evident with "Norwegian Wood" (from *Rubber Soul*), continued with songs such as "Lucy in the Sky with Diamonds" and the quintessential "A Day in the Life" (from *Sgt. Pepper*) and the singles "Strawberry Fields Forever/Penny Lane" and "I Am the Walrus."

Having ceased live performances with their August 1966 U.S. tour (recorded live performances at the Hollywood Bowl in 1964 and 1965 were eventually released in 1977), The Beatles focused their attention on recording, and, later on individual endeavors. *Sgt. Pepper's Lonely Hearts Club Band*, the group's first studio production album, was released in June 1967, with advance sales of one million plus. The record, the music industry's first recognized "concept album," was highly acclaimed by critics and was perhaps the high point of The Beatles' recording career. The album included "With a Little Help from My Friends" (sung by Ringo), Harrison's self-consciously philosophical "Within You, Without You" (Harrison playing sitar), and the quintessential Sixties studio production, "A Day in the Life."

Individual endeavors in 1967 included the solo acting debuts of John Lennon and Ringo Starr in the films *How I Won the War* and *Candy*, respectively. During the year, The Beatles scripted, cast, directed, and edited the made-for-television movie, *Magical Mystery Tour*, a conspicuous failure in its poor editing and photography. The soundtrack album, issued in November, included "The Fool on the Hill," "I Am the Walrus," and "All You Need Is Love." During 1968 Harrison composed, arranged, and recorded his own music for the soundtrack to the film *Wonderwall*. Lennon, now with Yoko Ono, recorded with her the controversial *Two Virgins* album. In April The Beatles formed their own record company, Apple; the double-record set entitled *The Beatles*, released in November, was the first album on the new label. Disjointed and showing the tell-tale signs of a Lennon–McCartney rift, the album contained such diverse songs as "Back in the U.S.S.R.," "Blackbird," "Revolution #1," and Harrison's superlative "While My Guitar Gently Weeps" (recorded, without credit, with Eric Clapton). "Hey Jude," issued in August, was the first single on the Apple label. In July 1968 the animated film *Yellow Submarine* premiered. This film was probably the most artistically and critically successful movie with which The Beatles were associated. Furthermore, it was one of the best "psychedelic" movies to come out in the late Sixties. The soundtrack album, released the following January, included the title song and "All You Need Is Love" again.

During most of 1969, the individual Beatles worked apart. Ringo appeared in the movie *The Magic Christian*. The soundtrack included a solo McCartney composition, "Come and Get It," performed by Badfinger. In March John Lennon married Yoko Ono and Paul McCartney married Linda Eastman. These marriages seemed to mark the informal end of The

Beatles. John Lennon became the first Beatle to perform publicly outside the group, in September in Toronto with The Plastic Ono Band. The only Beatle album release of 1969, *Abbey Road*, came out in November and included Harrison's "Something" and "Here Comes the Sun," Ringo's "Octopus' Garden," and "She Came In through the Bathroom Window." The *Abbey Road* album was actually the final Beatles recording. *Let It Be*, produced initially by George Martin and later reworked by Phil Spector and eventually issued in May 1970, was held up by re-mixing disputes and film editing problems. *Hey Jude* assembled single releases not previously contained on any American album ("Rain," "Lady Madonna," "Paperback Writer," "Hey Jude," and others). The film *Let It Be* premiered in May, and the soundtrack album included the title song, "Get Back," and "The Long and Winding Road," The Beatles' final single release. By the end of 1970, all four of The Beatles had issued solo recordings. In early 1971, Paul McCartney sued for dissolution of The Beatles' partnership, which legally ended on December 30, 1974. Subsequent Beatles album releases were four double-record anthology sets, the aforementioned *Live at the Hollywood Bowl* and *Live at the Star Club*, and 1980's collection, *Rarities*. Throughout the Seventies, rumors persisted that The Beatles would reunite for recordings or performances at the behest of some ambitious promoter, but such speculation was finally and tragically halted with the murder of John Lennon in New York City on December 8, 1980. The remaining three, plus Linda McCartney, did jointly record the 1981 tribute to Lennon, "All Those Years Ago," written by George Harrison.

EARLY BEATLES RECORDINGS

The Beatles with Tony Sheridan and Their Guests (4 songs)	MGM	SE–4215	February '64	
reissued as This Is Where It Started	Metro	MS–563	April '66	
Live at the Star Club	2-Lingasong	2–7001	June '77	
In the Beginning	Polydor	244504	May '70	
Introducing . . . The Beatles	VeeJay	VJLP–1062	January '64	
Jolly What! The Beatles and Frank Ifield	VeeJay	VJLP–1085	February '64	
Songs, Pictures and Stories of The Fabulous Beatles	VeeJay	VJLP–1092	October '64	
The Beatles vs. The Four Seasons	2-VeeJay	VJDX–30	October '64	
Ain't She Sweet	Atco	SD33–169	October '64	
The Early Beatles*	Capitol/Apple	ST–2309	March '65	A

PETE BEST

Best of The Beatles	Savage	71(M)	July '66

THE BEATLES

Meet The Beatles! *	Capitol/Apple	ST–2047	January '64	A
The Beatles' Second Album *	Capitol/Apple	ST–2080	April '64	A
A Hard Day's Night (soundtrack)	United Artists reissued on Capitol	UAS–6366 SW–11921	June '64 May '79	A A
Something New *	Capitol/Apple	ST–2108	July '64	A
The Beatles' Story *	2-Capitol/ Apple	STBO– 2222	November '64	A
Beatles '65 *	Capitol/Apple	ST–2228	December '64	A
Beatles VI *	Capitol/Apple	ST–2358	June '65	A
Help! (soundtrack) *	Capitol/Apple	SMAS– 2386	August '65	A
Rubber Soul *	Capitol/Apple	SW–2442	December '65	A
Yesterday . . . and Today *	Capitol/Apple	ST–2553	June '66	A
Revolver *	Capitol/Apple	SW–2576	August '66	A
Live at the Hollywood Bowl **	Capitol	SMAS– 11638	May '77	A
Sgt. Pepper's Lonely Hearts Club Band *	Capitol/Apple	SMAS– 2653	June '67	A
Magical Mystery Tour *	Capitol/Apple	SMAL– 2835	November '67	A
The Beatles *	2-Apple/ Capitol	SWBO– 101	November '68	A
Yellow Submarine (soundtrack) *	Apple/Capitol	SW–153	January '69	A
Abbey Road *	Apple/Capitol	SO–383	October '69	A
Hey Jude *	Apple/Capitol	SW–385	February '70	A
Let It Be *	Apple reissued on Capitol	ARS–34001 SW–11922	May '70 May '79	A A
1962–1966 *	2-Apple/ Capitol	SKBO– 3403	April '73	A
1967–1970 *	2-Apple/ Capitol	SKBO– 3404	April '73	A
Rock 'n' Roll Music **	2-Capitol	SKBO– 11537	June '76	
Rock 'n' Roll Music, Volume 1	Capitol	SN–16020		A
Rock 'n' Roll Music, Volume 2	Capitol	SN–16021		A
Love Songs *	2-Capitol	SKBL– 11711	October '77	A
Rarities	Capitol	SHAL– 12060	April '80	A

JEFF BECK. British lead guitarist extraordinaire, Jeff Beck is one of rock music's most outstanding, intelligent, and innovative guitarists. One of the first electric guitarists to utilize a fuzztone device, make extensive use of feedback while playing, and introduce both modal and East Indian tonalities into rock (with The Yardbirds), Beck also has the dubious distinction of being one of the first rock musicians to destroy equipment on stage. Beck is also known for introducing vocalist Rod Stewart to American audiences with his first Jeff Beck Group. Moreover, with his *Blow by Blow* album (and those subsequent), Jeff Beck helped redefine and revitalize the more challenging and ambitious sound of so-called "fusion music," a Seventies phenomenon not strictly classifiable as jazz or rock but containing elements of both.

Replacing Eric Clapton in The Yardbirds during the spring of 1965, Jeff Beck (born in Surrey, England, on June 24, 1944) played lead guitar with the group through its greatest hit-making period ("I'm a Man," "Heartful of Soul," "Over Under Sideways Down," and others). Leaving The Yardbirds in December 1966, he formed the first of several Jeff Beck Groups in late 1967. The members: Beck, Rod Stewart (vocals), Ron Wood (bass, harmonica), and Micky Waller (drums). The group proved enormously successful with its blues-oriented material during its May 1968 tour of the United States. That tour introduced American audiences to Rod Stewart, who had been singing almost anonymously with various blues aggregations in Britain for years. The group expanded in October 1968 with the addition of sessions keyboardist Nicky Hopkins. However, in early 1969, Beck fired Wood and Waller when on the verge of an American tour that was later cancelled. Following a second outstanding album, *Beck-ola*, the group fragmented, with Stewart and Wood joining The Faces and Hopkins moving to California to join Quicksilver Messenger Service.

Attempts to form a new band with Tim Bogert and Carmine Appice of Vanilla Fudge failed, and a subsequent car crash left Beck out of commission for 18 months. He re-emerged in late 1971 with his second Jeff Beck Group, with Bob Tench (vocals), Max Middleton (piano), Clive Chaman (bass), and Cozy Powell (drums). Recording two undistinguished albums, this second Jeff Beck Group disbanded during 1972. With the demise of their second-generation band, Cactus, Carmine Appice (drums) and Tim Bogert (bass) joined Beck for the short-lived Beck/Bogert/Appice aggregation.

After a two-year layoff, Jeff Beck returned to the music scene with 1975's *Blow by Blow* album, a surprising yet intriguing change of musical direction for Beck. Made with former Beatles' producer George Martin, the all-instrumental album had a distinctive jazz (and occasionally disco) flavor, and, curiously, was certified gold-award the year of its release. *Wired*, recorded with Czech jazz keyboard wizard Jan Hammer, similarly went gold-award in 1976. Subsequently Beck toured with Hammer, releasing a live set from the tour in 1977. Indulging in another "sabbatical" from music for three years, Jeff Beck re-emerged in 1980 with a new band, a new album, and another round of touring as an all-instrumental unit.

JEFF BECK

| Early Anthology | Accord | SN–7141 | December '81 | A |

THE JEFF BECK GROUP

Truth	Epic	PE–26413	August '68	A
Beck-ola	Epic	BXN–26478	June '69	A
Truth/Beck-ola	2-Epic	BG–33779	October '75	A
Rough and Ready	Epic	PE–30973	October '71	A
Jeff Beck Group	Epic	PE–31331	April '72	A

BECK, BOGERT, AND APPICE

Beck, Bogert and Appice	Epic	PE–32140	March '73	A

JEFF BECK

Blow by Blow *	Epic	PE–33409	March '75	A
Wired *	Epic	PE–33849	June '76	A

JEFF BECK AND JAN HAMMER

Live	Epic	PE–34433	March '77	A

JEFF BECK

There and Back	Epic	FE–35684	July '80	A

THE BEE GEES. Perhaps the most popular rock group of the mid- to late Seventies, the three brothers Gibb were one of the first rock groups to tour with a full orchestra (in 1968). Sustaining their early career with surreal ballads featuring strong melodies and thick harmonies, as exemplified by "Massachusetts" and "I Started a Joke," The Bee Gees survived a bitter mid-career crisis to become international stars on the basis of their own near-formulaic disco-style songs, beginning with 1975's "Jive Talkin'." The *Saturday Night Fever* soundtrack album, most of it written and much of it performed by the brothers, appears destined to become the best selling album in music history. Buoyed by his siblings' enormous popularity, younger brother Andy Gibb launched his own successful recording/performing career in 1977. In 1980 Barry Gibb bolstered Barbra Streisand's career by producing and writing songs for her top hit album, *Guilty*.

Barry Gibb and twin brothers Robin and Maurice were born in Douglas on the Isle of Man, England, on September 1, 1946, and December 22, 1949, respectively. They began their professional careers in the mid-Fifties in Manchester, England, when Barry was nine and twins Maurice and Robin seven; they subsequently emigrated with their family to Australia in 1958. After becoming radio and television stars, The Bee Gees, as they were now called, were signed to Australia's Festival Records in August 1962. On the strength of their first number one Australian single, "Spicks and Specks," the group returned to England in February 1967, quickly signing with Robert Stigwood. Within two months, the haunting "New York Mining Disaster 1941," composed by Barry and Robin, had become a hit. It was typical of The Bee Gee's hits over the next two years: a maudlin ballad possessing a strong melody, written and produced by the brothers, and characterized by Robin's vocal quaver, wispy nasal harmonies, and lush, almost heavy-handed orchestral arrangements. With Barry playing rhythm guitar and Robin playing bass, subsequent hits included "To Love Somebody," "Holiday," "Massachusetts," "I've Gotta Get a Message to You," and perhaps their two finest compositions, "Words" and "I Started a Joke." Their 1968 English tour created a rock music milestone as The Bee Gees performed with a full orchestra.

The Bee Gee's popularity, however, seemed to falter somewhat in 1969 as their ambitious concept album, *Odessa*, was issued virtually unnoticed. Former accompanists Vince Melouney (guitar) and Colin Peterson (drums) had departed in 1968 and August 1969, respectively. In March 1969 Robin had announced his intention to leave the group; he subsequently recorded *Robin's Reign*, while Barry and Maurice recorded *Cucumber Castle*. Reuniting in August 1970, The Bee Gees hit the comeback trail with the smash hits "Lonely Days" and "How Can You Mend a Broken Heart." However, the years 1972 through 1974 were dismal ones for the Gibbs, so they enlisted veteran producer Arif Mardin for another album of typical ballads, *Mr. Natural*.

Mardin's second (and last) production for The Bee Gees put the group back on track. *Main Course* included two disco-styled smash hits, "Jive Talkin'" and "Nights on Broadway," and established the pattern to be followed by the brothers and two new producers. The group hit consistently throughout the late Seventies with songs such as "You Should Be Dancing" and "Love So Right" from *Children of the World*, a platinum-award album the year of its release. The group's first live album similarly was certified platinum-award in 1977, during which younger brother Andy (born in Manchester, England, on March 5, 1958) scored top hits with Barry's "I Just Want To Be Your Everything" and "(Love Is) Thicker than Water." Massive success came to The Bee Gees with the *Saturday Night Fever* soundtrack. Almost entirely composed by the brothers Gibb, the album included three top hits by The Bee Gees, "How Deep Is Your Love," "Stayin' Alive," and "Night Fever," as well as the hit "If I Can't Have You," performed by Yvonne Elliman and written and produced by the brothers. During 1978, The Bee Gees co-starred with Peter Frampton and sang five songs in the contrived fairytale-like *Sgt. Pepper's Lonely Hearts Club Band* movie. In the meantime, they wrote smash hit songs for Samantha Sang ("Emotion"), Frankie Valli (the title song to the movie *Grease*), and brother Andy ("Shadow Dancing"). In early 1979, The Bee Gees, in conjunction with mentor Robert Stigwood and co-producer/host David Frost, staged a UNICEF (United Nations International Children's Economic Fund) benefit at the U.N., televised by NBC, with all revenues in excess of expenses going to UNICEF. The total revenues may eventually exceed $50 million. Subsequently, The Bee Gees issued yet another hit album *(Spirits Having Flown)* and three more top hit singles ("Too Much Heaven," "Tragedy," and "Love You Inside Out"), while brother Andy hit with "An Everlasting Love" and "(Our Love) Don't Throw It All Away." During 1980, Andy Gibb scored major hits with "Desire," "I Can't Help

It" (in duet with Olivia Newton-John), and "Time Is Time." Barry Gibb produced and wrote the songs for Barbra Streisand's *Guilty* album, which yielded the top hit "Woman in Love" and the smash hit title song duet by Barry and Ms. Streisand. Embroiled in on-again, off-again legal disputes with Robert Stigwood and RSO Records since late 1980, The Bee Gees eventually issued *Livin' Eyes* in 1982, and Andy Gibb was announced as the replacement for Dionne Warwick as the host for the popular syndicated television music show "Solid Gold."

THE BEE GEES

First	Atco	SD33–223	August '67	
Horizontal	Atco	SD33–233	January '68	
Idea	Atco	SD33–253	August '68	
Rare, Precious, and Beautiful	Atco	SD33–264	November '68	
Best*	Atco reissued on	SD33–292	July '69	
	RSO	874		
Odessa	2–Atco	2–702	February '69	
Odessa (condensed)	RSO	3007	December '76	A
Rare, Precious, and Beautiful— Volume 2	Atco	SD33–321	March '70	

ROBIN GIBB

Robin's Reign	Atco	SD33–323	May '70	

THE BEE GEES

Cucumber Castle	Atco	SD33–327	April '70	
Two Years On	Atco	SD33–353	December '70	
Melody (soundtrack)	Atco	33–363	June '71	
Trafalgar	Atco	SD–7003	August '71	
To Whom It May Concern	Atco	SD–7012	October '72	
Life in a Tin Can	RSO	SO–870	February '73	
Best, Volume 2	RSO	SO–875	August '73	
Mister Natural	RSO	SO–4800	May '74	
Main Course*	RSO	SO–4807 later 3024	May '75 June '77	A
Children of the World**	RSO	3003	September '76	A
Gold, Volume 1*	RSO	RS–1–3006	November '76	A
Here at Last . . . Live**	2-RSO	RS–2–3901	May '77	A
Saturday Night Fever (soundtrack)**	RSO	4001	November '77	A
Sgt. Pepper's Lonely Heart's Club Band (soundtrack)**	2-RSO	4100	July '78	
Spirits Having Flown**	RSO	RS–1–3041	January '79	A

| Greatest Hits** | 2–RSO | RS2–4200 | November '79 | A |
| Livin' Eyes | RSO | 3098 | January '82 | A |

ANDY GIBB

Flowing Rivers**	RSO	RS–1–3019	June '77	
Shadow Dancing**	RSO	RS–1–3034	May '78	
After Dark*	RSO	3069	February '80	A
Greatest Hits	RSO	3091	December '80	

CHUCK BERRY. Certainly the single most influential and important black person in the history of rock-and-roll, Chuck Berry is arguably the single most important figure, regardless of race, in the entire history of rock. As the first major rock artist to write virtually all his own songs, Berry provided songs that were aggressive, exuberant, and wry (in contrast to the vapid fluff popular in the mid- to late Fifties), reflecting the romance between rock-and-roll and the youth culture and its concerns (school, cars, girls, dancing). He is often cited as rock's first folk poet. With his lyrics, music, and uncommonly clear diction, Berry became the first black artist to gain mass popularity with young white audiences. Moreover, his innovative use of boogie-woogie and shuffle rhythms in his guitar playing and his distinctive off-time, double-note lead playing and alternating chord changes set the standard for rock guitar and did much to popularize the electric guitar. Despite his own personal penchant for the blues, Chuck Berry's primary influence comes through his up-tempo rock songs. The Beatles, The Rolling Stones, The Kinks, and other English groups recorded his songs during their early careers, and The Beach Boys' "Surfin' U.S.A." is an obvious reworking of "Sweet Little Sixteen." Bob Dylan's first rock hit, "Subterranean Homesick Blues," bears a remarkable resemblance to Berry's "Too Much Monkey Business," whereas many later groups such as Creedence Clearwater Revival and The Electric Light Orchestra, to name just two, continue to cover his material.

Born in St. Louis, Missouri, on October 18, 1926, Charles "Chuck" Berry began singing in a local church choir at age six, later taking up guitar while in high school and forming his first group in 1952. In early 1955, he traveled to Chicago and played with blues great Muddy Waters, who recommended he contact Leonard Chess of Chess Records. Signed immediately after the presentation of his first demonstration record, Berry's first single, "Maybelline," ostensibly co-authored by disc jockey Alan Freed, became a huge hit, one of rock-and-roll's first. Excelling in performance, his now-signature "duck walk" was fortuitously introduced into his act in New York in 1956. Hits continued through 1959, with "Roll Over, Beethoven," "School Days," "Rock and Roll Music," "Sweet Little Sixteen," and the biographical "Johnny B. Goode."

Unfortunately, in late 1959 Chuck Berry was busted for violation of The Mann Act, and, after a much-sensationalized trial, entered federal prison in February 1962. Released in 1963, he came back with "Nadine," "No Particular Place to Go," and "You Never Can Tell." His minor hit from late 1964, "Promised Land," has been recorded by a wealth of artists, including Elvis Presley. After moving to Mercury Records in 1966, Berry weathered a dismal period before returning to Chess in 1969. More in a blues vein, *Back Home*, *San Francisco Dues*, and *Bio* for Chess are considered among Berry's finest albums. His first certified gold-award single came in 1972 with the childishly risque "My Ding-a-Ling" from *The London Chuck Berry Sessions*, his only non-anthology gold-award album. Imprisoned for four months during 1979 on income tax evasion charges, Chuck Berry re-emerged with a new round of touring and his first album of new material in four years, *Rockit*.

CHUCK BERRY

After School Sessions	Chess	LP–1426 (M)	September '58
		later 1426 (E)	November '72
One Dozen Berrys	Chess	LP–1432 (M)	September '58
		later 1432 (E)	
Chuck Berry Is on Top	Chess	LP–1435 (M)	
		later 1435 (E)	November '72
Rockin' at the Hops	Chess	LP–1448 (M)	
New Juke Box Hits	Chess	LP–1456 (M)	
More Chuck Berry	Chess	1465(M)	
		later 1465 (E)	November '72
Chuck Berry on Stage	Chess	LP–1480 (M)	September '63
		later 1480 (E)	November '72
St. Louis to Liverpool	Chess	LP–1488	December '64
Chuck Berry in London	Chess	LP–1495	June '65
Fresh Berrys	Chess	LPS–1498	

CHUCK BERRY AND HOWLIN' WOLF

Pop Origins	Chess	1544(M)	

CHUCK BERRY AND BO DIDDLEY

Two Great Guitars	Checker	2991(M)	August '64
		later 2991 (E)	November '72

CHUCK BERRY

In Memphis	Mercury	61123	September '67
Live at The Fillmore	Mercury	SR–61138	October '67

From St. Louis to Frisco	Mercury	SR–61176	October '68	
Concerto in B. Goode	Mercury	SR–61223	July '69	
St. Louis to Frisco to Memphis	2-Mercury	SRM2–6501	November '72	
Back Home	Chess	1550	November '70	
San Francisco Dues	Chess	CH–50008	September '71	
The London Chuck Berry Sessions*	Chess	CH–60020	May '72	
Bio	Chess	CH–50043	August '73	
Chuck Berry	Chess	CH–60032	February '75	A
Rockit	Atco	SD38–118	August '79	A

CHUCK BERRY ANTHOLOGIES AND COMPILATIONS

Greatest Hits	Chess	1485(M)	May '64	
		later 1485 (E)	November '72	
Golden Decade	2-Chess	1514	March '67	
Golden Decade, Volume 2	2-Chess	2CH–60023	February '73	
Golden Decade, Volume 3	2-Chess	2CH–60028	April '74	
Golden Hits	Mercury	SR–61103	March '67	A
Flashback	Pickwick	2061		A
Johnny B. Goode	Pickwick	3327		
Sweet Little Rock and Roller	Pickwick	3345		
Wild Berrys	Pickwick	3392		
Greatest Hits	Archive of Folk and Jazz Music	321	October '76	A
Best	Gusto	0004(M)	August '78	A

BLOOD, SWEAT AND TEARS. The first major rock group success-fully to augment its sound with horns, Blood, Sweat and Tears displayed an early amalgamation of jazz and rock elements. Inadvertently, Blood, Sweat and Tears encouraged the independent development of so-called "fusion music," a form successfully pursued by Miles Davis, Herbie Hancock, and Weather Report in the late Sixties. After the departure of Al Kooper, Blood, Sweat and Tears evolved into an enormously popular, highly arranged, pop vocal–dominated band that set the standard for the blending together of rock, pop, and quasi-jazz music.

Blood, Sweat and Tears was formed by Al Kooper (born February 5, 1944, in Brooklyn, New York), Steve Katz (also born in Brooklyn, on May 9, 1945), and Bobby Colomby (born in New York City on December 20, 1944) following Katz and Kooper's departure from The Blues Project in 1967. With these founders recruiting additional personnel, the initial lineup was: Al Kooper (keyboards, vocals), Steve Katz (guitar, vocals), Bobby Colomby (drums, vocals), Jim Fielder (bass), Jerry Weiss and Randy Brecker (trumpets, flügelhorns), Fred Lipsius (alto saxophone, piano), and Dick Halligan (trombone, flute, keyboards). Though their first album, *Child Is Father to the Man*, was certified gold-award in 1969, no hit singles emerged from it. Nonetheless, the album contained a number of excellent Al Kooper compositions ("I Love You More than You'll Ever Know," "My Days Are Numbered," and "I Can't Quit Her") as well as early versions of Harry Nilsson's "Without Her" and Randy Newman's "Just One Smile."

In mid-1968, Kooper left Blood, Sweat and Tears to accept a lucrative offer from Columbia Records to become a producer. Weiss and Brecker also left, being replaced by Lew Soloff and Chuck Winfield (trumpets, flügelhorns) and Jerry Hyman (trombone, recorder). The lead vocalist role was taken over by Canadian singer David Clayton-Thomas (born September 13, 1941) for three gold-award albums. Clayton-Thomas had worked around Toronto for ten years, recording five Canadian gold-award records with The Bossmen. The new alignment's first album exploded onto the music scene in early 1969. As well as including Steve Katz' beautiful "Sometimes in Winter" and a remake of Billie Holiday's "God Bless the Child," the album yielded *three* smash hit singles: Laura Nyro's "And When I Die" and Clayton-Thomas' "Spinning Wheel" and "You've Made Me So Very Happy." The next album contained two hit singles, "Hi-De-Ho" and "Lucretia MacEvil," in addition to the elaborately arranged "Symphony/Sympathy for the Devil" and "40,000 Headmen." The group's follow-up album, their final gold-award album of new material, included only one moderate hit, "Go Down Gamblin'."

A series of desertions soon struck Blood, Sweat and Tears, effectively crippling the group. Clayton-Thomas departed in late 1971 to pursue an undistinguished solo career. Lipsius and Halligan also left, followed by Katz and Winfield in 1973. Using a succession of lead vocalists—Bobby Doyle, Jerry Fisher, and Jerry La Croix—the band added Larry Willis (keyboards), George Wadenius (guitar), Lou Marini, Jr. (saxophones), and later, Tom Malone (trumpet, flügelhorn, saxophones). Again appearing with Blood, Sweat and Tears at Mister Kelly's in Chicago in late 1974, David Clayton-Thomas subsequently rejoined the group. By then, only Bobby Colomby remained from the original group. Personnel shifts continued to plague Blood, Sweat and Tears, and, on January 31, 1978, one-year member Gregory Herbert was found dead in an Amsterdam hotel room during the group's European tour. By 1978, Blood, Sweat and Tears had switched to ABC Records for *Brand New Day*, and Clayton-Thomas also recorded a solo album for ABC before year's end. By 1980, David Clayton-Thomas was the only "original" member left in the group.

BLOOD, SWEAT AND TEARS

Child Is Father to the Man *	Columbia	PC–9619	March '68	A
Blood, Sweat and Tears *	Columbia	PC–9720	January '69	A
3 *	Columbia	KC–30090	July '70	
4 *	Columbia	KC–30590	June '71	
Greatest Hits *	Columbia	PC–31170	March '72	A

DAVID CLAYTON-THOMAS/LINDA RONSTADT

Back on the Street Again	Pickwick	SPC-3245

DAVID CLAYTON-THOMAS

I Got a Woman	Decca	75146	September '69
Magnificent Sanctuary Band	Columbia	KC-31000	April '72
Tequila Sunrise	Columbia	KC-31700	September '72
Harmony Junction	RCA	APL1-0173	September '73

BLOOD, SWEAT AND TEARS
(WITHOUT DAVID CLAYTON-THOMAS)

New Blood	Columbia	KC-31780	October '72	
No Sweat	Columbia	C-32180	August '73	A
Mirror Image	Columbia	KC-32929	August '74	

BLOOD, SWEAT AND TEARS (AGAIN WITH DAVID CLAYTON-THOMAS)

New City	Columbia	PC-33484	April '75	
More Than Ever	Columbia	PC-34233	June '76	
Brand New Day	ABC	1015	January '78	
Blood, Sweat and Tears	MCA	3227	May '80	A

DAVID CLAYTON-THOMAS

Clayton	ABC/MCA	AA-1104	October '78	A

MIKE BLOOMFIELD. One of the first white musicians to achieve popular acclaim as a blues guitarist, Mike Bloomfield was in the forefront of the late Sixties blues revival with The Paul Butterfield Blues Band and The Electric Flag before recording with Al Kooper (including the *Super Session* album that inaugurated the concept of the "supergroup") and pursuing a variety of independent musical projects.

BLOOMFIELD, KOOPER, AND STILLS

Super Session *	Columbia	PC-9701	August '68	A

MIKE BLOOMFIELD AND AL KOOPER

Live Adventures of Mike Bloomfield and Al Kooper	2-Columbia	PG-6	February '69

MIKE BLOOMFIELD

It's Not Killing Me	Columbia	CS-9883	September '69
	later Harmony	KH-30395	March '71

MIKE BLOOMFIELD, JOHN PAUL HAMMOND, AND DR. JOHN

Triumvirate	Columbia	KC–32172	May '73

MIKE BLOOMFIELD

Try It Before You Buy It	Columbia	PC–33173	May '75

MIKE BLOOMFIELD WITH KGB

KGB	MCA	2166	February '76

MIKE BLOOMFIELD

If You Love These Blues, Play 'em as You Please	Guitar Player	3002	February '77	A
Analine	Takoma	7059	October '77	A
Michael Bloomfield	Takoma	7063	July '78	A
Between the Hard Place and the Ground	Takoma	7070	December '79	A
Cruisin' for a Bruisin'	Takoma	7091	March '81	A
Count Talent and The Originals	Clouds	8805	May '78	A
Living in the Fast Lane	Waterhouse	11	March '81	A

MIKE BLOOMFIELD AND WOODY HARRIS

Gospel Duets	Kicking Mule	164	January '80	A

BLUE OYSTER CULT. Considered by some as America's foremost exponent of so-called "heavy metal music," Blue Oyster Cult combines a deafening, if frequently melodic, double-guitar attack with lyrics usually preoccupied with destruction, sado-masochism, and, on the lighter side, astronomy.

BLUE OYSTER CULT

Blue Oyster Cult	Columbia	PC–31063	February '72	A
Tyranny and Mutation	Columbia	PC–32017	February '73	A
Secret Treaties	Columbia	PC–32858	April '74	A
On Your Feet or on Your Knees*	2-Columbia	KG–33371	March '75	A
Agents of Fortune**	Columbia	PC–34164	June '76	A
Spectres*	Columbia	JC–35019	October '77	A
Some Enchanted Evening*	Columbia	PC–35563	September '78	A
Mirrors	Columbia	JC–36009	July '79	A

Cultosaurus Erectus	Columbia	JC–36550	July '80	A
Fire of Unknown Origin	Columbia	FC–37389	July '81	A

THE BLUES PROJECT. Perhaps the first band to bring electricity to both the blues and folk music, The Blues Project achieved both underground success and an above-ground reputation despite never having a hit single. Lasting less than three years, The Blues Project reunited in the early Seventies; former member Andy Kulberg formed Seatrain, one of the first rock bands to inject country-style music into rock.

THE BLUES PROJECT

"Live" at the Cafe Au Go Go	Verve/ Folkways	FTS–3000	April '66	
Projections	Verve/ Folkways	FTS–3008	December '66	
"Live" at Town Hall	Verve/ Forecast	FTS–3025	August '67	
Planned Obsolescence	Verve/ Forecast	FTS–3046	December '68	
Kooper, Blumenfeld, Kalb, Flanders, Katz, Kulberg of The Blues Project	Verve/ Forecast	FTS–3069	April '69	
The Best of the Blues Project	Verve/ Forecast	FTS–3077	July '69	
The Blues Project	MGM	GAS–118	October '70	
Archetypes	MGM	4953	August '74	

DANNY KALB AND STEFAN GROSSMAN

Crosscurrents	Cotillion	SD–9007	June '69

SEATRAIN

Seatrain	A&M	SP–4171	May '69	
Seatrain	Capitol	ST–659	January '71	A
Marblehead Messenger	Capitol	SMAS–829	October '71	A
Watch	Warner Brothers	2692	March '73	

THE BLUES PROJECT

Lazarus	Capitol	ST–782	September '71	
The Blues Project	Capitol	SMAS– 11017	June '72	
Reunion at Central Park	2-MCA	2–8003	October '73	A

THE BONZO DOG BAND. One of the first groups to explore the visual, the theatrical, and the humorous within the rock format, The Bonzo Dog Band parodied everything from Fifties rock-and-roll to the English music hall tradition while satirizing many aspects of contemporary life.

THE BONZO DOG DOODAH BAND

| Gorilla | Imperial | 12370 | March '68 | |

THE BONZO DOG BAND

Urban Spaceman	Imperial	12432	June '69	
Tadpoles	Imperial	12445	November '69	
Keynsham	Imperial	12457	August '70	
The Beast of The Bonzoes	United Artists	UAS–5517	August '71	A
Let's Make Up and Be Friendly	United Artists	UAS–5584	May '72	
The History of The Bonzo Dog Band	2-United Artists	LA321	September '74	A

ROGER RUSKIN SPEAR

| Electric Shocks | United Artists | LA097 | '72 | |

GRIMMS ROCKIN' DUCK (WITH NEIL INNES)

| Grimms Rockin' Duck | Antilles | AN–7012 | May '76 | |

NEIL INNES AND ERIC IDLE

| Rutland Weekend Songbook | Passport | PPSD–98018 | October '76 | |

NEIL INNES, ERIC IDLE, AND OTHERS

| The Rutles | Warner Brothers | HS–3151 | March '78 | |

BOOKER T. AND THE MGS. Perhaps the last rock group to issue completely instrumental hit records (a trend sorely missing in the Seventies), Booker T. and The MGs are probably best remembered for their creation of the so-called "Memphis sound" featured on most of the Stax-Volt Records hit releases of the Sixties. Featuring a cohesive yet spare instrumental sound, the group also produced a number of memorable hits in their own right, including their debut "Green Onions" and 1969's "Time Is Tight."

In 1962 Booker T. and The MGs (for *Memphis Group*) formed as the "house band" for Memphis' Stax Records. The members: keyboardist–multi-instrumentalist Booker T. Jones (born November 12, 1944, in Memphis), lead and rhythm guitarist Steve Cropper (born October 21, 1941, in Willow Springs, Missouri), drummer Al Jackson, Jr. (born November 27, 1935, in Memphis), and, later, bassist Donald "Duck" Dunn (born November 24, 1941, in Memphis). Dunn and Cropper had been members of The Mar-Keys since the late Fifties, and had both played on the group's 1961 hit single, "Last Night." Dunn continued with The Mar-Keys until 1964 while also playing as part of The MGs. In the early Sixties Booker T. and The MGs provided the instrumental backing for hits by Carla Thomas ("Gee Whiz") and her father Rufus Thomas ("Walking the Dog"). Their reputation as a band in their own right was established in 1962 with the smash hit instrumental, "Green Onions." Over the next seven years, the group continued to back various Stax artists and record independently while individual members pursued a variety of solo projects. Jones worked with artist–producer William Bell during 1965, co-authoring the oft-recorded "Born under a Bad Sign" with him. In 1966 Booker T. received his degree in applied music from the University of Indiana. In the mean-time, Steve Cropper supervised the recordings of Otis Redding and co-wrote hits by Wilson Pickett ("In the Midnight Hour"), Eddie Floyd ("Knock on Wood"), and, later, Redding ("Dock of the Bay"). Al Jackson also produced recordings by blues guitarist Albert King. Booker T. and The MGs served as the backing band for the above-mentioned hits as well as for Sam and Dave's two biggest hits, "Hold On! I'm Comin'" and "Soul Man." Successes on their own included the major hits "Groovin'" (1967) and "Soul Limbo" (1968) and the near-smashes "Hang 'em High" (1968) and "Time Is Tight" (1969), the last from the soundtrack to *Uptight*, scored by Booker T. Jones. In 1969 Steve Cropper recorded a solo album in addition to a "jam" album with Albert King and "Pop" Staples.

By 1970 Booker T. and The MGs had abandoned their position as Stax house band, disbanding officially in 1972. Jones moved to California, join-ing A&M Records as a staff producer. There he supervised recording ses-sions for Rita Coolidge, his wife Priscilla (Rita's sister), and Bill Withers (*Just as I Am*). During the early Seventies, Booker T. recorded three albums in collaboration with Priscilla before recording *Evergreen* solo in 1974. In the meantime, Cropper continued with sessions and production chores until moving to Los Angeles in 1975 following the demise of Stax/Volt Records. Dunn and Jackson had earlier recorded an album as The MGs with two other musicians.

The original members of Booker T. and The MGs were planning a reunion when Al Jackson was shot to death in Memphis on October 1, 1975. Subsequently the band did reunite, with Willie Hall succeeding Jackson on drums, for *Universal Language*. Booker T. again recorded solo, and he, Cropper, and Dunn recorded with others as The RCO All Stars behind The Band's Levon Helm. More recently, Cropper and Dunn have recreated their distinctive Sixties sound behind the Blues Brothers on tours and albums, as well as in the popular *Blues Brothers* movie of 1980. Booker T. Jones produced Willie Nelson's 1978 album *Stardust* and recently recorded *The Best of You* and *Booker T. Jones* for A&M Records, whereas

Steve Cropper issued *Playin' My Thang,* his second solo album, on MCA in 1981.

BOOKER T. AND THE MGS

Green Onions	Stax	701(M)	November '62	
	later Atlantic	7701		
Soul Dressing	Stax	705	April '65	
	later Atlantic	7705		
And Now!	Stax	711	January '67	
	later Atlantic	7711		
In the Christmas	Stax	713		
Spirit	later Atlantic	7713	December '69	
Hip Hug-Her	Stax	717	May '67	
	later Atlantic	7717		
Back to Back (with	Stax	720		
The Mar-Keys)	later Atlantic	7720		
Doin' Our Thing	Stax	724	April '68	
	later Atlantic	7724		
Soul Limbo	Stax	STS-2001	August '68	
		reissued as		
		4113	October '78	A
Uptight	Stax	STS-2006	February '69	
(soundtrack)				
Set	Stax	STS-2009	June '69	
McLemore Avenue	Stax	STS-2027	May '70	
Greatest Hits	Stax	STS-2033	November '70	
Melting Pot	Stax	STS-2035	January '71	
Best	Atlantic	SD-8202	November '68	A
Free Ride	Stax	4104	March '78	A

STEVE CROPPER

With a Little from	Volt	VOS-6006	July '69	
My Friends				
Playin' My Thang	MCA	5171	February '81	A

STEVE CROPPER/ALBERT KING/POP STAPLES

Jammed Together	Stax	2020	July '69

PRISCILLA JONES

Gypsy Queen	A&M	SP-4297	May '71

BOOKER T. AND PRISCILLA JONES

Booker T. and	2-A&M	SP-3504	August '71
Priscilla			
Home Grown	A&M	4351	June '72
Chronicles	A&M	4413	October '73

THE MGS

The MGs	Stax	STS-3024	December '73

BOOKER T. (JONES)

Evergreen	Epic	E–33143	October '74	A
Try and Love Again	A&M	4720	September '78	A
The Best of You	A&M	4798	June '80	A
Booker T. Jones	A&M	4874	September '81	A

BOOKER T. AND THE MGS

Universal Language	Asylum	1093	January '77

LEVON HELM AND THE RCO ALL STARS (WITH BOOKER T., STEVE CROPPER, AND DONALD "DUCK" DUNN)

Levon Helm and The RCO All Stars	ABC	AA–1017	November '77

THE BLUES BROTHERS (BACKED BY STEVE CROPPER AND DONALD "DUCK" DUNN)

Briefcase Full of Blues **	Atlantic	19217	December '78	A
The Blues Brothers (soundtrack) *	Atlantic	16017	June '80	A
Made in America	Atlantic	16025	December '80	A
Best	Atlantic	19331	December '81	A

DAVID BOWIE. Rock's master of image manipulation, from 1971's heavily made-up hermaphrodite, to 1972's alienated space-age rock-and-roller, Ziggy Stardust, to 1975's Philadelphia soul brother of *Young Americans*, David Bowie was probably the first star of so-called "glitter rock," with its bizarre costuming and cosmetics, contrived theatricality, and elaborate stage lighting and presentation. Attempting to revitalize the careers of pioneer "punk" rockers Iggy Pop and Lou Reed, Bowie has lately experimented on albums with British avant-gardist Brian Eno, yet his most recent recognition has come with the title role in the hit play, *The Elephant Man*.

Born David Jones in South London on January 8, 1947, he took up saxophone at age 12, later forming a number of groups, including David Jones and The Lower Third. Scoring several minor English hits in 1967, he changed his name to David Bowie to avoid confusion with Davy Jones of The Monkees. After a first album heavily influenced by British music hall singer–songwriter Anthony Newley, Bowie shifted to a "flower-power" image for his first episode in science fiction, *Space Oddity*, an album not released in the United States until 1972. The title cut single reached into the British top five and eventually became Bowie's first major American hit in 1973, yet he "retired" to run an Arts Lab in Beckenham, South London, for 18 months. Prevailed upon to return to the studio, Bowie recorded *The Man Who Sold the World* with guitarist Mick Ronson and drummer

Woody Woodmansey. With the English cover (banned in the United States) depicting Bowie as a drag queen bearing a striking resemblance to Lauren Bacall, the album earned him the beginnings of an English following and initiated the use of the term "glitter rock." His first album for RCA Records, *Hunky Dory*, recorded with Ronson, Woodmansey, and bassist Trevor Bolder, evoked Bowie's first major critical attention; it included the minor hit single "Changes," a moderate hit when re-released in 1974.

Subsequently, the first of four conceptual albums, *The Rise and Fall of Ziggy Stardust and The Spiders From Mars*, brought him widespread publicity and acclaim and the first recognition from American audiences. With Bowie becoming Ziggy Stardust and Ronson, Bolder, and Woodmansey becoming The Spiders From Mars, the album featured a minor hit, "Starman," and Bowie classics such as "Star," "Sufragette City," and "Rock 'n' Roll Suicide." The 1972 Ziggy Stardust tour of the United States introduced American audiences to Bowie's peculiar, camp mixture of makeup, costume and set changes, and elaborate lighting and staging. The next album, *Aladdin Sane*, proved a disappointment compared to *Ziggy* but did contain the minor hit "Genie Jean."

Earlier, Bowie had composed and produced Mott The Hoople's first hit, "All The Young Dudes," and produced Lou Reed's *Transformer* album. In 1973 Bowie produced Iggy Pop's *Raw Power* album. Following the release of *Pin Ups*, a collection of his versions of a number of English favorites from the 1964–67 era and his final album with The Spiders From Mars, and the conclusion of his English tour in 1973, Bowie announced his "retirement." However, by October he was filming an NBC–TV "Midnight Special." Subsequently, his first album without the services of Mick Ronson, *Diamond Dogs*, was issued. The album, often described as Orwellian, included the minor hit "Rebel Rebel." The year 1974 proved to be Bowie's most popular, with *David Live*, *Diamond Dogs*, and *Ziggy Stardust* all being certified gold during the year. Also, in 1976, The Spiders From Mars recorded an album of their own for Pye Records.

Young Americans revealed another image shift, with Bowie embracing the soul sound of Philadelphia. Certified gold-award the year of its release, the album contained the major hit title song and the top hit "Fame," co-authored by John Lennon. Bowie maintained his soul orientation with 1976's *Station to Station* album and the hit "Golden Years." Later that year, he showed an unexpected talent for acting in the title role to Nicholas Roeg's *The Man Who Fell to Earth*, portraying a space voyager stranded on Earth. Following the release of the anthology set, *Changesonebowie*, Bowie recorded his next three albums, save the live double-record set *Stage*, with "avant-gardist" Brian Eno. Although his appearance in the film *Just a Gigolo* was denigrated when it was eventually released in the United States in 1981, Bowie received rave reviews for his performance as the grossly deformed John Merrick on tour and on Broadway in Bernard Pomerance's *The Elephant Man* in 1980. In fact, his success in that role delayed a promotional tour scheduled in support of *Scary Monsters*, recorded without Brian Eno but with former King Crimson guitarist Robert Fripp.

DAVID BOWIE

The World of David Bowie	Deram	DES–18003	September '67	
Images 1966–67	2-London	BP–628/9	February '73	
Starting Point	London	50007	September '77	A
David Bowie	Mercury	SR–61246	December '69	
later issued as Space Oddity	RCA	AQL1–4813	November '72	A
The Man Who Sold the World	Mercury later RCA	SR–61325 AFL1–4816	December '70 November '72	
Hunky Dory	RCA	AFL1–4623 reissued as AYL1–3844	November '71	A

DAVID BOWIE AND THE SPIDERS FROM MARS

The Rise and Fall of Ziggy Stardust and The Spiders From Mars*	RCA	AFL1–4702 reissued as AYL1–3843	June '72	A
Aladdin Sane	RCA	AFL1–4852 reissued as AYL1–3890	April '73	A
Pin Ups	RCA	AQL1–0291	October '73	A

THE SPIDERS FROM MARS

The Spiders From Mars	Pye	12125	February '76	

DAVID BOWIE

Diamond Dogs*	RCA	AFL1–0576 reissued as AYL1–3889	May '74	A
David Live*	2-RCA	CPL2–0771	October '74	A
Young Americans*	RCA	AQL1–0998	March '75	A
Station to Station*	RCA	AQL1–1327	January '76	A
Changesonebowie**	RCA	AQL1–1732	May '76	A
Low	RCA	CPL1–2030 reissued as AYL1–3856	January '77	A

Heroes	RCA	AFL1–2522	October '77	
		reissued as AYL1–3857		A
Stage	2-RCA	CPL2–2913	October '78	
Lodger	RCA	AQL1–3254	May '79	A
Scary Monsters	RCA	AQL1–3647	September '80	A
Changestwobowie	RCA	AFL1–4202	November '81	A

BREAD. Another so-called "soft-rock" group to achieve major success in the Seventies, Bread consistently hit with romantic songs such as "Make It with You" and "Baby, I'm-a Want You," written and chiefly sung by David Gates, that appealed to both rock and easy-listening audiences.

Sessions musician David Gates met James Griffin and Robb Royer while working with a group called Pleasure Faire. The three banded together to form Bread in late 1968, signing with Elektra Records. On their first album were: David Gates (vocals, guitar, bass, keyboards), James Griffin (vocals, guitar), Robb Royer (vocals, guitar), and sessions musician Jim Gordon (drums). Though critically acclaimed, the album didn't sell well. With Mike Botts replacing Gordon on drums, *On the Waters* featured the top hit, "Make It with You," composed by Gates. "It Don't Matter to Me," from the first album, became the group's second hit. *Manna* included two hit singles written by Gates, "Let Your Love Go" and the smash hit "If." Royer left the group before the next album and was replaced by veteran sessions keyboardist Larry Knechtel. The hits nonetheless continued through 1973 with "Baby, I'm-a Want You," "Everything I Own," "Diary," "The Guitar Man," "Sweet Surrender," and "Aubrey." Though five of their first six albums had been certified gold-award, Bread disbanded in the spring of 1973 amidst disputes between Gates and Griffin. Both subsequently recorded solo albums; Gates fared better, scoring minor hits with "Clouds" and "Sail around the World." After another solo set and the moderate hit "Never Let Her Go," Gates reunited with Griffin and Royer for the gold-award album *Lost Without Your Love* and its near-smash hit title single. By 1977, David Gates was again recording solo, scoring a major hit with the film theme song to Neil Simon's *Goodbye Girl*. In 1981 James Griffin was reportedly recording with former Hollies vocalist Terry Sylvester.

BREAD

Bread	Elektra	EKS–74044	September '69	A
On the Waters*	Elektra	74076	August '70	A

Manna*	Elektra	EKS–74086	March '71	A
Baby, I'm-a Want You*	Elektra	EKS–75015	February '72	A
The Guitar Man*	Elektra	EKS–75047	November '72	A
The Best of Bread*	Elektra	EKS–75056 reissued as 108	March '73	A
Best, Volume 2*	Elektra	7E–1005 reissued as 110	May '74	A

DAVID GATES

| First | Elektra | EKS–75066 | October '73 | A |
| Never Let Her Go | Elektra | 7E–1028 | February '75 | A |

JAMES GRIFFIN

| Breakin' Up Is Easy | Polydor | 6018 | February '74 | |

BREAD

| Lost Without Your Love* | Elektra | 7E–1094 | January '77 | A |

DAVID GATES

Goodbye Girl	Elektra	148	July '78	A
Falling in Love Again	Elektra	251	February '80	A
Take Me Now	Arista	9563	October '81	A

DAVID BROMBERG. One of the most talented multi-instrumentalists recording today, David Bromberg can play everything from rock-and-roll to folk and from jazz to blues and country with finesse and precision, to the delight of his listeners. Having performed as a sideman on more than 75 albums, Bromberg has recently begun attending violin-making school.

DAVID BROMBERG

David Bromberg	Columbia	C–31104	January '72	A
Demon in Disguise	Columbia	PC–31753	November '72	A
Wanted—Dead or Alive	Columbia	PC–32717	January '74	A
Midnight on the Water	Columbia	PC–33397	May '75	A
Best: Out of the Blues	Columbia	PC–34467	April '77	A

VASSAR CLEMENTS AND DAVID BROMBERG

| Hillybilly Jazz | 2-Flying Fish | 101 | September '74 | A |

DAVID BROMBERG

How Late'll Ya Play 'Til?	2-Fantasy	F–79007	September '76	A
Reckless Abandon	Fantasy	9540	October '77	A
Bandit in a Bathing Suit	Fantasy	9555	May '78	A
My Own House	Fantasy	9572	December '78	A
You Should See the Rest of the Band	Fantasy	9590	March '80	A

JAMES BROWN. Probably the single most popular black artist among blacks, James Brown is one of the few rhythm-and-blues stars of the Fifties to retain his popularity as a soul act in the Sixties and Seventies. He may very well be the last vaudeville performer with his high-powered, histrionic, and intensely dramatic stage show. His classic live 1962 album *"Live" at the Apollo*, recently reissued, is regarded by some as the greatest in-concert album ever recorded and was likely the first album bought in mass quantities by blacks. One of the first entertainers to gain complete control of his own career, James Brown is certainly the first black artist to achieve independence from his record company in matters of arrangement, production, and packaging. In emphasizing polyrhythms during the mid-Sixties with "Out of Sight" and subsequent recordings, Brown helped Africanize American rhythm-and-blues. Moreover, James Brown was one of the first blacks to raise the banner of black self-pride and heightened political consciousness in the Sixties, while at the same time becoming one of the nation's first black entrepreneurs. Enduring declining record sales and concert attendance since the mid-Seventies, James Brown experienced a revival of interest in his music with his role in 1980's *Blues Brothers* movie.

Born on May 3, 1928, and raised in Augusta, Georgia, James Brown took up keyboards, then drums and bass, at an early age. He formed his first group, a gospel group, in the early Fifties. Changing their name to The Famous Flames and concentrating on rhythm-and-blues music, the group came to the attention of King Records of Cincinnati which quickly signed them after hearing their first demonstration record. Re-recorded, the song "Please, Please, Please" became a big rhythm-and-blues hit in 1956. Brown quickly became the undisputed leader, but James Brown and The Famous Flames had little to distinguish themselves from hundreds of other acts on the so-called "chitlin' circuit." However "Try Me," a rhythm-and-blues hit in 1958, filtered into the pop charts. A series of rhythm-and-blues hits followed, including "Think," "I Don't Mind," "Baby, You're Right," and "Night Train." Brown organized the James Brown Revue with 40 singers, dancers, and musicians and, with a well-rehearsed stage act polished to near-perfection, the show played to sell-out, box-office record crowds in ghetto areas across the country during the early Sixties. The live recording of their show at Harlem's Apollo Theater on October 24, 1962, reflects Brown's mastery of showmanship, and the resulting album, considered an in-performance masterpiece and one of the first to sell in large quantities to blacks, was eventually reissued on the independent label Solid Smoke in 1980.

During 1962 James Brown reluctantly recorded several songs with vocal chorus and strings at the insistence of King Records. One of the songs, "Prisoner of Love," eventually reached high into the pop charts. By 1964, however, Brown had de-emphasized vocals in favor of strong hard polyrhythms. He brought a set of recently recorded tapes in this new style to Smash Records of Chicago. One of the songs, "Out of Sight," did well in the pop charts and became Brown's first record to sell in large quantities to whites. Brown eventually returned to King with complete control over all aspects of his recording career, with releases on Smash restricted to instrumentals and records by members of the Revue. Eschewing club engagements in favor of concert auditoriums around 1965, Brown placed five songs in the pop charts' top ten through 1968: "Papa's Got a Brand New Bag," "I Got You (I Feel Good)," "It's a Man's Man's Man's World," "Cold Sweat," and "I Got the Feelin'."

By the late Sixties, James Brown was producing the whole show for the Revue—songs, costumes, routines, choreography, and lighting. Credited with quelling riots after the assassination of Dr. Martin Luther King, Jr., Brown issued one of the first anthems of black pride in 1968, "Say It Loud I'm Black and I'm Proud." After hits with "Give It Up or Turnit a Loose" and "I Don't Want Nobody to Give Me Nothing," Brown returned to more conventional dance-music hits including "Mother Popcorn" in 1969, "Get Up I Feel Like Being a Sex Machine" and "Super Bad" in 1970, "Hot Pants" in 1971, "Get on the Good Foot" in 1972, "I Got Ants in My Pants" in 1973, and "The Payback" and "My Thang" in 1974. Signing with Polydor Records in 1971, Brown recorded two soundtracks during 1973; his 1974 *Payback* album became his first and only certified gold-award album. Experiencing diminished popularity since the mid-Seventies, Brown used an outside producer for the first time for *The Original Disco Man* and *People* in 1979–80. Touring the rock club circuit for the first time in 1980, James Brown was introduced to a new generation of music fans and enjoyed a renewed interest in his music with his appearance in *The Blues Brothers* movie.

JAMES BROWN

Please, Please, Please	King	610(M) later 909 (M)	January '59
Try Me	King	635(M)	August '60
Think!	King	683(M)	December '60
The Always Amazing James Brown	King	743(M)	

Jump Around/ Night Train	King	771(M)		
Shout and Shimmy/Good Good Twistin'	King	780(M)	April '62	
James Brown and His Famous Flames Tour the U.S.A.	King	804(M)	September '62	
The James Brown Show—"Live" at the Apollo	King	826(M)	July '63	
reissued as Live and Lowdown at the Apollo, Volume 1	Solid Smoke	8006	October '80	A
Prisoner of Love	King	851(M)	August '63	
Pure Dynamite!	King	883(M)	February '64	
Unbeatable	King	919(M)		
Papa's Got a Brand New Bag	King	938	September '65	
I Got You (I Feel Good)	King	946	January '66	
Mighty Instrumentals	King	961		
It's a Man's World	King	985	September '66	
Christmas Songs	King	1010		
Raw Soul	King	1016	April '67 reissued May '70	
Live at the Garden	King	1018	June '67	
Cold Sweat	King	1020	September '67	
Live at the Apollo, Volume 2	2-King	1022		
I Can't Stand Myself When You Touch Me	King	1030	March '68	
I Got the Feelin'	King	1031	May '68	
Nothing But Soul	King	1034	August '68	
Thinking About Little Willie John and a New Nice Thing	King	1038		
Say It Loud, I'm Black and I'm Proud	King	1047	April '69	
Gettin' Down to It	King	1051	May '69	
Popcorn	King	1055	August '69	
It's a Mother	King	1063	September '69	
Ain't It Funky	King	1092	February '70	
It's a New Day	King	1095	July '70	
Soul on Top	King	1100	May '70	
Sex Machine	2-King	1115	September '70	
Sho Is Funky Down Here	King	1110	April '71	

Hey America—Christmas	King	1124	December '71	
Super Bad	King	1127	January '71	
Showtime	Smash	SRS–67054	May '64	
Grits and Soul	Smash	SRS–67057	April '65	
Today and Yesterday	Smash	SRS–67072	December '65	
Plays New Breed	Smash	SRS–67080	April '66	
Handful of Soul	Smash	SRS–67084	December '66	
Presenting . . . The James Brown Show	Smash	SRS–67087	December '66	
Plays the Real Thing	Smash	67093	June '67	
Sings out of Sight	Smash	67109	October '68	
Hot Pants	Polydor	PD–4054	September '71	
Revolution of the Mind	Polydor	3003	December '71	
Soul Classics, Volume 1	Polydor	5401	June '72	
There It Is	Polydor	PD–5028	July '72	
Get on the Good Foot	2-Polydor	PD2–3004	December '72	
Black Caesar (soundtrack)	Polydor	6014	March '73	
Slaughter's Big Rip-Off (soundtrack)	Polydor	PD–6015	July '73	
Soul Classics, Volume 2	Polydor	SD–5402	November '73	
The Payback*	2-Polydor	3007	January '74	
It's Hell	2-Polydor	PD2–9001	July '74	
Reality	Polydor	PD–6039	January '75	
Sex Machine Today	Polydor	PD–6042	May '75	
Everybody's Doin' the Hustle. . .	Polydor	6054	October '75	
Hot	Polydor	6059	April '76	
Get Up Offa That Thing	Polydor	6071	August '76	
Body Heat	Polydor	6093	January '77	
Mutha's Nature	Polydor	6111	September '77	
Sex Machine Recorded Live at Home	2-Polydor	9004	November '77	
Jam 1980s	Polydor	6140	April '78	
Take a Look at Those Cakes	Polydor	6181	January '79	
The Original Disco Man	Polydor	PD1–6212	August '79	A
People	Polydor	6258	April '80	A
Live . . . Hot on the One	2-Polydor	PD2–6290	August '80	A
Nonstop	Polydor			
Best	Polydor	6340	November '81	A

JACKSON BROWNE.   Perhaps the most stimulating and profound male song poet of the Seventies, Jackson Browne has written subtle, honest songs with recurrent romantic and apocalyptic themes and played them with a feeling for both folk and rock music.

Born in Heidelberg, Germany, on October 9, 1948, and raised in Los Angeles, Jackson Browne first sang at "hoots" in Orange County in 1966. His first song written while still in high school, he was signed to a songwriting contract in September 1966 by Elektra Records, only to be released from it later. He played folk clubs around New York during the winter of 1967, often accompanying Nico (of Velvet Underground fame), and returned to Los Angeles and served a brief tenure with The Nitty Gritty Dirt Band. Folksinger Tom Rush became the first major artist to showcase Browne's songs, recording "Shadow Dream Song" in 1967 and "These Days" in 1968. Browne's first performing success came in the fall of 1969, when he opened for Linda Ronstadt at Los Angeles' Troubadour Club. He completed his first concert tour in 1970, opening for Laura Nyro.

By 1971, Jackson Browne had initiated his own successful recording career with the invaluable assistance of multi-instrumentalist David Lindley (formerly with Kaleidoscope). "Doctor My Eyes" became a smash hit single from Browne's debut album, which also contained "Jamaica Say You Will" and "Rock Me on the Water." During the spring of 1972, he toured with songstress Joni Mitchell. Later that year, his "Take It Easy" (co-authored by Glenn Frey) launched The Eagles on their enormously successful career. Browne's second album release, coming nearly two years after the first, included the minor hit "Redneck Friend" as well as his own versions of "Take It Easy" and "These Days." By 1974 Browne was touring as a headline act with a band formed around David Lindley the previous year. Browne's *Late for the Sky* album, though yielding no hit single, was his most poignant and penetrating album, with visions of death, apocalypse and, most importantly, resigned hope; it contained most notably "Fountain of Sorrow," "The Late Show," "For a Dancer," and "Before the Deluge" and became his first certified gold-award album. Another two-year period elapsed before the release of *The Pretender*. Though displaying a degree of melodic and rhythmic repetition, the album again contained a number of honest and moving songs, from the hit "Here Comes Those Tears Again" to "The Fuse" and the title song. Yet another year passed before the issuance of the live set, *Running On Empty*, with its wide-ranging choice of moods and material. This album yielded a near-smash hit with the title song and a major hit with a modified re-make of Maurice Williams' top 1960–61 hit "Stay."

A leader of the antinuclear movement, Jackson Browne helped found MUSE (Musicians United for Safe Energy) in 1979 and was one of the major backers of the *No Nukes* movie and album. His 1980 album *Hold Out*, with its preoccupation with love relationships, was received equivocally by critics yet included the major hits "Boulevard" and "That Girl Could Sing." Having earlier produced and co-produced Warren Zevon's debut and second albums respectively, Browne co-produced David Lindley's debut solo album *El Rayo X* and appeared at several shows on Lindley's first solo tour. In September 1981, Jackson Browne was one of the demonstrators arrested at California's Diablo Canyon nuclear power plant.

JACKSON BROWNE

Jackson Browne*	Asylum	SD–5051	January '72	A
For Everyman*	Asylum	SD–5067	October '73	A
Late for the Sky*	Asylum	7E–1017	September '74	A
The Pretender**	Asylum	7E–1079 reissued as 107	October '76	A
Running On Empty**	Asylum	6E–113	December '77	A
Hold Out**	Asylum	511	July '80	A

THE BUFFALO SPRINGFIELD. One of the first American groups to combine electric instrumentation and drums with distinctive, incisive songwriting and intricate vocal harmonies, The Buffalo Springfield (along with the previously formed Byrds and The Mamas and The Papas) left music critics scrambling for a new term to describe this new sound and style. Thus was born the first hyphenated descriptive phrase to be applied to a new type of rock music, "folk-rock." Though the group helped pioneer the three-guitar format, they failed to enjoy major commercial success during their existence, perhaps due to their inability to transfer the dynamism of their live shows onto recordings. The Buffalo Springfield nonetheless became a near-legend in rock, and the influence of its key members is still felt today through various aggregations and solo endeavors.

Also known as The Herd in its early days, The Buffalo Springfield formed in Los Angeles in the spring of 1966. The members: Neil Young (first lead guitar, keyboards, vocals), Stephen Stills (second lead guitar, keyboards, vocals), Richie Furay (rhythm guitar, vocals), Bruce Palmer (bass), and Dewey Martin (drums). Neil Young, born in Toronto, Ontario, Canada, on November 12, 1945, had done solo work and played with The Mynah Birds in the Detroit area before moving to Los Angeles in 1965. Steve Stills, born in Dallas, Texas, on January 3, 1945, and folk musician Richard Furay, born on May 9, 1944, in Yellow Springs, Ohio, had been members of the New York based Au Go Go Singers. Canadian-born Bruce Palmer had been with The Mynah Birds, and Dewey Martin, born in Chesterville, Ontario, Canada, on September 30, 1942, had played with the bluegrass group The Dillards as well as drummed at the Grand Ole Opry and toured with Roy Orbison.

Featured at a July 1966 Hollywood Bowl concert, The Buffalo Springfield toured with The Byrds and The Beach Boys later in the year. Soon they embarked on a long stay at Los Angeles' Whiskey A Go Go. Though their first two single releases went generally unnoticed, their third, Stills'

"For What It's Worth," became the group's best selling single and launched their popular recording career. Their first album contained seven Stills songs, including the country-flavored "Go and Say Goodbye" and "Hot Dusty Roads," and five Neil Young songs, including the beautiful love song "Do I Have to Come Right Out and Say It" and "Flying on the Ground Is Wrong," both sung by Richie Furay. The gutsier *Buffalo Springfield Again* contained a wider range of material, from rock-and-roll (Young's psychedelic "Mr. Soul" and Stills' "Bluebird" and "Rock & Roll Woman") to the major production effort of Young's "Broken Arrow." Jim Messina handled part of the engineering duties while bass chores were shared among Jim Fielder, Bobby West, and the soon-to-depart Palmer. Released amidst reports of dissension and group in-fighting, the third album was produced by Jim Messina, who also played bass, sang, and contributed "Carefree Country Day." Outstanding songs on this final album included "On the Way Home" and "I Am a Child" by Neil Young, "Pretty Girl Why" and "Four Days Gone" by Steve Stills, and Richie Furay's "Kind Woman." Clashes between Stills and Young intensified, with Young quitting the group at least twice before leaving permanently. The Buffalo Springfield performed their last concert at Long Beach in May 1968.

Subsequently, all group members have pursued a variety of musical projects. Bruce Palmer and Dewey Martin each recorded a solo album before dropping out of sight. Jim Messina and Richie Furay formed Poco, whereas Young recorded solo before joining Stills in Crosby, Stills, Nash and Young. Later Stills recorded solo and Messina joined Kenny Loggins. In the mid-Seventies, Furay helped form The Souther–Hillman–Furay Band, and later formed his own band.

THE BUFFALO SPRINGFIELD

Buffalo Springfield	Atco	SD33–200	January '67	A
Buffalo Springfield Again	Atco	SD33–226	November '67	A
Last Time Around	Atco	SD33–256	July '68	A
Retrospective	Atco	SD33–283 reissued as 38–105	January '69	A
Buffalo Springfield	2-Atlantic	2–806	November '73	A

DEWEY MARTIN

| Medicine Ball | Uni | 73088 | October '70 | |

BRUCE PALMER

| The Cycle Is Complete | Verve/Fore-cast | FTS–3086 | March '71 | |

JIMMY BUFFETT. One of the more amusing of the Seventies singer–song-writers, Jimmy Buffett appeals to both country-and-western and rock audiences with an intriguing variety of songs about sailing and the Caribbean, drugs, womanizing, and drinking as well as the occasional finely crafted ballad.

JIMMY BUFFETT

Down to Earth	Barnaby	Z–30093	September '70	
High Cumberland Jubilee	Barnaby	6014	April '77	
Before the Salt: Early Jimmy Buffett	2-Barnaby	6019	February '79	
A White Sports Coat and a Pink Crustacean	Dunhill reissued on MCA	50150 37026	June '73	A
Living and Dying in 3/4 Time	Dunhill reissued on MCA	50132 37025	February '74	A
A1A	Dunhill reissued on MCA	50183 37027	December '74	A
Rancho Deluxe (soundtrack)	United Artists	LA466	July '75	A
Havana Day- dreamin'	ABC reissued on MCA	914 37023	February '76	A
Changes in Latitudes, Changes in Attitudes**	ABC/MCA	AB–990	February '77	A
Son of a Son of a Sailor**	ABC reissued on MCA	AA–1046 37024	March '78	A
You Had to Be There*	2-ABC reissued on MCA	AK–1108 AK2–1008	November '78	A
Volcano*	MCA	5102	September '79	A
Coconut Telegraph	MCA	5169	March '81	A

JOHNNY BURNETTE. Leader of an early and generally overlooked "rockabilly" group during the Fifties, Johnny Burnette later scored several pop hits before dying accidentally in 1964.

JOHNNY BURNETTE AND THE ROCK AND ROLL TRIO

Johnny Burnette and The Rock and Roll Trio	Coral reissued on Solid Smoke	CRL– 57080 (M) SS–8001	December '56 April '78	A

JOHNNY AND DORSEY BURNETTE

Together Again	Solid Smoke		December '80	A

JOHNNY BURNETTE

Dreamin'	Liberty	LST–7179	September '60
Johnny Burnette	Liberty	LST–7183	January '61
Johnny Burnette Sings	Liberty	LST–7190	May '61
Roses Are Red	Liberty	LST–7255	September '62
Hits and Other Favorites	Liberty	LST–7206	November '63
The Johnny Burnette Story	Liberty	LST–7389	January '66
Dreamin'	Sunset	SUS–5179	October '67
The Very Best of Johnny Burnette	United Artists	LA432	August '75

PAUL BURLISON

| Johnny Burnette's Rock and Roll Trio and Their Friends from Memphis | Rock-A-Billy | 1001 | April '81 | A |

JERRY BUTLER. One of the most popular soul music singer–songwriters to emerge in the late Fifties, Jerry Butler continues to pursue his on-again, off-again career, one of the longest in the music business. His once-fading career was bolstered in the late Sixties by the now-famous production–songwriting team of Kenny Gamble and Leon Huff, who later were mainstays of Philadelphia International Records, to which Butler has recently moved.

Born in Sunflower, Mississippi, on December 8, 1939, and raised in Chicago, Jerry Butler began singing with gospel groups as a child. By the age of 12 he was touring with the Northern Jubilee Gospel Singers. During 1957, he joined The Roosters, who later added Curtis Mayfield. By 1958 they had changed their name to The Impressions and signed with VeeJay Records. Featuring Butler's rich mellifluous baritone, The Impressions' first single, "For Your Precious Love," co-authored by Butler, became a big hit. Leaving the group after the solitary hit, Butler floundered for some time in his solo career, scoring a smash hit in late 1960 with "He Will Break Your Heart," co-written by Butler and Mayfield. Several years of hits followed, with "Find Another Girl," "I'm-a Telling You," Henry Mancini's pop "Moon River," "Make It Easy on Yourself," and "Need to Belong." Subsequently, Butler languished with VeeJay for several years, eventually achieving a smash hit with "Let It Be Me," recorded with Betty Everett in 1964, and later writing "I've Been Loving You Too Long (to Stop Now)" for and with Otis Redding.

With the demise of VeeJay Records in 1966, Jerry Butler moved to Mercury Records, where he worked with songwriter–producers Kenny Gamble and Leon Huff. The collaboration resulted in a number of hits for

Butler, including "Never Give You Up," "Hey Western Union Man," the smash "Only the Strong Survive," "Moody Woman," and "What's the Use of Breaking Up." Butler stayed with Mercury when Gamble and Huff moved to Columbia Records in 1970, and his career again seemed to fade despite recording *One and One* with Gene Chandler and hitting with "Ain't Understanding Mellow," recorded with Brenda Lee Eager. Switching to Motown Records during 1976, Butler finally scored a minor hit with "I Wanna Do It to You" in 1977. Recording a total of three solo albums and two albums with Thelma Houston for Motown, Jerry Butler has moved to Philadelphia International Records, where he has been reunited with the Gamble–Huff Team.

JERRY BUTLER AND THE IMPRESSIONS

For Your Precious Love	VeeJay	1075(M)	'63

JERRY BUTLER

Jerry Butler Esquire	Abner reissued on	2001(M)	
	VeeJay	1027(M) reissued as 1034 (M)	May '61
He Will Break Your Heart	VeeJay	1029(M)	May '61
Aware of Love	VeeJay	1038	January '62
Moon River	VeeJay	1046	June '63
Folk Songs	VeeJay	1057	May '63
Giving Up on Love/Need to Belong	VeeJay	1076	'63

JERRY BUTLER AND BETTY EVERETT

Delicious Together	VeeJay	1099	October '64
Starring Jerry Butler and Betty Everett	Tradition	2073	December '68
Together	Buddah	BDS–7507	June '70

JERRY BUTLER

Soul Artistry	Mercury	61105	March '67
Mr. Dream Merchant	Mercury	61146	January '68
Golden Hits (Live)	Mercury	61151	February '68
The Soul Goes On	Mercury	61171	July '68
The Ice Man Cometh	Mercury	SR–61198	January '69
Ice on Ice	Mercury	SR–61234	October '69
You and Me	Mercury	SR–61269	July '70
Jerry Butler Sings Assorted Sounds	Mercury	SR–61320	December '70

Sagittarius Movement	Mercury	SR–61347	October '71	
Spice of Life	2-Mercury	SRM2–7502	June '72	
Power of Love	Mercury	SRM1–689	February '74	
Sweet Sweet Sixteen	Mercury	SRM1–1006	July '74	
Gift of Love	Sunset	5216	August '68	
Melinda (soundtrack)	Pride	0006		

JERRY BUTLER ANTHOLOGIES AND COMPILATIONS

Best	VeeJay	1048	June '63	
More of the Best	VeeJay	1119	'64	
Very Best	Buddah	4001	May '69	
Best	Mercury	SR–61281	July '70	
Starring Jerry Butler	Tradition	2068		A
All Time Hits	Up Front	124(M)		
Jerry Butler!	Pickwick	SPC–3202		
All Time Hits	2–Trip	8011		
Best	United Artists	LA498	April '76	

JERRY BUTLER AND GENE CHANDLER

One and One	Mercury	61330	March '71

JERRY BUTLER AND BRENDA LEE EAGER

The Love We Have	Mercury	SRM1–660	July '73

JERRY BUTLER

Love's on the Menu	Motown	6–850	September '76	
Suite for the Single Girl	Motown	6–878	March '77	
It All Comes Out in My Song	Motown	6–892	December '77	
Nothing Says I Love You Like I Love You	Philadelphia International	JZ–35510	October '78	
The Best Love I Ever Had	Philadelphia International	JZ–36413	July '80	A

JERRY BUTLER AND THELMA HOUSTON

Thelma and Jerry	Motown	6–887	June '77
Two to One	Motown	7–903	July '78

PAUL BUTTERFIELD. Perhaps the first group of American white musicians to popularize the work of many unrecognized black blues artists, The Paul Butterfield Blues Band, along with Cream and The Electric Flag, sparked a massive wave of interest in blues music that spawned dozens of white blues bands and brought much-deserved recognition to many black blues performers. One of the first groups to play the blues at rock tempo and volume, The Paul Butterfield Blues Band was the first band to bring electrified instrumentation to the Newport Folk Festival, in 1965. "East–West," from the band's second album, was one of the first recordings to attempt a fusion of Western and Eastern musical styles. Reorganized after the second album, the band was one of the first electric bands to be augmented by horns. Finally, Paul Butterfield was considered one of America's leading white blues harmonica players.

THE PAUL BUTTERFIELD BLUES BAND

The Paul Butterfield Blues Band	Elektra	EKS–7294	October '65	A
East–West	Elektra	EKS–7315	August '66	A
Resurrection of Pig Boy Crabshaw	Elektra	74015	November '67	A
In My Own Dream	Elektra	EKS–74025	July '68	
Keep On Moving	Elektra	EKS–74053	October '69	
Live	Elektra	7E–2001	December '70	A
Sometimes I Feel Like Smiling	Elektra	75013	August '71	
Golden Butter	Elektra	7E–2005	May '72	A

SAM LAY

In Bluesland	Blue Thumb	BTS–14	April '70

PAUL BUTTERFIELD'S BETTER DAYS

Better Days	Bearsville	BR–2119	January '73
It All Comes Back	Bearsville	BS–2170	October '73

PAUL BUTTERFIELD

Put It in Your Ear	Bearsville	BR–6960	February '76	
North South	Warner Brothers	6995	January '81	A

THE BYRDS. The Los Angeles-based group that revolutionized the American popular music scene with their unique blend of folk and rock styles, The Byrds presented the first substantial challenge to the popularity of The Beatles and other English groups in the mid-Sixties. Their recording of Bob Dylan's "Mr. Tambourine Man" marked virtually the first time his still acoustic music had been adapted to rock and launched a new sound on the contemporary music scene, dubbed by critics as "folk-rock"; it ostensibly inspired Dylan to take up electric guitar. Moreover, The Byrds' 1966 hit "Eight Miles High" was probably the first recorded "psychedelic" song, and their 1968 *Sweetheart of the Rodeo* album introduced Gram Parsons and initiated a new sound labeled by critics as "country-rock." McGuinn, perhaps the finest twelve-string electric lead guitar player in rock, endured as The Byrds' only original member between late 1968 and early 1973, subsequently performing solo or with a new band until reuniting with Chris Hillman and, briefly, Gene Clark, in 1979–80. David Crosby had formed the hugely popular Crosby, Stills, Nash (and Young) aggregation, and Gram Parsons and Chris Hillman had formed The Flying Burrito Brothers. Both Clark and Hillman recorded solo, and Hillman helped man Steve Stills' Manassas and The Souther–Hillman–Furay Band.

The Byrds formed in Los Angeles in the summer of 1964. The members: Jim McGuinn (lead twelve-string guitar, vocals), Gene Clark (harmonica, guitar, vocals), David Crosby (rhythm guitar, vocals), Chris Hillman (bass, vocals), and Mike Clarke (drums). McGuinn, born in Chicago on July 13, 1942, had made his debut at The Gate of Horn in Chicago in the late Fifties, later backing The Limelighters; he performed as a solo folk artist in Greenwich Village and joined The Chad Mitchell Trio for two years. After backing Bobby Darin, he returned to solo work in early 1964. Born in Tipton, Missouri, on November 17, 1944, Gene Clark had been a member of The New Christy Minstrels, whereas David Crosby (born in Los Angeles on August 14, 1941) had been a member of Les Baxter's Balladeers and a folk singer of five years' experience. Chris Hillman, born on December 4, 1942, in Los Angeles, had fronted his own country and bluegrass group, The Hillmen, in 1963–64, while Mike Clarke (born June 3, 1944, in New York) had backed musicians such as Dino Valenti.

During 1964, with the help of producer Jim Dickson, The Byrds cut a demonstration tape at World Pacific Studios which was later issued as *Preflyte*. Initially signed to Elektra Records as The Beefeaters, the group's first single flopped and they subsequently signed with Columbia Records in September 1964, thus becoming the first rock band signed by the label. Preparing their first album for release, The Byrds recorded Bob Dylan's "Mr. Tambourine Man" at the urging of Dickson. Ironically, only McGuinn actually played for the recording, on his electric twelve-string. With McGuinn singing the lead vocal and Crosby and Clark providing the background vocals, the instrumentation was done by three of Los Angeles' finest sessions musicians, Hal Blaine, Larry Knechtel, and Leon Russell. The single, issued in March 1965, was a top hit and launched The Byrds into international prominence. Debuting that same month to mixed reactions at Ciro's in Los Angeles, the original group remained far more effective as a recording group than as performers.

All of The Byrds actually played on their debut album, save on "Mr. Tambourine Man" and "I Knew I'd Want You." Containing four Dylan songs, the album also included Clark's "I'll Feel a Whole Lot Better" and Jackie DeShannon's "Don't Doubt Yourself, Babe." The second album yielded the top hit "Turn, Turn, Turn" (adapted from the Bible by Pete Seeger) and contained two more Dylan songs and Clark's "Set You Free

This Time." Conflicts within the group soon became apparent as Crosby and McGuinn frequently disagreed on The Byrds' direction, often coming to actual blows. However, the first defection was Gene Clark in March 1966; he later recorded with The Gosdin Brothers before joining Doug Dillard in Dillard and Clark. Having lost a singer and their principal songwriter, the group realigned itself, with Hillman singing and McGuinn and Crosby writing more songs. At the same time, The Byrds started looking toward more sophistication in their work, with McGuinn immersing himself in the stylizations of jazz saxophonist John Coltrane. The result was the hit single "Eight Miles High," recorded shortly before Clark's departure. With three-part harmony and an almost imperceptible melody, the song featured McGuinn's outstanding twelve-string lead guitar played modally (rather than in a major or minor scale). Perhaps the first recorded "psychedelic" song, with its obvious reference to the then-popular drug LSD, "Eight Miles High" had the curious distinction of being one of the first Sixties singles to be banned from airplay. The eclectic album from which the song came included several other "psychedelic" songs as well as standard folk fare and the bluesy "Hey Joe."

Increasing musical sophistication became totally evident with the release of *Younger than Yesterday*. Though marred by two overdone production numbers, the album yielded two hits, Dylan's "My Back Pages" and McGuinn and Hillman's embitteredly satiric "So You Want to Be a Rock 'n' Roll Star," while including Crosby's beautiful love song "Everybody's Been Burned," two McGuinn–Crosby collaborations, "Why" and "Renaissance Faire," and four Hillman songs. By late 1967, however, the rift between McGuinn and Crosby had become irreparable. When Crosby refused to sing two Goffin–King compositions, he was summarily paid off and fired in October. Later Crosby produced Joni Mitchell's debut album and helped form Crosby, Stills, and Nash. Recorded with the assistance of outside musicians, most notably guitarist-singer Clarence White, *The Notorious Byrd Brothers* was critically hailed but only moderately successful and marked the beginning of a trend toward simplicity rather than sophistication in The Byrds' music.

Gene Clark returned briefly, only to leave again; Mike Clarke departed in November 1967, to be replaced by Hillman's cousin Kevin Kelly. Singer–songwriter–guitarist Gram Parsons was added, lending a country music orientation to The Byrds. The next album, *Sweetheart of the Rodeo*, openly embraced country-and-western music and was hailed as the first "country-rock" album. However, the album was too far ahead of its time and was a commercial flop. The Byrds subsequently began to deteriorate. Gram Parsons quit in mid–1968, followed in October by Hillman, who helped form The Flying Burrito Brothers with Parsons and Chris Ethridge. McGuinn, now using the first name Roger and the only original member left, put a new group together with Clarence White, drummer–singer Gene Parsons (no relation to Gram), and bassist–singer John York. Though *Dr. Byrds and Mr. Hyde* proved unspectacular, The Byrds' nosedive into obscurity was arrested by the overwhelming popularity of the Peter

Fonda–Dennis Hopper film, *Easy Rider*. The soundtrack album featured three songs sung by McGuinn, and the appropriately entitled followup. *The Ballad of Easy Rider*, yielded the minor hit "Jesus Is Just All Right." John York left after the album, to be replaced by Skip Battin. Years before, Battin had been half of the duo Skip and Flip, who hit with "Cherry Pie" in 1960. *(Untitled)*, half live and half studio material, included "Truck Stop Girl" (by Lowell George and Bill Payne of Little Feat) and several McGuinn–Jaques Levy collaborations, most notably "Lover of the Bayou" and "Chestnut Mare." *Byrdmaniax* contained an early version of Jackson Browne's "Jamaica Say You Will." *Farther Along* became The Byrds' final album of new material.

Gene Clark recorded his first solo album for A&M Records during 1971 as The Byrds continued to fragment, with Gene Parsons leaving in August 1972, followed by Clarence White in February 1973. Gene Parsons later recorded a solo LP, but White died in July 1973 of injuries sustained in an auto accident. Skip Battin also recorded a solo album after leaving The Byrds. Finally, in 1973, McGuinn disbanded the group for a solo performing and recording career. However, before McGuinn embarked on his solo career, the original Byrds reunited for a single album. A rather crass commercial venture, the album included two Neil Young songs as well as songs by each member except Clarke, with McGuinn's "Born to Rock 'n' Roll" standing out.

After debuting at the Troubadour, Roger McGuinn toured for nearly a year as a solo act in support of *Roger McGuinn* before assembling a backup band for *Peace on You*. Meanwhile, Gene Clark recorded his first album in three years for Asylum Records. After *Roger McGuinn and Band*, McGuinn toured with Bob Dylan's Rolling Thunder Revue in 1975 and 1976. That spring he released the acoustic *Cardiff Rose*, which contained two previously unrecorded songs, Joni Mitchell's "Dreamland" and Bob Dylan's "Up to Me." At the same time, Chris Hillman was back on the scene with *Slippin' Away*, following stints with Steve Stills' Manassas and the equivocal Souther–Hillman–Furay Band. During 1977, McGuinn formed a new band, Thunderbyrd, for an album of the same name; Gene Clark recorded an album for RSO Records, and Hillman a second for Asylum. In the spring Hillman's band toured Europe with Gene Clark's band and McGuinn's Thunderbyrd, leading to a jam session among the three at London's Hammersmith Odeon. Later, back in the States, Clark joined McGuinn onstage at The Troubadour; received enthusiastically, they later toured as a duo. Soon joined by Hillman, the trio, playing acoustic guitars, opened the Canadian leg of Eric Clapton's *Slowhand* tour. Then, during late 1978, the three recorded the highly polished, commercially oriented *McGuinn, Clark, and Hillman* album for Capitol Records, which yielded a moderate hit with "Don't You Write Her Off." The three toured for ten months and recorded *City* for Capitol, then Clark elected to stop touring. During 1980 Jim McGuinn and Chris Hillman recorded an album together, and Gene Parsons recorded his second solo album for Sierra Records.

THE HILLMEN

The Hillmen	Together	1012	'69

THE BYRDS

Preflyte	Together	STT–1001	September '69	
	reissued on			
	Columbia	C–32183	May '73	A
Mr. Tambourine Man	Columbia	PC–9172	June '65	A
Turn! Turn! Turn!	Columbia	CS–9254	December '65	A
Fifth Dimension	Columbia	CS–9349	August '66	A
Younger than Yesterday	Columbia	CS–9442	March '67	A
Notorious Byrd Brothers	Columbia	CS–9575	February '68	A
Sweetheart of the Rodeo	Columbia	PC–9670	August '68	A
Dr. Byrds and Mr. Hyde	Columbia	CS–9755	February '69	A
Ballad of Easy Rider	Columbia	CS–9942	November '69	
(Untitled)	2-Columbia	CG–30127	October '70	A
Byrdmaniax	Columbia	KC–30640	July '71	
Farther Along	Columbia	KC–31050	November '71	
Gene Clark, Chris Hillman, David Crosby, Roger McGuinn, Michael Clarke	Asylum	SD–5058	March '73	

THE BYRDS ANTHOLOGIES, COMPILATIONS, AND REISSUES

Greatest Hits*	Columbia	PC–9516	September '67	A
The Best of The Byrds (Greatest Hits, Volume 2)	Columbia	PC–31795	November '72	A
Mr. Tambourine Man/Turn! Turn! Turn!	2-Columbia	CG–33645	October '75	A
The Byrds Play Dylan	Columbia	PC–36293	December '79	A
The Original Singles 1965–1967	Columbia	FC–37335 (E)	May '81	A

GENE CLARK

Early L.A. Sessions	Columbia	KC–31123	June '72
Gene Clark with The Gosdin Brothers	Columbia	CS–9418	February '67

THE GOSDIN BROTHERS

Gene Clark	A&M	SP–4292	September '71	A
No Other	Asylum	1016	October '74	
Two Sides to Every Story	RSO	RS1–3011	February '77	

CHRIS HILLMAN

Cherokee	ABC	719	February '71	
Slippin' Away	Asylum	7E–1062	June '76	A
Clear Sailin'	Asylum	1104	May '77	

SKIP BATTIN

Skip Battin	Signpost	SP–8408	January '73	

GENE PARSONS

Kindling	Warner Brothers	BS–2687	August '73	
Melodies	Sierra	8703	February '80	A

ROGER McGUINN

Roger McGuinn	Columbia	C–31946	June '73	A
Peace on You	Columbia	KC–32956	September '74	
Roger McGuinn and Band	Columbia	PC–33541	June '75	
Cardiff Rose	Columbia	PC–34154	May '76	
Thunderbyrd	Columbia	PC–34656	March '77	

McGUINN, CLARK, AND HILLMAN

McGuinn, Clark, and Hillman	Capitol	SW–11910	January '79	A
City	Capitol	ST–12043	January '80	A

McGUINN AND HILLMAN

McGuinn and Hillman	Capitol	SOO–12108	October '80	A

J.J. CALE. An outstanding guitarist with a haunting yet lazy playing style, John "J.J." Cale (not to be confused with John Cale, formerly with The Velvet Underground) is best known as a Seventies singer–songwriter, authoring such popular songs as "After Midnight," "Magnolia," and "Cocaine."

J.J. CALE

Naturally	Shelter	SW–8908	November '71	
		reissued as 2122	October '74	
		later reissued as 52009		A
Really	Shelter	SW–8912	December '72	
		reissued as 52012		A
Okie	Shelter	SR–2107	May '74	
		reissued as 52015		A
Troubadour	Shelter	SRL–52002	September '76	A
5	MCA	ST–3163	September '79	A
Shades	MCA	5158	February '81	A

CANNED HEAT. A sixties white American blues-and-boogie band, Canned Heat created its own distinctive style by adapting old country-blues material in a fresh, exciting manner without the addition of a horn section, a practice favored by contemporary Chicago and New York white blues bands.

Originally formed as a jug band in Los Angeles during 1965 by blues enthusiast Bob "The Bear" Hite (born February 26, 1943, in Torrance, California), Alan "Blind Owl" Wilson (born July 4, 1943, in Boston, Massachusetts), and Frank Cook, Canned Heat became a white blues band with the addition of Henry Vestine (born December 25, 1944, in Washington, D.C.) and Larry Taylor (born June 26, 1949, in Brooklyn, New York). The members: Bob Hite (lead vocals, harmonica), Alan Wilson (guitar, harmonica, vocals), Henry Vestine (lead guitar), Larry Taylor (bass), and

Frank Cook (drums). Wilson had majored in music at Boston University and was a skilled arranger and recognized blues authority; Vestine had played briefly with The Mothers of Invention, and Taylor had played bass behind Jerry Lee Lewis in the Fifties.

Canned Heat's enthusiastic reception at The Monterey Pop Festival in June 1967 catapulted the band into national prominence. Signed to Liberty Records, the group's first album contained the underground favorite "Rollin' and Tumblin'." The second album, on which Fito de la Parra (born February 8, 1946, in Mexico City, Mexico) replaced Cook, featured "Amphetamine Annie" and the major hit "On the Road Again." Touring Europe in the fall of 1968, Canned Heat received an even more enthusiastic response there than in the States. Their third album, *Livin' the Blues*, continued the band's hit-making ways with "Going Up the Country." In July 1969 Vestine departed and was replaced by Chicago sideman Harvey Mandel. The following May Taylor left, and Vestine returned. On September 3, 1970, founding member Alan Wilson was found dead. Within weeks, Canned Heat scored another major hit with a remake of Wilbert Harrison's "Let's Work Together."

Subsequently, Joel Scott Hill took over on rhythm and lead guitar, Mandel quit, and Antonio de la Barreda joined on bass. During 1971, the band teamed with one of the legendary black blues artists, John Lee Hooker, for the recording of *Hooker 'n' Heat*. Thereafter a series of confusing personnel changes ensued: de la Barreda left, Larry Taylor returned, Joel Scott Hill quit, and Jamie Shane joined. With the band's popularity on the wane, they continued to record through 1974's *One More River to Cross*. Never disbanding, Canned Heat continued to follow a rigorous touring schedule. After recording an album for Takoma Records in 1979 as the only founding member still performing with Canned Heat, Bob "The Bear" Hite died of an accidental drug overdose on April 5, 1981, at age 38, in Venice, California.

CANNED HEAT

Live at Topanga	Wand	WDS–693		
	reissued on			
	Pickwick	3364		
Canned Heat	Liberty	LST–7526	August '67	
Boogie with	Liberty	LST–7541	January '68	
Canned Heat	reissued on			
	Pickwick	3614	April '78	A
	reissued on	LN–10105	April '80	A
	Liberty			
Livin' the Blues	2-Liberty	LST–	October '68	
	reissued on	27200		
	United			
	Artists	9955	October '71	
Hallelujah	Liberty	LST–7618	July '69	
Cookbook (The	Liberty	LST–11000	December '69	
Best of Canned		reissued as	April '81	A
Heat)		LN–		
		10106		
Future Blues	Liberty	LST–11002	September '70	

CANNED HEAT AND JOHN LEE HOOKER

Hooker 'n' Heat	2-Liberty	35002	February '71	

CANNED HEAT

Vintage Canned Heat	Janus	JLS–3009	January '70	
Collage	Sunset	SUS–5298	April '71	
Live in Europe	United Artists	5509	July '71	
Historical Figures and Ancient Heads	United Artists	UAS–5557	February '72	
The New Age	United Artists	LA049	March '73	
The Very Best of Canned Heat	United Artists	LA431	September '75	
One More River to Cross	Atlantic	SD–7289	January '74	
Canned Heat	Springboard International	4026	June '75	
Human Condition	Takoma	7066	July '79	A
Captured Live	Accord	SN–12179	December '81	A

CAPTAIN BEEFHEART AND THE MAGIC BAND. An unusual aggregation of musicians that played a distinctive mix of delta blues, rock-and-roll, and avant-garde jazz, Captain Beefheart and The Magic Band, after almost 15 years in the entertainment business, may still be years ahead of their time. The band's unique sound, passed over by all but the most progressive of fans, is characterized by Beefheart's incredible voice (growling and gravelly, with at least a four and one-half octave range), intricate arrangements, enigmatic lyrics (generally written by Beefheart), and early use of the theremin, an electronic instrument. Perhaps best known for 1969's *Trout Mask Replica*, the album that made Captain Beefheart an "underground" favorite, Captain Beefheart and The Magic Band recorded *Doc at the Radar Station*, which was received enthusiastically by critics in 1980 as members of the "new wave" acknowledged his influence.

Born in Glendale, California, on January 15, 1941, as Don Van Vliet, Captain Beefheart moved to the desert town of Lancaster at age 13. There, in high school, he became friends with Frank Zappa. Playing harmonica and saxophone, Beefheart performed with several rhythm-and-blues bands before forming The Magic Band in 1964. Gaining a reputation in Southern California desert towns, the group recorded Bo Diddley's "Diddy Wah Diddy" for A&M Records, and the song became a regional hit. However, material for a first album was rejected by A&M as "too negative," and Van Vliet retreated to Lancaster. During 1965 he brought the rejected material to Buddah Records, who released it as *Safe as Milk*. Winning considerable critical acclaim in the U.S. and Europe, the album spurred a successful tour of Europe in early 1966. With the departure of lead guitarist Ry Cooder, Captain Beefheart and The Magic Band were crippled, since the lead guitar parts, complex and erratic, were personally taught by Van Vliet over long periods of time. Alex St. Claire was brought on for *Mirror Man*, an album not released until years later.

Sessions for *Strictly Personal* began in April 1968, under producer Bob Krasnow, with Van Vliet, St. Claire, Jeff Cotton (guitar), Jerry Handley (bass), and John French (drums). The album was released on Krasnow's own label, Blue Thumb, in altered form while the band was touring Europe that summer. The disappointed Van Vliet later accepted Frank Zappa's offer to make a new album, free of all artistic restrictions, on Zappa's Straight Records. Following Van Vliet's lead, the members of the re-organized Magic Band took on bizarre names: guitarist–flutist Bill Harkleroad became Zoot Horn Rollo; guitarist Jimmy Simmons became Antennae Jimmy Semens; bassist Mark Boston became Rockette Morton. John French (Drumbo) was the uncredited drummer, whereas the still-unidentified Mascara Snake sang and played clarinet. The double-record set, *Trout Mask Replica*, produced by Zappa, was hailed as one of the most advanced concepts in rock music but proved a dismal commercial failure.

In late 1970, more than a year later, *Lick Off My Decals, Baby* was released initially on Straight, before Beefheart switched to Reprise Records. During 1971, Captain Beefheart and The Magic Band made one of its infrequent tours of the U.S. to befuddled fans, subsequently adding Art Tripp (also known as Ed Marimba) on drums and marimba for *The Spotlight Kid* and *Clear Spot*. Moving to Mercury Records, the band issued the "softer" and more accessible *Unconditionally Guaranteed* during 1974. The follow-up, *Bluejeans and Moonbeams*, fared poorly and, in 1975, Beefheart and The Magic Band parted company. Subsequently, Bill Harkleroad and Mark Boston formed Mallard, recording for Virgin Records in the late Seventies.

Later in 1975, Captain Beefheart recorded *Bongo Fury* with Frank Zappa and The Mothers. By 1976, Van Vliet had reassembled The Magic Band for occasional club appearances. The members included Jeff Tepper and Denny Walley (guitars), Bruce "Fossil" Fowler (trombone), Eric Kitabu Feldman (bass, keyboards), and Robert "Wait for Me" Williams (drums). During 1977 and 1978, the re-formed group concluded a successful tour of Europe and played sold-out engagements at New York's Bottom Line and Hollywood's Roxy. Finally, in late 1978, the group issued *Shiny Beast (Bat Chain Puller)* on Warner Brothers Records. In 1980, Captain Beefheart and The Magic Band's next release, *Doc at the Radar Station*, was issued on Virgin Records, received favorable reviews, and was hailed as perhaps the best of Beefheart's career.

CAPTAIN BEEFHEART AND THE MAGIC BAND

Safe as Milk	Buddah	BDS–5001	late '65
		reissued as	
		5063	May '69
Mirror Man	Buddah	BDS–5077	January '71
Strictly Personal	Blue Thumb	BTS–1	October '68

Trout Mask Replica	2-Straight reissued on	STS-1053	June '69	
	Reprise	2027	September '70	A
Lick Off My Decals, Baby	Reprise	RS-6420	September '70	
The Spotlight Kid	Reprise	MS-2050	February '72	
Clear Spot	Reprise	MS-2115	November '72	A
Unconditionally Guaranteed	Mercury	SRM1-709	March '74	
Bluejeans and Moonbeams	Mercury	SRM1-1018	November '74	

CAPTAIN BEEFHEART/FRANK ZAPPA/THE MOTHERS

| Bongo Fury | DiscReet | DS-2234 | October '75 | |

MALLARD

| In a Different Climate | Virgin | PZ-34489 | May '77 | |

CAPTAIN BEEFHEART AND THE MAGIC BAND

| Shiny Beast (Bat Chain Puller) | Warner Brothers | 3256 | November '78 | A |
| Doc at the Radar Station | Virgin | 13148 | October '80 | A |

JOHNNY CASH. One of the first "rockabilly" stars along with Sun Records stablemates Carl Perkins, Jerry Lee Lewis, and Elvis Presley, Johnny Cash later recorded folk-oriented material before establishing himself firmly in the country and pop fields in the Sixties. Cash brought an almost unprecedented social consciousness to country music with 1964's "The Ballad of Ira Hayes" from *Bitter Tears*, his monumental tribute to the American Indian. Moreover, in the early Seventies he encouraged compassion toward and sympathy with youthful protesters with "What Is Truth" and "Man in Black." Johnny Cash has thus been particularly influential in broadening the scope of country-and-western music and in popularizing country music with rock fans. Perhaps the first international country star, Cash was instrumental in introducing Bob Dylan and Kris Kristofferson to broad public acceptance; he appeared with and recorded the songs of each of them early in their careers.

Born in Kingsland, Arkansas, on February 26, 1932, Johnny Cash traveled to Memphis, Tennessee, after his Air Force discharge in July 1954, there to meet guitarist Luther Perkins and bassist Marshall Grant. With Cash playing guitar and singing in a deep baritone voice of exceptionally low and narrow range, the three practiced together, eventually auditioning for Sam Phillips of Sun Records in March 1955. Signed to Sun as Johnny Cash and The Tennessee Two, their first single, "Cry, Cry, Cry" backed with "Hey Porter," became a moderate country hit. Their first big pop hit came in 1956 with Cash's own "I Walk the Line." Subsequent Sun hits to make the pop charts included "Ballad of a Teenage Queen," "Guess Things Happen That Way," and "The Ways of a Woman in Love." During 1958, Cash's backing group became The Tennessee Three with the addition of W.S. Holland, one of country music's first drummers. That August the four switched to Columbia Records and soon hit with "Don't Take Your Guns to Town."

After moving to California in 1958, Johnny Cash began feeling the strain of constant touring by the early Sixties. The collapse of his first marriage and the death of friend Johnny Horton were serious personal blows, and he started taking amphetamines and tranquilizers to cope with his busy life. Nonetheless, he scored his first major hit with Columbia in 1963 with "Ring of Fire," soon followed by "Understand Your Man." His *Ring of Fire* anthology album became his first certified gold-award album in 1965. Hanging out on the periphery of the Greenwich Village folk scene, Cash appeared with Bob Dylan at 1964's Newport Folk Festival. During this time, Cash recorded a number of folk songs such as Peter LaFarge's "The Ballad of Ira Hayes" and Bob Dylan's "Don't Think Twice, It's Alright" and "It Ain't Me Babe," another country and folk hit.

Despite increasing popular success, Cash's life seemed to deteriorate. In October 1965 he was arrested at El Paso International Airport in possession of hundreds of stimulants and tranquilizers. After being found near death in a small Georgia town in 1967, Cash decided to reform. With June Carter of country music's famed Carter family providing moral support, he cleaned up his act. Subsequently, the two hit the country charts with "Jackson" before marrying in 1968. In 1970 the couple hit the pop charts with Tim Hardin's "If I Were a Carpenter."

Though Luther Perkins died accidentally in 1968, Johnny Cash persevered, replacing him with Bob Wooten. A series of successful television appearances had begun in 1967 and his 1968 *Johnny Cash at Folsom Prison* revitalized his career and made him an international country star. The album was certified gold-award the year of its release, as was another live album, 1969's *Johnny Cash at San Quentin*. His first network television show, broadcast on ABC–TV, featured a film of Cash and Bob Dylan recording "Girl from the North Country," which later appeared on Dylan's first country album, *Nashville Skyline*. Later shows featured artists such as Gordon Lightfoot, Kris Kristofferson, Waylon Jennings, and Joni Mitchell. Cash's biggest pop hit occurred in 1969 with Shel Silverstein's novelty song "A Boy Named Sue." During that year's Newport Folk Festival, Cash introduced Kris Kristofferson, later recording his "Sunday Morning Coming Down" and launching his nascent career. Subsequently Cash again demonstrated his social consciousness with "What Is Truth" and "Man in Black." Through the Seventies, he co-starred with Kirk Douglas in the film *A Gunfight*, narrated and co-produced the soundtrack to the Christian epic *Gospel Road*, and played Las Vegas without benefit of opening comedian or house orchestra. He also assisted in the production of *The Trail of Tears*, a dramatization of the tragedy of the Cherokee Indians, broadcast on public television (PBS). Johnny Cash continues to do television, tour, and record, regularly placing in the country charts and occasionally making the pop charts, as with 1976's "One Piece at a Time." In 1978 he hit the country charts with "There Ain't No Good Chain Gang," recorded with Waylon Jennings. In 1979–80, Johnny Cash scored major country hits with his recollection of his early Sun days, "I Will Rock with You," a remake of "(Ghost) Riders in the Sky," and, with Waylon Jennings again, "I Wish I Was Crazy Again."

JOHNNY CASH

Johnny Cash with His Hot and Blue Guitar	Sun	1220(M)
Sings the Songs That Made Him Famous	Sun	SLP–1235 (M)
Greatest!	Sun	SLP–1240 (M)
Sings Hank Williams	Sun	SLP–1245 (M)
Now Here's Johnny Cash	Sun	1255(M)
All Aboard the Blue Train	Sun	1270(M)
Original Sun Sound of Johnny Cash	Sun	1275(M)

JOHNNY CASH AND JERRY LEE LEWIS

Sunday Down South	Sun	119(M) reissued as 119(E)	November '70	A
Sing Hank Williams	Sun	125(M) reissued as 125(E)	September '71	A

JOHNNY CASH

The Fabulous Johnny Cash	Columbia	1253(M) later CS–8122	November '58 March '59	
Hymns by Johnny Cash	Columbia	CS–8125	April '59	A
Songs of Our Soil	Columbia	CS–8148	July '59	
Ride This Train	Columbia	CS–8255	August '60	
Now, There Was a Song!	Columbia	CS–8254	November '60	
Hymns from the Heart	Columbia	CS–8522	May '62	
Sound of Johnny Cash	Columbia	CS–8602	July '62	
Blood, Sweat and Tears	Columbia	CS–8730	January '63	

Christmas Spirit	Columbia	CS–8917	October '63	
I Walk the Line*	Columbia	CS–8990	June '64	A
Bitter Tears	Columbia	CS–9048	November '64	
Orange Blossom Special	Columbia	CS–9109	March '65	A
Ballads of the True West	2-Columbia	C2S–838	August '65	
Mean as Hell	Columbia	CS–9246	February '66	
Everybody Loves a Nut	Columbia	CS–9292	May '66	
That's What You Get for Lovin' Me	Columbia	CS–9337	October '66	
From Sea to Shining Sea	Columbia	CS–9447	February '68	
At Folsom Prison*	Columbia	PC–9639	June '68	A
The Holy Land	Columbia	KCS–9726	February '69	
At San Quentin*	Columbia	PC–9827	July '69	A
Hello, I'm Johnny Cash*	Columbia	KCS–9943	January '70	
The Johnny Cash Show	Columbia	KC–30100	November '70	
I Walk the Line (soundtrack)	Columbia	30397	December '70	
Man in Black	Columbia	C–30550	June '71	
A Thing Called Love	Columbia	KC–31332	April '72	
America: A 200-Year Salute in Story and Song	Columbia	KC–31645	September '72	
Any Old Wind That Blows	Columbia	KC–32091	February '73	A
Gospel Road (soundtrack)	2-Columbia	KG–32253	May '73	
That Ragged Old Flag	Columbia	KC–32917	June '74	
Five Feet High and Rising	Columbia	C–32951	July '74	
The Junkie and the Juicehead Minus Me	Columbia	KC–33086	November '74	
Sings Precious Memories	Columbia	C–33087	March '75	A
John R. Cash	Columbia	KC–33370	May '75	
Look at Them Beans	Columbia	KC–33814	November '75	
Strawberry Cake	Columbia	KC–34088	March '76	
One Piece at a Time	Columbia	PC–34193	June '76	
Last Gunfighter Ballad	Columbia	PC–34314	March '77	
The Rambler	Columbia	PC–34833	August '77	
I Would Like to See You Again	Columbia	KC–35313	May '78	
Gone Girl	Columbia	PC–35646	November '78	A

Silver	Columbia	JC–36086	August '79	A
A Believer Sings the Truth	Cachet	2–9001	December '79	
Rockabilly Blues	Columbia	JC–36779	October '80	A
Classic Christmas	Columbia	JC–36866	November '80	A
The Baron	Columbia	FC–37179	June '81	A
Encore	CBS	FC–37355	July '81	A

JOHNNY CASH AND JUNE CARTER

Carryin' On	Columbia	CS–9528	September '67	
Johnny Cash and His Woman	Columbia	C–32443	September '73	A
Give My Love to	Harmony	KH–31256	July '72	
The Johnny Cash Family Christmas	Columbia	C–31754	December '72	

THE TENNESSEE THREE

The Sound Behind Johnny Cash	Columbia	C–30220	June '71	

JOHNNY CASH ANTHOLOGIES, COMPILATIONS, AND REISSUES

Original Golden Hits, Volume 1	Sun	100(E)	September '69	A
Original Golden Hits, Volume 2	Sun	101(E)	September '69	A
Get Rhythm	Sun	105(E)	November '69	A
Story Songs of the Trains and Rivers	Sun	104(E)	December '69	A
Showtime	Sun	106(E)	December '69	A
The Singing Storyteller	Sun	115(E)	May '70	
Living Legend	2-Sun	118(E)	September '70	
Rough Cut King of Country Music	Sun	122(E)	November '70	
The Man, the World, His Music	2-Sun	126(E)	August '71	
Original Golden Hits, Volume 3	Sun	127(E)	February '72	A
I Walk the Line	Sun	139(M)		A
Folsom Prison Blues	Sun	140		A
Blue Train	Sun	141		A
Greatest Hits	Sun	142(M)		A
Superbilly (1955–1958)	Sun	1002(M)	August '78	A
The Original	Sun	1006		A
Sun Story, Volume 1	Sunnyvale	901(M)	November '77	
Johnny Cash	Harmony	11342	August '69	

Walls of a Prison	Harmony	KH–30138	November '70	
Johnny Cash Songbook	Harmony	KH–31602	October '72	
Ballad of the American Indians	Harmony	KH–32388	September '73	
Folsom Prison Blues	Hilltop reissued on	6116	April '72	
	Pickwick	6114		
I Walk the Line	Nashville	2108	May '73	
I Walk the Line/ Rock Island Line	2-Pickwick	2045		
Johnny Cash	2-Pickwick	2052		A
I Walk the Line	Pickwick	6097		
Rock Island Line	Pickwick	6101		
Big River	Pickwick	6118		
Country Gold	Power Pak	246(E)		A
Johnny Cash	Archive of Folk and Jazz Music	278		
Ring of Fire *	Columbia	CS–8853	July '63	A
Greatest Hits *	Columbia	PC–9478	July '67	A
The World of Johnny Cash *	2-Columbia	CG–29	June '70	A
Collection: His Greatest Hits, Volume 2 *	Columbia	PC–30887	October '71	A
At Folsom Prison and San Quentin	2-Columbia	CG–33639	October '75	A
Greatest Hits, Volume 3	Columbia	KC–35637	October '78	A

HARRY CHAPIN. A popular singer–songwriter–guitarist, Harry Chapin composed a new breed of Seventies songs best described as story songs, long narrative-style tales of loneliness and disappointment. He attained success on the basis of tireless touring, frequently at benefit concerts, rather than through his recordings, and died accidentally in 1981.

THE CHAPIN BROTHERS

Chapin Music	Rockland Music		'64

HARRY CHAPIN

Heads and Tales	Elektra	75023	March '72	A
Sniper and Other Love Songs	Elektra	EKS– 75042	September '72	A
Short Stories	Elektra	75065	December '73	A
Verities and Balderdash *	Elektra	7E–1012	September '74	A
Portrait Gallery	Elektra	1041	October '75	A

Greatest Stories: Live *	2-Elektra	2009 reissued as 6003	April '76	A
On the Road to Kingdom Come	Elektra	1082	October '76	A
Dance Band on the Titanic	2-Elektra	9E–301	August '77	A
Living Room Suite	Elektra	142	June '78	
Legends of the Lost and Found— New Greatest Stories Live	2-Elektra	703	October '79	A
Sequel	Boardwalk	FW–36872	October '80	A

RAY CHARLES. A multi-talented blind black musician, Ray Charles opened the way for the "soul" sound that became popular among both blacks and whites during the late Fifties and early Sixties. In secularizing certain facets of gospel music (chord changes, call-and-response techniques, vocal screams, wails, and moans) and combining them with blues-based lyrics, Charles devised a new genre of music. His gospel-based vocal style influenced virtually all the soul singers of the Sixties as well as many of the white English singers of the Sixties and Seventies (Mick Jagger, Eric Burdon, Joe Cocker, Rod Stewart, and others). Along with musicians such as Horace Silver, Charles was instrumental in leading many jazz musicians away from the abstracted and relatively inaccessible music of "be-bop" back to the roots of so-called "funk" or "soul" music. In using the electric piano on his first major pop hit, "What'd I Say," Charles was one of the first musicians to use the instrument that was to become so popular in both jazz and rock in the Sixties and Seventies. Moreover, the vocal work of Charles' female back-up group, The Raeletts, set the standard for black vocal groups that was so successfully exploited by Motown Records in the Sixties. Finally, in applying his gospel-oriented style to country-and-western material in the early Sixties, Ray Charles became the first black musician to have hits in the country field and the first black singer to make a major impact on the white adult market.

Born in Albany, Georgia, on September 23, 1930, as Ray Charles Robinson, Ray Charles was blinded by glaucoma at age 6, later learning the fundamentals of music at St. Augustine (Florida) School for the Blind. Starting with piano, he later took up clarinet and alto saxophone while learning both composition and arranging. Orphaned at 15, Charles went on the road to earn his livelihood at music. He joined Lowell Fulson's blues band for a year on the road before settling in Seattle in 1947 or 1948. There he formed The Maxim Trio, a Nat "King" Cole–style group who recorded on the small, Los Angeles-based Swingtime label beginning in 1948. Ray Charles' first rhythm-and-blues hit came in 1951 with "Baby Let Me Hold Your Hand." Switching to the New York-based rhythm-and-blues Atlantic label in 1952, he began regularly producing rhythm-and-blues hits in 1954, having shed his Nat "King" Cole stylizations and adapted gospel music techniques to blues lyrics. In early 1955 this new sound hit on both the popular and rhythm-and-blues markets with Charles' own composition, "I've Got a Woman."

Using top-flight studio musicians such as David "Fathead" Newman and the vocal back-up group, The Raeletts, Ray Charles scored consistently on the rhythm-and-blues charts throughout the late Fifties. He also became popular among jazz fans, recording two highly acclaimed albums with Modern Jazz Quartet vibist Milt Jackson and performing a startling set at the Newport Jazz Festival in July 1958. Finally, in 1959, Charles established himself as a highly successful popular artist with the release of his own smash hit composition, "What'd I Say." Sensing that Atlantic was still basically a rhythm-and-blues organization, he moved to ABC–Paramount Records in late 1959. Through 1961 he scored with the top pop hits "Georgia on My Mind" and "Hit the Road Jack" and major pop hits "Ruby" and "Unchain My Heart." In early 1961 Charles recorded *Genius + Soul = Jazz*, with arrangements by Quincy Jones played by the Count Basie Band. This album brought Charles an increasing measure of popularity with jazz fans, black and white, and even yielded a near-smash hit single, "One Mint Julep."

By 1962 Ray Charles was utilizing 40-piece orchestras and large vocal choruses for his recordings. With this full, commercial sound, his *Modern Sounds in Country and Western* became phenomenally popular. The album quickly became Charles' first certified gold-award album and yielded the smash hit singles "I Can't Stop Loving You" backed with "Born to Lose" and "You Don't Know Me." Within a year, *Volume II* of country-and-western material appeared with the near-smash hit singles "You Are My Sunshine" backed with "Your Cheating Heart" and "Take These Chains from My Heart." Major hit singles occurred through the Sixties with "Busted" and "That Lucky Old Sun" in 1963, "Crying Time" in 1965, "Together Again" and "Let's Go Get Stoned" in 1966, and "Here We Go Again" and Paul McCartney's "Yesterday" in 1967. During 1968, *Country and Western, Volume II, Greatest Hits*, and the anthology *A Man and His Soul* were all certified gold-award.

In the late Sixties and Seventies, Ray Charles continued to tour regularly, record for ABC, and appear frequently on television. He recorded for his own independent Crossover label after 1973 and returned to Atlantic in 1977. During 1976 Ray Charles also recorded *Porgy and Bess* with English songstress Cleo Laine for RCA Records.

PRE–ATLANTIC RAY CHARLES

Ray Charles with Arbee Stidham, Lil Son Jackson, and James Wayne	Mainstream	MRL–310	September '71

Ray Charles	Archive of Folk and Jazz Music	FS–244(E)	May '70	A
Ray Charles, Volume II	Archive of Folk and Jazz Music	FS–292(E)	September '74	A
14 Hits: The Early Years	King	5011(M)	December '77	A

RAY CHARLES

Hallelujah I Love Her So	Atlantic	8006(M)	August '57	
The Great Ray Charles	Atlantic	1259(M) reissued as 1259	September '57 June '60	A
Ray Charles at Newport	Atlantic	1289	October '58	
Yes Indeed!	Atlantic	8025(M)	October '58	
What'd I Say	Atlantic	8029(M)	September '59	
The Genius of Ray Charles	Atlantic	SD–1312	October '59	A
Ray Charles in Person	Atlantic	8039(M)	May '60	
The Genius After Hours	Atlantic	1369(M)	August '61	
The Genius Sings the Blues	Atlantic	8052(M)	August '61	
Live	2-Atlantic	SD2–503	April '73	A

RAY CHARLES AND MILT JACKSON

Soul Brothers	Atlantic	1279	July '58	A
Brothers in Soul— Soul Meeting	Atlantic	SD–1360	December '62	A

RAY CHARLES

Genius + Soul = Jazz	Impulse	A–2	January '61	
Original Ray Charles	Hollywood	504(M)	July '62	
Fabulous Artistry	Hollywood	505(M)	January '63	
Great Ray Charles	Premier	2004	December '62	
Fabulous Ray Charles	Premier	2005	December '62	
Ray Charles	Design	145	October '62	
Ray Charles	2-Time Volumes	2,4	March '63	
Incomparable Ray Charles	Strand	1086	April '63	
Ray Charles	Coronet	CX–173		
Memories of a Middle-Aged Man	Atco	33–263	November '68	

The Genius Hits the Road	ABC	335	July '60	
Dedicated to You	ABC	ABCS–355	January '61	
Ray Charles and Betty Carter	ABC	385	June '61	
Modern Sounds in Country and Western*	ABC	ABCS–410	January '62	
Modern Sounds in Country and Western, Volume II*	ABC	ABCS–435	October '62	
Ingredients in a Recipe for Soul	ABC	ABCS–465	June '63	
Sweet and Sour Tears	ABC	ABCS–480	February '64	
Have a Smile with Me	ABC	ABCS–495	July '64	
Live in Concert	ABC	ABCS–500	January '65	
Together Again (Country and Western Meets Rhythm and Blues)	ABC	520	August '65	
Crying Time	ABC	ABCS–544	January '66	
Ray's Moods	ABC	550	July '66	
Ray Charles Invites You to Listen	ABC	595	May '67	
A Portrait of Ray	ABC	625	March '68	
I'm All Yours	ABC	675	April '69	
Doing His Thing	ABC	695	June '69	
Love Country Style	ABC	707	July '70	
Volcanic Action of My Soul	ABC	726	March '71	
Cryin' Time	ABC	744	January '71	
A Message from the People	ABC	755	April '72	
Through the Eyes of Love	ABC	ABCX–765	October '72	
All-Time Great Country and Western Hits	2-ABC	ABCX–781/2	February '73	
My Kind of Jazz	Tangerine/ABC	TRCS–1512	June '70	
Jazz Number II	Tangerine/ABC	TRC–1516	February '73	
Come Live with Me	Crossover	CR–9000	February '74	
Renaissance	Crossover	CR–9005	June '75	
My Kind of Jazz, Part 3	Crossover	CR–9007	December '75	

RAY CHARLES AND CLEO LAINE

Porgy and Bess	2-RCA	CPL2–1831	November '76	A

RAY CHARLES

True to Life	Atlantic	SD–19142	November '77	
Love and Peace	Atlantic	19199	October '78	
Ain't It So	Atlantic	19251	October '79	A
Brother Ray Is at It Again	Atlantic	19281	October '80	A

RAY CHARLES ANTHOLOGIES

Best	Atlantic	SD–1543	reissued April '70	A
The Greatest Ray Charles (Do the Twist with Ray Charles)	Atlantic	SD–8054	December '61	A
The Ray Charles Story, Volume I	Atlantic	8063(M)	July '62	
The Ray Charles Story, Volume II	Atlantic	8064(M)	July '62	
The Ray Charles Story, Volumes I and II	2-Atlantic	2–900	July '62	
The Ray Charles Story, Volume III	Atlantic	8083(M)	June '63	
The Ray Charles Story, Volume IV	Atlantic	8094	June '64	
Great Hits of Ray Charles	Atlantic	7101	July '64	
Greatest Hits*	ABC	ABCS–415	July '62	
A Man and His Soul*	2-ABC	590	January '67	
25th Anniversary Salute	3-ABC	ABCH–731	October '71	
Rockin' with Ray	Archive of Folk and Jazz Music	358	November '80	A

CHEECH AND CHONG.   The first major stand-up comedy act of rock music and of the counter-culture, Cheech and Chong project a street-wise sense of humor concerned primarily with ethnicity and drugs and have sold more records than has any other comedy act. Buoyed by the astounding success of their 1978 film *Up in Smoke*, Cheech and Chong have subsequently concentrated on stoned-out comedy films.

CHEECH AND CHONG

Cheech and Chong*	Ode reissued on	77010	September '71	
	Warner Brothers	3250	October '78	A

Big Bambu*	Ode	SP–77014	June '72	
	reissued on			
	Warner	3251	October '78	A
	Brothers			
Los Cochinos*	Ode	77019	August '73	
	reissued on			
	Warner	3252	October '78	A
	Brothers			
Wedding Album*	Ode	77025	October '74	
	reissued on			
	Warner	3253	October '78	A
	Brothers			
Sleeping Beauty	Ode	77040	June '76	
	reissued on			
	Warner	3254	October '78	A
	Brothers			
Up in Smoke (soundtrack)	Warner Brothers	3249	October '78	A
Let's Make a New Dope Deal	Warner Brothers	HS–3391	March '80	A
Greatest Hits	Warner Brothers	3614	September '81	A

CHICAGO. A big-band rock group that initially utilized jazz-style improvisations, Chicago quickly degenerated into a pop group of huge popularity, issuing album after album of formulaic, predictable, middle-of-the-road fare. Amazingly, *every* Chicago album except their most recent has been certified gold-award, with three having been certified platinum-award during their years of release.

CHICAGO TRANSIT AUTHORITY

Chicago Transit Authority*	2-Columbia	PG–8	April '69	A

CHICAGO

Chicago*	2-Columbia	PG–24	February '70,	A
Chicago III*	2-Columbia	C2–30110	January '71	A
Live at Carnegie Hall*	4-Columbia	K4X– 30865	April '71	A
Chicago V*	Columbia	PC–31102	July '72	A
Chicago VI*	Columbia	PC–32400	June '73	A
Chicago VII*	2-Columbia	C2–32810	March '74	A

ROBERT LAMM

Skinny Boy	Columbia	KC–33095	August '74	

CHICAGO

Chicago VIII*	Columbia	PC–33100	March '75	A
Chicago IX— Chicago's Greatest Hits*	Columbia	JC–33900	November '75	A

Chicago X *	Columbia	PC–34200	June '76	A
Chicago XI *	Columbia	JC–34860	September '77	A
Hot Streets **	Columbia	FC–35512	September '78	A
Chicago XIII *	Columbia	FC–36105	August '79	A
Chicago XIV	Columbia	FC–36517	August '80	A
Greatest Hits, Volume 2	Columbia	FC–37682	December '81	A

PETER CETERA

Peter Cetera	Full Moon	3624	October '81	A

ERIC CLAPTON. Guitarist extraordinaire Eric Clapton is one of the two finest lead guitar players to emerge during the Sixties (Jimi Hendrix, of course, is the other). A member of three of the most influential English blues groups active in the Sixties (The Yardbirds, John Mayall's Bluesbreakers, and Cream), Clapton established the standard for the "clean" school of lead playing with his tasty, precise yet fluid guitar work. Cream, rock music's first powerhouse vocal and instrumental trio, made virtuoso playing an art form within rock and sparked the late-Sixties blues revival. The short-lived Blind Faith continued the improvisatory tradition, as did Clapton's first group, Derek and The Dominoes. Eric Clapton's subsequent solo work has emphasized the songs and ensemble performance rather than his lead playing and has incorporated a number of distinctly Seventies' rock phenomena, most notably reggae and country music.

Born in Ripley, Surrey, England, on March 30, 1945, Eric Clapton began playing guitar around the age of 16, later performing with a number of different bands before joining The Metropolis Blues Quartet in October 1963. The group later changed their name to The Yardbirds and Clapton stayed on with the group through March 1965. Put off by the increasingly commercial nature of The Yardbirds, Clapton sought out musicians more into a traditional blues "bag," joining John Mayall's Bluesbreakers in April 1965. There Clapton received extensive adulation as England's finest guitarist before leaving in July 1966 to form Cream. As the first "supergroup," Cream revolutionized rock music with their patented improvisational jams and inspired the blues revival of the late Sixties. With internal strains becoming increasingly evident by mid-1968, Cream announced their intention to disband and performed their final concert at London's Royal Albert Hall in December.

Almost immediately, another "supergroup," Blind Faith, was formed by Cream alumni Eric Clapton and Ginger Baker with Traffic's Stevie Winwood and Family's Rick Grech. Destined never to meet the promise of their overly enthusiastic publicity, Blind Faith completed one English and one American tour and one album before disbanding at the end of 1969. The interesting, if flawed, gold-award album featured Winwood's "Sea of Joy" and "Can't Find My Way Home" as well as Clapton's "In the Presence of the Lord." Subsequently Clapton participated in a number of sessions for other artists before joining the Delaney and Bonnie and Friends tour of 1970. Many of these "friends" later assisted Clapton with his first solo album. Included were Delaney and Bonnie, Leon Russell, Rita Coolidge, Steve Stills, drummer Jim Gordon, bassist Carl Radle, organist Bobby Whitlock, saxophonist Bobby Keys, and trumpeter Jim Price. The album contained the major hit single "After Midnight," composed by J.J. Cale, and featured outstanding lead guitar work on songs such as "Blues Power" and "Let It Rain."

In May 1970 Eric Clapton formed Derek and The Dominoes on the U.S. West Coast with Gordon, Radle, Whitlock, and Allman Brothers' Duane Allman. The group's first album, *Layla*, was certified gold-award during 1971. It included excellent double-lead guitar work on songs such as "Layla," "Bell Bottom Blues," "Keep on Growing," and Jimi Hendrix's "Little Wing." In 1971 Derek and The Dominoes toured without Allman; live recordings from the tour were issued in 1973. However, by 1972, the group had disbanded and Clapton, disillusioned by the death of Duane Allman and the failure of the "Layla" single on its first release (it became a near-smash hit when re-released in 1972), went into near-retirement. During this time, Clapton emerged only three times for live performances: in August 1971 at George Harrison's Bangla Desh Concert, in December 1971 for Leon Russell's Rainbow Theater engagement, and in January 1973 at The Rainbow Theater at the behest of The Who's Pete Townshend.

Clapton's first album of new material, *461 Ocean Boulevard*, was issued in 1974. The musicians included second guitarist George Terry, keyboardist Albhy Galuten, organist Dick Sims, bassist Radle, drummer Jamie Oldaker, and vocalist Yvonne Elliman. Clapton showcased his modest vocal talents, relegating his guitar playing to a secondary role. The album yielded one of Clapton's biggest hit singles, "I Shot the Sheriff," composed by reggae artist Bob Marley. Clapton toured the United States again during 1974 and 1975, featuring George Terry on second lead. Live recordings from the tour were released as *E.C. Was Here* several months after *There's One in Every Crowd*. During 1976 Clapton toured England for the first time in five years, issuing *No Reason to Cry* that fall. Clapton appears to be well on his way to regained widespread popularity; both *Slowhand* and *Backless* were certified platinum-award, and during 1978–79 he scored the smash hit "Lay Down Sally," the major hit "Wonderful Tonight," and the near-smash "Promises." During 1979 Eric Clapton again toured the United States with Radle, Oldaker, Sims, and British sessions guitarist Albert Lee, achieving a moderate hit with "Watch Out for Lucy." In 1980 Eric Clapton hit with "Tulsa Time/Cocaine," switching to Warner Brothers in late 1981.

ERIC CLAPTON WITH THE YARDBIRDS

For Your Love	Epic	BN–26167	June '65
Having a Rave Up	Epic	BN–26177	November '65
(side two only)			

Live with Sonny Boy Williamson	Mercury	SR–61071	March '66	
Eric Clapton and The Yardbirds	Springboard International	4036	November '75	

ERIC CLAPTON WITH JOHN MAYALL'S BLUESBREAKERS

Bluesbreakers	London	PS–492 reissued as	January '67	
		50009	February '78	A

BLIND FAITH

Blind Faith *	Atco reissued on	SD33–304	August '69	
	RSO	3016	February '77	A

ERIC CLAPTON WITH DELANEY AND BONNIE AND FRIENDS

On Tour	Atco	SD33–326	April '70	A

ERIC CLAPTON

Eric Clapton	Atco reissued on	SD33–329	July '70	
	RSO	3008	February '77	A
History of Eric Clapton *	2-Atco	SD2–803	April '72	A
Eric Clapton at His Best	2-Polydor	PD–3503	October '72	
Clapton	Polydor	PD–5526	February '73	

DEREK AND THE DOMINOES

Layla *	2-Atco reissued on	SD2–704	November '70	
	Polydor reissued on	PD–3501		
	RSO	3801	February '77	A
In Concert *	2-RSO	SO2–8800	January '73	

THE RAINBOW CONCERT

Eric Clapton's Rainbow Concert *	RSO	SO–877	September '73	

ERIC CLAPTON

461 Ocean Boulevard *	RSO	SO–4801	July '74	
There's One in Every Crowd	RSO	SO–4806	March '75	
E.C. Was Here	RSO	SO–4809	August '75	
No Reason to Cry	RSO	RS1–3004	August '76	
Slow Hand *	RSO	RS1–3030	November '77	A

Backless**	RSO	3039	November '78	
Just One Night*	2-RSO	2–4202	April '80	
Another Ticket*	RSO	3095	March '81	A

THE DAVE CLARK FIVE. One of the few groups led by a drummer, The Dave Clark Five capitalized on their English origin following the impact of The Beatles. They produced a number of mundane hits, particularly in the United States, before fading into oblivion in the late Sixties.

THE DAVE CLARK FIVE

Glad All Over*	Epic	BN–26093	April '64
Return!	Epic	BN–26104	July '64
American Tour	Epic	BN–26117	September '64
Coast to Coast	Epic	BN–26128	February '65
Weekend in London	Epic	BN–26139	April '65
Having a Wild Weekend (soundtrack)	Epic	BN–26162	July '65
I Like It like That	Epic	BN–26178	December '65
Greatest Hits*	Epic	BN–26185	March '66
Try Too Hard	Epic	BN–26198	July '66
Satisfied with You	Epic	BN–26212	September '66
More Greatest Hits	Epic	BN–26221	November '66
5 by 5	Epic	BN–26236	March '67
You Got What It Takes	Epic	BN–26312	July '67
Everybody Knows	Epic	BN–26354	February '68
The Dave Clark Five	Epic	EG–30434	November '71
Glad All Over Again (All-Time Greatest Hits)	2-Epic	KEG–33459	April '75

DICK CLARK. Host of ABC-TV's long run music-and-dance program "American Bandstand," Dick Clark helped promote the careers of most of the rock-and-rollers of the Fifties, both the talents and no-talents, while exploiting his position in the music industry through song copyright, record label and music publishing co-ownerships, and crass merchandising. Escaping most of the ill effects of the payola scandal of 1959, Dick Clark survived the furor and maintained his only slightly tarnished position in popular media, whereas many others (such as Alan Freed) were totally ruined by the investigation.

Born in Mount Vernon, New York, on November 30, 1929, Dick Clark became a radio station disc jockey at Syracuse University's campus station while majoring there in business administration. After graduation he worked at his uncle's upstate New York radio station before becoming a radio announcer at Philadelphia's WFIL in 1952. In 1956 Clark became host of WFIL–TV's dance-and-music show, "Philadelphia Bandstand," originally created by disc jockey Bob Horn. Thirteen months later, Clark persuaded officials of ABC to broadcast the show over the entire network as "American Bandstand" on weekday afternoons when students would be returning home from school. The format usually included one or two guest stars synchronizing their lip movements to their recorded songs, teenagers dancing to the records, and small-talk and record ratings by members of the audience. The show became enormously popular and a number of Philadelphia teenagers who regularly appeared as dancers became household celebrities. During the late Fifties, Clark became a full partner in Philadelphia-based record labels such as Jamie and Swan while promoting local "talents" such as Fabian, Frankie Avalon, Bobby Rydell, and Chubby Checker. Also during this time, Clark headed a number of tours presenting Dick Clark's Cavalcade of Stars at venues across the country.

Called before the Senate investigating committee probing so-called "payola" activities among disc jockeys, Dick Clark admitted to accepting a fur stole and expensive jewelry from a record company president. Clark was admonished for only this single transgression, despite the fact that songs and artists in which he held a significant interest were frequently featured on "American Bandstand." Clark had apparently divested himself of his music business holdings at a crucial time—before appearing to testify.

Dick Clark subsequently returned to his "Bandstand" show, moving in 1964 to Los Angeles, where he hosted "Where the Action Is" in the late Sixties. During the Seventies, Clark expanded his media exploits, producing TV specials and issuing a best-selling anthology rock-and-roll album under his name. Dick Clark's 1978 variety series "Live Wednesday" was quickly canceled, yet he has since served as host of the quiz show "$50,000 Pyramid" as well as the continuing "Bandstand" series, written the health book *Looking Great, Staying Young,* and produced TV specials such as "The Birth of The Beatles" and "The 30th Anniversary of American Bandstand."

DICK CLARK

Dance with Dick Clark, Volume 1	ABC–Paramount	ABC–258 (M)	
Dance with Dick Clark, Volume 2	ABC–Paramount	ABC–288	October '59
20 Years of Rock n' Roll *	2-Buddah	BDS–5133	July '73

JIMMY CLIFF.   The most accessible singer–songwriter to emerge from Jamaica's burgeoning reggae scene, Jimmy Cliff achieved his greatest success as the lead actor in the film *The Harder They Come.*

JIMMY CLIFF

Can't Get Enough of It	Veep	VPS–16536	April '69	
Wonderful World, Beautiful People	A&M	SP–4251	March '70	A

JIMMY CLIFF AND OTHERS

The Harder They Come (soundtrack)	Mango	SMAS–7400	February '73	
	reissued on Island/Mango	9202	March '75	A

JIMMY CLIFF

Unlimited	Reprise	2147	August '73	
Struggling Man	Island	SW–9343	June '74	
	reissued on Island/Mango	9235		A
Music Maker	Reprise	2188	September '74	
Follow My Mind	Reprise	MS–2218	October '75	
In Concert: The Best of Jimmy Cliff	Reprise	MS–2256	November '76	A
Give Thankx	Warner Brothers	3240	October '78	A
I Am the Living	MCA	5153	December '80	A
Give the People What They Want	MCA	5217	December '81	A

THE COASTERS. Rock-and-roll's first consistently successful comedy–vocal group, The Coasters issued a number of wry songs of adolescent pathos under the direction of the premier songwriting-production team of the Fifties, Jerry Leiber and Mike Stoller. One of the first black rhythm-and-blues vocal groups to achieve widespread popularity among white youth, The Coasters featured the unerringly ballsy saxophone playing of King Curtis on virtually all of their recordings, jointly producing a characteristic sound of almost unparalleled distinction.

The Coasters evolved out of The Robins, a rhythm-and-blues vocal group originally formed on the West Coast in 1950. Signed to Jerry Leiber and Mike Stoller's Los Angeles-based Spark Records, The Robins first drew the attention of New York's Atlantic Records with Leiber and Stoller's "Smokey Joe's Cafe" in 1955. Subsequently, the Spark catalog was sold to Atlantic and Leiber and Stoller signed probably the first independent production deal with Atlantic's subsidiary, Atco. The Robins' management balked at the prospective deal that would take the group to Atco, so Leiber and Stoller convinced lead singer Carl Gardner (born in Texas on April 29, 1928) and bass singer Bobby Nunn to form a new group. Joined by tenors Billy Guy (born in Hollywood on June 20, 1936) and Leon Hughes, they became The Coasters, first making the rhythm-and-blues charts in early 1956 with "Down in Mexico." Their first pop success came during 1957 with the two-sided hit "Youngblood/Searchin'."

During 1958 Leon Hughes left the group to be replaced first by Young Jessie, then Cornell Gunter, and finally by Earl Carroll (born November 2, 1937), formerly of The Cadillacs ("Speedo"). Around the same time, Will "Dub" Jones of The Cadets ("Stranded in the Jungle") took over for the retiring Bobby Nunn. Through the late Fifties, The Coasters hit the pop charts regularly with Leiber and Stoller songs such as "Yakety Yak," "Charlie Brown," "Along Came Jones," and "Poison Ivy." By late 1959, however, the group began to falter, as "Run Red Run" and "What About Us" became only minor hits. The outstandingly funky "Shoppin' for Clothes," featuring an unusually lewd saxophone break by King Curtis, fared even less well. The Coasters' final major hit came in 1961 with "Little Egypt," yet another Leiber and Stoller song. By the mid-Sixties, the group had left Atlantic and Ronnie Bright (born October 18, 1938) replaced Will Jones. Appearing in various shows during the rock-and-roll revival of the early Seventies, The Coasters reunited with Leiber and Stoller for 1973's *On Broadway* for King Records. Today Carl Gardner, Earl Carroll, Ronnie Bright, and new member Jimmy Norman continue to perform as The Coasters, while Cornell Gunter tours with a group as Cornell Gunter and The Coasters. In April 1981 a mutilated body found nearly a year earlier was identified as that of latter-day Coasters member Nathaniel "Buster" Wilson.

THE COASTERS

The Coasters	Atco	33–101(M)	January '58	
The Coasters' Greatest Hits	Atco	33–111(M)	December '59	A
One by One	Atco	33–123	December '60	
Coast Along with The Coasters	Atco	33–135	August '62	
Their Greatest Recordings/The Early Years	Atco	SD–33–371 (M)	November '71	A
It Ain't Sanitary	Trip	TLP–8028	December '72	
On Broadway	King	1146	May '73	
Greatest Hits	Power Pak	310(M)	August '78	A

EDDIE COCHRAN. One of rock-and-roll's first "legends" due to his early accidental death, Eddie Cochran was a distinguished guitarist and one of the first white rock-and-rollers. Moreover, he helped pioneer the studio technique of overdubbing as evidenced by his two biggest hits, "Summertime Blues" and "C'mon Everybody."

EDDIE COCHRAN

Singin' to My Baby	Liberty	LRP–3061 (M)	August '57	
		reissued as LN–10137	November '81	A
Eddie Cochran	Liberty	LRP–3172 (M)	June '60	
Never to Be Forgotten	Liberty	LRP–3220 (M)	November '63	
Summertime Blues	Sunset	SUM–1123 (M)	August '58	
Eddie Cochran	Sunset	SUS–5123	August '69	
Legendary Masters, Volume IV	2-United Artists	UAS–9959	November '71	A
Very Best (15th Anniversary Album)	United Artists	LA428	September '75	

JOE COCKER. An English rhythm-and-blues style vocalist whose jerky body movements in performance brought him notoriety during the late Sixties and early Seventies, Joe Cocker achieved his greatest popularity with his 1969 appearance at the Woodstock Festival and his 1970 Mad Dogs and Englishmen tour.

Born in Sheffield, England, on May 20, 1944, as John Cocker, Joe Cocker began playing drums during the late Fifties. By 1963, he was lead vocalist for Vance Arnold and The Avengers, who recorded an unsuccessful version of Lennon and McCartney's "I'll Cry Instead" in 1964. Returning to Sheffield, Cocker and musical mentor Chris Stainton hit in England with Stainton's "Majorine" in 1968. Signed to A&M Records, Cocker recorded a slow blues version of Lennon and McCartney's "With a Little Help from My Friends" with Stainton. The record became a big English hit and marked Cocker's first entry into the American charts. The subsequent album of the same title featured English musicians such as Jimmy Page and Stevie Winwood and included a driving version of Dave Mason's "Feelin' Alright." The album, certified gold-award in 1970, effectively launched Cocker's career.

In 1969 Stainton and Cocker formed The Grease Band for a successful U.S. tour that culminated in Cocker's much-heralded appearance at Woodstock. During the tour Cocker met sessions pianist Leon Russell, who subsequently played on and produced *Joe Cocker!* The gold-award album contained a minor hit version of Russell's "Delta Lady" and Cocker's first substantial U.S. hit, "She Came in Through the Bathroom Window." In March 1970, despite being on the verge of an American tour, Cocker and Stainton dismissed The Grease Band. Leon Russell then assembled a touring band of more than 40 members which included himself, a full horn section recently departed from Delaney and Bonnie, and a vocal chorus numbering from 6 to 11 which included Rita Coolidge. The band was called Mad Dogs and Englishmen and the tour proved immensely successful. The double-record set of recordings from the tour were quickly certified gold-award and eventually yielded four hit singles: "The Letter," "Cry Me a River," "High Time We Went," and "Feelin' Alright." The tour launched the popular careers of Leon Russell and Rita Coolidge and marked the high point of Cocker's career.

After the tour, Cocker disappeared for 18 months amidst a variety of uncomplimentary rumors. After *Joe Cocker* and the major hit "Midnight Rider," he again dropped out of sight; Stainton departed in early 1973. Cocker re-emerged in 1974 with *I Can Stand a Little Rain*, which featured Jimmy Webb's "The Moon Is a Harsh Mistress" and the smash hit single, "You Are So Beautiful." However, his 1974 U.S. tour was a virtual disaster, and his two subsequent albums sold only moderately, yielding no hit singles. During 1978, Joe Cocker again toured the United States, this time somewhat successfully, and switched to Elektra/Asylum Records for *Luxury You Can Afford.*

JOE COCKER

With a Little Help from My Friends *	A&M	SP–4182 reissued as 3106	May '69	A
Joe Cocker! *	A&M	SP–4224	November '69	A

THE GREASE BAND

The Grease Band	Shelter	8904	April '71

JOE COCKER

Mad Dogs and Englishmen *	2-A&M	SP–6002	August '70	A
Joe Cocker	A&M	SP–4368	November '72	A
I Can Stand a Little Rain	A&M	SP–3633	August '74	A
Jamaica Say You Will	A&M	SP–4529	August '75	
Stingray	A&M	SP–4574	May '76	A
Greatest Hits	A&M	4670	December '77	A
Luxury You Can Afford	Elektra/ Asylum	145	August '78	A

LEONARD COHEN. Canadian-born poet and novelist turned singer–songwriter, Leonard Cohen was one of the most powerful song poets to emerge in the Sixties. Despite the limited musical effectiveness of his weak, monotonic voice and sparse musical settings, his poetics, legitimately described as bleak and stark, even depressing, more than compensate in that his lyrics ultimately succeed through the underlying intensity of their humanity.

Born on September 21, 1934, and raised in his native Montreal, Canada, Leonard Cohen studied English Literature at McGill and Columbia Universities and published his first book of poetry in 1955. During the Sixties, he published a number of books of poetry as well as two novels, *The Favorite Game* and *Beautiful Losers*. The second, now standard college literary fare, was published in 1966 and had sold over 300,000 copies by the end of the decade.

Taught the classics of music as a child, Leonard Cohen began playing guitar and singing at 15 and performed with a barn dance group called The Buckskin Boys during his late teens. He started writing songs around 1964 but received little popular acclaim until Judy Collins recorded one of his most romantic compositions, "Suzanne," for her 1966 *In My Life* album. He began his performing career that year, his reputation enhanced by appearances in 1967 at the Newport Folk Festival and New York's Central park (with Ms. Collins). Signed to Columbia Records, Cohen's debut album included "Suzanne," the alienated "Stranger Song," the sorrowful "Hey, That's No Way to Say Goodbye," and the compassionate "Sisters of Mercy." The latter three songs had previously appeared on Judy Collins' *Wildflowers* album. A year later, Cohen successfully toured North America and Europe and issued *Songs From a Room*, which contained the oft-recorded classic "Bird on a Wire." Retiring from public performance at the end of 1970, he released *Songs of Love and Hate* during 1971. It contained songs such as "Dress Rehearsal Rag," "Diamonds in the Mine," and "Love Calls You by Your Name."

During Cohen's prolonged retirement, he published yet another volume of poetry, *The Energy of Slaves*, and Columbia issued live versions of previously released material in 1973. Finally, in 1974 he emerged for an album of new material, *New Skin for the Old Ceremony*, subsequently touring again in 1975. Later he switched to Warner Brothers Records, where he collaborated with songwriter–producer extraordinaire Phil Spector for the disappointing *Death of a Ladies' Man* in 1977. During 1979 Leonard Cohen recorded *Recent Songs*, issued on Columbia.

LEONARD COHEN

Songs of Leonard Cohen	Columbia	PC–9533	January '68	A
Songs from a Room	Columbia	CS–9767	April '69	A
Songs of Love and Hate	Columbia	C–30103	April '71	A
Live Songs	Columbia	KC–31724	May '73	
New Skin for the Old Ceremony	Columbia	C–33167	October '74	A
Best of Leonard Cohen	Columbia	JC–34077	April '76	A
Death of a Ladies' Man	Warner	BS–3125	November '77	A
Recent Songs	Columbia	PC–36264	October '79	A

JUDY COLLINS. A Denver-raised pianist–guitarist–singer, with her high clear voice Judy Collins, along with Joan Baez, set the standard for female folk artists in the early Sixties. Popular as a protest singer after her second album, Ms. Collins subsequently demonstrated impeccable taste in her selection of material during the mid- and late Sixties, popularizing songs by then-obscure songwriters such as Gordon Lightfoot, Joni Mitchell, Randy Newman, and Leonard Cohen. Additionally, she was instrumental in launching the career of Cohen by recording his "Suzanne" in 1966. Toward the late Sixties, she began writing songs of her own and, with the recent success of "Send in the Clowns" and "Hard Time for Lovers," is on the verge of becoming a pop star.

Born in Seattle, Washington, on May 1, 1939, Judy Collins moved to Boulder, Colorado, with her family while young. She started ten years of classical piano training at age seven and studied for eight years under female symphony conductor Antonia Brico. Taking up guitar at 16, she played traditional folk songs at local clubs within a few years. By the beginning of the Sixties, she had moved to New York where she became immersed in the burgeoning Greenwich Village folk music scene. Signed to Elektra Records, Collins recorded two albums of standard folk fare before starting to record protest songs. Subsequently she began to use material by then-unknown songwriters. *Concert* contained Tom Paxton's "The Last Thing on My Mind," and *5th Album* included Richard Farina's "Pack Up Your Sorrows," Eric Andersen's "Thirsty Boots," and Gordon Lightfoot's "Early Morning Rain," as well as three Bob Dylan songs.

With *In My Life*, Judy Collins broke away from the folksinger stereotype and established herself as an exceptional performer of a wide range of contemporary material. Eventually certified gold-award, the album contained Dylan's "Tom Thumb's Blues," Farina's "Hard Lovin' Loser," Randy Newman's "I Think It's Gonna Rain Today," and two Leonard Cohen songs. The popularity of one of these songs, "Suzanne," effectively launched the musical career of Cohen. *Wildflowers*, which contained Collins' first songs of her own writing, also included two more Cohen songs as well as two songs by Joni Mitchell. One of these, "Both Sides Now," became Collins' first major hit single and spurred the career of Ms. Mitchell. *Who Knows Where the Time Goes*, certified gold-award within a few months of its release, continued the presentation of outstanding contemporary material by featuring Cohen's "Bird on a Wire," Robin Williamson's "The First Boy (Girl) I Loved," Ian Tyson's "Someday Soon," and Sandy Denny's title cut.

Recollections contained live recordings, whereas *Whales and Nightingales*, another gold-award album, included Collins' second substantial hit single, the traditional gospel song "Amazing Grace." After three subsequent album releases in slightly over a year, Collins ceased her music career to produce and co-direct a documentary film on the life of her former piano teacher, Antonia Brico. The film, entitled *Antonia: A Portrait of the Woman*, premiered in September 1974 and was nominated for an Academy Award in 1975. During 1975 she resumed her performing and recording career and issued *Judith*, yet another gold-award album, in

March. Stephen Sondheim's "Send in the Clowns" was a moderate hit single that year, destined to become an even bigger hit when re-released in 1977. *Bread and Roses*, from 1976, didn't sell particularly well despite regular touring by Collins. Thus, Judy Collins took 1978 off, returning in 1979 with *Hard Time for Lovers*, its minor hit title single, and another tour, which included her debut in the Nevada Casino milieu.

JUDY COLLINS

A Maid of Constant Sorrow	Elektra	EKS–7209	November '61	A
Golden Apples of the Sun	Elektra	EKS–7222	August '62	A
#3	Elektra	EKS–7243	November '63	A
Concert	Elektra	EKS–7280	September '64	A
5th Album	Elektra	EKS–7300	September '65	A
In My Life *	Elektra	EKS–7320 reissued as EKS– 74027	December '66	A
False True Lovers	Folkways	3564(M)	March '67	
Wildflowers *	Elektra	EKS– 74012	November '67	A
Who Knows Where the Time Goes *	Elektra	EKS– 74033	November '68	A
Recollections	Elektra	EKS– 74055	August '69	A
Whales and Night- ingales *	Elektra	EKS– 75010	December '70	A
Living	Elektra	EKS– 75014	October '71	A
Colors of the Day *	Elektra	EKS– 75030	May '72	A
True Stories and Other Dreams	Elektra	EKS– 75053	January '73	A
Judith *	Elektra	7E–1032 reissued as 111	March '75	A
Bread and Roses	Elektra	EKS–1076	August '76	A
So Early in the Spring: The First Fifteen Years	2-Elektra	6002	July '77	A
Hard Time for Lovers	Elektra	171	March '79	A
Running for My Life	Elektra	253	April '80	A
Times of Our Lives	Elektra	60001	January '82	A

COMMANDER CODY AND HIS LOST PLANET AIRMEN. A transplanted Midwestern band, Commander Cody and His Lost Planet Airmen were instrumental in turning hippies on to straight country music by playing a refreshing mixture of rock-and-roll classics, country-and-western standards, and originals frequently concerned with dope smoking.

COMMANDER CODY AND HIS LOST PLANET AIRMEN

Lost in the Ozone	Paramount	PAS–6017	October '71	A
Hot Licks, Cold Steel, and Truckers' Favorites	Paramount	PAS–6031	August '72	A
Country Casanova	Paramount	PAS–6054	May '73	A
Live from Deep in the Heart of Texas	Paramount	PAS–1017	January '74	A
Commander Cody and His Lost Planet Airmen	Warner Brothers	BS–2847	February '75	
Tales from the Ozone	Warner Brothers	BS–2883	September '75	
We've Got a Live One Here	2-Warner Brothers	2LS–2939	July '76	A

THE COMMANDER CODY BAND

Rock and Roll Again	Arista	AL–4125	August '77	

THE MOONLIGHTERS

The Moonlighters	Amherst	AMH–1009	October '77	

COMMANDER CODY

Flying Dreams	Arista	4183	June '78	

RY COODER. An exceptional sessions guitarist, Ry Cooder has managed, without a hit single, to build a devoted following through his outstanding bottleneck and slide guitar and mandolin playing on widely varying material, from folk to blues and country as well as various forms of ethnic music.

RY COODER

Ry Cooder	Reprise	RS–6402	December '70	A
Into the Purple Valley	Reprise	MS–2052	December '71	A
Boomer's Story	Reprise	MS–2117	October '72	A
Paradise and Lunch	Reprise	MS–2179	May '74	A
Chicken Skin Music	Reprise	MS–2254	September '76	A

Showtime	Warner Brothers	BS–3059	July '77	A
Jazz	Warner Brothers	BSK–3197	May '78	A
Bop Till You Drop	Warner Brothers	BSK–3358	July '79	A
Borderline	Warner Brothers	3489	November '80	A

SAM COOKE. One of the most popular and influential black singers to emerge in the late Fifties, Sam Cooke was perhaps the first black recording artist successfully to synthesize a blend of gospel and pop musics. Eschewing the harsher shouting vocal style of Ray Charles and emphasizing his own high, clear, sensual tenor voice, Cooke helped establish the "soul" sound so evident in the Motown releases of the early and mid-Sixties. Inspiring a number of young black singers to turn to professional music, most notably Otis Redding, Cooke demonstrated early broad social concerns with two of his own songs, "Bring It on Home to Me" and "A Change Is Gonna Come."

Born in Chicago on January 22, 1935, the son of Reverend Charles Cooke, Sam Cooke was a member of a family gospel quartet known as The Singing Children by age nine. Performing with a brother in a gospel group called The Highway Q.C.s while still in high school, Cooke joined The Soul Stirrers, one of the most popular gospel quartets of the Forties, in 1954. Later, he became lead singer of The Pilgrim Travellers, a group which also included Lou Rawls. During 1956, Cooke began recording pop material, initially for Specialty Records. In mid-1957 his contract was sold to Keen Records. Keen's first two single releases didn't do much, but the third, "You Send Me," became a top pop hit in 1957–58. Subsequent major Keen hits for Cooke included "I'll Come Running Back to You," "Only Sixteen," and "Wonderful World."

In 1959 Same Cooke co-founded his own record label, SAR Records, for gospel-style recordings by The Soul Stirrers and Johnnie Taylor among others, and later in the year accepted a lucrative offer from RCA Records, where he was initially recorded with typical pop techniques (strings, horns, etc.). Between 1960 and 1964, Cooke recorded a string of hit singles, two of them smash hits, "Chain Gang" in 1960 and "Twistin' the Night Away" in 1962. Other major hits included "Cupid" in 1961, "Bring It on Home to Me" backed with "Having a Party" and "Nothing Can Change This Love" in 1962, "Send Me Some Lovin'," "Another Saturday Night" (written by Sam), "Frankie and Johnny," and "Little Red Rooster" in 1963, and "(Ain't That) Good News" (written by Sam) and "Good Times" in 1964. His career was certainly secure by 1964, with much promise for the future, but on December 11, 1964, he was shot to death in Los Angeles. Posthumously, Sam Cooke's "Shake" became a near-smash hit in 1965, followed by one of his finest compositions, "A Change Is Gonna Come," only a few days later.

SAM COOKE AND THE SOUL STIRRERS

The Soul Stirrers Featuring Sam Cooke	Specialty	2106(M) reissued as 2106(E)	November '59	A
Gospel Soul	Specialty	2116(E)	April '70	A
Gospel Soul, Volume 2	Specialty	2128(E)	January '71	A
Original	Specialty	2137(E)	January '71	A
That's Heaven to Me	Specialty	2146(E)	June '72	A

SAM COOKE

Two Sides of Sam Cooke	Specialty	SP-2119 (E)	reissued November '70	A
Sam Cooke Sings	Keen	2001(M)	February '58	
Encore	Keen	2003(M)		
Tribute to the Lady	Keen	2004		
Hit Kit	Keen	86101(M)		
I Thank God	Keen	86103(M)		
Wonderful World	Keen	86106(M)	June '61	
Sam's Songs	Famous	502(M)		
Only Sixteen	Famous	505(M)		
So Wonderful	Famous	508(M)		
You Send Me	Famous	509(M)		
Right On	Cherie	1001(M)		
Cooke's Tour	RCA	LSP-2221	May '60	
Hits of the 50s	RCA	LSP-2236	August '60	
Sam Cooke	RCA	LSP-2293	March '61	
My Kind of Blues	RCA	LSP-2392	October '61	
Twistin' the Night Away	RCA	LSP-2555	April '62	
The Best of Sam Cooke	RCA	LSP-2625 reissued as AYL1-3863	August '62	A
Mister Soul	RCA	LSP-2673	February '63	
Night Beat	RCA	LSP-2709	September '63	
Ain't That Good News	RCA	LSP-2899	March '64	
At the Copa	RCA	LSP-2970 reissued as ANL1-2658	October '64 March '78	
Shake	RCA	LSP-3367	February '65	
Best of Sam Cooke, Volume 2	RCA	LSP-3373	July '65	
Try a Little Love	RCA	LSP-3435	October '65	
The Unforgettable Sam Cooke	RCA	LSP-3517	March '66	
The Man Who Invented Soul	RCA	LSP-3991	April '68	

This Is Sam Cooke	2-RCA	VPS–6027 (E)	September '70	A
Interprets Billie Holiday	RCA	APL1– 0899	August '75	
One and Only	Camden	2264	September '68	
Sam Cooke	Camden	2433	October '70	
The Unforgettable Sam Cooke	Camden	2610	April '73	
You Send Me	Camden	ACL–0445	January '75	
Golden Sound	2-Trip	8030–2	January '73	
Sam Cooke Sings the Billie Holiday Story	Up Front	160	May '73	

RITA COOLIDGE. A pianist–vocalist who emerged from sessions work to tour with Delaney and Bonnie and the famed Mad Dogs and English-men before starting a solo career, Rita Coolidge has chosen excellent material and recruited exceptional musicians to augment her thin but pure voice.

Born in Nashville, Tennessee, on May 1, 1945, to a white Southern Baptist minister father and Cherokee Indian mother, Rita Coolidge, sisters Priscilla and Linda, and parents later moved to Memphis. The sisters began performing while still in high school, with Priscilla and Rita later working local clubs and recording radio jingles. Moving to Los Angeles in 1968, Priscilla met Stax Records house keyboardist Booker T. Jones, whom she later married, while Rita became acquainted with Leon Russell and Delaney and Bonnie. Rita even scored a regional hit in 1969 with "Turn Around and Love You" on Pepper Records. During the next two years, Rita Coolidge recorded with Delaney and Bonnie, Russell, Joe Cocker, Eric Clapton, Steve Sills, and Dave Mason as a background vocalist. She toured several times with Delaney and Bonnie and, in 1970, became a member of the famed Mad Dogs and Englishmen–Joe Cocker tour of the United States and Europe. On that tour, Coolidge frequently received standing ovations for her performance of the Delaney Bramlett–Leon Russell composition "Superstar," later popularized by The Carpenters. After the tour, she returned to sessions work.

Signed to A&M Records in late 1970, Rita Coolidge's debut album in-cluded two excellent songs written by unknown songwriter Marc Benno, "Second Story Window" and "(I Always Called Them) Mountains." Suc-cessfully touring the U.S., Canada, and Europe with The Dixie Flyers in 1971, she issued *Nice Feelin'* by year's end. The album featured Marc Ben-no's title cut and Graham Nash's "Better Days." *The Lady's Not for Sale*, from 1972, included Benno's "Inside of Me" and the title song (co-written by Kris Kristofferson) and yielded the minor hit single "Fever/My Crew," the second written by her sister and brother-in-law.

During 1973 Rita teamed with Kris Kristofferson, whom she had met two years earlier, for touring and recording. Their *Full Moon* album, certified gold-award in 1975, was released a month after their August 19th marriage. The album featured "I've Never Had It So Good" (co-written by Paul Williams), "Take Time to Love" (composed by Donnie Fritts and Tony Joe White), Tom Jans' "Loving Arms," and two Kristoffer-son–Coolidge collaborations. She subsequently recorded *Fall into Spring* solo before again joining Kristofferson for *Breakaway*. *It's Only Love,* solo, wasn't particularly successful, but *Anytime . . . Anywhere* became enormously popular in 1977, sporting three hit singles, Jackie Wilson's "Higher and Higher," Boz Scagg's "We're All Alone," and the Motown classic, "The Way You Do the Things You Do." Certified gold-, then platinum-award during the year, the album propelled her career, and *Love Me Again* yielded a major hit with "You." Rita Coolidge and Kris Kristofferson again teamed up for 1979's *Natural Act.* In 1979–80 Rita Coolidge scored a moderate hit with "I'd Rather Leave While I'm in Love," later achieving another moderate hit in duet with Glen Campbell on "Somethin' 'Bout You Baby I Like."

RITA COOLIDGE

Rita Coolidge	A&M	SP-4291 reissued as 3107	March '71	A
Nice Feelin'	A&M	SP-4325 reissued as 3130	November '71	A
The Lady's Not for Sale	A&M	SP-4370	October '72	A
Fall into Spring	A&M	SP-3627	May '74	A
It's Only Love	A&M	SP-4531	November '75	A
Anytime . . . Any-where**	A&M	4616	March '77	A
Love Me Again*	A&M	SP-4699	June '78	A
Satisfied	A&M	SP-4781	September '79	A
Greatest Hits	A&M	4836	March '81	A
Heartbreak Radio	A&M	3727	August '81	A

RITA COOLIDGE AND KRIS KRISTOFFERSON

Full Moon*	A&M	SP-4403	September '73	A
Breakaway	Monument/ Columbia	PZ-33278	December '74	A
Natural Act	A&M	4690	January '79	A

ALICE COOPER. Both the name of a Seventies rock band and the pseudonym of its vocalist–protagonist, Alice Cooper established their reputation through the onstage simulation of the primary fodder of American films and television, sex and violence. Group leader Cooper, often dressed in clothes intended to imply bisexuality and transvestism, acted out on stage such fantasies as necrophilia, infanticide, and execution (by gallows, electric chair, or guillotine). Initially rejected en masse by audiences, the group actually cultivated a perverse and repulsive image under the guidance of manager Shep Gordon. Sensationalized adverse publicity alienated the parents of adolescents who came to adore the highly negative image. Thus Alice Cooper became the first rock act to achieve widespread popularity *because of* an intentionally encouraged distasteful image, predating the now-faltering wave of late Seventies "punk" groups and antedated perhaps only by Iggy Pop and The Stooges. Moreover, Alice Cooper was one of the first rock groups consciously to dupe the unwitting media into promulgating a totally negative image for commercial gain. Nonetheless, Alice Cooper was one of the first rock acts to utilize huge and extravagant stage sets and did produce several classic rock-and-roll songs with "Eighteen," "School's Out," and "No More Mr. Nice Guy." Subsequently protagonist Cooper disbanded the group, while retaining the enormous and elaborate stage sets for the first strictly "hard-rock" performance at Nevada gambling casinos in 1975 and continued touring.

Group protagonist Vincent Furnier was born in Detroit on February 4, 1948, eventually settling in Phoenix, Arizona, in the early Sixties with his family. During high school, in 1964, Furnier formed his first band, The Earwigs, with friends Glen Buxton (born November 10, 1947), Dennis Dunaway (born December 9, 1948), and two others who left by the end of 1966. By the autumn of 1965, the group had changed its name to The Spiders and added Michael Bruce (born March 16, 1948). Playing local Arizona dates in 1966, the band next adopted the name The Nazz, re-grouped, and added Neal Smith (born September 23, 1947). The members: Vincent Furnier (lead vocals), Glen Buxton (lead guitar), Dennis Dunaway (bass), Michael Bruce (guitar and keyboards), and Neal Smith (drums).

Making forays into Los Angeles by 1967 in search of club dates and a recording contract, the band again changed its name, since a Philadelphia group led by Todd Rundgren was also using the name The Nazz. Vincent Furnier became Alice Cooper and the group as a whole took the name as its own. Alice Cooper first came to notoriety in Los Angeles as a result of per-forming at the memorial birthday party for Lenny Bruce. Thousands of people left the show shortly after the band took the stage, but two impor-tant individuals stayed for the show—Frank Zappa and Shep Gordon. Shortly thereafter, Zappa signed Alice Cooper to his new label, Straight Records, and Gordon became the group's manager. In 1968 the group moved to Los Angeles and recorded *Pretties for You*, which was released virtually unnoticed by the press in 1969. The group's second album, *Easy Action*, was similarly ignored upon release.

During 1970, Alice Cooper began playing engagements across the United States, eventually settling in Detroit and signing with Warner Brothers Records. Under producer Bob Ezrin, they recorded *Love It to Death*, which yielded one major hit, "Eighteen." The follow-up album, *Killer*, produced only minor hits, but both albums were nonetheless cer-tified gold-award during 1972. Now receiving intense publicity for their stage act, Alice Cooper next scored a near-smash hit with the title song to *School's Out*, yet another gold-award album in 1972. *Billion Dollar Babies*, an enormous album success, featured three hits, "Elected," "Hello Hurray," and "No More Mr. Nice Guy," and the subsequent 1973 tour became one of the biggest money-making tours of rock history.

Unable to top or even match the Billion Dollar Babies tour, protagonist Alice Cooper disbanded the group in 1974, replacing them with a band producer Ezrin had earlier assembled to back Lou Reed. Members of the original backing group, including Michael Bruce, Dennis Dunaway, and Neal Smith, later used the name The Billion Dollar Babies for their 1977 album, *Battle Axe*. After *Muscle of Love* and *Greatest Hits*, Cooper recorded for Atlantic Records *Welcome to My Nightmare*, which formed the basis for an hour-long television special and his Nevada gambling casino appearances. The album featured the un–Cooper-like ballad "Only Women (Bleed)," another major hit. *Alice Cooper Goes to Hell* and *Lace and Whiskey* each yielded one major hit, "I Never Cry" and "You and Me," respectively, but *Live at the Aladdin Theatre* proved a dismal failure. In late 1978 Alice Cooper returned with the major hit "How You Gonna See Me Now" and *From the Inside*, which formed the basis for his 1979 Madhouse Rock tour. Both concerned Cooper's much-publicized alchohol rehabilitation, with stage props for the tour including giant liquor bottles, an enormous syringe, and various hanging hospital equipment. *Flush the Fashion*, from 1980, yielded a moderate hit with "Clones (We're All)" and was followed by 1981's *Special Forces*.

ALICE COOPER

Pretties to You	Straight reissued on	STS–1051	June '69	
	Warner Brothers	1840	October '70	
Easy Action	Straight reissued on			
	Warner Brothers	1845	March '70	
Love It to Death *	Warner Brothers	1883	February '71	A
Killer *	Warner Brothers	BS–2567	November '71	A
School's Out *	Warner Brothers	BS–2623	June '72	A
Billion Dollar Babies *	Warner Brothers	BS–2685	February '73	A
Muscle of Love *	Warner Brothers	BS–2748	November '73	

THE BILLION DOLLAR BABIES

Battle Axe	Polydor	6100	April '77

ALICE COOPER

Greatest Hits*	Warner Brothers	2803	August '74	
		reissued as 3107		A
Welcome to My Nightmare*	Atlantic	SD–18130 reissued as 19157	February '75	A
Alice Cooper Goes to Hell*	Warner Brothers	BS–2896	July '76	A
Lace and Whiskey	Warner Brothers	K–3027	April '77	
Live at the Aladdin Theatre, Las Vegas	Warner Brothers	K–3138	November '77	A
From the Inside	Warner Brothers	3263	December '78	A
Flush the Fashion	Warner Brothers	3436	May '80	A
Special Forces	Warner Brothers	3581	August '81	A

ELVIS COSTELLO. One of the few new headline acts to emerge in rock during the late Seventies, singer–songwriter Elvis Costello has become the most critically and commercially successful of England's so-called "new wave" artists. An enigmatic figure, appearing both demanding and aloof in performance, Costello writes biting songs that usually reflect a vituperative and enraged stance, a stark and refreshing contrast to the over-produced and "disco-fied" musics dominating the contemporary scene.

Early biographical data on Elvis Costello is scant at best; apparently he was born Declan McManus and raised in Liverpool. He seems to have taken up guitar and song writing early in life, spending months, if not years, securing his first recording contract. Costello was the first artist to submit a demonstration tape to England's Stiff Records, a small, independent label formed in 1976. His first album, recorded with the expatriate Marin County-based band Clover, was released in England around May 1977. That fall Costello completed his first English tour with The Attractions, a backup band composed of drummer Pete Thomas, bassist Bruce Thomas (no relation), and keyboardist Steve Naive, an obvious if not typical "punk" moniker.

When the co-founders of Stiff Records split up in late 1977, Elvis Costello switched to Columbia Records, which released his first brilliant album, *My Aim Is True*, on the verge of his American debut at San Francisco's Old Waldorf. The album, produced by Nick Lowe, became the first "new wave" album to make a substantial dent in the American charts and featured songs such as "Less Than Zero," "Waiting for the End of the

World," and the atypical love ballad "Alison." The latter song was included on Linda Ronstadt's 1978 *Living in the USA* album. Without a hit single, Costello achieved an underground following with his late 1977 and early 1978 American tours. His enigmatic reputation was enhanced by *This Year's Model*, recorded with The Attractions and produced by Nick Lowe; the album included "Radio, Radio," "Lipstick Vogue," and "No Action." Elvis Costello's early 1979 American tour was equivocal at best, frequently alienating curious American rock artists, promoters, and audiences alike; but *Armed Forces*, again recorded with The Attractions and produced by Nick Lowe, became his best selling album to date and his first to be certified gold-award. *Get Happy*, which included an incredible 20 songs, was quickly followed by *Taking Liberties*, which contained B-sides to English and American singles and previously unreleased recordings such as "Girls Talk" (a minor hit for Dave Edmunds in 1979), "Talking in the Dark" (recorded by Linda Ronstadt), and "Stranger in the House" (recorded by country star George Jones). After *Trust*, which featured "Watch Your Step," Elvis Costello revealed his country-style leanings with *Almost Blue*, composed entirely of nonoriginal country favorites such as "Tonight the Bottle Let Me Down" and Hank Williams's "Why Don't You Love Me Like You Used to Do."

ELVIS COSTELLO

My Aim Is True*	Columbia	JC–35037	November '77	A
This Year's Model	Columbia	JC–35331	March '78	A
Armed Forces*	Columbia	JC–35709	January '79	A
Get Happy!!	Columbia	JC–36347	March '80	A
Taking Liberties	Columbia	JC–36839	October '80	A
Trust	Columbia	JC–37051	February '81	A
Almost Blue	Columbia	FC–37562	October '81	A

COUNTRY JOE AND THE FISH/COUNTRY JOE McDONALD. One of the most distinctive acts to emerge from the late-Sixties San Francisco Bay area scene, Country Joe and The Fish combined humor, street theater, radical politics, and jug band, folk, and psychedelic musics into a recognizable sound. Prominently featured at both protest rallies and love-ins in the highly politicized years of 1966 and 1967, Country Joe and The Fish helped create a direct link between people's music and people's politics. Their LSD commercial, Fish Cheer, and the anti-war litany, "I-Feel-Like-I'm-Fixin'-to-Die Rag," became classics of the era. More recently, Country Joe McDonald has recorded a number of potent ecology-oriented songs and the anthem-like "A Viet Nam Veteran's Still Alive."

COUNTRY JOE AND THE FISH

Electric Music for the Mind and Body	Vanguard	79244	May '67	A

I-Feel-Like-I'm-Fixin'-to-Die	Vanguard	79266	November '67	A
Together	Vanguard	79277	July '68	
Here We Are Again	Vanguard	VSD–79299	June '69	
Greatest Hits	Vanguard	6545	January '70	
C.J. Fish	Vanguard	VSD–6555	April '70	A
Life and Times—From Haight-Ashbury to Woodstock	2-Vanguard	27/8	October '71	A

BARRY MELTON

Bright Sun Is Shining	Vanguard	VSD–6551	June '70	
Melton, Levy, and The Dey Brothers	Columbia	KC–31279	August '72	
We are Like the Ocean	Music Is Medicine	9007	June '78	
Level with Me	Music Is Medicine	9014	October '80	A

COUNTRY JOE McDONALD

The Early Years	Piccadilly	3309	September '80	A
Thinking of Woody Guthrie	Vanguard	VSD–6546	January '70	
Tonight I'm Singing Just for You	Vanguard	6557	August '70	A
Quiet Days in Clichy (soundtrack)	Vanguard	79303	February '71	
Hold On It's Coming	Vanguard	79314	June '71	
War, War, War	Vanguard	VSD–79315	August '71	
Incredible! Live!	Vanguard	79316	February '72	A
Paris Sessions	Vanguard	VSD–79328	June '73	
Country Joe	Vanguard	79348	February '75	
Essential	2-Vanguard	85/6	June '76	A
Paradise with an Ocean View	Fantasy	F–9495	October '75	A
Love Is a Fire	Fantasy	9511	July '76	A
Goodbye Blues	Fantasy	9525	February '77	A
Rock 'n' Roll Music from Planet Earth	Fantasy	F–9544	February '78	A
Leisure Suite	Fantasy	F–9586	January '80	A

COUNTRY JOE AND THE FISH

Reunion	Fantasy	9530	June '77	A

CREAM. Arguably the second most influential English group of the Sixties, Cream was the first rock band to improvise extensively and often to perform extended pieces, thus elevating virtuoso instrumental playing within rock to an art form. Whereas The Beatles revolutionized rock by shifting the consuming public's attention from singles to albums through the consistency of their songwriting, Cream reinforced that shift on the basis of their instrumental prowess. Though all three members demonstrated exceptional talents on their respective instruments, Jack Bruce was the real musical pioneer; he established the use of the repeated musical figure or ostinato (the so-called "heavy riff") on bass, around which he was able to play lead lines, thus liberating the instrument from its strictly rhythmic role. Ginger Baker instituted the long drum solo into rock, a phenomenon now almost obligatory, particularly in performance. Eric Clapton unwittingly created the cult of the superstar guitarist, a role that was to plague him for some years after the dissolution of Cream. Furthermore, in openly acknowledging their debt to many obscure black American bluesmen, Cream inspired the blues revival of 1968. As the first rock group to utilize the trio format, Cream established the viability of the three-man instrumental lineup, a configuration later used by groups such as The Jimi Hendrix Experience, Grand Funk Railroad, and Robin Trower's group. Ostensibly the first "super-group," though neither Bruce nor Baker were particularly well-known in the United States, Cream also sparked the fusion of jazz and rock musics, a movement that was to revitalize jazz in the Seventies. Other noteworthy accomplishments include one of the first "underground" albums to achieve gold-award status *(Disraeli Gears)* and one of the first double-record sets of previously unreleased material *(Wheels of Fire)*.

Cream was formed in the summer of 1966 by lead guitarist Eric Clapton (born on March 30, 1945, in Ripley, Surrey, England), bassist Jack Bruce (born on May 14, 1943, in Glasgow, Scotland), and drummer Peter "Ginger" Baker (born on August 19, 1940, in Lewisham, London). Clapton had previously played with The Yardbirds and John Mayall's Bluesbreakers, whereas Baker had played with Graham Bond, and Bruce with Bond and Manfred Mann. Signed almost immediately by Atlantic Records, Cream's first album, *Fresh Cream*, was issued in early 1967. Though the album contained little of the improvisation that characterized the group in performance, it did include the English hit "I Feel Free." Undeniably more exciting in concert than on records, Cream soon completed enormously successful tours of England and the United States. *Disraeli Gears*, the group's second album, established Cream's improvisational format. Rather than playing a song straight through, Clapton, Bruce, and Baker would set up the basic "riff" to a song, then take off into individual improvisatory jams. Their material consisted of standard blues material as well as original songs composed by Bruce and Clapton, frequently in collaboration with lyricist Peter Brown. In fact, Brown was a frequent co-author with Bruce of much of Cream's original material. "Sunshine of Your Love," composed by Clapton, Bruce, and Brown, was a moderate hit from the album, later to become a major hit when re-released in the summer of 1968. Other outstanding cuts included "Strange Brew," "Tales of Brave Ulysses," "Take It Back," and "Swlabr."

Wheels of Fire, the double-record set released during 1968, included one disc of live recordings. Among the extended live pieces were Robert Johnson's "Crossroads," Willie Dixon's "Spoonful," and "Toad," on which Baker soloed for over ten minutes. The album also contained Booker T. Jones' "Born under a Bad Sign" and originals "Badge," composed by Clapton and George Harrison, and "Politician" and "White Room," both written by Jack Bruce and Peter Brown. By mid-1968, internal strains within Cream became increasingly evident and, coupled with the limited amount of mutually acceptable material, lead to their announcement of plans to disband at year's end. After a farewell tour of America in October and November and a final album, *Goodbye* (which contained little new material), Cream made their final public appearance at London's Royal Albert Hall on November 26, 1968. By 1969 all four original albums as well as *Best* had been certified gold-award.

Almost immediately Clapton and Baker formed yet another "super-group" with Traffic's Stevie Winwood and Family's Rick Grech. Completing one English and one American tour, Blind Faith recorded one interesting, if flawed, gold-award album. Noteworthy cuts included Winwood's "Sea of Joy" and "Can't Find My Way Home" and Clapton's "In the Presence of the Lord." Clashes between Winwood and Baker tore the group apart, and Blind Faith disbanded by the end of 1969. Clapton subsequently pursued sessions work and a solo career chronicled elsewhere.

In January 1970, drummer Ginger Baker formed Air Force with Winwood, Grech, Chris Wood, Denny Laine, Graham Bond, and a host of others for two unsuccessful albums. Baker subsequently pursued a growing interest in African music, later building a recording studio in Nigeria which opened in January 1973 (Paul McCartney's *Band on the Run* was recorded there). Earlier, Baker had performed sporadically and recorded with Fela Ransome-Kuti. In late 1974 Baker joined Gurvitz brothers Adrian and Paul to form The Baker–Gurvitz Army. The group lasted until 1976, after which Baker recorded *11 Sides of Baker*.

Jack Bruce, the odd-man-out in the formation of Blind Faith, subsequently completed one tour with Mike Mandel, guitarist Larry Coryell, and drummer Mitch Mitchell before pursuing a solo career in conjunction with lyricist Peter Brown. Despite receiving much praise, particularly in England, *Songs for a Tailor* and *Harmony Row* were largely overlooked. In the meantime, Bruce joined ex-Miles Davis drummer Tony Williams and guitarist extraordinaire John McLaughlin in Williams' Lifetime for touring and two albums, *Ego* apparently issued without crediting him. During 1972 Bruce joined Corky Laing and Leslie West of Mountain in the marginally successful Cream-like power trio, West, Bruce, and Laing, for two studio albums before dropping out during the summer of 1973. *Live 'n' Kickin'*, an album of live performances by the group, was issued after its demise.

During 1973 and 1974, Jack Bruce recorded two albums with the Jazz

Composer's Orchestra Association: keyboardist Carla Bley's ambitious three-record set, *Escalator over the Hill*, and Mike Mantler's *No Answer*. In 1974 Bruce recorded *Out of the Storm*, again with help from lyricist Peter Brown, before enlisting ex-Rolling Stones guitarist Mick Taylor, Carla Bley, and others toward the end of the year for the ill-fated Jack Bruce Band. The group completed one stormy European tour and were scheduled for studio recording in mid-1975, but both Bley and Taylor quit only days before the scheduled date. Subsequently Jack Bruce formed yet another band for *How's Tricks*, again utilizing Peter Brown's lyrics, and an American tour. In 1980 Bruce recorded *I've Always Wanted to Do This* with former Humble Pie guitarist Dave "Clem" Clempson, keyboardist Dave Sancious, and "fusion" pioneer percussionist Billy Cobham, and toured briefly with the group late that year. Other recent recordings by Jack Bruce include *B.L.T.* with Bill Lordan and Robin Trower, *Over the Top* with Clempson and former Rainbow drummer Cozy Powell, and *Truce* with Trower.

CREAM

Fresh Cream *	Atco	SD33–206	January '67	
	reissued on			
	RSO	3009	February '77	A
Disraeli Gears *	Atco	SD33–232	December '67	
	reissued on			
	RSO	3010	February '77	A
Wheels of Fire *	2-Atco	SD2–700	June '68	
	reissued on			
	RSO	3802	February '77	A
Goodbye *	Atco	SD–7001	February '69	
	reissued on			
	RSO	3013	February '77	A
Best *	Atco	SD33–291	July '69	
Live Cream	Atco	SD33–328	March '70	
	reissued on			
	RSO	3014	February '77	A
Live Cream, Volume 2	Atco	SD–7005	February '72	
	reissued on			
	RSO	3015	February '77	A
Heavy Cream	2-Polydor	PD–3502	October '72	
Off the Top	Polydor	PD–5529	September '73	

BLIND FAITH

Blind Faith *	Atco	SD33–304	August '69	
	reissued on			
	RSO	3016	February '77	A

GINGER BAKER

Ginger Baker's Air Force	2-Atco	SD2–703	April '70
Ginger Baker's Air Force—2	Atco	SD33–343	December '70
Stratavarious	Atco	SD–7013	August '72

Fela Ransome-Kuti and Africa '70 with Ginger Baker—Live!	Signpost	SP–8401	October '72
At His Best	2-Polydor	3504	November '72

BAKER–GURVITZ ARMY

Baker–Gurvitz Army	Janus	JXS–7015	January '75
Elysian Encounters	Atco	36–123	November '75
Hearts on Fire	Atco	36–137	June '76

GINGER BAKER

11 Sides of Baker	Sire	SA–7532	June '77

JACK BRUCE

At His Best	2-Polydor	3505	October '72
Songs for a Tailor	Atco	SD33–306	September '69
Harmony Row	Atco	SD33–365	August '71

TONY WILLIAMS' LIFETIME WITH JACK BRUCE

(Turn It Over)	Polydor	244021	July '70
Ego	Polydor	244065	May '71

WEST, BRUCE, AND LAING

Why Dontcha	Windfall reissued on Columbia	KC–31929 C–31929	October '72	A
Whatever Turns You On	Windfall reissued on Columbia	KC–32216 C32216	July '73	A
Live 'n' Kickin'	Windfall	KC–32899	April '74	

CARLA BLEY WITH JACK BRUCE

Escalator over the Hill	3-JCOA	3–LP– EOTH	November '73

MIKE MANTLER WITH JACK BRUCE

Now Answer	Watt	2	August '74

JACK BRUCE

Out of the Storm	RSO	SO–4805	November '74
How's Tricks	RSO	RS1–3021	April '77

JACK BRUCE AND FRIENDS

I've Always Wanted to Do This	Epic	JE–36827	November '80	A

JACK BRUCE, BILL LORDAN, AND ROBIN TROWER

B.L.T.	Chrysalis	1324	April '81	A

COZY POWELL (WITH JACK BRUCE)

Over the Top	Polydor	6312	May '81	A

JACK BRUCE AND ROBIN TROWER

Truce	Chrysalis	1352	January '82	A

CREEDENCE CLEARWATER REVIVAL. One of the most popular American rock bands of the late Sixties, Creedence Clearwater Revival was immensely successful with a series of Fifties-style rock-and-roll singles in an era dominated by album-oriented groups.

Originally formed in 1959 as The Blue Velvets by three El Cerrito, California, junior high school students—John Fogerty (born on May 28, 1945, in Berkeley, California), Stu Cook and Doug Clifford (both born on April 24, 1945, Cook in Oakland and Clifford in Palo Alto, California)—the group later became Tom Fogerty and The Blue Velvets with the addition of John's brother Tom (born on November 9, 1941, in Berkeley). Playing local engagements for years, the band recorded unsuccessfully on the local Kristy and Orchestra labels before securing a recording contract with Berkeley's Fantasy Records in 1964. With a name change to The Golliwogs, the group released a series of unsuccessful singles between 1965 and 1967. Subsequently, Paul Zaentz took over Fantasy in 1967 and the group decided to change their name to Creedence Clearwater Revival as of the beginning of 1968.

The group: John Fogerty (songwriting, production, lead guitar, lead vocals, keyboards, harmonica), Tom Fogerty (rhythm guitar, piano, vocals), Stu Cook (electric bass, piano), and Doug Clifford (drums). Creedence Clearwater Revival's self-titled debut album, released in the middle of 1968, contained a mixture of rock standards and John Fogerty originals. Their first single release, a reworking of Dale Hawkins' "Suzie Q," became a top nationwide hit and launched the band on a recording career that yielded regular hit singles, many of them two sided. *Bayou Country* produced the smash hit "Proud Mary" and also included "Born on the Bayou." *Green River* had two-sided hits, the smash "Bad Moon Rising" backed by "Lodi" and the smash "Green River" backed by "Commotion," and contained the ballad "Wrote a Song for Everyone." The hits continued with the smash "Down on the Corner/Fortunate Son" from *Willy and the Poor Boys* and three two-sided smash hit singles from *Cosmo's Factory*, "Travelin' Band/Who'll Stop the Rain," "Up Around the Bend/Run Through the Jungle," and "Lookin' Out My Back Door/Long As I See the Light." *Pendulum* yielded the near-smash "Have You Ever Seen the Rain/Hey Tonight." During 1970 Creedence Clearwater Revival successfully toured Europe, and all six Fantasy albums were certified gold-award during the year.

John Fogerty's creative dominance of the group led to dissension among the other members, with Tom Fogerty leaving in February 1971. The remaining trio subsequently toured Europe during 1971; John later shared the songwriting responsibilities with the other members for *Mardi Gras,* which contained two final hit singles, the smash "Sweet Hitchhiker" and "Someday Never Comes." In October 1972 Creedence Clearwater Revival disbanded. Several months earlier, Doug Clifford had issued *Cosmo* on Fantasy and Tom Fogerty had released the first of four solo albums on Fantasy in May 1972. John Fogerty recorded *Blue Ridge Rangers,* on which he played all instruments and sang all parts. Primarily composed of country material, the album yielded a minor hit with "Hearts of Stone" in early 1973. Later he switched to Asylum Records, with his self-titled debut album including the moderate hit "Rockin' All Over the World." Later Asylum issued *Hoodoo* by John Fogerty, and Stu Cook and Doug Clifford became the rhythm section for The Don Harrison Band, whereas Tom Fogerty formed Ruby. Doug Clifford later manned California Gold with sessions keyboardist Bobby Whitlock, and Tom Fogerty joined Festival in 1979. With Creedence Clearwater Revival experiencing an international renewal of interest in the early Eighties, Fantasy issued a 1970 live set, initially released incorrectly as *The Royal Albert Hall Concert,* which was re-released as *The Concert* in late 1980.

GOLLIWOGS

Pre-Creedence	Fantasy	9474	February '75	A

CREEDENCE CLEARWATER REVIVAL

Creedence Clearwater Revival*	Fantasy	8382	June '68	A
Bayou Country*	Fantasy	8387	January '69	A
Green River*	Fantasy	8393	August '69	A
Willy and the Poor Boys*	Fantasy	8397	November '69	A
The Concert	Fantasy	4501	November '80	A
Cosmo's Factory*	Fantasy	8402	July '70	A
Pendulum*	Fantasy	8410	December '70	A
Mardi Gras*	Fantasy	9404	April '72	A
Gold*	Fantasy	9418	November '72	A
More Creedence Gold	Fantasy	9430	July '73	A
Live in Europe	2-Fantasy	79001 reissued as CCR1	November '73	A
Chronicle	2-Fantasy	CCR2	March '76	A

CREEDENCE CLEARWATER REVIVAL REISSUES

1968/1969	2-Fantasy	CCR68	October '78	A
1969	2-Fantasy	CCR69	October '78	A
1970	2-Fantasy	CCR70	October '78	A

TOM FOGERTY

Tom Fogerty	Fantasy	9407	May '72	
Excalibur	Fantasy	9413	January '73	A
Zephyr National	Fantasy	9448	March '74	
Myopia	Fantasy	9469	December '74	
Deal It Out	Fantasy	9611	November '81	A

DOUG CLIFFORD

Cosmo	Fantasy	9411	August '72

JOHN FOGERTY

Blue Ridge Rangers	Fantasy	9415	May '73	A
John Fogerty	Asylum	7E–1046	September '75	A
Hoodoo	Asylum	1081	November '76	

THE DON HARRISON BAND WITH DOUG CLIFFORD AND STU COOK

The Don Harrison Band	Atlantic	SD–18171	April '76
Red Hot	Atlantic	SD–18208	January '77

RUBY WITH TOM FOGERTY

Ruby	PBR International	7001	March '77	A
Rock and Roll Madness	PBR International	7004	February '78	A

JIM CROCE. One of America's finest singer–songwriters of the Seventies, known for his amusing character songs and gentle love songs, Jim Croce died in an airplane accident just as he was beginning to receive much-deserved recognition.

Born on January 10, 1942 (or 1943) and raised in his native Philadelphia, Jim Croce began playing music professionally at the University of Villanova in 1964. In 1967 he moved to New York, where he played coffeehouses on the advice of college friend Tommy West. Signed to Capitol Records, Croce recorded one unsuccessful album with wife Ingrid before returning to Pennsylvania. During 1970, Maury Muehleisen, who later became Croce's lead guitarist, recorded an album, also on Capitol. In 1971 Tommy West and his partner Terry Cashman recorded a demonstration tape of Croce which eventually led to a recording contract with ABC Records. His first album yielded two major hit singles, "You Don't Mess Around with Jim" and "Operator (That's Not the Way It Feels)," and included "Time in a Bottle," a top hit when issued in late 1973. "One Less Set of Footsteps" was a moderate hit in early 1973, but "Bad Bad Leroy Brown," also from *Life and Times*, established Croce as a singer–songwriter. However, he and Muehleisen were killed on September 20,

1973, when their chartered plane crashed on takeoff near Natchitoches, Louisiana. *I Got a Name*, released posthumously, yielded three hit singles, "I Got a Name" in 1973, and "I'll Have to Say I Love You in a Song" and "Workin' at the Car Wash Blues" in 1974. All three of Croce's albums were certified gold-award during 1973, as was the anthology *Photographs and Memories* in 1974. During 1977 all of Jim Croce's albums were re-released on Tommy West and Terry Cashman's Lifesong Records.

JIM AND INGRID CROCE

Jim and Ingrid Croce	Capitol	ST–315	September '69
Another Day, Another Town	Pickwick	SPC–3332	'76

MAURY MUEHLEISEN

Gingerbread	Capitol	ST–644	December '70

JIM CROCE

You Don't Mess Around with Jim*	ABC reissued on Lifesong	ABCX–756 JZ–34993	June '72 December '77
Life and Times*	ABC reissued on Lifesong	ABCX–769 JZ–35008	February '73 December '77
I Got a Name*	ABC reissued on Lifesong	ABCX–797 JZ–35009	November '73 December '77
Photographs and Memories: Jim Croce's Greatest Hits*	ABC reissued on Lifesong	ABCD–835 JZ–35010	September '74 December '77
The Faces I've Been	2-Lifesong	LS–900	October '75
Time in a Bottle: Jim Croce's Greatest Love Songs	Lifesong	6007 reissued as JZ–35000	February '77 December '77
Bad Bad Leroy Brown: Jim Croce's Greatest Character Songs	Lifesong	JZ–35571	October '78

DAVID CROSBY/CROSBY, STILLS, NASH (AND YOUNG). Quintessential vocal harmony, acoustic guitar songwriting trio of the late Sixties, Crosby, Stills, and Nash combined their talents to produce an outstanding album of gentle melodic songs before adding the harder-edged sound of Neil Young for one diverse studio album and one double-record live album. With each member retaining his own distinctive musicial personality, the quartet became the darlings of the hippie movement with songs alternately mystical, communal, political, and romantic. More an aggregation of three (and four) individuals than a group, Crosby, Stills, Nash (and Young) created a characteristic sound that the three original members have attempted to maintain, somewhat equivocally, into the late-Seventies.

Ex-Byrd David Crosby (born in Los Angeles on August 14, 1941) and ex-Buffalo Springfield member Steve Stills (born in Dallas, Texas, on January 3, 1945) met Graham Nash (born in Blackpool, Lancashire, England, on February 2, 1942) of The Hollies during 1968. An informal jam in Los Angeles so impressed the three that they decided to form a group as soon as Nash could sever relations with the English group. He left The Hollies toward the end of 1968, and the three began recording for Atlantic Records in 1969. Their first album, *Crosby, Stills, and Nash,* released that spring, yielded two moderate hit singles, Nash's "Marrakesh Express" and Stills' "Suite: Judy Blue Eyes." With Dallas Taylor on drums, Crosby on rhythm guitar, and Stills dubbing-in lead guitar, organ, and bass, the album featured the precise vocal harmonies of Nash and Crosby. Included were two excellent Crosby songs, the resigned but optimistic "Long Time Gone" and the beautiful love song "Guinnevere," as well as Nash's "Lady of the Island," Stills' simple "Helplessly Hoping," and the mystical "Wooden Ships," composed by Crosby, Stills, and Paul Kantner (uncredited).

In an effort to fill out the acoustic sound, ex-Buffalo Springfield member Neil Young (born in Toronto, Ontario, Canada, on November 12, 1945), already pursuing a successful solo career, joined the group; they debuted at New York's Fillmore East less than a month before the quartet's celebrated appearance at the Woodstock Festival in August 1969. By the end of the year, however, the "good vibes" that had produced such magnificent results on the first album were dashed, as Stills broke up with Judy Collins, Nash broke up with Joni Mitchell, and Crosby's girlfriend was killed in an auto accident. Young admirably took up the slack for *Deja Vu,* perhaps the group's most successful album. It featured three hit singles, an electric version of Joni Mitchell's "Woodstock" and two Graham Nash songs, "Teach Your Children" and "Our House." The album also contained Crosby's "Almost Cut My Hair" and title cut, Stills' self-pitying "4 and 20," and Neil Young's three-part production effort, "Country Girl."

By the fall of 1970, Crosby, Stills, Nash, and Young had shattered in four directions, but not before issuing Young's brilliant "Ohio," an outraged response to the Kent State murders of May 1970. Nash subsequently compiled the double-record live set, *Four Way Street,* which included Young classics such as "On the Way Home," "Cowgirl in the Sand," and "Southern Man" (as well as "Ohio"), and two beautiful Crosby songs, "Triad" and "The Lee Shore." Stills and Young pursued solo careers chronicled elsewhere, whereas Crosby recorded *If I Could Only Remem-*

ber My Name with Nash, Young, Joni Mitchell, and various members of the San Francisco Bay area's musical community, including Jerry Garcia, Paul Kantner, and Grace Slick. Featuring several songs comprised of wordless vocal harmonies, the album contained Crosby's "Laughing" and "Traction in the Rain," as well as Nash, Young, and Crosby's "Music Is Love" and the conspiratorial "What Are Their Names."

Graham Nash recorded his first solo album, *Songs for Beginners*, during 1971 with Crosby, Garcia, Dave Mason, and the vocal assistance of Rita Coolidge. Two political songs, "Chicago" and "Military Madness," became moderate hits from the album that included the old Hollies' song, "I Used to Be a King," and Nash's "Better Days." In 1972 Nash and Crosby reunited for touring and one album. Later Nash recorded his second solo album, the much-maligned and under-promoted *Wild Tales*, with the assistance of Crosby, Dave Mason, Joni Mitchell, and multi-instrumentalist David Lindley. Persistent rumors of the reunion of Crosby, Stills, Nash, and Young were confirmed in 1974, when the quartet completed a summer-long tour. However, they fragmented again, with Crosby and Nash then joining forces for touring and recording. Though the duo's *Wind on the Water* and *Whistling down the Wire* yielded no major hit singles, both albums were certified gold-award the year of their release. Crosby, Stills, and Nash reunited under a low profile in December 1976 for touring and the platinum-award *CSN* album. It produced one hit single, Nash's "Just a Song Before I Go," and included Stills' "Dark Star." Stills has since recorded solo; both a live and a best of set have been issued for Nash and Crosby. Nash, a founding director of the antinuclear power Musicians United for Safe Energy (MUSE), later recorded the poorly received yet environmentally concerned *Earth & Sky* and was working on a duet set with Steve Stills in 1981.

CROSBY, STILLS, AND NASH

Crosby, Stills, and Nash *	Atlantic	SD–8229 reissued as 19117	May '69	A

CROSBY, STILLS, NASH, AND YOUNG

Deja Vu *	Atlantic	SD–7200 reissued as 19118	March '70	A
Four Way Street *	2-Atlantic	SD2–902	April '71	A
So Far *	Atlantic	18100 reissued as 19119	August '74	A

DAVID CROSBY

If I Could Only Remember My Name *	Atlantic	SD–7203	February '71	A

GRAHAM NASH

Songs for Begin- ners*	Atlantic	SD–7204	June '71	A
Wild Tales	Atlantic	SD–7288	December '73	A

DAVID CROSBY AND GRAHAM NASH

Graham Nash/ David Crosby*	Atlantic	SD–7220	April '72	A
Wind on the Water	ABC reissued on MCA	ABCD–902 37007	October '75	A
Whistling down the Wire*	ABC	ABCD–956	July '76	
Live	ABC	AA–1042	November '77	
The Best of David Crosby and Graham Nash	ABC reissued on MCA	1102 37008	October '78	A

CROSBY, STILLS, AND NASH

CSN**	Atlantic	SD–19104	May '77	A
Replay	Atlantic	16026	January '81	A

GRAHAM NASH

Earth & Sky	Capitol	SWAK– 12014	March '80	A

THE CRYSTALS. Phil Spector's first "girl group," The Crystals recorded his first Philles Records million-selling single ("He's a Rebel") and were the object of his increasingly adventuresome productions in the early Sixties before he turned his attentions to The Ronettes and The Righteous Brothers.

Born and raised in Brooklyn, the members of The Crystals started singing locally as a quintet around 1961. The members: Lala Brooks, Mary Thomas, Barbara Alston, Pat Wright, and Dee Dee Kenniebrew. Auditioned by Phil Spector during 1961, the group was the first signing to his newly formed Philles label. Their first release, "There's No Other," co-authored by Spector, became a major hit before the end of the year, with "Uptown," written by Barry Mann and Cynthia Weil, becoming their second major hit. Mary Thomas left the group in 1962, and The Crystals continued as a quartet. Their biggest success came in September 1962 with the Gene Pitney composition "He's a Rebel," a top hit. Ironically, none of the actual Crystals sang on the recording; lead vocals were handled by Darlene Love, who subsequently had solo hits with "(Today I Met) The Boy I'm Gonna Marry" and "Wait 'Til My Bobby Gets Home" for Philles in 1963. The Crystals' next major hit came with "He's Sure the Boy I Love," another Barry Mann and Cynthia Weil composition. "Da Doo Ron Ron," written by Spector, Ellie Greenwich, and Jeff Barry, was a smash hit in early 1963 and is one of Spector's classic production efforts. The group's final smash hit was "Then He Kissed Me," yet another Spector, Greenwich, and Barry collaboration. Subsequently, The Crystals' popularity faded despite the release of singles on United Artists and Michelle, and the group broke up in the late Sixties, only to reunite for the rock-and-roll revival of the early Seventies.

THE CRYSTALS

Twist Uptown	Philles	PHLP–4000(M)	'62
He's a Rebel	Philles	PHLP–4001(M)	March '63
Greatest Hits, Volume 1	Philles	PHLP–4003(M)	'63

THE CHARLIE DANIELS BAND. Another Southern boogie-and-blues band utilizing the double lead-guitar and double drums format popularized by The Allman Brothers, The Charlie Daniels Band has achieved its popularity more from their tight, hard-driving playing in performance and on albums than from the usual series of hit singles.

Born in Wilmington, North Carolina, on October 28, 1936, Charlie Daniels took up guitar at age 15, later playing in a bluegrass band called The Misty Mountain Boys. Between 1958 and 1967, he was a member of The Jaguars, who played regularly throughout the South. At the urging of producer Bob Johnston, Daniels went to Nashville in 1967, subsequently working under Johnston on Bob Dylan's *Nashville Skyline, Self Portrait*, and *New Morning* albums. He also played on three Leonard Cohen albums and Ringo Starr's 1970 *Beaucoups of Blues* album, while producing four records for The Youngbloods. Recording one album for Capitol Records in 1971, Daniels later assembled his band and switched to Kama Sutra Records, where they first achieved popularity with *Honey in the Rock* and the "Uneasy Rider" single. Maintaining a rigorous touring schedule, The Charlie Daniels Band had its biggest early success with 1974's *Fire on the Mountain* album, which yielded two hit singles, "The South's Gonna Do It Again" and "Long Haired Country Boy." The personnel on the album were: Charlie Daniels (lead guitar, banjo, violin, vocals), Barry Barnes (second guitar, vocals), Joel DiGregorio (keyboards, vocals), Mark Fitzgerald (bass), and Fred Edwards and Gary Allen (drums). That year Tom Crain became second guitarist and Charlie Hayward bassist, with Don Murray and then Jim Marshall replacing Gary Allen as second drummer. The band was twice invited to perform on the "Grand Ole Opry" (August 1976 and April 1978), and also played at President Carter's Inaugural Ball. Switching to Epic Records in 1976, The Charlie Daniels Band eventually scored a top country and smash pop hit with "The Devil Went down to Georgia," featuring Daniels' incendiary fiddle playing, from *Million Mile Reflections,* the group's first platinum-award album. *Full Moon*, from 1980, yielded a major hit with the patriotic "In America" and the moderate hit "The Legend of Wooley Swamp."

THE CHARLIE DANIELS BAND

The Charlie Daniels Band	Capitol	ST–790 reissued as ST– 11414 reissued as SN– 16039	September '71 August '75	 A
TeJohn, Grease, and Wolfman	Kama Sutra reissued on Epic	2060 JE–34665	September '72 March '78	 A
Honey in the Rock reissued as Uneasy Rider	Kama Sutra Epic	KSBS–2071 PE–34369	April '73 December '76	 A
Way Down Yonder reissued as Whis- key	Kama Sutra Epic	 PE–34664	January '74 June '77	 A
Fire on the Moun- tain*	Kama Sutra reissued on Epic	KSBS–2603 JE–34365	December '74 December '76	 A
Nightrider	Kama Sutra reissued on Epic	2607 PE–34402	September '75 December '76	 A
Essential	2-Kama Sutra	2612	November '76	
Saddletramp*	Epic	PE–34150	April '76	A
High Lonesome	Epic	PE–34377	November '76	A
Midnight Wind	Epic	PE–34970	October '77	A
Million Mile Re- flection**	Epic	JE–35751	May '79	A
Full Moon**	Epic	FE–36571	August '80	A

BOBBY DARIN. Briefly a late-Fifties rock-and-roller, Bobby Darin encouraged the return of rock to the pop mainstream through the recording of middle-of-the-road material, including the definitive version of "Mack the Knife," before trying country-and-western and folk music and ending his career in obscurity on the Motown label.

Born Robert Walden Cassotto on May 14, 1936, in a tough area of the Bronx, New York, Bobby Darin learned to play drums, piano, and guitar as a child. After studying drama for a short time at Hunter College in New York, he decided to enter show business, thus changed his name. Signed and quickly dropped by Decca Records, Darin then signed with Atco Records, a subsidiary of the then rhythm-and-blues label Atlantic. His first hit came with his own composition, "Splish Splash," in 1958, soon followed by "Queen of the Hop." He successfully broadened his base of popularity during 1959 with the smash hit "Dream Lover" and the top hit version of Kurt Weill's "Mack the Knife," taken from *The Threepenny Opera*. *That's All* and *This Is Darin* became best-sellers, establishing

Darin in a pop role similar to that of Frank Sinatra and launching his highly successful night club career. *At the Copa* was yet another best-seller, as were the singles "Beyond the Sea," "Clementine," "Won't You Come Home Bill Bailey," "Artificial Flowers," "You Must Have Been a Beautiful Baby," "Irresistible You" (backed by "Multiplication"), and "Things." Switching to Capitol Records in 1962, Darin at first recorded country-and-western style hits such as "You're the Reason I'm Living" and "18 Yellow Roses." Returning to the pop mold, he found little success; his career faded dramatically through the mid-Sixties. He then returned to Atlantic, where he had a near-smash folk-style hit with Tim Hardin's "If I Were a Carpenter" in 1966. He subsequently took on the trappings of a folk artist with little success, later recording for his own record label, Direction, before joining Motown Records in 1971. On December 20, 1973, Bobby Darin died while undergoing an operation for a heart condition that had existed since childhood.

BOBBY DARIN

Bobby Darin	Atco	33–102(M)	December '58	
That's All	Atco	SD33–104	March '59	
This Is Darin	Atco	SD33–115	February '60	
At the Copa	Atco	SD33–122	August '60	
For Teenagers Only	Atco	1001(M)	October '60	
It's You or No One	Atco	33–124		
25th Day of December	Atco	33–125		
Two of a Kind (with Johnny Mercer)	Atco	33–126	March '61	
The Bobby Darin Story	Atco	33–131	May '61	A
Love Swings	Atco	SD33–134	July '61	
Twist with Bobby Darin	Atco	33–138	January '62	
Bobby Darin Sings Ray Charles	Atco	33–140	March '62	
Things and Other Things	Atco	SD33–146	September '62	
Bobby Darin Winners	Atco	SD33–167	July '64	
Oh! Look at Me Now	Capitol	SW–1791	October '62	
You're the Reason I'm Living	Capitol	ST–1866	March '63	
Earthy	Capitol	ST–1826	August '63	
18 Yellow Roses	Capitol	ST–1942	August '63	
Golden Folk Hits	Capitol	ST–2007	February '64	
From Hello Dolly to Goodbye Charlie	Capitol	ST–2194	November '64	
Venice Blue	Capitol	ST–2322	May '65	

The Best of Bobby Darin	Capitol	ST–2571	September '66	
The Shadow of Your Smile	Atlantic	8121	May '66	
In a Broadway Bag	Atlantic	SD–8126		
If I Were a Carpenter	Atlantic	SD–8135	January '67	
Inside Out	Atlantic	SD–8142	June '67	
Doctor Dolittle	Atlantic	SD–8154	October '67	
Bobby Darin	Direction	1936	'68	
Commitment	Direction	1937	'69	
Bobby Darin	Motown	753	'72	
1936–1973	Motown	813	March '74	A

DEEP PURPLE. Formed in the late Sixties, Deep Purple was a seminal high-decibel, "heavy metal" English rock band during the Seventies. They issued the classic "Smoke on the Water" and two gold-award albums before launching the solo career of Ritchie Blackmore with Rainbow.

Born in Weston-super-Mare, England, on April 14, 1945, Ritchie Blackmore took up guitar at 11 and was playing English sessions by the age of 17. He played with Screaming Lord Sutch for several years before moving to Hamburg, Germany, where he formed Deep Purple in March 1968. The members: lead guitarist Blackmore, organist Jon Lord (born in Leicester, England, on June 9, 1941), vocalist Rod Evans (born in Edinburgh, Scotland, on January 19, 1945), bassist Nick Simper (born in Norwood Green, England, on November 3, 1946), and drummer Ian Paice (born in Nottingham, England, on June 29, 1948). Lord had previously played for four years with The Artwoods, which included Keef Hartley. Their first single, a loud version of Joe South's "Hush," was a smash hit in America during the summer of 1968. *Shades of Deep Purple* became a best-seller, and the band toured the States before the end of the year. Several pop-type singles were minor hits, and Deep Purple's second album, *Book of Taliesyn,* sold quite well. Evans and Simper were replaced by two former members of Episode Six, Ian Gillan (born on August 19, 1945, in Hounslow, England) and Roger Glover (born on November 30, 1945, in Brecon, South Wales), respectively, in July 1969. That same year Jon Lord composed a concerto for rock band and symphony orchestra which was recorded that September and released on their new label, Warner Brothers, as *Deep Purple/The Royal Philharmonic Orchestra* in 1970.

Fireball became a best-seller in 1971, only to be surpassed by 1972's *Machine Head,* which was certified gold-award the year of its release. *Who Do We Think We Are* and *Made in Japan* were both also certified gold-award shortly after release. The second contained the group's smash hit single "Smoke on the Water," now regarded as a classic high-decibel song. However, in June 1973 both vocalist Gillan and bassist Glover quit the band, to be replaced by unknown David Coverdale and Glenn Hughes, respectively. Glover later recorded *The Butterfly Ball* and *Elements* in the late Seventies before joining Rainbow, whereas Gillan recorded *Child in Time*, *Scarabus*, and *Glory Road* through 1980. The regrouped Deep Purple's *Burn* and *Stormbringer* albums both subsequently became gold-award records without benefit of a hit single. In 1974 Jon Lord recorded *First of the Big Bands* with vocalist–keyboardist Tony Ashton, formerly of Family. By 1975 Ritchie Blackmore had become bored with his role in Deep Purple and dropped out in May. He was replaced on lead guitar by American Tommy Bolin, who had recorded one solo album and two albums with The James Gang. *Come Taste the Band*, Bolin's first album with Deep Purple, contained seven songs which he had either written or co-written. The album sold quite well, but in 1976, Deep Purple disbanded.

Tommy Bolin subsequently recorded a second solo album, *Private Eyes*, and was on tour promoting it when he died in Miami on December 4, 1976, of a drug overdose. Jon Lord later joined Tony Ashton, former Deep Purple drummer Ian Paice, and bassist Paul Martinez for *Malice in Wonderland*. In the meantime, Ritchie Blackmore had formed Rainbow for a successful, if not spectacular, recording career with the Polydor and Oyster labels. Experiencing numerous personnel changes, Rainbow added drummer Cozy Powell in September 1975 and bassist Roger Glover in April 1979. Powell left the group in 1981 to record *Over the Top* with former Cream bassist Jack Bruce and former Humble Pie guitarist Dave "Clem" Clempson. In January 1978 David Coverdale formed Whitesnake, adding Jon Lord that August and later recruiting Ian Paice.

DEEP PURPLE

Shades of Deep Purple	Tetragram- maton	T–102	September '68	
Book of Taliesyn	Tetragram- maton	T–107	December '68	
Deep Purple	Tetragram- maton	T–119 reissued as 5005	July '69	
Deep Purple/The Royal Philhar- monic Orchestra	Warner Brothers	1860	May '70	
Deep Purple in Rock	Warner Brothers	WS–1877	September '70	A
Fireball	Warner Brothers	2564	August '71	A
Machine Head*	Warner Brothers	BS–2607 reissued as 3100	March '72	
Purple Passages	2-Warner Brothers	2LS–2644	October '72	A
Who Do We Think We Are?*	Warner Brothers	BS–2678	January '73	A
Made in Japan*	2-Warner Brothers	2WS–2701	April '73	A

ROGER GLOVER

The Butterfly Ball	UK	56000	January '76	
Elements	Polydor	PD–6137	April '78	

IAN GILLAN

Child in Time	Oyster	1602	July '76	
Scarabus	Island	9511	January '78	
	reissued on Antilles	7066		A
Glory Road	Virgin	13146	October '80	

DEEP PURPLE

Burn*	Warner Brothers	2766	February '74	A
Stormbringer*	Warner Brothers	PR–2832	November '74	A
Come Taste the Band	Warner Brothers	PR–2895	December '75	A
Made in Europe	Warner Brothers	PR–2995	November '76	A
When We Rock, We Rock; When We Roll, We Roll	Warner Brothers	3223	September '78	A
Deepest Purple/The Very Best of Deep Purple	Warner Brothers	3486	October '80	A

TONY ASHTON AND JON LORD

First of the Big Bands	Warner Brothers	BS–2778	May '74

TOMMY BOLIN

Teaser	Nemperor	436	November '75	A
Private Eyes	Columbia	PC–34329	September '76	A

RITCHIE BLACKMORE/RAINBOW

Rainbow	Polydor	PD–6049	August '75	A
Rainbow Rising	Oyster	OY1–1601	May '76	A
On Stage	2-Oyster	OY2–1801	June '77	A
Long Live Rock 'n' Roll	Polydor	6143	May '78	A
Down to Earth	Polydor	PD1–6221	August '79	A
Difficult to Cure	Polydor	6316	May '81	A
Jealous Lover	Polydor	PX–502	December '81	A

PAICE, ASHTON, AND LORD

Malice in Wonder-land	Warner Brothers	BS–3038	June '77

DAVID COVERDALE AND WHITESNAKE

Snakebite	United Artists	LA915	August '78	
Trouble	United Artists	LA937	March '79	
Love Hunter	United Artists	LT–981	October '79	
Ready an' Willing	Mirage	19276	August '80	A
Live in the Heart of the City	Mirage	19292	December '80	A
Come an' Get It	Atlantic	16043	June '81	A

COZY POWELL

Over the Top	Polydor	6312	May '81	A
Tilt	Polydor	6342	January '82	A

RICK DERRINGER. Prime mover in the Sixties group The McCoys as a teenager, Rick Derringer was later a member of both Johnny Winter's back-up band and brother Edgar Winter's White Trash. An active sessions musician and producer, Derringer played on albums by Richie Havens, Alice Cooper, Todd Rundgren, and Steely Dan, while eventually producing four albums for each of the Winter brothers. Initiating a solo recording career in 1973, Derringer finally formed his own group in 1976.

THE McCOYS

Hang On Sloopy	Bang	212	November '65
You Make Me Feel So Good	Bang	213	'66
Infinite McCoys	Mercury	SR–61163	June '68
Human Ball	Mercury	SR–61207	March '69

RICK DERRINGER AND THE McCOYS

Outside Stuff	2-Mercury	SRM2–7506	March '74

RICK DERRINGER AND JOHNNY WINTER

Johnny Winter And	Columbia	PC–30221	August '70	A
Johnny Winter And Live*	Columbia	PC–30475	February '71	A
Johnny Winter And/Live	2-Columbia	CG–33651		A
John Dawson Winter III	Blue Sky	PZ–33292	November '74	

RICK DERRINGER WITH EDGAR WINTER

White Trash	Epic	E–30512	April '71	A
Roadwork*	2-Epic	PEG–31249	March '72	A
They Only Come Out at Night*	Epic	PE–31584	November '72	A

| Jasmine Night-dreams | Blue Sky | PZ–33483 | May '75 | |
| Edgar Winter Group with Rick Derringer | Blue Sky | PZ–33798 | October '75 | |

RICK DERRINGER

| All American Boy | Blue Sky | PZ–32481 | November '73 | A |
| Spring Fever | Blue Sky | PZ–33423 | March '75 | |

DERRINGER

Derringer	Blue Sky	PZ–34181	June '76	A
Sweet Evil	Blue Sky	PZ–34470	February '77	
Live	Blue Sky	PZ–34848	June '77	A
If I Weren't So Romantic, I'd Shoot You	Blue Sky	JZ–35075	June '78	
Guitars and Women	Blue Sky	JZ–36092	October '79	
Face to Face	Blue Sky	JZ–36551	October '80	A

NEIL DIAMOND. A prolific songwriter in the Tin Pan Alley tradition since the mid-Sixties, Neil Diamond is a highly successful singles artist, enormously popular in the pop field with his ballads and gentle rock songs.

Born in Coney Island, New York, on January 24, 1941, Neil Diamond began writing songs early in life, signing a songwriting contract with Sunbeam Music in the mid-Sixties. There he wrote "I'm a Believer" and "A Little Bit of You, a Little Bit of Me," big hits for The Monkees in 1966 and 1967, respectively. In and out of publishing houses for a number of years, Diamond eventually joined songwriters Jeff Barry and Ellie Greenwich in a publishing firm. After writing "Solitary Man" and "Cherry, Cherry" at his first session, he was brought by Barry to Jerry Wexler of Atlantic Records, who subsequently turned him over to Bert Berns of Bang Records. "Solitary Man" was only a minor hit in May 1966, but "Cherry, Cherry" became a huge hit before the end of the year. A string of hit singles for Bang continued through 1967 with "I Got the Feelin' (Oh, No, No)," "You Got Me," "Girl, You'll Be a Woman Soon," "I Thank the Lord for the Night Time," and "Kentucky Woman." In 1966 Diamond signed with MCA's Uni label and moved to Los Angeles. His first album for Uni, *Brother Love's Travelling Salvation Show*, yielded two hit singles, the title cut and "Sweet Caroline." His second album for Uni, *Touching You Touching Me*, produced the hit "Holly Holy," and became his first certified gold-award album. During 1970, "Shilo" and "Solitary Man" on the Bang label and "Soolaimon," "Cracklin' Rosie," and The Hollies' "He Ain't Heavy, He's My Brother" from *Tap Root Manuscript* were substantial hits for Diamond. Subsequent hits on Uni included "I Am . . . I Said," one of his finest compositions, "Stones" from *Stones*, and "Song Sung Blue," "Play Me," and "Walk on Water" from *Moods*.

In the fall of 1972, Neil Diamond announced a sabbatical from touring that was to last 40 months. He subsequently signed what at the time was the biggest single-artist deal in recording history with Columbia Records, where his debut album, *Jonathan Livingston Seagull*, yielded the hit single "Be" and became one of the biggest-selling soundtrack albums in history, only to be surpassed later by *Saturday Night Fever*. Diamond's second Columbia album, issued a full year later, sported two hit singles, "Longfellow Serenade" and "I've Been This Way Before." His third, *Beautiful Noise*, not released until a year and a half later and produced by The Band's Robbie Robertson, became Diamond's first certified platinum-award album. The album was issued only days before his return to live performance, at the opening of Las Vegas' Aladdin Theatre. Subsequent live recordings at Los Angeles' Greek Theater were released as *Love at the Greek*, followed by *I'm Glad You're Here with Me Tonight* and *You Don't Bring Me Flowers*, featuring the smash hit single title cut, sung with Barbra Streisand. Recent hits for Neil Diamond include "Forever in Blue Jeans," the title song to *September Morn*, and the smash "Love on the Rocks," from the soundtrack to the poorly received movie, *The Jazz Singer*, in which he made his motion picture debut.

NEIL DIAMOND

The Feel of Neil Diamond	Bang	214	September '66	A
Just for You	Bang	217	July '67	A
Greatest Hits	Bang	219	June '68	A
Shilo/Solitary Man	Bang	221	September '70	A
Do It!	Bang	224	February '71	A
Double Gold	2-Bang	227	January '73	A
Velvet Gloves and Spit	Uni reissued on MCA	73030 2010 reissued as 37056	November '68	A
Brother Love's Travelling Salvation Show	Uni reissued on MCA	73047 2011 reissued as 37057	May '69	A
Touching Me Touching You*	Uni reissued on MCA	73071 2006 reissued as 37058	December '69	A
Gold*	Uni reissued on MCA	73084 2007	August '70	A
Tap Root Manuscript*	Uni reissued on MCA	73092 2013	November '70	A
Stones*	Uni reissued on MCA	93106 2008	November '71	A
Moods*	Uni reissued on MCA	93136 2005	July '72	A

Rainbow*	MCA	2103	August '73	
		reissued as 37059		A
Hot August Night*	2-MCA	2-8000	December '72	A
His 12 Greatest Hits*	MCA	2106	June '74	A
And the Singer Sings His Songs	MCA	2227	October '76	
		reissued as 37060		A
Jonathan Livingston Seagull (soundtrack)*	Columbia	JS–32550	October '73	A
Serenade*	Columbia	PC–32919	October '74	A
Beautiful Noise**	Columbia	JC–33965	June '76	A
Love at the Greek**	2-Columbia	KC2–34404	February '77	A
I'm Glad You're Here with Me Tonight**	Columbia	PC–34990	November '77	A
You Don't Bring Me Flowers**	Columbia	FC–35625	November '78	A
September Morn**	Columbia	FC–36121	January '80	A
On the Way to the Sky	Columbia	TC–37628	November '81	A
The Jazz Singer (songs from the soundtrack)**	Capitol	SWAV–12120	November '80	A
Love Songs	MCA	5239	September '81	A

DION AND THE BELMONTS/DION DiMUCCI. One of the most popular white "doo-wop" vocal groups to emerge from New York's street-corner scene of the Fifties, Dion and The Belmonts scored with several hit singles before Dion left the group to pursue a successful solo career through 1963. Dion subsequently faded from the scene during the English invasion and re-emerged in 1968 as a folk-style artist.

Born in the Bronx, New York, on July 18, 1939, Dion DiMucci began making appearances playing acoustic guitar around the age of 11. He formed Dion and The Timberlanes briefly in early 1957, which was superseded by Dion and The Belmonts later that year. The Belmonts, also from the Bronx, were first tenor Angelo D'Aleo (born February 3, 1940), second tenor Fred Milano (born August 22, 1939), and bass singer Carlo Mastrangelo (born October 5, 1938). Signing with Laurie Records in February 1958, Dion and The Belmonts had their first hit with "I Wonder Why" in May. "No One Knows" followed, but D'Aleo left to join the navy in late 1958 and was not replaced. Subsequently, "A Teenager in Love" and the Rodgers and Hart classic "Where or When" became smash hits for the group in 1959 and 1960, respectively.

Dion left the group to pursue a solo career in October, 1960, as The Belmonts, rejoined by D'Aleo in 1961, recorded for their own Sabina label, scoring two moderate hits, "Tell Me Why" and "Come On, Little Angel," in 1961 and 1962, respectively. Dion's career, in the meantime, had taken off with "Lonely Teenager" in October 1960. Later hits for Dion on Laurie included the top hit "Runaround Sue" and the smash "The Wanderer," both co-written by Dion and Ernie Maresca, "Lovers Who Wander," "Little Diane," "Love Came to Me," and "Sandy," through 1963. In late 1962 Dion switched to Columbia Records for the smash hit singles "Ruby Baby," "Donna, the Prima Donna," and "Drip Drop." Thereafter, Dion met with little recording success until returning to Laurie in 1968. The previous year he had reunited with The Belmonts for *Together Again* on ABC Records. Back at Laurie, Dion recorded Dick Holler's ode to assassinated leaders, "Abraham, Martin, and John," a smash hit during 1968 and Dion's last major hit. Dion then toured the college-and-coffeehouse circuit as a folk-style, acoustic guitar artist, switching to Warner Brothers in 1970. During 1972 he reunited again with The Belmonts, Frank Lyndon having replaced Carlo Mastrangelo years earlier, for a concert at Madison Square Garden, recordings of which were issued on Warner Brothers in 1973. The Belmonts' final album, the a capella *Cigars, Accapella, and Candy*, was also issued that year. In 1974, Dion recorded *Born to Be with You* under producer-extraordinaire Phil Spector; but the album, when eventually released in 1975, was apparently issued in England only. After *Streetheart* for Warner Brothers, Dion formed the five-man Street Heart Band in early 1977, recording *Return of the Wanderer* with the band in 1978. Dion DiMucci's most recent album, *Inside Job*, was recorded for the Christian label, DaySpring.

DION AND THE BELMONTS

Presenting	Laurie	1002(M)	March '60	
When You Wish upon a Star	Laurie	2006(M)	September '60	
By Special Request: Together on Record	Laurie	2016(M)	September '66	
Together Again	ABC	ABCS–599	February '67	
Greatest Hits	Columbia	C–31942	February '73	A
Reunion—Dion and The Belmonts at Madison Square Garden, 1972	Warner Brothers	BS–2664	February '73	
Doo-Wop	Pickwick	3521	May '76	

THE BELMONTS

Carnival of Hits	Sabina	5001	October '62
Summer Love	Dot	DLP–25949	September '69
Cigars, Accapella, and Candy	Buddah	BDS–5123	March '73

DION (DiMUCCI)

Alone with Dion	Laurie	2004(M)		
Runaround Sue	Laurie	2009(M)	December '61	
Lovers Who Wander	Laurie	2012(M)	July '62	
Sings His Greatest Hits	Laurie	2013(M)	December '62	
Love Came to Me	Laurie	2015(M)		
Dion Sings to Sandy	Laurie	2017(M)	June '63	
Dion Sings the 15 Million Sellers	Laurie	2019(M)		
More Greatest Hits	Laurie	2022(M)		
Dion	Laurie	2047	November '68	
Ruby Baby	Columbia	CS–8810	March '63	
		reissued as C–35577	February '79	A
Donna, the Prima Donna	Columbia	CS–8907	November '63	
		reissued as C–35995	May '79	A
Wonder Where I'm Bound	Columbia	CS–9773	January '69	
Sit Down, Old Friend	Warner Brothers	1826	February '70	
You're Not Alone	Warner Brothers	1872	February '71	
Sanctuary	Warner Brothers	WS–1945	December '71	
Suite for Late Summer	Warner Brothers	BS–2642	November '72	
Born to Be with You	Warner/ Spector	9102	May '75	
Streetheart	Warner Brothers	2954	July '76	

DION AND THE STREET HEART BAND

Return of the Wanderer	Lifesong	JZ–35356	April '78	A

DION

Inside Job	DaySpring	4022	November '80	A

DOCTOR HOOK (AND THE MEDICINE SHOW). Breaking into the music scene on the basis of several Shel Silverstein songs, Doctor Hook (and The Medicine Show) endured a number of marginally successful albums before returning to the charts with rock standards and gentle country-style ballads, while retaining Silverstein's humorous bent.

Formed originally as The Chocolate Paupers in the late Sixties in New Jersey, Doctor Hook played local bars and clubs until "discovered" by songwriter Shel Silverstein, perhaps best known as the author of Johnny Cash's "A Boy Named Sue." The members: vocalist–guitarist Ray Sawyer (born February 1, 1937, in Chickasaw, Alabama), vocalist–guitarist Dennis Locorriere (born June 13, 1949, in Union City, New Jersey), steel guitarist George Cummings (born July 28, 1938), keyboardist William Francis (born January 16, 1942, in Sacramento, California), guitarist Richard Elswit (born July 6, 1945, in New York City), bassist Jance Garfat (born March 3 or 20, 1944, in San Francisco, California), and drummer John David, replaced by John Walters (born April 28, 1945, in Fort Meade, Maryland). The group subsequently appeared and performed in a movie Silverstein was scoring, *Who Is Harry Kellerman and Why Is He Saying Those Terrible Things about Me?*, starring Dustin Hoffman, before signing with Columbia Records in 1971. Their first two albums consisted entirely of Silverstein songs and one song from each became major hits, "Sylvia's Mother" and the classic "The Cover of the Rolling Stone." After backing Silverstein on his 1973 *Freakin' at the Freakers Ball* album, Doctor Hook began introducing their own material on *Belly Up*. The group soon went bankrupt and were released by Columbia, eventually signing with Capitol Records in 1975. Their appropriately titled Capitol debut, *Bankrupt,* yielded a smash hit single with the thinly sung remake of Sam Cooke's "Only Sixteen." The follow-up, *A Little Bit More*, produced a major hit with the title-song ballad and a minor hit with the tongue-in-cheek ballad "If Not You." In 1977 Ray Sawyer recorded an overlooked solo album for Capitol. By 1978 Doctor Hook was back on the hit-making trail, scoring with yet another ballad "Sharing The Night Together," from *Pleasure and Pain*, their first certified gold-award album. In 1979 the group scored a smash hit with "When You're in Love with a Beautiful Woman," followed by the major hit "Better Love Next Time" and the smash "Sexy Eyes" from *Sometimes You Win. . . .* By late 1980 Doctor Hook had switched to Casablanca Records for the moderate hit "Girls Can Get It" and *Rising*.

DOCTOR HOOK (AND THE MEDICINE SHOW)

Doctor Hook and The Medicine Show	Columbia	C–30898	April '72	A
Sloppy Seconds	Columbia	PC–31622	November '72	A
Belly Up	Columbia	C–32270	October '73	A
Revisited—The Best of Doctor Hook	Columbia	PC–34147	May '76	A
Bankrupt	Capitol	ST–11397 reissued as SN–16179	May '75	A
A Little Bit More	Capitol	ST–11522 reissued as SN–16180	April '76	A

RAY SAWYER

Ray Sawyer	Capitol	11591	February '77

DOCTOR HOOK

Makin' Love and Music	Capitol	ST–11632	November '77	A
Pleasure and Pain *	Capitol	SW–11859 reissued as SN–16181	October '78	A
Sometimes You Win . . .	Capitol	SOO–12023	November '79	A
Greatest Hits	Capitol	SOO–12122	December '80	A
Live	Capitol	ST–12114	December '81	A
Rising	Casablanca	7251	December '80	A

DOCTOR JOHN. Long a New Orleans and Los Angeles sessions guitarist and pianist, Doctor John assumed a voodoo persona for his initial Atco recordings, later de-emphasizing the role with *Gumbo* for subsequent rhythm-and-blues style recordings for several different labels.

DOCTOR JOHN

Doctor John and His New Orleans Congregation	Ace	2020(M)	
Gris-Gris	Atco	SD33–234	February '68
Babylon	Atco	SD33–270	March '69
Remedies	Atco	SD33–316	April '70
The Sun, Moon, and Herbs	Atco	SD33–362	August '71
Gumbo	Atco	7006	May '72
In the Right Place	Atco	SD–7018	February '73
Desitively Bon- naroo	Atco	SD–7043	April '74

DOCTOR JOHN, JOHN PAUL HAMMOND, AND MIKE BLOOMFIELD

Triumvirate	Columbia	C–32172	May '73

DOCTOR JOHN

Anytime, Anyplace	Barometer	67001	May '74
Hollywood, by Thy Name	United Artists	LA552	November '75
Zu Zu Man	Trip	9518	
Superpak	2-Trip	3507	February '76
Night Tripper at His Best	Power Pak	263(E)	
One Night Late	Karate	5404	February '78

City Lights	Horizon	732	December '78	
Tango Palace	Horizon	SP-740	September '79	A
Love Potion	Accord	SN-7118	November '81	A
Plays	Clean Cuts	705	January '82	A

FATS DOMINO. One of the most popular of the Fifties rock-and-rollers, selling tens of millions of records by 1960, Fats Domino successfully made the transition from rhythm-and-blues to rock-and-roll, focused attention on the music of New Orleans, and inspired other Southern black singers, most notably Little Richard and Lloyd Price, to pursue careers in popular music.

Born in New Orleans as Antoine Domino on February 26, 1928, "Fats" Domino started playing piano at age six, debuting professionally at age ten. Around 1949 he took a job with David Bartholomew's local dance band. Bartholomew was to become Fats' arranger and producer, co-author of many of Fats' hits, and would play trumpet behind him on recordings until 1956. Domino's first recording session after signing with Imperial Records yielded a substantial rhythm-and-blues hit with "The Fat Man," from which his nickname came, in 1950. Rhythm-and-blues hits with "Every Night about This Time," "Rockin' Chair," and "Goin' Home" followed, with Fats becoming the most popular performer and record seller around New Orleans by 1952. White audiences first took note of Domino in 1955 after Pat Boone covered his "Ain't That a Shame," a hit single for both men. Subsequent smash pop hits included "I'm in Love Again" backed with "My Blue Heaven," "Blueberry Hill," and "Blue Monday" in 1956, "I'm Walkin' " in 1957, "Whole Lotta Loving" in 1958, and "I Want to Walk You Home" backed with "I'm Gonna Be a Wheel Someday" in 1959. Other major hits included "When My Dreamboat Comes Home," "Valley of Tears" backed with "It's You I Love," "Wait and See," "I'm Ready," and "Be My Guest."

Although his popularity began to fade in the early Sixties, Fats Domino managed a smash hit with "Walkin to New Orleans" backed with "Don't Come Knockin' " in 1960, and scored major hits with "Country Boy," "Three Nights a Week," "My Girl Josephine," "What a Price," "It Keeps Rainin'," "Let the Four Winds Blow," "What a Party," and the Hank Williams' classics "Jambalaya (On the Bayou)" and "You Win Again" through 1962. In 1963 he signed with ABC–Paramount Records, where he was recorded with large orchestral backing and big vocal choruses, a practice already being used by the label with Lloyd Price and Ray Charles. His tenure lasted about two years, after which he signed with Mercury Records. In the meantime, Domino had established himself by the end of 1965 as a part of the Las Vegas scene, where he still plays three months a year. Achieving little recording success at Mercury, he switched to Reprise Records in 1968, placing *Fats Is Back* on the album charts and scoring a minor hit, his last, with The Beatles' "Lady Madonna." Through the Seventies, Fats Domino continued to tour up to ten months a year, recreating his old hits for appreciative audiences across the country. In 1980–81 he managed a minor country hit with "Whiskey Heaven."

FATS DOMINO

Fats Domino	Archive of Folk and Jazz Music	280(M)	July '74	A
Fats Domino, Volume 2	Archive of Folk and Jazz Music	330(M)	November '77	A
Rock and Rollin' with Fats Domino	Imperial	LP-9004 (M)	April '56	
Rock and Rollin'	Imperial	LP-9009 (M)	September '56	
This Is Fats Domino!	Imperial	LP-9028 (M)	January '57	
Here Stands Fats Domino	Imperial	LP-9038 (M)	April '57	
This Is Fats	Imperial	LP-9040 (M)	May '57	
Fabulous Mr. D	Imperial	LP-9055 (M)	September '58	
	reissued on Liberty	LN-10136	November '81	A
Fats Domino Swings 12,000,000 Records	Imperial	LP-9062 (M)	January '59	
Let's Play Fats Domino	Imperial	LP-9065 (M)	October '59	
	reissued on Liberty	LN-10135	November '81	A
Million Record Hits	Imperial	LP-9103 (M)	February '60	
A Lot of Dominos	Imperial	LP-12066	November '60	
I Miss You So	Imperial	9138(M)	February '61	
Let the Four Winds Blow	Imperial	LP-12073	July '61	
What a Party	Imperial	LP-9164 (M)	November '61	
Twistin' the Stomp	Imperial	LP-9170 (M)	March '62	
Million Sellers by Fats	Imperial	LP-9195 (M)	June '62	
	reissued on United Artists	LM-1027	April '80	A
Just Domino	Imperial	LP-9208 (M)	October '62	
Walking to New Orleans	Imperial	LP-9227 (M)	February '63	
Let's Dance with Domino	Imperial	LP-9239 (M)	June '63	

Here He Comes Again!	Imperial	LP–9248 (M)	September '63	
Here Comes Fats Domino	ABC-Paramount	ABCS–455	July '63	
Fats on Fire	ABC-Paramount	ABCS–479	February '64	
Getaway with Fats Domino	ABC-Paramount	ABCS–510	January '66	
'65	Mercury	SR–61039	October '65	
Southland U.S.A.	Mercury	SR–61065	February '66	
Fats Domino	Sunset	5103	May '66	
Stompin' Fats Domino	Sunset	5158	June '67	
Trouble in Mind	Sunset	5200	August '69	
Ain't That a Shame	Sunset	5299	April '71	
Fats Domino	Grand Award	267	June '68	
Fats Is Back	Reprise	RS–6304	September '68	
Fats	Reprise	6439	April '71	
Fats Domino	Pickwick	2031		
Blueberry Hill	Pickwick	3111	January '69	
My Blue Heaven	Pickwick	3295	June '72	
Fats' Hits	Pickwick	5005(M)		
When I'm Walking	Harmony	11343	September '69	
	reissued on Columbia	C–35996	May '79	A
30 Hits—The Fats Domino Sound	United Artists	104(M)		
Legendary Masters	United Artists	UAS–9958	February '72	
Superpak	2-United Artists	LA122	'73	A
Very Best	United Artists	LA233	August '74	
Play It Again, Fats	United Artists	LA380	March '75	

TOM DONAHUE. An early Sixties concert promoter, record company manager, and disc jockey in the San Francisco region, "Big Daddy" Tom Donahue created America's first alternative to banal AM-radio programming at FM-radio station KMPX in 1967. By playing album cuts rather than Top-40 singles, re-introducing live music broadcasts, and utilizing the airwaves as a true public service to its listeners, Donahue proved that FM-radio need not cater to limited audiences as it had done in the past. In thus founding "underground radio," Donahue showed that radio audiences would gratefully accept a nonfrenetic approach to recorded musical presentation that eschewed the limited singles playlist concept, the use of offensive and inane commercials, and the abhorrence of controversy and public access to the airwaves. He inspired the formation of underground FM-radio stations across the country, virtually forced AM-radio stations to revise their programming, and encouraged the development of what is referred to today as "album-oriented rock" (AOR) radio.

Born in South Bend, Indiana, on May 21, 1928, Tom Donahue first worked as a disc jockey during the late Forties in Charleston, West

Virginia. He later worked at Washington, D.C.'s WINX and Philadelphia's WIBG before being hired by San Francisco radio station KYA in 1961. In early 1964 he and fellow disc jockey Bobby Mitchell formed Autumn Records, hiring Sly Stone as its only producer. Autumn released a number of hits by San Francisco's first major group, The Beau Brummels, as well as one by Bobby Freeman ("C'mon and Swim"), and signed Grace Slick's first group, The Great Society. Donahue and Mitchell presented rock concerts in the Bay area at least two years before Bill Graham did, including The Beatles' final public performance in 1966.

On April 7, 1967, Tom Donahue took over the 8 PM-to-midnight shift at FM-radio station KMPX. The station, formerly a foreign language outlet, allowed Donahue to play album cuts, broadcast live music, refuse certain commercials, make public announcements of a political or general interest nature, and generally get involved with the community at large and its concerns. KMPX thus became the nation's first full-time, album-cut, reasonably intelligent FM-radio station. The format proved enormously popular and was picked up by hundreds of FM stations across the country, thus liberating contemporary music fans from the banality and myopia of AM-radio programming. After a bitter strike against KMPX during 1968, Donahue and nearly the entire staff defected to KSAN–FM, formerly a classical music station. The station was subsequently virtually unchallenged as the area's top progressive rock station, and Donahue became the station's general manager in 1972. On the verge of becoming the general manager and part-owner of the recently sold KMPX station, "Big Daddy" Tom Donahue died of a heart attack on April 28, 1975, at age 46.

DONOVAN. After initial appearances in the mix-Sixties as an English folk artist strongly resembling America's Bob Dylan, Donovan later embraced benificent psychedelia and naive spiritualism for a series of hit singles and best-selling albums before fading into near-obscurity by the Seventies.

Born in Glasgow, Scotland, as Donovan Leitch on May 10, 1946, Donovan took up guitar as a teenager. Performing on BBC–TV's "Ready, Steady, Go" in early 1965, he signed with Hickory Records for several folk-style hits, two of his own compositions, "Catch the Wind" and "Colours," and Buffy Sainte-Marie's "Universal Soldier." Subsequently abandoning the Dylan-like image, Donovan signed with Epic Records for a number of psychedelic, quasi-mystical hits through the late Sixties. His first Epic album release, *Sunshine Superman*, yielded the top hit single title cut and featured perhaps his finest composition, the ominous "Season of the Witch." The follow-up, *Mellow Yellow*, included the smash hit single title cut as well as the haunting "Young Girl Blues." *A Gift from a Flower to a Garden*, a double-record set and Donovan's only non-anthology, certified gold-award album, was also released as two separate single albums, *Wear Your Love like Heaven* and *For Little Ones*. The first yielded the title cut

hit single, whereas the second contained the major hit, "Epistle to Dippy."
Donovan continued to have hit singles through the late Sixties with "There
is a Mountain," from *In Concert*, "Jennifer Juniper" and the smash
"Hurdy Gurdy Man" from *Hurdy Gurdy Man*, and "Lalena." *Baraba-
jagal*, recorded with guitarist Jeff Beck, featured two moderate hits, the
title cut and "To Susan on the West Coast Waiting." Since 1969's "Atlan-
tis," Donovan has encountered little success, save 1973's best-selling
Cosmic Wheels album. *Essence to Essence*, *7-Tease* (recorded in
Nashville), and *Slow Down World* managed to penetrate the lower levels
of the album charts, but 1977's *Donovan*, on his new label Arista, didn't
even make the charts.

DONOVAN

Catch the Wind	Hickory	123	July '65	
Fairy Tales	Hickory	127	December '65	
The Real Donovan	Hickory	135	September '66	
Like It Is, Was, and Evermore Shall Be	Hickory	143	January '67	
The Best of Donovan	Hickory	149	November '69	
Sunshine Superman	Epic	BN–26217	August '66	A
Mellow Yellow	Epic	BN–26239	January '67	
A Gift from a Flower to a Garden*	2-Epic	B2N–171	November '67	A
Wear Your Love Like Heaven	Epic	BN–26349	December '67	
For Little Ones	Epic	BN–26350	December '67	
In Concert	Epic	BN–26386	July '68	A
Hurdy Gurdy Man	Epic	BN–26420	October '68	A
Greatest Hits*	Epic	PE–26439	February '69	A
Barabajagal	Epic	BN–26481	August '69	A
Open Road	Epic	E–30125	July '70	
Donovan P. Leitch	2-Janus	3022	November '70	
Hear Me Now	Janus	3025	June '71	
World—Physical/ Spiritual	2-Epic	KEG– 31210	April '72	
Cosmic Wheels	Epic	KE–32156	March '73	
Essence to Essence	Epic	E–32800	January '74	
7-Tease	Epic	PE–33245	November '74	
Barabajagal/Hurdy Gurdy Man	2-Epic	BG–33731	September '75	
Sunshine Super- man/In Concert	2-Epic	BG–33734	September '75	
Slow Down World	Epic	PE–33945	May '76	
History of British Pop	Pye	502	January '76	
History of British Pop, Volume 2	Pye	507	September '76	
Donovan	Arista	4143	August '77	

THE DOOBIE BROTHERS. One of the more popular of the California singles bands of the Seventies, The Doobie Brothers have recorded a series of hard-driving rock albums, often utilizing the double lead-guitar format, while enduring a number of personnel changes, to become one of America's top live acts by 1978. As The Doobie Brothers became dominated by Michael McDonald, particularly after the 1979 departure of Jeff "Skunk" Baxter, former chief singer and songwriter Tom Johnston embarked on a modest solo career.

In 1969 drummer John Hartman moved to San Jose, California, from West Virginia, ostensibly to join the re-formed Moby Grape. The project fell through, but ex-Grape member Skip Spence introduced Hartman to guitarist–songwriter Tom Johnston, and the two subsequently formed Pud with bassist Greg Murphy, who was quickly replaced by Dave Shogren. The group became a quartet with the addition of former folk guitarist Pat Simmons and adopted the name The Doobie Brothers for engagements throughout the San Francisco Bay area. Signed to Warner Brothers Records, the group recorded one ill-received album before replacing Shogren with Tiran Porter and adding a second drummer in the person of Mike Hossack. The members: Tom Johnston (lead vocals, guitar, keyboards, songwriting), Pat Simmons (guitar, harmony vocals, songwriting), John Hartman (drums), Tiran Porter (bass, harmony vocals), and Mike Hossack (drums).

Using the double guitar, double drums format popularized by The Allman Brothers, The Doobie Brothers recorded *Toulouse Street*. The album, the first of a continuing series of gold-award albums, yielded the smash hit single, "Listen to the Music," written by Johnston, and a moderate hit, "Jesus Is Just Alright," as well as containing "Rockin' Down the Highway." Their next album, *The Captain and Me*, produced two major hit singles, "Long Train Runnin' " and "China Groove," both written by Johnston. No major hit emerged until Simmons' "Black Water" from *What Were Once Vices Are Now Habits* became a smash single at the end of 1974. The beginning of 1974 had seen the departure of Mike Hossack, who was replaced by drummer–vocalist Keith Knudsen. Ex-Steely Dan and sessions guitarist–vocalist Jeff "Skunk" Baxter, who had recorded and toured with The Doobie Brothers for six months on a part-time basis, joined the group full time by the end of 1974. *Stampede*, the band's first album with Baxter as a full-time member, featured three hits: one major, "Take Me in Your Arms (Rock Me);" one moderate, "Sweet Maxine;" and one minor, "I Cheat the Hangman." Nonetheless, Baxter continued sessions and tour work with James Taylor, Elton John, and Hoyt Axton.

Near the beginning of The Doobie Brothers' spring tour of 1975, Tom Johnston collapsed and returned to his home in order to recover from health problems, only rejoining the band intermittently and ultimately leaving the group officially in January 1977. With their chief songwriter disabled, the group enlisted former Steely Dan keyboardist–vocalist Mike McDonald in the fall of 1975. McDonald's "Takin' It to the Streets" became the hit single from the album of the same name, with his "It Keeps You Runnin' " becoming only a moderate hit. With two former Steely Dan members as part of the group, The Doobie Brothers began to explore a more sophisticated and jazz-oriented sound, only to score minor hits from 1977's *Livin' on the Fault Line*. During 1978 Carly Simon scored a smash hit with "You Belong to Me," co-written with McDonald and, by 1979, The Doobie Brothers had returned to its hit-making ways with the heavily rhythm-and-blues influenced *Minute by Minute* album, which yielded the top hit "What a Fool Believes" (co-written by McDonald and Kenny Loggins) and the major hits "Minute by Minute" and "Dependin' on You" during the year. Also in 1979 founding member John Hartman dropped out, whereas Jeff Baxter departed to return to studio work. The Doobie Brothers subsequently re-aligned with McDonald, Simmons, Porter, Knudsen, and new members John McFee (steel guitar, rhythm guitar, dobro, violin), Cornelius Bumpus (keyboards, saxophone), and Chet Mc-Cracken (drums). McFee had previously been in Clover, and Bumpus was a latter-day member of Moby Grape. The new lineup's first album, *One Step Closer*, produced the smash hit "Real Love," co-written by McDonald, and the major hit title song, written by McFee, Knudsen, and Carlene Carter, by the end of 1980. During the year, Tiran Porter left the group and was replaced by sessions bassist Willie Weeks.

In the meantime, Tom Johnston had taken more than a year to record his solo debut, *Everything You've Heard Is True*. However, the album produced only one moderate hit, "Savannah Nights," despite a tour by Johnston in the album's support. *Still Feels Good*, from 1981, fared little better.

THE DOOBIE BROTHERS

The Doobie Brothers	Warner Brothers	1919	May '71	A
Toulouse Street*	Warner Brothers	BS–2634	March '72	A
The Captain and Me*	Warner Brothers	BS–2694	March '73	A
What Were Once Vices Are Now Habits*	Warner Brothers	2750	February '74	A
Stampede*	Warner Brothers	2835	April '75	A
Takin' It to the Streets**	Warner Brothers	BS–2899	March '76	A
The Best of the Doobies**	Warner Brothers	BS–2978 reissued as 3112	November '76	A
Livin' on the Fault Line*	Warner Brothers	BSK–3045	August '77	A
Minute by Minute**	Warner Brothers	3193	December '78	A
One Step Closer**	Warner Brothers	HS–3452	September '80	A

THE DOORS / 141

The Best of The Doobies, Volume II	Warner Brothers	3612	October '81	A

TOM JOHNSTON

Everything You've Heard Is True	Warner Brothers	3304	September '79	A
Still Feels Good	Warner Brothers	3527	August '81	A

THE DOORS. One of the first rock groups to achieve initial popularity "underground" by means of FM-radio play, The Doors were also one of the first rock groups to record extended pieces that were later edited down for release as a single ("Light My Fire"). An outstanding improvisatory group, The Doors were fronted by the near-legendary Jim Morrison, who contributed powerful pieces of surreal poetry frequently preoccupied with sex and death. In acting out his poetry with carefully devised theatrics in concert, Jim Morrison and The Doors became perhaps the first rock group to consciously inject serious and often compelling theatrics and poetics into their act. As a result, The Doors were one of the first rock bands to be discussed and criticized in terms of rock music, lyrics, and performance as art. Although 1978's *An American Prayer* failed to win Jim Morrison much-deserved recognition as a true poet, The Doors nonetheless experienced a remarkable revival of interest, particularly after the 1980 publication of the best-selling tome, *No One Here Gets Out Alive.*

Jim Morrison was born into a naval family in Melbourne, Florida, on December 8, 1943, and eventually enrolled in the theater arts department of UCLA in 1964, majoring in film. Chicago-born on February 12, 1943, Ray Manzarek, who was sidelining with the blues-style band Rick and The Ravens, met Morrison during 1965 while also attending film classes at UCLA. The two quickly contacted jazz drummer John Densmore, born in Los Angeles on December 1, 1945, about forming a group, and The Doors' lineup was completed with the subsequent addition of Robbie Krieger, born in Los Angeles on January 8, 1946. The members: Jim Morrison (lead vocals, songwriting), Robbie Krieger (guitar, songwriting), Ray Manzarek (organ, piano), and John Densmore (drums).

After several months of rehearsal, The Doors were hired as house band for Los Angeles' Whisky A Go-Go for four months. Signed to Elektra Records, the group began recording their debut album during 1966. The self-titled album was an instant success through widespread FM-radio play, thus becoming one of the first rock albums popularized by the "alternative" media. The album contained Morrison's psychosexual epic "The End" and sported a number of hard-driving rock songs such as "Break on Through," "Back Door Man," "Take It as It Comes," and Krieger's "Light My Fire." Shortened from its original nearly 7-minute length for single release, "Light My Fire" became a huge hit by mid-1967 and broadened the Doors' base of popularity beyond the underground. Their second album, *Strange Days*, retained the format of the first while exhibiting more sophisticated musical arrangements. It contained another extended Morrison piece (the 11-minute "When the Music's Over") and a number of potent rock songs ("My Eyes Have Seen You" and "Love Me Two Times") as well as several haunting ballads ("Strange Days" and "Unhappy Girl"). "People Are Strange" and "Love Me Two Times" became the hit singles from the album.

Though not as powerful as prior releases, *Waiting for the Sun* featured the printed words of yet another epic Morrison poem, "The Celebration of the Lizard," which found musical expression only in "Not to Touch the Earth." Krieger's puerile "Hello, I Love You" was the big hit from the album, whereas "Unknown Soldier" became only a moderate hit. Morrison's anarchistic "Five to One" bore stark contrast to the album's shallow ballads. In the meantime, given Morrison's penchant for drama in performance, The Doors became an enormous concert attraction by the end of 1968. As audiences grew larger, Morrison increased his theatricality, but performances were erratic by 1969, culminating in Morrison's indecent exposure bust in Miami in March of that year. Many subsequent concerts turned into outrageous fiascos due to Morrison's antics.

The Soft Parade, probably The Doors' weakest album with Morrison, was dominated by Krieger's juvenile lyrics and sported one major hit, "Touch Me." Nonetheless, *Morrison Hotel* saw The Doors return to straight rock with songs such as "Roadhouse Blues" and "You Make Me Real," though the album yielded no major hit singles. Following its release, The Doors even completed a successful tour largely free of problems. With *Absolutely Live*, featuring the complete "Celebration of the Lizard," and *13* intervening, *L. A. Woman* was the last Doors album with Jim Morrison. The album contained two hits, "Love Her Madly" and "Riders on the Storm," as well as the excellent title cut.

In March 1971 a disillusioned and weary Jim Morrison, beset by legal problems and years of alcohol abuse, moved to Paris, France, for rest and recuperation, only to die of a heart attack under mysterious circumstances on July 3, 1971. The three remaining members of The Doors persevered through *Other Voices* and *Full Circle* before disbanding in 1973. Ray Manzarek subsequently recorded two obscure solo albums for Mercury Records before forming Nite City with vocalist Noah James around the end of 1976. Robbie Krieger and John Densmore formed The Butts Band for two albums on Blue Thumb Records, with Krieger later recording solo in 1977.

Near the end of 1978, Elektra issued *An American Prayer*. A living document of Jim Morrison's predilection for poetry and drama, the album featured material he had recorded primarily on his last birthday, December 8, 1970. The remaining original Doors, Robbie Krieger, Ray Manzarek, and John Densmore, had edited many hours of tape and added musical backing for this final testament to one of rock music's finest poets, Jim Morrison. With the use of "The End" in the film *Apocalypse Now* and the publication of Danny Sugarman and Jerry Hopkins' best-selling *No One Here Gets Out Alive,* The Doors enjoyed an astounding renewal of interest in the early Eighties that saw *Greatest Hits* quickly certified platinum-award. In the meantime, former Doors Robbie Krieger and Ray Manzarek had produced recordings for several different Los Angeles bands, and John Densmore turned his attention to modern dance and acting.

THE DOORS

The Doors *	Elektra	EKS–74007	January '67	A
Strange Days *	Elektra	EKS–74014	October '67	A
Waiting for the Sun *	Elektra	EKS–74024	August '68	A
The Soft Parade *	Elektra	EKS–75005	July '69	A
Morrison Hotel *	Elektra	EKS–75007	February '70	A
Absolutely Live *	2-Elektra	EKS–9002	July '70	A
13 *	Elektra	EKS–74079	November '70	A
L.A. Woman *	Elektra	EKS–75011	April '71	A
Other Voices	Elektra	EKS–75017	November '71	
Weird Scenes Inside the Gold Mine *	2–Elektra	8E–6001	November '71	A
Full Circle	Elektra	EKS–75038	July '72	
The Best of The Doors	Elektra	EQ–5035	September '73	A

THE BUTTS BAND

The Butts Band	Blue Thumb	BTS–63	January '74	
Hear and Now	Blue Thumb	6018	January '75	

RAY MANZAREK

The Golden Scarab	Mercury	SRM1–703	March '74	
The Whole Thing Started with Rock and Roll	Mercury	SRM1–1014	January '75	

NITE CITY

Nite City	20th Century	528	February '77	

ROBBIE KRIEGER

Robbie Krieger and Friends	Blue Note	LA664	September '77	

JIM MORRISON AND THE DOORS

An American	Elektra	502	December '78	A
Prayer				
Greatest Hits**	Elektra	515	October '80	A

THE DRIFTERS. Not to be confused with The Drifters led by Clyde McPhatter and Johnny Moore between 1953 and 1958, this "new" Drifters initially featured Ben E. King on lead vocals. It was this and subsequent groupings of The Drifters that created an early "soul" sound with gospel-style singing, pop-oriented material, and lush orchestral backgrounds. Though these Drifters were not the first rhythm-and-blues vocal group to utilize strings for recordings (that claim probably goes to The Orioles of "Crying in the Chapel" fame), The Drifters popularized the format, a format subsequently used by many rhythm-and-blues and soul acts.

The original Drifters were formed in 1953 around lead vocalist Clyde McPhatter. He departed the group in late 1954, to be replaced by Johnny Moore, who was replaced by Bobby Hendricks in 1958. Johnny Moore and Bobby Hendricks were the lead singers on *Rockin' and Driftin'*. Manager George Treadwell, owner of The Drifters' name, fired what was left of the group in June 1958 and enlisted The Crowns as the "new" Drifters. The members: Ben E. King (lead baritone), Charles Thomas (tenor), Doc Green (baritone), and Ellsbury Hobbs (bass).

Born Benjamin Nelson on September 28, 1938, in Henderson, North Carolina, Ben E. King co-authored The Drifters' first hit single "There Goes My Baby" with manager Treadwell. The recording, a smash hit single in 1959 in both the rhythm-and-blues and pop fields, had been produced by legendary producer–songwriters Jerry Leiber and Mike Stoller, who produced many of the subsequent Drifter hits. "Dance with Me," co-written by Treadwell, was the next in the series of hit singles essentially aimed at white audiences. Brill Building professional songwriters "Doc" Pomus and Mort Shuman provided The Drifters' next four hit singles: "(If You Cry) True Love, True Love" in 1959, and "This Magic Moment," "Save the Last Dance for Me," and "I Count the Tears" in 1960.

By 1961 Ben E. King had left The Drifters to pursue a solo career. His first hit came with a song written by Jerry Leiber and then apprentice-producer Phil Spector, "Spanish Harlem." Later hits included "Stand by Me" (co-authored by King) and "Amor" in 1961, "Don't Play That Song" in 1962, and "I (Who Have Nothing)" in 1963. In the meantime, The Drifters were enjoying their greatest hit-making period with Rudy Lewis (born August 23, 1936) on lead vocals. Their 1961 hits included Carole King and Gerry Goffin's "Some Kind of Wonderful" as well as "Please Stay" and "Sweets for My Sweet." With Tommy Evans replacing Ellsbury Hobbs as bass singer, The Drifters scored with "When My Little Girl Is Smiling," the Goffin–King classic "Up on the Roof," and two Barry Mann–Cynthia Weil compositions, "On Broadway" and "I'll Take You Home." Rudy Lewis died in 1963 and was replaced by original Drifter

Johnny Moore (born in Selma, Alabama, in 1934) for the group's final hits in 1964, "Under the Boardwalk" and "Saturday Night at the Movies."

The Drifters continued to record into the early Seventies, but met with little success. Several different groupings of The Drifters exist to this day, one led by Johnny Moore, another by original Drifter Bill Pinckney, and a third by Charles Thomas. Johnny Moore's Drifters had a substantial English hit in 1974 with "Kissin' in the Back Row of the Movies."

Absent for a number of years, Ben E. King re-emerged in 1974 with Atlantic Records. "Supernatural Thing—Part 1" was a big hit for King from *Supernatural* in early 1975 and, despite the poor showing of the follow-up *I Had a Love, Benny and Us*, recorded with the white Scottish rhythm-and-blues band, The Average White Band, became a best-seller in 1977. Atlantic has since issued three albums for Ben E. King.

THE DRIFTERS

Rockin' and Driftin'	Atlantic	8022(M)	November '58	
Greatest Hits	Atlantic	8041(M)	October '60	
Save the Last Dance for Me	Atlantic	SD–8059	February '62	
Up on the Roof	Atlantic	SD–8073	February '63	
Our Biggest Hits	Atlantic	SD–8093	July '64	
Under the Board-walk	Atlantic	SD–8099	August '64	
The Good Life with The Drifters	Atlantic	SD–8103	February '65	
I'll Take You Where the Music's Playing	Atlantic	SD–8113	October '65	
Golden Hits	Atlantic	SD–8153	December '67	A
The Drifters Now	Bell	219		
Best	Arista	4111	February '77	

BEN E. KING

Spanish Harlem	Atco	SD33–133	August '61	
Sings for Soulful Lovers	Atco	SD33–137	August '62	
Don't Play That Song	Atco	SD33–142	June '62	
Greatest Hits	Atco	SD33–165	July '64	A
7 Letters	Atco	SD33–174	February '65	
Rough Edges	Maxwell	88001	September '70	
Beginning of It All	Mandala	3007	November '72	
Supernatural	Atlantic	SD–18132	April '75	
I Had a Love	Atlantic	SD–18169	May '76	

BEN E. KING/THE AVERAGE WHITE BAND

Benny and Us	Atlantic	SD–19105	July '77

BEN E. KING

Let Me Live in Your Life	Atlantic	19200	September '78	
Music Trance	Atlantic	19269	May '80	
Street Tough	Atlantic	19300	April '81	A

BOB DYLAN. Certainly the most important single figure in contemporary music during the Sixties, Bob Dylan was the first and most significant song poet to emerge from the folk music scene, inspiring a whole generation of folk artists and later rock artists to explore the vast potential of songwriting in matters socially conscious, personal, philosophical, and intellectual. Established as a powerful political folk-style singer–songwriter with his second and third albums, Dylan's "Blowin' in the Wind" and "The Times They Are A-Changin' " became anthems of the youth-protest movement. Having successfully made the transition from traditional folk music to penetrating highly political, socially conscious protest music, Dylan subsequently revitalized folk music and songwriting with his highly personal, intense song poetics permeated with acute literary and philosophical references. Though generally unrecognized, Bob Dylan also displayed an early virtuosity on harmonica more typical of the blues scene than of the folk scene.

Seemingly one step ahead of his audience at critical philosophical and personal as well as musical junctures, Bob Dylan has somehow managed to avoid becoming type-cast by fans and critics alike at progressive stages of his career to maintain his status as contemporary music's most independent, elusive, and enigmatic figure. The prime mover in the development of so-called "folk-rock" music during 1965 inasmuch as his "Mr. Tambourine Man" was the smash debut single of The Byrds, Dylan was severely criticized by folk fans and critics for his move into rock music with *Bringing It All Back Home* and his Newport Folk Festival appearance, backed by the electrified Paul Butterfield Blues Band. Nonetheless, with that album Dylan began successfully to reinvigorate rock with his emotionally evocative, vituperative, and surrealistic song poetics, while vastly expanding the concepts and concerns of contemporary music and song writing, thus laying the groundwork for the singer–songwriter movement of the late Sixties and early Seventies. Dylan virtually demolished the standard a–b–a song structure and instituted almost singlehandedly the free verse stanza. Having challenged almost an entire generation of folk and rock fans to re-examine their values and attitudes, Dylan, with *Bringing It All Back Home,* soon came to be presumptuously hailed by critics and the media as the spokesman for his generation. Moreover, whereas The Beatles were establishing the album as the unit of public consumption of music, Dylan was establishing the album as the unit of personal musical expression.

With *Highway 61 Revisited,* Bob Dylan brought song poetry into the classrooms and onto the streets and, with later assistance from The Beatles, made rock music intellectually respectable and promoted the view of rock music and lyrics as a valid art form as well as popular entertainment. With the 6-minute "Like a Rolling Stone," his first major hit single and perhaps his finest composition, Dylan permanently broke the recording industry's 3-minute song-length rule and thus encouraged dozens of groups and individual artists to at least occasionally abandon the restrictive format. *Blonde on Blonde*, probably the first non-anthology double-record set by a major contemporary artist, revealed an unprecedented level of performance and lyrical invention, marked the beginning of Dylan's break with the purely rock-and-roll audience in favor of a more intellectual audience, and firmly brought an existential stance to rock music. Through his widespread popularity Dylan also encouraged a number of artists to use their marginally adequate singing voices on recordings, most notably Jimi Hendrix, inasmuch as the entire body of Dylan's work to date had been sung in a harsh, strident, adenoidal voice lacking sophisticated musical nuances.

Retreating to upstate New York following a serious motorcycle accident in the summer of 1966, Bob Dylan assembled his most recent touring band for relatively informal recordings. The recordings, somehow pirated and issued illegally on so-called "bootleg" albums, became some of the earliest and best-selling albums of the genre. The backing group, eventually known as The Band, were later launched on their own successful career, not on the basis of the usual intensive touring or hit single but as the result of a word-of-mouth reputation and stunning debut album. The recordings, finally released officially in 1975 as *The Basement Tapes*, were critically acclaimed as one of the greatest albums in the history of American popular music.

At last Bob Dylan re-emerged with *John Wesley Harding*, an album that perplexed and overwhelmed many of his fans. Much of the vituperation and anger exhibited earlier was gone, and the album reflected a conscious concern with vanity, arrogance and pride, resignation, perseverance, and resurrection in the real world. A marked contrast to the prevailing trend towards complexity, the album's final two cuts presaged the next unanticipated shift in Dylan's music toward a "pop" sensibility. *Nashville Skyline*, critically attacked by most writers, contained simple, gentle songs in a "country-pop" mold that rejected both the vitriolic and alienated vision of *Bringing It All Back Home, Highway 61 Revisited,* and *Blonde on Blonde*, and the profound personal and philosophical concerns of *John Wesley Harding*. Certainly not the first so-called "country-rock" album, *Nashville Skyline* nonetheless represented a reconciliation between country and rock musics and encouraged the popular acceptance of this new musical fusion among fans in both fields.

With his career subsequently in eclipse during the early Seventies, Bob Dylan was being discounted as a major force in contemporary music by 1974. However, he again confounded his critics following his 1974 tour with The Band by re-establishing himself as a song poet of immense stature and talent with *Blood on the Tracks*. Furthermore, he substantiated his popularity with pop as well as rock audiences with 1975's *Desire* album.

Beginning in 1979, Dylan once more bewildered and mystified fans and critics by recording simplified "born-again" Christian material. Discounted and castigated many times during his career, Bob Dylan may yet again astound and confuse his critics and audiences with another uncanny musical work.

In the oft-accounted story, Bob Dylan was born Robert Zimmerman in Duluth, Minnesota, on May 24, 1941, moving with his family to Hibbing when he was six. Taking up guitar around age 12, he later formed several groups while still in high school. After graduation, he attended the University of Minnesota for several months, dropping out in late 1960 to travel to New York to visit his idol Woody Guthrie, hospitalized with Huntington's disease. Dylan began performing in Greenwich Village folk clubs in early 1961, debuting professionally at Gerde's Folk City that April. First noticed by *New York Times* critic Robert Shelton that September, Dylan was soon signed to Columbia Records by John Hammond. His first album, released in March 1962, featured traditional folk and blues songs such as "Man of Constant Sorrow" and "House of the Rising Sun," as well as Eric Von Schmidt's "Baby, Let Me Follow You Down" and the original "Song to Woody." The follow-up album, *The Freewheelin' Bob Dylan*, contained all his own material and effectively established him as a songwriter. The songs included a number of potent "protest" and anti-war songs such as "Masters of War," "A Hard Rain's A-Gonna Fall," and "Blowin' in the Wind." During 1963, the folk group Peter, Paul, and Mary popularized two songs from the album, "Blowin' in the Wind" and "Don't Think Twice, It's All Right," consecutive major hits for the group.

The Times They Are A-Changin', from early 1964, featured several songs concerning the treatment of blacks in America ("The Lonesome Death of Hattie Carroll" and "Only a Pawn in Their Game"), the anti-war "With God on Our Side," and the title song, adopted by the youth-protest movement as a political anthem as had been the earlier "Blowin' in the Wind." The more personal *Another Side* included a number of songs later recorded by others in the so-called "folk-rock" mold: "It Ain't Me, Babe" (by The Turtles), "All I Really Want to Do" (by The Byrds and Cher), and "Chimes of Freedom" and "My Back Pages" (by The Byrds).

Bob Dylan began to leave the folk-protest movement behind with 1965's *Bringing It All Back Home* album. Half acoustic and half electric, the album contained a number of songs written in a stream-of-consciousness style and pervaded with incisive, evocative, surreal images such as "Gates of Eden" and "Subterranean Homesick Blues." Other inclusions were the provocative "It's Alright Ma (I'm Only Bleeding)" and "It's All Over Now, Baby Blue," and the underrated love songs "She Belongs to Me" and "Love Minus Zero/No Limit." "Subterranean Homesick Blues" became Dylan's first hit single, and "Mr. Tambourine Man" was soon recorded by The Byrds as the first "folk-rock" song. Having become an international celebrity, Dylan was soon being hailed by fans and critics as the spokesman of his disillusioned, alienated generation.

Bob Dylan decisively left his folk audience behind during 1965.

Already dismayed by the electric rock sound of "Subterranean Homesick Blues," these fans and critics were positively shocked by that summer's *Highway 61 Revisited* album, "Like a Rolling Stone" single, and Dylan's appearance at the Newport Folk Festival backed by the electrified Paul Butterfield Blues Band. The album, recorded with Mike Bloomfield on electric guitar and Al Kooper on keyboards, created an unmistakable sound and featured some of Dylan's most startling songwriting efforts. Filled with surreal images, stimulating existential observations, and emotionally evocative song poetry, the album contained a number of classics of Sixties songwriting: "Ballad of a Thin Man," "Queen Jane Approximately," and the tour de force "Desolation Row." Indeed, the album was remarkably consistent in the high level of its songwriting and performance, and Dylan effectively made the entire album, rather than single songs, the unit of his expression. The quintessential "Like a Rolling Stone," arguably his finest composition, became Dylan's first smash hit single and established his credibility with a new rock audience.

During the summer of 1965, Bob Dylan contacted a Canadian group known as Levon and The Hawks, then touring the United States' East Coast. Between the fall of 1965 and the summer of 1966, the group, later to become known simply as The Band, toured with Dylan but without the group's recalcitrant drummer and leader, Levon Helm. In the fall of 1966, Columbia issued one of the first non-anthology double-record sets in rock history for Dylan as *Blonde on Blonde.* Considered by many as Dylan's most fully realized album, the recording was made with outstanding Nashville sessions musicians such as Wayne Moss, Charlie McCoy, Kenneth Buttrey, and Hargus "Pig" Robbins, as well as keyboardist Al Kooper and The Band's Robbie Robertson. An immensely wide-ranging album in terms of the songwriting, *Blonde on Blonde* yielded three moderate hit singles, "Rainy Day Women # 12 & 35," "I Want You," and "Just Like a Woman." Another remarkably consistent set in terms of musical performance and lyrical invention, the album also included the desolate "Visions of Joanna," the vituperative "Most Likely You'll Go Your Way and I'll Go Mine," and the side-long "Sad Eyed Lady of the Lowlands," composed in the studio as the musicians waited.

On July 30, 1966, Bob Dylan was seriously injured in a motorcycle accident; he subsequently retreated to upstate New York to recuperate amidst a variety of wild and irresponsible rumors. He summoned all the members of The Band and rehearsed and recorded with them during his public absence. The recordings, made between June and September of 1967, were somehow pirated and released on so-called "bootleg" albums. Among the material were a number of previously unrecorded Dylan songs such as "Million Dollar Bash," "Lo and Behold!," and "Please, Mrs. Henry." Several of the songs were later recorded by other groups: "Too Much of Nothing" by Peter, Paul, and Mary in 1967, and "You Ain't Goin' Nowhere" and "Nothing Was Delivered" by The Byrds on their *Sweetheart of the Rodeo* album from 1968. The Band's debut album featured "Tears of Rage" and "This Wheel's on Fire." The recordings were eventually released in 1975 as *The Basement Tapes.*

Bob Dylan finally re-emerged with *John Wesley Harding* in early 1968, though he was not to tour again until 1974. This album also befuddled many of his fans. The harsh strident voice was replaced with a mellow pleasing voice, and the songs contained little of the vituperation and anger of his previous album releases. Instead, the songs were concerned with resignation, regeneration, and resurrection, and an almost religious wariness. Moreover, the songs exhibited little of the rock-and-roll raunch earlier evident in that they were recorded with only Charlie McCoy on bass and Kenneth Buttrey on drums. The album yielded no hit singles, yet featured a number of profoundly moving existential pieces, including one of Dylan's later classics, "All Along the Watchtower," later recorded in its definitive version by Jimi Hendrix. The album's final two songs, "Down Along the Cove" and "I'll Be Your Baby Tonight," presaged another Dylan shift that was to find full fruition in 1969's *Nashville Skyline*—a move into a "country-pop" kind of sound.

Recorded with the same basic personnel as used earlier (Buttrey and McCoy as well as Peter Drake and Charlie Daniels), *Nashville Skyline* once again turned critics and fans' heads in confused dismay. Attacked by many critics as sentimental and simplistic, the album included a duet with Johnny Cash on an early Dylan song, "Girl from the North Country," and a number of songs written in an almost Tin Pan Alley mold. "Lay Lady Lay" became a substantial hit from the album. The next album, the dis-jointed *Self Portrait*, contained a variety of different material, including live recordings with The Band ("Like a Rolling Stone" and "The Mighty Quinn") and cover versions of songs written by Paul Simon and Gordon Lightfoot. Almost universally panned, the album was hastily followed by *New Morning*, which contained ditties such as "If Dogs Run Free," "Time Passes Slowly," and "If Not for You."

After *New Morning*, Bob Dylan was largely out of the public eye for several years. He had appeared at the January 1968 Woody Guthrie Memorial concert and the fall 1969 Isle of Wight Festival, but he emerged only once in the early Seventies for George Harrison's Concert for Bangla Desh. His only recordings of the period were five songs for the anthology *Greatest Hits, Volume II*, and the singles "Watching the River Flow" and "George Jackson," the second a brief return to protest music. During 1973, he finally reappeared in a small part in the film, *Pat Garrett and Billy The Kid*, for which he wrote and performed the soundtrack music. "Knockin' on Heaven's Door" was a pop and easy-listening hit single from the sound-track, but his next album, *Dylan*, again primarily featured cover versions of songs such as Jerry Jeff Walker's "Mr. Bojangles" and Joni Mitchell's "Big Yellow Taxi."

By 1974 Bob Dylan was back on the scene, first with *Planet Waves*, recorded with The Band, on Asylum Records. Again Dylan received a critical drubbing, though songs such as "Going, Going, Gone," "Something There Is About You," and "Forever Young" were finely crafted. In January and February 1974, he toured for the first time in eight years, again with The Band. The tour was nearly an instant sellout and yielded the double-record set, *Before the Flood*, by midyear. Dylan convincingly re-established himself as a powerful songwriter with *Blood on the Tracks*. The album included a diversity of material, from the vituperative "Idiot Wind" to a number of moving songs such as "Tangled Up in Blue," "Simple Twist of Fate," and "Shelter from the Storm," as well as the epic Western tale, "Lily, Rosemary, and The Jack of Hearts," befitting film presentation.

In an effort to re-establish "grass roots" contact with his audience, Bob Dylan assembled the Rolling Thunder Revue for generally unannounced engagements in the Northeast. Participants varied greatly, with appearances made by Roger McGuinn, Joan Baez, Ramblin' Jack Elliott, Ronnie Hawkins, Mick Ronson, Scarlet Rivera, and others. Though it was to continue into 1976, the tour of the Rolling Thunder Review culminated in the December 8, 1975, benefit performance at Madison Square Garden for ex-boxer Rubin "Hurricane" Carter, who was alleged to have been unjustly convicted of three murders in New Jersey in 1974. Several weeks earlier, Dylan had issued the highly controversial "Hurricane" single that sought to bring attention to Carter's plight. The song was extracted from *Desire*, possibly Dylan's best selling album and legitimately his first certified platinum-award album. Recorded with bassist Rob Stoner, violinist Scarlet Rivera, and background vocalist Emmylou Harris, the album featured seven songs written by Dylan in collaboration with Jacques Levy. His next album, *Hard Rain*, merely compiled new recordings of Dylan songs from "Maggie's Farm" to "Idiot Wind."

In early 1978 Bob Dylan released the 3-hour 52-minute film *Renaldo and Clara*, shot during the Rolling Thunder Revue tour. Written, produced, directed, and co-edited by Dylan, the film assembled 56 songs from the tour within a series of confusing and widely careening parables revolving around Renaldo (Dylan), Clara (then-wife Sara), The Woman In White (Joan Baez), and Dylan (played by Ronnie Hawkins). Greeted by disparaging reviews, the film was later withdrawn for re-editing, though subsequent versions have yet to spark the imagination of a large-scale audience. Beginning in February, Dylan made his first appearances outside the United States in more than 11 years at concerts in Japan, Australia, New Zealand, and western Europe. By midyear the erratic *Street Legal* was issued to mixed reviews, though it was soon certified gold-award. In September Dylan inaugurated a 3-month tour of the U.S. and Canada that also met with mixed reviews, perhaps the first negative reviews of any Dylan tour during his career. *Bob Dylan at Budokan* (Japan), a double-record live set, was issued in the spring of 1979. It contained reworked versions of 22 of Bob Dylan's songs. That fall Columbia issued Dylan's first album of essentially Christian material, *Slow Train Coming*, recorded with Dire Straits guitarist Mark Knopfler. A remarkable best-seller, again stirring the ire of many critics, the album yielded a major hit with "Gotta Serve Somebody" while containing "When You Gonna Wake Up," "Gonna Change My Way of Thinking," and "When He Returns."

Restricting himself primarily to his religious material, Dylan played fourteen shows at San Francisco's Warfield Theater in late 1979, drawing mixed reactions from his audience. Featuring looser song structures and much lyrical repetition, *Saved* sold far less well than *Slow Train Coming*, yet did include two excellent nonreligious songs, "What Can I Do for You" and "Solid Rock." Again playing the Warfield Theater in late 1980 and touring Europe during the summer of 1981, Bob Dylan achieved somewhat of a comeback with *Shot of Love*, noteworthy for its intelligent and poetic lyrics, newfound sense of melody, and restrained religiosity.

BOB DYLAN

Bob Dylan	Columbia	PC–8579	March '62	A
Freewheelin' *	Columbia	PC–8786	May '63	A
The Times They Are A-Changin'	Columbia	PC–8905	January '64	A
Another Side of Bob Dylan	Columbia	PC–8993	August '64	A
Bringing It All Back Home *	Columbia	JC–9128	March '65	A
Highway 61 Revisited *	Columbia	JC–9189	August '65	A
Blonde on Blonde *	2-Columbia	C2S–841	May '66	A

BOB DYLAN AND THE BAND

The Basement Tapes	2-Columbia	C2–33682	July '75	A

BOB DYLAN

Greatest Hits *	Columbia	JC–9463	March '67	A
John Wesley Harding *	Columbia	JC–9604	January '68	A
Nashville Skyline *	Columbia	JC–9825	April '69	A
Self Portrait *	2-Columbia	P2X–30050	June '70	A
New Morning *	Columbia	PC–30290	October '70	A
Greatest Hits, Volume II *	2-Columbia	PG–31120	November '71	A
Pat Garrett and Billy The Kid (soundtrack)	Columbia	PC–32460	August '73	A
Dylan *	Columbia	PC–32747	December '73	A

BOB DYLAN AND THE BAND

Planet Waves *	Asylum	7E–1003	January '74	
Before the Flood *	2-Asylum	AB–201	July '74	

BOB DYLAN

Blood on the Tracks *	Columbia	JC–33235	January '75	A
Desire **	Columbia	JC–33893	December '75	A
Hard Rain *	Columbia	JC–34349	September '76	A
Street Legal *	Columbia	JC–35453	June '78	A

Bob Dylan at Budokan	2-Columbia	PC2–36067	May '79	A
Slow Train Coming**	Columbia	FC–36120	August '79	A
Saved	Columbia	FC–36553	July '80	A
Shot of Love	Columbia	TC–37496	August '81	A

THE EAGLES. The most popular Seventies rock band to create a distinctive country sound with rock instrumentation, The Eagles based their music on easily identifiable melodies, strong vocal harmonies, and engaging lyrics, mostly of their own composition. Highly successful as both a singles and an album band, The Eagles have issued consecutive certified gold-award albums. Their second, *Desperado*, had a certain conceptual consistency in its being grounded in the outlaws-of-the-old-and-new-West theme. Since the addition of guitarist Joe Walsh, The Eagles have shown a greater instrumental vitality in their music.

The Eagles were formed in August 1971 in Los Angeles. Glen Frey (born in Detroit, Michigan, on November 6, 1948) and J. D. Souther had formed Longbranch/Pennywhistle in the late Sixties, recording one album for the now-defunct Amos label. Frey later served as backup musician to Linda Ronstadt. Don Henley (born in Linden, Texas, on July 22, 1947) had been a member of Shiloh, who also recorded an album for Amos. Randy Meisner (born in Scottsbluff, Nebraska, on March 8, 1946) had been an original member of Poco before joining Rick Nelson's Stone Canyon Band for two years. Bernie Leadon (born July 19, 1947, in Minneapolis, Minnesota) recorded one album each with Hearts and Flowers and Dillard and Clark and two with The Flying Burrito Brothers prior to working with Linda Ronstadt. The members of The Eagles: Glen Frey (guitar, keyboards, vocals), Bernie Leadon (guitar, banjo, mandolin, slide and steel guitars, vocals), Randy Meisner (bass, vocals), and Don Henley (drums, vocals).

Signed to Asylum Records, The Eagles recorded their first album in London. "Take It Easy," written by Frey and Jackson Browne, was the group's first big hit, followed by the Henley–Leadon composition "Witchy Woman" and Jack Tempchin's "Peaceful Easy Feeling." The debut album also contained "Train Leaves Here This Morning," originally included on the first Dillard and Clark album. *Desperado*, also recorded in London, was somewhat of a "concept" album, based on the theme of the rock band as old-and-new-West outlaws. Nonetheless, the album yielded only two minor hits, the title composition written by Henley and Frey and David Blue's "Outlaw Man." During 1973 The Eagles toured throughout the United States successfully, though the band showed little instrumental punch. While recording *On the Border*, the band added sessions musician

Don Felder (guitar, banjo, pedal steel, vocals) to fill out the instrumental sound. Felder, born September 21, 1947, in Topanga, California, had previously recorded one album with the jazz band Flow for CTI. *On the Border* contained three songs by outside writers, Paul Craft's "Midnight Flyer," Tom Waits' "Ol' 55," and Jack Tempchin's "Already Gone" (a moderate hit), and included The Eagles' first smash single, the tender and delicate "Best of My Love."

In 1974, the first three Eagles albums were all certified gold-award. The group's popularity was solidified with 1975's *One of These Nights*. The album produced three smash singles, all written by group members, with the title cut, "Lyin' Eyes," and "Take It to the Limit." During the year, the band toured internationally in support of the album, only to see the departure of Bernie Leadon by year's end. Guitarist–vocalist Joe Walsh, born November 20, 1947, in Cleveland, Ohio, and previously with The James Gang and a solo recording artist, was added to provide a more dynamic, rough-edged quality to the group's instrumental sound, which had been frequently criticized as the band's weakest aspect. His contribution was much in evidence on *Hotel California*. Though the album's first hit single, "New Kid in Town," resembled much of the group's earlier material, the later hits, "Hotel California" and "Life in the Fast Lane," featured the excellent lead guitar playing of Walsh and revealed a biting existential bent to the lyrics; "The Last Resort" expressed a deep if pessimistic concern with ecology.

The Eagles successfully toured the United States, England, and Europe during 1977. In August of that year, Randy Meisner left The Eagles, to be replaced by former Poco bassist Tim Schmit, born in Sacramento, California, on October 30, 1947. During 1977–78, Bernie Leadon recorded an album with Michael Georgiades, and Randy Meisner recorded an unsuccessful solo album. In late 1978 The Eagles issued the moderate hit "Please Come Home for Christmas," as they continued to work on their much-delayed follow-up to *Hotel California*.

Eventually released in late 1979, *The Long Run* quickly yielded the top hit "Heartache Tonight" (written by Henley and Frey with Bob Seger and J. D. Souther) and the near-smashes "The Long Run" and "I Can't Tell You Why," the latter with lead vocals by Schmit. Touring with opening act Roy Orbison during 1980, The Eagles scored a major hit with Steve Young's "Seven Bridges Road" from the double-record set *Live*. As the members of The Eagles pursued various solo projects, Randy Meisner scored major hits with "Deep Inside My Heart" and "Hearts on Fire" from *One More Song*, on which he had been aided by songwriters Eric Kaz and Wendy Waldman.

LONGBRANCH/PENNYWHISTLE (WITH GLEN FREY)

Longbranch/ Pennywhistle	Amos	7007	'69

SHILOH (WITH DON HENLEY)

Shiloh	Amos	7015	'70

HEARTS AND FLOWERS (WITH BERNIE LEADON)

Of Horses, Kids, and Forgotten Women	Capitol	ST–2868	June '68	

FLOW (WITH DON FELDER)

Flow	CTI	1003	June '70	

THE EAGLES

The Eagles*	Asylum	SD–5054	June '72	A
Desperado*	Asylum	SD–5068	April '73	A
On the Border*	Asylum	7E–1004	February '74	A
One of These Nights*	Asylum	7E–1039	June '75	A
Their Greatest Hits—1971–1975**	Asylum	7E–1052 reissued as 105	January '76	A
Hotel California**	Asylum	7E–1084 reissued as 103	November '76	A
The Long Run**	Asylum	508	October '79	A
Live**	2-Asylum	BB–705	November '80	A

THE BERNIE LEADON–MICHAEL GEORGIADES BAND

Natural Progressions	Asylum	7E–1107	September '77	

RANDY MEISNER

Randy Meisner	Elektra	140	June '78	A
One More Song	Epic	JE–36478	October '80	A

EARTH, WIND AND FIRE. A Seventies all-black band of widespread popularity among both blacks and whites, Earth, Wind and Fire has created a fusion of rhythm-and-blues and jazz musics with layers of percussion, punchy horn arrangements, and smooth ensemble vocals. Augmented by lyrics expressing a hopeful philosophical stance of happiness and brotherhood, Earth, Wind and Fire has produced a series of best-selling, high-energy singles and albums.

Originally conceived in Los Angeles in 1970 as a co-operative musical ensemble by Maurice White (born in Memphis, Tennessee, on December 19, 1941), Earth, Wind and Fire recorded two marginally successful albums for Warner Brothers Records before switching to Columbia. Maurice White had previously been a sessions drummer at Motown and Chess Records, later touring with pianist Ramsey Lewis for three years. Other members of Earth, Wind and Fire while with Warner Brothers were White's brother, bassist Verdine White (born in Chicago on July 25, 1951), guitarists Ronney Laws and Roland Bautista, vocalist Jessica Cleaves, and pianists Wade Flemons and Donald Whitehead. With the move to Columbia, Flemons and Whitehead were dropped and percussionist–vocalist Phillip Bailey (born May 8, 1951, in Denver, Colorado) and keyboardist Larry Dunn (born June 19, 1953, in Denver) were added. The Columbia debut, *Last Days and Times*, was only moderately successful, and guitarists Laws and Bautista were subsequently dropped in favor of guitarists Al McKay (born February 2, 1948, in Los Angeles) and Johnny Graham (born August 3, 1951, in Louisville, Kentucky). Other additions were horn player Andrew Woolfolk (born in Denver on October 11, 1950) and percussionist Ralph Johnson (born in Los Angeles on July 4, 1951). The members: Maurice White (kalimba, drums, lead vocals), Verdine White (bass, percussion, vocals), Jessica Cleaves (vocals), Phillip Bailey (congas, percussion, vocals), Larry Dunn (keyboards), Al McKay (guitar, percussion), Johnny Graham (guitar), Ralph Johnson (drums, percussion, vocals), and Andrew Woolfolk (flute, tenor and soprano saxophones).

Earth, Wind and Fire's second Columbia release, *Head to the Sky*, yielded two minor hits, "Evil" and "Keep Your Head to the Sky," and was certified gold-award during 1973. Jessica Cleaves left prior to the group's recording of *Open Our Eyes*, an album which produced two moderate hit singles, "Mighty Mighty" and "Devotion." In early 1975 Earth, Wind and Fire added White brother Fred (born in Chicago on January 13, 1955) on drums and percussion. *That's the Way of the World* firmly established the band, providing two big hit singles, the title cut and the smash "Shining Star." *Gratitude*, a two-record set, featured three live sides and one studio side of all new material. Two songs from the studio side became hit singles, "Sing a Song" and "Can't Hide Love." *Spirit*, dedicated to the group's late musical mentor and co-producer Charles Stepney, was the band's first certified platinum-award album and yielded two major hit singles, "Getaway" and "Saturday Nite." "Serpentine Fire" and "Fantasy" became hits from the group's second platinum-award album, *All 'n' All*. During 1978, Earth, Wind and Fire's version of "Gotta Get You into My Life" from the soundtrack to *Sgt. Pepper's Lonely Hearts Club Band* became a substantial hit, as did one of the two new songs on *Best, Volume I*, "September." The latter album was on Earth, Wind and Fire's newly formed ARC label, distributed by Columbia.

In 1979 the group scored smash hits with "Boogie Wonderland" (recorded with The Emotions) and the ballad "After the Love Has Gone," and a platinum-award certification for *I Am*. *Faces*, from late 1980, failed to produce a major pop hit. During 1981 original guitarist Roland Bautista rejoined Earth, Wind and Fire, replacing the departed Al McKay.

EARTH, WIND AND FIRE

Earth, Wind and Fire	Warner Brothers	WS–1905	April '71
The Need of Love	Warner Brothers	1958	November '71
Another Time	2-Warner Brothers	2798	August '74

Last Days and Times	Columbia	PC–31702	October '72	A
Head to the Sky*	Columbia	PC–32194	June '73	A
Open Our Eyes*	Columbia	PC–32712	March '74	A
That's the Way of the World*	Columbia	PC–33280	March '75	A
Gratitude*	2-Columbia	PG–33694	November '75	A
Spirit**	Columbia	PC–34241	September '76	A
All 'n' All**	Columbia	JC–34905	November '77	A
The Best of Earth, Wind and Fire, Volume I**	ARC/ Columbia	FC–35647	December '78	A
I Am**	ARC/ Columbia	FC–35730	June '79	A
Faces*	2-ARC/ Columbia	KC2– 36795	October '80	A
Raise!	ARC/ Columbia	TC–37548	November '81	A

DAVE EDMUNDS. Welsh guitarist–producer who, during the late Sixties, perfected studio techniques that effectively recreated the sounds of the Fifties and early Sixties, Dave Edmunds has sparked a return to a simpler recorded sound in the Seventies. A stark contrast to the over-production used by The Bee Gees and Fleetwood Mac, among others, this less dense, uncomplicated sound has been favored by the so-called "punk" bands emerging first in England in the late Seventies.

DAVE EDMUNDS

Rockpile	MAM	3	'72	
Subtle as a Flying Mallet	RCA	LPL1– 5003	November '75	
		reissued as AYL1– 4238	January '82	A
Get It	Swan Song	SS–8418	April '77	A
Tracks on Wax 4	Swan Song	8505	September '78	A
Repeat when Necessary	Swan Song	SS–8507	July '79	A
Twangin'. . .	Swan song	16034	May '81	A
Best	Swan Song	8510	December '81	A

ROCKPILE

Seconds of Pleasure	Columbia	JC–36886	November '80	A

THE ELECTRIC FLAG. An American rock group that reflected the blues revival of 1968, The Electric Flag was one of the first rock groups to utilize a horn section. Remaining together for approximately one year, The Electric Flag disintegrated after only two albums. Members Mike Bloomfield and Buddy Miles were able to maintain a level of popularity after disbanding, Miles initially on the basis of his powerhouse drumming, later through his association with Jimi Hendrix and Carlos Santana.

THE BARRY GOLDBERG BLUES BAND

Blowing My Mind	Epic	BN–26199	July '66	

THE ELECTRIC FLAG

A Long Time Comin'	Columbia	CS–9597	March '68	A
An American Music Band	Columbia	CS–9714	December '68	
Best	Columbia	C–30422	March '71	
The Band Kept Playing	Atlantic	SD–18112	October '74	

BARRY GOLDBERG

The Barry Goldberg Reunion	Buddah	BDS–5012	September '68
Two Jews Blues	Buddah	BDS–5029	January '69
Street Man	Buddah	5051	November '70
Blasts from My Past	Buddah	5081	
Barry Goldberg	Atco	SD–7040	March '74

NICK GRAVENITES

My Labors	Columbia	CS–9899	September '69

BIG BROTHER AND THE HOLDING COMPANY WITH NICK GRAVENITES

Be a Brother	Columbia	C–30222	November '70
How Hard It Is	Columbia	C–30738	August '71

THE BUDDY MILES EXPRESS

Expressway to Your Skull	Mercury	SR–61196	November '68
Electric Church	Mercury	61222	June '69

THE BAND OF GYPSYS WITH BUDDY MILES

The Band of Gypsys*	Capitol	STAO–472	March '70	A

BUDDY MILES

Them Changes	Mercury	SR–61280	July '70	A
We Got to Live Together	Mercury	SR–61313	November '70	
A Message to the People	Mercury	SRM1–608	April '71	
Live	2-Mercury	SRM2–7500	September '71	

BUDDY MILES AND CARLOS SANTANA

Live! *	Columbia	PC–31308	June '72	A

BUDDY MILES

Chapter VII	Columbia	KC–32048	February '73
Booger Bear	Columbia	KC–32694	November '73
All the Faces of Buddy Miles	Columbia	KC–33089	October '74
More Miles Per Gallon	Casablanca	7019	July '75
Bicentennial Gathering of the Tribes	Casablanca	7024	June '76

KGB WITH BARRY GOLDBERG

KGB	MCA	2166	February '76
Motion	MCA	2221	September '76

ROGER TROY

Roger Troy	RCA	APL1–1910	December '76

THE BUDDY MILES REGIMENT

Sneak Attack	2-Atlantic	2–4000	August '81	A

THE ELECTRIC LIGHT ORCHESTRA/THE MOVE. Formed out of The Move, an enigmatic and controversial Sixties English singles band, The Electric Light Orchestra brought to fruition Roy Wood's conception of a fully electric rock band augmented by a classical string section. Ironically, Wood left the group after only a single album to pursue revived Fifties rock-and-roll music. Nonetheless, despite the fact that the integration of the string section produced little more than gratuitous four- or eight-bar introductions and a lush orchestral sound, The Electric Light Orchestra has been hailed as one of the most successful "progressive" groups of the Seventies. Certainly one of the world's top concert attractions by the late Seventies, The Electric Light Orchestra constructed a massive stage structure for many of the shows of their fall 1978 American tour, a stunning tribute to today's technology and the public's apparent demand for progressively extravagant stage presentation.

Formed in late 1965 by a number of English musicians from the Birmingham area, The Move quickly drew the attention of the London underground by means of their dramatic and often violent stage presentations. The members: Carl Wayne (vocals), Roy Wood (guitar, vocals), Trevor Burton (guitar, vocals), Richard Tandy (keyboards, bass), Ace Kefford (bass), and Bev Bevan (drums). Roy Wood, born in Birmingham on

November 8, 1946, had previously manned Gerry Levene and The Avengers with Graeme Edge (later with The Moody Blues) and Mike Sheridan and The Nightriders. Trevor Burton, born in Birmingham on March 9, 1949, had played lead guitar with Danny King and The Mayfair Set, whereas Bev Bevan, born in Birmingham on November 25, 1946, had drummed with Denny Laine (later with Paul McCartney's Wings) and The Diplomats and Carl Wayne and The Vikings, which included Carl Wayne (born near Birmingham on August 18, 1944) and Ace Kefford (born in Birmingham on December 10, 1946). Keyboardist Richard Tandy was born in Birmingham on March 26, 1948. With Wood writing virtually all The Move's material, the band scored a series of English hits. The first was "Night of Fear" in early 1967; subsequent hit singles included "I Can Hear the Grass Grow," "Flowers in the Rain," "Fire Brigade," and "Blackberry Way." Involved in a legal dispute with then-Prime Minister Harold Wilson and notorious for smashing TV sets and pianos on stage, The Move recorded only two albums in their first four years of existence.

Though a popular singles band in England, The Move was virtually unrecognized in the United States until later, eventually cultivating a serious underground following. In the meantime, a series of personnel changes started with the April 1968 departure of Ace Kefford. Trevor Burton left in February 1969, as did Richard Tandy, and Rick Price was brought on to handle the bass chores. Vocalist Carl Wayne dropped out in January 1970, and guitarist–vocalist Jeff Lynne (born December 30, 1947, in Birmingham) was added for the avowed reason of forming an outfit that would combine classical strings and rock instrumentation. Lynne had previously played with the obscure group The Idle Race for nearly four years, recording *The Birthday Party* with the group. With The Move's lineup reduced to Wood, Bevan, and Lynne, the group issued its final album of totally new material, *Message from the Country*, in 1971. The Move's last album, *Split Ends*, contained seven songs from the prior album as well as the group's only American chart entry, "Do Ya," composed by Lynne. During 1969 Richard Tandy and Trevor Burton played in Balls with Denny Laine and Steve Gibbons. Tandy later joined The Electric Light Orchestra and Burton later manned The Steve Gibbons Band.

Roy Wood had originally conceived of The Electric Light Orchestra as a parallel outfit to The Move, but contractual entanglements of the latter led to its demise. Recorded over a lengthy period of time with the same lineup as on *Message from the Country*, The Electric Light Orchestra's debut album, *No Answer*, was critically acclaimed and yielded one English hit single, "10538 Overture." However, by 1972, Wood had lost interest in the project and left the group to form Wizzard with ex-Move bassist Rick Price. Earlier Wood had recorded, produced, and engineered *Boulders*, on which he played all the instruments. The album, recorded in 1970, wasn't issued until 1973, several months after the release of Wizzard's debut album, *Wizzard's Brew*. Wood, as the central figure in Wizzard, painted his hair garish colors and wore elaborate makeup in an apparent effort to appeal to younger audiences. With the nucleus of Wizzard, Wood later recorded *Eddy and The Falcons*, a tribute to Fifties rock-and-roll. Eventually he returned to solo recording with *Mustard* in 1976 and *Super Active Wizzo* in 1977.

What some consider as the true beginning of The Electric Light Orchestra's career came with *ELO II*. Jeff Lynne assumed the primary role as producer, arranger, composer, lead vocalist, and lead guitarist, and the album secured the band's position in the forefront of so-called "classical-rock." Lynne and Bevan had added keyboardist Richard Tandy, a bassist, and three former members of the London Symphony Orchestra (2 cellists and 1 violinist). The album yielded The Electric Light Orchestra's first, albeit minor, American hit with a trite remake of Chuck Berry's "Roll Over, Beethoven." In the summer of 1973, the band completed its first of many American tours, issuing *On the Third Day* before year's end. Though the album included several minor hits, *Eldorado* was the album that firmly established ELO. "Can't Get It Out of My Head" became the group's first major American hit, and the album was certified gold-award in 1975.

The band's personnel finally stabilized with *Face the Music*. In addition to Lynne, Bevan, and Tandy, the group included bassist–vocalist Kelly Groucutt (born in Coseley, Staffordshire, on September 8, 1945), cellists Hugh McDowell (born in London on July 31, 1953) and Melvyn Gale (born in London on January 15, 1952), and violinist Mik Kaminski (born in Yorkshire, England, on September 2, 1951). The album featured two major hit singles, "Evil Woman" and "Strange Magic." *Ole ELO* compiled the group's earlier hits, whereas *A New World Record*, their first certified platinum-award album, yielded the hits "Livin' Thing" and "Telephone Line." The double-record set *Out of the Blue* contained two major hit singles, "Turn to Stone" and "Sweet Talkin' Woman," as well as Lynne's first extended piece of work since *Eldorado*, the side-long "Concerto for a Rainy Day."

For their 1978 American tour, The Electric Light Orchestra assembled one of the most spectacular and grandiose stage presentations in the history of rock music. For approximately half of the tour's shows, the band utilized a white, 5-ton, 60-foot-wide fiberglass structure resembling a space ship, the top half of which ascended 40 feet to reveal the band hidden inside. Complete with synchronized lasers, the production (if not the music) represented a remarkable tribute to showmanship and technology.

During 1979, The Electric Light Orchestra switched to Columbia Records. Their debut album on the new label, *Discovery*, featured a 42-piece German orchestra and a 30-voice all-male choir, an ambitious attempt to expand the "classical-rock" fusion. The album yielded two smash hits, "Shine a Little Love" and "Don't Bring Me Down," before year's end. In 1980, The Electric Light Orchestra recorded much of the music for the Gene Kelly–Olivia Newton-John film soundtrack *Xanadu*, scoring major hits with "I'm Alive" and "All Over the World," and a smash hit with the title song, sung by Newton-John. During 1981 the group achieved yet another smash hit with the rockabilly-style, soundtrack-like "Hold On Tight," perhaps the finest song of their career.

THE IDLE RACE

| The Birthday Party | Liberty | 7603 | February '69 | |

THE MOVE

The Move	A&M			
Shazam	A&M	SP–4259	April '70	
The Best of The Move	2-A&M	3625	May '74	
Looking On	Capitol	ST–658	May '71	
Message from the Country	Capitol	ST–811	August '71	
Split Ends	United Artists	UAS–5666	February '73	

ROY WOOD

Wizzard's Brew	United Artists	LA042	May '73	
Boulders	United Artists	LA168	October '73	
Introducing Eddy and The Falcons	United Artists	LA219	September '74	A
Mustard	United Artists	LA575	January '76	
Super Active Wizzo	Warner Brothers	3065	October '77	A
On the Road	Warner Brothers	3247	August '81	A
One Man Band	Townhouse	SN–7127	November '81	A

THE ELECTRIC LIGHT ORCHESTRA

No Answer	United Artists	UAS–5573	June '72	
	reissued on Jet	PZ–35524	September '78	A
ELO II	United Artists	LA040	March '73	
	reissued on Jet	PZ–35533	September '78	A
On the Third Day	United Artists	LA188	December '73	
	reissued on Jet	PZ–35525	September '78	A
Eldorado *	United Artists	LA339	October '74	
	reissued on Jet	PZ–35526	September '78	A
Face the Music *	United Artists	LA546	October '75	
	reissued on Jet	PZ–35527	September '78	A
Ole ELO *	United Artists	LA630	June '76	
	reissued on Jet	PZ–35528	September '78	A
A New World Record **	United Artists	LA679	October '76	
	reissued on Jet	PZ–35529	September '78	A
Out of the Blue **	2-Jet/United Artists	LA823	October '77	
	reissued on Jet	KZ2–35530	September '78	A
Discovery **	Jet	FZ–35769	June '79	A
Greatest Hits **	Jet	FZ–36310	December '79	A
A Box of Their Best	4-Jet	Z4X–36966	December '80	A
Time *	Jet	FZ–37371	August '81	A

OLIVIA NEWTON–JOHN/THE ELECTRIC LIGHT ORCHESTRA

| Xanadu (sound-track) ** | MCA | 6100 | July '80 | A |

EMERSON, LAKE, AND PALMER/THE NICE. One of the first English rock bands to pursue classical music regularly and actively within a rock format during the Sixties, The Nice never achieved in America the success they encountered in England and Europe. Reduced to a trio after a single album, The Nice was perhaps the first rock group to explore the trio format utilizing keyboards rather than electric guitar as the primary focus. Moreover, The Nice, fronted by multi-keyboardist Keith Emerson, became one of the most powerful and dynamic concert attractions in the world by 1969. Soon disbanding, The Nice were superseded by Emerson, Lake, and Palmer, one of the first "supergroups" of the Seventies. The three continued to pursue the "classical-rock" and keyboard-based power-trio formats, as Emerson effectively introduced the synthesizer into rock music. One of the biggest concert attractions in the United States by 1974, Emerson, Lake, and Palmer have nonetheless met with little subsequent success in their native England. One of the first rock bands to tour with a truly quadraphonic sound system (in 1974), Emerson, Lake, and Palmer attempted to tour with a full symphony orchestra during 1977. By 1979 Emerson, Lake, and Palmer had disbanded, with Emerson subsequently working on film soundtracks.

Formed in 1967 as a backing group for soul singer Pat Arnold, The Nice began touring on their own in October 1967. The members: keyboardist–vocalist Keith Emerson (born November 2, 1944), guitarist–vocalist David O'List, bassist–guitarist–vocalist Lee Jackson, and drummer Brian "Blinky" Davison. Signed to Andrew Oldham's Immediate label, The Nice's first album featured Emerson's rousing "Rondo," apparently based on Dave Brubeck's "Blue Rondo a la Turk." With the subsequent departure of O'List, the group's primary singer and songwriter, Emerson became the musical and visual focus of The Nice. His flamboyant stage act, which included stabbing and assaulting his electric organ, brought the group widespread notoriety in England and Europe. Utilizing the power-trio format of Cream and The Jimi Hendrix Experience (but replacing the electric lead guitar with a variety of keyboards), The Nice's second album, *Ars Longa Vita Brevis*, showcased the title composition performed in four movements with coda. By 1970 the group was on the verge of an American breakthrough, but elected to disband. Ironically, The Nice thereafter finally placed in the American album charts with *Five Bridges Suite*, perhaps their finest work.

During late 1969 in San Francisco, Keith Emerson, still with The Nice, met guitarist–bassist–vocalist Greg Lake (born in Bournemouth, England, on November 10, 1948), a founding member of King Crimson (with Robert Fripp). With the demise of The Nice, they formed Emerson, Lake, and Palmer with drummer Carl Palmer (born March 20, 1947), formerly with The Crazy World of Arthur Brown and Atomic Rooster. With Emerson now exploring the sounds created by the synthesizer, the group debuted at the 1970 Isle of Wight Festival, gaining a reputation for their furious stage act and virtuoso abilities. Emerson, Lake, and Palmer's first two albums, both issued in 1971, were instantly successful, both being certified gold-award before year's end. The first included the somber ballad

"Lucky Man," which became a minor hit single. Their third album was an ambitious live recording based on Modest Mussorgsky's classical composition, *Pictures at an Exhibition*. The follow-up, *Trilogy*, featured Aaron Copland's "Hoedown" and Maurice Ravel's "Bolero," and yielded a moderate hit with the subtle and intricate "In the Beginning."

After a layoff of nearly a year and a half, Emerson, Lake, and Palmer recorded *Brain Salad Surgery* for their own label, Manticore. In 1974 they completed a four-month American tour—traveling with 36 tons of equipment. Emerson using six Moog synthesizers as well as two organs, a Steinway, and an electric piano. Each drum of Palmer's drum kit had its own synthesizer, and his equipment included two timpani, two gongs, chimes, and a large church bell. Additionally, the tour used the first truly quadraphonic sound system. The triple-record live set, *Welcome Back*, was soon issued and certified gold-award by year's end.

Emerson, Lake, and Palmer subsequently withdrew from both the concert and recording scenes to pursue solo projects. Their next album, the double-record set *Works, Volume I*, was finally released in 1977. Each member used one side for a solo effort, and all three played together on the final side. The haunting "C'est la Vie," composed by Greg Lake, became a minor hit from the album. That May, Emerson, Lake, and Palmer embarked on a come-back tour of America with a 57-piece orchestra and 6-person vocal choir. The cost, estimated at $250,000 per week, proved prohibitive and the orchestra was dismissed after 15 concerts. Before year's end, an album consisting of apparent outtakes from the previous work and five single sides previously unavailable on an album was released as *Works, Volume 2*. Late 1978's *Love Beach* was greeted by scathingly hostile reviews. By 1979 Emerson, Lake, and Palmer had disbanded. Emerson subsequently scored the soundtrack to the Sylvester Stallone film *Nighthawks*, recording the vocal to an updated version of Stevie Winwood's "I'm a Man."

THE NICE

The Thoughts of Emerlist Davjack	Immediate	Z–1252004	February '68	
Ars Longa Vita Brevis	Immediate	Z–1252020	March '69	
The Nice	Immediate	Z–1252022	November '69	
Five Bridges Suite	Mercury	SR–61295	August '70	
Elegy	Mercury	SR–61324	May '71	
Keith Emerson with The Nice	2-Mercury	SRM2–6500	February '72	A
Autumn to Spring	Charisma	CAS–1	May '73	
Immediate Story, Volume 1	2-Sire	3710	January '76	

EMERSON, LAKE, AND PALMER

Emerson, Lake, and Palmer*	Cotillion reissued on Atlantic	SD–9040 SD–19120	January '71	A

Tarkus*	Cotillion	SD–9900	June '71	
	reissued on Atlantic	SD–19121		A
Pictures at an Exhibition*	Cotillion	ELP–66666	January '72	
	reissued on Atlantic	SD–19122		A
Trilogy*	Cotillion	9903	July '72	
	reissued on Atlantic	SD–19123		A
Brain Salad Surgery*	Manticore	MS–66669	November '73	
	reissued on Atlantic	SD–19124		A
Welcome Back*	3-Manticore	MC3–200	August '74	A
Works, Volume 1*	2-Atlantic	SD2–7000	March '77	A
Works, Volume 2*	Atlantic	SD–19147	November '77	A
Love Beach*	Atlantic	SD–19211	December '78	
In Concert	Atlantic	SD–19255	November '79	A
The Best of Emerson, Lake, and Palmer	Atlantic	19283	November '80	A

KEITH EMERSON

Nighthawks (soundtrack)	MCA	5196	April '81	A

GREG LAKE

Greg Lake	Chrysalis	1357	November '81	A

THE EVERLY BROTHERS. Producing one of the most distinctive and memorable sounds of the rock-and-roll Fifties, The Everly Brothers were essentially a country vocal duet accompanied by drums and their own guitar playing. Singing songs concerned with teenage subjects such as parents, school, and young love, The Everly Brothers appealed to "easy listening" audiences as well as teenagers and country-and-western fans. As a result, they scored a consistent string of hits between 1957 and 1962, placing many singles high in the rhythm-and-blues and country-and-western charts as well as the pop charts. Their unique vocal sound, characterized by their whining, nasally, yet precise and polished close-harmony singing, has been emulated by everyone from The Beatles to The Beach Boys and The Byrds, and from The Hollies to Crosby, Stills, Nash, and Young.

The sons of established country-and-western artists, Don and Phil Everly (born in Brownie, Kentucky, on February 1, 1937, and January 19, 1939, respectively) were playing guitars at a very early age, debuting on their parents' radio show from KMA in Shenandoah, Iowa, when Don was age eight and Phil six. During summers, the brothers would tour the country circuit with their parents; they continued to perform on radio during the school year. After high school, The Everly Brothers moved to Nashville where they were signed briefly to Columbia Records and, more importantly, met the songwriting team of Felice and Boudleaux Bryant and met Chet Atkins, who was to produce many of their records. Switching to Cadence Records, the brothers' first hit came with the Bryants' "Bye, Bye, Love" in 1957. This song, one of the classics of Fifties rock-and-roll, started a string of smash hits, many of which were successes in the country-and-western and rhythm-and-blues as well as pop fields, that would last until 1962. The Everly Brothers' hits included the Bryants' "Wake Up, Little Susie" in 1957, Boudleaux Bryant's "All I Have to Do Is Dream" and "Bird Dog" (backed with "Devoted to You"), and the Bryants' "Problems" in 1958. They successfully toured Britain for the first time in 1958 and continued the string of hits on their return with "Take a Message to Mary" backed with "Poor Jenny" (both by Felice and Boudleaux Bryant), and Don's "('Til) I Kissed You," recorded with The Crickets in 1959. Later hits on Cadence included the ballad "Let It Be Me," their first recording with strings, and Phil's "When Will I Be Loved."

In 1960 The Everly Brothers were the first artists signed to the newly established Warner Brothers label. No longer using the services of the songwriting Bryants and producer Chet Atkins, the brothers nonetheless continued their succession of hits with their own composition, "Cathy's Clown," and "So Sad" backed with "Lucille" in 1960, and the two-sided hit "Walk Right Back/Ebony Eyes" in 1961. Their last major hits came in 1962 with the Howie Greenfield–Carole King song, "Crying in the Rain," and "That's Old Fashioned." That year Don and Phil Everly joined the Marine Corps Reserve, serving six months active duty. The brothers' personal relationship seems to have deteriorated after their time with the marines, but they returned to touring and recording, with Phil suffering a nervous breakdown during their 1963 tour of Great Britain. They eventually managed to score moderate hits with "Gone, Gone, Gone" in 1964 and "Bowling Green" in 1967, but they never became the potent force they had been years before. Nonetheless, *Roots* was hailed as an excellent return to their country origins, and *Stories We Could Tell*, on RCA, featured the assistance of John Sebastian, Delaney and Bonnie, and David Crosby and Graham Nash. The Everly Brothers finally split up in 1973, with each pursuing a rather lackluster solo career. Don Everly managed minor country hits in 1977 with "Since You Broke My Heart" and "Brother Juke-Box," whereas brother Phil recorded for several different labels before achieving a minor country hit with "Dare to Dream Again" on Curb Records in 1980–81. The Everly Brothers' legacy continues to this day as hit recordings of their songs still appear regularly, such as Linda Ronstadt's "When Will I Be Loved" in 1975 and Carly Simon and James Taylor's "Devoted to You" and Anne Murray's "Walk Right Back," both from 1978.

THE EVERLY BROTHERS

The Everly Brothers	Cadence	CLP–3003(M)	January '58
Songs Our Daddy Taught Us	Cadence	CLP–3016(M)	

Best	Cadence	CLP–3025(M)	March '59	
The Fabulous Style of The Everly Brothers	Cadence	25040	August '60	
Folk Songs	Cadence	25059		
15 Everly Hits	Cadence	25062		
It's Everly Time	Warner Brothers	WS–1381	May '60	
A Date with The Everly Brothers	Warner Brothers	WS–1395	November '60	
Top Vocal Duet	Warner Brothers	WS–1418	December '61	
Instant Party	Warner Brothers	WS–1430	March '62	
Golden Hits	Warner Brothers	WS–1471	June '62	A
Christmas with The Everly Brothers	Warner Brothers	WS–1483		
Sing Great Country Hits	Warner Brothers	WS–1513	October '63	
Very Best	Warner Brothers	WS–1554		A
Gone, Gone, Gone	Warner Brothers	WS–1585	January '65	
Rock 'n' Soul	Warner Brothers	WS–1578	March '65	
Beat 'n' Soul	Warner Brothers	WS–1605	August '65	
In Our Image	Warner Brothers	WS–1620	March '66	
Two Yanks in England	Warner Brothers	WS–1646	December '66	
Hit Sound	Warner Brothers	WS–1676	February '67	
The Everly Brothers Sing	Warner Brothers	WS–1708	July '67	
Roots	Warner Brothers	WS–1752	November '68	
The Everly Brothers Show	Warner Brothers	WS–1858		
Wake Up, Little Susie	Harmony	11304	February '69	
Chained to a Memory	Harmony	11388	May '70	
Original Greatest Hits	2-Barnaby	350	July '70	
End of an Era	2-Barnaby	ZG–30260	March '71	
History of The Everly Brothers	2-Barnaby	15008	May '73	
Greatest Hits	2-Barnaby	6006	September '74	
Greatest Hits, Volume 1	Barnaby	4004	May '79	
Greatest Hits, Volume 2	Barnaby	4005	May '79	

Greatest Hits, Volume 3	Barnaby	4006	May '79
Stories We Could Tell	RCA	LSP–4620	March '72
Pass the Chicken and Listen	RCA	LSP–4781	November '72

DON EVERLY

Don Everly	Ode	SP–77005	February '71
Sunset Towers	Ode	77023	August '74
Brother Juke-Box	Hickory	44003	April '77

PHIL EVERLY

Star-Spangled Springer	RCA	APL1– 0092	May '73
Phil's Diner	Pye	12104	January '75
Mystic Line	Pye	12121	October '75
Living Alone	Elektra	213	July '79

THE FACES/THE SMALL FACES.

THE FACES/THE SMALL FACES. A successful English singles band of the mid- to late Sixties that remained generally unrecognized in the United States, in 1968 The Small Faces issued probably the first album packaged in a round rather than square jacket, *Ogdens' Nut Gone Flake.* Following Steve Marriott's departure to form Humble Pie with Peter Frampton, The Small Faces enlisted Ron Wood and, later, Rod Stewart from the first Jeff Beck Group to form The Faces. Under separate contracts, Stewart recorded both solo and with The Faces (through 1975), with his solo career overshadowing that of The Faces. Following The Faces' breakup, Rod Stewart went on to become a true "superstar"; Ron Wood toured and recorded with The Rolling Stones, officially joining that group in July 1977. Bassist Ronnie Lane formed his own group, Slim Chance, later to record the dynamic *Rough Mix* with Pete Townshend, who was then languishing through a dismal period with The Who. In mid-1976 Steve Marriott re-formed The Small Faces, only to see drummer Kenney Jones join The Who in late 1978.

THE SMALL FACES

There Are But Four Small Faces	Immediate	Z–1252002	March '68
Ogden's Nut Gone Flake	Immediate reissued on ABKCO	Z–1252008 4225	September '68 March '73
Early Faces	Pride	0001	August '72
History of The Small Faces	Pride	0014	
Archetypes	MGM	4955	August '74
Immediate Story, Volume 2	2-Sire	3709	January '76

THE FACES

First Step	Warner Brothers	WS–1851	April '70
Long Player	Warner Brothers	WS–1892	January '71

A Nod Is as Good as a Wink . . . to a Blind Horse*	Warner Brothers	BS–2574	November '71	
Ooh La La	Warner Brothers	BS–2665	April '73	
Snakes and Ladders: Best	Warner Brothers	BS–2897	May '76	

ROD STEWART AND THE FACES

Live	Warner Brothers	BS–2572		
Coast to Coast: Overture and Beginners	Mercury	SRM1–697	December '73	
Rod Stewart and The Faces	Springboard International	4030	September '75	

RON WOOD

I've Got My Own Album to Do	Warner Brothers	BS–2819	September '74	
Now Look	Warner Brothers	BS–2872	July '75	
Gimme Some Neck	Columbia	PC–35702	May '79	A

RONNIE LANE/SLIM CHANCE

Ronnie Lane/Slim Chance	A&M	SP–3638	May '75	

RON WOOD AND RONNIE LANE

Mahoney's Last Chance (soundtrack)	Atco	SD36–126	August '76	

RONNIE LANE AND PETER TOWNSHEND

Rough Mix	MCA	2295	September '77	A

THE SMALL FACES

Playmates	Atlantic	19113	August '77	
78 in the Shade	Atlantic	19171	October '78	

IAN McLAGEN

Troublemaker	Mercury	SRM1–3786	January '80	A
Bump in the Night	Mercury	4007	May '81	A

FAIRPORT CONVENTION. Though sorely neglected in the United States, Fairport Convention was probably the first English group to combine traditional English folk music, compelling original songs, and rock instrumentation to become that country's first "folk-rock" group. Established as one of the top British female vocalists during her tenure with Fairport Convention, Sandy Denny also became recognized as an outstanding songwriter, primarily on the strength of "Who Knows Where the Time Goes," popularized by Judy Collins in 1968–69. Mainstay Dave Swarbrick, with the group since their third album, was one of the first musicians to play the violin as a lead instrument within the rock band format. A seminal group, Fairport Convention launched the solo careers of Denny, Richard Thompson (popular in England but generally unrecognized in the United States), and Ian Matthews, who had a major hit with "Shake It" in late 1978.

Formed in 1967, Fairport Convention's initial lineup was Simon Nicol (lead guitar), Richard Thompson (guitar, songwriting), Ashley "Tyger" Hutchings (bass), Judy Dyble (vocals), and Martin Lamble (drums). Soon augmented by vocalist Ian Matthews (born Ian McDonald in Lincolnshire, England), Fairport Convention recorded one English album before singer–songwriter Sandy Denny (born in Wimbledon, England, on January 6, 1947), briefly a member of The Strawbs, replaced Dyble in May 1968. Moving into traditional British folk music with the arrival of Denny and her stunning contralto voice, the group's first American album release, on A&M Records, featured Denny's "Fotheringay," Thompson's "Meet on The Ledge," and a moving version of Bob Dylan's previously unrecorded "I'll Keep It with Mine," as well as the obscure Joni Mitchell song "Eastern Rain." The album went virtually unnoticed in the United States, and Matthews left to pursue a solo career before the release of *Unhalfbricking.* For that album, Fairport Convention was assisted by virtuoso violinist Dave Swarbrick (born April 5, 1941), who soon joined the group on a permanent basis. The album included Thompson's "Genesis Hall" and an 11-minute version of the traditional folk song "A Sailor's Life," in addition to Denny's best known composition, "Who Knows Where the Time Goes," and their first major English hit, Bob Dylan's "If You Gotta Go, Go Now," sung by Denny in French.

Killed in a wreck of the group's van, Martin Lamble was replaced by Dave Mattacks on drums for *Liege and Lief,* the album that garnered Fairport's first substantial recognition. However, both Sandy Denny and Ashley Hutchings left the group in late 1969, Hutchings to form Steeleye Span and Denny to form the short-lived Fotheringay with vocalist–guitarist Trevor Lucas (born on December 25, 1943 or 1945) and drummer Gerry Conway, both former members of Eclection. Bassist Dave Pegg (born November 2, 1947) was brought in for Fairport Convention's *Full House,* recorded without a recognized vocalist. Personnel changes continued to plague Fairport Convention as Richard Thompson quit the band in January 1971 to work with Matthews and Denny, later to record solo. *Angel Delight* and *"Babbacombe Lee,"* Fairport's first two American album chart entries, were recorded as a mere quartet (Nicol, Mattacks, Swarbrick, and Pegg), after which both Nicol and Mattacks dropped out.

Meanwhile, Ian Matthews had formed Matthews' Southern Comfort for two inauspicious albums, finally breaking through with *Later That Same Year* in 1971. The album featured a thinly sung remake of Joni Mitchell's "Woodstock" that became a major pop and easy listening hit in America as well as a smash English hit. However, Matthews abruptly left the group in November 1970, later to record two solo albums for Vertigo Records before forming the short-lived Plainsong during 1972. Thereafter moving to the United States, Matthews was again recording solo by 1973, first the marginally successful countrified *Valley Hi*, followed by three obscure albums through 1977.

Fotheringay, formed in March 1970 by Sandy Denny, Trevor Lucas, lead guitarist Jerry Donahue (born September 24, 1946), bassist Pat Donaldson, and drummer Gerry Conway, recorded only one album. Although it featured an excellent Denny–Lucas composition, "Peace in the End," the album failed to gain any significant commercial success. During 1971 Denny recorded *The North Star Grassman and the Ravens* as a solo, with the assistance of Lucas, Donaldson, Conway, and Richard Thompson. Poorly produced, the album included one fine Denny composition, "Crazy Lady Blues," but did not sell. Denny subsequently recorded a number of early rock-and-roll songs with Thompson and Hutchings as The Bunch, before recording the Lucas-produced *Sandy* as a solo. At the same time Reprise issued Thompson's first solo album, *Henry, the Human Fly*. Several years later Thompson recorded two albums with wife Linda before quitting the music business. *Live (More or Less)* compiled eight years of Richard Thompson's performances and, given the couple's English popularity (they remained unknown in the United States), they resumed recording in 1978 with *At First Light*.

Earlier, in August 1972, Dave Swarbrick and Dave Pegg had enlisted former Fotheringay members Trevor Lucas and Jerry Donahue for yet another edition of Fairport Convention. Dave Mattacks also rejoined for a while, to be replaced by drummer Bruce Rowland. *Rosie* (recorded with Sandy Denny), *Nine*, and *A Movable Feast* were again ignored. Denny's outstanding *Like an Old-Fashioned Waltz*, recorded with Lucas, Thompson, and Donahue, contained seven excellent Denny originals but was also generally overlooked. Sandy Denny and Trevor Lucas both joined Fairport for *Rising for the Moon*, but in January 1976 they both departed. Jerry Donahue also left for sessions work on the United States' West Coast and *Gottle o' Geer*, Fairport Convention's final American album, was recorded by Swarbrick, Pegg, and Rowland. Another solo album by Sandy Denny was issued in 1977; on April 21, 1978, she died at the age of 31 as the result of a cerebral hemorrhage after suffering a fall. Ian Matthews, seemingly destined for obscurity, finally re-emerged in late 1978 with a major hit, "Shake It," from *Stealin' Home*, followed in 1979 by the minor hit "Give Me an Inch." Later that year, Fairport Convention formally disbanded; Dave Pegg replaced John Glascock in Jethro Tull and Dave Swarbrick subsequently recorded a solo album for TransAtlantic.

FAIRPORT CONVENTION

Fairport Convention	A&M	SP–4185	July '69	A
Unhalfbricking	A&M	SP–4206	April '70	
Fairport Convention	Cotillion	SD–9024	May '70	
Liege and Lief	A&M	SP–4257	July '70	A
Full House	A&M	SP–4265	September '70	
Angel Delight	A&M	SP–4319	November '71	
"Babbacombe Lee"	A&M	SP–4333	February '72	

MATTHEWS' SOUTHERN COMFORT

Matthews' Southern Comfort	Decca	75191	
2nd Spring	Decca	75242	December '70
Later That Same Year	Decca	75264	April '71

IAN MATTHEWS

If You Saw Thro' My Eyes	Vertigo	1002	June '71
Tigers Will Survive	Vertigo	1010	February '72

PLAINSONG

In Search of Amelia Earhart	Elektra	EKS–75044	November '72

IAN MATTHEWS

Valley Hi	Elektra	EKS–75061	August '73	A
Some Days You Eat the Bear . . . and Some Days the Bear Eats You	Elektra	EKS–75078	March '74	A
Go for Broke	Columbia	PC–34102	May '76	A
Hit and Run	Columbia	PC–34671	March '77	

ECLECTION

Eclection	Elektra	74023	September '68

FOTHERINGAY

Fotheringay	A&M	SP–4269	September '70

SANDY DENNY

The North Star Grassman and the Ravens	A&M	SP–4317	November '71	A
Sandy	A&M	SP–4371	November '72	A

THE BUNCH

Rock On	A&M	SP–4354	June '72	A

RICHARD THOMPSON

Henry, the Human Fly	Reprise	MS–2112	December '72
Live (More or Less)	2-Island	9421	February '77

RICHARD AND LINDA THOMPSON

Hokey Pokey	Island	9305	June '75
Pour Down like Silver	Island	9348	February '76
At First Light	Chrysalis	1177	October '78

FAIRPORT CONVENTION

Rosie	A&M	SP–4386	May '73	
Nine	A&M	SP–3603	February '74	A
Fairport Chronicles	2-A&M	SP–3530	July '76	A
A Movable Feast	Island	9285	October '74	
Rising for the Moon	Island	9313	July '75	
Gottle o' Geer	Island	9389	October '76	
	reissued on Antilles	7054		A

SANDY DENNY

Like an Old-Fashioned Waltz	Island	9340 reissued as 9258	June '74	
Rendezvous	Island	9433	July '77	A

IAN MATTHEWS

Stealin' Home	Mushroom	MES–5012	September '78

DAVE SWARBRICK

Swarbrick	TransAtlantic	337	August '80	A

RICHARD AND MIMI FARINA. Prominent members of the Sixties Greenwich Village folk music scene, Richard and Mimi Farina recorded two excellent albums of Richard's songs, including the classic "Pack Up Your Sorrows." He died tragically in a motorcycle accident shortly after the publication of his classic tale of the early "hippie" era, *Been Down So Long, It Looks Like Up to Me.* Recording one album with songwriter-guitarist Tom Jans and one unreleased album for Columbia Records, Mimi Farina formed the nonprofit Bread and Roses organization in northern

California's Marin County in 1974 for benefit performances at various institutions. Since 1977 Bread and Roses has staged annual festivals of acoustic music in Berkeley, California, one of the few acoustic music festivals still extant.

RICHARD AND MIMI FARINA

Celebrations for a Grey Day	Vanguard	VSD–79174	May '65	A
Reflections in a Crystal Wind	Vanguard	VSD–79204	February '66	A
Memories	Vanguard	VSD–79263	January '69	A
Best	2-Vanguard	VSD–21/22	May '71	A

MIMI FARINA AND TOM JANS

| Take Heart | A&M | SP–4310 | July '71 | A |

BREAD AND ROSES

| The Bread and Roses Festival of Acoustic Music | 2-Fantasy | F–79009 | September '79 | A |
| The Bread and Roses Festival of Music | 2-Fantasy | 79011 | March '81 | A |

THE FIFTH DIMENSION. One of the more popular black vocal groups of the late Sixties and early Seventies, The Fifth Dimension utilized essentially pop material, by Jimmy Webb and Laura Nyro in particular, for their warm, lush harmonies of widespread appeal. During the latter half of the Seventies, The Fifth Dimension endured a series of personnel changes and limited record sales, while originals Billy Davis, Jr., and Marilyn McCoo initiated their own recording and performing career with the certified gold-award album, *I Hope We Get to Love on Time.*

Lamonte McLemore (born in St. Louis on September 17, 1939) formed a vocal group, The Hi-Fi's, in Los Angeles during the mid-Sixties with Marilyn McCoo (born in Jersey City, New Jersey, on September 30, 1944) and two others. McCoo, raised in Los Angeles, had been performing for audiences since the age of 12. The Hi-Fi's came to the attention of Ray Charles, who took them on the road, but the group broke up. McCoo and McLemore subsequently formed a new group with Florence LaRue (born February 4, 1943, in Plainfield, New Jersey), Ron Townson (born January 20, 1943, in St. Louis) and McLemore's cousin from St. Louis, Billy Davis, Jr. Davis had formed his first group while still in high school and later served with The Emeralds and The St. Louis Gospel Singers. Signed to Johnny Rivers' Soul City Records in 1966, the group adopted the name The Fifth Dimension before year's end.

After a moderate hit with John Phillips' "Go Where You Wanna Go," The Fifth Dimension scored their first major hit (a near-smash) in mid-1967 with Jimmy Webb's "Up, Up and Away." Their second album, *The Magic Garden*, was a concept album made with Webb which yielded moderate hits with "Paper Cup" and "Carpet Man." *Stoned Soul Picnic* effectively established The Fifth Dimension as a popular all-vocal group, producing two hits with Laura Nyro songs, "Sweet Blindness" and the title cut (a smash hit), as well as the major hit "California Soul." The group's first certified gold-award album, *The Age of Aquarius*, contained two top hits, a medley from *Hair*, "Aquarius/Let the Sun Shine In," and Nyro's "Wedding Bell Blues," in addition to the major hits "Workin' on a Groovy Thing" and "Blowing Away." Switching to Bell Records, The Fifth Dimension continued to have major hits through 1971 with "Puppet Man" and Nyro's "Save the Country" from *Portrait*, Burt Bacharach and Hal David's "One Less Bell to Answer" (a smash hit), and "Never My Love." *Individually and Collectively* yielded hits with "(Last Night) I Didn't Get to Sleep at All" and "If I Could Reach You"; *Greatest Hits on Earth* became the group's final gold-award album, with subsequent album and singles releases faring poorly. Their last moderate hit came in 1973 with "Living Together, Growing Together."

Married in 1969, Marilyn McCoo and Billy Davis, Jr., announced their departure from The Fifth Dimension in June 1975. They stayed on through November as the group recorded another concept album, *Earthbound*, with Jimmy Webb for ABC Records. McCoo's replacement was later replaced by Terri Bryant, and, still later, Pat Bass. Davis' place was taken over by Danny Beard, who was superseded by Lou Courtney. Compounding the personnel shifts, Ron Townson quit the group to be replaced by Mic Bell. Florence LaRue and Lamonte McLemore remain from the original group and, despite the assortment of personnel changes, The Fifth Dimension are still quite popular on the nightclub circuit. By 1981 Ron Townson had rejoined The Fifth Dimension.

Initiating their own pop-oriented night club career in 1976, Marilyn McCoo and Billy Davis, Jr., debuted at San Francisco's Fairmont Hotel in March. Recording for ABC Records, they had a smash hit with "You Don't Have to Be a Star (to Be in My Show)" from their gold-award debut album in the fall of 1976. They had a major hit with "Your Love" in 1977, the year they hosted a prime-time summer television series, but subsequent releases have fared less well, prompting a switch to Columbia Records in 1978.

THE FIFTH DIMENSION

Up, Up and Away *	Soul City	92000	May '67
The Magic Garden	Soul City	92001	December '67
Stoned Soul Picnic	Soul City	92002	August '68
The Age of Aquarius *	Soul City	92005	May '69
Greatest Hits *	Soul City	33900	May '70

The July 5th Album	Soul City	33901	August '70
Portrait*	Bell	6045	May '70
Love's Lines, Angles, and Rhymes*	Bell	6060	March '71
Live!!*	2-Bell	9000	October '71
Reflections	Bell	6065	November '71
Individually and Collectively	Bell	6073	March '72
Greatest Hits on Earth*	Bell reissued on Arista	1106 4002	September '72
Living Together, Growing To-gether	Bell	1116	March '73
Soul and Inspira-ation	Bell	1315	January '75
Earthbound	ABC	897	August '75
Star Dancing	Motown	896	February '78
High on Sunshine	Motown	914	February '79

MARILYN McCOO AND BILLY DAVIS, JR.

I Hope We Get to Love on Time*	ABC	952	September '76
Two of Us	ABC	1026	August '77
Marilyn and Billy	Columbia	JC–35603	October '78

ROBERTA FLACK. A multi-talented black musician, Roberta Flack achieved her first recognition in conjunction with Donny Hathaway, establishing herself on her own in 1972 with the belated smash hit "The First Time Ever I Saw Your Face." Functioning as composer and arranger as well as pianist and singer, Roberta Flack has retained her popularity with rock, easy-listening, and rhythm-and-blues fans into the Eighties.

Born in Black Mountain, North Carolina, on February 10, 1940, into a musical family, Roberta Flack moved with her family to the suburbs of Washington, D.C., at the age of four. Starting classical piano lessons at nine, she graduated from high school at 15 and received her baccalaureate in music education from Howard University at 19. Returning to the Washington area after a year in North Carolina, Flack taught high school and moonlighted as a piano accompanist to opera singers at the Tivoli Club, later renamed Mr. Henry's. Also working piano bars in the area, she was "discovered" in 1968 by jazz pianist Les McCann, who assisted her in securing an Atlantic Records recording contract. Her debut album, *First Take*, which she arranged, languished for more than six months before finally entering the album charts. Flack's second album, *Chapter Two*, though yielding no hit single, became her first certified gold-award album in 1971. Her first successful single came that year with Carole King's "You've Got a Friend," recorded with Donny Hathaway.

Recognized by the end of 1971, Roberta Flack was firmly established in 1972. The Clint Eastwood film, *Play Misty for Me,* featured her version of Ewan McColl's folksong, "The First Time Ever I Saw Your Face." Released as a single, the song became an instant smash hit in both the rock and easy-listening fields. "Where Is the Love," taken from her best-selling duet album with Donny Hathaway, was also a major hit in 1972, the year both her first and third albums were certified gold-award. Assisted by her almost constant touring around the world, Flack's next album, *Killing Me Softly,* yielded the smash hit title cut as well as a moderate hit with Janis Ian's "Jesse." She subsequently co-produced and arranged *Feel Like Makin' Love,* which included the smash hit title song composed by Gene McDaniels. Taking a year off from touring and recording, Flack returned with *Blue Lights in the Basement* and the smash hit "The Closer I Get to You," recorded with Donny Hathaway. However, 1978's *Roberta Flack* fared less well, despite yielding the moderate hit "If Ever I See You Again," composed by Joe Brooks, author of "You Light Up My Life." A second duet album with Donny Hathaway from 1980 yielded two minor hits with "You Are My Heaven" and "Back Together Again." Following the duet set with Peabo Bryson, *Live & More,* Roberta Flack worked on the soundtrack to the Richard Pryor–Cicely Tyson film *Bustin' Loose.*

ROBERTA FLACK

First Take*	Atlantic	SD–8230	June '69	A
Chapter Two*	Atlantic	SD–1569	August '70	A
Quiet Fire*	Atlantic	SD–1594	November '71	A

ROBERTA FLACK AND DONNY HATHAWAY

Roberta Flack and Donny Hath- away*	Atlantic	SD–7216	April '72	A
Roberta Flack Featuring Donny Hathaway*	Atlantic	16013	March '80	A

ROBERTA FLACK

Killing Me Softly*	Atlantic	SD–7271 reissued as SD– 19154	August '73	A
Feel Like Makin' Love	Atlantic	SD–18131	March '75	
Blue Lights in the Basement*	Atlantic	SD–19149	December '77	A
Roberta Flack	Atlantic	SD–19186	September '78	A
Roberta Flack	Atlantic	19317	December '81	A

ROBERTA FLACK AND PEABO BRYSON

Live & More	2-Atlantic	2–7004	December '80	A

FLEETWOOD MAC. Weathering numerous personnel changes and legal and financial difficulties, Fleetwood Mac has progressed from its status as an English blues band of the late Sixties with a strong cult following to become an enormously popular pop-oriented group of the late Seventies. Formed by three former members of John Mayall's Bluesbreakers, Fleetwood Mac initially pursued a successful English career as a blues band during the late-Sixties blues revival. For a time sporting an unusual three guitar front line with Peter Green, Jeremy Spencer, and Danny Kirwan, Fleetwood Mac gradually left the blues behind following the departure of co-founder Green. Subsequently creating a softer, more harmonic sound utilizing widely divergent material with *Kiln House*, the album which first brought the group large-scale recognition in the United States, Fleetwood Mac strengthened their pop-oriented repertoire with the addition of singer–songwriter Christine McVie (nee Perfect) from Chicken Shack in 1970. After the exit of guitarist–songwriter Jeremy Spencer, Fleetwood Mac began to transform into an English-Californian band with the addition of singer–songwriter Bob Welch. With only Mick Fleetwood and John McVie remaining from the original group, Fleetwood Mac endured a series of confusing personnel changes following the stunning *Bare Trees* album, only to become mired in financial and legal problems during 1973.

Following the departure of Bob Welch for a marginal career with the power trio Paris, Fleetwood Mac was able to re-group for 1975's landmark *Fleetwood Mac* best-seller. Truly an English-Californian band with the recruitment of Californians "Stevie" Nicks and Lindsey Buckingham for *Fleetwood Mac* (the group's first gold-award album), Fleetwood Mac has become one of the biggest concert attractions and best-selling groups in the world, primarily on the strength of the visual and musical focus provided by Stevie Nicks and Christine McVie and the slick production of their recent albums. *Rumours*, a year in the works, became one of the largest selling albums in music history, selling over 14 million copies, whereas *Tusk*, nearly two years in the works, exhibited a high degree of eclecticism and marked the creative ascendancy of Buckingham. During 1980–81, the various members of Fleetwood Mac pursued solo projects; Stevie Nicks established herself as a solo artist with the best-selling *Bella Donna* album.

Former members of Fleetwood Mac have generally not fared well. Danny Kirwan has issued a series of obscure albums for DJM Records; both Jeremy Spencer and Peter Green released their first solo albums in years during 1979. Undoubtedly the most successful former member is Bob Welch, whose debut solo album, *French Kiss*, was certified platinum-award in 1978.

Fleetwood Mac was formed in July 1967 by two former members of John Mayall's Bluesbreakers, guitarist–songwriter Jeremy Spencer (born July 4, 1948, in West Hartlepool, England), and bassist Bob Brunning, who was replaced in September by former Mayall bassist John McVie (born November 26, 1945, in London). Guitarist–songwriter Peter Green (born in Bethnal Green, London, on October 29, 1946) had joined Mayall following Eric Clapton's mid-1966 departure to form Cream and appeared on Mayall's *A Hard Road* album. Green had previously been a member of Peter B's Looners and Shotgun Express, as had drummer Mick Fleetwood (born in Redruth, England, on July 24, 1947). Fleetwood, a drummer since the age of 13, shared drumming duties with Aynsley Dunbar in John Mayall's group during 1966 and 1967. Originally known as Peter Green's Fleetwood Mac, the group debuted at the British National Jazz and Blues Festival on August 12, 1967, and soon signed to Mike Vernon's Blue Horizon label. Issued on Epic Records in the United States, the group's debut album included songs by Elmore James, Howlin' Wolf, and Sonny Boy Williamson as well as blues-oriented originals by Green and Spencer. Only marginally successful in the United States, the album proved surprisingly popular in England; the group soon scored their first English hit with Green's instrumental "Albatross."

In August 1968 Peter Green brought on a third guitarist–vocalist, Danny Kirwan (born May 13, 1950), and Fleetwood Mac's second American album, *English Rose*, contained songs by all three guitarists, including Green's "Black Magic Woman," popularized by Santana in 1970. Green's "Man of the World" became the group's second English hit in 1969, the year the group's members recorded two albums that were initially released as *Blues Jam in Chicago, Volumes 1* and *2*, with blues greats such as Otis Spann and Willie Dixon. Switching to Reprise Records, Fleetwood Mac recorded *Then Play On* without the assistance of Jeremy Spencer. Leaving much of the blues influence behind, the album featured a number of pop-oriented songs by Green. Before the end of 1969, Fleetwood Mac scored their first American singles chart entry with Green's "Oh, Well." Early the next year, the departed Spencer released a solo album in England, recorded with the help of Kirwan, McVie, and Fleetwood. The real surprise occurred that April when Green announced he would be leaving Fleetwood Mac the next month.

Fleetwood Mac's first album without Peter Green, *Kiln House*, confirmed the group's move into a softer, more harmonic and pop-oriented type of music. Containing widely divergent material, the album included Spencer's Western parody, "Blood on the Floor," Kirwan's rousing "Tell Me All the Things You Do," and the collaborative "Station Man" and "Jewel-Eyed Judy," both featuring lead vocals by Kirwan. The album became the group's first major album success in the United States and inspired popularity far exceeding the cult following that had attended their marginally successful American tours since 1968. For the album, Fleetwood Mac was assisted by John McVie's wife Christine. Married in August 1968, the former Christine Perfect (born in Greenodd, Lancashire, on July 12, 1943) had been a member of Chicken Shack, playing piano and singing the group's 1969 English hit, "I'd Rather Go Blind." Leaving Chicken Shack for the domesticity of married life, Christine McVie soon returned to the music scene with a solo album, later reissued as *The Legendary Christine Perfect Album*, and a new short-lived band. Having occasionally added piano for earlier Fleetwood Mac recordings, she officially joined the group in August 1970, shortly before the release of *Kiln House*.

In the meantime, Peter Green recorded a single solo album, *The End of the Game*, before totally withdrawing from the music scene. He eventually resurfaced in late 1979 with *In the Skies,* on Sail Records. Then, in February 1971, during Christine McVie's first American tour with Fleetwood Mac, Jeremy Spencer abruptly left the group while in Los Angeles. Joining a Christian colony, Spencer later recorded *Jeremy Spencer and The Children of God* with various members of the religious group; he was not to record again until 1979, when *Flee* was issued on Atlantic Records.

Fleetwood Mac, now comprised of Kirwan, Fleetwood, and the McVies, auditioned for a replacement for Spencer. Bob Welch (born in Los Angeles on either August 31, 1945, or July 31, 1946), a lead guitarist, singer, and songwriter, was the eventual choice, joining in April 1971. Welch, a veteran of both the Los Angeles club scene and the Las Vegas nightclub scene, had been a member of a multi-racial rhythm-and-blues band, The Seven Sons. When that group broke up in 1969, Welch moved to Paris and formed yet another rhythm-and-blues band before successfully auditioning for Fleetwood Mac. With the departures of Green and Spencer, Fleetwood Mac switched to ballads and softer rock songs for *Future Games,* Christine McVie and Bob Welch's debut recording with the group. The album yielded no hit singles, but the follow-up, *Bare Trees,* proved to be the group's second successful American album. Again containing widely divergent material, the album included Kirwan's "Dust" and "Bare Trees," Christine's "Spare Me a Little," and Welch's "Sentimental Lady." However, in October 1972, Danny Kirwan left Fleetwood Mac, later recording obscure albums for DJM Records which were released in 1975, 1977, and 1979.

Danny Kirwan was replaced by vocalist Dave Walker, formerly of Savoy Brown, and lead and slide guitarist Bob Weston, from "Long" John Baldry's band. The new lineup recorded the equivocal *Penguin* album, which oddly fared rather well in the American album charts. Walker was then dismissed, and *Mystery to Me* was recorded with Welch, Weston, Fleetwood, and the McVies. Containing songs written primarily by Welch and Christine McVie, the album fared well in the United States. Bob Weston subsequently left the group in October 1973. *Heroes Are Hard to Find,* regarded as Fleetwood Mac's first album as a transplanted Los Angeles band, was recorded by Welch, Fleetwood, and the McVies, yielding an underground hit with Welch's "Bermuda Triangle." However, a protracted period of legal and financial problems beset the group as manager Clifford Davis, claiming control of the Fleetwood Mac name, assembled a group of unknowns to tour America under that name. Litigation was instituted as the real Fleetwood Mac moved to Los Angeles and Mick Fleetwood assumed the group's management. The release of *Heroes Are Hard to Find* was held up, and the group was advised to abandon touring. Eventually vindicated by the courts, the real Fleetwood Mac suffered yet another personnel change when Bob Welch left at the end of 1974. He subsequently formed the power trio Paris with ex-Jethro Tull bassist Glen Cornick and drummer Thom Mooney. After a marginally successful debut album, Mooney left Paris to be replaced by Hunt Sales. The group disbanded in 1977.

Reduced to a trio, Fleetwood Mac recruited Stephanie "Stevie" Nicks (born in Phoenix, Arizona, on May 26, 1948) and Lindsey Buckingham (born in Palo Alto, California, on October 3, 1949), to whom the group had been earlier introduced by producer Keith Olsen. The much-traveled Stevie Nicks had ended up in the San Francisco area after dropping out of San Jose State College to join a group called Fritz in 1968. Fritz, whose bassist and second vocalist was Lindsey Buckingham, persevered for over three years before disbanding in 1971. Nicks and Buckingham remained together as a duo, moving to Los Angeles and eventually signing with Polydor Records. Having recorded one album, the two came to the attention of Fleetwood Mac before Welch's departure. With Buckingham and Nicks joining Fleetwood Mac in January 1975, this newest lineup recorded *Fleetwood Mac* in Los Angeles. Once again featuring three independent singer–songwriters, Fleetwood Mac was well on its way to becoming the quintessential English-Californian rock band. The album yielded three hit singles, Christine's "Over My Head" and "Say You Love Me" and Nicks' "Rhiannon," and also contained Christine's "Warm Ways" and Nicks' "Landslide." Spurred by the visual and musical focus provided by Christine McVie and Stevie Nicks, the subsequent six-month promotional tour made Fleetwood Mac a massively popular concert attraction and established the group as one of the prime purveyors of pop-oriented, harmonically rich, and extravagantly produced contemporary music.

The self-produced follow-up to *Fleetwood Mac*, *Rumours*, reinforced the group's burgeoning popularity despite the fact that John and Christine McVie and Buckingham and Nicks split up as couples. The album produced four hit singles—Buckingham's "Go Your Own Way," Nicks' "Dream," and Christine's "Don't Stop" and "You Make Loving Fun"— and eventually sold over 14 million copies. A 10-month, 10-country world tour following the release of *Rumours* undoubtedly strengthened Fleetwood Mac's reputation as a concert attraction.

During 1977 Bob Welch initiated a solo career under the auspices of Mick Fleetwood. Welch's debut album, *French Kiss*, saw Welch playing guitar and bass and performing lead and background vocals on virtually every track, with drummer Alvin Taylor providing the only major assistance. A remake of "Sentimental Lady," recorded with Lindsey Buckingham, Christine McVie, and Mick Fleetwood, became a major hit before the end of 1977, followed by "Ebony Eyes" and "Hot Love, Cold World" in 1978. Touring with Fleetwood Mac in promotion of *French Kiss*, Welch later recorded *Three Hearts* with drummer Alvin Taylor and keyboardist David Adelstein. In early 1979, Welch scored another major hit with "Precious Love."

During 1979 former Fleetwood Mac members Jeremy Spencer and Peter Green were both back with new albums. However, the year's big news was the October release of the double-record Fleetwood Mac set, *Tusk*. Recorded over a two-year period at the cost of over $1 million, the album was an instant best-seller. Overlong and disjointed, *Tusk* indicated the creative ascendancy of Lindsey Buckingham, whose odd, near-smash hit title cut, recorded with the USC Marching Band, was the album's first singles release. An exhaustive American tour was completed by Fleetwood

Mac before the end of 1979, as Nicks' "Sara" became the album's second near-smash, followed in 1980 by the major hit "Think About You." Conducting a nine-month world tour during 1980, Fleetwood Mac issued the double-record set *Live* (taken from the *Tusk* tour) at year's end as the various members subsequently pursued solo projects. While Mick Fleetwood recorded *The Visitor* for RCA in Ghana, Africa, with local talent, and Lindsey Buckingham recorded the eccentric yet accessible *Law & Order* for Asylum, largely by himself, Stevie Nicks cut *Bella Donna* for the recently formed Modern label. An instant best-seller, *Bella Donna* quickly yielded two smash hits with "Stop Draggin' My Heart Around" (in duet with author and bandleader Tom Patty) and "Leather and Lace" (in duet with Eagle Don Henley), and virtually established Nicks as a solo act. Around the same time, Buckingham hit with "Trouble."

FLEETWOOD MAC

Fleetwood Mac	Epic	BN–26402	July '68	
The Original Fleet- wood Mac (recorded '67)	Sire	SR–6045	November '77	A
English Rose	Epic	BN–26446	January '69	
English Rose/ Fleetwood Mac	2-Epic	BG–33740	October '75	
Black Magic Woman	2-Epic	KEG– 30632	September '71	
Vintage Years: Best	2-Sire	3706 reissued as 2XS– 6006	February '75	A
Blues Jam in Chicago, Volume 1	Blue Horizon	BH–4803	'69	
Blues Jam in Chicago, Volume 2	Blue Horizon	BH–4805	'69	
Fleetwood Mac in Chicago (reissue of above)	2-Blue Horizon reissued on Sire	BH–3801 3715 reissued as 2XS– 6009	'70 January '76	A
Then Play On	Reprise	RS–6368	October '69	A
Kiln House	Reprise	RS–6408	September '70	A

CHICKEN SHACK (WITH CHRISTINE McVIE)

40 Blue Fingers Freshly Packed and Ready to Serve	Epic	BN–26414	January '69
O. K., Ken?	Blue Horizon	BH–7705	April '69

CHRISTINE McVIE

The Legendary Christine Perfect Album	Sire	7522 reissued as 6022	July '76	

PETER GREEN

End of the Game	Reprise	RS–6436	February '71	
In the Skies	Sail	0110	November '79	
Little Dreamer	Sail	0112	October '80	A

JEREMY SPENCER

Jeremy Spencer and The Children of God	Columbia	KC–31990	November '72	
Flee	Atlantic	SD–19236	June '79	

FLEETWOOD MAC

Future Games	Reprise	RS–6465	October '71	A
Bare Trees*	Reprise	MS–2080 reissued as 2278	April '72	A

DANNY KIRWAN

Second Chapter	DJM	1	November '75	
Danny Kirwan	DJM	9	May '77	
Hello There, Big Boy	DJM	22	May '79	

FLEETWOOD MAC

Penguin	Reprise	MS–2138	April '73	A
Mystery to Me*	Reprise	MS–2158 reissued as 2279	October '73	A
Heroes Are Hard to Find	Reprise	MS–2196	September '74	A

PARIS (WITH BOB WELCH)

Paris	Capitol	ST–11464	January '76	
Big Town, 2061	Capitol	ST–11560	September '76	

LINDSEY BUCKINGHAM AND STEVIE NICKS

Buckingham/Nicks	Polydor	PD–5058	October '73	A

FLEETWOOD MAC

Fleetwood Mac*	Reprise	MS–2225 reissued as 2281	July '75	A
Rumours**	Warner Brothers	BSK–3010	February '77	A

| Tusk** | 2-Warner Brothers | 2HS–3350 | October '79 | A |
| Live* | 2-Warner Brothers | 2WB–3500 | December '80 | A |

BOB WELCH

French Kiss**	Capitol	ST–11663 reissued as SN– 16125	October '77	A
Three Hearts*	Capitol	SO–11907 reissued as SN– 16126	March '79	A
The Other One	Capitol	SW–12017 reissued as SN– 16127	November '79	A
Man Overboard	Capitol	SOO– 12107	October '80	A
Bob Welch	RCA	AFL1– 4107	October '81	A

MICK FLEETWOOD

| The Visitor | RCA | AFL1– 4080 | June '81 | A |

STEVIE NICKS

| Bella Donna* | Modern | 38–139 | August '81 | A |

LINDSEY BUCKINGHAM

| Law & Order | Asylum | 5E–561 | September '81 | A |

THE FLYING BURRITO BROTHERS/GRAM PARSONS. Though virtually unrecognized in their own time, The Flying Burrito Brothers, particularly in the person of Gram Parsons, exerted a tremendous influence on rock music in the late Sixties and early Seventies by successfully combining rock and country instrumentation, rock amplification, and typically plaintive country-style lyrics. Though The Byrds' *Sweetheart of the Rodeo* album (on which original Flying Burrito Brothers Chris Hillman and Gram Parsons played) is generally regarded as the first major "country-rock" album, some claim that Parsons' International Submarine Band LP, *Safe at Home*, was actually the first album of the genre. Parsons' two albums with The Flying Burrito Brothers, *The Gilded Palace of Sin* and *Burrito Deluxe*, though critically acclaimed, yielded no hit singles and sold only marginally. Nonetheless, these albums and Parsons' two subsequent solo albums exerted an enormous influence on the sensibilities of rock musicians and fans, opening the way for the later successes of a number of

Los Angeles-based "country-rock" bands such as Poco and The Eagles. Rick Roberts, Gram Parsons' replacement in The Flying Burrito Brothers, also endured the fate of being ignored, both with the group and solo, until he eventually received recognition with Firefall in the latter half of the Seventies. Gram Parsons' legacy, unrecognized during his lifetime (he died in September 1973), has been upheld by Emmylou Harris, co-vocalist on his two solo albums, in the late Seventies.

Born in Winterhaven, Florida, on November 5, 1946, Gram Parsons grew up in Waycross, Georgia, and obtained his first guitar while in his early teens. After playing with several Georgia bands, he formed the folk-style quartet The Shilos in New York's Greenwich Village and toured the East Coast college and coffeehouse circuit between 1963 and 1965. In 1979 archive recordings of The Shilos were issued on Sierra Records. After briefly studying theology at Harvard University, Parsons formed perhaps the first "country-rock" band, The International Submarine Band, in 1965 in the Cambridge region. Having recorded *Safe at Home* with the band on Lee Hazlewood's LHI label, Parsons soon joined The Byrds for their much-celebrated *Sweetheart of the Rodeo* album. Later hailed as the first "country-rock" album, the LP included two Gram Parsons songs, "Hickory Wind" (co-authored by International Submarine Band member Bob Buchanan) and "One Hundred Years from Now." Leaving The Byrds after only three months, Parsons was soon followed by Chris Hillman (born December 4, 1942, in Los Angeles). Around the end of 1968 the two formed The Flying Burrito Brothers. The original members: Gram Parsons (rhythm guitar, keyboards, vocals), Chris Hillman (rhythm guitar, mandolin, vocals), "Sneaky" Pete Kleinow (pedal steel guitar), and Chris Ethridge (bass, piano).

Signed to A&M Records, The Flying Burrito Brothers recorded their debut album, *The Gilded Palace of Sin*, for 1969 release. Picturing the members in elaborate country-and-western style Nudie suits (Parsons' suit prominently featured marijuana leaves), the album contained some of Parsons' finest songwriting efforts, including "Sin City" (co-authored by Hillman) and "Hot Burrito #1" (co-authored by Ethridge), with lead vocals by Parsons. During 1969 Chris Ethridge exited for sessions work and was replaced by Bernie Leadon (guitar, banjo), formerly with Dillard and Clark, with Hillman switching to bass. Ex-Byrd Michael Clarke became the group's drummer that year following the departure of Jon Corneal. *Burrito Deluxe*, their next album, featured a fine countrified version of Jagger and Richard's "Wild Horses" as well as a number of songs written or co-written by Parsons, including "High Fashion Queen" and "Lazy Days." Gram Parsons left The Flying Burrito Brothers the month *Burrito Deluxe* was issued and was replaced by Rick Roberts (born August 31, 1949, in Clearwater, Florida), who led the group through a variety of incarnations into 1972. "Sneaky" Pete Kleinow and Bernie Leadon both departed in 1971 and, by October, the group was virtually reconstituted with Roberts, Hillman, Clarke, pedal steel guitarist Al Perkins, and three members of Country Gazette—fiddler Byron Berline, guitarist Kenny Wertz, and bassist Roger Bush. This grouping recorded the live set, *The Last of the*

Red Hot Burritos, but, before a late 1971 European tour, Clarke, Hillman, and Perkins dropped out. The tour, undertaken as The Hot Burrito Revue with Country Gazette, saw the addition of Alan Munde (guitar, banjo), Don Beck (guitar, pedal steel guitar), and Erik Dalton (drums). Following the tour the group disbanded, with *Hot Burritos* and *Close Up the Honky Tonks* being issued after the group's demise.

By late 1972 Gram Parsons was recording again, with the vocal assistance of Emmylou Harris, fiddler Berline, steel guitarist Perkins, and James Burton, Ricky Nelson's early and Elvis Presley's latter-day guitarist. His first solo album, *GP*, included "Kiss the Children," co-authored by Parsons and Rick Grech (a former member of Family and Blind Faith). *Grievous Angel*, also recorded with Emmylou Harris, contained another Parsons–Grech collaboration, "Las Vegas," as well as the Parsons originals "In My Hour of Darkness" and "Brass Buttons," earlier recorded by Poco on their *Crazy Eyes* album. However, several months before the release of *Grievous Angel*, Gram Parsons died at the age of 26, apparently from multiple drug use, on September 19, 1973, at Joshua Tree, California. Never fully recognized in his own lifetime, Gram Parsons lives on in the work of Emmylou Harris, whose popularity, ironically, is primarily in the country field rather than in the rock field.

During 1974 The Flying Burrito Brothers re-formed with originals "Sneaky" Pete and Chris Ethridge plus Louisiana fiddler Gib Guilbeau, ex-Byrds drummer Gene Parsons (no relation), and ex-Canned Heat vocalist–guitarist Joel Scott Hill. *Flying Again* proved marginally successful, but, following the departure of Ethridge in early 1976, *Airborne* fared dismally. Without a recording contract for three years, The Flying Burrito Brothers, with Kleinow, Guilbeau, and guitarist Greg Harris, re-emerged in 1980 with the minor country hit "White Line Fever" and *Live from Tokyo* on the Regency label.

GRAM PARSONS

Early Years, Volume 1 (1963–65)	Sierra	SRS–8702	February '79	A

THE INTERNATIONAL SUBMARINE BAND

Safe at Home	LHI	12001	'67

THE BYRDS (WITH GRAM PARSONS AND CHRIS HILLMAN)

Sweetheart of The Rodeo	Columbia	PC–9670	August '68	A

THE FLYING BURRITO BROTHERS

The Gilded Palace of Sin	A&M	SP–4175 reissued as 3122	March '69	A
Burrito Deluxe	A&M	SP–4258	April '70	A

The Flying Burrito Brothers	A&M	SP–4295	June '71	A
Last of the Red Hot Burritos	A&M	SP–4343	May '72	A
Hot Burritos	A&M	SP–8070		
Close Up the Honky Tonks	2-A&M	SP–3631	June '74	A

GRAM PARSONS

GP	Reprise	2123	January '73	A
Grievous Angel	Reprise	2171	January '74	A

GRAM PARSONS/THE FLYING BURRITO BROTHERS

Sleepless Nights	A&M	SP–4578	May '76	A

THE FLYING BURRITO BROTHERS

Flying Again	Columbia	PC–33817	October '75
Airborne	Columbia	PC–34222	June '76
Live from Tokyo	Regency	79001	January '80

FOGHAT. An offshoot of the English blues-and-boogie band Savoy Brown, Foghat achieved widespread popularity in the United States, particularly following the release of *Energized*, while remaining virtually unknown in their native country. Touring almost constantly, Foghat has far out-distanced Savoy Brown by issuing a number of moderate hit singles and a string of gold-award albums between 1975 and 1978.

"Lonesome" Dave Peverett (born in London on April 10, 1950), Tony Stevens, and Roger Earl (born in London on May 16, 1946) had been members of Savoy Brown since 1967. In late 1970 the three departed that group, auditioned guitarists and formed Foghat with Rod Price (born in London on November 22, 1947). The initial members: Dave Peverett (guitar, vocals), and Rod Price (slide and electric guitar), Tony Stevens (bass), and Roger Earl (drums). Signed to Bearsville Records, Foghat's debut album yielded the group's first, albeit minor, hit with "I Just Want to Make Love to You" in late 1972. Touring the United States almost constantly, Foghat soon became one of the most sought-after opening acts in the early Seventies. The band made its breakthrough in 1974 with *Energized*, the first of a consecutive series of gold-award albums. Born in Columbia, Missouri, on December 5, 1950, multi-instrumentalist Nick Jameson subsequently produced *Rock and Roll Outlaws* and *Fool for the City*, playing bass on the latter album. *Fool for the City* yielded Foghat's first major hit single with "Slow Ride," as well as a minor hit with "Fool for the City." Tony Stevens abruptly left the group in 1975, and Jameson took over his bass position. However, Jameson departed for a solo career before *Night Shift*, with Craig McGregor (born in Milford, Connecticut, on October 13, 1949) assuming the bass chores for Foghat. Jameson later produced *Foghat Live*, the group's only certified platinum-award album.

Foghat subsequently ceased touring for six months, returning with *Stone Blue* in 1978 and *Boogie Motel* in 1979, the latter yielding a major hit with "Third Time Lucky (First Time I Was a Fool)." Jameson's first solo album, on which he played virtually every instrument, was released on Warner Brothers in late 1977.

FOGHAT

Foghat*	Bearsville	BR-2077	July '72	A
Foghat: Rock and Roll	Bearsville	BR-2136	March '73	A
Energized*	Bearsville	BR-6950	January '74	A
Rock and Roll Outlaws*	Bearsville	BR-6956	October '74	A
Fool for the City*	Bearsville	BR-6959 reissued as BR-6980	October '75	A
Night Shift*	Bearsville	BR-6962	November '76	A
Live**	Bearsville	K-6971	August '77	A
Stone Blue*	Bearsville	K-6977	May '78	A
Boogie Motel	Bearsville	BHS-6990	September '79	A
Tight Shoes	Bearsville	HS-6999	June '80	A
Girls to Chat and Boys to Bounce	Bearsville	3578	July '81	A

NICK JAMESON

Already Free	Warner Brothers	BR-6972	October '77

FOREIGNER. A late Seventies "hard rock" band comprised, in part, of former members of King Crimson and Spooky Tooth, Foreigner quickly became a successful singles and album band and a popular touring attraction.

Formed in early 1976 by Britons Mick Jones and Ian McDonald, Foreigner was originally a six-piece rock band. The members: Mick Jones (lead guitar, vocals), Ian McDonald (guitar, keyboards, horns, vocals), Lou Gramm (lead vocals), Al Greenwood (keyboards, synthesizer), Ed Gagliardi (bass, vocals), and Dennis Elliott (drums). Jones (born December 27, 1944 or 1947, in Butleigh, Somerset, England), a sessions musician and songwriter, had been a member of King Crimson, appearing on the group's sensational debut album. He later recorded *McDonald and Giles* with King Crimson original Mike Giles before pursuing sessions and production work. In the early Seventies Lou Gramm (born Lou Grammtico on May 2, 1950 or 1951, in Rochester, New York) co-founded Black Sheep, who eventually recorded two albums for Capitol Records. Al Greenwood (born in New York City on October 20, 1951) had been in a group called Storm, whereas Englishman Dennis Elliott (born in London on August 18, 1950) was a sessions drummer who had played on Ian

Hunter's debut solo album. Ed Gagliardi (born in Brooklyn, New York, on February 13, 1952) was the last to join Foreigner.

Foreigner rehearsed for several months before signing with Atlantic Records and initiating the recording of their debut album in November 1976. *Foreigner*, released the next March, proved immensely popular and yielded three major hit singles, "Feels Like the First Time," "Cold as Ice," and "Long, Long Way from Home," and was certified platinum-award by August. Touring the United States virtually nonstop between April and October 1977, Foreigner entered the studio to record their second album following the tour. Launching a worldwide tour in March 1978, the group's *Double Vision* album was issued in June. The album again produced three hit singles—"Hot Blooded," "Double Vision," and "Blue Morning, Blue Day"—and was certified platinum-award the month of its release. In September 1979 Foreigner issued *Head Games*, another instant best-seller, which yielded hits with "Dirty White Boy" and "Head Games" before year's end. Earlier in April, Ed Gagliardi had been replaced by Rick Wills (bass, vocals), a former member of Peter Frampton's Camel and Steve Marriott's re-formed Small Faces. In early 1980 Foreigner scored a moderate hit with the sexist "Women," but that September Ian McDonald and Al Greenwood were dismissed from the group. Employing two synthesizer specialists, the four-piece Foreigner subsequently recorded perhaps their finest album, 4, which yielded a major hit with "Urgent," featuring an exciting saxophone solo by Junior Walker.

McDONALD AND GILES

McDonald and Giles	Cotillion	9042	February '71	

BLACK SHEEP

| Black Sheep | Capitol | ST–11369 | February '75 | A |
| Encouraging Words | Capitol | ST–11447 | October '75 | |

FOREIGNER

Foreigner**	Atlantic	SD–18215 reissued as SD–19109	March '77	A
Double Vision**	Atlantic	SD–19999	June '78	A
Head Games**	Atlantic	SD–29999	September '79	A
4**	Atlantic	16999	August '81	A

THE FOUR SEASONS. The most successful East Coast white vocal group of the Sixties, The Four Seasons issued a series of smash singles during the decade featuring the shrill piercing falsetto lead voice of Frankie Valli. One of the few major white American musical challenges to The

Beatles other than The Beach Boys, The Four Seasons became so popular that they were able to score a hit record as The Wonder Who in 1965 and launch Valli on a successful simultaneous solo recording career in 1966. Totally reconstituted, save Valli, by the Seventies, The Four Seasons rapidly faded after Valli's departure in 1977, only to be reunited for a 1980 tour.

The evolution of The Four Seasons began during the mid-Fifties in the Newark, New Jersey, area with the formation of The Varietones by drummer Frankie Valli (born in Newark on May 3, 1937, as Frank Castelluccio), guitarist brothers Nick and Tommy De Vito (born in Belleville, New Jersey, on June 19, 1935) and bassist Hank Majewski. Changing their name to The Four Lovers in 1965, the group signed with RCA Records and scored a minor hit that year with "You're the Apple of My Eye." Producing no more hits, The Four Lovers subsequently languished on the New Jersey lounge circuit for several years. In the meantime another New Jersey group, initially formed in 1957 as an instrumental group under the name The Royal Tones, had a major hit as The Royal Teens with the novelty song "Short Shorts" in early 1958. Among the members were songwriter-keyboardist Bob Gaudio (born in the Bronx, New York, on November 17, 1942).

In 1960 Hank Majewski left The Four Lovers to be replaced by Nick Massi (born Nicholas Macioci on September 19, 1935, in Newark). Shortly thereafter Nick De Vito departed, being replaced by Bob Gaudio. With a name change to The Four Seasons in 1961, the group—Valli, Gaudio, Tommy De Vito, and Massi—recorded the flop single "Bermuda" for George Goldner's Gone label. The Four Seasons later left Goldner and, with the assistance of writer–performer turned producer Bob Crewe, the group signed with VeeJay Records. With Gaudio and Crewe splitting the songwriting duties, The Four Seasons first hit big with "Sherry" in August 1962. Through 1967 The Four Seasons, featuring Frankie Valli's falsetto lead vocals, were consistently in the top ten. Smash hits on VeeJay included "Big Girls Don't Cry" in 1962 and "Walk like a Man" and "Candy Girl" in 1963, followed by moderate hits with "Stay" and "Alone" in 1964. Near the end of 1964 VeeJay assembled early recordings by The Beatles and several Four Seasons' hits as *The Beatles versus The Four Seasons*, today a rare and expensive collectors' item.

By 1964 The Four Seasons had switched to Philips Records, where the hits continued with "Dawn," "Ronnie," the classic "Rag Doll," "Save It for Me," and "Big Man in Town." By the end of 1965, following hits with "Bye, Bye Baby" and "Let's Hang On," The Four Seasons' sound was so popular that the group was able to score a major hit with a dreadful version of Bob Dylan's "Don't Think Twice" as The Wonder Who. During 1966 Frankie Valli initiated a solo recording career that culminated in the 1967 smash, "Can't Take My Eyes off You."

With rock music becoming increasingly sophisticated by the mid-Sixties, The Four Seasons recorded *Sing Big Hits by Burt Bacharach . . .*

Hal David . . . Bob Dylan, certainly one of the worst albums of the Sixties and enough to make even the most casual Dylan fan cringe with revulsion. An attempt at social consciousness in 1968, *The Genuine Imitation Life Gazette*, sold rather poorly. Producer-songwriter Bob Crewe subsequently parted company with The Four Seasons, as Bob Gaudio assumed the group's production chores. By 1970 The Four Seasons were encountering difficulty in scoring hit records. Leaving Philips, the group moved to Mowest Records in 1972. By then the group had been entirely reconstituted behind Valli, as Massi had left in 1965, De Vito had retired in 1970, and Gaudio had departed in 1972, though he continued to record with the group.

Frankie Valli, signing as a solo act with Private Stock Records in 1974, scored a smash hit later that year with "My Eyes Adored You." During 1975 both Valli and The Four Seasons had major hits, The Four Seasons with the smash hits "Who Loves You" and "December, 1963 (Oh, What a Night)" on Warner Brothers, and Valli with "Swearin' to God" and "Our Day Will Come." In 1977 Frankie Valli finally left The Four Seasons after a seven-month farewell tour, to score yet another smash hit the following year with the title song to the film *Grease*, composed by several of The Bee Gees. That year Valli switched to Warner Brothers records for *Frankie Valli . . . Is the Word*. By 1980 Frankie Valli had moved to MCA Records, rejoining The Four Seasons for a reunion tour that saw pianist Jerry Corbetta and drummer Gerry Polci injured in a freak on-stage accident in Philadelphia on July 5, 1980. The tour produced *Reunited Live* on Warner/Curb Records in 1981.

THE FOUR LOVERS

Joyride	RCA	1317(M)	

THE FOUR SEASONS

Sherry	VeeJay	SR–1053	October '62
Four Seasons Greetings	VeeJay	SR–1055	
Big Girls Don't Cry	VeeJay	SR–1056	February '63
Ain't That a Shame	VeeJay	SR–1059	July '63
Stay and Other Great Hits reissued as Folk-Nanny	VeeJay	SR–1082	June '64
Girls, Girls, Girls, We Love Girls	VeeJay	SR–1121	
Recorded Live on Stage	VeeJay	SR–1154	

THE FOUR SEASONS AND THE BEATLES

The Beatles versus The Four Seasons	2-VeeJay	DXS–30	October '64

THE FOUR SEASONS

Born to Wander	Philips	PHS–600129	February '64
Dawn (Go Away)	Philips	PHS–600124	March '64
Rag Doll	Philips	PHS–600146	August '64
The Four Seasons Entertain You	Philips	PHS–600164	April '65
Sing Big Hits by Burt Bacharach . . . Hal David . . . Bob Dylan	Philips	PHS–600193	December '65
Working My Way Back to You	Philips	PHS–600201	January '66
Lookin' Back	Philips	PHS–600222	December '66
Four Seasons' Christmas Album	Philips	PHS–600223	December '66
New Gold Hits	Philips	PHS–600243	June '67
The Genuine Imitation Life Gazette	Philips	PHS–600290	December '68
Half and Half	Philips	PHS–600341	May '70
Chameleon	Mowest	108	May '72
Who Loves You	Warner Brothers	2900	November '75
Helicon	Warner Brothers	3016	May '77

FOUR SEASONS ANTHOLOGIES AND COMPILATIONS

Golden Hits of The Four Seasons	VeeJay	SR–1065	September '63
More Golden Hits of The Four Seasons	VeeJay	SR–1088	September '64
Gold Vault of Hits*	Philips	PHS–600196	December '65
Second Vault of Golden Hits*	Philips	PHS–600221	November '66
Edisione D'Oro (Gold Edition— 29 Golden Hits)*	2-Philips	PHS2–6501	December '68
The Four Seasons Story	2-Private Stock	7000	December '75
Brotherhood of Man	Pickwick	3223	

A

FRANKIE VALLI

Solo	Philips	PHS–600247	July '67

Timeless	Philips	PHS–600274	August '68	
Inside You	Motown	852	November '75	
Motown Super-star Series, Volume 4	Motown	5–104	'81	A
Closeup	Private Stock	2000	March '75	
Gold	Private Stock	2001	December '75	
Our Day Will Come	Private Stock	2006	December '75	
Valli	Private Stock	2017	February '77	
Lady Put the Light Out	Private Stock	7002	May '78	
Frankie Valli Hits	Private Stock	7012	May '78	
Frankie Valli . . . Is the Word	Warner Brothers	3233	August '78	
The Very Best of Frankie Valli	MCA	3198	December '79	A
Heaven Above Me	MCA	5134	September '80	A

FRANKIE VALLI AND THE FOUR SEASONS

Reunited Live	2-Warner/ Curb	2WB–3497	February '81	A

THE FOUR TOPS. One of several male vocal groups recording for Motown Records in the latter half of the Sixties, The Four Tops had a series of hit singles, almost all written by the songwriting–production team of Brian Holland, Lamont Dozier, and Eddie Holland. Noted for their polished singing, precise choreography, and complex stage routines, The Four Tops became perhaps the most popular Motown act in Great Britain; they were overshadowed by The Supremes in the United States. The Four Tops managed several hits in 1968 after the departure from Motown of Holland–Dozier–Holland, only to switch to ABC–Dunhill in 1972; initially under songwriter–producers Dennis Lambert and Brian Potter, they attained modest recording success at best, hitting again with their classic sound on "She Used to Be My Girl" in 1981.

Born and raised in Detroit, the members of The Four Tops began singing together as high school students and later spent three years on the area's nightclub and concert circuits. The members: lead vocalist Levi Stubbs, Abdul "Duke" Fakir, Renaldo "Obie" Benson, and Lawrence Payton, Jr. Originally known as The Four Aims, the group became The Four Tops upon signing with Chess Records in 1956. Their sole single for the label did not sell, and the group subsequently recorded unsuccessfully for Columbia and Riverside before signing with the infant Motown Records aggregation in March 1963. Initially recording for Motown's short-lived jazz-oriented Workshop label, The Four Tops later switched to Motown, where they achieved their first hit with Holland–Dozier–Holland's "Baby I Need Your Loving" in August 1964. Following the early 1965 hit "Ask the Lonely," one of the few Four Tops' hits not written by H–D–H, the group scored with one of their most popular singles, the classic "I Can't Help Myself (Sugar Pie, Honey Bunch)." Subsequent hits included "It's the Same Old Song," "Something About You," and "Shake Me, Wake Me (When It's Over)," followed by the smash hits "Reach Out, I'll Be There," "Standing in the Shadows of Love," and "Bernadette," all written by H–D–H. Moderate hits ensued with "Seven Rooms of Gloom" and "You Keep Running Away" but, by 1968, The Four Tops were covering The Left Banke's "Walk Away Renee" and Tim Hardin's "If I Were a Carpenter." No more major hits occurred for The Four Tops until 1970, when they finally scored again with a remake of "It's All in the Game" and Smokey Robinson and Frank Wilson's "Still Water (Love)."

Renaldo "Obie" Benson co-authored the title track to Marvin Gaye's best-selling *What's Going On* album, but in 1972 The Four Tops switched to ABC–Dunhill Records. Initially co-produced by songwriters Dennis Lambert and Brian Potter, the group had hits with "Keeper of the Castle," "Ain't No Woman (Like the One I've Got)," and "Are You Man Enough," from the film *Shaft in Africa*. Recording for ABC beginning in 1975, The Four Tops eventually scored a smash hit in 1981 with "She Used to Be My Girl" on Casablanca Records.

THE FOUR TOPS

The Four Tops	Motown	622	February '65	
Volume 2	Motown	634	November '65	
On Top	Motown	647	August '66	
Live!	Motown	654	December '66	
On Broadway	Motown	657	April '67	
Reach Out	Motown	660	August '67	
Greatest Hits	Motown	662	September '67	A
Yesterday's Dreams	Motown	669	September '68	
Now!	Motown	675	July '69	
Soul Spin	Motown	695	December '69	
Still Waters Run Deep	Motown	704	April '70	
Changing Times	Motown	721	October '70	
Greatest Hits, Volume 2	Motown	740	September '71	
Nature Planned It	Motown	748	May '72	
Best of The Four Tops	2-Motown	764	May '73	
Anthology	3-Motown	809	July '74	A
Motown Superstar Series, Volume 14	Motown	5–114		A

THE FOUR TOPS AND THE SUPREMES

The Magnificent Seven	Motown	717	October '70
The Return of the Magnificent Seven	Motown	736	June '71
Dynamite	Motown	745	January '72

THE FOUR TOPS

Keeper of the Castle	Dunhill	DSX–50129	November '72	
Main Street People	Dunhill	DSX–50144	September '73	
Meeting of the Minds	Dunhill	DSD–50166	April '74	
Live and In Concert	Dunhill	DSD–50188	October '74	
I Can't Help Myself	Pickwick	3381	January '75	
Night Lights Harmony	ABC	862	May '75	
Catfish	ABC	968	October '76	
The Show Must Go On	ABC	1014	November '77	
At the Top	ABC/MCA	AA–1092	October '78	A
Tonight	Casablanca	7258	October '81	A

PETER FRAMPTON. Talented British guitarist who first gained attention with The Herd in the late Sixties, Peter Frampton later formed Humble Pie with ex-Small Face Steve Marriott, only to depart before the release of the group's first certified gold-award album, *Rockin' the Fillmore.* Languishing in a solo recording and performing career for years, Peter Frampton was eventually recognized as an early "hard rock" romanticist in his songwriting. He finally broke through with the totally unexpected success of 1976's *Frampton Comes Alive!,* which prominently featured his use of the "voice-box," a synthesizer-type device that seemed to make the guitar emanate words. The album, quickly certified gold- and platinum-award, became both the best-selling live album and the best-selling double-record set in music history, eventually selling over 15 million copies worldwide. However the album's huge sales created problems as critics sought to explain its popularity, leading to Frampton's status as one of the most misunderstood rock stars since Bruce Springsteen. Peter Frampton's tours, singles, and albums since 1977 have fared less well, possibly due to his appearance in the inane *Sgt. Pepper's Lonely Hearts Club Band* movie with The Bee Gees and a layoff necessitated by a serious automobile accident in 1978.

Born in Beckenham, Kent, England, on April 22, 1950, Peter Frampton obtained his first guitar at the age of eight and debuted professionally at 12. By 16, he was a member of The Herd with keyboardist Andy Bown, bassist Gary Taylor, and drummer Andrew Steele, scoring several English hit singles and recording one album for Fontana Records. In 1968 Frampton left The Herd to form Humble Pie with ex-Small Face Steve Marriott, ex-Spooky Tooth bassist Greg Ridley, and drummer Jerry Shirley. After two albums for Andrew Oldham's Immediate label, Humble Pie began to display a harder and louder sound on their first two albums for A&M Records, thus thwarting Frampton's gentler, more romantic style. He quit the group in the fall of 1971 before the release of *Rockin' the Fillmore*, Humble Pie's first gold-award album, recorded in April 1971.

Peter Frampton then pursued sessions work, assisting in the recording of George Harrison's *All Things Must Pass*, Harry Nilsson's *Son of Schmilsson*, and John Entwhistle's *Whistle Rhymes*. In 1972 Frampton recorded his first solo album, *Wind of Change*, playing most of the instruments himself. Intent on concentrating his touring efforts on the United States rather than on his native England, he subsequently formed a group with keyboardist Mick Gallagher, bassist Rick Wills, and drummer John Siomos. As Frampton's Camel, the band recorded one album, which included the earliest version of "Do You Feel like We Do," and toured the United States before disbanding in 1974. Frampton then recorded *Somethin's Happening* with Wills and drummer John Headley Down, playing keyboards, guitar, guitar synthesizer, and percussion and singing on the album. Working intensively in the United States with a road band comprised of drummer Siomos and former Herd member Andy Bown, the group recorded *Frampton*, his first album to sell in significant quantities. Though released as singles, neither "Show Me the Way" nor "Baby, I Love Your Way" from the album became major hits.

Peter Frampton finally broke through in the United States with the live double-record set, *Frampton Comes Alive!*, recorded at San Francisco's Winterland. Compiling much of his earlier material, the album yielded three major hit singles with "Show Me the Way," "Baby, I Love Your Way," and "Do You Feel like We Do," while also containing "All I Want to Be (Is by Your Side)." "Do You Feel like We Do" featured Frampton using a so-called "voice-box," a device which sends the electric guitar signal through a tube in his mouth, making the guitar "sing" synthesized words. The album took critics totally by surprise as it quickly was certified gold-, then platinum-award, eventually selling in excess of 15 million copies. Frampton, previously just another hard-working English rock musician, became a "superstar" almost overnight, playing at baseball stadiums filled with adulating fans throughout the summer of 1976 and into 1977.

The follow-up to *Frampton Comes Alive!*, *I'm in You*, was released in mid-1977, yielding a smash hit with the title song; but the subsequent single releases, "Signed, Sealed, Delivered (I'm Yours)" and "Tried to Love," fared progressively less well. Though ultimately certified platinum-award, the album's sales were only a fraction of those of *Comes Alive!* During the rest of 1977 and much of 1978, Frampton worked on the $12 million Robert Stigwood film production of *Sgt. Pepper's Lonely Hearts Club Band*. Co-starring with The Bee Gees, Frampton filled the role of Billy Shears in this abysmal fairy tale–like musical featuring 29 Beatles songs. Poorly received by critics and public alike, the film ran for only a short time before being relegated to the cheap movie-house circuit. To add injury to insult, Frampton suffered severe injuries in an automobile accident in the Bahamas shortly before the movie's release, necessitating a two-and-a-half month period of recuperation. His career seemed to have suffered a serious loss of momentum, inasmuch as his 1979 return to touring saw him playing 10,000 seat halls rather than baseball stadiums.

Moreover, *Where Should I Be* yielded only one major hit with "I Can't Stand It No More." Two years later, in 1981, Frampton recorded *Breaking All The Rules* and toured midsized halls.

THE HERD

Lookin' Through You	Fontana	SRF–67579	October '68	

PETER FRAMPTON

Wind of Change	A&M	SP–4348 reissued as 3133	June '72	A
Frampton's Camel	A&M	SP–4389 reissued as 3138	May '73	A
Somethin's Hap- pening	A&M	SP–3619	March '74	
Frampton*	A&M	SP–4512	March '75	A
Frampton Comes Alive!*	2-A&M	SP–3703	January '76	A
I'm in You**	A&M	SP–4704	June '77	A
Where Should I Be*	A&M	SP–3710	June '79	A
Breaking All the Rules	A&M	3722	June '81	A

PETER FRAMPTON, THE BEE GEES, AND OTHERS

Sgt. Pepper's Lonely Hearts Club Band**	2-RSO	4100	July '78

ARETHA FRANKLIN. Initially an authentic gospel singer touring with her father Reverend C. L. Franklin's evangelistic troupe as a teenager, Aretha Franklin languished for years as a "commercial" singer at Columbia Records, where seemingly no one was able to arrange, produce, and choose material appropriate to her undeniably powerful and emotive vocal style. Switching to Atlantic Records in 1966, she immediately found sympathetic treatment from veteran producer Jerry Wexler that resulted in a series of pop and rhythm-and-blues hit singles and best-selling albums including her Atlantic debut, *I Never Loved a Man the Way I Love You,* the classic *Lady Soul,* and *Aretha Now.* Acclaimed as the most popular female artist in rock music in the late Sixties, Aretha Franklin endured a set of personal problems that retarded her career for a while, only to come back with cover versions of other people's hits. By the early Seventies, she had re-established herself with *Live at Fillmore West* (recorded with Ray Charles), *Young, Gifted, and Black,* and *Amazing Grace,* a return to her gospel heritage and one of the few gospel albums ever to be certified gold-award. In the late Seventies Aretha Franklin continued her best-selling ways with *Sparkle*, written and produced by Curtis Mayfield.

Born in Memphis, Tennessee, on March 25, 1942 (or 1943), the daughter of well-known evangelist preacher Reverend C. L. Franklin, Aretha Franklin was raised in Detroit, where she began singing in her father's New Bethel Baptist Choir at the age of 8. By 14 she was a featured performer on his evangelistic tour, continuing on the gospel circuit for four years and recording *The Gospel Sound of Aretha Franklin* on Checker Records at age 16. In 1960, with the encouragement of her father and Teddy Wilson bassist Major "Mule" Holly, Franklin auditioned for Columbia Records a&r chief John Hammond, who immediately signed her. Making her night club debut at The Trade Winds in Chicago, she toured the upper echelons of the so-called "chitlin circuit" as Hammond guided her in the direction of classic jazz and blues singers such as Bessie Smith and Billie Holiday. She managed a moderate hit with "Rock-A-Bye Your Baby with a Dixie Melody" in 1961, but when subsequent records failed to sell, Columbia began handing her Tin Pan Alley–style material. Several of her albums, *Runnin' Out of Fools* in particular, sold modestly but, in general, her career with Columbia was unspectacular.

In November 1966 Aretha Franklin switched to Atlantic Records and was personally supervised by veteran producer Jerry Wexler. Recorded in Muscle Shoals, Alabama, with Ms. Franklin on piano and King Curtis on saxophone, her first Atlantic single, "I Never Loved a Man (the Way I Love You)," became an instant pop and rhythm-and-blues hit. Certified gold-award the year of its release, the *I Never Loved a Man the Way I Love You* album also contained Aretha Franklin favorites such as "Do Right Woman—Do Right Man" and "Dr. Feelgood," while yielding yet another smash hit with Otis Redding's "Respect." *Aretha Arrives* produced only one hit with "Baby, I Love You," but *Lady Soul*, perhaps her finest album ever, contained four hits: Carole King and Gerry Goffin's "(You Make Me Feel like) A Natural Woman," sister Carolyn Franklin's "Ain't No Way," "(Sweet, Sweet Baby) Since You've Been Gone" (co-authored by Aretha), and the smash "Chain of Fools," written by Don Covay. The follow-up, *Aretha Now*, yielded three hits with Aretha's own "Think," "I Say a Little Prayer," and "See-Saw," whereas *Aretha in Paris* was recorded during her triumphant European tour of May 1968.

During late 1968 and 1969, while in the midst of marital and career-related alcohol problems, Aretha Franklin began recording other people's hits. In 1969 she had hits with Robbie Robertson's "The Weight" and Lennon and McCartney's "Eleanor Rigby" but, fortunately, she was back to more appropriate material with Ben E. King's "Don't Play That Song" and the title song to *Spirit in the Dark*, both major hits. By the fall of 1970 Franklin had dropped her 16-piece band in favor of a tighter combo of sessions players directed by saxophonist King Curtis. *Live at Fillmore West*, recorded with surprise guest Ray Charles, became her fourth certified gold-award album, yielding a hit with Simon and Garfunkel's "Bridge over Troubled Water." Following a smash hit with "Spanish Harlem,"

Young, Gifted, and Black produced hits with "Rock Steady" and "Day Dreaming" while also containing Otis Redding's "I've Been Loving You Too Long" and the title song.

In early 1972 Aretha Franklin returned to her gospel roots, recording the double-record set *Amazing Grace* at the New Temple Missionary Baptist Church in Watts, California, with perennial gospel favorite Reverend James Cleveland and his Southern California Community Choir. Surprisingly, the album was certified gold-award during the year, thus becoming one of the few gospel albums to sell in such large quantities. Franklin subsequently flirted with more of a jazz sound with *Hey, Now, Hey (The Other Side of the Sky)*, which she co-produced with jazz arranger Quincy Jones. The album produced a hit with sister Carolyn's "Angel," whereas *Let Me in Your Life* yielded hits with "I'm in Love" and Stevie Wonder's "Until You Come Back to Me." Ms. Franklin's next two albums sold only modestly, but the album from the Warner Brothers' film *Sparkle*, composed and produced by Curtis Mayfield, sold well; it was certified gold-award in 1976 and included her last major hit, "Something He Can Feel." Neither *Sweet Passion*, produced by Lamont Dozier, nor *Almighty Fire*, composed and produced by Curtis Mayfield, did particularly well, and 1979's *La Diva* revealed a decidedly disco orientation. By 1980 she had switched to Arista Records for *Aretha* and the minor pop hit "United Together." Well-established on the supper club and Nevada casino circuit, Aretha Franklin remains one of the most popular and passionate of soul singers.

ARETHA FRANKLIN

The Gospel Sound of Aretha Franklin	Checker	10009	October '64	
Aretha (with The Ray Bryant Trio)	Columbia	CS–8412	April '61	
reissued as The First 12 Sides	Columbia	KC–31953	January '73	
Electrifying	Columbia	CS–8561	January '62	
Tender, Moving, Swinging	Columbia	CS–8676	September '62	
Laughing on the Outside	Columbia	CS–8879	September '63	
Unforgettable	Columbia	CS–8963	April '64	A
Runnin' Out of Fools	Columbia	CS–9081	December '64	
Yeah!!!	Columbia	CS–9151	June '65	
Soul Sister	Columbia	CS–9321	June '66	
Take It like You Give It	Columbia	CS–9429	March '67	
Take a Look	Columbia	CS–9554	October '67	
Aretha Franklin	2-Columbia	GP–4	November '68	
Soft and Beautiful	Columbia	CS–9776	May '69	
Today I Sing the Blues	Columbia	CS–9956	February '70	

I Never Loved a Man the Way I Love You*	Atlantic	SD–8139	April '67	A
Aretha Arrives	Atlantic	SD–8150	August '67	
Lady Soul*	Atlantic	SD–8176	February '68	
Aretha Now*	Atlantic	SD–8186	July '68	
Aretha in Paris	Atlantic	SD–8207	October '68	
Soul '69	Atlantic	SD–8212	February '69	
This Girl's in Love with You	Atlantic	SD–8248	February '70	
Spirit in the Dark	Atlantic	SD–8265	September '70	
Live at Fillmore West (with Ray Charles)*	Atlantic	SD–7205	May '71	
Young, Gifted, and Black*	Atlantic	SD–7213	January '72	
Amazing Grace (with James Cleveland)*	2-Atlantic	SD2–906	June '72	A
Hey, Now, Hey (The Other Side of the Sky)	Atlantic	SD–7265	July '73	
Let Me in Your Life	Atlantic	SD–7292	February '74	
With Everything I Feel in Me	Atlantic	SD–18116	December '74	
You	Atlantic	SD–18151	October '75	
Sparkle	Atlantic	SD–18176	June '76	
Sweet Passion	Atlantic	SD–19102	May '77	
Almighty Fire	Atlantic	SD–19161	April '78	
La Diva	Atlantic	SD–19248	September '79	A
Aretha	Arista	9538	October '80	A
Love All the Hurt Away	Arista	9552	September '81	A

ARETHA FRANKLIN ANTHOLOGIES AND COMPILATIONS

Greatest Hits	Columbia	CS–9473	May '67	
Greatest Hits, Volume 2	Columbia	CS–9601	March '68	A
Queen of Soul	Harmony	11274	August '68	
Once in a Lifetime	Harmony	11349	November '69	
2 Sides of Love	Harmony	11418	September '70	
Greatest Hits, 1960–65	Harmony	KH–30606	August '71	
In the Beginning: The World of Aretha Franklin (1960–67)	2-Columbia	KG–31355	June '72	
The Legendary Queen of Soul	2-Columbia	C2–37377	September '81	A
Aretha's Gold	Atlantic	SD–8227	July '69	A
Aretha's Greatest Hits	Atlantic	SD–8295	September '71	A

Best of Aretha Franklin	Atlantic	SD–8305	
10 Years of Gold	Atlantic	SD–18204	December '76

ALAN FREED. One of the most important popularizers of rock-and-roll during the Fifties, Alan Freed was the first disc jockey and concert producer of rock-and-roll. Often credited with coining the term "rock-and-roll" in 1951, ostensibly to avoid the stigma attached to rhythm-and-blues and so-called "race" music, Alan Freed opened the way to the white acceptance of black music as a disc jockey in Cleveland, Ohio, and later in New York City, eschewing white "cover" versions in favor of rhythm-and-blues originals. A staunch defender of rock-and-roll and rhythm-and-blues at a time when the record industry sought only to malign and restrict those musics, Alan Freed began producing rock-and-roll concerts in 1952 with an ill-fated Cleveland show. Indulging in the questionable but almost standard practices of taking unsubstantiated songwriting credits and accepting money to play certain records, Alan Freed was ruined by the "payola" investigation of 1959–60. He was made the scapegoat of the entire scandal, as others, most notably the more established Dick Clark, escaped virtually unscathed. Dying ignominiously and impoverished in 1965, Alan Freed finally received some recognition as a result of the fictionalized 1978 film, *American Hot Wax.*

Born in Johnstown, Pennsylvania, on December 15, 1922, Alan Freed grew up in Salem, Ohio, performing his first radio work while attending Ohio State College. Following jobs as announcer at WKST and disc jockey at WAKR, he moved to Cleveland's WJW in 1951, where, prompted by record shop owner Leo Mintz, he began playing black rhythm-and-blues records. The songs, played as "rock-and-roll" to avoid any racial stigma, proved unexpectedly popular among white youth and, as a consequence, Freed started producing rock-and-roll concerts. His first, staged in Cleveland in March 1952, was oversold and subsequently canceled, leading to rock-and-roll's first riot. In September 1954 Freed moved to New York's WINS, where his rock-and-roll show made the station the city's most popular among white audiences. During the mid-Fifties, he began taking partial songwriting credit for songs such as The Moonglows' "Sincerely" and Chuck Berry's "Maybellene." Freed's concert promotion activities culminated in the establishment of box office records at New York's Paramount Theater in 1957. He also appeared in some of the earliest rock-and-roll movies, including *Rock Around the Clock.*

However, Alan Freed's decline began in March 1958, when a stabbing and a number of beatings occurred at one of his concerts in Boston. Rock-and-roll shows were subsequently banned in several cities and Freed was charged with inciting to riot and unlawful destruction of property, charges that were finally dismissed 17 months later. He quit WINS and switched to New York's WABC, only to be fired in November 1959 for refusing "on principle" to sign statements denying his acceptance of bribes for playing records. Becoming the brunt of the entire anti-rock-and-roll movement, Freed was indicted in 1960 for accepting $30,000 in "payola" and eventually pleaded guilty in March 1963 for taking $2700 from two companies. Run out of New York City, he worked briefly for KDAY in Los Angeles. Charged with income tax evasion in 1964, Freed died in ignominy and obscurity on January 20, 1965, at the age of 42, in Palm Springs, California. Some belated recognition of his contribution to rock-and-roll came with the 1978 release of the Paramount Pictures film *American Hot Wax*, a fictionalized "week in the life of rock-and-roll," with Alan Freed as its central character.

THE FUGS. Composed of three Beat-generation poets, The Fugs sought to stir Sixties audiences with outrageous and iconoclastic poetry, satire, and outright obscenity in their songs primarily concerned with sex, drugs, and politics. One of the earliest rock satire groups and certainly the first "underground" group, The Fugs' pioneering efforts paved the way for the premeditated offensiveness of Frank Zappa's Mothers of Invention, The Stooges, Alice Cooper, and the Seventies "punk rockers," and the silliness of Flo and Eddie and Cheech and Chong.

Conceived by Beat poets Ed Sanders and Tuli Kupferberg near the end of 1964, The Fugs also included poet–drummer Ken Weaver and a variety of guitarists, bassists, keyboard players, and other musicians. Kansas City-raised Sanders, a former classical languages major at New York University, had published *Poem from Jail* in 1963 and served as editor of "Fuck You" and as owner–manager of the Peace Eye Bookstore in New York's Lower East Side. Missourian Kupferberg, an avowed anarchist, had published *Snow Job; Poems: 1946–1959* in 1959. Debuting at Greenwich Village's Folklore Center, the ever-changing Fugs later occupied the Players Theater on MacDougal Street, logging some 900 consecutive performances there. Their first album for the small Broadside label, later reissued on the esperanto label ESP, included a sampling of their songs concerned with sex, drugs, and contemporary life such as "Slum Goddess," "I Couldn't Get High," "Boobs a Lot," and "Nothing." Their self-titled second album (undoubtedly their best seller) contained Sanders' "Group Grope" and "Dirty Old Man," Kupferberg's anti-war "Kill for Peace," and the uncommonly lyrical "Morning, Morning," composed by Kupferberg and included on Richie Havens' *Mixed Bag* album. The postponed or repressed *Virgin Fugs*, eventually released in 1968, sported Fugs classics such as "Caca Rock," "Coca Cola Douche," and "New Amphetamine Shriek."

Seemingly on the verge of a major breakthrough, The Fugs switched to Reprise Records. Their debut for the label, *Tenderness Junction*, fared poorly, but *It Crawled into My Hand, Honest* at least managed modest sales. The latter album included "Johnny Pissoff Meets the Red Angel," "Burial Waltz," and "National Haiku Contest." However, by the release of

Belle of Avenue A, The Fugs' had disbanded, to see the posthumous release of the live set, *Golden Filth*, in 1970. Weaver subsequently returned to the Southwest, whereas Sanders remained with Reprise for two obscure albums. Kupferberg, who had recorded *No Deposit, No Return* for ESP, later compiled the book, *Listen to the Mockingbird: Satiric Songs to Tunes You Know*, published in 1973. Ed Sanders returned to writing in 1971 with *The Family*, chronicling the story of the Charlie Manson commune, and *Tales of Beatnik Glory*, published in 1975. He resurfaced in 1979 with the irreverent two-hour "Karen Silkwood Cantata," performed at the Creative Musical Studio near Woodstock, New York.

THE FUGS

Ballads of Contemporary Protest, Point of Views, and General Dissatisfaction	Broadside	304(M)	February '66	
reissued as The Fugs' First Album	ESP	1018	October '66	
The Fugs	ESP	1028	June '66	
The Virgin Fugs	ESP	1038	September '68	
Rounder's Score (with Holy Modal Rounders 4)	ESP	2018	August '75	
Tenderness Junction	Reprise	6280	January '68	
It Crawled into My Hand, Honest	Reprise	6305	September '68	
Belle of Avenue A	Reprise	6359	November '69	
Golden Filth	Reprise	6396	August '70	A

TULI KUPFERBERG

No Deposit, No Return	ESP	1035	

ED SANDERS

Sanders' Truckstop	Reprise	RS–6374	February '70
Beer Cans on the Moon	Reprise	MS–2105	September '72

MARVIN GAYE. One of the most popular singles artists for the Tamla–Motown organization during the Sixties, Marvin Gaye was teamed with several of Motown's female singers during the decade, most successfully with the late Tammi Terrell. Perhaps the most flexible Motown artist, Marvin Gaye made a smooth transition from early gospel-style recordings to a rather pop-oriented sound that emphasized his smooth, sensual tenor voice. Still later he stunned both music fans and his wary record company with 1971's *What's Going On* album. Probably the first "concept" album by a black artist, *What's Going On* revealed a poignant and passionate concern with urban decay, ecological crises, and spiritual impoverishment without being overbearing or didactic. Thus established as a songwriter, producer, and album artist, Marvin Gaye was able to become one of the first Motown artists to achieve a measure of independence from the label. Eschewing social commentary in favor of straightforward romantic material for *Let's Get It On*, possibly his most popular album, Marvin Gaye is one of the few Motown acts to maintain popularity throughout the Seventies while remaining with the label. Certainly one of today's premier soul singer–songwriters, Marvin Gaye, along with Stevie Wonder, has managed to forge an identity separate from the corporate one—in contrast to Motown's other remaining top artist, Diana Ross, who seems subservient to the will of overlord Berry Gordy, Jr.

Born on April 2, 1939, and raised in his native Washington, D.C., Marvin Gaye played organ and sang in his father's church choir. During high school he studied piano while learning drums as well. In the mid-Fifties he was a member of the local vocal group, The Rainbows, which also included Don Covay and Billy Stewart. Gaye later formed his own group, only to join Harvey Fuqua's reconstituted Moonglows around 1958. Spotted performing in Detroit in 1961 by Berry Gordy, Jr., Gaye was signed to the fledgling family of Motown labels, where he initially acted as a sessions drummer; he later toured with Smokey Robinson and The Miracles for six months. He started recording solo on the Tamla label and had his first moderate hit with "Stubborn Kind of Fellow," recorded with The Vandellas, in late 1962. A string of major hits in both the rhythm-and-blues and pop fields followed with "Hitch Hike," "Pride and Joy" (which Gaye co-wrote), and "Can I Get a Witness" in 1963. A more pop-oriented sound emerged in 1964 for the hits "You're a Wonderful One" (by

Holland–Dozier–Holland), "Try It Baby," the overlooked "Baby, Don't You Do It," and "How Sweet It Is to Be Loved by You" (by H–D–H).

During 1964 Marvin Gaye began with Mary Wells a series of associations with Motown organization female singers. The duet produced the two-sided hit "What's the Matter with You, Baby/Once upon a Time," whereas Gaye and Kim Weston had a minor hit with "What Good Am I Without You" later that year. An established singles artist by 1965, Gaye continued his hit-making ways with "I'll Be Doggone" and "Ain't That Peculiar," both co-written by Smokey Robinson. After hitting with "It Takes Two" in tandem with Kim Weston in early 1967, Gaye started recording with Tammi Terrell. Their hits over the next two years included four Nicholas Ashford–Valerie Simpson compositions, "Ain't No Mountain High Enough," "Your Precious Love," "Ain't Nothing Like the Real Thing," and "You're All I Need to Get By," as well as "If I Could Build My Whole World Around You." At the end of 1968 Gaye had a solo hit with the definitive version of Barrett Strong and Norman Whitfield's "I Heard It through the Grapevine," recorded by Gladys Knight and The Pips a year earlier. Subsequent hits by Gaye included "Too Busy Thinking about My Baby" and "That's the Way Love Is," but in 1969 he ceased touring after Tammi Terrell collapsed in his arms on stage. She died in March 1970 of a brain tumor.

After a protracted period of seclusion, Marvin Gaye re-emerged to demand more independence from the Motown organization. Eschewing the rigid singles format, he recorded and produced *What's Going On*, which featured sophisticated string and horn arrangements. The album, which revealed Gaye's growing concern with inner-city decay, ecology, and spiritual poverty, was reluctantly released on Tamla in mid-1971. With all songs either written or co-written by Gaye, the album ironically became one of Motown's best-selling albums, yielding smash singles with the title song (co-authored by Gaye, Alfred Cleveland, and The Four Tops' "Obie" Benson), "Mercy, Mercy Me (the Ecology)" and "Inner City Blues (Make Me Wanna Holler)." Gaye followed up the stunning success of *What's Going On* with the largely instrumental soundtrack to the film *Trouble Man*, from which the title song was yet another major hit.

In 1973 Marvin Gaye co-authored, co-produced, and recorded *Let's Get It On*, perhaps his most popular album. A dramatic contrast to *What's Going On*, *Let's Get It On* shunned social commentary in favor of straightforward romantic material. The title cut became a smash hit single, and other hit singles from the album included "Come Get to This" and "Distant Lover." Later that year Gaye was teamed with Diana Ross for an album that produced one major hit single, "My Mistake (Was to Love You)." Finally, in early 1974, Gaye returned to live performance at the Oakland (California) Coliseum, from which *Marvin Gaye Live!* resulted. *I Want You* produced the hit single title song, whereas *Live at the London Paladium*, a double-record set, yielded the smash hit "Got to Give It Up, Part 1." During 1979, bankrupt and the subject of divorce proceedings, Marvin Gaye issued the rather embittered double-record set, *Here, My Dear*.

MARVIN GAYE

Soulful Sounds of Marvin Gaye	Tamla	221(M)	'62	
"That Stubborn Kinda Fellow"	Tamla	239(M)	March '63	
Live on Stage	Tamla	242(M)	November '63	
When I'm Alone, I Cry	Tamla	251(M)	June '64	
Hello, Broadway	Tamla	259	January '65	
How Sweet It Is (to Be Loved by You)	Tamla	258	February '65	
A Tribute to the Great Nat King Cole	Tamla	261	February '66	
Moods of Marvin Gaye	Tamla	266	July '66	
In the Groove	Tamla	285	October '68	
M.P.G.	Tamla	292	June '69	
That's the Way Love Is	Tamla	299	October '69	

MARVIN GAYE AND MARY WELLS

Marvin and Mary Together	Motown	613(M)	May '64	

MARVIN GAYE AND KIM WESTON

It Takes Two	Tamla	270	October '66	

MARVIN GAYE AND TAMMI TERRELL

United	Tamla	277	October '67	
You're All I Need to Get By	Tamla	284	September '68	
Easy	Tamla	294	October '69	
Greatest Hits	Tamla	7–302	June '70	A
Motown Superstar Series, Volume 2	Motown	5–102		A

MARVIN GAYE, TAMMI TERRELL, MARY WELLS, AND KIM WESTON

His Girls	Tamla	293	June '69	

MARVIN GAYE

What's Going On	Tamla	7–310	June '71	A
Trouble Man (soundtrack)	Tamla	5–322	December '72	
Let's Get It On	Tamla	7–329	August '73	A

MARVIN GAYE AND DIANA ROSS

Diana and Marvin/ Ross and Gaye	Motown	7–803	October '73	A

MARVIN GAYE

Live!	Tamla	6–333	June '74	
I Want You	Tamla	6–342	March '76	
Live at the London Palladium	2-Tamla	7–352	March '77	
Here, My Dear	2-Tamla	13–364	January '79	A
Love Man	Tamla	8–369	February '80	
In Our Lifetime	Tamla	8–374	February '81	A

MARVIN GAYE ANTHOLOGIES AND COMPILATIONS

Greatest Hits	Tamla	7–252	April '64	A
Greatest Hits, Volume 2	Tamla	278	September '67	
Super Hits	Tamla	7–300	November '70	
Anthology	3-Motown	9–791	March '74	A
Greatest Hits	Tamla	7–348	September '76	A
Motown Superstar Series, Volume 15	Motown	5–115		A

THE J. GEILS BAND. Hard-driving Seventies rock and blues band from the Boston region, The J. Geils Band are more effective in front of an audience than on recordings. In the process of becoming one of America's premier live acts through more than ten years of touring, The J. Geils Band has scored only one major hit single, yet four gold-award albums.

Formed around 1967 in the Boston area as The J. Geils Blues Band, the group developed a devoted local following before signing with Atlantic Records in 1969. The members: guitarist J. Geils (born February 20, 1946), lead vocalist Peter Wolf (born March 7, 1946), harmonica player Magic Dick (born May 13, 1945), keyboardist Seth Justman, bassist Danny Klein, and drummer Stephen Bladd. The band's self-titled debut album was virtually overlooked, although it did contain the underground favorite, "First I Look at the Purse." Their second, *The Morning After*, did yield the group's first moderate hit with "Looking for a Love." As the band continually criss-crossed the United States in search of a wider audience, they recorded the live *Full House* set. *Bloodshot*, The J. Geils Band's first certified gold-award album, produced a moderate hit with "Give It to Me," but *Ladies Invited* sold far less well. *Nightmares* fared much better, yielding the group's only major hit, "Must of Got Lost." After *Hotline* and yet another live set, *Blow Your Face Out*, the band became merely Geils for their final Atlantic album, the self-produced *Monkey Island*. In 1978 the group switched to EMI–America for *Sanctuary* and the moderate hit "One Last Kiss." They have resumed using the name J. Geils Band. *Love Stinks*, from 1980, yielded the moderate hits "Come Back" and "Love Stinks."

THE J. GEILS BAND

The J. Geils Band	Atlantic	SD–8275	January '71	A
The Morning After	Atlantic	SD–8297	October '71	A
Full House*	Atlantic	SD–7241	October '72	A
Bloodshot*	Atlantic	SD–7260	April '73	A
Ladies Invited	Atlantic	SD–7286	November '73	
Nightmares and Other Tales from the Vinyl Jungle	Atlantic	SD–18107	October '74	A
Hotline	Atlantic	SD–18147	September '75	
Blow Your Face Out	2-Atlantic	SD2–507	May '76	A

GEILS

Monkey Island	Atlantic	SD–19103	June '77	A

THE J. GEILS BAND

Best	Atlantic	SD–19234	June '79	A
Best, Volume 2	Atlantic	19284	November '80	A
Sanctuary*	EMI–America	SO–17006	December '78	
Love Stinks*	EMI–America	SOO–17016	February '80	A
Freeze Frame	EMI–America	SOO–17062	December '81	A

GENESIS. One of several so-called "progressive-rock" groups from England active during the Seventies, Genesis favored a variety of keyboards and synthesizers, as did Yes and Emerson, Lake, and Palmer. However, inasmuch as Genesis was originally formed as a songwriters' collective, the emphasis was on the songs rather than on virtuoso musicianship. Achieving their first significant British press coverage with frontman Peter Gabriel's use of mime and costuming in performance during 1972, Genesis attempted their American breakthrough as a headline act rather than as a supporting act. Indeed, Genesis has always headlined on tour in the United States. Following *Selling England by the Pound*, in which the group explored their favorite themes of myth, legend, and fantasy, Genesis recorded their tour de force, *The Lamb Lies Down on Broadway*, an elaborate album combining a story line with surreal lyrics and hailed by some as the definitive concept album. Employing progressively ambitious stage presentations for subsequent tours, Genesis' success can be credited as much to their visual and theatrical in-concert performances as to their songwriting and musicianship. Oddly, following the departure of Gabriel, Genesis became even more popular, much to the surprise of critics, as Gabriel pursued his own successful solo career.

Genesis was formed in January 1967 as a songwriters' collective by four students at England's Charterhouse School—Peter Gabriel (born May 13,

1950), Tony Banks (born March 27, 1950, in East Hoathly, England), Mike Rutherford (born October or November 2, 1950, in Guilford, England), and Anthony Phillips. During 1968, under producer Jonathan King the group recorded their first album, which was initially released in the United States as *In the Beginning*, later reissued as *From Genesis to Revelation*, and finally reissued under the original U.S. title. The album was generally overlooked and the group was released from its recording contract after a year. With the addition of John Mayhew (drums), Genesis was Peter Gabriel (lead vocals), Anthony Phillips (lead guitar), Tony Banks (keyboards, 12-string guitar, backup vocals), and Mike Rutherford (bass, 12-string guitar, backup vocals). This grouping recorded *Trespass* for the ABC subsidiary Impulse in the United States (Charisma in England), after which Phillips and Mayhew departed. Drummer–backup vocalist Phil Collins (born January 30 or 31, 1951, in London) was recruited and, several months later, lead and 12-string guitarist Steve Hackett (born February 12, 1950) joined Genesis.

For *Nursery Cryme*, on Charisma Records, Genesis featured extensive use of the mellotron. The album contained two Genesis favorites, "Musical Box" and "Return of the Giant Hogweed," garnered rave reviews in England, and helped expand the group's cult following in the United States. Around the same time, the band began experimenting with visuals and theatrics in performance that later became the group's trademark. Peter Gabriel came to be the visual focus of Genesis, utilizing mime, costuming, and lengthy song introductions on stage. *Foxtrot* included several Genesis favorites such as "Watcher of the Skies" and the 23-minute "Supper's Ready," the latter employing elaborate costuming by Gabriel and spectacular lighting in performance. In December 1972 Genesis, attempting to generate a following beyond its cult status, debuted in the United States as a headline act. The group's reputation at home was enhanced by a subsequent British tour, though their next album, *Genesis Live*, was held up for a year before American release.

Genesis' first major breakthrough into the American market came with *Selling England by the Pound*. Featuring further songwriting developments on themes from myth, legend, and fantasy as well as Banks' synthesizer work and several songs in odd time signatures, the album contained the group's first English hit, "I Know What I Like." With their reputation secure as a major British band by 1974, Genesis switched to Atlantic Records for the double-record "concept" album, *The Lamb Lies Down on Broadway*. Written in its entirety by Peter Gabriel, the album traced the surreal contemporary adventures of its hero, Rael, in the harsh New York City environment. The subsequent British and American tours virtually duplicated the album in performance, with Gabriel portraying Rael through a series of odd costume changes.

However, in May 1975, Peter Gabriel, weary from near-constant touring and recording, departed from Genesis. Inasmuch as Gabriel had been (incorrectly) assumed to be the band's musical leader and chief songwriter, critics began predicting the demise of Genesis. Phil Collins soon took over the lead vocal chores for subsequent recordings, the first of which, *A Trick of the Tail,* proved even more successful than *The Lamb Lies Down on Broadway.* For the first time, the songs were credited to individual members rather than to the group as a whole. In the meantime Steve Hackett had recorded his first solo album, *Voyage of the Acolyte,* with Rutherford and Collins, and Phil Collins did sessions and worked with yet another band, Brand X.

In order to free Collins from his drumming duties, Genesis recruited former King Crimson and Yes drummer Bill Bruford for their 1976 tours of North America, England, and Europe. The group's next album, *Wind and Wuthering,* recorded in Holland, astoundingly fared even better than *A Trick of the Tail* and yielded Genesis' first American singles chart entry with "Your Own Special Way." For their worldwide 1977 tour, they used all new sound and lighting equipment, this time enlisting the services of drummer Chester Thompson (born in Baltimore, Maryland, on December 11, 1948). The 1976 and 1977 tours were later documented on *Seconds Out.* However, shortly before its release, Steve Hackett dropped out to concentrate on a solo career. During 1977 original Genesis guitarist Anthony Phillips initiated a solo recording career, with his first album produced by Mike Rutherford. Moreover, after 18 months of recuperation and keyboard training, Peter Gabriel was back with his surprisingly successful debut solo album, which included the minor hit "Solsbury Hill."

Reduced to a trio and augmented by Thompson and new guitarist Daryl Stuermer (born in Milwaukee, Wisconsin, on November 27, 1952), Genesis recorded the appropriately titled *. . . And Then There Were Three,* with Rutherford playing all guitar and bass parts. The album was certified gold-award the year of its release and yielded a major hit single with "Follow You, Follow Me." Around the same time Chrysalis Records issued the modestly successful *Please Don't Touch* for Steve Hackett, whereas Passport Records released *Wise after the Event* for Anthony Phillips. Also, Peter Gabriel recorded a second surprisingly successful self-titled album with producer–guitarist Robert Fripp. In 1979 further releases included Hackett's *Spectral Mornings* and Tony Banks' solo debut, *A Curious Feeling.* During 1980 Gabriel scored a moderate hit with "Games Without Frontiers," as Genesis achieved a major hit with "Misunderstanding" from the gold-award *Duke.* Phil Collins' *Face Value* was certified gold-award the year of its release, 1981.

GENESIS

In the Beginning	Mercury	61175	November '68	
reissued as From Genesis to Revelation	London	643	October '74	
reissued as In the Beginning	London	50006	September '77	A
Trespass	Impulse	AS–9205	September '70	
	reissued on ABC/MCA	AB–816		A
Nursery Cryme	Charisma	CAS–1052	September '71	
Foxtrot	Charisma	CAS–1058	October '72	

The Best (reissue of above two albums)	2-Buddah	5659	April '76	
Nursery Cryme/ Foxtrot	2-Charisma	2701	November '79	
Selling England by the Pound	Charisma/ Famous	FC–6060	November '73	A
Genesis Live	Charisma	CAS–1666	May '74	
The Lamb Lies Down on Broadway	2-Atlantic	401	November '74	A
A Trick of the Tail	Atco	SD36–129 reissued as SD38–101	March '76	A

BRAND X (WITH PHIL COLLINS)

Unorthodox Behaviour	Passport	9819	November '76	A
Moroccan Roll	Passport	9822	April '77	A
Livestock	Passport	9824	November '77	A
Masques	Passport	9829	October '78	A
Product	Passport	9840	December '79	A
Do They Hurt	Passport	9845	July '80	A

GENESIS

Wind and Wuthering	Atco	SD36–144	January '77	
Seconds Out	2-Atlantic	9002	November '77	A
. . . And Then There Were Three*	Atlantic	SD–19173	March '78	A
Duke*	Atlantic	16014	April '80	A
Abacab	Atlantic	19313	October '81	A

STEVE HACKETT

Voyage of the Acolyte	Chrysalis	CHR–1112	April '76	A
Please Don't Touch	Chrysalis	CHR–1176	April '78	A
Spectral Mornings	Chrysalis	CHR–1223	June '79	A
Defector	Charisma	3103	August '80	A
Cured	Epic	FE–37632	October '81	A

PETER GABRIEL

Peter Gabriel	Atco	SD36–147	February '77	A
Peter Gabriel	Atlantic	SD–19181	June '78	
Peter Gabriel	Mercury	3848	June '80	A

ANTHONY PHILLIPS

The Geese and the Ghost	Passport	98020	February '77	

Wise after the Event	Passport	9828	July '78	A
Sides	Passport	9834	July '80	A

TONY BANKS

A Curious Feeling	Charisma	CA1–2207	December '79	A

MIKE RUTHERFORD

Smallcreep's Day	Passport	9843	April '80	A

PHIL COLLINS

Face Value*	Atlantic	16029	March '81	A

STEVE GOODMAN. A Seventies writer of songs alternately poignant and humorous, singer–guitarist Steve Goodman is best known as the author of Arlo Guthrie's 1972 hit, "City of New Orleans." An energetic and enthusiastic performer projecting an impish sense of humor on stage, Steve Goodman has yet to receive much-deserved recognition, despite his obvious songwriting talents and boisterous stage presence.

STEVE GOODMAN

Steve Goodman	Buddah	BDS–5096	January '72	
Somebody Else's Troubles	Buddah	BDS–5121	December '72	
The Essential Steve Goodman	2-Buddah	BDS–5665	November '76	
Jessie's Jig and Other Favorites	Asylum	7E–1037	July '75	
Words We Can Dance To	Asylum	7E–1061	April '76	A
Say It in Private	Asylum	7E–1118	October '77	A
High and Outside	Asylum	6E–174	March '79	A
Hot Spot	Asylum	297	October '80	A
Gathering at the Earl of Old Town	Mountain Railroad	670	'80	

BERRY GORDY, JR. Founder–owner of the Tamla–Motown family of record labels, Berry Gordy, Jr., in conjunction with William "Smokey" Robinson, established Motown Records as an important independent record label in the early Sixties through a series of rhythm-and-blues–style hit singles by groups such as The Marvelettes, Martha and The Vandellas, and Robinson's own Miracles. With Motown Records becoming the largest and most successful independent record company in the United States by 1964, Gordy, Robinson, and the Brian Holland–Lamont Dozier–Eddie

Holland team subsequently created a sophisticated commercial blend of gospel and pop musics recognized as distinct from raunchier rhythm-and-blues. This new sound, effectively labeled as "soul" music, proved enormously popular with white as well as with black audiences and encouraged the ascendancy of black vocal groups throughout the Sixties. Berry Gordy, Jr.'s, role in the rise of Motown Records resulted from his astute sense of business administration, his uncanny sense of the country's musical taste, and his ability to recognize talent and inspire it to its fullest potential. Creatively, much credit is due to the songwriting and production efforts of Smokey Robinson and the Holland–Dozier–Holland team for actually developing the new sound.

Berry Gordy, Jr., exercised an unprecedented degree of control over the careers of his acts, subjecting them to rigorous discipline and directing that they be taught how to dance, dress, and present themselves as stars. With Motown Records firmly established in the singles market by the mid-Sixties, Gordy transformed many of his essentially teen-oriented singers into artists of widespread appeal. Thus his acts were introduced into the American supper club and prime-time television fields and promoted on a worldwide basis, all the while projecting an image of respectability and wholesomeness. However, by 1966 his acts were displaying a high degree of homogeneity in their sound, and during 1967 he was being seriously challenged in the rhythm-and-blues/soul field by Stax–Volt acts such as Sam and Dave and Otis Redding and by Atlantic's Aretha Franklin and Wilson Pickett. Gordy suffered a major setback in 1968, when Holland–Dozier–Holland left the company, which led to experimentation with so-called "psychedelic soul" music for The Temptations under producer Norman Whitfield. The apparent creative exhaustion of Smokey Robinson by 1969 also did not bode well for the company; Gordy was nonetheless able to establish Diana Ross, whose every career step he had personally supervised, as a solo act following her departure from The Supremes in 1970.

Bolstered by the success of the teen-oriented Jackson Five, which eventually became Motown's best-selling singles act, Berry Gordy, Jr., moved the Motown family of record labels from Detroit to Hollywood in 1970. He was able to maintain the position of Motown Industries, as it then became known, by the emergence of Marvin Gaye and Stevie Wonder (the first acts granted artistic independence) as album-oriented singer–songwriters with *What's Going On* (1971) and *Music of My Mind* (1972), respectively. Moreover, the establishment of Diana Ross as the company's first all-around entertainer—in supper clubs, on television and film (*Lady Sings the Blues* in 1972), as well as with recordings—upheld the company's reputation in the entertainment industry. However, in the mid-Seventies many major artists left the company in reaction to its allegedly oppressive artistic policy. Martha Reeves of The Vandellas and The Four Tops moved to new record labels in 1974, as did Gladys Knight and The Pips and The Jackson Five in 1975. Though again seriously challenged in the mid-Seventies, this time by Kenny Gamble and Leon Huff's Philadelphia International Records (particularly with their act The O'Jays), and enduring continued defections (The Temptations in 1976, The Miracles in 1977),

Motown was able to further its successes with acts such as The Commodores.

NOTE: Berry Gordy's aloofness from the entertainment industry is well documented. Readers should be aware that the Motown family of record labels (Tamla, Motown, Gordy, Soul) have only recently submitted sales figures to the Recording Industry Association of America. The RIAA is the organization that certifies gold- and platinum-award records. Thus, few Motown records have ever been so certified, despite extensive sales.

Detroit-born on November 28, 1929, Berry Gordy, Jr., dropped out of high school to become a featherweight boxer. Drafted into the army, upon his discharge in 1953 he set up a record store which soon went bankrupt. Subsequently working on a Ford Motor Company assembly line, Gordy began writing songs during the mid-Fifties. His first song sale, to Decca, was "Reet Petite," Jackie Wilson's first, albeit minor, pop hit in 1957. Gordy's earliest major songwriting success came with "Lonely Teardrops," also recorded by Jackie Wilson, in 1958. With funds provided by that hit, Gordy began producing records for Eddie Holland and Marv Johnson, and Johnson scored a big hit with Gordy's "You Got What It Takes" in 1959. Encouraged by songwriter–friend William "Smokey" Robinson, Gordy borrowed money from his family to found Tammie Records, soon changed to Tamla Records. The label's first significant success occurred as distributor of Barrett Strong's "Money," on his sister's Anna label. Later in 1960, "Shop Around," co-written by Gordy and Robinson, became Tamla's first smash hit for Robinson's Miracles, establishing Tamla as an important independent record label. Eddie Holland's brother Brian subsequently collaborated on early hits by The Marvelettes, as Robinson worked with Mary Wells for a series of hits in 1962 on the newly formed Motown label. Before year's end, The Contours scored with the raucous "Do You Love Me," written by Gordy, on yet another label, Gordy.

As the Motown family of labels developed local Detroit talent, Brian and Eddie Holland teamed with songwriter Lamont Dozier in 1963 to create a distinctive pop sound that appealed to white as well as black audiences. Initially working with the rather raw-sounding Martha and The Vandellas, Holland–Dozier–Holland achieved massive songwriting and production success with The Supremes between 1964 and 1967. The team also wrote and produced major hits for Marvin Gaye, The Four Tops, and Martha and The Vandellas during that time. In the meantime, Smokey Robinson was writing hits for Mary Wells, The Temptations,- Marvin Gaye, and his own Miracles. Gordy concentrated his attentions on Diana Ross, front person of The Supremes, seeking to establish her as a major pop star by personally supervising every stage of her career.

Recognized by 1964 as the largest independent record company through its successes in the singles market, Motown diversified into an entertainment complex. The previously established Jobete Music Company handled song publishing and copywriting, whereas Hitsville, U.S.A. controlled the company's recording studios, and International Talent Management trained artists in matters of deportment. Berry Gordy, Jr.'s, unprecedented concern with career management, coupled with the rigorous discipline imposed on artists, alienated some of his acts and led to the company's first defection in 1964 by Mary Wells. Nonetheless, between 1964 and 1967 Motown became respectable as acts originally aimed at teen audiences were groomed for the adult pop market. Thus acts were introduced into the American supper club and prime-time television fields while the company was simultaneously establishing itself internationally. A high degree of homogeneity in the sound of Motown acts was recognizable after 1966 (with Jr. Walker and The All Stars and Gladys Knight and The Pips being the primary exceptions on yet another label, Soul), leading to serious challenges by Atlantic and Stax–Volt artists in the pop and rhythm-and-blues/soul fields. During 1967, to create a higher degree of visibility of several of its singers, three Motown acts were renamed: The Supremes became Diana Ross and The Supremes; The Miracles, Smokey Robinson and The Miracles; and Martha and The Vandellas, Martha Reeves and The Vandellas. Later, Motown experimented with so-called "psychedelic soul" for The Temptations under songwriter–producer Norman Whitfield, initially in collaboration with Eddie Holland, later in collaboration with Barrett Strong following the bitter departure of Holland–Dozier–Holland in 1968.

As he endured the loss of Holland–Dozier–Holland and the apparent exhaustion of Smokey Robinson's songwriting abilities, Berry Gordy, Jr., continued to concentrate on the career of Diana Ross as a solo act separate from The Supremes, beginning in 1970. Maintaining the company's success with the astounding popularity of the teen-oriented Jackson Five (eventually Motown's best selling singles act), Gordy moved to Los Angeles in 1970 and established Motown Industries, expanding his interests to a Broadway musical and films in addition to previous recording and performing concerns. Bolstered by the success of Marvin Gaye and Stevie Wonder (the first acts to achieve considerable independence from the company) as album-oriented singer–songwriters with *What's Going On* (1971) and *Music of My Mind* (1972), respectively, Motown was nonetheless challenged in the pop and soul fields by Kenny Gamble and Leon Huff's Philadelphia International Records by 1973, particularly by The O'Jays. During the first half of the Seventies, Diana Ross was established as Motown's first all-around entertainer by her achieving success in supper clubs and films—*Lady Sings the Blues* in 1972, *Mahogany* in 1975—as well as through recordings. However, Motown suffered a series of major defections during the mid-Seventies. Martha Reeves began recording solo on a variety of labels in 1974, and The Four Tops switched to ABC–Dunhill. In 1975 The Jackson Five moved to Epic and Gladys Knight and The Pips to Buddah. The Miracles without Smokey Robinson (Robinson had pursued a conspicuously unsuccessful solo career since 1973) switched to Columbia in 1977, and The Temptations went to Atlantic. Nevertheless, Berry Gordy, Jr., has maintained the status of Motown Industries as the largest black-owned and operated company in America on the strength of the careers of Diana Ross, Marvin Gaye, and Stevie Wonder, and recent acts such as The Commodores.

BILL GRAHAM. Rock music's most famous entrepreneur and concert promoter of the Sixties and Seventies, Bill Graham established the first and most famous ballroom at San Francisco's Fillmore Auditorium in 1966. While booking virtually every major rock act except The Beatles over the next five years, Graham encouraged and, in part, inspired the growth of the so-called "San Francisco sound" in the late Sixties. With the openings of Fillmore West in San Francisco and Fillmore East in New York City during 1968, Bill Graham advanced the ballroom rock concert scene that spread across the country in the late Sixties and died off in the early Seventies due to increased expenses. An early enthusiast for both rock poster art and "light shows," Graham effectively established the standards by which all rock concert promotions were subsequently judged. Bill Graham, one of the last rock concert promoters to close his small-sized hall, maintained his medium-sized Winterland hall through the end of 1979, when the popularity of huge festivals and baseball stadium concerts, in conjunction with exorbitant artists' demands and obnoxious audience behavior, led to the obsolescence of such venues. Now again involved in concert promotions and the management of several major rock acts, Graham must also be credited with attempting to enlarge the musical spectrum of rock fans by booking such non-rock acts as Miles Davis, Rahsaan Roland Kirk, and The Staples Singers into his halls.

Born Wolfgang Grajonca in Berlin, Germany, in 1931, Bill Graham moved to the United States in 1941, formally changing his name in 1949 when granted citizenship. He later served in the U.S. Army and graduated from New York City College before moving to the San Francisco Bay area. Leaving his executive position with a farm equipment company, Bill Graham took over management of the radical street-theater improvisational group, The Mime Troupe, in 1965. To raise funds for The Mime Troupe, he promoted a benefit concert of Bay area musicians at San Francisco's Longshoremen's Hall on November 6, 1965. On December 10, 1965, Graham promoted another benefit concert at the Fillmore Auditorium in one of San Francisco's black ghettos with The Jefferson Airplane, The Great Society (with Grace Slick), and The Warlocks (later The Grateful Dead). The financial and artistic success of the benefits, along with his subsequent promotion of the now-legendary Trips Festival at the Longshoremen's Hall in January 1966, led Graham to the regular presentation of rock shows at the Fillmore Auditorium. By year's end, he was also presenting concerts at the larger 5400-seat Winterland Arena and managing, if briefly, The Jefferson Airplane. The concerts became astoundingly successful and featured both unknown local talent and big-name outside acts.

In early 1968 the disgruntled Jefferson Airplane and Grateful Dead took over an old dance hall on San Francisco's Market Street called The Carousel. Bill Graham, who had opened Fillmore East in New York City in March 1968, assumed management of The Carousel as Fillmore West in August 1968, following his departure from the original Fillmore. Over the next three years, he presented virtually every major rock act at the

Fillmores while also giving unknown acts a chance to perform and booking a number of non-rock acts such as Miles Davis and The Staples Singers. Graham's enormous success with the Fillmores encouraged the establishment of ballrooms such as his across the country and marked the heyday of concert rock. He opened the talent booking agency, Millard, in October 1968, and established Fillmore and San Francisco Records in February 1969, recording Cold Blood and Elvin Bishop before dissolving the labels at the beginning of 1972. The Woodstock Festival of August 1969, however, presaged the demise of the ballroom concert scene, as audiences grew larger and expenses increased. As ballrooms across the country folded in 1970–71, Graham announced his intention to close the Fillmores.

By July 1971 both Fillmore East and Fillmore West had been closed, and a weary Bill Graham "retired" from the concert promotion business. Nonetheless, he was back by 1972, producing The Rolling Stones' tour. He subsequently booked acts into the Winterland Arena and later produced Bob Dylan's come-back tour and Crosby, Stills, Nash, and Young's reunion tour, both in 1974. By 1978 the Winterland venue had also become obsolete, giving way to the impersonal and lucrative festivals and stadium concerts. On New Year's Eve 1978–79, The New Riders of the Purple Sage, The Blues Brothers, and The Grateful Dead played the final performance at Winterland, a hall once castigated as overly large and acoustically unsound, but now sorely missed. Today Bill Graham remains active in the rock music business by presenting shows in northern California, running a lighting, sound, and staging service, and managing the careers of Ronnie Montrose, Eddie Money, Bobby Bare, and Carlos Santana. During 1980 Graham entered the nightclub business for the first time, purchasing San Francisco's most successful club, the Old Waldorf.

GRAND FUNK RAILROAD. Blisteringly loud American "heavy metal" band of the Seventies, the power trio Grand Funk Railroad scored an astounding series of 11 consecutive gold-award albums despite minimal radio airplay and scathingly hostile critical reception. One of the earliest American "heavy metal" bands, Grand Funk Railroad has the dubious distinction of being one of the first bands to attain massive popularity through "hype" and constant touring rather than through exceptional musical talent or a series of best-selling singles. Disbanding in 1976, Grand Funk re-formed under Mark Farner in 1981.

TERRY KNIGHT AND THE PACK

Terry Knight and The Pack	Lucky Eleven	8000	November '66
The Best of Mark Farner, Terry Knight, and Donnie Brewer	Lucky Eleven	8001	

Reflections	Cameo	C–2007		
Mark, Don, and Terry—1966–1967	ABKCO	AB–4217	November '72	

GRAND FUNK RAILROAD

On Time*	Capitol	ST–307 reissued as SN–16178	October '69	A
Grand Funk*	Capitol	SKAO–406 reissued as SN–16177	January '70	A
Closer to Home*	Capitol	SKAO–471 reissued as SN–16176	July '70	A
Live Album*	Capitol	SWBB–633	December '70	A
Survival*	Capitol	SW–764	April '71	A
E Pluribus Funk*	Capitol	SW–853	November '71	A
Mark, Don, and Mel 1969–1971*	2-Capitol	SABB–11042	May '72	
Phoenix*	Capitol	SMAS–11099	October '72	
We're an American Band*	Capitol	SMAS–11207	August '73	A
Shinin' On*	Capitol	SWAE–11278	March '74	
All the Girls in the World, Beware!!!*	Capitol	SO–11356	December '74	
Caught in the Act	2-Capitol	SABB–11445	September '75	A
Born to Die	Capitol	ST–11482	January '76	
Grand Funk Hits	Capitol	ST–11579 reissued as SN–12010 reissued as SN–16138	November '76 October '79	A
Good Singin', Good Playin'	MCA	2216	July '76	

MARK FARNER

Mark Farner	Atlantic	SD–18232	November '77	
No Frills	Atlantic	SD–19196	September '78	

GRAND FUNK RAILROAD

Lives	Full Moon/ Epic	3625	October '81	A

THE GRATEFUL DEAD. One of America's best-loved and most enduring bands since its inception during the heyday of "psychedelia" in San Francisco, The Grateful Dead has staunchly maintained an anticommercial show business stance that has nonetheless produced several durable and popular albums (though never a major hit single). Essentially a live band which performed marathon sets of two to five hours, often starting off sluggishly and ending spectacularly, The Grateful Dead have introduced as much free-form music into the body of rock as has any other essentially improvisatory group, their contribution based on the extraordinary lead guitar playing of Jerry Garcia and the virtuoso bass playing of Phil Lesh. Building an underground reputation by playing regularly and often for free (usually in San Francisco's Golden Gate Park), The Grateful Dead concentrated on live performances as most other area bands signed recording contracts. A true people's band, actually living in the Haight-Ashbury district during the "psychedelic" era, The Grateful Dead continue to approach rock music on their own terms, dividing funds communally and supporting a massive "family" entourage while eschewing virtually all the trappings of the rock stars they nonetheless became.

Initial recording success for The Grateful Dead naturally came with several live albums, but, following the enlistment of lyricist Robert Hunter, the group recorded two fine country-flavored albums that were eventually certified gold-award, *Workingman's Dead* and *American Beauty*. As one of rock music's least known major songwriters (along with Procol Harum's Keith Reid), Robert Hunter has been favorably compared to The Band's Robbie Robertson in his concern with the plight of the "little man" in the history and folklore of America during the last century. A remarkably independent and democratic band, The Grateful Dead's members have always retained the freedom to work in separate musical settings. Virtually all the members have recorded outside the group, most notably Jerry Garcia with The New Riders of the Purple Sage and with Old and In The Way, as well as solo, and Bob Weir with Kingfish and solo. Having developed the most loyal and devoted following in rock music— known as Deadheads—The Grateful Dead became the first rock band totally to finance their own independent record labels, with Grateful Dead Records in July 1973 and Round Records in January 1974, only to abandon the experiment in June 1975 because of distribution problems. Constantly turning profits back into their music in the form of new and advanced instruments and improved sound systems, The Grateful Dead toured throughout 1974 with a massive state-of-the-art sound system of remarkable clarity that has since been cannibalized and sold. Finally employing outside producers for 1977's *Terrapin Station* (Keith Olsen) and 1978's *Shakedown Street* (Lowell George of Little Feat), The Grateful Dead's current recorded sound includes elements of jazz and atonal improvisation, often underpinned with disco-style rhythms. In keeping with their reputation as a band regularly playing benefit concerts for free, The Grateful Dead played in Egypt at the foot of the Great Pyramids in September 1978, incurring expenses of approximately $500,000.

Born in San Francisco on August 1, 1942, Jerry Garcia obtained his first guitar, an electric guitar, at the age of 15. Dropping out of high school, he served a brief stint in the Army before returning to the Palo Alto area and forming a duo with Robert Hunter to play the local coffeehouse circuit in the early Sixties. Forming The Wildwood Boys with Hunter and David Nelson (later of The New Riders of the Purple Sage), Garcia, Hunter, and Nelson were later members of The Hart Valley Drifters, who won an amateur bluegrass contest at the Monterey Folk Festival in 1963. Garcia next helped form Mother McCree's Uptown Jug Champions, a jug band, with harmonica player Ron "Pig Pen" McKernan (born September 8, 1945, in San Bruno, California), guitarist Bob Weir (born October 16, 1947, in San Francisco), John "Marmaduke" Dawson (also later with The New Riders of the Purple Sage), and Bob Matthews, who later formed the electronic equipment development firm that provided The Grateful Dead's sound system, Alembic. The jug band went electric and Pig Pen switched to organ, and, by July 1965, the group had evolved into The Warlocks, with Garcia, Weir, Pig Pen, drummer Bill Kreutzman (born June 7, 1946, in Palo Alto, California), and Phil Lesh (born March 15, 1940, in Berkeley, California), a classically trained violinist and composer of 12-tone and electronic music. The Warlocks played at Bill Graham's first rock event at the Fillmore Auditorium in late 1965 and later at The Trips Festival and author Ken Kesey's infamous Acid Tests, chronicled in Tom Wolfe's *Electric Kool-Aid Acid Test.* Performing frequently, often for free in San Francisco's Golden Gate Park with The Jefferson Airplane and other area bands, The Warlocks became The Grateful Dead around the time the group moved into 710 Ashbury Street in the heart of the Haight-Ashbury district in June 1966. The members: Jerry Garcia (lead guitar, vocals), Bob Weir (rhythm guitar, vocals), Ron "Pig Pen" McKernan (harmonica, keyboards, vocals), Phil Lesh (bass), and Bill Kreutzman (drums).

Concentrating on live performances, The Grateful Dead eventually signed with Warner Brothers Records. Their self-titled debut album featured Pig Pen's gruff lead vocals on essentially blues-based material such as "Good Morning, Little School Girl" and "Morning Dew." During the summer of 1967 keyboardist Tom Constanten joined the group, as did percussionist–drummer Mickey Hart, thus freeing Lesh from his strictly rhythmic function on bass. The Grateful Dead's second album, *Anthem of the Sun,* released almost 18 months after the first, was again primarily blues-oriented. During 1969 keyboardist Tom Constanten departed the group, and they recruited Robert Hunter as full-time nonperforming lyricist. *Aoxomoxoa* contained several band favorites such as "St. Stephen" and "China Cat Sunflower," with lyrics by Hunter. In an effort to cash in on their reputation as a performing band, the group recorded the double-record live set, *Live Dead,* but the album fared no better than did prior releases.

In 1970 The Grateful Dead dropped their blues- and improvisatory-based sound in recording for a country-flavored, vocally rich, and much simplified sound that resulted in what many regard as the group's finest two albums, *Workingman's Dead* and *American Beauty*. The two albums featured some of Robert Hunter's most striking efforts as a songwriter. *Workingman's Dead* included the group's first, albeit minor, hit, "Uncle John's Band," as well as "Easy Wind," "Casey Jones," and "New Speedway Boogie," their "official" statement regarding the December 1969 debacle at Altamont Speedway with The Rolling Stones. Recorded with the assistance of The New Riders of the Purple Sage and featuring Jerry Garcia on pedal steel guitar, *American Beauty* included a number of Grateful Dead classics such as Pig Pen's "Operator," Weir and Hunter's "Sugar Magnolia," and the Hunter–Garcia collaborations "Candyman," "Till the Morning Comes," and "Truckin'," the group's second minor hit and one of their anthem songs.

By 1970 the remarkably diffuse outside activities of the members of The Grateful Dead had started. Having taken up pedal steel guitar several years earlier, Jerry Garcia played the instrument with former associates David Nelson and John "Marmaduke" Dawson in the countrified New Riders of the Purple Sage beginning that spring. While performing and recording with keyboardist Howard Wales, ex-Creedence Clearwater Revival member Tom Fogerty, and "funk" keyboardist Merl Saunders (as well as playing sessions for Crosby, Stills, Nash, and Young and The Jefferson Airplane), Garcia remained with The New Riders into 1971. He appeared on their debut Columbia album and subsequently recorded his first solo album for Warner Brothers. With Garcia playing all instruments except drums, *Garcia* featured "Deal" and the minor hit "Sugaree."

The Grateful Dead's first major album success came with *Grateful Dead*, a double-record live set certified gold-award the year of its release, 1971. It contained widely divergent material, from Merl Haggard's "Mama Tried" and John Phillips' "Me and My Uncle" to Fifties rock-and-roll classics such as "Johnny B. Goode," as well as the next in a series of "band" songs, "Playing in the Band." However, during 1971, Pig Pen fell ill, seldom toured with the group, and was replaced by keyboardist–vocalist Keith Godchaux (born in San Francisco on July 19, 1948) by year's end. In 1972, a thinly disguised Grateful Dead album was released as Bob Weir's debut solo album, *Ace*. Showcasing the songs of Weir and John Barlow, the album employed Keith Godchaux, introduced his vocalist–wife Donna Godchaux (a former Muscle Shoals sessions vocalist), and included Weir's "One More Saturday Night" and the definitive version of "Playing in the Band."

By the time of The Grateful Dead's first major European tour in the spring of 1972, Mickey Hart had left the group and Pig Pen had rejoined. Donna Godchaux was added to the band, and the two-month tour yielded The Grateful Dead's second certified gold-award album, the triple-record set *Europe '72*. The album featured several Dead classics such as "Ramble on Rose" and the earliest recorded version of Hunter and Garcia's "Brown-Eyed Women." During the year Mickey Hart recorded the solo album, *Rolling Thunder*, with the assistance of Garcia, Grace Slick, Steve Stills, and The Tower of Power horn section. Sadly, on March 8, 1973, founding member Ron "Pig Pen" McKernan was found in his Marin County apartment, dead at the age of 27.

In July 1973 The Grateful Dead financed the establishment of their own independent record label, Grateful Dead Records. The label's first release, *Wake of the Flood*, contained more Hunter–Garcia songs such as "Row Jimmy," and sold well, if not spectacularly. The following January Round Records was founded for outside recordings by members of the group. By May Round Records had issued Jerry Garcia's second solo album and Robert Hunter's first, *Tales of the Great Rum Runners*, which included "It Must Have Been the Roses" and "Keys to the Rain."

On March 23, 1974, at the Cow Palace south of San Francisco, The Grateful Dead unveiled the $400,000-plus state-of-the-art sound system they were to use through October. With each instrument having its own complete and independent sound unit, the mammoth 30-foot-high system utilized 480 speakers powered by amplifiers producing over 25,000 watts (RMS). Emitting a loud, clear, and clean sound, the system did not produce the distorted, bone-crushing noise normally associated with such a powerful system. That June the group issued *Live from Mars Hotel*, which featured "U.S. Blues" and the Dead classic "Ship of Fools." Following a tour of Europe, The Grateful Dead played five consecutive nights at San Francisco's Winterland in October before "retiring" from live performance for over a year. Recorded remote and filmed by seven camera crews, edited performances from this run were eventually released in film form in June 1977 as *The Grateful Dead Movie*.

During The Grateful Dead's hiatus, the various members pursued a variety of independent projects. During 1975 Round Records issued *Old and In The Way*, recorded in the fall of 1973. This bluegrass aggregation, which had played around the San Francisco Bay area in 1973 and 1974, included Jerry Garcia on banjo and two musicians extraordinaire, fiddler Vassar Clements and mandolinist David Grisman. Other 1975 releases on Round included *Keith and Donna* (by the Godchaux's), Robert Hunter's *Tiger Rose*, and *Seastones* (Phil Lesh and composer–synthesizer wizard Ned Lagin). In June The Grateful Dead signed an agreement with United Artists for worldwide distribution of both Round and Grateful Dead Records.

Following the return of percussionist Mickey Hart, The Grateful Dead recorded *Blues for Allah*, a decidedly jazz-oriented venture that included the Hunter–Garcia–Kreutzman collaboration "Franklin's Tower" and the minor hit "The Music Never Stopped," by Weir and John Barlow. Weir subsequently hooked up with Kingfish, formed by former New Rider Dave Torbert, and assisted in the recording of the group's debut Round album. Also in early 1976 Round issued Garcia's third solo album, *Reflections*. By that June The Grateful Dead were ready to tour again. Thus Weir dropped out of Kingfish, The Dead issued the poorly mixed live set, *Steal Your Face*, and The Diga Rhythm Band, featuring Mickey Hart and tabla player Zakir Hassain, released *Diga*.

In 1977 The Grateful Dead switched to Arista Records, for the first

THE GRATEFUL DEAD / 225

time employing the services of an outside producer, Keith Olsen of
Fleetwood Mac fame, for *Terrapin Station.* Prominently featuring horns,
strings, and vocal choruses, the album included "Estimated Prophet,"
"Samson and Delilah," and the side-long "Terrapin." Bob Weir's *Heaven
Help the Fool,* produced by Olsen and recorded with guitarist Bobby
Cochran and keyboardist Brent Mydland, was issued in early 1978,
yielding the minor hit "Bombs Away." Within two months, The Jerry Garcia Group's *Cats under the Stars* was released, again showcasing the lyrics
of Robert Hunter. In September The Grateful Dead spent $500,000 to ship
25 tons of equipment and to play at the foot of the Great Pyramids of Egypt
in a benefit performance for the Egyptian Department of Antiquities and
the Faith and Hope Society, a charitable organization. Before year's end,
the group's *Shakedown Street* was issued. Produced by Lowell George of
Little Feat, the album revealed a distinctive, sophisticated, and almost
discofied sound. In March 1979 Keith and Donna Godchaux left The
Grateful Dead to pursue solo projects. Keyboardist Brent Mydland, a
former touring and recording partner of Bob Weir, debuted with the
group in April. In the meantime, Mickey Hart had in part scored the music
to the epic if equivocal 1979 Vietnam War movie *Apocalypse Now.* Other
recordings featuring exotic percussion instruments from Hart's extensive
collection that were not used in the film surfaced in late 1980 as *The
Rhythm Devils Play River Music.*

The flurry of activities by The Grateful Dead and its members continued into the Eighties. The group's *Go to Heaven,* produced by Gary
Lyons, sold quite well and even yielded a minor hit with the Garcia–
Hunter composition "Alabama Getaway." Unfortunately, former member
Keith Godchaux died on July 23, 1980, in Ross, California, of injuries suffered in an automobile accident two days prior. The Dead toured again in
1980 and, by early 1981, Bob Weir had formed Bobby and The Midnites
with guitarist Bobby Cochran, Dead keyboardist Brent Mydland, and "fusion" drummer Billy Cobham, among others, for a brief tour and an
eponymous album on Arista Records. Later that year, Mickey Hart assembled High Noon with harmonica player Norton Buffalo and keyboardist Merl Saunders for engagements around the Bay area. As for The
Grateful Dead, they issued two double-record live sets during the year, the
acoustic *Reckoning* and the electric *Dead Set.* Also, near year's end, Relix
Records issued another solo album by lyricist Robert Hunter.

THE GRATEFUL DEAD

The Grateful Dead	Warner Brothers	WS–1689	April '67	A
Anthem of the Sun	Warner Brothers	WS–1749	August '68	A
Aoxomoxoa	Warner Brothers	WS–1790	June '69	A
Live Dead	2-Warner Brothers	2WS–1830	December '69	A
Workingman's Dead *	Warner Brothers	WS–1869	June '70	A

American Beauty*	Warner Brothers	WS-1893	November '70	A
Grateful Dead*	2-Warner Brothers	2WS-1935	September '71	A
Europe '72*	3-Warner Brothers	3WX-2668	October '72	A

GRATEFUL DEAD ANTHOLOGIES AND COMPILATIONS

Vintage Grateful Dead	Sunflower	5001	October '70	
Historic Dead	Sunflower	5004	June '71	
History	Pride	0016		
History of The Grateful Dead (Volume 1)— Bear's Choice	Warner Brothers	BS-2721	June '73	A
Skeletons from the Closet/The Best of The Grateful Dead*	Warner Brothers	W-2764	February '74	A
Best	2-Warner Brothers	2W-3091	November '77	A

NEW RIDERS OF THE PURPLE SAGE (WITH JERRY GARCIA)

| N.R.P.S. | Columbia | PC-30888 | August '71 | A |

JERRY GARCIA AND HOWARD WALES

| Hooteroll? | Douglas | KZ-30859 | October '71 | |

JERRY GARCIA

Garcia	Warner Brothers	BS-2582	January '72	
Compliments of Garcia	Round	RX-102	May '74	A
Reflections	Round	LA565	January '76	

JERRY GARCIA AND MERL SAUNDERS

| Live at Keystone | Fantasy | F-79002 | December '73 | A |

BOB WEIR

| Ace | Warner Brothers | BS-2627 | May '72 | |

MICKEY HART

| Rolling Thunder | Warner Brothers | BS-2635 | September '72 | |

THE GRATEFUL DEAD

| Wake of the Flood | Grateful Dead | GD-01 | October '73 | |
| Live from Mars Hotel | Grateful Dead | GD-102 | June '74 | |

| Blues for Allah | Grateful Dead | LA494 | August '75 | |
| Steal Your Face | 2-Grateful Dead | LA620 | June '76 | |

ROBERT HUNTER

Tales of the Great Rum Runners	Round	RX–101	May '74	
Tiger Rose	Round	RX–105	March '75	
Jack O' Roses	Relix		November '81	A

OLD AND IN THE WAY (WITH JERRY GARCIA)

| Old and In The Way | Round | RX–103 | February '75 | A |

KEITH AND DONNA (GODCHAUX)

| Keith and Donna | Round | RX–104 | February '75 | |

SEASTONES (WITH PHIL LESH)

| Seastones | Round | RX–106 | April '75 | |

KINGFISH (WITH BOB WEIR)

| Kingfish | Round | LA564 | February '76 | |

THE DIGA RHYTHM BAND (WITH MICKEY HART)

| Diga | Round | LA600 | July '76 | |

THE GRATEFUL DEAD

Terrapin Station	Arista	AL–7001	August '77	A
Shakedown Street	Arista	AB–4198	December '78	A
Go to Heaven	Arista	9508	May '80	A
Reckoning	2-Arista	8604	April '81	A
Dead Set	2-Arista	8606	September '81	A

BOB WEIR

| Heaven Help the Fool | Arista | AB–4155 | February '78 | A |

THE JERRY GARCIA GROUP

| Cats under the Stars | Arista | AB–4160 | March '78 | |

THE RHYTHM DEVILS

| Play River Music | Passport | 9844 | September '80 | |

BOBBY AND THE MIDNITES

| Bobby and The Midnites | Arista | 9568 | November '81 | A |

AL GREEN. One of the premier soul singers of the first half of the Seventies, based in large part on his high, sensual voice and the production of veteran Willie Mitchell, Al Green was recognized as one of America's top male vocalists. However, his popularity has diminished since he became a minister and produced his own recent, religiously oriented albums.

Born on April 13, 1946, in Forrest City, Arkansas, Al Green moved with his family to Grand Rapids, Michigan, when he was nine. For the next seven years he sang with his brothers in the gospel group The Green Brothers, forming the pop group The Creations about 1964. They toured the so-called "chitlin circuit" for three years before breaking up, with several members later joining Jr. Walker and The All-Stars. At the end of 1967 Green had a major rhythm-and-blues and minor pop hit with "Back Up Train" as Al Greene, but the concurrent album failed to sell. He soon found himself back on the chitlin circuit, where he was spotted by bandleader–producer Willie Mitchell in Midland, Texas, during 1969. Signed to the Memphis-based Hi label, Green scored several moderate rhythm-and-blues/soul hits in 1970 and 1971 featuring the sparse sound of Memphis studio musicians and the careful production of Mitchell. He had his first major pop hit in mid-1971 with his own "Tired of Being Alone."

At the end of 1971 Al Green's "Let's Stay Together" became a smash hit, and the album of the same name was certified gold-award the following year. Writing his own material, either alone or in collaboration with either Willie Mitchell or Al Jackson of Booker T. and the MGs, Green's *I'm Still in Love with You* yielded two smash hits, "Look What You've Done for Me" and the title song. "You Ought to Be with Me," "Call Me (Come Back Home)," and "Here I Am (Come and Take Me)" were major hits from *Call Me*, as were "Livin' for You" in 1974, and "L–O–V–E (Love)" and "Full of Fire" in 1975. By then, however, both the production and vocal delivery had become formulaic, and "Keep Me Crying" was only a moderate hit at the end of 1976. Green and Mitchell parted company in early 1977, shortly after Green had become a minister and bought his own Memphis church, the Full Gospel Tabernacle. Green's subsequent self-produced religious albums, *The Belle Album* and *Truth 'n Time*, fared poorly, failing to yield another major hit single. Nonetheless, the "new wave" band Talking Heads scored a moderate hit at the end of 1978 with Green's "Take Me to the River."

AL GREENE

Back Up Train	Hot Line	1500	July '68

AL GREEN

Green Is Blue	Hi	SHL–32055	October '69
Al Green Gets Next to You	Hi	SHL–32062	April '71
Let's Stay To-gether*	Hi	SHL–32070	February '72

I'm Still in Love with You*	Hi	XSHL–32074	September '72	
Call Me*	Hi	XSHL–32077	May '73	
Livin' for You*	Hi	ASHL–32082	December '73	
Al Green Explores Your Mind*	Hi	SHL–32087	November '74	
Al Green Is Love	Hi	SHL–32092	August '75	
Full of Fire	Hi	SHL–32097	March '76	
Have a Good Time	Hi	SHL–32103	November '76	
The Belle Album	Hi (Cream)	6004	December '77	A
Truth 'n Time	Hi (Cream)	6009	December '78	A
Love Ritual	London	710	June '78	
Highway to Heaven	Myrrh	6661	November '80	A

AL GREEN REISSUES AND ANTHOLOGIES

Al Green	Bell	6076	September '72	
Greatest Hits	Hi	SHL–32089	March '75	A
Greatest Hits, Volume 2	Hi	SHL–32105	June '77	A
Tired of Being Alone	Hi (Cream)	8000	December '77	A
Can't Get Next to You	Hi (Cream)	8001	December '77	A
Let's Stay Together	Hi (Cream)	8007	June '78	A

DAVID GRISMAN. From the seminal Sixties group, The Even Dozen Jug Band, to Earth Opera and the short-lived Old and In The Way, David Grisman has quietly pursued a curious and exciting admixture of bluegrass, jazz, and classical musics as a virtuoso mandolinist in the Seventies. His *David Grisman Quintet* album, from 1976, became one of the best-selling independently distributed albums in music history, leading to a major label contract with the Horizon subsidiary of A&M Records and *Hot Dawg*, which enjoyed surprising popularity among jazz fans.

THE EVEN DOZEN JUG BAND

The Even Dozen Jug Band	Elektra	EKS–7246	December '63

EARTH OPERA

Earth Opera	Elektra	EKS–74016	May '68

The Great American Eagle Tragedy	Elektra	EKS– 74038	March '69	

OLD AND IN THE WAY

Old and In The Way	Round	RX–103	February '75	A

DAVID GRISMAN

Early Dawg	Sugar Hill	3713	April '81	
The David Grisman Rounder Album	Rounder	0069	August '76	A
The David Grisman Quintet	Kaleidoscope	5	May '77	A
Hot Dawg	Horizon	SP–731	January '79	A
Quintet '80	Warner Brothers	3469	August '80	A
Mondo Mando	Warner Brothers	3618	October '81	A

DAVID GRISMAN AND STEPHANE GRAPPELLI

Live	Warner Brothers	3550	May '81	A

THE GUESS WHO. Popular North American singles band of the late Sixties and early Seventies, The Guess Who were the first Canadian band to achieve major success in the United States. Superseded by Bachman–Turner Overdrive around the middle of the Seventies, The Guess Who endured numerous personnel changes before dissolving at the end of 1975, as lead vocalist–songwriter Burton Cummings subsequently pursued a modestly successful solo career. In 1979 The Guess Who were reconstituted behind original member Jim Kale.

The Guess Who began their evolution in the Winnipeg, Manitoba, region of Canada in the early Sixties, in the persons of vocalist Chad Allen and guitarist Randy Bachman (born September 27, 1943). Chad Allen and The Expressions became The Guess Who in 1965 when Allen dropped out to attend college. The members: guitarist Bachman, lead vocalist–keyboardist–rhythm guitarist Burton Cummings (born December 31, 1947), bassist Jim Kale (born August 11, 1943), and drummer Gary Peterson (born May 26, 1945). During 1965 the group scored a major hit with "Shakin' All Over," after which they established a national reputation with their weekly Canadian television show, "Where It's At." Releasing over a dozen Canadian singles in 1967 and 1968, The Guess Who secured stateside distribution of their recordings through RCA Records in 1969. They had their first major hit with the Bachman–Cummings composition "These Eyes," from *Wheatfield Soul. Canned Wheat* yielded the two-sided hit "Laughing/Undun" and the smash hit "No Time," another Bachman–Cummings collaboration. As "American Woman/No Sugar Tonight" was climbing the charts on its way to becoming another smash hit in 1970, Randy Bachman left the group to form Brave Belt with Chad Allen and, later, the enormously popular Bachman–Turner Overdrive.

After recruiting Canadian guitarists Kurt Winter and Greg Leskiw, The Guess Who hit with "Hand Me Down World" and "Share the Land" from *Share the Land*. Other hit singles included "Albert Flasher/Broken" and "Rain Dance," but in 1972 Leskiw and Kale left the group. Adding two Winnipeg musicians, guitarist Dan McDougall and bassist Billy Wallace, The Guess Who weathered several years of diminishing popularity. During 1974 Winter was replaced by guitarist Domenic Troiano, a former member of The James Gang with two solo albums to his credit. In 1974 the group scored two moderate hits, "Star Baby" and "Dancin' Fool," and one smash hit, "Clap for the Wolfman," but at the end of 1975 The Guess Who disbanded.

Domenic Troiano later recorded three undistinguished solo albums for Capitol Records, while lead vocalist Burton Cummings pursued a solo recording career as the first artist signed to the Columbia Records subsidiary, Portrait. His first single, "Stand Tall," was a major hit at the end of 1976, but later singles fared poorly. *My Own Way to Rock*, recorded with Randy Bachman, sold moderately, but the self-produced *Dream of a Child* sold far less well. By 1979 a reconstituted Guess Who, with original bassist Jim Kale, had recorded the dismal *All This for a Song*.

THE GUESS WHO

Shakin' All Over	Scepter	SCE–533	December '66
	reissued on MGM	SE–4645	July '69
	reissued on Springboard International	4022	June '75
Wheatfield Soul	RCA	LSP–4141	March '69
		reissued as ANL1–1171	November '75
Canned Wheat Packed by The Guess Who	RCA	LSP–4157	October '69
		reissued as ANL1–0983	July '75
American Woman*	RCA	LSP–4266	February '70
		reissued as AFL1–4266	
		reissued as AYL1–3673	
Share the Land*	RCA	LSP–4359	October '70
Sown and Grown in Canada	Wand	WDS–691	March '71

A

The Guess Who Play The Guess Who	P.I.P.	6806	May '71
So Long, Bannatyne	RCA	LSP-4574	August '71
Rockin'	RCA	LSP-4602 reissued as ANL1-2683	March '72 March '78
Live at the Paramount	RCA	LSP-4779	August '72
Artificial Paradise	RCA	LSP-4830	January '73
Number 10	RCA	APL1-0130	July '73
Road Food	RCA	APL1-0405	April '74
Flavours	RCA	CPL1-0636	January '75
Power in the Music	RCA	APL1-0995	July '75
The Way They Were	RCA	APL1-1778	July '76

THE GUESS WHO ANTHOLOGIES AND COMPILATIONS

The Best of The Guess Who*	RCA	LSPX-1004 reissued as AYL1-3662	April '71 June '80	A
The Best of The Guess Who, Volume 2	RCA	APL1-0269	December '73	
The Greatest of The Guess Who	RCA	APL1-2253 reissued as AYL1-3746	April '77	A
The Guess Who	Pickwick	SPC-3246		

DOMENIC TROIANO

Domenic Troiano	Mercury	SRM1-639	August '72	
Tricky	Mercury	SRM1-670	May '73	
Burnin' at the Stake	Capitol	ST-11665	August '77	
The Joke's on Me	Capitol	SW-11772	June '78	
Fret Fever	Capitol	ST-11932	June '79	A

BURTON CUMMINGS

Burton Cummings	Portrait	PR-34261	November '76	A
My Own Way to Rock	Portrait	PR-34698	July '77	
Dream of a Child	Portrait	JR-35481	July '78	

THE GUESS WHO

All This for a Song	Hilltak	19227	April '79

ARLO GUTHRIE. Son of folk music legend Woody Guthrie, Arlo Guthrie received near-instantaneous acclaim with his humorous and satiric talking-blues song, "Alice's Restaurant," in 1967. Starring in the Arthur Penn-directed film of the same name, Guthrie later popularized Steve Goodman's classic train song, "City of New Orleans," in 1972. Arlo Guthrie continues to tour and record regularly, while living with the possibility that he may have inherited his father's fatal, incurable malady, Huntington's chorea.

ARLO GUTHRIE

Alice's Restaurant *	Reprise	RS–6267	October '67	A
Arlo	Reprise	RS–6299	October '68	
Running down the Road	Reprise	RS–6346	October '69	
Alice's Restaurant (soundtrack)	United Artists	5195	October '69	
Washington County	Reprise	RS–6411	September '70	
Hobo's Lullaby	Reprise	MS–2060	May '72	A
Last of the Brooklyn Cowboys	Reprise	MS–2142	April '73	A
Arlo Guthrie	Reprise	MS–2183	May '74	

ARLO GUTHRIE AND PETE SEEGER

Together in Concert	2-Reprise	2R–2214	May '75	A

ARLO GUTHRIE

Amigo	Reprise	MS–2239	September '76	A
The Best of Arlo Guthrie	Warner Brothers	K–3117	December '77	A
One Night	Warner Brothers	3232	September '78	A
Outlasting the Blues	Warner Brothers	3336	June '79	A
Power of Love	Warner Brothers	3558	June '81	A

BILL HALEY. The first international rock-and-roll star, Bill Haley, along with his group The Comets, fused certain elements of country music, Western swing, and black rhythm-and-blues to produce some of the earliest rock-and-roll song hits. Featuring standup acoustic bass and the saxophone playing of Rudy Pompelli, Bill Haley and The Comets scored only a moderate hit with the initial release of "Rock Around the Clock" in 1954, after which they became probably the first white artists to place a rock-and-roll single on the rhythm-and-blues charts with "Dim, Dim the Lights" at the beginning of 1955. Coupled with teenage rebellion as the opening song to the 1955 film *Blackboard Jungle*, "Rock Around the Clock," upon re-release, became perhaps the best-selling single of the rock-and-roll Fifties (over 22 million copies) and one of the best-selling singles of all time. Always much more popular in England than in the United States, Bill Haley's success was cut short stateside by the ascendancy of Elvis Presley in 1956.

BILL HALEY

Rock with Bill Haley and The Comets	Essex	202(M)	
Bill Haley and His Comets	Decca	8225(M) DL–78225	January '56 December '62
He Digs Rock and Roll	Decca	8315(M) DL–78315	
Rock and Roll Stage Show	Decca	8345(M) DL–78345	August '56
Rockin' the Oldies	Decca	8569(M) DL–78569	September '57
Rockin' Around the World	Decca	8692(M) DL–78692	
Rockin' the Joint	Decca	8775(M) DL–78775	September '58

Bill Haley's Chicks	Decca	DL–78821	February '59	
Strictly Instru- mental	Decca	DL–78964	December '59	
Greatest Hits!	Decca	75027	July '68	
	reissued on MCA	161(E)		A
Golden Hits	2-Decca	DXSE– 7211(E)	May '73	
	reissued on MCA	4010		A
Bill Haley and His Comets	Warner Brothers	WS–1378	March '60	
Haley's Juke Box	Warner Brothers	WS–1391	August '60	
Rock 'n' Roll Revival	Warner Brothers	WS–1831	March '70	
Twistin' Knights at the Round Table	Roulette	SR–25174	July '62	
Bill Haley with His Comets	Vocalion	3696(M)	March '63	
Scrapbook	Kama Sutra	KSBS–2014	June '70	
The King of Rock and Roll	Alshire	5202	November '70	
Razzle-Dazzle	2-Janus	JX2S–7003	November '71	
Travelin' Band	Janus	JXS–3035	December '72	
Bill Haley and The Comets	Pickwick	3256		A
Rock and Roll Revival	Pickwick	3280		A
Rock and Roll	GNP Crescendo	GNPS– 2077	April '74	A
Rock Around the Country	GNP Crescendo	GNPS– 2097	March '76	A
Rockin' & Rollin'	Accord	SN–7125	November '81	A

DARYL HALL AND JOHN OATES. Veteran "Philadelphia soul" sessions musicians of the late Sixties, Daryl Hall and John Oates formed their singer–songwriter duo in the early Seventies and recorded a number of overlooked rhythm-and-blues inflected albums for Atlantic Records before scoring nearly consecutive gold-award albums and smash hit singles with "Sara Smile" and "Rich Girl" on RCA in the latter half of the Seventies.

Daryl Hall (born in Pottstown, Pennsylvania, on October 11, 1948) and John Oates (born in New York City on April 7, 1949) met around 1967 in Philadelphia. Both had early musical training, Hall in voice and classical piano, Oates on accordion and, later, guitar. Each worked as a sessions musician at Sigma Sound in Philadelphia under songwriter–producers Kenny Gamble and Leon Huff, playing with soul groups such as The Delfonics and The Stylistics. The two began writing songs together and formed Gulliver for one album on Elektra Records before breaking up in 1970. They subsequently started performing together as a duo, eventually signing with Atlantic Records in 1972. Their primarily acoustic debut album, *Whole Oates*, was overlooked, but their second, *Abandoned Luncheonette*, yielded the minor hit "She's Gone." The song became a smash soul hit for The Tavares in 1974, the year Hall and Oates recorded their final Atlantic album, the rather electronic *War Babies*, under producer Todd Rundgren.

Daryl Hall and John Oates switched to RCA Records in April 1975, and their debut album for the label produced a smash hit with Hall's "Sara Smile." Spurred by that success, Atlantic re-released "She's Gone" and the single became another smash hit, leading to the belated gold-award certification of *Abandoned Luncheonette* in 1976. During that year *Bigger Than Both of Us* yielded the smash hit "Rich Girl" and the moderate hit "Back Together Again." In 1977 Atlantic issued the anthology set *No Goodbyes* for Hall and Oates, whereas RCA released the best-selling *Beauty on a Back Street*. Following the live set, *Livetime*, the duo recorded *Along the Red Ledge* with their road band which included guitarist Caleb Quaye, bassist Kenny Passarelli, and drummer Roger Pope. Harder rocking than previous rhythm-and-blues oriented albums, *Along the Red Ledge* contained the major hit "It's a Laugh" and the minor hit "I Don't Wanna Lose You." During 1979 Daryl Hall and John Oates recorded the disco-influenced *X-Static*, an album which de-emphasized both their rhythm-and-blues roots and their fine vocal harmonies. Following the release of Hall's controversial and esoteric *Sacred Songs*, recorded in 1977 with Robert Fripp, the duo established themselves as superstars with *Voices*, which yielded four hits with "How Does It Feel to Be Back," a remake of The Righteous Brothers' top 1965 hit "You've Lost That Lovin' Feeling," "You Make My Dreams Come True," and the top hit "Kiss on My List."

GULLIVER

Gulliver	Elektra	EKS–74070	August '70	

DARYL HALL AND JOHN OATES

Past Times Behind (recorded 1971–2)	Chelsea	547	July '77	
Whole Oates	Atlantic	SD–7242	October '72	A
Abandoned Luncheonette *	Atlantic	SD–7269 reissued as SD–19139	December '73	A
War Babies	Atlantic	SD–18109	October '74	A
No Goodbyes	Atlantic	SD–18213	March '77	
Daryl Hall and John Oates *	RCA	AFL1–1144 reissued as AYL1–3836	August '75	A

Bigger Than Both of Us*	RCA	APL1–1467	August '76	
		reissued as AYL1–3866		A
Beauty on a Back Street*	RCA	AFL1–2300	August '77	
		reissued as AYL1–4230	January '82	A
Livetime	RCA	AFL1–2802	May '78	
Along the Red Ledge*	RCA	AFL1–2804	August '78	
		reissued as AYL1–4231	January '82	A
X-Static	RCA	AFL1–3494	October '79	
Voices*	RCA	AQL1–3646	August '80	A
Private Eyes	RCA	AFL1–4028	October '81	A

DARYL HALL

Sacred Songs	RCA	AFL1–3573	March '80	

EMMYLOU HARRIS. Emerging from the remnants of the East Coast folk scene in the late Sixties, Emmylou Harris received her first major exposure with the now-legendary Gram Parsons, singing backup on his two solo albums. Initiating a solo recording career approximately a year after Parsons' unexpected death in September 1973, Emmylou Harris has recorded a series of best-selling albums as a song interpreter, featuring her thin, fragile, and understated voice. Her American popularity is primarily among straightforward country music fans, whereas she is curiously quite popular in England and Europe, where she headlines concerts. One of the most successful Seventies promoters of country music with a rock sound, Emmylou Harris' success is due in large part to the excellence of her Hot Band, whose members have included former Ricky Nelson and Elvis Presley guitarist James Burton and songwriter Rodney Crowell.

Born in Birmingham, Alabama, in 1949, Emmylou Harris moved with her family to the Washington, D.C., area and obtained her first guitar at the age of 16. She started her musical career in 1967, performing around Washington and New York at the tail end of the East Coast folk movement. Signed to Jubilee Records in 1969, Harris recorded one album before retiring for a time after the birth of her first child. After unsuccessfully attempting to break through in Nashville during the latter half of 1970, she returned to Washington, formed a small band, and performed locally. "Discovered" at The Cellar Door by members of The Flying Burrito Brothers, Harris was asked to join the group shortly before its second incarnation dissolved. Introduced to Gram Parsons in late 1971, she was later summoned to Los Angeles to sing backup on his debut solo album, *GP*. She toured with Parsons in the spring of 1973 and assisted with his *Grievous Angel* album that summer.

However, Gram Parsons died unexpectedly on September 19, 1973, and Emmylou Harris decided to stay in Washington, where she formed her Hot Band. The members: James Burton (guitar), songwriter Rodney Crowell (rhythm guitar), Glen D. Hardin (keyboards), Hank DiVito (pedal steel guitar), Emory Gordy (bass), and John Ware (drums). Signed to Warner Brothers Records in mid-1974, Harris recorded her first two albums for the label's subsidiary, Reprise. Her debut Reprise album, *Pieces of the Sky*, contained standard country-and-western material, including the smash country hit "If I Could Only Win Your Love" (by The Louvin Brothers), as well as Lennon and McCartney's "For No One," and the original "Boulder to Birmingham," co-written with Bill Danoff (of "Take Me Home, Country Roads" fame). After singing background vocals on Bob Dylan's *Desire* album, Harris recorded *Elite Hotel*, her first certified gold-award album. It included three Gram Parsons songs ("Wheels," "Sin City," and "Ooh, Las Vegas") and yielded three country hit singles with Buck Owens' "Together Again," Don Gibson's "Sweet Dreams," and "One of These Days." Other inclusions were "Feelin' Single—Seein' Double" and the Rodney Crowell–Emmylou Harris collaboration, "Amarillo."

After a triumphant tour of Europe and England in 1976, Emmylou Harris recorded *Luxury Liner* for Warner Brothers, replacing James Burton with Briton Albert Lee. The album contained Gram Parsons' title song and two country hits, "Making Believe" and Chuck Berry's "C'est la Vie." *Quarter Moon in a Ten-Cent Town*, recorded with the Hot Band, this time with the assistance of James Burton and Willie Nelson, included three country hits, Dolly Parton's "To Daddy," "Two More Bottles of Wine," and "Easy from Now On," as well as Rodney Crowell's "I Ain't Living Long Like This." In February 1978 Harris began work on an album with Dolly Parton and Linda Ronstadt, but the project, with its promise of the first female country "super-group," was later abandoned, apparently due to scheduling conflicts and rushed recording. During 1979, Harris' *Blue Kentucky Girl* was issued; essentially her first album consisting entirely of country material, the LP included Gram Parsons' "Hickory Wind," Rodney Crowell's "Even Cowgirls Get the Blues" (with harmonies by Ronstadt and Parton), and the smash country hits "Save the Last Dance for Me" and "Beneath Still Waters." During 1980 she scored country hits with "Wayfaring Stranger" and Paul Simon's "The Boxer" from the bluegrass-style *Roses in the Snow* and a minor country hit with "That Lovin' You Feeling Again" with Roy Orbison. *Evangeline* featured Ronstadt and Parton harmonizing on the country hit remake of "Mister Sandman."

EMMYLOU HARRIS

Gliding Bird	Jubilee	12052	'70	
Pieces of the Sky	Reprise	MS–2213	March '75	A
		reissued as		
		K–2284		

Elite Hotel*	Reprise	MS–2236 reissued as K–2286	January '76	A
Luxury Liner*	Warner Brothers	BS–2998 reissued as 3115	January '77	A
Quarter Moon in a Ten-Cent Town	Warner Brothers	BSK–3141	January '78	A
Profile: The Best of Emmylou Harris*	Warner Brothers	BSK–3258	November '78	A
Blue Kentucky Girl*	Warner Brothers	BSK–3318	April '79	A
Roses in the Snow*	Warner Brothers	3422	May '80	A
Light of the Stable—The Christmas Album	Warner Brothers	3484	November '80	A
Evangeline*	Warner Brothers	3508	January '81	A
Cimarron	Warner Brothers	3603	December '81	A

GEORGE HARRISON.   Neither the most prolific nor the most successful of the former Beatles, George Harrison was the member most involved in Indian music and culture, later regularly espousing spiritualism and humanitarianism in his solo work. His first post-Beatles album, *All Things Must Pass*, has been hailed by some as one of the rock masterpieces of the Seventies despite its occasional lapses into didacticism and pedantry. Harrison's humanitarian impulses produced perhaps the crowning achievement of his career in 1971 with the benefit show, Concert for Bangladesh. Forming his own record company, Dark Horse, in 1974, George Harrison was the first former Beatle to tour America, also in 1974. While he continued to record the infrequent hit single and gold-award album, George Harrison bridged into other fields during the late Seventies. In 1978 he appeared in The Beatles-parody television special "All You Need Is Cash"; more recently, he acted as financer and executive producer of the Monty Python film, *Life of Brian*.

Born in Wavertree, Liverpool, England, on February 25, 1943, George Harrison bought his first guitar at the age of 13, met Paul McCartney in 1958 and soon joined the skiffle group, The Quarrymen, with McCartney and John Lennon. When The Quarrymen disbanded around the end of 1959, Harrison, Lennon, and McCartney formed The Moondogs, later changing their name to The Silver Beatles. Regularly performing at the Cavern Club in Liverpool after January 1961 (making the occasional foray into Germany), The Beatles' lineup was completed with the August 1962 addition of drummer Ringo Starr. The Beatles' story, of course, is chronicled elsewhere. Harrison, generally overshadowed by songwriters Lennon and McCartney, made his songwriting debut with "Don't Bother Me" from *Meet The Beatles* (1964). Later songwriting efforts by Harrison during the course of The Beatles' career included "If I Needed Someone," "Taxman," "Within You, Without You," the classic "While My Guitar Gently Weeps," "Something," and "Here Comes the Sun." While The Beatles were still intact, Harrison recorded *Wonderwall*, an Eastern-sounding film soundtrack, and the experimental *Electronic Sound* album, one of the few releases on the short-lived Zapple label.

Although Paul McCartney did not sue for dissolution of The Beatles until December 1970, George Harrison was essentially independent of the group by the May 1970 release of *Let It Be*, the stormy Beatles' film and recording finale. Harrison's debut solo album, the three-record set *All Things Must Pass*, was co-produced by Phil Spector and recorded with Eric Clapton, Dave Mason, Bobby Whitlock, and Billy Preston. It became a surprise instant best-seller, yielding hits with "My Sweet Lord/Isn't It a Pity" and "What Is Life," while including other excellent songs such as "Wah-Wah," "If Not for You," "Beware of Darkness," and "Apple Scruffs." During July 1971 Harrison, concerned with the famine engulfing Bangladesh, organized two benefit performances staged in New York's Madison Square Garden. Enlisting the services of Ringo Starr, Billy Preston, and Leon Russell (among others), Harrison was able to coax both Bob Dylan and Eric Clapton (both in semiretirement) into performing at the charity show. Though seemingly delayed unnecessarily, the resulting three-record set, *Concert for Bangladesh*, was eventually issued in early 1972 and accrued hundreds of thousands of dollars for relief of the heinous situation in Bangladesh.

In the meantime, George Harrison took nearly two years in completing his second solo album, *Living in the Material World*. Finally released in mid-1973, the album was critically lambasted despite yielding the smash hit "Give Me Love (Give Me Peace on Earth)." Other songs included the satiric "Sue Me, Sue You Blues," ironic in the light of difficulties caused by the remarkable similarities of "My Sweet Lord" and The Chiffons' "He's So Fine" (later the subject of prolonged litigation). In June 1974 Harrison announced the formation of Dark Horse Records (with distribution handled by A&M), the first signing being long-time friend Ravi Shankar. During November 1974, Harrison became the first former Beatle to tour the United States, with Ravi Shankar. However, the tour (his only tour) was met with scathing reviews, due in large part to voice problems and a muddled sound mix. Issued in December, *Dark Horse* took another critical drubbing. The album contained two moderate hits, "Dark Horse" and "Ding Dong, Ding Dong," and a rewritten version of The Everly Brothers' "Bye, Bye, Love," an apparent indictment of Eric Clapton's cuckolding of Harrison.

In the fall of 1975 George Harrison's *Extra Texture* was released, yielding the hit "You" and including an obvious reworking of one of Harrison's Beatles classics as "This Guitar (Can't Keep from Crying)." During January 1976 he switched to his own Dark Horse label, issuing *33 & 1/3* before year's end. The album produced the hits "This Song" (a musical comment on his problems with "My Sweet Lord" and "She's So Fine") and

"Crackerbox Palace." Inactive during much of 1977, Harrison finally re-emerged in December to appear on NBC–TV's "Saturday Night Live" with Paul Simon. The following March he appeared in a small part in the television special, "All You Need Is Cash," Monty Python alumnus Eric Idle's Beatles parody. During 1978 Harrison switched distribution of Dark Horse to Warner Brothers Records and became partial financer and executive producer of Monty Python's controversial *Life of Brian* film, released in September 1979. Released earlier in the year, *George Harrison* produced a major hit with "Blow Away." In 1981 Harrison scored a smash hit with the tribute to slain John Lennon, "All These Years Ago," recorded with Ringo Starr and Paul and Linda McCartney, as the film *The Time Bandits*, scripted by Monty Python's Terry Gilliam and Michael Palin and partially financed by Harrison, was released.

GEORGE HARRISON

Wonderwall Music	Apple	ST–3350	November '68	
Electronic Sound	Zapple	ST–3358	May '69	
All Things Must Pass *	3-Apple/ Capitol	STCH–639	November '70	A

GEORGE HARRISON AND FRIENDS

Bangladesh *	3-Apple	STCX– 3385	January '72

GEORGE HARRISON

Living in the Material World *	Apple/Capitol	SMAS– 3410	May '73	
	reissued on Capitol	SN–16216		A
Dark Horse *	Apple/Capitol	SMAS– 3418	December '74	
	reissued on Capitol	SN–16055		A
Extra Texture *	Apple/Capitol	SW–3420	September '75	
	reissued on Capitol	SN–16217		A
Best *	Capitol	ST–11578	November '76	A
33 & 1/3 *	Dark Horse	DH–3005	November '76	A
George Harrison *	Dark Horse	DH–3255	February '79	A
Somewhere in England	Dark Horse	3492	May '81	A

RONNIE HAWKINS. Considered by some as the last of the original American rock-and-rollers, Ronnie Hawkins is best known in the United States as the leader of The Hawks, one edition of which eventually became The Band. Known in the States for little else, Ronnie Hawkins established himself as a star in Canada during the Sixties, eventually recording for Cotillion and Monument Records in the early Seventies.

RONNIE HAWKINS

Ronnie Hawkins	Roulette	SR–25078	August '59	
Ronnie Hawkins and The Hawks—Mr. Dynamo	Roulette	SR–25102	January '60	
The Folk Ballads of Ronnie Hawkins	Roulette	SR–25120	June '60	
Ronnie Hawkins Sings the Songs of Hank Williams	Roulette	SR–25137	November '60	
Ronnie Hawkins with The Band	Roulette	42045	November '70	
Ronnie Hawkins	Cotillion	SD–9019	February '70	
The Hawk	Cotillion	SD–9039	May '71	
Rock and Roll Resurrection	Monument	KZ–31330	September '72	
The Giant of Rock 'n' Roll	Monument	KZ–32940	September '74	
The Giant of Rock 'n' Roll/Rock and Roll Resurrection	2-Monument	BZ–33855	December '75	
Hawk	United Artists	LA968	October '79	A

ISAAC HAYES. Accompanist to Otis Redding and author (with David Porter) of most of Sam and Dave's hits, Isaac Hayes came into his own with 1969's gold-award *Hot Buttered Soul* album. The album (which featured long introductory "raps," elaborate arrangements, and the 15-minute "By the Time I Get to Phoenix") established the "rap" introduction format later exploited by Barry White, broke soul music's preoccupation with the three-minute-length song, and brought an unprecedented level of musical sophistication and complexity to soul music. Arranged, performed, and partially written by Isaac Hayes, 1971's *Shaft* soundtrack was the first massively successful soundtrack to the first of a spate of Seventies black-oriented movies, establishing both the "scratch" guitar rhythm and the "wah-wah" bass in soul music. Established on the supper club circuit complete with the "Black Moses" persona, Isaac Hayes has met with only modest success since 1975's *Chocolate Chip* album, despite recording duet albums with Dionne Warwick in 1977 and Millie Jackson in 1979.

Born in Covington, Tennessee, on August 20, 1943 (or August 6, 1938), Isaac Hayes began singing with The Morning Stars vocal group after moving to Memphis with his family. Later taking up piano and saxophone, he worked at Stax Records as a sideman, composer, and producer after meeting Floyd Newman of The Mar-Keys. As keyboard accompanist to Otis Redding (an association that lasted until Redding's death in 1967), Hayes played organ on Redding's first major hit, "I've Been Loving You

Too Long (to Stop Now)." In collaboration with David Porter, Hayes wrote "B–A–B–Y" for Carla Thomas and three Sam and Dave hits, "Hold On! I'm Comin'," "Soul Man," and "I Thank You." Initiating his solo recording career in 1967, Hayes hit big with his second album, *Hot Buttered Soul*, in 1969. The best-selling album featured "rap" introductions, elaborately orchestrated pop-style arrangements, and lengthy song renditions that became standard soul music practices (and eventually clichés), while yielding the two-sided hit, "Walk On By/By the Time I Get to Phoenix." His next two albums sold quite well, but 1971's soundtrack to the film *Shaft* sold spectacularly. Issued a year before Curtis Mayfield's *Super Fly*, *Shaft* was the first of a series of best-selling soundtracks to black-oriented movies, producing a smash hit with the title song.

Assuming the persona of "Black Moses," replete with shaven head, gold chains, and an entourage of beautiful women, Isaac Hayes was soon established on the supper club circuit, as the gold-award *Live at the Sahara Tahoe* attested. The title song to the gold-award *Joy* album became a major hit, after which he recorded two poorly received soundtracks, *Tough Guys* and *Truck Turner*, starring in both films. Forming Hot Buttered Soul Records under the affiliation of ABC Records in 1975, his debut album for the label, *Chocolate Chip*, was a best-seller, but later releases fared less well. Following *A Man and a Woman*, recorded with Dionne Warwick, Isaac Hayes moved to Polydor Records, where he recorded *Royal Rappin's* with Millie Jackson in 1979. After scoring a major hit that year with the title song to *Don't Let Go*, Hayes appeared as a prison gang leader in the 1981 film *Escape from New York*.

ISAAC HAYES

Presenting Isaac Hayes	Enterprise	13–100	February '68	
In the Beginning	Atlantic	SD–1599	February '72	
Hot Buttered Soul *	Enterprise	ENS–1001	July '69	
	reissued on Stax	4114	October '78	A
Isaac Hayes Movement	Enterprise	ENS–1010	April '70	
	reissued on Stax	4129	March '80	A
To Be Continued . . .	Enterprise	ENS–1014	November '70	
	reissued on Stax	4133	March '80	A
Shaft (soundtrack)	2-Enterprise	ENS2–5002	August '71	A
	reissued on Stax	88002	October '78	A
Black Moses	2-Enterprise	ENS–5003	November '71	
Live at the Sahara Tahoe *	2-Enterprise	ENX2–5005	May '73	
Joy *	Enterprise	ENS–5007	October '73	
Tough Guys (soundtrack)	Enterprise	7504	May '74	
Truck Turner (soundtrack)	2-Enterprise	7507	July '74	

The Best of Isaac Hayes	Enterprise	7510	August '75	
Enterprise: His Greatest Hits	2-Stax	88003	August '80	A
Chocolate Chip*	Hot Buttered Soul	874	June '75	
Groove-a-Thon	Hot Buttered Soul	925	February '76	
Juicy Fruit (Disco Freak)	Hot Buttered Soul	953	July '76	

ISAAC HAYES AND DIONNE WARWICK

| A Man and a Woman | 2-ABC reissued on MCA | 996 10012 | February '77 May '80 | A |

ISAAC HAYES

New Horizon	Polydor	PD1-6120	December '77	A
Hotbed	Stax	4102	April '78	A
For the Sake of Love	Polydor	PD1-6164	November '78	A
Don't Let Go*	Polydor	PD1-6224	September '79	A
And Once Again	Polydor	6269	May '80	A
Lifetime Thing	Polydor	6329	November '81	A

ISAAC HAYES AND MILLIE JACKSON

| Royal Rappin's | Polydor | PD1-6229 | October '79 | A |

JIMI HENDRIX. One of the two "superstar" guitarists of the Sixties, Jimi Hendrix is revered by some as *the* master virtuoso of the electric guitar. Undoubtedly the most adventurous and daring electric guitarist of the Sixties, Hendrix enormously expanded the possibilities of the instrument, masterfully manipulating devices such as the wah-wah pedal, fuzz-box, Uni-Vibe, and tape-delay mechanism to produce sounds sometimes gentle and melodic, but more often loud and "psychedelic," even extraterrestial and aquatic. Jimi Hendrix's carefully controlled use of distortion and feedback laid the foundations for all the "heavy metal" guitarists of the Seventies while inspiring jazz musicians such as Miles Davis to adopt certain elements of rock music, thus leading to the development of so-called "fusion" music.

A left-handed guitarist, Jimi Hendrix astoundingly played a right-handed guitar upside down and backwards, rather than using a left-handed guitar. One of rock music's most outstanding showmen during his days with The Jimi Hendrix Experience, Hendrix resurrected old bluesmen's show-stopping techniques such as playing the guitar behind his back or head, playing the guitar with his teeth, and aggressively carressing, humping, and attacking his guitar with such sexual lewdness as to become instantly legendary. Ironically achieving his first mass popularity in

England rather than his native United States, Jimi Hendrix was launched in America with his breathtaking performance at the 1968 Monterey Pop Festival. As rock music's first black "superstar," Hendrix was the first black musician to shatter the record industry's preoccupation with blacks as singles artists. Inspired to take up singing by the success of the poor-voiced Bob Dylan, Jimi Hendrix later recorded the definitive version of Dylan's "All Along the Watchtower," The Jimi Hendrix Experience's only major hit single.

Seeking to alter his image of showman and black "super stud" by 1968, Jimi Hendrix sought to be recognized simply as a guitarist (as with Chuck Berry, Hendrix's blues-based recordings have been sorely overlooked) and to relegate his flamboyance and outrageous stage demeanor to his past, much to the consternation of perplexed and often hostile fans. Somewhat out of the public eye following the breakup of The Experience in 1969, Hendrix played at the Woodstock Festival that August, performing a stirring and controversial version of "The Star Spangled Banner," replete with the sounds of rockets and bombs that accurately portrayed the violence of both past and contemporary American cultures. After the short-lived Band of Gypsys in early 1970, Jimi Hendrix continued to tour and record, and opened his own Electric Ladyland studio in New York City shortly before his August appearance at the Isle of Wight Festival. Seeking to expand the limits of contemporary popular music further, Hendrix had logged over 800 hours of studio tapes with musicians such as John McLaughlin and other "avant garde" jazz figures in an effort to create a fusion of jazz, rhythm-and-blues, and contemporary rock, only to die unnecessarily and unfulfilled on September 18, 1970.

Born in Seattle, Washington, on November 27, 1942, Jimi Hendrix obtained his first acoustic guitar at the age of 11 and graduated to electric guitar at 12. Playing in a number of Seattle area rock bands by 14, he dropped out of high school to join the Army, where he met and jammed with bassist Billy Cox. Discharged from the Army after sustaining a back injury in a parachute jump, Hendrix toured the South's "chitlin" circuit, backing artists such as B. B. King, Sam Cooke, and Jackie Wilson. He then worked for Little Richard and Ike and Tina Turner before moving to New York in 1964 to back The Isley Brothers and King Curtis and to record with Curtis Knight and Lonnie Youngblood. During 1965 Hendrix formed his own group, Jimmy James and The Blue Flames, for engagements around Greenwich Village in 1966. "Discovered" there by former Animals bassist Bryan "Chas" Chandler, Hendrix went to England at Chandler's behest in September 1966, forming The Jimi Hendrix Experience with guitarist–turned-bassist Noel Redding (born in Folkstone, England, on December 25, 1945) and drummer Mitch Mitchell (born in London on July 9, 1946). A power trio with the same basic lineup as Cream (which was formed only months earlier), The Jimi Hendrix Experience was an immediate success in Europe, scoring major hits in England with "Hey Joe," "Purple Haze," and "The Wind Cries Mary" in early 1967.

Commencing their first British tour at the end of March, The Jimi Hendrix Experience's debut album, *Are You Experienced*, was riding high on the British charts when they debuted in the United States at the Monterey Pop Festival in June. The performance (part of which is featured in D. A. Pennebaker's *Monterey Pop* film) included Dylan's "Like a Rolling Stone" and the breathtaking finale of "Wild Thing," culminating in the ignition of Hendrix's lighter-fluid drenched guitar. Word of Hendrix's flamboyant Monterey appearance spread rapidly, and *Are You Experienced*, upon American release in August, became an instant best-seller despite yielding no major hit single. The album included early Hendrix classics such as "Purple Haze," "Hey Joe," and "Foxey Lady," as well as the poignantly lyrical "The Wind Cries Mary." Following an abortive tour with The Monkees (a mismatch if ever there were one), Hendrix returned to England and toured America regularly in 1968 and 1969 to sell-out crowds.

The Jimi Hendrix Experience's *Axis: Bold as Love*, released stateside in early 1968, was another instant best-seller, containing the masterful "Little Wing" and the ominous "If 6 Was 9," later included in Peter Fonda and Dennis Hopper's *Easy Rider* film and soundtrack. *Electric Ladyland*, The Experience's final album, was arguably their finest recording although some critics have denigrated it as self-indulgent. Included on the two-record set were the vituperative "Crosstown Traffic," the long jam "Voodoo Chile" (featuring Stevie Winwood on organ), and the group's only major hit single, Dylan's "All Along the Watchtower," in what is generally acknowledged as its definitive version. Tours by The Experience in 1968 saw Hendrix retreating from his role as psychedelic flash guitarist–showman, much to the chagrin of inflexible fans. In November 1968 The Jimi Hendrix Experience announced their intention to break up, though contractual obligations kept the group together into 1969. Noel Redding later formed Fat Mattress in 1969, Road in 1971, and The Noel Redding Band in 1975. Drummer Mitch Mitchell continued to play on-and-off with Hendrix until his death, briefly becoming a member of Ramatam with ex-Iron Butterfly guitarist Mike Pinera in 1972.

During 1969 Jimi Hendrix began building his own studio, Electric Ladyland, in New York City, while seldom performing publicly and eventually logging over 800 hours of studio tapes with "avant garde" jazz musicians such as John McLaughlin. In August Hendrix, backed by Mitch Mitchell and Army buddy Billy Cox, played the Woodstock Festival. The performance culminated in the stunning and controversial version of "The Star Spangled Banner," which appropriately segued in "Purple Haze" and was later included on the first *Woodstock* album. On New Year's Eve 1969–70, the all-black Band of Gypsys (Hendrix, Cox, and drummer Buddy Miles) debuted at Bill Graham's Fillmore East. The performance, recorded and later released in album form, included Miles' "(Them) Changes" and Hendrix's 12-minute-plus "Machine Gun." However, the group never really worked out, perhaps due to Miles' overbearing drumming style.

Jimi Hendrix was soon recording his next album with Mitchell and Cox. During the spring and summer of 1970 Hendrix toured with them, opening his Electric Ladyland studio shortly before their August appearance at the Isle of Wight. On September 18, 1970, Jimi Hendrix died of "inhalation of vomit due to barbiturate intoxication" in London at the age of 27. *The Cry of Love*, issued posthumously, featured Buddy Miles on "Ezy Rider" and Noel Redding on "My Friend" and included two excellent but overlooked slow blues-style songs, "Drifting" and "Angel." Before the end of 1971 Reprise had issued the soundtrack to *Rainbow Bridge*, which contained "Dolly Dagger," "Pali Gap," and the live "Hear My Train a Comin'." *Hendrix in the West*, regarded by some as his finest album since *Are You Experienced*, assembled live performances apparently recorded during 1970 such as Chuck Berry's "Johnny B. Goode" and the Hendrix originals "Red House," "Little Wing," and "Voodoo Chile." The posthumously released *Soundtrack Recordings from the Film "Jimi Hendrix"* serves as an excellent compilation of Hendrix's live recordings. In 1978 and 1979 Reprise issued two anthology sets as *The Essential Jimi Hendrix*.

JIMI HENDRIX AND LITTLE RICHARD

Roots of Rock	Archive of Folk and Jazz Music	296(E)	September '74	
Together	Pickwick	3347		

JIMI HENDRIX WITH THE ISLEY BROTHERS

In the Beginning	T-Neck	TNS–3007	May '71

JIMI HENDRIX AND CURTIS KNIGHT

Get That Feeling	Capitol	ST–2856	December '67
Flashing	Capitol	ST–2894	June '68
Get That Feeling/ Flashing	2-Capitol	SWBB–659	January '71

JIMI HENDRIX AND LONNIE YOUNGBLOOD

Together	Maple	6004	March '71

THE JIMI HENDRIX EXPERIENCE/OTIS REDDING

Historic Performances at the Monterey International Pop Festival*	Reprise	MS–2029	August '70	A

THE JIMI HENDRIX EXPERIENCE

Are You Experienced*	Reprise	RS–6261	August '67	A
Axis: Bold as Love*	Reprise	RS–6281	February '68	A
Electric Ladyland*	2-Reprise	2RS–6307	August '68	A

FAT MATTRESS (WITH NOEL REDDING)

Fat Mattress	Atco	SD33–309	November '69
Fat Mattress II	Atco	SD33–347	January '71

THE NOEL REDDING BAND

Clonakilty Cowboys	RCA	APL1– 1237	December '75
Blowin'	RCA	APL1– 1863	September '76

RAMATAM (WITH MITCH MITCHELL)

Ramatam	Atlantic	SD–7236	August '72

THE BAND OF GYPSYS

The Band of Gypsys*	Capitol	STAO–472	March '70	A

JIMI HENDRIX

The Cry of Love	Reprise	MS–2034	February '71	
Rainbow Bridge (soundtrack)	Reprise	MS–2040	October '71	
Hendrix in the West	Reprise	MS–2049	February '72	
War Heroes	Reprise	MS–2103	November '72	
Soundtrack Re- cordings from the Film "Jimi Hendrix"	2-Reprise	2RS–6481	June '73	A
Crash Landing	Reprise	MS–2204	February '75	A
Midnight Light- ning	Reprise	MS–2229	November '75	A
Nine to the Universe	Warner Brothers	HS–2299	April '80	A

VARIOUS OTHER JIMI HENDRIX RELEASES INCLUDING ANTHOLOGIES AND COMPILATIONS

The Jimi Hendrix Experience: Smash Hits*	Reprise	MS–2025 reissued as MS– 2276	July '69	A
In the Beginning	Shout	502	September '72	
Rare Hendrix	Trip	9500	August '72	
Roots of Hendrix	Trip	9501	January '73	
The Genius of Jimi Hendrix	Trip	9523	August '74	
Superpak	2-Trip	3509	February '76	
Before London	Accord	SN–7101	April '81	A
Free Spirit	Accord	SN–7112	April '81	A
Cosmic Feeling	Accord	SN–7139	November '81	A

In Concert	Springboard International	4031		
The Very Best of Jimi Hendrix	United Artists	LA505	April '76	
Jimi	Pickwick	3528	May '76	
The Essential Jimi Hendrix	2-Reprise	2RS–2245	July '78	A
The Essential Jimi Hendrix, Volume II	Reprise	HS–2293	July '79	A

HERMAN'S HERMITS. Following on the heels of The Beatles, Herman's Hermits toured the United States in 1965 shortly after their first single, "I'm Into Something Good," became an American hit. Through 1968 Herman's Hermits released a series of hit novelty songs, "cover" songs, and teen-oriented songs that brought them greater popularity in the United States than in Great Britain. Though the original group broke up in 1971, Herman's Hermits were later reconstituted, whereas lead vocalist Peter Noone eventually formed the "new wave" style Tremblers in 1980.

Formed in 1962 by Peter Noone as The Heartbeats, Peter became Herman and the group became Herman's Hermits at the behest of producer Mickie Most. The members: vocalist, pianist, and guitarist Peter Noone (born in Manchester, England, on November 5, 1947), guitarists Keith Hopwood (born October 26, 1946, in Manchester) and Derek Leckenby (born May 14, 1945 or 1946, in Leeds, England), bassist Karl Green (born July 31, 1946 or 1947, in Salford, England), and drummer Barry Whitwam (born July 21, 1946, in Manchester). The group first hit with Carole King and Gerry Goffin's "I'm Into Something Good," on which the group actually played their instruments, in late 1964. Future Led Zeppelin members Jimmy Page and John Paul Jones handled much of the subsequent guitar and bass work, respectively. In early 1965 Herman's Hermits had their first smash hit with "Can't You Hear My Heartbeat," followed by "Silhouettes" and the ditty "Mrs. Brown You've Got a Lovely Daughter." Around the same time the group successfully toured America, due in large part to their simple, gentle songs and Noone's adolescent good looks. Other hit singles from 1965 were "Wonderful World," "I'm Henry VIII, I Am," "Just a Little Better," and "A Must to Avoid." Their hits continued into 1968, but only "Dandy" (by The Kinks' Ray Davies) from 1966 and the two-sided hit, "There's a Kind of Hush/No Milk Today," from 1967, merit mention. Herman's Hermits remained together despite waning popularity until 1971, when Herman went solo under his real name. Herman's Hermits were reconstituted by originals Green, Leckenby, and Whitwam in 1973, as Noone pursued neglected recording and acting careers. Peter Noone eventually re-emerged in 1980 as vocalist and rhythm guitarist for the Los Angeles-based Tremblers, whose debut album was the first release on Beach Boys associate Tom Johnston's Johnston Records.

HERMAN'S HERMITS

Introducing Herman's Hermits*	MGM	SE–4282	February '65
On Tour*	MGM	SE–4295	June '65
Hold On!	MGM	SE–4342	February '66
Both Sides of Herman's Hermits	MGM	SE–4386	August '66
There's a Kind of Hush All Over the World*	MGM	SE–4438	March '67
Blaze	MGM	SE–4478	September '67
Mrs. Brown, You've Got a Lovely Daughter	MGM	SE–4548	September '68

HERMAN'S HERMITS ANTHOLOGIES AND COMPILATIONS

The Best of Herman's Hermits*	MGM	SE–4315	November '65	
The Best of Herman's Hermits, Volume II	MGM	SE–4416	November '66	
The Best of Herman's Hermits, Volume III	MGM	SE–4505	December '67	
Their Greatest Hits	2-ABKCO	4227	September '73	A

THE TREMBLERS

Twice Nightly	Johnston	JZ–36532	August '80	A

DAN HICKS AND HIS HOT LICKS. Evolving out of The Charlatans, one of the first San Francisco bands of the "psychedelic" era, Dan Hicks and His Hot Licks recorded one album for Epic, followed by three for Blue Thumb in the early Seventies, that effectively combined elements of Forties jazz, blues, Western swing, country, and jug band musics in a nonelectric setting. Featuring the outstanding fiddle work of Sid Page, the wry songs of leader Hicks, and the precise harmonies of various female vocalists (known as The Lickettes), Dan Hicks and His Hot Licks never had a hit single but nonetheless inspired later "nostalgia" acts such as The Pointer Sisters and Manhattan Transfer. Ironically Hicks disbanded the group just as *Last Train to Hicksville* was becoming their most successful album.

THE CHARLATANS

The Charlatans	Philips	600309	July '69

TONGUE AND GROOVE

Tongue and Groove	Fontana	67593	May 69

DAN HICKS AND HIS HOT LICKS

Original Recordings	Epic	BN–26464	September '69	A
Where's the Money	Blue Thumb	BTS–29	September '71	
Striking It Rich!	Blue Thumb	BTS–36	May '72	A
Last Train to Hicksville	Blue Thumb	BTS–51	May '73	A

DAN HICKS

It Happened One Bite	Warner Brothers	BSK–3158	February '78

HOLLAND–DOZIER–HOLLAND. Motown Records' premier songwriting-production team, rivaled only by William "Smokey" Robinson in the early Sixties and Norman Whitfield–Barrett Strong in the late Sixties, Brian Holland, Lamont Dozier, and Eddie Holland were largely responsible for the "Motown sound," having devised a highly popular synthesis of pop and gospel musics. Utilizing an excellent team of sessions musicians and sophisticated studio equipment, Holland–Dozier–Holland (hereafter referred to as H–D–H) created the songs and the sound that thrust "soul" music into the forefront of American popular music in the Sixties, causing it to register widespread popularity with whites as well as blacks. Between 1963 and 1967, H–D–H composed and produced over 25 top-ten hits, primarily for The Four Tops and The Supremes. Severing relations with Motown in 1968, H–D–H continued their hit-making ways as producers in the early Seventies on their own labels, Invictus and Hot Wax, for artists such as Chairmen of the Board, Honey Cone, and Freda Payne. In 1973 Lamont Dozier quit the team to pursue his own marginally successful recording career, thus breaking up one of the most popular and influential songwriting-production teams in rock history.

Detroit-born on June 16, 1941, Lamont Dozier began singing as a child in his grandmother's church choir, writing his first song at the age of ten. He made his recording debut with The Romeos at 15, but the group soon broke up. Having met Berry Gordy, Jr., in 1958, Dozier joined the staff of the fledgling Motown organization in the early Sixties. Detroit-born on October 30, 1939, Eddie Holland dropped out of college to work for Berry Gordy and later became a recording artist in his own right, scoring a moderate hit with "Jamie" in early 1962 and recording one album on

Motown. Brian Holland, Detroit-born on February 15, 1941, was introduced to Gordy by his brother Eddie in the early Sixties. Brian collaborated on two early hits on Tamla for The Marvelettes, "Please Mr. Postman" and "Playboy."

In 1963 Brian and Eddie Holland and Lamont Dozier teamed up as a songwriting-production unit. Between 1963 and the end of 1967, H–D–H wrote and produced the majority of Motown's hit singles, including over 25 top-ten records. Their hit songs included "Heat Wave," "Quicksand," and "Nowhere to Run" for Martha and The Vandellas, "Mickey's Monkey" for Smokey Robinson's Miracles, and "How Sweet It Is (to Be Loved by You)" for Marvin Gaye. Much of their finest material was provided to The Four Tops and The Supremes. H–D–H song hits for The Four Tops included "Baby I Need Your Loving," "I Can't Help Myself," "It's the Same Old Song," "Reach Out, I'll Be There," "Standing in the Shadows of Love," and "Bernadette." Nevertheless, H–D–H's biggest successes came with The Supremes, regarded by many as Motown's premier act. The team wrote and produced at least ten number-one hits for The Supremes, as well as numerous top-ten hits. These included "Where Did Our Love Go," "Baby Love," "Come See About Me," "Stop! In the Name of Love," "Back in My Arms Again," "I Hear a Symphony," "My World Is Empty Without You," "Love Is Like an Itching in My Heart," "You Can't Hurry Love," "You Keep Me Hangin' On," "Love Is Here and Now You're Gone," and "The Happening" (with Frank DeVol). H–D–H extended their string of hits for the group as Diana Ross and The Supremes in 1967 with "Reflections" and "In and Out of Love." Earlier, during 1966, Eddie Holland had collaborated with Norman Whitfield on several major hits for The Temptations, including "Ain't Too Proud to Beg," "Beauty Is Only Skin Deep," and "(I Know) I'm Losing You."

However, in 1968, Brian Holland, Lamont Dozier, and Eddie Holland bitterly quit Motown to form their own record labels, Invictus (distributed by Capitol) and Hot Wax (distributed by Buddah). A series of lawsuits ensued between H–D–H and Motown, and the team was enjoined from writing songs after May 1969. Nonetheless, they produced a number of hits in the early Seventies. Invictus hits included "Give Me Just a Little More" and "Pay to the Piper" by Chairmen of the Board, and "Band of Gold" and the controversial "Bring the Boys Home" by Freda Payne. Hits on Hot Wax included "Somebody's Been Sleeping" by 100 Proof Aged in Soul, and "Want Ads," "Stick-Up," and "One Monkey Don't Stop No Show" by Honey Cone. Following an out-of-court settlement of the Motown—H–D–H lawsuits in early 1972, Brian Holland and Lamont Dozier returned to active recording, scoring minor hits together with "Why Can't We Be Lovers" and "Don't Leave Me Starvin' for Your Love" on Invictus. In 1973 Dozier left the Hollands to pursue his own solo recording career, hitting with "Trying to Hold On to My Woman" and "Fish Ain't Bitin' " in 1974 on ABC Records. Dozier later switched to Warner Brothers Records for several generally overlooked albums. In 1979 Bonnie Pointer scored a major hit with H–D–H's "Heaven Must Have Sent You," a minor hit for The Elgins 13 years earlier.

EDDIE HOLLAND

Eddie Holland	Motown	604(M)	April '63

LAMONT DOZIER

Out Here on My Own	ABC	804	January '74	
Black Bach	ABC	839	December '74	
Love and Beauty	Invictus	KZ–33134	December '74	
Right There	Warner Brothers	BS–2929	July '76	
Peddlin' Music on the Side	Warner Brothers	BS–3039	June '77	
Bittersweet	Warner Brothers	BS–3282	December '78	
Working on You	Columbia	ARC–37129	May '81	A

THE HOLLIES. One of the most popular English singles bands to surface in the wake of The Beatles, The Hollies achieved their mid-Sixties success on the basis of Allan Clarke's distinctive lead vocals, the whining, high-pitched and sometimes harsh harmonies of Graham Nash and Tony Hicks, and the songwriting of Graham Gouldman (later with 10 c.c.) and the Clarke–Hicks–Nash team. Never able to make serious inroads as an album-oriented group and essentially restricted to pop-style material, The Hollies continued despite the 1968 departure of Nash (see Crosby, Stills, Nash). The group's hits became more infrequent during the Seventies, and Allan Clarke's on-again off-again membership with the group became permanently off in 1977.

Allan Clarke (born in Salford, England, on April 5, 1942) and Graham Nash (born in Blackpool, England, on February 2, 1942) became friends in elementary school and later sang together as The Two Teens, Ricky and Dane, and with the groups The Fourtones and The Deltas. During 1962 the two teamed with Tony Hicks (born in Nelson, England, on December 16, 1945), Eric Haydock, and Don Rathbone, debuting at the Oasis Club in Manchester. By 1963 Rathbone had been replaced by Bobby Elliot (born December 8, 1942, in Burnley, England) and the group had become The Hollies. The members: Allan Clarke (lead vocals, harmonica), Graham Nash (harmony vocals, guitar), Tony Hicks (lead guitar, vocals, banjo), Eric Haydock (bass), and Bobby Elliot (drums). Signed to a recording contract in early 1963, the group scored several English hits, making their first American chart entry with "Just One Look" in 1964. Although "I'm Alive" was a smash English hit in the spring of 1965, The Hollies did not have their first major American hit until late that year with Graham Gouldman's "Look Through Any Window." The group toured the United States for the first time in the spring of 1965, replacing Eric Haydock with Bernie Calvert (born September 16, 1942, in Burnley) in early 1966. Years earlier Calvert had been a member of The Dolphins with Tony Hicks and Bobby Elliot.

The years 1966 and 1967 were perhaps The Hollies' most successful. After hitting with Graham Gouldman's "Bus Stop" in mid-1966, they scored hits with "Stop! Stop! Stop!" "On a Carousel," "Pay You Back with Interest," and "Carrie Anne," all Clarke–Hicks–Nash collaborations, the last on Epic Records. An attempt to make inroads in the album market with *Dear Eloise/King Midas in Reverse* fared dismally and Nash, unhappy with the prospect of recording an album of Dylan songs, left the group in late 1968 to join David Crosby and Steve Stills. Nash was replaced by vocalist–rhythm guitarist Terry Sylvester (born January 8, 1947, in Liverpool, England), a former member of The Swinging Blue Jeans. Ironically, the Dylan album sold poorly.

In early 1970 the rather maudlin ballad, "He Ain't Heavy, He's My Brother," became a major hit for The Hollies, and the album of the same name sold quite well. In October 1971 The Hollies fired Allan Clarke, who went on to pursue a solo career and released *My Real Name Is 'Arold* at the end of 1972. Ironically, *Distant Light*, Clarke's last album with The Hollies, yielded the smash American hit "Long Cool Woman (in a Black Dress)" some months after his departure. Swedish vocalist Mikael Rickfors was added to the group, but Clarke was back for 1974's *The Hollies*, which included the smash hit (The Hollies' last), "The Air That I Breathe." Terry Sylvester recorded a solo album during 1974 and The Hollies did not record another album for more than two years after 1975's *Another Night*. Clarke recorded another solo set, eventually leaving The Hollies in 1977. He had a moderate hit with "(I Will Be Your) Shadow in the Street" early that year, followed by the minor hit "Slipstream" in 1980. Terry Sylvester left The Hollies in June 1981 to record with former Bread vocalist James Griffin, and Bernie Calvert also quit the group shortly thereafter.

THE HOLLIES

Hear! Hear!	Imperial	LP–12299	January '66	
Here I Go Again	Imperial	LP–12265	January '66	
The Hollies—Beat Group	Imperial	LP–12312	July '66	
Bus Stop	Imperial	LP–12330	October '66	
Stop! Stop! Stop!	Imperial	LP–12339	February '67	
Evolution	Epic	BN–26315	July '67	
Dear Eloise/King Midas in Reverse	Epic	BN–26344	January '68	
Words and Music by Bob Dylan	Epic	BN–26447	August '69	
He Ain't Heavy, He's My Brother	Epic reissued on Columbia Special Products	BN–26538 EN–13092	March '70 November '76	
Moving Finger	Epic	E–30255	February '71	
Distant Light	Epic	E–30958	June '72	A
Romany	Epic	E–31992	January '73	A

The Hollies	Epic	KE–32574	April '74	
Another Night	Epic	PE–33387	February '75	
Clarke, Hicks, Sylvester, Elliot, Calvert	Epic	PE–34714	June '77	
Crazy Steal	Epic	PE–35334	May '78	A

HOLLIES ANTHOLOGIES AND COMPILATIONS

Greatest Hits	Imperial	LP–12350	May '67	
Greatest Hits	Epic	PE–32061	September '73	A
Very Best	United Artists	LA329	March '75	
The Hollies' Greatest	Capitol	N–16056	December '80	A

ALLAN CLARKE

My Real Name Is 'Arold	Epic	KE–31757	November '72	
I've Got Time	Asylum	7E–1056	February '76	A
I Wasn't Born Yesterday	Atlantic	SD–19175	May '78	A
Legendary Heroes	Curb	267	April '80	A

TERRY SYLVESTER

| Terry Sylvester | Epic | KE–33076 | September '74 | |

BUDDY HOLLY. One of the two great singer–songwriter–guitarists of the Fifties (along with Chuck Berry), Buddy Holly was probably the first rock performer to concern himself with virtually every aspect of his music, as singer (with his distinctive "hicupping" vocal style), guitarist, songwriter, and arranger. With The Crickets, Holly established the standard lineup for the rock band (two guitars, bass, and drums) and set the precedent for the self-contained rock-and-roll band, writing their own material and choosing what and how to record. One of the first rock musicians from a country-and-western background to use drums, Holly was among the first white musicians to apply the heavy backbeat of black rhythm-and-blues to country and pop-style material. One of the earliest innovators of rock-and-roll, Buddy Holly pioneered the studio technique of "overdubbing" and "double-tracking" under producer Norman Petty, later utilizing the services of saxophonist King Curtis, vocal choirs, and a studio orchestra. With the use of vocal choirs and the studio orchestra, Holly became one of the originators of the modern "pop" song within the rock tradition. Probably the first rock-and-roll "legend" due to his early accidental death, Buddy Holly's legacy lives on in the recorded work of numerous contemporary artists (Linda Ronstadt in particular), despite a career that lasted just over two years.

Born Charles Hardin Holley in Lubbock, Texas, on September 7, 1936, Buddy Holly took up violin as a youngster, later switching to guitar. By the age of 13, he was performing with friend Bob Montgomery, playing "western and bop" music. The duo sang country-and-western songs on their own radio show on station KDAV in Lubbock between 1953 and 1955, recording a number of songs later released as *Holly in the Hills*. Spotted opening a Lubbock rock show by a talent scout, Holly was soon signed to Decca Records. Three times during 1956, he traveled to Nashville to record under veteran producer Owen Bradley, the second time accompanied by The Three Tunes—guitarist Sonny Curtis (born in Meadow, Texas, on May 9, 1937), drummer Jerry Allison (born in Hillsboro, Texas, on August 31, 1939) and bassist Don Guess. These sessions, eventually issued in 1958 as *That'll Be the Day* (later re-released on Vocalion and MCA Records as *The Great Buddy Holly*), included an early version of "That'll Be the Day," as well as "Rock Around with Ollie Vee" and "Midnight Shift." However, none of Decca's 1956 singles releases for Holly ever made the charts.

Subsequently released by Decca, Buddy Holly started recording at producer Norman Petty's studio in Clovis, New Mexico, in early 1957. The first session, recorded with guitarist Niki Sullivan, bassist Larry Welborn, and Three Tunes drummer Jerry Allison, yielded another version of the Holly–Allison collaboration, "That'll Be the Day." Submitted to and rejected by Roulette Records, the demonstration tape found its way to Bo Thiele. He released the song on Brunswick Records under the name The Crickets and quickly signed the group. By September "That'll Be the Day" had become a smash American and English hit. Earlier that year, in the spring, The Crickets had come together with Sullivan, Allison, and standup bassist Joe Mauldin. Norman Petty took over the career of Buddy Holly and The Crickets as manager, producer, sessions leader, and occasional keyboardist, negotiating separate contracts for The Crickets with Brunswick and for Holly with Coral Records. Holly soon hit with the classic rock song "Peggy Sue" (backed with "Everyday"), while The Crickets scored major hits with "Oh, Boy" (backed with "Not Fade Away") and "Maybe Baby." The debut Crickets album was released at the end of 1957, but Sullivan left the group in December. Reduced to a trio, Holly was obliged to play guitar as both a rhythm and lead instrument on tours of the United States and, in early 1958, Australia and England.

During 1958 The Crickets hit with "Think It Over" and Buddy Holly with "Rave On" and Bobby Darin's "Early in the Morning," the latter recorded in New York without The Crickets but with vocal choir and saxophonist Sam "The Man" Taylor. However, "It's So Easy" and "Heartbeat," recorded with guitarist Tommy Allsup, fared poorly and, by October, The Crickets had split from Holly and Holly had left Norman Petty. Holly subsequently recorded "True Love Ways," "Raining in My Heart," and Paul Anka's "It Doesn't Matter Anymore" in New York under producer Dick Jacobs, utilizing Jacob's orchestra. Thus Holly was seemingly moving in a more "pop" direction. Holly then embarked on a tour of the Midwest with guitarist Allsup, drummer Charlie Bunch, and guitarist turned electric bassist Waylon Jennings. Following a concert at Clear Lake, Iowa, on February 2, 1959, Buddy Holly, then 22, Richie Valens ("Donna," "La Bamba"), and J.P. "The Big Bopper" Richardson ("Chantilly Lace") died when their chartered plane crashed shortly after takeoff. Jennings had apparently been bumped from his seat on the plane, and Dion and The Belmonts, also on the tour, had apparently made alternate travel arrangements.

"It Doesn't Matter Anymore" (backed with "Raining in My Heart") soon became a major hit and *The Buddy Holly Story*, issued within two months of Holly's death, became a best-selling album, eventually certified gold-award in 1969. Norman Petty assembled a variety of Buddy Holly albums and singles from old tapes, overdubbing strings and other instrumentation. The Crickets stayed together through 1965, recording several albums, including one with Bobby Vee. Sonny Curtis scored songwriting successes with "More Than I Can Say," co-written with Jerry Allison (a smash hit for Leo Sayer in 1980), and "I Fought the Law" (a near-smash for The Bobby Fuller Four in 1966), and recorded several albums in the late Sixties. He eventually re-emerged by the Eighties as a country artist, achieving moderate country hits with "The Real Buddy Holly Story" and "Love Is All Around." Tommy Allsup recorded an album for Reprise in 1965, and Bob Montgomery proved successful as a songwriter ("Misty Blue") and independent producer for Johnny Darrell and Bobby Goldsboro ("Honey"). Waylon Jennings struggled as a country-and-western artist through the latter half of the Sixties, finally achieving recognition as an "outlaw" country musician by 1976.

During the Sixties Buddy Holly's legacy was kept alive as The Rolling Stones scored their first American singles chart entry with his "Not Fade Away," Peter and Gordon hit with "True Love Ways," and The Bobby Fuller Four had a hit with Holly's "Love's Made a Fool of You." In the later half of the Seventies, Linda Ronstadt recorded a number of Holly's songs, scoring major hits with "That'll Be the Day" and "It's So Easy." Paul McCartney purchased the publishing rights to all of Holly's songs and Wings sideman Denny Laine recorded an entire album of his songs, *Holly Days*. In May 1978, *The Buddy Holly Story*, starring Gary Busey, was released and became a surprise film hit, sparking revitalized interest in Holly. The Beach Boys, Leo Sayer, and Santana had minor hits that year with "Peggy Sue," "Raining in My Heart," and "Well, All Right," respectively. Waylon Jennings' *I've Always Been Crazy* album featured a four-song Holly medley and, since 1979, Jennings has toured with the original Crickets.

BUDDY HOLLY AND BOB MONTGOMERY

Holly in the Hills	Coral	CRL–757463	February '65

BUDDY HOLLY

That'll Be the Day	Decca	8707(M)	May '58	
reissued as The	Vocalion	VL–73811(E)	November '67	
Great Buddy				
Holly	reissued on Coral/MCA	20101(E)		A

BUDDY HOLLY AND THE CRICKETS

The Chirping Crickets	Brunswick	BL–54038 (M)	December '57	
reissued as Buddy Holly and The Crickets	Coral	CRL–757405 (E)	May '62	

BUDDY HOLLY

Buddy Holly	Coral	CRL–57210 (M)	April '58	
The Buddy Holly Story *	Coral	CRL–57279 (M)	March '59	
The Buddy Holly Story, Volume 2	Coral	CRL–57326 (M)	April '60	
Reminiscing	Coral	CRL–757426	March '63	
Buddy Holly Showcase	Coral	CRL–757450	June '64	
The Best of Buddy Holly	Coral	7CX–8	May '66	
Greatest Hits	Coral	CRL–757492	April '67	
Giant	Coral	CRL–757504	January '69	
Good Rockin'	Vocalion	VL–73293 (E)	'71	
Buddy Holly: A Rock 'n' Roll Collection	2-Decca reissued on MCA	DXSE–7207(E) 4009(E)	September '72	A
Buddy Holly Complete	6–MCA	80000(M)	April '81	A

BUDDY HOLLY AND THE CRICKETS

20 Golden Greats	MCA	3040(M)	May '78	A

THE CRICKETS

In the Style with The Crickets	Coral	CRL–757320	January '61
Bobby Vee Meets The Crickets	Liberty	LST–7228	July '62
Somethin' Else!	Liberty	LST–7272	January '63
California Sun	Liberty	LST–7351	April '64
Rockin' 50's Rock and Roll	Barnaby	Z–30268	January '71
Remnants	Mercury	SRM1–695	January '74

TOMMY ALLSUP

The Buddy Holly Song Book	Reprise	RS–6182	November '65

SONNY CURTIS

Beatle Hits	Imperial	12276	January '66	
First	Viva	36012	March '68	
The Sonny Curtis Style	Viva	36021		
Sonny Curtis	Elektra	227	December '79	
Love Is All Around	Elektra	283	July '80	A
Rollin'	Elektra	349	July '81	A

HOT TUNA. An outgrowth of The Jefferson Airplane, Hot Tuna was formed at the end of the Sixties by Jack Casady and Jorma Kaukonen in pursuit of their own separate musical interests while still with the parent group. Casady, recognized as one of rock music's most inventive bassists, and Kaukonen performed and recorded acoustic and, later, electric blues frequently featuring extended improvisations. Remaining perhaps San Francisco's last important "psychedelic" band, Hot Tuna disbanded in 1978.

HOT TUNA

Hot Tuna	RCA	LSP–4353 reissued as AYL1–3864	June '70	A
Electric—Recorded Live ("First Pull Up, Then Pull Down")	RCA	LSP–4550 reissued as AYL1–3865	June '71	A
Burgers	Grunt	FTR–1004 reissued as BXL1–2591 reissued as AYL1–3951	March '72	A
Phosphorescent Rat	Grunt	BXL1–0348	January '74	A

JORMA KAUKONEN WITH TOM HOBSON

Quah	Grunt	BXL1–0209 reissued as AYL1–3747	September '74	A

HOT TUNA

America's Choice	Grunt	BXL1–0820	April '75	A
Yellow Fever	Grunt	BXL1–1238	November '75	

Hoppkorv	Grunt	BXL1–1920	October '76	
		reissued as AYL1–3950		A
Double Dose	2-Grunt	CYL2–2545	March '78	
Final Vinyl	Grunt	BXL1–3357	April '79	A

JORMA KAUKONEN

| Jorma | RCA | AFL1–3446 | October '79 | A |

JORMA KAUKONEN AND VITAL PARTS

| Barbeque King | RCA | AFL1–3725 | March '81 | A |

SVT

| No Regrets | MSI | 2002 | October '81 | A |

HUMBLE PIE. "Hard rock" English band of the Seventies, Humble Pie, lead by ex-Small Face Steve Marriott, featured singer–guitarist Peter Frampton in its initial incarnation. More effective live than on recordings, and eventually more successful as an album band than as a singles band, Humble Pie continued after Frampton's 1971 departure and disbanded in 1975, after which Marriott recorded solo and with the reconstituted Small Faces (who broke up by 1979).

HUMBLE PIE

Town and Country	Immediate	207	'69	
As Safe as Yesterday	Immediate	101	'69	
Lost and Found—Town and Country/Safe as Yesterday	2-A&M	SP–3513	September '72	A
Humble Pie	A&M	SP–4270	November '70	
		reissued as 3127		A
Rock On	A&M	SP–4301	May '71	A
Performance: Live Rockin' the Fillmore*	A&M	SP–3506	November '71	A
Smokin'*	A&M	SP–4342	March '72	
		reissued as 3132		A
Eat It	2-A&M	SP–3701	March '73	A
Thunderbox	A&M	SP–3611	February '74	A

Street Rats	A&M	SP-4514	March '75	
On to Victory	Atlantic	38-122	April '80	A
Go for the Throat	Atlantic	38-131	April '81	A

STEVE MARRIOTT

| Marriott | A&M | SP-4572 | March '76 |

THE SMALL FACES

| Playmates | Atlantic | SD-19113 | August '77 |
| 78 in the Shade | Atlantic | SD-19171 | October '78 |

ROUGH DIAMOND (WITH DAVE CLEMPSON)

| Rough Diamond | Island | 9490 | April '77 |

CHAMPION (WITH DAVE CLEMPSON)

| Champion | Epic | JE-35438 | August '78 |

JACK BRUCE AND FRIENDS (INCLUDING DAVE CLEMPSON)

| I've Always Wanted to Do This | Epic | 36827 | November '80 | A |

I

JANIS IAN. Singer–songwriter–multi-instrumentalist Janis Ian has really had two separate careers, one as the teenage folk-protest writer–performer of 1967's "Society's Child," the other as the sensitive singer–songwriter of 1975's "At Seventeen." In virtual retirement after the relative failures of her follow-ups to her debut album, Janis Ian developed her skills as musical arranger and mature, highly personal songwriter that led to her re-emergence in 1974. Nonetheless, her career since 1976's *Aftertones* has again seemed to be in eclipse, as subsequent albums sold progressively less well.

JANIS IAN

Janis Ian	Verve	FTS–3017	February '67	
For All the Seasons of Your Mind	Verve	FTS–3024	December '67	
The Secret Life of J. Eddy Fink	Verve	FTS–3048	July '68	
Who Really Cares	Verve	FTS–3063	October '71	
Present Company	Capitol	SM–683	March '71	A
Stars	Columbia	PC–32857	April '74	A
Between the Lines *	Columbia	PC–33394	March '75	A
Aftertones	Columbia	PC–33919	January '76	A
Miracle Row	Columbia	PC–34440	January '77	A
Janis Ian	Columbia	JC–35325	August '78	A
Night Rains	Columbia	JC–36139	October '79	A
Restless Eyes	Columbia	FC–37360	June '81	A

JANIS IAN REISSUES AND COMPILATIONS

Janis Ian	MGM	GAS–121	October '70
Janis Ian	Polydor	PD–6058	January '76

THE IMPRESSIONS. The soul group of the Sixties that presented one of the biggest challenges to the myriad of Tamla–Motown groups, the Chicago-based Impressions scored a number of hit singles featuring smooth, precise harmonies behind Curtis Mayfield's wispy falsetto lead vocals. Dominated by Mayfield as vocal and musical arranger and song-writer, The Impressions created a synthesis of pop and gospel musics that, while directed primarily at a black audience, also appealed to whites. Although Mayfield's lyrics had become overtly political by 1968, championing black self-pride and revealing a sense of social consciousness, his compositions were sometimes viewed as strident and didactic. Recording for Mayfield's own Curtom label after the fall of 1968, The Impressions experienced declining popularity after his departure to pursue a solo career in 1970 (chronicled elsewhere). Mayfield, of course, later achieved widespread success with his *Superfly* soundtrack. His replacement, Leroy Hutson, also went solo in 1973, as early members Sam Gooden and Fred Cash reconstituted The Impressions for a marginal recording career.

Mississippi-born Jerry Butler (December 8, 1939) and Chicago-born Curtis Mayfield (June 3, 1942) knew each other as early as 1956, when they were members of Chicago-based vocal groups—Butler with The Modern Jubilaires, Mayfield with The Alphatones. By 1957 Butler was working with The Roosters, a three-man rhythm-and-blues vocal group whose fourth member, tenor Fred Cash, had remained in the group's hometown of Chattanooga, Tennessee. During 1957 the four (Butler, brothers Arthur and Richard Brooks, and bass singer Sam Gooden) were joined by Curtis Mayfield and became The Impressions under manager Eddie Thomas. The group's first major hit came in 1958 with "For Your Precious Love," erroneously credited to Jerry Butler and The Impressions. Butler soon left The Impressions to pursue a successful solo career, and Mayfield assumed the lead vocal chores for the group. Curtis Mayfield continued to work with Butler as guitarist, co-authoring Butler's second hit, "He Will Break Your Heart," as The Impressions languished until rejuvenated by the addition of Fred Cash. Signed to ABC–Paramount in 1961, The Impressions scored their first pop hit with Mayfield's "Gypsy Woman" late that year. Subsequent single releases fared less well and, by 1963, the group was reduced to a trio with the departure of the Brooks brothers.

In the fall of 1963 the three-man Impressions (Mayfield, Gooden, and Cash) began an impressive string of hit records, virtually all written by Mayfield, with "It's All Right." Hits through 1965 included "Talking About My Baby," "I'm So Proud," "Keep on Pushing," "You Must Believe Me," "Amen," "People Get Ready," "Woman's Got Soul," and "You've Been Cheatin'." The Impressions' popularity waned a bit in the mid-Sixties but, by 1968, they were back with the prideful "We're a Winner." During that year Mayfield formed his own record label, Curtom Records, on which The Impressions subsequently recorded. The group's first two Curtom albums, *This Is My Country* and *Young Mod's Forgotten Story*, contained a number of socially conscious black-oriented songs such as "Mighty, Mighty Spade and Whitey" and the hits "This Is My Country" and "Choice of Colors."

Following the success of the group's "Check Out Your Mind" single, Curtis Mayfield left The Impressions for a solo career while continuing to record and produce the group. Leroy Hutson replaced Mayfield as lead vocalist, but the group had no major hits during his two-year tenure. By 1973 Hutson had departed to pursue his own marginally successful solo career on Curtom Records, and the two remaining Impressions, Sam Gooden and Fred Cash, recruited lead vocalist Reggie Torian and tenor Ralph Johnson for the group's last major hit, "Finally Got Myself Together." By 1979 The Impressions, again reduced to a trio (Gooden, Cash, and Torian), had switched to 20th Century-Fox Records.

EARLY IMPRESSIONS

In the Beginning	Checker	3014	
For Your Precious Love	VeeJay	1075	
Vintage Years	2-Sire	3717	February '77

THE IMPRESSIONS

The Impressions	ABC	450	August '63
Never Ending Impressions	ABC	468	March '64
Keep on Pushing	ABC	493	August '64
People Get Ready	ABC	505	February '65
One by One	ABC	523	September '65
Ridin' High	ABC	545	March '66
The Fabulous Impressions	ABC	606	June '67
We're a Winner	ABC	635	February '68
Versatile	ABC	668	July '69
This Is My Country	Curtom	8001	November '68
Young Mod's Forgotten Story	Curtom	8003	April '69
Check Out Your Mind	Curtom	8006	November '70
Times Have Changed	Curtom	8012	April '72
Preacher Man	Curtom	8016	May '73
Finally Got Myself Together	Curtom	8019	February '74
Three the Hard Way (sound-track)	Curtom	8602	August '74
Sooner or Later	Curtom	0103	June '75
First Impressions	Curtom	5003	July '75
Loving Power	Curtom	5009	March '76
It's About Time	Cotillion	9912	December '76
Come to My Party	20th Century-Fox	T–596	September '79
Fan the Fire	20 Century-Fox	624	June '81	A

THE IMPRESSIONS ANTHOLOGIES AND COMPILATIONS

Greatest Hits	ABC	515	March '65
Best	ABC	654	September '68

16 Greatest Hits	ABC	727	March '71	
	reissued on Pickwick	3602	April '78	A
Best Impressions— Curtis, Sam, Fred	Curtom	8004	November '70	
Chart Busters	Pickwick	3502		

CURTIS MAYFIELD

| His Early Years with The Impressions | 2-ABC | 780 | January '73 | |

LEROY HUTSON

Love, Oh, Love	Curtom	8017	June '73	
	reissued as 5020		January '78	
Leroy Hutson	Curtom	5002	April '75	
Feel the Spirit	Curtom	5010	March '76	
Hutson II	Curtom	5011	November '76	
Closer to the Source	Curtom	5018	March '78	
Unforgettable	RSO	3062	February '80	A

THE INCREDIBLE STRING BAND. Obscure esoteric Scottish folk-style group of the late Sixties and early Seventies, The Incredible String Band was essentially singer–songwriters Robin Williamson and Mike Heron. Utilizing exotic instrumentation and singing in a strange vocal drone, The Incredible String Band became identified with the British "psychedelic-counterculture" movement, but never progressed beyond their cult status. After the group's breakup in late 1974 Robin Williamson moved to Los Angeles, later forming his Merry Band for further esoteric recordings on Flying Fish Records, whereas Mike Heron eventually resurfaced on Casablanca Records in late 1979.

THE INCREDIBLE STRING BAND

The Incredible String Band	Elektra	EKS–7322	May '67	A
The 5000 Spirits or the Layers of the Onion	Elektra	EKS– 74010	December '67	A
The Hangman's Beautiful Daughter	Elektra	EKS– 74021	July '68	
Wee Tam	Elektra	EKS– 74036	March '69	A
The Big Huge	Elektra	EKS– 74037	March '69	A

Changing Horses	Elektra	EKS–74057	December '69	A
I Looked Up	Elektra	EKS–74061	July '70	
U	Elektra	7E–2002	December '70	A
Relics	2-Elektra	7E–2004	October '71	A
Liquid Acrobat as Regards the Air	Elektra	EKS–74112	February '72	
Earthspan	Reprise	MS–2122	October '72	
No Ruinous Feud	Reprise	MS–2139	April '73	
Hard Rope and Silken Twine	Reprise	MS–2198	June '74	

MIKE HERON

Smiling Men with Bad Reputations	Elektra	EKS–74093	July '71	
Mike Heron	Casablanca	7186	November '79	A

ROBIN WILLIAMSON

Journey's Edge	Flying Fish	033	May '77	A
American Stone-henge	Flying Fish	062	May '78	A
Songs of Love and Parting	Flying Fish	257	December '81	A

ROBIN WILLIAMSON AND HIS MERRY BAND

A Glint at the Kindling	Flying Fish	096	August '79	A

IRON BUTTERFLY. One of the first American "heavy metal" bands, Iron Butterfly burst onto the music scene in 1968 with their side-long epic "In-a-Gadda-da-Vida," one of the longest album cuts in rock music at the time. The *In-a-Gadda-da-Vida* album remained on the American charts for over two years and became one of the largest selling rock albums of the era. Subsequently suffering a number of personnel changes, Iron Butterfly never regained the glory surrounding the song and disbanded in 1971, to re-form briefly in 1975.

IRON BUTTERFLY

Heavy	Atco	SD33–227	February '68	
In-a-Gadda-da-Vida*	Atco	SD33–250	July '68	A
Ball*	Atco	SD33–280	February '69	
Live	Atco	SD33–318	March '70	A
Metamorphosis	Atco	SD33–339	August '70	
The Best of Iron Butterfly/Evolution	Atco	SD33–369	November '71	
Scorching Beauty	MCA	465	January '75	
Sun and Steel	MCA	2164	December '75	

THE ISLEY BROTHERS.   Long-lived rhythm-and-blues/soul vocal group, The Isley Brothers recorded for at least four different labels in a variety of styles following their first pop hit with "Twist and Shout" in 1962. Forming T-Neck Productions in 1964, which was briefly distributed by Atlantic, The Isley Brothers gained a large measure of artistic control after their stint with Tamla Records by resurrecting T-Neck in 1969. Thus the brothers became one of the first black acts (along with Marvin Gaye and Stevie Wonder) to achieve independence from a major record company. Joined by younger brothers Ernie and Marvin and brother-in-law Chris Jasper, The Isley Brothers became a self-contained band in 1969. With Ernie playing guitar in a style strongly reminiscent of Jimi Hendrix (some say he is the finest exponent of the Hendrix tradition now playing) and Jasper exploring keyboard-synthesizer possibilities pioneered by Stevie Wonder, The Isley Brothers successfully made the transition from singles band to album-oriented band with their 3 + 3 album from 1973. With the younger and newer members writing and arranging most of the material, The Isley Brothers have issued a series of gold- and platinum-award albums through the Seventies.

Isley Brothers Vernon, Ronald (born May 21, 1941), Rudolph (born April 1, 1939), and O'Kelly (born December 25, 1937) began singing as a quartet at churches in their hometown of Cincinnati and later toured churches throughout the Midwest. Reduced to a trio by the accidental death of Vernon, The Isley Brothers went to New York as teenagers in 1957, recorded several unsuccessful singles for Teenage and Gone Records, and debuted at the Howard Theater in Washington, D.C.. Switching to RCA Records in late 1958, the brothers scored their first minor pop hit with their own composition, "Shout," recorded under producers Hugo and Luigi (later producers of The Stylistics), in the fall of 1959. Following the release of *Shout* in 1960, they moved to Atlantic Records, working under producers Jerry Leiber and Mike Stoller. Finding little success, the brothers went to Florence Greenberg's Wand and Scepter labels and scored a major hit in 1962 with the raucous "Twist and Shout," written by Bert Berns and Phil Medley. Their travels nonetheless continued as they moved to United Artists in 1963, again with little success. The Isley Brothers subsequently toured the rhythm-and-blues circuit in the mid Sixties with then-unknown guitarist Jimi Hendrix. Recordings with Hendrix eventually surfaced as *In the Beginning* in 1971.

In 1964 The Isley Brothers formed their own production company, T-Neck (named after their adopted hometown, Teaneck, New Jersey), but a solitary release by the company, distributed by Atlantic, fared poorly. Later releases were issued on Atlantic and, in late 1965, the brothers moved to Motown's Tamla Records, where they were placed with songwriter–producers Holland–Dozier–Holland. "This Old Heart of Mine (Is Weak for You)" became a major pop hit for The Isley Brothers in early 1966, but releases through 1968 were essentially restricted to the rhythm-and-blues field.

By 1969 The Isley Brothers had revived T-Neck, working out a distribution deal with Buddah Records. Their first release on T-Neck, "It's Your

Thing," became a smash hit early that year, and younger brothers Ernie and Marvin and brother-in-law Chris Jasper soon joined the three vocalizing Isleys on drums, bass, and keyboards, respectively. Ernie later took up guitar, developing a playing style that owed much to Jimi Hendrix, whereas Jasper utilized synthesizers in addition to standard keyboard instruments. "I Turned You On" was a major pop hit for The Isleys in mid-1969, but their next did not come for two years, until they recorded Steve Stills' "Love the One You're With" from *Givin' It Back*, an album totally comprised of cover songs. After another major hit with "Pop That Thing" in mid-1972, The Isley Brothers switched distributorship of T-Neck to Columbia in 1973, firmly establishing themselves as album artists with the gold-award *3 + 3*, which yielded the smash hit "Who's That Lady," featuring Ernie's phase-shifter lead guitar work. *Live It Up* and *The Heat Is On* were both certified gold-award the year of their release, the latter including the smash hit "Fight the Power" and the major hit "For the Love of You." Later album releases attained the gold-award level, with *Go for Your Guns*, *Showdown*, and *Go All the Way* certified platinum-award during the years of release.

THE ISLEY BROTHERS

The Isley Brothers and Marvin and Johnny	Crown	CLP–5352		
Shout	RCA	LSP–2156	December '59	
Twist and Shout	Wand	653(M)	September '62	
Take Some Time Out	Scepter	552		
Twisting and Shouting	United Artists	UAS–6313	February '64	
In the Beginning (with Jimi Hendrix)	T-Neck	TNS–3007	May '71	
This Old Heart of Mine	Tamla	269	June '66	
Soul on the Rocks	Tamla	275	January '68	
It's Our Thing	T-Neck	TNS–3001	April '69	
Brothers Isley	T-Neck	TNS–3002	October '69	
Live at Yankee Stadium	T-Neck	TNS–3004	October '69	
Get Into Something	T-Neck	TNS–3006	January '71	
Givin' It Back	T-Neck	TNS–3008	September '71	
Brother, Brother, Brother	T-Neck	TNS–3009	May '72	
Live	2-T-Neck	TNS–3010	March '73	
3 + 3*	T-Neck	PZ–32453	August '73	A
Live It Up*	T-Neck	PZ–33070	August '74	A
The Heat is On*	T-Neck	PZ–33536	May '75	A
Harvest for the World*	T-Neck	PZ–33809	May '76	A
Go for Your Guns**	T-Neck	PZ–34432	April '77	A

Showdown **	T-Neck	JZ–34930	April '78	A
Winner Takes All *	2-T-Neck	PZ2–36077	June '79	A
Go All the Way **	T-Neck	FZ–36305	April '80	A
Grand Slam *	T-Neck	FZ–37080	April '81	A
Inside You	T-Neck	FZ–37533	October '81	A

ISLEY BROTHERS ANTHOLOGIES AND COMPILATIONS

Do Their Thing	Sunset	5257	July '69	
Doin' Their Thing	Tamla	287	April '70	
Motown Superstar Series, Volume 6	Motown	5–106		A
This Old Heart of Mine	Pickwick	3398		
Rock On, Brother	Camden	ACL1– 0126	May '73	
Country/Rock Around the Clock	Camden	ACL–0861	May '75	A
The Best	2-Buddah	BDS–5652	April '76	
The Very Best	United Artists	LA500	April '76	
Greatest Hits	T-Neck	TNS–3011	November '73	
Forever Gold	T-Neck	PZ–34452	August '77	
Timeless	T-Neck	KZ2–35650	October '78	

JAN AND DEAN. Early Sixties purveyors of innocuous fun songs concerning surfing, cars, high school, and girls, Jan and Dean were second only to The Beach Boys in their promotion of these southern California themes. In fact, The Beach Boys' Brian Wilson wrote several of Jan and Dean's biggest hits, including "Surf City" and "The New Girl in School." Issuing a series of hit singles between 1963 and 1965 featuring multi-tracked voices, sound effects, and sessions musicians Glen Campbell and Leon Russell, Jan and Dean were recording folk and Beatles songs by the mid-Sixties. However, in April 1966 Jan was nearly killed in a Los Angeles automobile wreck that left him in a coma for nearly a year. Suffering paralysis of his right side and impaired speech and memory, Jan spent years in physical therapy as Dean pursued a career as a graphic artist, designing album covers. An attempted 1973 reunion did not work out but, by 1978, Jan and Dean were again performing occasionally.

Los Angeles-born Jan Berry (April 3, 1941) and Dean Torrance (March 10, 1940) met in junior high school. Fascinated with the popular "doo wop" sound of the late Fifties, they began singing similarly styled material in The Barons while in high school. The group recorded "Jennie Lee" in Berry's garage and, upon release on Arwin Records, the song became a major hit in 1958, credited to Jan and Arnie (Dean was in the Army at the time). In 1959 Jan and Dean scored with another song recorded in Berry's garage, "Baby Talk," on Dore Records, but their next major success did not come until 1961 with their "doo wop" version of "Heart and Soul." Signed to Liberty Records by early 1962, they began a string of hit singles with Brian Wilson's "Linda" in early 1963. Wilson's "Surf City" was a smash hit for Jan and Dean during the summer of 1963 and subsequent hits included "Honolulu Lulu," "Drag City," the two-sided "Dead Man's Curve/The New Girl in School," the smash "The Little Old Lady from Pasadena," "Ride the Wild Surf," and Wilson's "Sidewalk Surfin'," a precursor of the Seventies skateboard rage.

By 1965 Jan and Dean had attempted to capitalize on the folk craze with the dismal *Folk 'n' Roll* album and soon recorded several Beatles songs on *Filet of Soul*. However, in April 1966 Jan Berry was nearly killed when his Corvette, allegedly traveling at 90 miles per hour, struck a parked truck. In a coma for nearly a year, Jan spent much of the next ten years undergoing intensive physical therapy for a condition that included paralysis of his right side and impairment of his speech, hearing, memory, and vision. Dean Torrance handled both vocal parts for *Save for a Rainy Day;* he later opened Kittyhawk Graphics, where he designed album covers. Jan ultimately returned to the studio in 1970, later performing with Dean at Hollywood's 1973 "Surfer's Stomp Reunion." As a result of interest created by the biographical "Dead Man's Curve" CBS television special in February 1978, and with Jan's condition apparently much improved, Jan and Dean appeared with The Beach Boys during the year. Though no permanent reunion was planned, Jan and Dean do occasionally perform in the Los Angeles and San Francisco regions.

JAN AND DEAN

Jan and Dean	Dore	101	
The Heart and Soul of Jan and Dean	Design	181	
Jan and Dean Take Linda Surfin'	Liberty	LST–7294	June '63
Surf City (and Other Swingin' Cities)	Liberty	LST–7314	August '63
Drag City	Liberty	LST–7339	January '64
Dead Man's Curve/ The New Girl in School	Liberty	LST–7361	May '64
Ride the Wild Surf	Liberty	LST–7368	October '64
The Little Old Lady from Pasadena	Liberty	LST–7377	October '64
Command Performance—"Live" in Person	Liberty	LST–7403	February '65
Folk 'n' Roll	Liberty	LST–7431	January '66
Filet of Soul	Liberty	LST–7441	May '66
Jan and Dean Meet Batman	Liberty	LST–7444	May '66
Save for a Rainy Day	Columbia	CS–9461	April '67

JAN AND DEAN ANTHOLOGIES AND COMPILATIONS

Jan and Dean's Golden Hits	Liberty	LST–7248	September '62	
Jan and Dean's Golden Hits, Volume 2	Liberty	LST–7417	September '65	
Jan and Dean's Golden Hits, Volume 3	Liberty	LST–7460	October '66	
Jan and Dean Legendary Masters #3	Sunset 2-United Artists	SUS–5156 UAS–9961	February '67 November '71	A

Gotta Take That One Last Ride	2-United Artists	LA341	October '74	
The Very Best of Jan and Dean, Volume 1	United Artists	LA443	September '75	
The Very Best of Jan and Dean, Volume 2	United Artists	LA515	April '76	
Dead Man's Curve	United Artists	LT–999 reissued as LN–10011	December '79	A
Best	Liberty	LN–10115	April '81	A

THE JEFFERSON AIRPLANE/STARSHIP.

Although not the first band of San Francisco's "hippie-psychedelic" era (that claim probably belongs to The Charlatans), The Jefferson Airplane was the first San Francisco group to secure a major label recording contract. The group's debut album, *Jefferson Airplane Takes Off*, though generally overlooked, was an exciting blend of the folk and rock idioms featuring compelling vocal harmonies, Marty Balin's romantic songwriting, and containing an early version of the hippie anthem "Let's Get Together." With the amplification of guitars and the replacement of original female vocalist Signe Anderson by Grace Slick of The Great Society, The Jefferson Airplane became transformed into San Francisco's first widely recognized "psychedelic" band. The first San Francisco group to score a national hit ("Somebody to Love"), The Jefferson Airplane followed up with one of the first drug-oriented hit singles, Slick's "White Rabbit." As with The Grateful Dead, San Francisco's other enduring major group, The Jefferson Airplane was a remarkably democratic band (at least initially), quickly establishing themselves with the local "counter-culture" community and frequently playing for free in Golden Gate Park.

Surrealistic Pillow, The Jefferson Airplane's first album with Grace Slick as a member, became an instant best-seller and launched the so-called "San Francisco sound" into national, indeed international, prominence while raising Grace Slick to the rank of female "superstar," to be rivaled at the time by only Janis Joplin. Having no major hit single after *Surrealistic Pillow*, the album established The Jefferson Airplane as an album-oriented group, a status reinforced with *After Bathing at Baxter's* and *Crown of Creation*, both of which contained songs alternately surreal, psychedelic, mellow, and romantic. However, by the time of *Volunteers*, Grace Slick and Paul Kantner had seized creative dominance of the group, and Balin was reduced to half the song credit of the title song, the radical political anthem from Balin's final album with The Jefferson Airplane. "We Can Be Together" extended the tradition established with "Let's Get Together" and, moreover, *Volunteers* presaged Kantner's later preoccupation with science fiction themes with "Wooden Ships," co-authored by David Crosby and Steve Stills.

By the spring of 1971, overwhelmed by Slick and Kantner and derided by Jack Casady and Jorma Kaukonen for his romantic bent, Marty Balin had left The Jefferson Airplane. The group subsequently endured a chaotic period of personnel changes, solo and joint ventures that saw the self-indulgent *Bark* and *Long John Silver* albums nonetheless become best-sellers. In August 1972 Casady and Kaukonen left The Jefferson Airplane to pursue the blues-oriented Hot Tuna full time, and the group was essentially reconstituted and revived as The Jefferson Starship in early 1974. Marty Balin sang lead vocals on "Caroline" from The Starship's debut album, *Dragonfly*, and returned to the group full time in early 1975. Featuring the group's first smash single in eight years (Balin's "Miracles"), *Octopus* re-established The Jefferson Starship as one of America's most popular recording bands. Bolstered by Balin's singing and songwriting, the group's next two albums, *Spitfire* and *Earth*, were both certified platinum-award during the year of release. However, by 1979, both Slick and Balin had left the group, and The Jefferson Starship was yet again realigned with Kantner as the only original member.

Cincinnati-born on January 30, 1942, as Martyn Jerel Buchwald, Marty Balin was performing around the San Francisco area with the folk group The Town Criers in 1964. During the spring of 1965 he took over a small San Francisco club called The Honeybucket, renaming it The Matrix. Over the next few months, Balin assembled a group of musicians, including guitarists Paul Kantner and Jorma Kaukonen, and vocalist Signe Toly. Named The Jefferson Airplane, the group debuted at The Matrix on August 13, 1965, performing a blend of rock and folk musics. The group's members: Balin, Kantner, Kaukonen, Toly, bassist Bob Harvey and drummer Jerry Pelequin. San Francisco-born on March 12, 1942, Paul Kantner had been living in Los Angeles with David Crosby and David Freiberg before moving to the Bay area. He met Kaukonen (born in Washington, D.C., on December 23, 1940) in Santa Cruz and, later, Balin while performing on 12-string guitar and banjo at The Drinking Gourd. Soon Harvey and Pelequin were replaced in The Jefferson Airplane by Alexander "Skip" Spence, a rhythm guitarist converted to drummer, and bassist Jack Casady (born in Washington, D.C., on April 13, 1944), a high school friend of Kaukonen's. On October 16, 1965, The Jefferson Airplane performed at San Francisco's first dance concert at Longshoremen's Hall, the precursor of the local concert scene developed by promoter Bill Graham that was later to spread across the nation.

Signed to RCA Records, thus becoming the first of many Bay area bands to secure a major label recording contract, The Jefferson Airplane recorded their debut album in Hollywood. Dominated by Balin's songwriting and smooth rich voice, *Jefferson Airplane Takes Off* featured the distinctive vocal harmonies of Balin, Kantner, and Signe Anderson (now married). Though not a best-seller, the album contained an early version of one of the anthems of the emerging "hippie" movement, "Let's Get Together," and Balin's dynamic "It's No Secret." Both Anderson and Spence left The Jefferson Airplane in 1966, she to have a baby and he to form Moby Grape. Drummer Spencer Dryden (born in New York City on April 7, 1943) and vocalist Grace Slick (born in Chicago on October 30, 1939) were recruited as replacements. Grace Slick, a former model, had been a member of the recently dissolved Great Society, which had been part of the local music scene since 1965 and often appeared with The Jefferson Airplane. The Great Society also included Slick's drummer husband Jerry Slick and his brother Darby Slick. Recordings made by The Great Society for Columbia Records were eventually issued in 1968, after the acknowledged success of The Jefferson Airplane.

Surrealistic Pillow, Grace Slick's first album with The Jefferson Airplane, contained two songs she had performed with The Great Society, Darby Slick's "Somebody to Love" and her own "White Rabbit." Both were major hits in 1967 and the album, certified gold-award by July, effectively launched the "San Francisco sound." The album also included two beautiful romantic ballads by Balin, "Today" (co-authored by Kantner) and "Comin' Back to Me," as well as Balin's frenetic "3/5 of a Mile in 10 Seconds" and his surreal "Plastic Fantastic Lover." Slick's piercing soprano voice, more rough and powerful than Anderson's, complemented Balin's high sensual tenor, and her flamboyant in-performance demeanor soon made her the visual and musical focus of The Jefferson Airplane. In fact, her presence soon began to overwhelm Balin, as *After Bathing at Baxter's* contained only one song by Balin, "Young Girl Sunday Blues," co-authored with Kantner. The album included "psychedelic" instrumental ruminations by Casady and Kaukonen, as on "Spare Chaynge," Kantner's "The Ballad of You and Me and Pooneil," and Slick's "Two Heads," as well as two mellower Kantner compositions, "Won't You Try" and "Saturday Afternoon."

Marty Balin contributed more to *Crown of Creation*, authoring one and co-authoring three songs, but most attention was directed at Kantner's title song, Slick's surreal "Lather" and "Greasy Heart," and David Crosby's previously unrecorded "Triad." During 1968 The Jefferson Airplane toured Europe for the first time, issuing *Bless Its Pointed Little Head*, which assembled live recordings, in early 1969. *Volunteers* was again dominated by Slick and Kantner. Although the stand-out cut from the album was Balin and Kantner's radical political title song, the album featured Kantner's "We Can Be Together" and David Crosby, Steve Stills, and Paul Kantner's mystical "Wooden Ships," a forerunner of the science fiction fantasies in which Kantner would soon indulge.

A chaotic period of solo and joint projects and personnel changes soon engulfed The Jefferson Airplane. Jorma Kaukonen and Jack Casady had been performing together as the blues-oriented Hot Tuna since 1969, often opening shows for The Jefferson Airplane. The first of many Hot Tuna albums appeared in mid-1970, some months after Spencer Dryden had quit the parent group and had been replaced by surf drummer Joe E. Covington. In October, at the urging of Covington, black electric violinist "Papa" John Creach (born on May 28, 1917, in Beaver Falls, Pennsylvania) joined The Jefferson Airplane, subsequently performing and recording with both The Airplane and Hot Tuna. In December the bombastic *Blows Against the Empire* was released under the name of Paul Kantner and The Jefferson Starship. Recorded by Kantner, Slick, Casady, and Covington with the assistance of Jerry Garcia, David Crosby, Graham Nash, David Freiberg, and Jorma's brother Peter Kaukonen, the album featured a number of Kantner science fiction songs, the most accessible of which, "Have You Seen the Stars Tonite," was co-written by Crosby. Conspicuously absent was Marty Balin, although he was listed as co-author of two songs.

By the spring of 1971 Marty Balin had left The Jefferson Airplane. By that September the group had formed their own independent label, Grunt Records, with manufacture and distribution handled by RCA. The label's first album release, *Bark*, credited to The Jefferson Airplane, yielded a minor hit with Covington's ditty, "As Pretty as You Feel," and was certified gold-award almost immediately. In November "Papa" John Creach's first solo album was issued on Grunt as was *Sunfighter*, credited to Paul Kantner and Grace Slick. Recorded by the then-current members of The Airplane plus Garcia, Nash, and Crosby and two members of Grunt Records' Steelwind, leader Jack Traylor and 16-year-old guitarist Craig Chaquico, the album sold modestly at best. By March 1972 Covington had left The Airplane, later to record a solo album on Grunt. He was replaced by John Barbata (born April 1, 1945, in Passaic, New Jersey), a sessions veteran who had been a member of The Turtles and toured with Crosby, Stills, Nash, and Young. That summer The Jefferson Airplane conducted a major American tour with Barbata and bassist–keyboardist–vocalist David Freiberg (born August 24, 1938, in Boston), a former member of Quicksilver Messenger Service. In August Jack Casady and Jorma Kaukonen left The Jefferson Airplane to pursue Hot Tuna full time. Recorded with three different drummers, *Long John Silver*, the final Jefferson Airplane album of new material, was issued in August, oddly selling quite well despite its apparent diffuse and undirected nature. In 1973 Freiberg recorded *Baron von Toolbooth and the Chrome Nun* with Kantner and Slick. The final Jefferson Airplane albums were the live *Thirty Seconds over Winterland*, *Early Flight* (recordings from 1966–67 that featured Signe Anderson's vocal on "High Flying Bird"), and the double-record anthology set, *Flight Log*.

During 1973 Marty Balin performed and recorded with a Marin county bar band, Bodacious D.F. Their RCA album, though generally overlooked by the public, featured Balin's fine lead vocals on leader Vic Smith's "Drivin' Me Crazy." In early 1974 Grace Slick's much maligned *Manhole* was issued, after which the group added Jorma Kaukonen's brother Peter on bass. In 1972 Peter Kaukonen had recorded a solo album on Grunt, but he remained with the group for less than six months, being replaced in mid-1974 by keyboardist–vocalist Peter Sears (born in Bromley, England, on May 27, 1948), whom Slick and Kantner had met during the sessions for *Manhole*. Lead guitarist Craig Chaquico (born in Sacramento, California, on September 26, 1954) joined permanently, and the group's first album as simply The Jefferson Starship, *Dragonfly*, contained Slick and Sears' "Hyperdrive" and yielded a minor hit with Slick and Kantner's "Ride the

Tiger." However, the feature cut of the album was Marty Balin and Paul Kantner's "Caroline," with lead vocals performed by Balin.

Marty Balin rejoined The Jefferson Starship for their spring 1975 tour and stayed with the group for over three years. The group's smash 1975 album, *Red Octopus*, yielded the group's first major hit in eight years, "Miracles," composed and sung by Balin, and exposed The Starship to a wide new audience. The album also included the minor hit "Play on Love," by Sears and Slick, and "Tumblin'," written by Balin, Freiberg, and Grateful Dead lyricist Robert Hunter. "Papa" John Creach subsequently left the group in order to pursue an inauspicious solo recording career on Buddah and DJM Records. *Spitfire*, The Jefferson Starship's first platinum-award album, contained "Cruisin'" (written by Charlie Hickox of Bodacious D.F.) and the major hit "With Your Love," co-written by Balin. In 1978 *Earth* yielded four hit singles of which two were major hits, Jesse Barish's "Count on Me" and "Runaway."

During the summer of 1978 The Jefferson Starship toured Europe for the first time in more than ten years. However, Grace Slick suddenly became ill before a scheduled appearance in Frankfurt, Germany, and the subsequent cancellation of the concert led to the destruction of virtually all of the group's equipment (valued at over $100,000) by incensed fans. Following a poor performance two nights later in Hamburg, Slick returned to the United States, not to perform with the group again for nearly three years. Marty Balin later gave a stellar performance with The Jefferson Starship minus Grace Slick at Knebworth Castle, England, but he, too, was soon to leave the group.

In October 1978 drummer John Barbata was critically injured in a northern California automobile accident and was replaced by well-traveled English drummer Aynsley Dunbar by the beginning of 1979. Dunbar had played with John Mayall, Jeff Beck, and Rod Stewart and fronted his own band for four years before joining Frank Zappa in 1970 and Journey in 1974. Subsequently rehearsing with former Elvin Bishop vocalist Mickey Thomas ("Fooled Around and Fell in Love"), The Jefferson Starship—minus both Slick and Balin—made an unannounced appearance at a free concert in San Francisco's Golden Gate Park in May 1979 and later played several local club engagements with this newest incarnation of the group. This lineup (Kantner, Freiberg, Chaquico, Sears, Dunbar, and Thomas) soon recorded the "hard rock" *Freedom at Point Zero*, which yielded a major hit with "Jane" and the minor hit "Girl with the Hungry Eyes." In November a rock musical entitled *Rock Justice*, co-written and co-directed by Marty Balin and Bob Heyman, premiered at San Francisco's Old Waldorf. The musical, in which a rock singer is prosecuted for not having a hit record, featured songs written by Balin, Heyman, and local guitarist Mike Varney. In late 1980 an original-cast album of *Rock Justice* was issued on EMI–America, followed the next year by Balin's first solo album, *Balin*, which yielded a smash hit with Jessie Barish's "Hearts." In the meantime Grace Slick had recorded two solo albums for RCA before rejoining The Starship for the aggressive *Modern Times* album and its resulting hit single, "Find Your Way Back." Mickey

Thomas, who had recorded a solo album between his stints with Elvin Bishop and The Jefferson Starship, completed a second solo album during 1981.

THE JEFFERSON AIRPLANE

Jefferson Airplane Takes Off	RCA	AFL1–3584	September '66	
		reissued as AYL1–3739		A
Early Flight	Grunt	CYL1–0437	March '74	

THE GREAT SOCIETY

Conspicuous Only in Its Absence	Columbia	CS–9624	April '68	A
How It Was—Collector's Item, Volume 2	Columbia	CS–9702	September '68	
Collector's Item	2-Columbia	CG–30459	March '71	A
Somebody to Love	Harmony	KH–30391	March '71	

THE JEFFERSON AIRPLANE

Surrealistic Pillow*	RCA	AFL1–3766	February '67	
		reissued as AYL1–3738		A
After Bathing at Baxter's	RCA	LSO–1511	December '67	
		reissued as AFL1–4545		A
Crown of Creation*	RCA	AFL1–4058	September '68	
		reissued as AYL1–3797		A
Bless Its Pointed Little Head	RCA	AFL1–4133	February '69	
		reissued as AYL1–3798		A
Volunteers*	RCA	AFL1–4238	November '69	
		reissued as AYL1–3867		A
The Worst of The Jefferson Airplane*	RCA	AFL1–4459	November '70	
		reissued as AYL1–3661	June '80	A

PAUL KANTNER AND THE JEFFERSON STARSHIP

Blows Against the Empire*	RCA	AFL1– 4448	December '70	
		reissued as AYL1– 3868		A

PAUL KANTNER AND GRACE SLICK

Sunfighter	Grunt	FTR–1002	November '71	

THE JEFFERSON AIRPLANE

Bark*	Grunt	FTR–1001	September '71	
Long John Silver*	Grunt	FTR–1007	July '72	
Thirty Seconds over Winterland	Grunt	BXL1– 0147	March '73	A
Flight Log	2-Grunt	CYL2– 1255	February '77	A

PETER KAUKONEN

Black Kangaroo	Grunt	FTR–1006	September '72	

PAUL KANTNER, GRACE SLICK, AND DAVID FREIBERG

Baron von Tool-booth and the Chrome Nun	Grunt	BXL1– 0148	June '73	
	reissued on RCA	AYL1– 3799		A

JOE E. COVINGTON'S FAT FANDANGO

Your Heart Is My Heart	Grunt	BFL1– 0149	June '73	

BODACIOUS D.F.

Bodacious D.F.	RCA	APL1– 0206	September '73	

GRACE SLICK

Manhole	Grunt	BXL1– 0347	January '74	
		reissued as AYL1– 3736		A
Dreams	RCA	AFL1– 3544	March '80	A
Welcome to the Wrecking Ball	RCA	AQL1– 3851	March '81	A

THE JEFFERSON STARSHIP

Dragonfly*	Grunt	BXL1– 0717	October '74	
		reissued as AYL1– 3796		A
Red Octopus*	Grunt	BXL1– 0999	July '75	
		reissued as AYL1– 3660	June '80	A
Spitfire**	Grunt	BXL1– 1557	June '76	
		reissued as AYL1– 3953		A
Earth**	Grunt	BXL1– 2515	February '78	A
Gold*	Grunt/RCA	BZL1– 3247	February '79	A

MARTY BALIN

| Rock Justice (original cast) | EMI–America | SWAK– 17036 | October '80 | A |
| Balin | EMI–America | ST–17054 | May '81 | A |

MICKEY THOMAS

| As Long as You Love Me | MCA | 2256 | May '77 | |
| Alive Alone | Elektra | 530 | September '81 | A |

THE JEFFERSON STARSHIP

| Freedom at Point Zero* | Grunt | BZL1– 3452 | November '79 | A |
| Modern Times* | Grunt | BZL1– 3848 | April '81 | A |

WAYLON JENNINGS. Along with Willie Nelson, Waylon Jennings leads the late Seventies "outlaw" country music movement that eschews the sophisticated orchestral production developed during the Sixties in Nashville for country-and-western artists. After years as a relatively obscure country artist, Waylon Jennings convinced RCA Records to grant him a measure of artistic independence for *Ladies Love Outlaws*, perhaps the first country-and-western album to feature simple songs unmarred by the usual elaborate string and horn backing arrangements. The anthology album, *The Outlaws*, with songs performed by Nelson and Jennings among others, effectively established this new approach and became the first country album to be certified platinum-award. Gaining acceptance in both the rock and pop fields, Waylon Jennings and Willie Nelson have done much to promote the growing popularity of country music since the late Seventies.

Born in Littlefield, Texas, on June 15, 1937, Waylon Jennings took up guitar as a teenager, later moving to Lubbock where he hosted his own show on radio station KLLL and met Buddy Holly, who was to produce Jennings' first recording, "Jole Blon." Performing on Holly's final 1959 tour playing electric bass, Jennings was "bumped" from his seat on the ill-fated plane that crashed the night of February 2, 1959, in rural Ohio, killing Holly, J. P. "The Big Bopper" Richardson, and Richie Valens. Jennings subsequently returned to Lubbock to work as a disc jockey; in the early Sixties, he moved to Phoenix, where he formed his backing group, The Waylors, and performed regularly at JD's Club. After early recordings later released on Vocalion and A&M, he was signed to RCA Records by Chet Atkins in 1965 and moved to Nashville the next year to pursue a modest career as a country-and-western artist. His country hits during the Sixties included "(That's What You Get) For Lovin' Me," "Only Daddy That'll Walk the Line," and "Brown-Eyed, Handsome Man." Touring 300 days a year, Jennings' first minor pop hit came in 1969 with "MacArthur Park," followed the next year by "The Taker."

In the early Seventies Waylon Jennings negotiated a record contract with RCA that allowed him to choose his own musicians and produce his own recordings. *Ladies Love Outlaws*, recorded, in part, with The Waylors, heralded a trend in country music towards exciting, raw, and more personalized music. *Honky Tonk Heroes*, comprised primarily of Billy Joe Shaver songs, even made the pop album charts. Jennings managed minor pop hits with "I'm a Ramblin' Man" in 1974, "Are You Sure Hank Done It This Way" in 1975, and "Can't You See" in 1976, but the RCA anthology album, *The Outlaws*, effectively established the "outlaw" country music movement. Assembling recordings by Jennings, Willie Nelson, Jennings' wife Jessi Colter, and Tompall Glaser, the album became a surprising best-seller, yielding a major pop hit with the Jennings–Nelson duet, "Good Hearted Woman." Certified platinum-award by November, the album also featured the Jennings–Colter duet, "Suspicious Minds," and Colter's "I'm Looking for Blue Eyes."

Having played rock venues such as The Troubadour in Los Angeles and The Bottom Line in New York (even opening for The Grateful Dead in San Francisco in 1973), Waylon Jennings soon established himself with rock and pop fans as well as country-and-western audiences with his own best-selling albums. *Ol' Waylon* yielded the major pop and top country hit "Luckenbach, Texas (Back to the Basics of Love)," recorded with Willie Nelson, and was certified platinum-award the year of its release. The duet album *Waylon and Willie* also became a major best-seller, producing a moderate pop and top country hit with "Mamas, Don't Let Your Babies Grow Up to Be Cowboys" and the top country hit "The Wurlitzer Prize." During 1978 Jennings scored country hits with Johnny Cash on "There Ain't No Good Chain Gangs" and on his own with "I've Always Been

Crazy" and the tongue-in-cheek "Don't You Think This Outlaw Bit's Got Out of Hand." The latter two songs came from *I've Always Been Crazy*, another best-seller that also included an exciting Buddy Holly medley. Reinforcing Holly's legacy, Waylon Jennings has toured with the original Crickets since 1979, the year he had top country hits with "Amanda" and "Come with Me." During 1980 Jennings scored a top country hit with Rodney Crowell's "I Ain't Living Long like This" and a top country and major pop hit with "Theme from 'The Dukes of Hazzard.' "

WAYLON JENNINGS

Waylon Jennings	Vocalion	73873(E)	August '69	A
Don't Think Twice	A&M	SP–4238	May '70	
Folk-Country	RCA	LSP–3523	April '66	
Leavin' Town	RCA	LSP–3620	October '66	
Nashville Rebel	RCA	LSP–3736	December '66	
Ol' Harlan	RCA	LSP–3660	March '67	
Love of the Common People	RCA	LSP–3825	August '67	
Hangin' On	RCA	LSP–3918	February '68	
Only the Greatest	RCA	LSP–4023	July '68	
Jewels	RCA	LSP–4085	January '69	
Just to Satisfy You	RCA	LSP–4137	April '69	
Country Folk	RCA	LSP–4180	September '69	
Waylon	RCA	LSP–4260	February '70	
Best	RCA	AFL1–4341	July '70	A
Singer of Sad Songs	RCA	AFL1–4418	December '70	A
The Taker/Tulsa	RCA	AFL1–4487	April '71	A
Cedartown, Georgia	RCA	LSP–4567	September '71	
Good-Hearted Woman	RCA	AFL1–4647	March '72	
		reissued as AYL1–3737		A

VARIOUS OTHER WAYLON JENNINGS ALBUMS

One and Only	Camden	CAS–2183	November '67	
Heartaches by the Number	Camden	CAS–2556	April '72	A
Ruby, Don't Take Your Love to Town	Camden	CAS–2608	April '73	A
Only Daddy That'll Walk the Line	Camden	ACL–0306	March '74	A

WAYLON JENNINGS

Ladies Love Outlaws	RCA	AFL1–4751	October '72	A

Lonesome, On'ry, and Mean	RCA	AFL1–4854	April '73	A
Honky Tonk Heroes	RCA	AFL1–0240	August '73	
		reissued as AYL1–3897		A
This Time	RCA	AFL1–0539	June '74	
		reissued as AYL1–3942		A
The Ramblin' Man	RCA	AFL1–0734	September '74	
		reissued as AYL1–4073		A
Dreaming My Dreams*	RCA	AFL1–1062	July '75	
		reissued as AYL1–4072		A

WAYLON JENNINGS, WILLIE NELSON, JESSI COLTER, AND TOMPALL GLASER

The Outlaws**	RCA	AFL1–1321	February '76	A

WAYLON JENNINGS

Are You Ready for the Country*	RCA	AFL1–1816	July '76	
		reissued as AYL1–3663	June '80	A
Live (1974)*	RCA	AFL1–1108	December '76	
		reissued as AYL1–4163	November '81	A
Ol' Waylon**	RCA	AFL1–2317	May '77	A
I've Always Been Crazy*	RCA	AAL1–2979	September '78	A
Greatest Hits**	RCA	AHL1–3378	May '79	A
What Goes Around Comes Around*	RCA	AHL1–3493	November '79	A
Music Man*	RCA	AAL1–3602	June '80	A

WAYLON JENNINGS AND WILLIE NELSON

Waylon and Willie**	RCA	AAL1–2686	January '78	A

WAYLON JENNINGS, WILLIE NELSON, AND VARIOUS ARTISTS

Honky Tonkin'	RCA	AHL1–3422	July '79	A

WAYLON JENNINGS AND JESSI COLTER

Leather and Lace*	RCA	AAL1–3931	March '81	A

JETHRO TULL. Initially a blues-oriented English band, Jethro Tull evolved into one of the earliest so-called "progressive" rock bands, opening the way for numerous other similarly labeled English and European bands by the early Seventies. Generally more popular in the United States than in their native country (and attracting the attention of jazz fans), Jethro Tull became firmly established as an album band with their first of a series of "concept" albums, *Aqualung*, a reputation enhanced by *Thick as a Brick*. Featuring leader Ian Anderson's manic stage presence in performance, Jethro Tull subsequently became increasingly theatrical in concert, culminating in the critically scorned but enormously popular *A Passion Play* album and tour. After retiring from touring for two years, Jethro Tull re-emerged in late 1974 with a hit single ("Bungle in the Jungle") and a sell-out "come-back" tour that re-established the band. Virtually all Jethro Tull albums have been certified gold-award.

During 1966 and 1967 future Jethro Tull members Ian Anderson (born August 10, 1947), John Evan (born March 28, 1948), Glenn Cornick (born April 24, 1947), Barriemore Barlow (born September 10, 1949), and Jeffrey Hammond-Hammond (born July 30, 1946) were at various times members of the John Evan Band, a group performing around their native Blackpool in northern England. In 1967 the band traveled to London where they hoped to establish themselves on the club circuit. As the other members gradually drifted off, Cornick and Anderson persevered, forming Jethro Tull before year's end. The members: Ian Anderson (flute, guitar, saxophone, lead vocals), bassist Glenn Cornick, guitarist Mick Abrahams (born April 7, 1943), and drummer Clive Bunker (born December 12, 1946), with Abrahams and Anderson as principle songwriters. An immediate success on the club circuit, Jethro Tull was well received at the 1968 National Jazz and Blues Festival. Signed to Island Records (Reprise in the United States), the group's blues-oriented debut album, *This Was*, sold modestly; but, in early 1969, Abrahams departed to form Blodwyn Pig. Briefly replaced by future Black Sabbath guitarist Tony Iommi, Abrahams' permanent replacement was guitarist Martin Barre (born November 17, 1946). Ian Anderson effectively took over as Jethro Tull's leader, abandoning Abrahams' penchant for blues-based material in favor of highly melodic songs often featuring wry, off-beat lyrics. *Stand Up*, regarded by some as Jethro Tull's classic album, contained group favorites such as "Bouree," "Look into the Sun," and "We Used To Know," and became a best-seller.

By 1970 Jethro Tull had established itself as one of the United States' top concert attractions by means of regular tours, perhaps to the detriment of their English popularity. Thus *Benefit* became the group's first certified gold-award American album, while in England it failed to sell as well as *Stand Up*. In 1971 Glenn Cornick left Jethro Tull to form Wild Turkey (in 1975 he turned up in Bob Welch's power trio Paris), to be replaced on bass by Jeffrey Hammond-Hammond, formerly of The John Evan Band. Moreover, Evan himself joined the group on keyboards during the year, debuting on the group's first concept album, *Aqualung*. Although attacked by some critics as bombastic and pretentious, the album sold well in both Great Britain and the United States and included Tull favorites such as "Cross-Eyed Mary," "Locomotive Breath," and "Aqualung." Clive Bunker departed the group before the end of 1971 to form Jude and later resurfaced with the re-formed Blodwyn Pig. He was replaced on drums by Barriemore Barlow, another veteran of The John Evan Band. Extensive touring, particularly of the United States, continued in 1971 and 1972 and *Thick as a Brick*, essentially an album-long ballad without individual cuts, sold spectacularly. Meanwhile, Anderson introduced stage props into the group's live performances.

Living in the Past assembled live performances and early songs unreleased in the United States in a two-record package on Jethro Tull's new label, Chrysalis, yielding the group's first major American hit, "Living in the Past," an English hit from 1969. Critically lambasted by virtually every rock critic, the group's final concept album, *A Passion Play*, sold poorly in England but massively in the United States. The subsequent American tour featuring the theatrically oriented performance of the album was greeted by record-breaking, sell-out attendance. Nonetheless, apparently road weary and ostensibly disillusioned by hostile press reviews, Jethro Tull announced their "retirement" from live performance in August 1973. The group retreated to Switzerland where they recorded *War Child* as the soundtrack to a movie. The movie was eventually abandoned as too costly, but the album yielded the group's second major American hit, "Bungle in the Jungle."

Jethro Tull resumed touring in late 1974, playing to sell-out crowds in both England and the United States. *Minstrel in the Gallery* continued the group's gold-award best-selling ways in America, but the album fared less well in England. In December 1975 Jeffrey Hammond-Hammond left Jethro Tull and was replaced by bassist John Glascock. *Too Old to Rock and Roll . . . Too Young to Die* broke the group's string of certified gold-award albums, and *Songs from the Wood* contained the group's final, albeit minor, hit, "The Whistler." By 1977 keyboardist David Palmer, the orchestrator of all Jethro Tull albums save *Benefit*, had joined the group. Subsequent Jethro Tull albums have sold quite well, and the group continued to tour America regularly. In the fall of 1979 Dave Pegg, a former member of Fairport Convention, replaced ailing John Glascock on bass. On November 17, 1979, John Glascock, who had been ill for some time, died in a London hospital at the age of 27. During 1980 Anderson dismissed Barlow, Evan, and Palmer, replacing them with keyboardist–violinist Eddie Jobson and drummer Mark Cramey.

JETHRO TULL

This Was	Reprise	RS–6336	February '69	
	reissued on Chrysalis	CHR–1041		A
Stand Up*	Reprise	RS–6360	October '69	
	reissued on Chrysalis	CHR–1042		A
Benefit*	Reprise	RS–6400	April '70	
	reissued on Chrysalis	CHR–1043		A

BLODWYN PIG (WITH MICK ABRAHAMS)

Ahead Rings Out	A&M	SP–4210	December '69
Getting to This	A&M	SP–4243	June '70

MICK ABRAHAMS

Mick Abrahams	A&M	4312	August '71

WILD TURKEY (WITH GLENN CORNICK)

Battle Hymn	Reprise	2070	March '72

JETHRO TULL

Aqualung*	Reprise	MS–2035	May '71	
	reissued on Chrysalis	CHR–1044		A
Thick as a Brick*	Reprise	MS–2072	April '72	
	reissued on Chrysalis	CHR–1003		A
Living in the Past*	2-Chrysalis	ZCH–1035	October '72	A
A Passion Play*	Chrysalis	CHR–1040	July '73	A
War Child*	Chrysalis	CHR–1067	October '74	A
M.U. (The Best of Jethro Tull)**	Chrysalis	CHR–1078	August '75	A
Minstrel in the Gallery*	Chrysalis	CHR–1082	September '75	A
Too Old to Rock and Roll . . . Too Young to Die	Chrysalis	CHR–1111	May '76	A
Songs from the Wood*	Chrysalis	CHR–1132	February '77	
Best, Volume 2	Chrysalis	CHR–1135	November '77	A
Heavy Horses*	Chrysalis	CHR–1175	April '78	A
Bursting Out*	2-Chrysalis	CHR–1201	September '78	A
Stormwatch*	Chrysalis	CHR–1238	October '79	A
"A"	Chrysalis	CHE–1301	September '80	A

BILLY JOEL. Classically trained pianist Billy Joel persevered through several New York rock bands and an obscure solo album during the late Sixties and early Seventies, finally to emerge in 1974 with the autobiographical "Piano Man." Unable to sustain public interest in his career, Billy Joel continued to write highly melodic, ballad-style songs, eventually establishing himself as a popular Seventies singer–songwriter with 1977's *The Stranger* and its four hit singles.

Billy Joel grew up in the suburban community of Hicksville, on New York's Long Island, where he was born on May 9, 1949, initiating a dozen years of classical piano training at the age of four. In 1964, as a teenager, he joined his first rock band The Echoes, which evolved into The Hassles by 1968. Following two obscure albums for United Artists, The Hassles disbanded and Joel and Hassles drummer Jon Small formed the power duo Attila for one album on Epic Records. Signed to Family Productions in 1971, Billy Joel recorded his first album of all original material, *Cold Spring Harbor*, for the label, but the poorly produced album failed to sell despite six months of touring to promote it. A live broadcast by Joel and his band in Philadelphia generated a regional favorite with "Captain Jack," and the song was played regularly on radio station WMMR–FM for months. Joel, embroiled in legal disputes with Family Productions, moved to Los Angeles, where he took up residence at the Executive Room piano bar as Bill Martin. On the strength of "Captain Jack," he was signed to Columbia Records in the spring of 1973, recording *Piano Man* in North Hollywood. The blatantly autobiographical title song became a major hit from the album in early 1974 but, despite two other minor hits, interest in Joel waned. "The Entertainer" was a moderate hit from *Streetlife Serenade*, after which Joel switched management and moved to upstate New York. *Turnstiles*, issued a year and a half later, was greeted by minimal sales despite the inclusion of "New York State of Mind" (covered by Barbra Streisand on her *Superman* album) and the Phil Spector-style "Say Goodbye to Hollywood."

Subsequently touring successfully for nearly a year, Billy Joel recorded *The Stranger* under producer Phil Ramone, well known in the industry for his work with Paul Simon and Phoebe Snow. The album yielded *four* hit singles, the smash "Just the Way You Are," "Movin' Out (Anthony's Song)," the controversial "Only the Good Die Young," and "She's Always a Woman." Certified platinum-award in January 1978, *The Stranger* was followed by *52nd Street*, also produced by Phil Ramone. Certified platinum-award the month of its release, the album included the smash hit "My Life," two other major hits, "Big Shot" and "Honesty," and another Phil Spector-style song, "Until the Night." *Glass Houses*, from 1980, included the near-smash "You May Be Right," the facile top hit "It's Still Rock and Roll to Me," and the major hit "Don't Ask Me Why."

THE HASSLES

| The Hassles | United Artists | UAS–6631 | March '68 | |
| | reissued on Liberty | LN–10138 | November '81 | A |

Hour of the Wolf	United Artists reissued on Liberty	UAS–6699 LN–10139	May '69 November '81	A

ATTILA

Attila	Epic	E–30030	July '70

BILLY JOEL

Cold Spring Harbor	Family Productions	2700	'72	
Piano Man*	Columbia	PC–32544	November '73	A
Streetlife Sere-nade*	Columbia	PC–33146	October '74	A
Turnstiles*	Columbia	PC–33848	May '76	A
The Stranger**	Columbia	PC–34987	September '77	A
52nd Street**	Columbia	FC–35609	October '78	A
Glass Houses**	Columbia	FC–36384	March '80	A
Songs in the Attic	Columbia	TC–37461	September '81	A

ELTON JOHN. Perhaps the first rock "superstar" of the Seventies, Elton John was launched on his highly popular recording and performing career with ecstatically received shows in 1970 in Los Angeles, New York, and Philadelphia which were accompanied by one of the most massive "hype" campaigns in rock history. In conjunction with lyricist Bernie Taupin, Elton John composed some of the most popular songs of the Seventies, characterized by Taupin's vaguely romantic and nostalgic and often obscure words and John's highly melodic music and ever-present "hook," or catchy repetitive motif. Exhibiting a flair for outrageous showmanship, wearing wild and often silly clothes, and performing in a flamboyant and flashy fashion, Elton John has been compared to Jerry Lee Lewis and, perhaps more accurately, to Liberace. Often identified with the so-called "glitter rock" movement, Elton John nonetheless retained a sense of tastefulness which avoided the garish and disconcerting image attached to David Bowie and others of the genre. With Taupin and John established as poignant songwriters with late 1970's "Your Song" and John established as a virtual rock institution by 1972, Elton John elicited perhaps the broadest appeal of any rock performer (rivaled only by Paul McCartney) with his penchant for showmanship and catchy melodies and his command of a variety of musical styles. Though critically reproached as lacking a defined musical character and regarded as a synthesizer rather than as an in-novator of musical styles, Elton John nevertheless bridged the gap between pop and rock with enormous success, particularly in the United States.

Forming Rocket Records with manager John Reid in 1973, Elton John launched the career of Kiki Dee and revived the career of Neil Sedaka on the label, recording hit singles with each. In the summer of 1974, Elton John negotiated probably the largest recording contract to date ($8,000,000) with MCA Records, later to be surpassed by Stevie Wonder with Motown in 1975. "Retiring" from live performance in 1976 and again in 1977, Elton John's popularity (though not sales) diminished after the single "Sorry Seems to Be the Hardest Word" from *Blue Moves*, essentially his last album in collaboration with Bernie Taupin. After the poorly received but best-selling *A Single Man* album (with lyricist Gary Osborne), Elton John returned to touring in February 1979, eschewing both his backing rock band and his earlier "glitter rock" stance. During May Elton John became the first rock superstar to play in Russia, performing well-received shows in Leningrad and Moscow. During 1979 Elton John attempted to re-establish his popularity with an EP (extended play record) recorded with "Philadelphia soul" producer Thom Bell, the discofied *Victim of Love* album, and tours of the United States between September and November for the first time in three years.

Born Reginald Dwight in Pinner, Middlesex, England, on March 25, 1947, Elton John began playing piano at the age of four. Winning a scholarship to the Royal Academy of Music in London at age 11, he later performed in a succession of local bands before joining Bluesology as a teenager. Taken over by "Long" John Baldry as his backing group by 1967, Bluesology frequently backed visiting American black acts such as Major Lance, Patti Labelle and The Bluebelles, and Billy Stewart. After the smash English hit with the "schmaltz" ballad "Let the Heartaches Begin" by Baldry, Bluesology disbanded and Reginald Dwight became Elton John. Unsuccessfully auditioning for Liberty Records, John was put in touch with lyricist Bernie Taupin (born in Lincoln, England, on May 22, 1950), and the two were later signed to a three-year songwriting contract with Dick James Music. As the team had little luck writing commercial material, John recorded an anonymous series of budget albums covering current hits. Urged by publicist Steve Brown to pursue their own course, Taupin and John assembled new material and recorded an album, *Empty Sky* (eventually released in the United States in 1975), but both the album and John's first single, "Lady Samantha," sold minimally in England. Subsequently employing arranger Paul Buckmaster and producer Gus Dudgeon, John recorded *Elton John*, but the album's first single, "Border Song," fared little better than did "Lady Samantha." John soon recruited drummer Nigel Olsson (born February 10, 1949, in Wallasey, England) and bassist Dee Murray, former members of The Spencer Davis Group, for a promotional tour of Britain's college circuit.

Undaunted by initial failures, Elton John's American record company, Uni (later absorbed by the parent company, MCA Records), launched a massive publicity campaign to "hype" John's American debut at The Troubadour in Los Angeles in August 1970. The tactic worked exceedingly well, and shows there, in New York, and in Philadelphia were greeted by ecstatic reviews. By the beginning of 1971, "Your Song," the second single from *Elton John* (and one of the duo's finest compositions), had become John's first major hit single and the album, which also included "Take Me to the Pilot," was certified gold-award in February. *Tumbleweed Connection*, revealing Taupin's fascination with the American Old West and containing the John favorite, "Country Comfort," was certified gold-award in March despite yielding no hit singles. During 1971 two Elton John albums were issued in rapid succession: the soundtrack to *Friends* (on Paramount) and the live *11–17–70* (on Uni). *Madman across the Water,* recorded with Nigel Olsson, Dee Murray, and guitarist Davey Johnstone, produced two moderate hits, "Levon" and "Tiny Dancer," but was greeted harshly by British critics. In the meantime, Nigel Olsson and Bernie Taupin recorded solo albums on Uni and Elektra, respectively, whereas Johnstone recorded his first solo album in 1973 on MCA Records.

Over the next two years, Elton John enjoyed what is generally regarded as the artistic highpoint of his career. In early 1972 he and his band (Olsson, Murray, and Johnstone) went to France to record *Honky Chateau,* on which massive string arrangements were de-emphasized and guitar was featured. "Rocket Man" and "Honky Cat" became smash hits from the album and effectively re-established John in Great Britain. *Don't Shoot Me, I'm the Piano Player* yielded two smash hits with the derivative "Crocodile Rock" and the poignant "Daniel," another of the duo's finest compositions. The double-record set *Goodbye Yellow Brick Road* included "Candle in the Rain" and featured three smash singles, "Saturday Night's Alright for Fighting," "Bennie and The Jets," and the title song. Also during 1973 percussionist Ray Cooper joined Elton John's band. Recorded in the United States, *Caribou* contained two more smash hits, "Don't Let the Sun Go Down on Me" and "The Bitch Is Back," and was followed by two smash hit single releases, "Lucy in the Sky with Diamonds" and "Philadelphia Freedom."

Earlier, in 1973, Elton John and manager John Reid had formed Rocket Records. In late 1974 Kiki Dee and early Sixties singer–songwriter Neil Sedaka had hits on the label, Dee with "I've Got the Music in Me" and Sedaka with "Laughter in the Rain." Sedaka's revitalized career with Rocket lasted through late 1976, when he switched to Elektra Records. Moreover, in June 1974, Elton John concluded a new recording contract with MCA Records valued at $8,000,000, the largest such deal in rock history until Stevie Wonder's $13,000,000 contract with Motown in August 1975. John appeared as The Pinball Wizard in Ken Russell's film *Tommy* in 1975, the year MCA belatedly issued *Empty Sky* in the United States. The autobiographical *Captain Fantastic and the Brown Dirt Cowboy,* which dealt with the early career of John and Taupin, featured the smash hit "Someone Saved My Life Tonight." During the spring, bassist Dee Murray and drummer Nigel Olsson left the Elton John Band; Olsson pursued a solo recording career on Rocket, Columbia, and Bang that yielded the major hit "Dancin' Shoes" and the moderate hit "Little Bit of Soap" in 1978–79. With guitarist Johnstone and percussionist Cooper remaining, the band brought in drummer Roger Pope from the recently dissolved Kiki Dee Band and debuted at Wembley Stadium in June. Featuring the smash hit "Island Girl," *Rock of the Westies* was an instant best-seller, as was the live set *Here and There*, but in August 1976 John announced he was disbanding his group and "retiring" from live performance. Having had an uncredited hit with Neil Sedaka in late 1975 with

"Bad Blood" and a credited smash hit with Kiki Dee in the summer of 1976 with "Don't Go Breaking My Heart," John recorded his final album in collaboration with Bernie Taupin during 1976. *Blue Moves* yielded a major hit with "Sorry Seems to Be the Hardest Word" and a moderate hit with "Bite Your Lip (Get Up and Dance)," but John did not have another top-ten hit for a year and a half.

Though critically attacked, Elton John's *A Single Man*, recorded in collaboration with lyricist Gary Osborne, was yet another best-seller. In February 1979 John returned to live performances, accompanied only by percussionist Ray Cooper, which culminated in several appearances in Russia that May. During the year John recorded a three-song EP with Philadelphia International producer Thom Bell (The Spinners, The Stylistics) that yielded a smash hit with "Mama Can't Buy You Love." He also recorded the inane discofied *Victim of Love* under songwriter–producer Pete Bellote (Donna Summer). Between September and November, Elton John toured the United States for the first time in three years, playing remarkably subdued concerts in medium-sized halls, accompanied by only percussionist Cooper. During 1980 Bernie Taupin recorded his second solo album; Elton John scored a smash hit with "Little Jeannie," toured again with Dee Murray and Nigel Olsson, and switched to Geffen Records.

ELTON JOHN

Empty Sky	MCA	2130	January '75	
		reissued as 3008		
		reissued as 620		A
Elton John *	Uni	73090	July '70	
	reissued on MCA	2012		
		reissued as 3000		A
		reissued as 37067		A
Tumbleweed Connection *	Uni	73096	January '71	
	reissued on MCA	2014		
		reissued as 3001		A
Friends (sound-track) *	Paramount	PAS–6004	March '71	
	reissued on Pickwick	3598	April '78	
11–17–70	Uni	93105	May '71	
	reissued on MCA	2015		
		reissued as 3002		
		reissued as 679		A
Madman across the Water *	Uni	93120	November '71	
	reissued on MCA	2016		
		reissued as 3003		A

NIGEL OLSSON

Drum Orchestra and Chorus	Uni	73113	October '71	
Nigel Olsson	Rocket	PIG–2158	November '75	
Nigel Olsson	Columbia	JC–35048	March '78	
Nigel	Bang	JZ–35792	February '79	
Changing Tides	Bang	JZ–36491	August '80	A

BERNIE TAUPIN

Bernie Taupin	Elektra	EKS–75020	March '72	
He Who Rides the Tiger	Asylum	263	May '80	A

DAVEY JOHNSTONE

Smiling Faces	MCA	340	August '73	A

ELTON JOHN

Honky Chateau*	Uni reissued on MCA	93135 2017 reissued as 3004 reissued as 37064	May '72	A
Don't Shoot Me, I'm the Piano Player*	MCA	2100 reissued as 3005	January '73	A
Goodbye Yellow Brick Road*	2-MCA	2–10003	October '73	A
Caribou*	MCA	2116 reissued as 3006 reissued as 37065	June '74	A
Greatest Hits*	MCA	2128 reissued as 3007	November '74	A
Captain Fantastic and the Brown Dirt Cowboy*	MCA	2142 reissued as 3009 reissued as 37066	June '75	
Rock of the Westies*	MCA	2163 reissued as 3011 reissued as 621	October '75	A
Here and There*	MCA	2197 reissued as 3010 reissued as 622	May '76	A

Blue Moves**	2-MCA	2-11004	October '76	A
Greatest Hits, Volume 2**	MCA	3027	October '77	A
A Single Man**	MCA	3065 reissued as 37068	October '78	A
Victim of Love	MCA	5104	October '79	
21 at 33*	MCA	5121	May '80	A
The Fox	Geffen	GHS-2002	May '81	A

JANIS JOPLIN. Probably the first female "superstar" of rock music, rivaled at the time only by Grace Slick, Janis Joplin is regarded by some as the greatest white female blues singer of all time. She certainly redefined the role of the female vocalist with her gutsy, physically and emotionally wrenching, and virtually sexual delivery, opening the way for female "shouters" in rock music. Along with The Jefferson Airplane and The Grateful Dead, Janis Joplin's first group, Big Brother and The Holding Company, formed the nucleus of San Francisco's burgeoning "counter-culture" music scene in the mid-Sixties, with Joplin emerging as one of the most powerful personalities of the era and essentially becoming a legend in her own time. Exploding out of the August 1967 Monterey Pop Festival into international prominence, Big Brother and The Holding Company recorded the certified gold-award *Cheap Thrills* album before the late 1968 departure of Joplin, much to the chagrin of critics and San Francisco associates. Subsequently performing and recording with backup bands (rather than with an integrated band), Janis Joplin recorded two more gold-award albums prior to her death from a heroin overdose in October 1970 at the age of 27.

Raised in Port Arthur, Texas, where she was born on January 19, 1943, Janis Joplin had discovered the blues by the age of 17. She began singing locally, primarily at Ken Threadgill's Austin bar, in 1961, sojourning briefly to San Francisco to perform at folk clubs and bars before returning to Texas to attend college. During 1965 musicians Sam Andrew (born in Taft, California, on December 18, 1941), Peter Albin (born in San Francisco on June 6, 1944), James Gurley (born in Detroit in 1941), and, later, David Getz (born in Brooklyn, New York, in 1938) were hanging out at Chet Helms' Haight-Ashbury residence. They subsequently formed Big Brother and The Holding Company with Andrew and Gurley on guitars, Albin on bass, and Getz on drums. While organizing dances at the Avalon Ballroom, Helms became the group's manager and successfully recruited Texan friend Janis Joplin as vocalist for the band. Backed by screeching "psychedelic" guitars, she sang, almost shouted, in the style of blues singers such as Bessie Smith, investing her performances with intense, passionate involvement. Debuting at the Avalon Ballroom in June 1966, Big Brother and The Holding Company signed a recording contract with the small Chicago-based Mainstream label which released the group's poorly pro-duced debut album (essentially a demonstration tape) in September 1967.

Big Brother and The Holding Company were launched into international prominence by their much-celebrated appearance at the Monterey International Pop Festival in August 1967. Their soon-released debut Mainstream album featured Janis Joplin's stunning performances of "Women Is Losers" and "Down on Me," as well as the whole band's overlooked "Blindman." Signed to a management contract with Albert Grossman (then Bob Dylan's manager) in January 1968, the group switched to Columbia Records for their only other album with Janis Joplin, *Cheap Thrills*. "Piece of My Heart" emerged as the hit single from the album which also included "Big Mama" Thornton's "Ball and Chain," Janis' own "Turtle Blues," and a moving rendition of George Gershwin's "Summertime." With Joplin garnering the majority of the media attention, rumors of the group's breakup began to spread in November and were confirmed on December 1 with Joplin's final appearance with the group at Chet Helms' Family Dog.

Retaining guitarist Sam Andrew, Janis Joplin formed a new band, alternately known as Squeeze and The Janis Joplin Revue, with organist Bill King, bassist Brad Campbell, drummer Ron Markowitz, and a horn section. Debuting equivocally at the Memphis Sound Party on December 18, 1968, the group soon suffered a variety of personnel changes. After recording one certified gold-award album, *Kozmic Blues*, with the group, Janis Joplin performed her final concert with this band on December 29, 1969, at Madison Square Garden. In April 1970 she again appeared with Big Brother and The Holding Company, which was reconstituted with Sam Andrew and singer–songwriter Nick Gravenites, at Fillmore West. Big Brother (without Janis Joplin) subsequently recorded two albums for Columbia, the first featuring Gravenites' tongue-in-cheek ode to Merle Haggard, "I'll Change Your Flat Tire, Merle."

Forming a new band, Full-Tilt Boogie, in May, Janis Joplin debuted the group at Freedom Hall in Louisville, Kentucky, on June 12, 1970. The members included guitarist John Till (a later-day member of her prior band) and bassist Brad Campbell. By September they had nearly finished recording their album, but on October 4, 1970, Janis Joplin was found dead at the age of 27 in her Hollywood hotel, the victim of a heroin overdose. Released posthumously, *Pearl* yielded a smash hit with Kris Kristofferson's "Me and Bobby McGee" and included "Cry Baby," Joplin's own satirical ditty, "Mercedes Benz," and one of her theme songs, "Get It While You Can." Columbia subsequently issued a double-record live set with Big Brother and Full-Tilt Boogie in 1972, a greatest hits package in 1973, a double-record soundtrack album to the film *Janis* in 1975, and *Farewell Song* in 1982.

BIG BROTHER AND THE HOLDING COMPANY

Big Brother and The Holding Company	Mainstream reissued on Columbia	6099 C–30631	September '67 May '71	
Cheap Thrills*	Columbia	PC–9700	August '68	A
Be a Brother	Columbia	C–30222	November '70	
How Hard It Is	Columbia	C–30738	August '71	

JANIS JOPLIN

Kozmic Blues*	Columbia	PC–9913	September '69	A
Pearl*	Columbia	KC–30322	January '71	A
Janis Joplin in Concert*	2-Columbia	C2X–31160	May '72	A
Greatest Hits*	Columbia	PC–32168	July '73	A
Janis (soundtrack)	2-Columbia	PG–33345 (M)	April '75	A
Farewell Song	Columbia	PC–37569	January '82	A

KALEIDOSCOPE. Probably the most eclectic American rock band of the late Sixties, Kaleidoscope featured multi-instrumentalists David Lindley, Chris Darrow, and Solomon Feldthouse. Playing such exotic stringed instruments as the saz, bouzouki, and oud, Kaleidoscope performed spectacularly live, producing music that revealed influences of rock, bluegrass, jazz, and classical musics as well as the folk musics of many countries (India, Greece, and Turkey). Chris Darrow left in 1968, later to pursue a neglected solo recording career and, following Kaleidoscope's breakup in 1970, Lindley, a sessions musician and member of Jackson Browne's band, became the prime exponent of the lap steel guitar during the Seventies.

KALEIDOSCOPE

Sidetrips	Epic	BN–26304	May '67	
Beacon from Mars	Epic	BN–26333	December '67	
Kaleidoscope	Epic	BN–26467	May '69	
Bernice	Epic	BN–26508	March '70	
When Scopes Collide	Pacific Arts	7–102	March '76	

CHRIS DARROW

Artist Proof	Fantasy	F–9403	March '72	
Chris Darrow	United Artists	LA048	March '73	
Under My Own Disguise	United Artists	LA242	June '74	
Fretless	Pacific Arts	7–132	June '79	

DAVID LINDLEY

El Rayo-X	Asylum	524	May '81	A

CHRIS DARROW AND MAX BUDA

Eye of the Storm	Takoma	7092	June '81	A

B.B. KING. The single most popular, successful, and influential black bluesman, B.B. King has never compromised his role as a blues performer for the sake of mere popularity. One of the most innovative of the urban blues singers, B.B. King has remained true to the blues through 20 years of touring the so-called "chitlin" circuit of small black rhythm-and-blues clubs 300 days a year, through the rise of rock-and-roll, and through his eventual success in the late Sixties. One of the world's greatest guitar soloists, B.B. King developed a manner of playing featuring his trademark "bent" note stylizations that has influenced virtually every guitarist in the blues and rock fields, an influence frequently acknowledged by white guitarists during the late Sixties, most notably Eric Clapton and Mike Bloomfield. With his style introduced to a mass white audience by Clapton, Bloomfield, and myriad other guitarists, with well-received appearances at venues such as the Fillmores East and West, and with the conspicuous success of "The Thrill Is Gone" in the wider arena of pop music in 1970, B.B. King became established as a singer and guitarist of enormously wide appeal. Elevated to the exclusive Nevada casino and supper club circuit by the Seventies, B.B. King became the first black bluesman to tour Russia, in 1979.

Born Riley B. King on a plantation in rural Mississippi on September 16, 1925, B.B. King started playing guitar with his first group, The Elkhorn Singers, at an early age. Performing in local black clubs for several years, he was drafted in 1943, moving to Memphis in 1947 after his discharge. There he moved in with his cousin, country blues artist Bukka White, and later secured a ten-minute mid-afternoon show on radio station WDIA with the assistance of the second Sonny Boy Williamson (real name: Rice Miller). King subsequently formed The Beale Streeters, whose members at times included Bobby "Blue" Bland and Johnny Ace, and became known as "The Beale Street Blues Boy," later shortened to "B.B." After initial recordings for the small Nashville-based Bullet label in 1949, he was signed to the Los Angeles-based Modern/RPM label by Ike Turner. Scoring his first smash rhythm-and-blues hit with "Three O'Clock Blues" in 1952, King formed a band that included a small horn section (a regular feature of his band throughout his career) and began tirelessly touring the "chitlin" circuit of small black rhythm-and-blues clubs. Subsequent rhythm-and blues hits on RPM included "You Know I Love You" in 1952, "Please Love Me" in 1953, "You Upset Me" in 1954, "Every Day I Have the Blues" (his signature song) in 1955, and "Sweet Little Angel" in 1956. B.B. King's first pop chart entry occurred in 1957 with "Be Careful with a Fool." Following the discontinuation of the RPM label by 1958, King recorded singles on Kent, with albums issued on the budget label Crown and reissued on United and Custom. Rhythm-and-blues hits on Kent included "Please Accept My Love" and "Sweet Sixteen," with "Rock Me Baby" becoming a moderate pop hit in 1964 after his departure.

In 1961 B.B. King signed with ABC Records, recording for both ABC and its subsidiary Bluesway label. His early recordings did not sell, although his *Live at the Regal* album, from 1965, is often considered to be one of his finest albums. "Don't Answer the Door" was a smash rhythm-and-blues hit in late 1966, and "Paying the Cost to Be the Boss" became a major rhythm-and-blues and moderate pop hit in 1968. By then, King had successfully appeared at the Fillmores West and East and had received laudatory comments concerning his playing by popular white guitarists such as Eric Clapton and Mike Bloomfield. *Lucille* became King's first album chart entry and *Live at The Village Gate—Well at the Hit Factory*, recorded under rock producer Bill Szymczyk, sold quite well. However, *Completely Well*, featuring the major pop hit "The Thrill Is Gone," was the album that established King with white audiences. His next two albums, *Indianola Mississippi Seeds*, recorded with Joe Walsh and Leon Russell, and *Live at Cook County Jail*, became best-sellers.

Established on the supper club and Nevada casino circuit by the early Seventies, B.B. King began recording exclusively for ABC with *Indianola Mississippi Seeds*. He soon recorded a series of modestly selling albums such as *B.B. King in London* (with Steve Marriott, Peter Green, and Ringo Starr), *L.A. Midnight* (with Joe Walsh and Taj Mahal), and *To Know You Is to Love You* (with Stevie Wonder on keyboards). The last album yielded moderate pop hits with "I Like to Live the Love" and the title song, but King's biggest commercial success came in collaboration with Bobby "Blue" Bland, *Live Together for the First Time*, certified gold-award in 1975. Another collaboration by the two fared less well in 1976 and, by 1979, King had switched to MCA Records for *Take It Home*. In February and March of 1979 he performed about 20 shows in Russia, becoming the first black bluesman to tour that country. Later, B.B. King became one of the few artists to perform live (rather than "lip-synching" a recording) on Dick Clark's "American Bandstand."

EARLY B.B. KING

Original Folk Blues, 1949–1950	United	7788(M)
Singin' the Blues	Crown	5020(M)
	also United	7726(M)
The Blues	Crown	5063(M)
	also United	7732(M)
B.B. King Wails	Crown	5115(M)
	also Crown	147
reissued as I Love You So	United	7711(M)
	also Custom	1049(M)
B.B. King Sings Spirituals	Crown	5119(M)
	also Crown	152
	also United	7723(M)
	also Custom	1059(M)
The Great B.B. King	Crown	5143(M)
	also United	7728(M)
King of the Blues	Crown	5157(M)
	also Crown	195
	also United	7730
My Kind of Blues	Crown	5188(M)
	also United	7724(M)
Blues for Me	Crown	5230(M)
	also United	7708(M)
	also Custom	1046(M)

Easy Listening	Crown	5286(M)		
Blues	also United	7705(M)		
Blues in My Heart	Crown	5309(M)		
	also United	7703(M)		
	also Custom	1040(M)		
The Soul of B.B.	Crown	5359(M)		
King	also United	7714(M)		
	also Custom	1052(M)		
	also Kent	539(M)	April '70	
Swing Low, Sweet	United	7721		
Chariot				
Rock Me, Baby	United	7733(M)		
Let Me Love You	United	7734(M)		
Live! B.B. King	United	7736(M)		
on Stage				
The Jungle	United	7742(M)		
Boss of the Blues	United	7750(M)		
The Incredible	United	7756(M)		
Soul of B.B.				
King				
Turn On with B.B.	United	7763(M)		
King				
Greatest Hits,	United	7766(M)		
Volume 1				
Better Than Ever	United	7771(M)		
The Original Sweet	United	7773(M)		
Sixteen				
Best	Galaxy	8202	June '63	
16 Greatest Hits	Galaxy	8208		

LATTER–DAY B.B KING

Mr. Blues	ABC	456	August '63	
Live at the Regal	ABC	509	February '65	
	MCA	reissued as AB–724	September '71	A
	reissued on Pickwick	3593	April '78	A
Confessin' the	ABC	528	December '65	
Blues				
Blues Is King	Bluesway	6001	February '67	
	reissued on ABC	704		
Blues on Top of	Bluesway	6011	February '68	
Blues	reissued on ABC	709		
Lucille	Bluesway	6016	October '68	
	reissued on ABC	712		
Live at The Village	Bluesway	6031	June '69	
Gate—Well at	reissued on ABC/MCA	AB–819		A
the Hit Factory				
Completely Well	Bluesway	6037	December '69	
	reissued on ABC/MCA	AB–868		A

Indianola Missis- sippi Seeds	ABC	713	October '70	
Live at Cook County Jail	ABC/MCA	AB–723	January '71	A
In London	ABC	730	October '71	
L.A. Midnight	ABC	743	February '72	
Guess Who	ABC	759	September '72	
To Know You Is to Love You	ABC	794	August '73	

B.B. KING AND BOBBY "BLUE" BLAND

Live Together for the First Time*	2-Dunhill	50190	October '74	A
Together Again . . . Live	Impulse	9317	July '76	A

B.B. KING

Lucille Talks Back	ABC	898	October '75	
King Size	ABC	977	February '77	
Midnight Believer	ABC/MCA	AA–1061	May '78	A
Take It Home	MCA	3151	August '79	A
Live at Ole Miss	2-MCA	8016	April '80	A
There Must Be a Better World Somewhere	MCA	5162	March '81	A

LATTER–DAY B.B. KING ANTHOLOGIES AND COMPILATIONS

Electric B.B./ His Best	Bluesway reissued on ABC/MCA	6022 AB–813	June '69	A
Back in the Alley: The Classic Blues of B.B. King	Bluesway reissued on ABC/MCA	6050 AB–878	January '73	A
Paying the Cost to Be the Boss	Pickwick	3385	January '75	

CAROLE KING. In collaboration with then-husband Gerry Goffin, Carole King wrote an astounding series of best-selling songs while working as a professional songwriter at New York's famed Brill Building during the Sixties. Prolific writers, Goffin and King wrote nearly as many hits as did Beatles Lennon and McCartney and scored over 70 chart entries by 1970, including the smash hits "Will You Love Me Tomorrow" by The Shirelles, "Take Good Care of My Baby" by Bobby Vee, "Go Away, Little Girl" by Steve Lawrence, and "The Loco-Motion" by Little Eva. With the Goffin–King team breaking up in 1967, Carole King eventually embarked on a solo career in 1970 at the encouragement of Lou Adler. With songs revealing a maturity and sophistication not generally evident in her earlier songs, *Writer* sold modestly, but her follow-up, *Tapestry*, sold spectacularly and heralded the rise of the singer–songwriter. The album eventually sold over

14 million copies, becoming the best selling pop album in history during its nearly six years on the album charts. (*Tapestry* was later challenged in sales by *Frampton Comes Alive* and Fleetwood Mac's *Rumours* and exceeded by the soundtracks to *Saturday Night Fever* and *Grease*.) Not surprisingly, *Tapestry* overshadowed Carole King's subsequent recording career. Nonetheless, all her later albums through 1977 (save the album to the children's television special "Really Rosie") have been certified gold-award. Switching from Lou Adler's Ode Records to Capitol Records by 1977, Carole King has not fared well since then.

Born in Brooklyn as Carole Klein on February 9, 1941, Carole King began singing and taking piano lessons at the age of four. She formed the female vocal group The Co-Sines at age 14 and met songwriter Gerry Goffin (born in Queens, New York, on February 11, 1939) in 1958 while attending Queens College. Signed as a staff songwriter to Al Nevins and Don Kirshner's Aldon Music at 17, she soon married Goffin and initiated their collaborative songwriting career at New York's famed Brill Building. First brought to the attention of the public as the subject of Neil Sedaka's late 1959 hit, "Oh! Carol," King, with Goffin, scored their first hit, a smash, in late 1960 with "Will You Love Me Tomorrow," recorded by The Shirelles. Through 1963 Goffin and King wrote a number of hits recorded by a variety of artists. These included "Some Kind of Wonderful," "When My Little Girl Is Smiling," and the smash "Up on the Roof" for the Drifters, the smash "Take Good Care of My Baby" and "Sharing You" for Bobby Vee, "Crying in the Rain" (with Howie Greenfield) for The Everly Brothers, "Her Royal Majesty" for James Darren, "Point of No Return" for Gene McDaniels, the smash "One Fine Day" for The Chiffons, "Hey, Girl" for Freddie Scott, and "I Can't Stay Mad at You" for Skeeter Davis. During 1963 Goffin and King provided Steve Lawrence and Eydie Gorme with a number of hits, beginning with the smash "Go Away, Little Girl" by Lawrence. The team also contributed hits to two English groups during the mid-Sixties, "I'm Into Something Good" for Herman's Hermits in 1964 and "Don't Bring Me Down" for The Animals in 1966. The duo also collaborated with Phil Spector on "Just Once in My Life" for The Righteous Brothers in 1965.

In 1962 Don Kirshner formed Dimension Records, as Gerry Goffin learned production and Carole King arranging. Dimension's first release, "The Loco-Motion," written by Goffin and King and recorded by Little Eva, became a smash hit in midyear. Carole King's version of "It Might as Well Rain until September," originally written for Bobby Vee, was Dimension's second hit, followed by Little Eva's "Keep Your Hands Off My Baby," and two songs performed by The Cookies, "Chains" and "Don't Say Nothin' (Bad about My Baby)," with all songs written by Goffin–King. During 1963 the label issued *The Dimension Dolls*, an anthology of material performed by King, Little Eva, and The Cookies. King's four cuts on the album were assembled from demonstration tapes.

During the mid-Sixties, Gerry Goffin and Carole King formed their own record label, Tomorrow, but singles by King and The Myddle Class failed to reach the charts. In 1967 King and Goffin contributed hit songs to Kirshner's own Monkees ("Pleasant Valley Sunday") and to Aretha Franklin ("[You Make Me Feel like] A Natural Woman"), while providing The Byrds with "Goin' Back" and "Wasn't Born to Follow." King subsequently broke up the songwriting team, divorcing Goffin and marrying the bass player from The Myddle Class, Charles Larkey. Goffin later surfaced with his own solo album, *It Ain't Exactly Entertainment*, in 1973. King moved to Los Angeles, where she formed The City with Larkey and guitarist Danny Kortchmar and recorded one album, *Now That Everything's Been Said*, for Lou Adler's Ode Records. The album failed to sell but did include "Wasn't Born to Follow" and Goffin and King's "Hi-De-Ho," a major hit for Blood, Sweat and Tears in 1970.

By 1970 Carole King had initiated a solo career, assisting James Taylor with *Sweet Baby James* and recording her debut solo album, *Writer*, with Larkey, Kortchmar, and Taylor. The album contained the Goffin–King songs "Up on the Roof," "Goin' Back," and "No Easy Way Down," but sold only modestly. In 1971 King recorded *Tapestry* and the album proved enormously successful. As James Taylor's version of King's "You've Got a Friend" was climbing the charts, so was her own double-sided smash hit, "It's Too Late/I Feel the Earth Move." The album later yielded another major two-sided hit with "So Far Away/Smackwater Jack," while also including "Way Over Yonder" and two earlier Goffin–King compositions, "Will You Love Me Tomorrow" and "A Natural Woman." This collection of mature, sophisticated songs (in contrast to the earlier teen melodramas) ultimately appealed to virtually every sector of the record-buying public. The album eventually sold more than 14 million copies and remained for nearly six years on the album charts.

Carole King's next two albums, *Carole King Music* and *Rhymes and Reasons*, sold well, each yielding a hit single ("Sweet Seasons" and "Been to Canaan," respectively) but somehow lacking *Tapestry's* magic. *Fantasy* was somewhat more socially conscious, producing moderate hits with "Believe in Humanity" and "Corazon," but *Wrap Around Joy*, with most lyrics provided by David Palmer, was decidedly jazz-oriented and revealed a change in musical direction. The album's smash hit, "Jazzman," featured an exciting saxophone solo by Tom Scott and was followed by "Nightingale." After "Really Rosie," an animated television show based on the children's books of Maurice Sendak and using Sendak's lyrics, King recorded *Thoroughbred* with the vocal assistance of Graham Nash, David Crosby, and James Taylor. The album included four Goffin–King songs and yielded a major hit with "Only Love Is Real." At the end of 1976 King severed relations with Lou Adler's Ode Records, switching to Capitol for *Simple Things* and the moderate hit, "Hard Rock Cafe." By then separated from Charles Larkey, she collaborated with songwriter Rick Evers for the album's material and utilized the services of the Boulder, Colorado, club band Navarro in recording. King later married Evers but, on March 21, 1978, he died from a cocaine overdose in Los Angeles. *Welcome Home* became Carole King's first album to sell only modestly since *Writer*, and 1979 saw the release of *Touch the Sky*. During 1980, *Pearls*, a collection of her versions of many of the Goffin–King classics of the Sixties, yielded a major hit with "One Fine Day."

THE DIMENSION DOLLS (CAROLE KING, LITTLE EVA, THE COOKIES)

The Dimension Dolls	Dimension	DLP–6001 (M)	November '63	

THE CITY

Now That Every-thing's Been Said	Ode	Z–1244012	March '69	

GERRY GOFFIN

It Ain't Exactly Entertainment	2-Adelphi	AD–4102	January '73	

CAROLE KING

Writer: Carole King	Ode	SP–77006 reissued as PE–34944	August '70 October '78	A
Tapestry*	Ode	SP–77009 reissued as PE–34946	February '71 October '78	A
Carole King Music*	Ode	SP–77013 reissued as PE–34949	November '71 October '78	A
Rhymes and Reasons*	Ode	SP–77016 reissued as PE–34950	October '72 October '78	A
Fantasy*	Ode	SP–77018 reissued as PE–34962	June '73 October '78	A
Wrap Around Joy*	Ode	SP–77024 reissued as PE–34953	September '74 October '78	A
Really Rosie (TV soundtrack)	Ode	SP–77027 reissued as PE–34945	February '75 October '78	A
Thoroughbred*	Ode	SP–77034 reissued as PE–34963	January '76 October '78	A
Simple Things*	Capitol	SMAS–11667 reissued as SN–16057	August '77	A

Greatest Hits*	Epic	JE–34967	November '77	A
Welcome Home	Capitol	SW–11785	June '78	
		reissued as SN–16058		A
Touch the Sky	Capitol	SW–11953	June '79	
		reissued as SN–16059		A
Pearls—Songs of Goffin and King	Capitol	SOO–12073	June '80	A

KING CRIMSON. Seminal British "progressive" band of the late Sixties and first half of the Seventies, King Crimson attained the status of "superstars" in England and Europe but remained essentially a cult band in the United States. Showcasing the somewhat pretentious songwriting of Pete Sinfield and the guitar and mellotron playing of Robert Fripp, one of the most eccentric and enigmatic figures to emerge from British rock, King Crimson's debut album, *In the Court of the Crimson King*, was a best-seller. Virtually reconstituted thereafter, King Crimson and Fripp endured through six more albums, including the celebrated *Lark's Tongue in Aspic* (featuring percussionist Jamie Muir) before disbanding in late 1974. One-time members of King Crimson include Greg Lake (later with Emerson, Lake, and Palmer), Ian McDonald (later with Foreigner), Boz Burrell (later with Bad Company) and John Wetton (later with Uriah Heep, now with U.K.). Following two esoteric albums with ex-Roxy Music member Brian Eno, Robert Fripp initiated an unusual solo career with *Exposure* and his American "anti-tour" of 1979, utilizing so-called "Frippertronics," a tape delay system for solo guitar.

Robert Fripp, born in Wimbourne, Dorset, in 1946, started playing guitar at the age of 11 and worked with his first music group at age 14. In 1967 he helped form the trio Giles, Giles, and Fripp, with Giles brothers Mike and Pete on drums and bass, respectively. Their only album failed to sell and, by the fall of 1968, the group had broken up. Mike Giles (born in Bournemouth in 1942) and Fripp began rehearsing a new band called King Crimson the following January and debuted that April in London. The members: guitarist Fripp, drummer–vocalist Giles, lead vocalist–bassist Greg Lake (born in Bournemouth on November 10, 1948), and multi-instrumentalist Ian McDonald (born in London on June 25, 1946), with Pete Sinfield providing lyrics. The group's underground reputation was soon enhanced by a July appearance in Hyde Park at a free Rolling Stones concert. King Crimson's debut album, *In the Court of the Crimson King*, was greeted with near-unanimous critical acclaim and was eventually certified gold-award in 1977. The album featured five extended pieces, including the underground favorites "Epitaph," "21st Century Schizoid Man" and, of course, the title song. However, after the group's first American tour, in December 1969, Giles and McDonald left the band, later to record the overlooked *McDonald and Giles*. Reduced to a trio,

King Crimson began recording their second album, only to see Greg Lake depart to join Keith Emerson and Carl Palmer during those sessions. *In the Wake of Poseidon*, much akin to their first album, was completed with Gordon Haskell (vocals, bass), Mel Collins (reeds), the Giles brothers (who sat in while replacements were found), with Fripp taking over on mellotron. The album sold quite well despite its remarkable resemblance to their debut album.

By late 1970 Mel Collins and Gordon Haskell had become permanent members of King Crimson, as had drummer Andy McCulloch. Nonetheless, Haskell quit shortly before the final sessions for *Lizard*, later to record a solo album on Atco. Ian Wallace replaced McCulloch, and Fripp recruited bassist Boz Burrell for *Islands*. Again, after a second American tour in early 1972, King Crimson disintegrated. Collins, Wallace and Burrell left briefly to join Alexis Korner, and Fripp dismissed lyricist Pete Sinfield, who also eventually recorded a solo album. After several months' layoff, Robert Fripp reconstituted King Crimson with avant garde percussionist Jamie Muir, violin and mellotron player David Cross, bassist–vocalist John Wetton (from Family), and drummer Bill Bruford (from Yes). This grouping recorded *Lark's Tongue in Aspic*, regarded by many as the group's finest later-day album, but Muir dropped out after the first tour. *Starless and Bible Black* was recorded by the remaining quartet, and *Red*, King Crimson's final studio album, was recorded without Cross but with the assistance of Mel Collins and Ian McDonald. Fripp dissolved King Crimson around October 1974, some months after completing an American tour that produced the live set, *U.S.A.*

Robert Fripp subsequently recorded two esoteric albums with Brian Eno, whereas John Wetton joined Uriah Heep for a year and Bill Bruford toured with Genesis in 1976. Wetton and Bruford later formed U.K., but Bruford dropped out to record the solo set, *Feels Good to Me*, and to form the four-piece Bruford in 1979. Brian Eno and Robert Fripp developed a system of music utilizing two tape recorders and solo guitar called "Frippertronics" that Fripp employed for his 1979 American "anti-tour." Robert Fripp launched his solo recording career that year with *Exposure*. Fripp later recorded *God Save the Queen* and *The League of Gentlemen* before re-forming King Crimson in 1981.

GILES, GILES, AND FRIPP

The Cheerful Insanity of Giles, Giles, and Fripp	Deram	18019	November '68	

KING CRIMSON

In the Court of the Crimson King*	Atlantic	SD–8245 reissued as SD–19155	October '69	A
In the Wake of Poseidon	Atlantic	SD–8266	September '70	A

Lizard	Atlantic	SD–8278	March '71	A
Islands	Atlantic	SD–7212	February '72	A
Lark's Tongue in Aspic	Atlantic	SD–7263	May '73	A
Starless and Bible Black	Atlantic	SD–7298	April '74	A
Red	Atlantic	SD–18110	November '74	
U.S.A.	Atlantic	SD–18136	May '75	A

McDONALD AND GILES

McDonald and Giles	Cotillion	9042	February '71	

GORDON HASKELL

It Is and It Isn't	Atco	SD33–378	December '71	

PETE SINFIELD

Still	Manticore	66667	October '73	

ROBERT FRIPP AND BRIAN ENO

No Pussyfooting	Island reissued on Antilles	16 7001	November '75	
Evening Star	Antilles	7018	June '76	
Evening Star	Editions EG	103	July '81	A

U.K.

U.K.	Polydor	PD1–6146	May '78	
Danger Money	Polydor	PD1–6194	March '79	
Night after Night	Polydor	PD1–6234	October '79	A

BILL BRUFORD

Feels Good to Me	Polydor	PD1–6149	May '78	A
One of a Kind	Polydor	PD1–6205	June '79	A
Gradually Going Tornado	Polydor	6261	March '80	A
Bruford Tapes	Editions EG	106	July '81	A

ROBERT FRIPP

Exposure	Polydor	PD1–6201	May '79	A
God Save the Queen/Under Heavy Manners	Polydor	4266	April '80	A
The League of Gentlemen	Polydor	6317	April '81	A

DARYL HALL (WITH ROBERT FRIPP)

Sacred Songs	RCA	AFL1–3573	March '80	

KING CRIMSON

| Discipline | Warner Brothers | 3629 | October '81 | A |

THE KINGSTON TRIO. The most successful folk group to emerge dur-ing the late Fifties (with six of their first seven albums certified gold-award by 1962), The Kingston Trio projected a clean-cut college image that enabled them to avoid the politically suspect stigma attached to early Fif-ties folk artists. In successfully bringing their "good time" acoustic music into the wider arenas of AM radio, television, and pop music, The Kingston Trio made folk music commercially viable and opened the way for the early Sixties folk movement that presented the public with Peter, Paul, and Mary, Joan Baez, Bob Dylan, and dozens of others. Placing vir-tually all of their albums on the album charts, The Kingston Trio dis-banded in 1967. Second-generation member John Stewart subsequently pursued a modest performing and recording career (chronicled elsewhere) that eventually blossomed in 1979. In the early Seventies, original Bob Shane, owner of The Kingston Trio name, reconstituted the group with new members for tours of the club and college circuits.

Collegians Dave Guard (born in San Francisco on October 19, 1934), Nick Reynolds (born in San Diego, California, on July 27, 1933), and Bob Shane (born in Hawaii on February 1, 1934) formed The Kingston Trio in Stanford, California, in 1957, playing coffeehouses around the San Fran-cisco Bay area. With all three members playing guitar and banjo and sing-ing, the group was signed to Capitol Records, releasing their debut album in 1958. The Kingston Trio scored their first major hit (and ultimately their biggest selling single) before year's end with "Tom Dooley." Before the dawn of the Sixties, they had major hits with "The Tijuana Jail," "M.T.A.," and "A Worried Man." Their early albums sold spectacularly, with six of their first seven albums being certified gold-award by 1962, and four of them remaining on the charts for more than two years. Dave Guard left The Kingston Trio in May 1961 and recorded a modest-selling album with The Whiskey Hill Singers the next year. He was replaced by John Stewart (born September 5, 1939, in San Diego, California) of The Cumberland Three, and the group's hits continued through 1963 with Pete Seeger's "Where Have All the Flowers Gone," Dave Guard's "Scotch and Soda" (only a minor hit, but standard lounge fare today), Hoyt Axton's "Greenback Dollar," and "Reverend Mr. Black." Although The Kingston Trio never had another hit single, their albums continued to sell quite well through 1964, after which they switched to Decca Records. Overwhelmed by the myriad of British groups invading the American music scene, The Kingston Trio disbanded in 1967, with John Stewart going on to a mod-estly successful performing and recording career. In 1969 and again in 1974, Bob Shane revived the group with new members for college concerts and club appearances. The present members are Shane, George Grove, and Roger Gambill. During the Seventies Dave Guard resurfaced for reunions of the reconstituted Limelighters and tours with The Steve Seskin Trio and The Modern Folk Quartet. In November 1981 Shane, Guard, Reynolds, Stewart, Grove, and Gambill united for a single Kingston Trio concert broadcast on public television in early 1982.

THE KINGSTON TRIO

The Kingston Trio*	Capitol	T–996(M)	June '58	
reissued as Tom Dooley	Capitol	N–16185 (M)		A
From the hungry i*	Capitol	T–1107(M) reissued as M–11968 (M)	January '59 September '79	A
Stereo Concert*	Capitol	ST–1183	March '59	
At Large*	Capitol	ST–1199	June '59	
reissued as "Scarlet Ribbons"	Capitol	SN–16186		A
Here We Go Again!*	Capitol	ST–1258	October '59	
Sold Out*	Capitol	ST–1352	April '60	
String Along*	Capitol	ST–1407	August '60	
The Last Month of the Year	Capitol	ST–1446	November '60	
Make Way!	Capitol	ST–1474	February '61	

DAVE GUARD AND THE WHISKEY HILL SINGERS

Dave Guard and The Whiskey Hill Singers	Capitol	ST–1728	June '62

THE KINGSTON TRIO

Goin' Places	Capitol	ST–1564	July '61
Close-Up	Capitol	ST–1642	October '61
College Concert	Capitol	ST–1658	February '62
Something Special	Capitol	ST–1747	July '62
New Frontier	Capitol	ST–1809	December '62
# 16	Capitol	ST–1871	March '63
Sunny Side!	Capitol	ST–1935	August '63
Sing a Song with The Kingston Trio	Capitol	SKAO–2005	December '63
Time to Think	Capitol	ST–2011	January '64
Back in Town	Capitol	ST–2081	May '64
Nick–Bob–John	Decca	74613	January '65
Stay Awhile	Decca	74656	June '65
Somethin' Else	Decca	74694	December '65
Children of the Morning	Decca	74758	June '66

KINGSTON TRIO ANTHOLOGIES AND COMPILATIONS

Encores	Capitol	DT–1612	September '61	
The Best of The Kingston Trio*	Capitol	SM–1705 reissued as SN–16183	April '62	A
Folk Era	3-Capitol	STCL–2180	December '64	
The Best of The Kingston Trio, Volume 2	Capitol	SM–2280 reissued as SN–16184	March '65	A
The Best of The Kingston Trio, Volume 3	Capitol	SM–2614	November '66	A
Tom Dooley/ Scarlet Ribbons	2-Capitol	STBB–513	July '70	
Once Upon a Time	2-Tetragram- maton	TD–5101	July '69	
Tom Dooley	Pickwick	3260	February '71	
The Kingston Trio	Pickwick	3297	March '72	
Where Have All the Flowers Gone	Pickwick	3323	October '72	

THE KINKS. One of the longest-lived groups of the early to mid-Sixties British invasion (rivaled only by The Who and The Rolling Stones), The Kinks have endured a remarkably erratic career of hit and flop singles, concept albums, and record company switches with leader Ray Davies and original members Dave Davies and Mick Avory. Following several hard-edged two- and three-chord hit singles, Ray Davies began writing amusing satirical songs of social comment such as "A Well Respected Man." Their American popularity suffered after their first United States tour in 1965, since the American Federation of Musicians prevented them from touring the country between 1966 and 1969. The Kinks attempted to come back with the boldly conceptual *Arthur* album (often favorably compared to The Who's *Tommy*, but generally neglected by fans), but they were re-established by the follow-up, *Lola versus Powerman and the Moneygo-round*. The album's title song is generally regarded as the first rock song to overtly deal with transvestism. Again touring the United States in late 1969 as their British popularity faded, The Kinks recorded an equivocal series of concept albums between 1973 and 1975 that were performed in their entirety in a theatrical manner during concurrent tours. Abandoning the conceptual/theatrical approach with their switch to Arista Records in 1976, The Kinks returned to the singles charts with songs from their best-selling *Sleepwalker*, *Misfits*, and *Low Budget* albums.

Born in Muswell Hill, London, on June 21, 1944, Ray Davies began playing music in the early Sixties with The Dave Hunt Band, whereas brother Dave Davies (born in Muswell Hill on February 3, 1947) formed The Ravens to play the local debutante circuit in 1962. Ray later joined The Ravens and, with the additions of Mick Avory (born in Hampton Court, Middlesex, on February 15, 1944) and Peter Quaife (born in Tavistock, Devonshire, on December 27, 1943), the band backed singer Robert Wace. Essentially formed in December 1963, The Kinks, as they had come to be known, were "discovered" by Shel Talmy, who secured them a recording contract with Pye Records. The members: Ray Davies (guitar, lead vocals), Dave Davies (lead and rhythm guitar, keyboards, vocals), Pete Quaife (bass, vocals), and Mick Avory (drums), with Ray as principle songwriter. The group's first two singles barely sold, but the third, "You Really Got Me" (released on Reprise in the United States), became a smash British and American hit. The like-sounding "All Day and All of the Night" was a major hit in early 1965, followed by the slower-paced "Tired of Waiting for You" and "Set Me Free." They toured the United States in 1965 but, due to an apparent oversight, the group was unofficially banned from appearing again by the American Federation of Musicians until 1969.

The moderate hit "Who'll Be the Next in Line" echoed the earlier raunchy sound, but "A Well Respected Man" marked the beginning of a new phase of astute satire in Ray Davies' songwriting. "Dedicated Follower of Fashion" poked fun at Carnaby Street fops, and the follow-up, "Sunny Afternoon," was decidedly mellow and melodic, even compassionate. The vaguely thematic *Face to Face* album, The Kinks' first conspicuously poor-selling album, also included Ray's "Dandy," a smash hit for Herman's Hermits in late 1966. Save two minor hits in 1967, The Kinks did not have another singles chart entry until 1970. After *Something Else*, The Kinks' final album with Shel Talmy as producer, Ray Davies produced the next two Kinks albums as well as scored the soundtracks to *The Virgin Soldiers* and *Percy*. Dave Davies managed a hit with the English solo single "Death of a Clown" but, during the late Sixties, The Kinks' albums and singles sold poorly in the United States, probably due to the group's limited touring. In March 1969 Pete Quaife left the group and was replaced by John Dalton (born May 21, 1943) on bass. The critically acclaimed, historically conscious concept album *Arthur (or The Decline and Fall of the British Empire)* sold modestly at best, despite yielding a minor hit with "Victoria."

The Kinks resumed touring in the United States in late 1969 with their usual sloppy stage presentation and, during May 1970, John Gosling was added to the group on keyboards and backup vocals. The Kinks finally re-established themselves at year's end with *Lola versus Powerman and the Moneygoround*, an acerbic look at the pop music industry and their situation within it. The album yielded a major hit with "Lola," apparently the first rock song to overtly deal with transvestism, and a minor hit with "Apeman." By 1971 The Kinks had switched to RCA Records. Reprise later issued *The Kink Kronikles* and *The Great Lost Kinks Album* in the United States only. The Kinks' RCA debut, *Muswell Hillbillies*, a decidedly countrified effort, sold only modestly despite the inclusion of Kinks favorites such as "Alcohol" and "Acute Schizoid Paranoid Blues." Subsequently augmented by a three-piece horn section, The Kinks' *Everybody's in Showbiz*, containing the excellent "Celluloid Heroes," fared somewhat better.

Ray Davies and The Kinks next embarked on a program of ambitious concept albums, complete with on-tour theatrical presentations. The character Mr. Flash from *The Village Green Preservation Society* was resurrected, but *Preservation* (released as *Act I* and the two-record set *Act II*) failed to sell in significant quantities. During 1974 Ray and Dave Davies formed Konk Records, distributed by ABC/Dunhill, as an outlet for productions outside the group, but recordings by Claire Hamill and Cafe Society proved unsuccessful. Construction of a 24-track recording studio in London was also begun in 1974. The Kinks' next two albums, *Soap Opera* and *Schoolboys in Disgrace*, sold rather well, but concurrent tours featuring theatrical performances of each album's material seemed to perplex rather than amuse American audiences.

By 1977 Andy Pyle had replaced John Dalton on bass and The Kinks had switched to Arista Records. Dismissing the horn section and abandoning the concept album format, the group recorded *Sleepwalker* as a mere collection of unrelated songs. The album, their best-selling in years, yielded the group's first, albeit minor, hit in six years with the title song. *Misfits* produced a moderate hit with "A Rock 'n' Roll Fantasy," but John Gosling and Andy Pyle left The Kinks in April 1978. They were replaced by bassist Jim Rodford (born in St. Albans, England, on July 7, 1945), a former member of Argent, and ex-Pretty Things keyboardist Gordon Edwards (born in Liverpool on December 26, 1946), who was later replaced by Ian Gibbons. In 1979, with originals Ray and Dave Davies and Mick Avory still remaining, The Kinks toured America again and recorded the gold-award *Low Budget*, which included the underground favorite "A Gallon of Gas" and the moderate hit "Superman."

THE KINKS

You Really Got Me	Reprise	RS–6143	December '64	
Kinks-Size	Reprise	RS–6158	March '65	
Kinda Kinks	Reprise	RS–6173	August '65	
Kinks Kinkdom	Reprise	RS–6184	December '65	
Kink Kontroversy	Reprise	RS–6197	April '66	
Face to Face	Reprise	RS–6228	January '67	
"Live" Kinks	Reprise	RS–6260	September '67	A
Something Else	Reprise	RS–6279	February '68	A
Four More Respected Gentlemen	Reprise	RS–6309	November '68	
The Kinks Are the Village Green Preservation Society	Reprise	RS–6327	March '69	A
Arthur (or The Decline and Fall of the British Empire)	Reprise	RS–6366	November '69	A

Lola versus Power-man and the Moneygoround	Reprise	RS–6423	November '70	A
Kink Kronikles	2-Reprise	2XS–6454	April '72	A
The Great Lost Kinks Album	Reprise	MS–2127	February '73	
Muswell Hillbillies	RCA	LSP–4644	December '71	
Everybody's in Showbiz	RCA	VPS–6065	August '72	A
Preservation, Act I	RCA	LPL1–5002	November '73	
Preservation, Act II	2-RCA	CPL2–5040	May '74	
Soap Opera	RCA	AFL1–5081	April '75	
		reissued as AYL1–3750		A
Schoolboys in Disgrace	RCA	AFL1–5102	November '75	
		reissued as AYL1–3749		A
Sleepwalker	Arista	AL–4106	February '77	A
Misfits	Arista	AB–4167	June '78	A
Low Budget*	Arista	AB–4240	July '79	A
One for the Road*	2-Arista	A2L–8401	June '80	A
Give the People What They Want	Arista	9567	September '81	A

DAVE DAVIES

AFL1–3603	RCA	AFL1–3603	July '80	A
Glamour	RCA	AFL1–4036	June '81	A

KINKS ANTHOLOGIES AND COMPILATIONS

Greatest Hits!*	Reprise	RS–6217	August '66	
Celluloid Heroes—The Kinks' Greatest	RCA	AFL1–1743	June '76	
		reissued as AYL1–3869		A
Second Time Around	RCA	AFL1–3520	August '80	A
History of British Pop, Volume 1	Pye	505	November '76	
History of British Pop, Volume 2	Pye	509	November '76	

KISS. Combining features of both so-called "glitter rock" and "heavy metal" musics (including garish costuming and makeup, spectacular on-stage special effects, and barely competent, over-loud, guitar-based music), Kiss established themselves as an enormously popular concert attraction and album band through an extensive media campaign by their record company, Casablanca, and a year and a half of nearly constant touring. Universally attacked by critics, Kiss nonetheless endeared themselves to legions of prepubescent fans (much to the chagrin of their parents) with gimmicks such as mock-blood vomiting, fire-breathing, explosions and fireworks, dry-ice fogs, and rocket-firing guitars in performance. To support a mythology perpetrated by numerous "fanzines," the members of Kiss have never appeared in public or been photographed without their full-face greasepaint makeup. A virtual rock industry unto themselves, Kiss merchandising includes T-shirts, comics, jewelry, and films as well as the series of nearly instantaneous platinum-level sales of albums since 1976. In late 1978 Kiss became the first rock band whose members simultaneously issued solo albums, backed by the largest advertising-promotion budget in music history ($2.5 million), resulting in platinum-level sales for each album.

KISS

Kiss*	Casablanca	NBLP–9001	March '74	
		reissued as NBLP–7001		A
Hotter Than Hell*	Casablanca	NBLP–7006	November '74	A
Dressed to Kill*	Casablanca	NBLP–7016	April '75	A
Alive!*	2-Casablanca	NBLP–7020	October '75	A
Destroyer**	Casablanca	NBLP–7025	March '76	A
The Originals	3-Casablanca	NBLP–7032	August '76	
Rock and Roll Over**	Casablanca	NBLP–7037	November '76	A
Love Gun**	Casablanca	NBLP–7057	June '77	
Alive II**	2-Casablanca	NBLP–7076	November '77	
Double Platinum**	Casablanca	NBLP–7100	May '78	
Dynasty**	Casablanca	NBLP–7152	June '79	A
Unmasked*	Casablanca	7225	June '80	A
Music from the Elders	Casablanca	7261	January '82	A

GENE SIMMONS

| Gene Simmons** | Casablanca | NBLP–7120 | September '78 | |

ACE FREHLEY

| Ace Frehley** | Casablanca | NBLP–7121 | September '78 | |

PETER CRISS

| Peter Criss** | Casablanca | NBLP–7122 | September '78 | |
| By Myself | Casablanca | 7240 | September '80 | A |

PAUL STANLEY

| Paul Stanley** | Casablanca | NBLP–7123 | September '78 | |

GLADYS KNIGHT AND THE PIPS. One of the longest-lived family acts in rock music, Gladys Knight and The Pips have been together professionally for over 25 years (save a year's absence by Gladys Knight in the early Sixties), scoring major hits on four different labels. With The Pips functioning as an integral part of the group rather than as mere vocal backup, Gladys Knight and The Pips featured the precise choreography of Cholly Atkins even before they (and he) joined the Motown organization. Despite the fact that Gladys Knight was favorably compared to Aretha Franklin, Gladys Knight (and The Pips) were ostensibly treated as a second-line act at Motown, leading to their switch to Buddah Records in 1973. Developing a reputation as *the* female-led group of the mid Seventies, Gladys Knight and The Pips became one of the few former Motown acts to retain (and even increase) their popularity and success after leaving the organization. Established as television and cabaret performers by 1974, Gladys Knight and The Pips continue to record and tour the exclusive Nevada casino and supper club circuit.

Gladys Knight (born May 28, 1944) began singing with the gospel group, The Morris Brown Choir, in her native Atlanta, Georgia, at the age of four, later touring with the group throughout the South. At age seven she won a competition on the "Ted Mack Amateur Hour" television show, thereafter touring with Mack for a year. In 1952, at the age of eight, Gladys Knight joined several close relatives to sing informally at brother Merald's birthday party. Thus was born the first incarnation of The Pips, with Gladys, Brenda, and Merald "Bubba" Knight (born September 2 or 4, 1942), and cousins Elenor and William Guest(the latter born June 2, 1941). The group soon began playing engagements around their native Atlanta, later touring the nation with Jackie Wilson and Sam Cooke in 1957. Initial recordings on Brunswick that year proved unsuccessful;

Elenor and Brenda dropped out of the group and were replaced by another cousin, Edward Patten (born August 2, 1939), and Langston George. Finally, in 1961, the group scored their first hit with the Johnny Otis ballad, "Every Beat of My Heart," on VeeJay as The Pips and on Fury as Gladys Knight and The Pips. They hit with "Letter Full of Tears" on Fury in early 1962, but the company soon went out of business and Gladys Knight returned to Atlanta for a year while The Pips did sessions work. Langston George left, and Ms. Knight rejoined the group in 1963, signing with Maxx Records and scoring a moderate hit with "Giving Up" in 1964.

The first signing to Motown's Soul label in 1965, Gladys Knight and The Pips languished with the company for several years before achieving a moderate hit in 1967 with "Everybody Needs Love." Later that year, under producer Norman Whitfield, the group had a smash hit with "I Heard It through the Grapevine," only to see Marvin Gaye score an even bigger hit with the song a year later. Subsequent hits on Soul included "The End of the Road" in 1968, "Friendship Train" and a remake of Shirley Ellis' "The Nitty Gritty" in 1969, and "You Need Love like I Do (Don't You)" in early 1970. The group adopted a more mellow sound for later-day Soul hits such as "If I Were Your Woman," "I Don't Want to Do Wrong," "Make Me the Woman That You Go Home To," "Neither One of Us" (a smash hit), and Gladys' own "Daddy Could Swear, I Declare." Their *Neither One of Us* album became a best-seller but, despite their consistent recording success and growing status as a live act, Gladys Knight and The Pips felt they were not being treated as a front-line act, and so defected to Buddah Records in March 1973.

Gladys Knight and The Pips' debut Buddah album, *Imagination*, yielded three smash hits with Tony Joe White's "Midnight Train to Georgia," Barry Goldberg and Gerry Goffin's "I've Got to Use My Imagination," and "Best Thing That Ever Happened to Me." The album was soon certified gold-award, as was the soundtrack to *Claudine*, recorded under songwriter–producer Curtis Mayfield. That album produced a smash hit with "On and On," and subsequent hits on Buddah included "I Feel a Song (in My Heart)," "The Way We Were," and "Part-Time Love." However, after 1975's *Second Anniversary*, singles and albums by Gladys Knight and The Pips fared modestly at best. By late 1976 Gladys Knight had made her acting debut with husband Barry Hankerson in *Pipe Dreams;* the soundtrack to the film was recorded by the group. In 1978 Gladys Knight signed with Columbia Records as a solo, whereas The Pips—"Bubba" Knight, William Guest, and Edward Patten—began recording for Casablanca Records. Allowed to work in clubs but prevented from recording together for more than two years by legal disputes, Gladys Knight and The Pips reunited for the Nicholas Ashford–Valerie Simpson-produced *About Love* and *Touch* albums for Columbia.

GLADYS KNIGHT AND THE PIPS

| Letter Full of Tears | Fury | F–1003(M) |

Tastiest Hits	Bell	6013	June '68	
In the Beginning	Bell	1323	February '75	
Every Beat of My Heart	Accord	SN–7103	April '81	A
Letter Full of Tears	Accord	SN–7105	April '81	A
Everybody Needs Love	Soul	706	October '67	
Feelin' Bluesy	Soul	707	June '68	
Silk and Soul	Soul	711	January '69	
Nitty Gritty	Soul	713	October '69	
All in a Knight's Work	Soul	730		
If I Were Your Woman	Soul	731	May '71	
Standing Ovation	Soul	7–736	January '72	A
Neither One of Us	Soul	7–737	March '73	A
All I Need Is Time	Soul	739	July '73	
Knight Time	Soul	741	March '74	
A Little Knight Music	Soul	744	April '75	
Imagination*	Buddah	BDS–5141	October '73	A
Claudine (soundtrack)*	Buddah	BDS–5602	March '74	
I Feel a Song*	Buddah	BDS–5612	October '74	A
Second Anniversary*	Buddah	BDS–5639	October '75	
Pipe Dreams (soundtrack)	Buddah	BDS–5676	November '76	
Bless This House	Buddah	BDS–5651	March '77	A
Still Together	Buddah	BDS–5689	April '77	
The One and Only	Buddah	BDS–5701	September '78	

GLADYS KNIGHT AND THE PIPS ANTHOLOGIES AND COMPILATIONS

Greatest Hits	Soul	723	April '70	
Anthology	2-Motown	7–792	February '74	A
Motown Superstar Series, Volume 13	Motown	5–113		A
Gladys Knight and The Pips	Up Front	UPF–130		
Best of Gladys Knight and The Pips	Buddah	BDS–5653	February '76	A
Every Beat of My Heart	Pickwick	3348		
It Hurt Me So	Pickwick	3374		
I Heard It through the Grapevine	Pickwick	3534	May '76	
The Very Best of Gladys Knight and The Pips	United Artists	LA503	April '76	

THE PIPS

At Last . . . The Pips	Casablanca	NBLP–7081	February '78	A
Callin'	Casablanca	NBLP–7113	August '78	A

GLADYS KNIGHT

Miss Gladys Knight	Buddah	BDS–5714	December '78	
Gladys Knight	Columbia	JC–35704	March '79	A

GLADYS KNIGHT AND THE PIPS

About Love	Columbia	JC–36387	May '80	A
Touch	Columbia	FC–37086	September '81	A

AL KOOPER. One of the most erratic figures in the history of American rock music, Al Kooper has been involved in projects great and small as teenage performer, songwriter, sessions musician, group member or leader, solo artist, and producer. As a teenage performer, Al Kooper was a member of The Royal Teens, who provided the novelty smash "Short Shorts" in 1958; as a songwriter, he co-authored Gary Lewis and The Playboys' first hit (a smash), "This Diamond Ring." As a sessions musician, Al Kooper recorded with Bob Dylan (*Highway 61 Revisited, Blonde on Blonde*), Tom Rush, Moby Grape, and, perhaps most importantly, Mike Bloomfield and Steve Stills (*Super Session*, probably the first "jam"-style recording of widespread popularity). As a member of The Blues Project, he helped bring electric instrumentation to white folk and blues music. As founder–member of Blood, Sweat and Tears, Al Kooper inducted the horn section into rock music and encouraged, indirectly, the development of so-called "jazz-rock." As a producer, he worked on Lynyrd Skynyrd's first three albums (all certified gold-award) as well as The Tubes' first album. However, as conspicuous as these successes and pioneering efforts are, they do not totally overshadow Al Kooper's failures: he was kicked out of Blood, Sweat and Tears after a single album, his solo recording career proved marginally successful at best, and many of the people he produced later denounced him.

AL KOOPER WITH THE BLUES PROJECT

"Live" at the Cafe Au Go Go	Verve	FTS–3000	May '66
Projections	Verve	FTS–3008	December '66
"Live" at Town Hall	Verve	FTS–3025	August '67

AL KOOPER WITH BLOOD, SWEAT AND TEARS

Child Is Father to the Man *	Columbia	PC–9619	February '68	A

KOOPER, BLOOMFIELD, AND STILLS

Super Session*	Columbia	PC–9701	August '68	A

AL KOOPER AND MIKE BLOOMFIELD

The Live Adventures of Mike Bloomfield and Al Kooper	2-Columbia	PG–6	February '69	A

AL KOOPER

I Stand Alone	Columbia	CS–9718	February '69	
You Never Know Who Your Friends Are	Columbia	CS–9855	September '69	
Kooper Session: Al Kooper Introduces Shuggie Otis	Columbia	CS–9951	January '70	A
Landlord (soundtrack)	United Artists	5209	August '70	
Easy Does It	2-Columbia	G–30031	September '70	
New York City (You're a Woman)	Columbia	C–30506	June '71	
A Possible Projection of the Future/Childhood's End	Columbia	KC–31159	March '72	
Naked Songs	Columbia	KC–31723	January '73	
Al's Big Deal/Unclaimed Freight: An Al Kooper Anthology	2-Columbia	PG–33169	March '75	
Act Like Nothing's Wrong	United Artists	LA702	November '76	

KRIS KRISTOFFERSON. Reinvigorating a staid Nashville country-and-western music scene by 1971 with his potent songwriting, Kris Kristofferson helped broaden the appeal of country music while drawing critical attention from folk and rock critics and fans and opening the way for a new generation of country songwriters such as Billy Joe Shaver, Jerry Jeff Walker, Guy Clark, and Rodney Crowell. Composing nearly instant classics such as "Sunday Mornin' Comin' Down," "Help Me Make It through the Night," and "Me and Bobby McGee," and recording several best-selling albums, Kris Kristofferson also enjoyed widespread popularity in collaboration with wife Rita Coolidge, particularly with their 1973 *Full Moon* album. However, Kristofferson's subsequent musical career suffered as he sought to establish himself as an actor with co-starring roles in films such as *Pat Garrett and Billy The Kid* (with James Coburn) and *A Star Is*

Born (with Barbra Streisand). At least partially re-established as musician and songwriter with 1978's *Easter Island* album, Kris Kristofferson continues to pursue his acting career, with hopes of eventually becoming a screenwriter and film director.

Born in Brownsville, Texas, on June 22, 1936, Kris Kristofferson moved frequently with his military family before eventually settling in California. A creative writing major at Pomona College, he won a Rhodes Scholarship to Oxford University upon graduation in 1958. A successful short story writer and unpublished book author, Kristofferson began pursuing songwriting as a sideline under the name Kris Carson while in England. Remaining at Oxford for less than two years, he joined the army and served as a helicopter pilot in Germany, where he played service clubs. Discharged after four and a half years (turning down an offer to teach literature at West Point), Kristofferson moved to Nashville in 1965, where he worked as a janitor at Columbia Records and met Johnny Cash. Later taking a variety of jobs, Kristofferson returned to Nashville, where he was eventually signed to a songwriting contract by Fred Foster. In 1969 he provided Roger Miller a major country hit with "Me and Bobby McGee," soon followed by a minor hit with "Sunday Mornin' Comin' Down" for Ray Stevens.

Signed to Fred Foster's Monument Records, Kris Kristofferson recorded his debut album in 1970, but it was generally overlooked by the consuming public. However, a number of established country-and-western artists began recording his songs, resulting in three smash country hits by early 1971: "For the Good Times" (also a major pop hit) by Ray Price, "Sunday Mornin' Comin' Down" by mentor Johnny Cash, and "Help Me Make It through the Night" (another major pop hit) by Sammi Smith. Making his first major club appearance at The Troubadour in Los Angeles in June 1970, Kristofferson performed a number of times during the year on Cash's television program. Kristofferson's popularity was soon broadened when Janis Joplin scored a smash pop hit with "Me and Bobby McGee" in early 1971. His debut album, reissued in 1971 and eventually certified gold-award in 1974, included all of the above hits as well as "To Beat the Devil," dedicated to Johnny Cash and his wife June Carter, and the satirical "Best of All Possible Worlds." During 1971 Kristofferson had his first moderate pop hit with "Loving Her Was Easier (Than Anything I'll Ever Do Again)" from *The Silver-Tongued Devil and I,* his first certified gold-award album. The album also contained "The Taker," "The Pilgrim—Chapter 33," and the tender "When I Loved Her." *Border Lord* was attacked by many critics, although it included two wry Kristofferson songs, "Gettin' By, High and Strange" and "Kiss the World Goodbye," yet yielded no major hits. *Jesus Was a Capricorn,* with the title song dedicated to John Prine, contained "Nobody Wins" and Kristofferson's second major pop hit, "Why Me."

Subsequent albums by Kris Kristofferson fared progressively poorly as he continued to pursue an acting career initiated with *Cisco Pike.* During 1973 he co-starred in *Pat Garrett and Billy The Kid* opposite veteran James Coburn, while touring and recording with Rita Coolidge, whom he had met two years earlier. Their best-selling *Full Moon* album was issued a month prior to their August wedding. Their second duet album, *Breakaway*, fared less well, as Kristofferson worked on films such as the highly acclaimed *Alice Doesn't Live Here Anymore*, and *The Sailor That Fell from Grace with the Sea*. During 1976 he co-starred with Barbra Streisand in an updated remake of *A Star Is Born*, and their soundtrack album was an instant best-seller, being certified platinum-award within a month of its release. Later Kristofferson recorded the modestly selling *Easter Island*, *Natural Act* with Rita Coolidge, and *Shake Hands with the Devil*, in the meantime co-starring with Burt Reynolds and Jill Clayburgh in *Semi-Tough*, with Ali McGraw in the poorly received *Convoy*, and with former heavyweight boxing champion Muhammad Ali in the made-for-TV movie, *Freedom Road*. In late 1979 Kris Kristofferson filed for divorce from Ms. Coolidge. He subsequently starred in the Michael Cimino debacle *Heaven's Gate*, and *Rollover*, opposite Jane Fonda.

KRIS KRISTOFFERSON

Kristofferson	Monument	SLP–18139	June '70	
reissued as Me and Bobby McGee*	Monument/ Columbia	PZ–30817	September '71	A
The Silver-Tongued Devil and I*	Monument/ Columbia	PZ–30679	July '71	A
Border Lord	Monument/ Columbia	KZ–31302	February '72	
Jesus Was a Capricorn*	Monument/ Columbia	PZ–31909	October '72	A

KRIS KRISTOFFERSON AND RITA COOLIDGE

Full Moon*	A&M	SP–4403	September '73	A
Breakaway	Monument/ Columbia	PZ–33278	December '74	A
Natural Act	A&M	SP–4690	January '79	A

KRIS KRISTOFFERSON

Spooky Lady's Sideshow	Monument/ Columbia	PZ–32914	May '74
Who's to Bless and Who's to Blame	Monument/ Columbia	PZ–33379	September '75
Surreal Thing	Monument/ Columbia	PZ–34254	July '76

KRIS KRISTOFFERSON AND BARBRA STREISAND

A Star Is Born (soundtrack)**	Columbia	JS–34403	December '76	A

KRIS KRISTOFFERSON

Songs of Kristof-ferson *	Columbia	PZ–34687	May '77	A
Easter Island	Columbia	PZ–35310	March '78	A
Shake Hands with The Devil	Columbia	JZ–36135	September '79	
To the Bone	Columbia	JZ–36885	January '81	A

PATTI LABELLE AND THE BLUEBELLES/LABELLE. Partially established members of the Sixties "girl group" scene (primarily on the strength of their 1962 hit "I Sold My Heart to the Junkman"), Pattie Labelle and The Bluebelles had dropped out of the charts by 1967 while with their third label. Under the auspices of former British television worker Vicki Wickham, the three female black vocalists became Labelle, left behind their slick and sleek image, and transformed into probably the first and perhaps the only major female group of "glitter rock." Wearing outlandish space-age costumes and blatantly emphasizing a kinky, camp sense of sexuality, Labelle developed a cult following, particularly among homosexuals. The first female group *and* the first black group to play New York's Metropolitan Opera House (in 1974), Labelle finally broke through in 1975 with the smash hit "Lady Marmalade," a sexually charged and controversial single banned by many radio stations. This success, however, did not sustain the group, as subsequent recordings fared progressively poorly and, by 1977, the three members of Labelle had split up to pursue modest solo careers.

PATTI LABELLE AND THE BLUEBELLES

The Apollo Presents The Bluebelles	Newtown	631(M)		
Sleigh Bells, Jingle Bells, and Bluebelles	Newtown	632(M)		
On Stage	Cameo	P–7043(M)	June '64	
Over the Rainbow	Atlantic	SD–8119	May '66	
Dreamer	Atlantic	SD–8147	August '67	
At the Apollo	Up Front	UPF–129		
Greatest Hits	Trip	8000	February '71	
Superpak	2-Trip	3508	February '76	
Very Best	United Artists	LA504	April '76	A

LABELLE

Labelle	Warner Brothers	WS–1943	September '71

Moonshadow	Warner Brothers	BS–2618	August '72	
Pressure Cookin'	RCA	APL1– 0205	August '73	
Nightbirds *	Epic	KE–33075	October '74	A
Phoenix	Epic	PE–33579	September '75	
Chameleon	Epic	PE–34189	August '76	

PATTI LABELLE

Patti Labelle	Epic	PE–34847	August '77	A
Tasty	Epic	JE–35335	June '78	A
It's Alright with Me	Epic	JE–35772	March '79	A
Released	Epic	JE–36381	February '80	A
Best of Patti Labelle	Epic	FE–36997	January '82	A
The Spirit's in It	Philadelphia International	FZ–37380	September '81	A

NONA HENDRYX

| Nona Hendryx | Epic | PE–34683 | October '77 | |

SARAH DASH

Sarah Dash	Kirshner	JZ–35477	November '78	
Oo-La-La, Sarah Dash	Kirshner	JZ–36207	April '80	
Close Enough	Kirshner	BFZ– 37659	November '81	A

LED ZEPPELIN. Prototype British "heavy metal" band of the Seventies, Led Zeppelin evolved out of one of the most seminal and influential of all British groups, The Yardbirds. In fact, the designation as the *first* "heavy metal" band more deservedly goes to The Yardbirds, Cream, The Jimi Hendrix Experience, or even to the early Who rather than to Led Zeppelin, although the term seems to have been invented after the debut of Led Zeppelin. Guitarist Jimmy Page, credited by some as having played on 50 to 90 percent of all British-released records between 1963 and 1965, originally joined The Yardbirds on bass but later, briefly, he played dual lead guitars with Jeff Beck in perhaps the first instance of the format later pursued by so many groups from The Allman Brothers on. Moreover Page, generally recognized as the most consistently successful British "superstar" guitarist, acquired that honor more by default than by actual achievement, given the erraticism of Jeff Beck and Eric Clapton. Also noteworthy is the fact that Page, unlike Clapton, has never acknowledged his debt to American black blues guitarists.

Often compared with The Who for their consummate employment of the three-instrument–lead vocalist format, Led Zeppelin inspired a glut of "heavy metal" imitators during the Seventies after their nearly instantaneous popularity. Often criticized for their "macho" and sexist lyrics, Led Zeppelin has seldom been held in high esteem by the American rock press, probably due to the fact that they were "hyped" into popularity by means of a massive promotional campaign sponsored by their record company, Atlantic. Probably the first foreign rock group to establish a worldwide reputation by concentrating on live engagements primarily in the United States, Led Zeppelin was breaking box office records regularly after 1969. Eventually receiving recognition in late 1971 with "Stairway to Heaven," certainly one of the definitive production arrangements of the Seventies, the band's popularity was finally acknowledged by the media in 1973. Led Zeppelin thereafter embarked on a policy of limiting their live appearances and album releases, thus lending an aura of mystique to the group. Forming their own record company, Swan Song, in 1974 with manager Peter Grant for releases by Bad Company, Maggie Bell, The Pretty Things, and themselves, Led Zeppelin last toured the United States in 1977. Following the September 1980 death of John Bonham, rivaled only by Keith Moon of The Who as rock music's most flamboyant and celebrated drummer of the Seventies, Led Zeppelin disbanded.

Jimmy Page (born on January 9, 1945, in Heston, Middlesex, England) took up guitar in his early teens, later playing with Neil Christian and The Crusaders before attending art college for two years. Upon returning to music, he quickly became a much sought-after sessions guitarist, allegedly playing on more than half of all the records released in England between 1963 and 1965. Early sessions credits included The Who's "I Can't Explain," Them's "Gloria," "Here Comes the Night," and "Baby, Please Don't Go," and unspecified recordings by The Kinks (disputed by Ray Davies), The Rolling Stones, and Herman's Hermits. Page turned down an offer to join The Yardbirds as replacement for Eric Clapton in 1965, the year Page served as house producer–arranger for Andrew Oldham's Immediate label. In mid-1966 he did join The Yardbirds, replacing departed bass player Paul Samwell-Smith, later to play twin lead guitar with Jeff Beck after Chris Dreja switched to bass. Yardbirds' recordings with Beck and Page apparently included "The Train Kept A-Rollin" from *Rave Up*, "Stroll On" from the soundtrack to the film *Blow-Up*, and "Happenings Ten Years Time Ago." Jeff Beck left The Yardbirds at the end of 1966 and Page continued as the group's lead guitarist for another 18 months. Finally, in July 1968, The Yardbirds broke up, and Page and Dreja unsuccessfully attempted to continue as The New Yardbirds with vocalist–guitarist Terry Reid and drummer Paul Francis. Reid, unavailable to join the group, suggested that Robert Plant (born in Birmingham on August 20, 1947 or 1948) from the Birmingham group The Band of Joy be recruited as lead vocalist. Plant in turn recommended former Band of Joy drummer John Bonham (born near Birmingham on May 31, 1947). Dreja later dropped out to pursue a career as a photographer, and sessions bassist–keyboardist John Paul Jones (born January 3, 1946, in Sidcup, Kent) was brought in as his replacement. Essentially formed in October 1968, Led Zeppelin quickly recorded their first album for Atlantic Records, soon fulfilling The Yardbirds' remaining obligations. Around this time, Jimmy Page also played sessions with Jeff Beck ("Beck's Bolero"), Donovan (*Hurdy Gurdy Man*) and Joe Cocker (*With a Little Help from My Friends*).

Led Zeppelin's debut album was an instant best-seller, featuring their first American singles chart entry "Good Times-Bad Times" and the classics, "Dazed and Confused" and "Communication Breakdown." In early 1969 the group completed their first American tour in support of Vanilla Fudge, soon returning as a headline act. Shortly thereafter a whole school of "heavy metal" rock developed in the wake of Led Zeppelin. *Led Zeppelin II* included the smash hit classic "Whole Lotta Love," as well as "Living Loving Maid (She's Just a Woman)," and "Ramble On." Concentrating their activities on the United States (they never released a single in Great Britain), Led Zeppelin were performing their fifth American tour by March 1970. *Led Zeppelin III* yielded the major hit "Immigrant Song," but *IV* was the album that finally brought the group critical recognition. In addition to containing the hits "Black Dog" and "Rock and Roll," the album included one of the definitive production arrangements of the Seventies, "Stairway to Heaven," which built from a subtle acoustic guitar and vocal to a thundering climax, ending with a gentle acoustic guitar–vocal reprise.

During the summer of 1972, Led Zeppelin again toured America, outdrawing The Rolling Stones in a number of cities. *Houses of the Holy*, recorded in 1972 but not issued until early 1973, was the first Led Zeppelin album to utilize string arrangements. Almost immediately certified gold-award, the album yielded a major hit with "D'Yer Mak'er." The group's 1973 American tour was an instant sellout, and they broke both the single-artist concert attendance and gross income records with their Tampa, Florida, show. With the rock press finally acknowledging their enormous popularity, Led Zeppelin formed Swan Song Records with manager Peter Grant in 1974, a year during which they were otherwise relatively inactive. In early 1975 *Physical Graffiti* was issued, yielding the moderate hit "Trampled under Foot," but lead vocalist Robert Plant was seriously injured later that year in an automobile accident in Greece, necessitating a layoff of more than a year. *Presence* became Led Zeppelin's first certified platinum-award album in 1976, without benefit of either a tour or single. The film (and soundtrack album) *The Song Remains the Same*, taken primarily from a 1973 concert at Madison Square Garden, was released as the group's first live album and movie, and the film became a cult attraction that still regularly plays at midnight showings across the country.

During 1977 Led Zeppelin again toured the United States, playing regular marathon three-hour sets to sellout crowds; but an ugly incident between shows at the Oakland Coliseum (in which three members of promoter Bill Graham's support crew were allegedly beaten up by manager Peter Grant, drummer John Bonham, and two members of the group's entourage) served to reinforce the notion that Led Zeppelin had become arrogant, insensitive, and smug. The group subsequently maintained a low profile and eventually re-emerged in 1979 with *In Through the Out Door* and the major hit "Fool in the Rain." That fall Led Zeppelin's first British appearance in four years at the Knebworth Festival was reviewed critically as perfunctory at best, obsolete at worst. On September 25, 1980, John Bonham was found dead in the Windsor home of Jimmy Page, the victim of inhalation of vomit after a drinking spree; on December 4 Led Zeppelin announced that it was disbanding.

LED ZEPPELIN

Led Zeppelin *	Atlantic	SD–8216 reissued as SD–19126	February '69	A
Led Zeppelin II *	Atlantic	SD–8236 reissued as SD–19127	August '69	A
Led Zeppelin III *	Atlantic	SD–7201 reissued as SD–19128	September '70	A
Led Zeppelin IV *	Atlantic	SD–7208 reissued as SD–19129	November '71	A
Houses of the Holy *	Atlantic	SD–7255 reissued as SD–19130	March '73	A
Physical Graffiti *	2-Swan Song	SS2–200	February '75	A
Presence **	Swan Song	SS–8416	March '76	A
The Song Remains the Same (soundtrack) **	2-Swan Song	SS2–201	November '76	A
In Through the Out Door **	Swan Song	SS–16002	September '79	A

BRENDA LEE. Possessing a voice equally adept at mournful ballads and at hard-belting rock songs, Brenda Lee was one of the most popular female vocalists of the early Sixties, accruing more than 25 singles chart entries between 1960 and 1963. Scoring her last major hit in 1966 with "Coming on Strong," Brenda Lee returned to country music in the Seventies while regularly playing clubs and Nevada casino engagements. In 1979–80 Brenda Lee achieved three near-smash country hits.

Born in Atlanta, Georgia, on December 11, 1944, as Brenda Mae Tarpley, Brenda Lee started singing at the age of four, winning a local television children's talent contest at age six, and subsequently appearing for three years on the local television show "TV Wranglers." Introduced to country star Red Foley in 1955, she later appeared on his television show "Ozark Jubilee." Signing with Decca Records in 1956, Brenda Lee had her first minor hit in early 1957 with "One Step at a Time" at the age of 12. Her first major hit came in early 1960 with "Sweet Nothin's," followed in midyear by the two-sided smash, "I'm Sorry/That's All You Gotta Do." Both of Lee's 1960 albums became best-sellers as the hits continued with "I Want to Be Wanted" and the oft-issued Christmas classic, "Rockin' around the Christmas Tree." During 1961 her hits included "Emotions," "You Can Depend On Me," "Dum Dum," and "Fool #1," followed by "Break It to Me Gently," "Everybody Loves Me but You," "Heart in Hand," and the smash "All Alone Am I" in 1962. After hits with "Losing You," "The Grass Is Greener," and "As Usual" in 1963, Brenda Lee's hits became less frequent. Later major hits included "Is It True" in 1964, "Too Many Rivers" in 1965, and her final major hit, "Coming on Strong," in 1966. She subsequently recorded contemporary material in an "easy listening" style before returning to her country music heritage with 1970's *Memphis Portrait*. Her Seventies albums on MCA Records sparked little interest, yet she continued to tour the night club circuit. In 1979–80 Brenda Lee scored near-smash country hits with "Tell Me What It's Like," "The Cowgirl and the Dandy," and "Broken Trust."

BRENDA LEE

Grandma, What Great Songs You Sang	Decca	DL–78873	August '59	
Brenda Lee	Decca	DL–74039	July '60	
This Is . . . Brenda Lee	Decca	DL–74082	November '60	
Emotions	Decca	DL–74104	May '61	
All the Way	Decca	DL–74176	August '61	
Sincerely	Decca	DL–74216	March '62	
That's All, Brenda	Decca	DL–74326	October '62	
All Alone Am I	Decca	DL–74370	March '63	
Let Me Sing	Decca	DL–74439	December '63	
By Request	Decca	DL–74509	June '64	
Merry Christmas from Brenda Lee	Decca reissued on MCA	DL–74583 232	December '64	
	reissued as 15021			A
Top Teen Hits	Decca	DL–74626	March '65	
Versatile	Decca	DL–74661	June '65	
Too Many Rivers	Decca	DL–74684	September '65	
Bye Bye, Blues	Decca	DL–74755	April '66	
Ten Golden Years	Decca reissued on MCA	DL–74757 107	June '66	
Coming on Strong	Decca	DL–74825	December '66	
Reflections in Blue	Decca	DL–74941	November '67	
Johnny One Time	Decca	DL–75111	May '69	
Memphis Portrait	Decca	DL–75232	November '70	

BRENDA LEE AND PETE FOUNTAIN

For the First Time	Decca	DL-74955	April '68

BRENDA LEE

Here's Brenda Lee	Vocalion	73795(E)	May '67	A
Let It Be Me	Vocalion reissued on	73890		
	Coral	20044		A
Brenda	MCA	305	May '73	A
The Brenda Lee Story	2-MCA	4012	September '73	A
New Sunrise	MCA	373	January '74	
Now	MCA	433	January '75	
Sincerely, Brenda Lee	MCA	477	June '75	
L.A. Sessions	MCA	2233	December '76	
Even Better	MCA	3211	January '80	A
Take Me Back	MCA	5143	November '80	A
Only When I Laugh	MCA	5278	December '81	A

JERRY LEIBER AND MIKE STOLLER. The single most significant, influential, and popular songwriting-production team of the Fifties and early Sixties, Jerry Leiber and Mike Stoller became the first independent producers in the history of rock music in 1955. Reconstituting The Robins as The Coasters for Atlantic Records, Leiber and Stoller provided that group with some of the first songs in rock music to incorporate satire and social comment. Indeed, they furnished The Coasters with more than a dozen hit songs. Later writing and producing some of Elvis Presley's finest post-Sun Records recordings, Leiber and Stoller were put in charge of the reconstituted Drifters in the late Fifties. That group's smash 1959 hit, "There Goes My Baby," produced and co-authored by Leiber and Stoller, established a precedent in black music through the use of Latin rhythms and quasi-classical strings behind Ben E. King's gospel-style lead vocal. That and subsequent recordings by The Drifters and Ben E. King proved so successful that virtually every subsequent black vocal group was backed by strings in recording, thus heralding the beginning of "soul" music. Leiber and Stoller's early Sixties productions (save those for The Coasters and The Drifters) fared less well; so, in 1964, they joined George Goldner in the formation of Red Bird Records. There the two used the compositions of professional songwriting teams such as Jeff Barry and Ellie Greenwich and Gerry Goffin and Carole King for over 20 hits by The Shangri-Las, The Dixie Cups, and others. Subsequently selling out to Goldner, Leiber and Stoller languished for a period with Columbia Records before retiring from studio work for three years. Investing in established music publishing firms, Jerry Leiber and Mike Stoller eventually re-emerged in the Seventies to produce Stealers Wheel and Procol Harum, among others.

Born in Baltimore on April 25, 1933, Jerry Leiber met Mike Stoller (born in New York City on March 13, 1933) in Los Angeles in 1949, soon teaming together to write and produce songs for blues artists such as Amos Milburn and Jimmy Weatherspoon. Their first rhythm-and-blues hit composition was "Hard Times" by Charles Brown in early 1952, followed the next year by "Hound Dog" by Willie Mae "Big Mama" Thornton (that song, of course, was revived by Elvis Presley in 1956). In 1953 Leiber and Stoller formed their own label, Spark Records, for recordings by The Robins such as "Smokey Joe's Cafe" and "Riot in Cell Block #9." Signed to the New York-based Atlantic label as independent producers in 1955, the two convinced Carl Gardner and Bobby Nunn of the otherwise recalcitrant Robins to form a new group for recordings on Atlantic's Atco subsidiary. The group was dubbed The Coasters and, between 1955 and 1961, Leiber and Stoller provided them with a series of hit songs which usually incorporated wry humor, satire, and social comment. "Down in Mexico," the group's first single as The Coasters, became a rhythm-and-blues hit, but 1957's "Searchin'" was the first of a series of pop hits for the group. Featuring the dynamic saxophone playing of King Curtis, subsequent hit recordings by The Coasters, virtually all composed by Leiber and Stoller, included "Young Blood," "Yakety Yak," "Charlie Brown," "Along Came Jones," "Poison Ivy," and "Little Egypt."

In 1955 Jerry Leiber and Mike Stoller furnished The Cheers with a major hit with "Black Denim Trousers and Motorcycle Boots." Elvis Presley scored smash hits with their "Hound Dog" and "Love Me" in 1956, after which Leiber and Stoller were contracted to supply songs for Presley's movies. The team wrote the title songs to *Jailhouse Rock, Loving You,* and *King Creole,* while providing other hit songs such as "Treat Me Nice" and "Don't." Their songs "Kansas City" and "Love Potion #9" were hits for Wilbert Harrison and The Clovers, respectively, in 1959.

During the late Fifties, Jerry Leiber and Mike Stoller were put in charge of Atlantic's reconstituted Drifters. For "There Goes My Baby," the two used Latin rhythms and a string section to back lead vocalist Ben E. King's stunning gospel-style voice. The song, a smash hit, effectively established the use of such eclectic ingredients (the strings in particular) in the recording of black vocal groups and ushered in "soul" music. The team's "Dance with Me" was a major hit for The Drifters in 1959, and they later provided Ben E. King with hits such as "Spanish Harlem" (their most often recorded song) and "Stand by Me" once he went solo. Apprentice producer Phil Spector, co-author with Leiber of "Spanish Harlem," was obviously inspired by the production-arrangement technique of the team, as evidenced by his own hit productions during the first half of the Sixties. In 1963 The Drifters scored a near smash with the moving "On Broadway," co-written by Leiber, Stoller, Barry Mann, and Cynthia Weil.

In 1964 Jerry Leiber and Mike Stoller met George Goldner and the three formed Red Bird and Blue Cat Records, utilizing the songwriting services of Jeff Barry and Ellie Greenwich, George "Shadow" Morton, and Gerry Goffin and Carole King. Red Bird hits included "Chapel of Love,"

"People Say," and "Iko, Iko" by The Dixie Cups and "Remember (Walkin' in the Sand)," "Leader of the Pack," and "Give Him a Great Big Kiss" by The Shangri-Las. By 1966, apparently weary of their largely administrative duties, Leiber and Stoller had sold out to Goldner. They moved to Columbia Records, but productions for The Coasters and others were handled poorly, leading Leiber and Stoller to terminate their agreement with the label. They subsequently retired from the studio for three years, investing in large music publishing firms such as Starday/King in 1970. In the meantime several of their songs became hits, "D.W. Washburn" for The Monkees in 1968 and "Is That All There Is?" for Peggy Lee in 1969.

Generally inactive during the early Seventies, Jerry Leiber and Mike Stoller returned to the studio in 1973 to produce albums for Stealers Wheel, The Coasters, and T-Bone Walker. Stealers Wheel scored a smash hit with "Stuck in the Middle with You," and Leiber and Stoller subsequently produced albums for Peggy Lee, Elkie Brooks, and *Procol's Ninth* for Procol Harum. During 1978 the odd set *Other Songs by Leiber and Stoller*, performed by mezzo-soprano Joan Morris, was issued on Nonesuch Records.

JERRY LEIBER BEAT BAND

Scooby Doo	Kapp	1127(M)	March '59

LEIBER–STOLLER BIG BAND

Yakety Yak	Atlantic	SD–8047	February '61

JOHN LENNON. The first of The Beatles to record and perform outside the group while it was still nominally intact, John Lennon was certainly the most controversial and unorthodox of the group's members; his 1966 statement that The Beatles were more popular than Jesus was only one of many examples. Sparking controversy by appearing nude with wife-to-be Yoko Ono on the cover of *Two Virgins*, Lennon scored major hits in 1969 with "Give Peace a Chance" (soon adopted as one of the anthems of the anti-war movement) and "Cold Turkey," recorded with the loosely assembled Plastic Ono Band (often including Eric Clapton). Those singles were eclipsed in 1970–71 by the stunningly profound and excruciatingly personal *John Lennon/Plastic Ono Band* album, arguably Lennon's most moving album. *Imagine*, essentially Lennon's first solo album, continued his profound personal inclination in songwriting, as demonstrated by the idealistic title song, the satirical "Crippled Inside," and the vitriolic attack on former songwriting partner Paul McCartney in "How Do You Sleep." Nonetheless John Lennon was unable (or unwilling) to keep pace with McCartney's popularity (particularly after *Band on the Run*), as Lennon devolved into political polemicism with *Sometime in New York City*. Lennon returned to the rock mainstream with *Mind Games* and *Walls and Bridges* but, by the end of 1975, he had retreated from the music business, ostensibly content that his mark had already been made. Brilliantly re-emerging in late 1980, John Lennon was murdered on December 8, 1980, as *Double Fantasy* and its first single were topping the charts.

During 1966, while The Beatles were still intact, John Lennon (born in Woolton, Liverpool, England, on October 9, 1940) met Japanese avant-garde artist Yoko Ono (born in Tokyo on February 18, 1933), with whom he recorded *Two Virgins*, the cover of which featured nude photos of the couple and sparked consternation among record retailers. In 1969 they recorded *Life with the Lions* (on the short-lived Zapple label) and, following their March marriage, *Wedding Album*. After the wedding, the couple caused the first of a series of controversies with their "Bed-In" for peace in Amsterdam. "Give Peace a Chance," recorded with the loosely aggregated Plastic Ono Band in a Montreal hotel room, became a major hit in July and was soon adopted by the anti-war movement as one of their anthems. That September, Lennon, Ono, and The Plastic Ono Band—Eric Clapton (guitar), Klaus Voorman (bass), and Alan White (drums)—played a rock-and-roll festival in Toronto, and recordings of the performance, issued as *Live Peace in Toronto 1969*, yielded a moderate hit with the ominous "Cold Turkey."

In February 1970 "Instant Karma (We All Shine On)," recorded under producer Phil Spector, became a smash hit for John Lennon, and he and Yoko later underwent "primal scream" therapy under radical psychologist Dr. Arthur Janov. That experience produced, at least in part, the intense raw emotionalism of *John Lennon/Plastic Ono Band*. The album included such highly personal songs as "Mother" and "Isolation," as well as the litany "God" and the caustic sociopolitical song "Working Class Hero," banned by some radio stations for its use of obscenity. In the meantime Yoko Ono recorded two albums with The Plastic Ono Band noteworthy only for the attempt to make her screams and screeches seem musical. In the spring of 1971 "Power to the People" became a major hit for the couple and, during the year, Lennon recorded *Imagine*, essentially his first solo album. An instant best-seller, the album yielded a smash hit with the title song and also contained the poignant "Jealous Guy," the satirical "Crippled Inside," and the vitriolic attack on McCartney, "How Do You Sleep."

Subsequently embroiled in legal proceedings by the U.S. Immigration and Naturalization Service which sought to deport him (ultimately resolved in Lennon's favor in 1976), John Lennon, Yoko Ono, and The Plastic Ono Band recorded *Sometime in New York City* with the New York-based band, Elephant's Memory. The politically charged album, featuring songs concerning the Attica prison riots, Northern Ireland, and the pro-feminist anthem "Woman Is the Nigger of the World," was critically attacked and sold only modestly at best. In 1973 two albums by Yoko Ono were issued, followed by Lennon's *Mind Games*. Although a best-seller, the album was not well received critically, yet it yielded a major hit with the title song. The follow-up, *Walls and Bridges*, fared better, producing hits with "Whatever Gets You through the Night" and "#9 Dream." A pet project of Lennon's, *Rock 'n' Roll*, contained rock-and-roll classics recorded over a two-year period such as the hit "Stand by Me."

Later in 1975 the anthology set *Shaved Fish* was issued. John Lennon and Yoko Ono thereafter retired from the music business, as Lennon regularly denied reports of a Beatles reunion while purchasing a dairy farm in New York state and a beachfront mansion in Florida.

During 1980 John Lennon began writing again, returning to the studio in August with Yoko Ono and a group of hand-picked sessions players to record *Double Fantasy*. Comprised of seven Lennon and seven Ono songs, the album and its first single, Lennon's "(Just Like) Starting Over," were instant top hits. The album also included Lennon's revealing "Watching the Wheels," the touching "Beautiful Boy," and another hit, "Woman," but on the night of December 8, 1980, Lennon was shot to death outside his luxury Manhattan apartment building. Covered by the media in a manner usually reserved for world statesmen, Lennon's death forever quelled rumors of a Beatles reunion and ended the career of one of this century's most respected and profound artists. In 1981 Yoko Ono re-emerged from her grief with the pop-style *Season of Glass*, largely produced by Phil Spector.

JOHN AND YOKO LENNON

Unfinished Music #1: Two Virgins	Apple	T–5001	November '68
Unfinished Music #2: Life with the Lions	Zapple	ST–3357	May '69
Wedding Album	2-Apple	SMAX–3361	October '69

JOHN LENNON/PLASTIC ONO BAND

Live Peace in Toronto 1969 *	Apple	SW–3362	December '69	
John Lennon/Plastic Ono Band *	Apple/Capitol	SW–3372	December '70	A
Sometime in New York City	2–Apple/ Capitol	SVBB–3392	June '72	A

YOKO ONO/PLASTIC ONO BAND

Plastic Ono Band	Apple	SW–3373	December '70
Fly	2-Apple	SVBB–3380	September '71

YOKO ONO

Approximately Infinite Universe	2-Apple	SVBB–3399	January '73
Feeling the Space	Apple	SW–3412	October '73

JOHN LENNON

Imagine *	Apple/Capitol	SW–3379	September '71	A

Mind Games*	Apple/Capitol	SW–3414	November '73	
	reissued on			
	Capitol	SN–16068		A
Walls and Bridges*	Apple/Capitol	SW–3416	September '74	A
Rock 'n' Roll	Apple/Capitol	SK–3419	February '75	
	reissued on			
	Capitol	SN–16069		A
Shaved Fish	Apple/Capitol	SW–3421	October '75	A

JOHN LENNON AND YOKO ONO

| Double Fantasy** | Geffen | GHS–2001 | December '80 | A |

YOKO ONO

| Season of Glass | Geffen | GHS–2004 | June '81 | A |

JERRY LEE LEWIS. The premier white piano and vocal stylist of the rock-and-roll Fifties, Jerry Lee Lewis performed one of the most dynamic, if calculated, stage shows of that (or any other) era while projecting an aura of arrogant self-confidence. His inimitable piano style, self-taught and virtually unaltered throughout his career, featured endless glissandos and furious hammering and banging of the instrument, often played with elbows and feet. Recording such rock-and-roll classics as "Whole Lotta Shakin' Going On" and "Great Balls of Fire," Jerry Lee Lewis never attained the stature of Chuck Berry or Elvis Presley primarily because he did not write his own material and he restricted himself to the immobile piano. Moreover, Lewis suffered a crippling blow to his career through adverse publicity surrounding his marriage to his 13-year-old cousin that led to the cancellation of his first English tour in 1958. Out of the singles charts for nearly three years, Jerry Lee Lewis covered pop and rhythm-and-blues hits during the early Sixties, again dropping off the charts for more than six years before re-establishing himself as a country-and-western artist in 1968 with "Another Place, Another Time," "What's Made Milwaukee Famous (Has Made a Loser out of Me)," and a continuing string of country hits including 1977's "Middle-Age Crazy."

Born in Ferriday, Louisiana, on September 29, 1935, Jerry Lee Lewis first began playing the piano around the age of 8, making his first public appearance at a local Ford dealership in 1949 around the age of 14. Performing locally on weekends for four years, usually playing drums and singing (though occasionally doubling on piano), Lewis built a solid regional following. In February 1956 he traveled to Memphis to audition for Sun Records, recording some demonstration tapes for Jack Clement in the absence of Sam Phillips. Returning to Memphis a month later, Lewis discovered that Phillips liked the recordings and he was soon signed to a contract. His first record, "Crazy Arms," became a moderate country hit, but his second, "Whole Lotta Shakin' Going On," became a smash country-and-western, rhythm-and-blues, and pop hit, bolstered by his appearance on the Steve Allen television show. "Great Balls of Fire," co-authored by Otis Blackwell, was a smash hit in all three fields in late 1957, as was Blackwell's "Breathless," and "High School Confidential," from the film of the same name. In May 1958 Lewis arrived in England for his first European tour, but it was cancelled by the fifth day after the British press revealed, in rather lurid terms, that he was traveling with his 13-year-old cousin–wife, Myra. Back home, his records were banned by many radio stations and Lewis was unable to score another major hit until 1961 with his own version of Ray Charles' "What'd I Say."

In 1963 Jerry Lee Lewis switched to the Smash subsidiary of Mercury Records, but commerical success eluded him as he criss-crossed the country playing county fairs, package shows, gymnasiums, and roadhouses. Finally, in 1968, he scored the first of a series of major country hits with "Another Place, Another Time," followed by the classic, "What's Made Milwaukee Famous (Has Made a Loser out of Me)." Other noteworthy country hits on Smash included "She Still Comes Around (to Love What's Left of Me)" and "She Even Woke Me Up to Say Goodbye." In 1970 Lewis recorded an album with sister Linda Gail Lewis, switching to the parent label Mercury that year, where he managed moderate pop hits with "Me and Bobby McGee" and "Chantilly Lace" in 1972 and "Drinking Wine Spo-Dee O'Dee" in 1973. That year, *Session in London*, recorded with guitarists Rory Gallagher, Alvin Lee, and Peter Frampton, became one of his best-selling albums. In 1977 Lewis had one of his finest later-day country hits with "Middle-Age Crazy," but after *Keeps Rockin'*, he moved to Elektra Records. His debut Elektra album contained the country hit that has become his theme song, "Rockin' My Life Away," and subsequent country hits included "Who Will the Next Fool Be," "When Two Worlds Collide," and "Over the Rainbow." One of contemporary music's most exciting performers, Jerry Lee Lewis continued to play over 250 engagements a year until his summer 1981 hospitalization for stomach problems.

SUN RECORDS AND SUN–RELATED RELEASES OF JERRY LEE LEWIS

Jerry Lee Lewis	Sun	LP–1230 (M)		
Jerry Lee's Greatest	Sun	LP–1265 (M)		
Rockin' Rhythm and Blues	Sun	107(M)		
Golden Cream of Country	Sun	108(M)		
Taste of Country	Sun	114(M)		
Memphis Rock and Roll	Sun	116(M)		
Ole Tyme Country Music	Sun	121		
Monsters	Sun	124(E)	December '75	A
Original Golden Hits, Volume 1	Sun	102(E)		A
Original Golden Hits, Volume 2	Sun	103(E)		A

Original Golden Hits, Volume 3	Sun	128(E)		A
From the Vaults of Sun	Power Pak	247(M)		A
Sun Story, Volume 5	Sunnyvale	905(M)	November '77	
Golden Rock and Roll	Sun	1000(M)	August '78	A
Duets	Sun	1011(M)	January '79	A
The Original	Sun	1005	May '79	A

JERRY LEE LEWIS AND JOHNNY CASH

Sunday Down South	Sun	119(E)		A
Sing Hank Williams	Sun	125(E)		A

JERRY LEE LEWIS, CHARLIE RICH, AND CARL PERKINS

And Friends	Sun	1018	January '80	A

LATER JERRY LEE LEWIS

Greatest Live Show on Earth	Smash	SRS–67056	December '64
The Return of Rock!	Smash also Mercury	SRS–67063 16340	May '65 July '67
Country Songs for City Folks	Smash	SRS–67071	December '65
Memphis Beat	Smash	SRS–67079	May '66
By Request	Smash	SRS–67086	December '66
Soul My Way	Smash	SRS–67097	December '67
Another Place, Another Time	Smash	SRS–67104	June '68
She Still Comes Around (to Love What's Left of Me)	Smash	SRS–67112	February '69
The Country Music Hall of Fame, Volume 1	Smash	SRS–67117	May '69
The Country Music Hall of Fame, Volume 2	Smash	SRS–67118	May '69
She Even Woke Me Up to Say Goodbye	Smash	SRS–67128	February '70

JERRY LEE LEWIS AND LINDA GAIL LEWIS

Together	Smash	SRS–67126	November '69

JERRY LEE LEWIS

Live at the International, Las Vegas	Mercury	61278	October '70
In Loving Memories	Mercury	61318	January '71

There Must Be More to Love Than This	Mercury	61323	January '71	
Touching Home	Mercury	61343	July '71	
Would You Take Another Chance on Me?	Mercury	61346	November '71	
This Old Piano	Mercury	61366	February '73	
The "Killer" Rocks On	Mercury	SRM1–637	April '72	
Session in London	2-Mercury	SRM2–803	March '73	
Sometimes a Memory Ain't Enough	Mercury	SRM1–677	November '73	
Southern Roots	Mercury	SRM1–690	January '74	
I-40 Country	Mercury	SRM1–710	August '74	
Boogie Woogie Country Man	Mercury	SRM1–1030	May '75	
Odd Man In	Mercury	SRM1–1064	February '76	
Country Class	Mercury	SRM1–1109	November '76	
Country Memories	Mercury	5004	December '77	A
Keeps Rockin'	Mercury	5010	August '78	
Jerry Lee Lewis	Elektra	6E–184	March '79	A
When Two Worlds Collide	Elektra	254	April '80	A
Killer Country	Elektra	291	September '80	A

JERRY LEE LEWIS ANTHOLOGIES AND COMPILATIONS (OTHER THAN SUN)

Golden Hits of Jerry Lee Lewis	Smash	SRS–67040 reissued as SL–7001	February '64 October '79	A
The Best of Jerry Lee Lewis	Smash	SRS–67131	May '70	
The Best of Jerry Lee Lewis, Volume 2	Mercury	5006	January '78	
Jerry Lee Lewis	Pickwick	2055		A
Drinkin' Wine Spo-Dee O'Dee	Pickwick	2344		
High Heel Sneakers	Pickwick	3224		
Roll Over, Beethoven	Pickwick	6110		
Rural Route #1	Pickwick	6120		
I Walk the Line	Accord	SN–7133	November '81	A

GORDON LIGHTFOOT. A prolific folk-style singer–songwriter, Gordon Lightfoot was initially known in the United States for his compositions "For Lovin' Me" and "Early Morning Rain," recorded by Ian and Sylvia and Peter, Paul, and Mary during the Sixties. Well known in his native Canada during the second half of the Sixties, Gordon Lightfoot finally established himself in the United States with his gold-award *Sit Down, Young Stranger* album and "If You Could Read My Mind" hit single in 1970. Regarded as one of the most consistent and prolific Canadian singer–songwriters of the Seventies (he has written over 400 songs), Gordon Lightfoot has recorded several gold-award albums, while artists as diverse as Bob Dylan, Elvis Presley, Barbra Streisand, and Waylon Jennings have recorded his songs.

Born in Orillia, Ontario, on November 17, 1938, Gordon Lightfoot started piano lessons at the age of eight or nine and switched to guitar during high school. Writing his first song at 17, he traveled to Los Angeles after graduation to study orchestration at Westlake College for over a year. Returning to Toronto, Lightfoot began playing bars, clubs, and coffeehouses. He spent 1963 in England and, after returning to Canada, dropped out of music for more than a year, finally re-emerging on the lounge circuit. Fellow Canadians Ian and Sylvia (Tyson) were the first to record any of Lightfoot's songs, but Peter, Paul, and Mary were the act that first scored hits with his "For Lovin' Me" and "Early Morning Rain," in 1965. Signed to United Artists Records, Lightfoot recorded four albums before finally registering an album chart entry with *Sunday Concert*. Quickly recognized in Canada, he remained in obscurity in the United States through the late Sixties despite the recording of a number of his own excellent compositions such as "The Way I Feel," "Ribbon of Darkness," "Canadian Railroad Trilogy," "The Last Time I Saw Her," and "Did She Mention My Name?"

Switching to Warner Brothers' Reprise label at the end of 1969, Gordon Lightfoot's debut album for the company yielded the smash hit "If You Could Read My Mind" while containing his other outstanding creations such as "Approaching Lavender," "Saturday Clothes," and "Sit Down, Young Stranger." Certified gold-award in 1971, the album was followed by several modestly selling albums. However, late 1973's *Sundown* became an instant best-seller, featuring "The Watchman's Gone" and the poignant "Too Late for Praying" and producing hits with "Sundown" and "Carefree Highway." Lightfoot's *Cold on the Shoulder* yielded the hit "Rainy Day People," whereas *Summertime Dream* generated a smash hit with the dirge-like "The Wreck of the Edmund Fitzgerald." *Endless Wire*, Gordon Lightfoot's fifth certified gold-award album, included the moderate hit, "The Circle Is Small (I Can See It in Your Eyes)," originally recorded nine years earlier.

GORDON LIGHTFOOT

| Lightfoot | United Artists | UAS–6487 reissued as LN– 10044 | May '66 | A |
| The Way I Feel | United Artists | UAS–6587 reissued as LN– 10042 | June '67 | A |

Did She Mention My Name?	United Artists	UAS–6649 reissued as LN–10041	February '68	A
Back Here on Earth	United Artists	UAS–6672 reissued as LN–10040	February '69	A
Sunday Concert	United Artists	UAS–6714 reissued as LN–10039	November '69	A
Sit Down, Young Stranger reissued as If You Could Read My Mind*	Reprise	RS–6392	May '70	A
Summer Side of Life	Reprise	RS–2037	April '71	A
Don Quixote	Reprise	MS–2056	February '72	A
Old Dan's Record	Reprise	MS–2116	October '72	
Sundown*	Reprise	MS–2177	December '73	A
Cold on the Shoulder	Reprise	MS–2206	February '75	A
Summertime Dream**	Reprise	MS–2246	May '76	A
Endless Wire*	Warner Brothers	BSK–3149	January '78	A
Dream Street Rose	Warner Brothers	HS–3426	March '80	A

GORDON LIGHTFOOT ANTHOLOGIES AND COMPILATIONS

Best	United Artists	UAS–6754 reissued as LN–10038	November '70	A
Classic Lightfoot— Best, Volume 2	United Artists	UAS–5510	June '71	
Best, Volume 3	United Artists	LA189		
Very Best	United Artists reissued as	LA243 LA381	July '74 March '75	
Very Best, Volume 2	United Artists	LA445	September '75	
Gord's Gold*	2-Reprise	MS–2237	October '75	A

LITTLE ANTHONY AND THE IMPERIALS. Black rhythm-and-blues vocal group initially formed in the late Fifties, Little Anthony and The Imperials had hits with "Tears on My Pillow" and the novelty song "Shimmy, Shimmy, Ko-Ko Bop." Hooking up with songwriter–producer Teddy Randazzo in the early Sixties, Little Anthony and The Imperials scored four major hits in 1964–65, including the often recorded "Goin' Out of My Head" and "Hurt So Bad."

THE IMPERIALS

We Are The Imperials	End	302(M)
Shades of the 40's	End	311(M)

LITTLE ANTHONY AND THE IMPERIALS

I'm on the Outside (Looking In)	DCP reissued on	6801	December '64	
	Veep	16510	July '67	
Goin' Out of My Head	DCP reissued on	6808	February '65	
	Veep	16511	July '67	
Payin' Our Dues	Veep	16513	December '66	
Reflections	Veep	16514	June '67	
Movie Grabbers	Veep	16516	October '67	
Forever Yours	Roulette	42007	September '69	A
Out of Sight, Out of Mind	United Artists	UAS–6720 reissued as LN–10117	October '69 April '80	A
On a New Street	Avco	AV–11012	'74	

LITTLE ANTHONY

Little Anthony	Sunset	5287	September '70	
Daylight	Song Bird	3245	September '80	A

LITTLE ANTHONY AND THE IMPERIALS
ANTHOLOGIES AND COMPILATIONS

Best	DCP reissued on	6809	March '66	
	Veep	16512	July '67	
Hits	Pickwick	3029	September '66	
Greatest Hits	Roulette	25294(M)	July '66	
Best, Volume 2	Veep	16519	March '68	
Very Best	United Artists	LA255 reissued as LA382	August '74 March '75	
Best	Liberty	LN–10133	November '81	A

LITTLE FEAT/LOWELL GEORGE. Quickly recognized by musicians and critics in the early Seventies as the best "unknown" band in America, Little Feat was led by Lowell George, who was often regarded as one of the most underrated singers, songwriters, and guitarists of the Seventies. Considered one of rock music's finest slide-guitar players (his distinctive style was produced by sliding down, rather than up, the guitar strings),

George wrote such classics as "Willin'" (later popularized by Linda Ronstadt), "Truck-Stop Girl," and "Dixie Chicken" for Little Feat. Ironically, Little Feat attained their first commercial success with 1974's *Feats Don't Fail Me Now*, an album that featured Lowell George's singing and playing, rather than songwriting. George retained a somewhat reduced profile during Little Feat's subsequent rise to popularity that culminated in 1978's gold-award live set, *Waiting for Columbus*. Striking out as a solo act in April 1979 to promote his own *Thanks, I'll Eat It Here*, Lowell George died of an accidental drug overdose on June 29, 1979.

Los Angeles-born, Lowell George made his show business debut on television's "Ted Mack Amateur Hour" at the age of six. Taking up guitar at 11, he haunted local coffeehouses and clubs before forming his first rock band, The Factory, with drummer Ritchie Hayward around 1966. When that group broke up, George played for a time with The Standells ("Dirty Water"), The Seeds ("Pushin' Too Hard") and The Mothers of Invention. In late 1969 he formed Little Feat with former Mothers' bassist Roy Estrada, Santa Barbara keyboardist Bill Payne, and friend Ritchie Hayward, who, in the meantime, had been a member of The Fraternity of Man ("Don't Bogart That Joint"). Signed to Warner Brothers Records on the strength of George's songwriting, Little Feat's debut album featured an acoustic version of George's often covered truck-driving classic, "Willin'," and "Truck-Stop Girl," co-written by Payne. Although quickly recognized by musicians and critics alike, the album failed to sell. *Sailin' Shoes*, regarded by many as the group's finest album, also sold poorly despite the inclusion of an electrifed version of "Willin'" and George songs such as "Trouble," "Easy to Slip," and "Teenage Nervous Breakdown." Estrada soon left Little Feat to join Captain Beefheart, and the group added guitarist Paul Barrere, bassist Ken Gradney, and conga player Sam Clayton. *Dixie Chicken*, produced by Lowell George, proved another commercial failure, although it did reveal the ascendancy of Payne and Barrere as songwriters and George as singer and musician.

Lowell George, having earlier produced albums by Bonnie Raitt and others, pursued sessions work as Little Feat broke up for a time. They regrouped for 1974's *Feats Don't Fail Me Now*, their first commercially successful album, which included George's "Rock and Roll Doctor" and "Long Distance Love." On the road for six months promoting the album, Little Feat successfully completed a tour of Europe in early 1975. Their next two albums, *The Last Record Album* (produced by George) and *Time Loves a Hero*, saw George contributing very few songs. However, the live double-record set *Waiting for Columbus* became the group's first and only certified gold-award album. During 1978 Lowell George produced The Grateful Dead's *Shakedown Street*, parting company with Little Feat in April 1979. His debut solo album, *Thanks, I'll Eat It Here*, nearly three years in the works and largely featuring the compositions of other songwriters, was released in March; but, while on a promotional tour with a new band, Lowell George died of an accidental drug overdose in Arlington, Virginia, on June 29, at the age of 34. Little Feat's *Down on the Farm*, released after George's death, contained five songs written or co-written by George, with vocal and instrumental overdubs provided by the other band members.

LITTLE FEAT

Little Feat	Warner Brothers	WS–1890	February '71	A
Sailin' Shoes	Warner Brothers	BS–2600	April '72	A
Dixie Chicken	Warner Brothers	BS–2686	February '73	A
Feats Don't Fail Me Now	Warner Brothers	BS–2784	August '74	A
The Last Record Album	Warner Brothers	BS–2884	October '75	A
Time Loves a Hero	Warner Brothers	BS–3015	April '77	A
Waiting for Columbus*	2-Warner Brothers	2BS–3140	February '78	A
Down on the Farm	Warner Brothers	HS–3345	November '79	A
Hoy–Hoy!	2-Warner Brothers	3538	August '81	A

LOWELL GEORGE

Thanks, I'll Eat It Here	Warner Brothers	BS–3194	March '79	A

LITTLE RICHARD. The on-again, off-again, self-styled "King of Rock-and-Roll," Little Richard was probably the first rock artist to achieve widespread popularity on the basis of a frantic and furious presence in recording and performing. An inspiration for the wild and boisterous stage acts of Jerry Lee Lewis and James Brown through Mick Jagger and Jimi Hendrix (Little Richard's one-time guitar accompanist), Little Richard's shouting gospel-style vocals were later emulated by Otis Redding and Joe Tex during the early stages of their careers. Scoring at least seven major hit singles between late 1955 and early 1958, Little Richard upheld his reputation as one of rock music's most erratic and unpredictable characters by denouncing rock-and-roll and joining the ministry in 1957. Re-emerging in 1964, Little Richard encountered little success as a contemporary soul act and eventually enjoyed renewed popularity with the rock-and-roll revival of the late Sixties and early Seventies. However, by the late Seventies Little Richard was again preaching against rock-and-roll.

Born on December 5, 1932, in Macon, Georgia, as Richard Penniman, Little Richard was singing on the streets of Macon by the age of seven and became the lead singer in a local church choir at age 14. Subsequently joining a traveling medicine show, he won an Atlanta talent contest in 1951 which resulted in an RCA recording contract. Encountering little success with his blues-based recordings for RCA, Little Richard switched to the Houston-based Peacock label in 1952, making his first recordings for the company in early 1953. A demonstration tape sent to Art Rupe of the Los Angeles-based Specialty Records in 1955 resulted in a new recording contract. Initial sessions recorded in New Orleans under producer "Bumps" Blackwell yielded a major hit with "Tutti Frutti" at the beginning of 1956 and later hits that year, recorded in Los Angeles, included the two-sided hit "Long Tall Sally/Slippin' and Slidin'" and "Rip It Up." In early 1957 Little Richard scored a minor hit with the title song to the film *The Girl Can't Help It* (in which he appeared), followed by "Lucille" (backed by the unusually soulful "Send Me Some Lovin'"), "Jenny, Jenny," and "Keep a Knockin'," probably his biggest hit.

"Good Golly, Miss Molly" became Little Richard's last major hit in early 1958; but earlier, while touring Australia, he announced his intention to leave rock-and-roll behind in favor of the ministry. Subsequently enrolling in Alabama's Oakwood College to study theology, Little Richard later recorded several gospel albums as Specialty continued to issue his prior recordings with little success. Returning to the music business around 1964, he recorded for VeeJay and, in a contemporary soul style, for Okeh and Modern. During this period Jimi Hendrix was briefly Little Richard's guitar accompanist—recordings of the two eventually surfaced during the Seventies. Enjoying renewed popularity with the rock-and-roll revival of the late Sixties, Little Richard signed with Reprise Records in early 1970 and scored a minor hit with "Freedom Blues" that year and even penetrated the album charts with 1971's *The King of Rock and Roll*. However, he seemed to be only a pale imitation of his former self; his self-serving and monomaniacal performances and television appearances did little to further his career. By 1977, Little Richard had again renounced the secular world in favor of tours of the gospel circuit.

LITTLE RICHARD

Here's Little Richard	Specialty	SP–2100 (M)	July '57	
Little Richard, Volume 2	Specialty	SP–2103 (M)	January '59	A
Fabulous Little Richard	Specialty	SP–2104 (M)	May '59	A
Well, Alright!	Specialty	2136(E)		A
Little Richard	Camden	CAL–420 (M)	April '58	
It's Real	Mercury	60656	December '61	
Little Richard Sings Spirituals	United	7723(M)		
Little Richard Sings Freedom Songs	Crown	5362(M)		
Clap Your Hands	Spin O Rama	119		
Coming Home	Coral	CRL– 757446	December '63	

King of the Gospel Singers	Mercury reissued on Pickwick	16288 3258	November '64
Recorded Live	United also Kent/ Modern	7775(M) 1000(M)	
Wild and Frantic Little Richard	United also Kent/ Modern	7777(M) 1003(M)	
Little Richard Is Back	VeeJay	1107	December '64
Explosive	Okeh	OKS– 14117	February '67
Little Richard	Buddah	BDS–7501	June '70
Every Hour with Little Richard	Camden	CAS–2430	August '70
The Rill Thing	Reprise	RS–6406	September '70
The King of Rock and Roll	Reprise	RS–6462	October '71
Second Coming	Reprise	MS–2107	October '72

LITTLE RICHARD AND JIMI HENDRIX

Roots of Rock	Archive of Folk and Jazz Music	296(E)	September '74
Together	Pickwick	3347	

LITTLE RICHARD ANTHOLOGIES AND COMPILATIONS

Little Richard's Biggest Hits	Specialty	SP–2111 (M)	January '64	A
Little Richard's Grooviest 17 Original Hits	Specialty	2113(E)		A
His Greatest Hits	VeeJay	1124	'64	
Greatest Hits	Okeh	OKS– 14121	July '67	
Little Richard	Kama Sutra	KSBS–2023	November '70	
Cast a Long Shadow	Epic	EG–30428	April '71	
Greatest Hits	2-Trip	8013	November '71	
Big Hits	GNP Crescendo	9033	January '75	A
Very Best	United Artists	LA497	April '76	
Tutti Frutti	Accord	SN–7123	November '81	A

KENNY LOGGINS AND JIM MESSINA.   Initially formed as an informal arrangement of Kenny Loggins *with* Jim Messina, the team's *Sittin' In* album proved so popular that they formed a road band to tour and record as Loggins *and* Messina. Messina was a veteran recording engineer, producer, and former member of two of America's early "country-rock" bands, The Buffalo Springfield and Poco. He provided first guitar and the harder-edged songs, whereas Loggins played second guitar and supplied gentle love songs such as the classics "Danny's Song" and "A Love Song." Spurred by the smash hit "Your Mamma Don't Dance," Loggins and Messina maintained a high level of popularity by touring extensively and emerged as a people's band rather than a critics' band. With all but one of their first seven albums being certified gold-award, Loggins and Messina parted company in the latter half of 1976. Kenny Loggins quickly established himself with both FM radio and "easy listening" audiences, whereas Messina waited more than two years to record his debut solo album, *Oasis*.

Born in Maywood, California, on December 5, 1947, Jim Messina formed several surf bands while still in high school. Recording two obscure surf-and-dragster albums as Jim Messina and The Jesters, Messina was first approached to produce recordings while still a senior in high school. Upon graduation, he immediately moved to Hollywood and learned the fundamentals of studio engineering at Harmony Recorders and, later, at Sunset Sound. Messina scored his first success as a studio musician on Jackie Lee's one-chord "Do the Duck," a hit in late 1965. Essentially a creature of the studio, Messina was oblivious to the burgeoning local "folk-rock" scene, but was introduced to it when he recorded Joni Mitchell's first demonstration tape at the behest of David Crosby. Through Crosby, word filtered down to Neil Young, who enlisted Messina to engineer "Hung Upside Down" and "Broken Arrow" from *Buffalo Springfield Again*. With the departure of Springfield bassist Bruce Palmer, Messina was recruited to play bass as well as to engineer and produce *Last Time Around*, to which he contributed "Carefree Country Day."

The stormy career of The Buffalo Springfield ended in the summer of 1968, and Jim Messina and Richie Furay formed Poco, with Messina staying on through the group's first three albums. Leaving Poco in November 1970, Messina became a staff producer at Columbia Records, meeting songwriter Kenny Loggins in December. Born in Everett, Washington, on January 7, 1948, Loggins (and family) moved to the Los Angeles suburb of Alhambra when he was about eight years of age. He started singing as a child, taking up guitar in high school and dropping out of Pasadena City College to concentrate on songwriting. Serving four years as a staff writer for ABC–Wingate Music, Loggins was also briefly a member of a later-day edition of The Electric Prunes ("Too Much to Dream Last Night"). He finally saw one of his compositions, "House at Pooh Corner," become a minor hit for The Nitty Gritty Dirt Band in early 1971.

Jim Messina was assigned to produce Kenny Loggins' debut solo album for Columbia, but Messina suggested that they record it together, with Messina informally *"Sittin' In."* The album did not yield any major hit singles but did contain a number of excellent songs by both artists. These included Messina's "Nobody but You," "Peace of Mind," and the politically oriented extended piece "Same Old Wine," and Loggins' "House at Pooh Corner" and the gently celebratory "Danny's Song," a major hit for

Anne Murray in early 1973. *Sittin' In* sold so well that Loggins and Messina decided to form a touring band, officially inaugurating their duo career with *Loggins and Messina*. That album became their first of many certified gold-award albums, yielding hits with "Your Mama Don't Dance" and "Thinking of You," while also containing the duo's "Angry Eyes." Touring regularly, Loggins and Messina eventually played over 700 engagements in five years. *Full Sail* produced their last major hit with "My Music" and included Loggins' "A Love Song" and Messina's "You Need a Man." After the double-record live set *On Stage*, the two recorded the ambitious *Mother Lode* album, which yielded minor hits with "Changes" and "Growin'"; *So Fine* was an oldies collection. After *Native Sons*, their final studio album, Loggins and Messina agreed to part company, completing their farewell tour in September 1976. Columbia later issued the anthology set, *The Best of Friends*, and another double-record live album, *Finale*, for Loggins and Messina.

Kenny Loggins soon recorded his debut solo album, *Celebrate Me Home*, for Columbia and it was certified gold-award without yielding a major hit single. In 1977 he toured with Fleetwood Mac, opening shows for the "superstar" group. Recorded with his touring band, Loggins' *Nightwatch* album produced a smash hit with "Whenever I Call You 'Friend'," co-written with Melissa Manchester and sung as a rather incongruous duet with Fleetwood Mac's Stevie Nicks. As *Nightwatch* sold in quantities requisite for platinum-award certification, Loggins performed at a wide variety of venues, including auditoriums, supper clubs, and Nevada casinos. Finally, in 1979, Jim Messina formed a new band in Santa Barbara, California, and recorded the rather bland *Oasis* album as his solo debut. Issued the same month as *Oasis*, Kenny Loggins' *Keep the Fire* yielded a major hit with "This Is It," co-written with The Doobie Brothers' Mike McDonald. In 1980 Loggins scored a near-smash hit with "I'm Alright."

JIM MESSINA AND THE JESTERS

Jim Messina and The Jesters	Thimble	TLP–3	
The Dragsters	Audio Fidelity	DFS–7037	December '64

KENNY LOGGINS AND JIM MESSINA

Sittin' In *	Columbia	PC–31044	February '72	A
Loggins and Messina *	Columbia	PC–31748	October '72	A
Full Sail *	Columbia	PC–32540	October '73	A
On Stage *	2-Columbia	PG–32848	April '74	A
Mother Lode *	Columbia	PC–33175	October '74	A
So Fine	Columbia	PC–33810	August '75	A
Native Sons *	Columbia	PC–33578	January '76	A
The Best of Friends *	Columbia	PC–34388	December '76	A
Finale	2-Columbia	JG–34167	October '77	A

KENNY LOGGINS

Celebrate Me Home**	Columbia	PC–34655	April '77	A
Nightwatch**	Columbia	JC–35387	July '78	A
Keep the Fire*	Columbia	JC–36172	October '79	A
Alive*	2-Columbia	C2X–36738	September '80	A

JIM MESSINA

Oasis	Columbia	JC–36140	October '79	
Messina	Warner Brothers	3559	June '81	A

LOVE/ARTHUR LEE.   One of the earliest Los Angeles rock groups of the Sixties, Love inspired a serious underground following in both the United States and England although they seldom performed outside the Los Angeles region. Their debut 1966 album featured an early version of the rock classic "Hey, Joe," whereas *Da Capo* contained the classic "Seven and Seven Is" (the group's only major hit) and "Revelation," one of the first side-long album cuts in rock music. Certainly one of the overlooked classics of Sixties rock, *Forever Changes* is one of the definitive production arrangements of the era, enhanced by biting surreal lyrics (primarily by Arthur Lee) that makes it one of the premier existentially oriented albums of rock. Never a particularly stable group, Love was reconstituted by Lee for *Four Sail*, an album noteworthy for its excellent powerhouse musicianship. Love's last album, *False Start*, included a dynamic performance by lead guitarist Jimi Hendrix, and Lee's solo debut, *Vindicator*, stands as a befitting tribute to the guitar stylings of Hendrix. Having developed a reputation for eccentricity and erraticism, Arthur Lee later dropped out of sight, although rumors circulated in 1979 that Love would re-form.

LOVE

Love	Elektra	EKS–74001	April '66	
Da Capo	Elektra	EKS–74005	February '67	
Forever Changes	Elektra	EKS–74013	December '67	A
Four Sail	Elektra	EKS–74049	August '69	
Revisited	Elektra	EKS–74058	September '70	
Out Here	2-Blue Thumb	BTS–9000	December '69	
False Start	Blue Thumb	BTS–8822	December '70	
Best	Rhino	800	May '80	A

ARTHUR LEE

Vindicator	A&M	SP–4356	June '72	
Reel-to-Real	RSO	SO–4804	November '74	
Arthur Lee	Rhino	020	August '81	A

THE LOVIN' SPOONFUL/JOHN SEBASTIAN. Another of America's challenges to the British predominance of popular music in the mid-Sixties, The Lovin' Spoonful created a distinctive mixture of folk, blues, and rock musics as modernized jug band music which became known as "good-time" music. Featuring a zany and extroverted stage act, The Lovin' Spoonful put as much emphasis on their instrumental playing as they did on their harmony singing to produce their fresh, exuberant, uncluttered sound. Also key to the success of The Lovin' Spoonful was John Sebastian's pop-style songwriting which dealt with romantic themes maturely and realistically rather than in the irritatingly naive manner of professional Tin Pan Alley songwriters. Despite a series of major hits between 1965 and 1967, including the classics "Do You Believe in Magic," "Summer in the City," and "Darling, Be Home Soon," the career of The Lovin' Spoonful was cut short when allegations were circulated that one of the members had turned drug informant upon threat of deportation. John Sebastian re-established himself with members of the so-called "counter-culture" through his celebrated appearance at the Woodstock Festival in 1969 and his excellent contractually delayed *John B. Sebastian* album, but his infrequent Seventies releases have fared modestly at best, save his smash 1976 single, "Welcome Back."

John Sebastian was born on March 17, 1944, in New York's Greenwich Village, the son of a renowned classical harmonica player. Taking up harmonica himself as a child and guitar at the age of 12, he later added piano and autoharp to his instrumental repertoire. Playing early recording sessions for Tim Hardin and Jesse Colin Young, Sebastian joined The Even Dozen Jug Band in 1963. That band also included Maria Muldaur, and Steve Katz, later with The Blues Project and Blood, Sweat and Tears. In 1964 Zalman Yanovsky (born in Toronto, Ontario, on December 19, 1944) was briefly a member of the New York-based Mugwumps, whose other members were singer–songwriter Jim Hendricks, and Denny Doherty and Cass Elliott, who later became half of The Mamas and The Papas. Yanovsky and Sebastian met during recording sessions by The Mugwumps that were eventually released in 1967 after the acknowledged success of both The Lovin' Spoonful and The Mamas and The Papas. Encouraged by producer Erik Jacobsen, John Sebastian formed The Lovin' Spoonful to record his songs. The members: John Sebastian (guitar, autoharp, piano, harmonica, vocals), Zalman Yanovsky (lead guitar, vocals), Steve Boone (born in Camp Lejune, North Carolina, on September 23, 1943) (bass, piano, vocals), and Joe Butler (born in Glen Cove, New York, on January

9, 1943, *or* in Great Neck, New York, on September 16, 1943) (drums, vocals).

Signed to Kama Sutra Records, with distribution handled by MGM, The Lovin' Spoonful recorded their debut album in 1965. Released near year's end, *Do You Believe in Magic* sported a fresh, clean, friendly sound for traditional folk and blues songs and Sebastian originals such as "Younger Girl," the hit classic "Do You Believe in Magic," and the smash hit "Did You Ever Have to Make Up Your Mind." *Daydream* became a best-seller, yielding a smash hit with the title song and containing a number of fine songs such as "Didn't Want to Have to Do It" and "You Didn't Have to Be So Nice." In between soundtrack albums to Woody Allen's *What's Up, Tiger Lily?* and Francis Ford Coppola's *You're a Big Boy Now*, The Lovin' Spoonful issued *Hums*, usually regarded as their most fully realized album. Producing a smash hit with the classic summertime song "Summer in the City," the album also included the hits "Rain on the Roof" and "Nashville Cats." Moreover, "Darling, Be Home Soon," one of Sebastian's strongest and most endearing songs, became a major hit in 1967, as did "Six O'Clock."

However, in late 1966, several members of The Lovin' Spoonful had been busted on drug charges in San Francisco, and Yanovsky, threatened with deportation, apparently incriminated at least one area resident. Yanovsky left the group in ignominy in July 1967 (later to record the ironically titled solo album, *Alive and Well in Argentina*), and The Lovin' Spoonful's image was permanently tarnished. Jerry Yester was recruited to replace Yanovsky for *Everything Is Playing*, which contained "Six O'Clock," "She Is Still a Mystery," and "Younger Generation" but, by the fall of 1968, John Sebastian had departed the group. Steve Boone also left, and Joe Butler reconstituted the group for *Revelation: Revolution '69* before dissolving the group in the summer of 1969.

In August 1969 John Sebastian re-established himself with members of the so-called "counter-culture" through his renowned appearance at the Woodstock Festival. However, he had become embroiled in legal disputes among his former management, MGM Records, and his new label, Reprise, that resulted in the delay of the release of his debut solo album. In fact, *both* MGM and Reprise issued *John B. Sebastian* in early 1970. Recorded with the assistance of Steve Stills, David Crosby, and Graham Nash, the album contained several good-time up-tempo songs, two gentle love songs, "She's a Lady" and "Magical Connection," and two songs of communal good will, "How Have You Been" and "I Had a Dream." Both MGM and Reprise issued marginally successful live albums by Sebastian, followed by *"The Four of Us"* on Reprise. His next album, *Tarzana Kid*, did not come until three years later, and it failed to sell despite the inclusion of Jimmy Cliff's "Sitting in Limbo," Lowell George's "Dixie Chicken," and Sebastian's own "Stories We Could Tell" (recorded by The Everly Brothers in 1972). Sebastian was back in 1976 with *Welcome Back*, and the album sold modestly at best, yet yielded a smash hit with the title song, which was used as the theme song to the hit television situation comedy "Welcome Back, Kotter."

THE EVEN DOZEN JUG BAND

The Even Dozen Jug Band	Elektra	EKS–7246	December '63

THE MUGWUMPS

The Mugwumps	Warner Brothers	WS–1697	July '67

THE LOVIN' SPOONFUL

Do You Believe in Magic	Kama Sutra	KLPS–8050	November '65
Daydream	Kama Sutra	KLPS–8051	March '66
What's Up, Tiger Lily? (soundtrack)	Kama Sutra	KLPS–8053	September '66
Hums of The Lovin' Spoonful	Kama Sutra	KLPS–8054	December '66
You're a Big Boy Now (soundtrack)	Kama Sutra	KLPS–8058	March '67
Everything Is Playing	Kama Sutra	KLPS–8061	December '67
Revelation: Revolution '69	Kama Sutra	KLPS–8073	November '68

LOVIN' SPOONFUL ANTHOLOGIES AND COMPILATIONS

Best*	Kama Sutra	KLPS–8056	February '67
Best, Volume 2	Kama Sutra	KLPS–8064	February '68
24 Karat Hits	2-Kama Sutra	750	September '68
John Sebastian Song Book	Kama Sutra	KSBS–2011	June '70
Very Best	Kama Sutra	KSBS–2013	June '70
Once Upon a Time	Kama Sutra	KSBS–2029	April '71
The Best	2-Kama Sutra	2608	April '76

ZALMAN YANOVSKY

Alive and Well in Argentina	Kama Sutra	KSBS–2030	'69

JOHN SEBASTIAN

John B. Sebastian	MGM	SE–4654	February '70
	also Reprise	RS–6379	February '70
Live	MGM	SE–4720	October '70
Real Live John Sebastian	Reprise	MS–2036	April '71
The Four of Us	Reprise	MS–2041	September '71
Tarzana Kid	Reprise	MS–2187	September '74
Welcome Back	Reprise	MS–2249	April '76

LYNYRD SKYNYRD. Another popular hard-working Southern rock band of the Seventies, Lynyrd Skynyrd was nonetheless more influenced by British groups such as The Rolling Stones and Cream than by their progenitors, The Allman Brothers. Usually propelled by a unique *three-guitar* front line and featuring the strong stage presence and prolific songwriting of leader Ronnie Van Zant, Lynyrd Skynyrd opened shows for The Who's late 1973 *Quadrophenia* tour, subsequently establishing themselves through years of rigorous touring. Scoring a number of hits with songs often sexually or regionally chauvinistic, Lynyrd Skynyrd recorded the outstanding "Free Bird," a jam-style radio classic of 1974–75. With all of their albums becoming best-sellers, Lynyrd Skynyrd were enjoying enormous popularity when their chartered plane crashed on October 20, 1977, in rural Mississippi, killing three members and injuring most of the others. In late 1979 five surviving members of Lynyrd Skynyrd bravely regrouped as The Rossington–Collins Band for further recordings.

Vocalist Ronnie Van Zant (born in Jacksonville, Florida, on January 15, 1948 or 1949) and guitarists Gary Rossington and Allen Collins (both born in Jacksonville, on December 4, 1951, and July 19, 1952, respectively) formed the first of a series of rock bands during the mid-Sixties. Experiencing frequent personnel changes, the band toured the Southern high school and bar circuit for six years. In 1972 the band's personnel stabilized with Van Zant, Rossington, Collins, keyboardist Billy Powell (born in Corpus Christi, Texas, on June 3, 1952), bassist Leon Wilkeson (born in Newport, Rhode Island, on April 2, 1952), guitarist Ed King, and drummer Bob Burns. Ed King had previously been a member of The Strawberry Alarm Clock, who scored a smash hit with "Incense and Peppermint" in late 1967. By 1972, having taken the name Lynyrd Skynyrd, the band was making occasional forays into Atlanta, Georgia, where they were "discovered" by producer Al Kooper. Signed to Kooper's newly formed Sounds of the South label (distributed by MCA), Lynyrd Skynyrd were well-received at MCA's Sounds of the South Party in Atlanta during July 1973. Initiating a rigorous touring schedule, Lynyrd Skynyrd's Kooper-produced debut album, usually referred to as *Pronounced Leh-nerd Skin-nerd*, was supported by a major promotional campaign by MCA. The album featured Van Zant's plea to the cuckolded man, "Gimme Three Steps," and the underground favorites, "Simple Man" and "Free Bird," the latter a major hit when released as a single in late 1974.

Offered the opening position for The Who's late 1973 American *Quadrophenia* tour, Lynyrd Skynyrd were exposed to their largest audiences to date, performing creditably. The Al Kooper-produced *Second Helping* became the band's first certified gold-award album and yielded a near-smash hit with the Southern anthem "Sweet Home Alabama." Touring exhaustively, Lynyrd Skynyrd's so-called Torture Tour of 1975 resulted in the departures of Ed King and Bob Burns. Kooper's final production for the band and King's final album with the band, *Nuthin' Fancy* on MCA Records, introduced drummer Artimus Pyle (born in Louisville, Kentucky, on July 15, 1948) and produced a major hit with "Saturday Night Special." Lynyrd Skynyrd continued with a two-guitar front line, adding the female backup vocal group The Honkettes (Cassie Gaines, Leslie Hawkins, and Jo Billingsley) in early 1976.

Gimme Back My Bullets, produced by Tom Dowd, fared less well than had Kooper's productions, and Cassie Gaines' guitarist–brother Steve (born in Miami, Oklahoma, on September 14, 1949) joined the group in June 1976. The live double-record set *One More for the Road* became Lynyrd Skynyrd's first certified platinum-award album, and the group took a respite from touring. They were back on the road in the fall of 1977 but, on October 20, 1977, their chartered plane crashed when it ran out of gas over rural Mississippi, killing Ronnie Van Zant and Steve and Cassie Gaines and injuring most of the others. *Street Survivors*, issued only days before the crash, featured a ghastly cover quickly withdrawn by MCA as being in poor taste. The album contained the ominously ironic "That Smell" and yielded a major hit with "What's Your Name." As band members recovered, convalesced, and attempted to return to a normal life style, MCA issued *Skynyrd's First . . . and Last*, originally recorded in 1970 and 1971 before the band had secured a recording contract. In the fall of 1979 five surviving members of Lynyrd Skynyrd—Gary Rossington, Allen Collins, Billy Powell, Leon Wilkeson, and Artimus Pyle—augmented by sessions guitarist Barry Harwood, reunited as The Rossington–Collins Band. Formally debuting in Atlanta in June 1980, the group soon scored a minor hit with "Don't Misunderstand Me."

LYNYRD SKYNYRD

Pronounced Leh-nerd Skin-nerd*	MCA/Sounds of the South reissued on MCA	363 3019	September '73	A
Second Helping*	MCA/Sounds of the South reissued on MCA	413 3020	April '74	A
Nuthin' Fancy*	MCA	2137 reissued as 3021 reissued as 37069	March '75	A
Gimme Back My Bullets*	MCA	2170 reissued as 3022 reissued as 37070	February '76	A
One More for the Road**	2-MCA	2-6001 reissued as 8011	September '76	A
Street Survivors**	MCA	3029	October '77	A
Skynyrd's First . . . and Last**	MCA	3047 reissued as 37071	September '78	A
Gold and Platinum**	2-MCA	2-11008	December '79	A

THE ROSSINGTON–COLLINS BAND

Anytime, Any-place, Anywhere*	MCA	5130	June '80	A
This Is the Way	MCA	5207	October '81	A

THE MAMAS AND THE PAPAS. One of the few American groups to receive widespread attention in a music scene dominated by British acts during the mid-Sixties, The Mamas and The Papas were one of the earliest "hippie" groups, wearing brightly-colored, odd-looking apparel and espousing in song the ethics of an open life-style and love *before* the crunch of San Francisco's "acid-rock." Though most of the members emerged from a folk music background, The Mamas and The Papas' success was due in large part to the slick pop-style Los Angeles production of manager Lou Adler and the intricate vocal arrangements of leader John Phillips. Featuring the excellent songwriting of Phillips, the impressive vocal harmonies of the four members and the outstanding playing of some of Los Angeles' finest studio musicians, The Mamas and The Papas enjoyed consistent popularity through three years of existence despite their infrequent live performances. Moreover, Phillips and Adler organized the 1967 Monterey Pop Festival, perhaps the first-ever rock music festival and certainly one of the most significant, launching the American careers of Jimi Hendrix, The Who, and Janis Joplin, among others. Following the group's breakup in 1968, Cass Elliot pursued a modest career as a pop-style cabaret entertainer, whereas John Phillips and Denny Doherty essentially dropped out after neglected solo albums. During the late Sixties, Cass Elliot's Laurel Canyon home was a hub of musical and social activities, with artists such as David Crosby, Steve Stills, Graham Nash, Joni Mitchell, and Eric Clapton being frequent visitors. In fact, Crosby, Stills, and Nash first joined voices there before formally forming their "superstar" group.

John Phillips, born August 30, 1935, on Paris Island, South Carolina, began performing in Greenwich Village folk clubs during the late Fifties with groups such as The Smoothies, which included Scott McKenzie. In 1961 Phillips, McKenzie, and Dick Weissman formed the folk trio The Journeymen, debuted at Gerde's Folk City that spring, and ultimately recorded three albums for Capitol Records. Denny Doherty, born November 29, 1941, in Halifax, Nova Scotia, Canada, recorded two albums for Epic while a member of the folk group The Halifax Three with Pat La Croix and Richard Byrne. Tim Rose, Cass Elliot (born Ellen Cohen on September 19, 1941, in Baltimore, Maryland) and her first husband James

Hendricks formed The Big Three in New York around 1963. Recording two albums for the FM label, The Big Three had evolved into The Mugwumps by the summer of 1964. Comprised of Doherty, Elliot, Hendricks, and Canadian Zalman Yanovsky (later a member of The Lovin' Spoonful), The Mugwumps recorded a single album that was eventually issued after the successes of The Mamas and The Papas and The Lovin' Spoonful.

With the dissolution of The Mugwumps, Denny Doherty joined John Phillips and his wife Michelle (born Holly Michelle Gilliam on June 4, 1945, in Long Beach, California) in the Virgin Islands. Subsequently joined by Cass Elliot, the four worked on perfecting their vocal sound (Michelle had been singing for less than three months) for five months during the spring and summer of 1965 before moving to Los Angeles. There Barry McGuire put them in touch with producer Lou Adler, who signed the group as The Mamas and The Papas to his newly formed Dunhill label. With John Phillips playing guitar and singing baritone, Michelle singing soprano, Doherty tenor, and Elliot contralto, they recorded their debut album with sessions musicians Larry Knechtel (keyboards), Joe Osborn (bass), and Hal Blaine (drums), with Adler providing slick pop-style production. The album, *If You Can Believe Your Eyes and Ears*, quickly yielded smash hits with John and Michelle's "California Dreamin'" and John's "Monday, Monday," while containing John's "Go Where You Wanna Go" and Lennon and McCartney's "I Call Your Name." The album was soon certified gold-award, as was *The Mamas and The Papas*, which produced smash hits with "I Saw Her Again" (by John Phillips and Doherty) and "Words of Love" (by John) and included "No Salt on Her Tail," "Dancing Bear," and "Strange Young Girls" (all by John) and "Trip Stumble and Fall" (by John and Michelle). Early 1967's *Deliver* yielded smash hits with "Dedicated to the One I Love" (a 1961 smash for The Shirelles) and John and Michelle's autobiographical "Creeque Alley."

During 1967 John Phillips and Lou Adler organized the Monterey International Pop Festival, perhaps the first and certainly one of the most successful rock music festivals of the late Sixties. Coinciding with the smash success of Phillips' "San Francisco (Be Sure to Wear Flowers in Your Hair)," as recorded by former associate Scott McKenzie, the festival (and the subsequent D.A. Pennebaker film) launched the enormously popular American careers of Jimi Hendrix, The Who, and Janis Joplin. Recordings of The Mamas and The Papas' performance there were eventually issued in 1971. In 1968 *The Papas and The Mamas*, produced by Adler and recorded with the same studio musicians, included a major hit with Phillips' "Twelve Thirty" as well as his excellent "Safe in My Garden" and an early version of Cass Elliot's first solo hit, "Dream a Little Dream of Me." However, "Glad to Be Unhappy" became the group's last major hit and, by mid-1968, The Mamas and The Papas had broken up.

Cass Elliot quickly recorded her debut solo album for Dunhill, which yielded the aforementioned hit, but she did not score another hit until 1969, when "It's Getting Better" and "Make Your Own Kind of Music" proved moderate successes. Pursuing a career as a nightclub and television performer, she later recorded an ill-received but underrated album with Dave Mason, who was coming off the huge success of his debut solo album, *Alone Together*. By then, both John Phillips and Denny Doherty had recorded solo albums, with Phillips managing a moderate hit with "Mississippi" in the summer of 1970, the year he and Michelle divorced. During 1971 The Mamas and The Papas reunited briefly for the John Phillips-produced *People Like Us* album; by 1972, Elliot had switched to RCA Records, where her recordings failed to sell significantly. After the successful completion of a two-week engagement at the Palladium Theater in London, Cass Elliot succumbed to a heart attack on July 29, 1974, at the age of 32. That year, Doherty recorded an album for the small Ember label and, early the next year, the Andy Warhol-produced musical *Man on the Moon*, featuring the music and lyrics of John Phillips, debuted and quickly closed in New York. In the meantime Michelle Phillips had concentrated on an acting career, appearing in the 1973 film *Dillinger* and co-starring opposite ballet star Rudolph Nureyev in the dismal 1976 film *Valentino*. After recording *Victim of Romance* for A&M Records, she returned to acting, appearing in the film *Bloodline* and starring in the television mini-series "Aspen" and "The French Atlantic Affair." In 1980, after years of absence from recording, John Phillips was indicted on serious drug charges by a federal grand jury in New York, only to be fined and sentenced to 30 days in jail.

THE JOURNEYMEN (WITH JOHN PHILLIPS)

The Journeymen	Capitol	ST–1629	October '61
Coming Attrac- tions—Live!	Capitol	ST–1770	August '62
New Directions in Folk Music	Capitol	ST–1951	August '63

THE HALIFAX THREE (WITH DENNY DOHERTY)

The Halifax Three	Epic	BN–26038	March '63
San Francisco Bay Blues	Epic	BN–26060	September '63

THE BIG THREE (WITH CASS ELLIOT)

The Big Three	FM	307	October '63
Live at the Recording Studio	FM	311	July '64
The Big Three Featuring Cass Elliot	Roulette	42000	August '69

THE MUGWUMPS (WITH CASS ELLIOT AND DENNY DOHERTY)

The Mugwumps	Warner Brothers	WS–1697	July '67

THE MAMAS AND THE PAPAS

If You Can Believe Your Eyes and Ears*	Dunhill	DS–50006	March '66	
The Mamas and The Papas*	Dunhill	DS–50010	September '66	
Deliver*	Dunhill	DS–50014	March '67	
Historic Performance at the Monterey International Pop Festival	Dunhill	DSX–50100	March '71	
Present The Papas and The Mamas	Dunhill	DS–50031	May '68	A
People Like Us	Dunhill	DSX–50106	October '71	

THE MAMAS AND THE PAPAS ANTHOLOGIES AND COMPILATIONS

Book of Songs	Dunhill	DS–50022	'67	
Farewell to the First Golden Era	Dunhill	DS–50025	November '67	A
Golden Era, Volume 2	Dunhill	DS–50038	September '68	A
16 Greatest Hits	Dunhill	DS–50064	September '69	A
Anthology—A Gathering of Flowers	Dunhill	DSY–50073	April '70	A
20 Golden Hits	Dunhill	DSX–50145	February '73	A
California Dreamin'	Pickwick	3357		
Monday, Monday	Pickwick	3380	January '75	
Biggest Hits	2-Pickwick	2076	January '75	A

CASS ELLIOT

Dream a Little Dream	Dunhill	DS–50040	October '68
Bubblegum, Lemonade, and Something for Mama	Dunhill	DS–50055	June '69
Make Your Own Kind of Music	Dunhill	DS–50071	November '69

CASS ELLIOT AND DAVE MASON

Dave Mason and Cass Elliot	Blue Thumb	BTS–8825	March '71

JOHN PHILLIPS

John Phillips	Dunhill	DS–50077	April '70

DENNY DOHERTY

Watcha Gonna Do	Dunhill	DS–50096	February '71

CASS ELLIOT

Cass Elliot	RCA	LSP–4619	March '72
The Road Is No Place for a Lady	RCA	LSP–4753	October '72
Don't Call Me Mama Anymore	RCA	APL1– 0303	December '73

CASS ELLIOT ANTHOLOGIES AND COMPILATIONS

Mama's Big Ones	Dunhill	DS–50093	December '70	A
Her Best Music	2-Pickwick	2075	January '75	A
Dream a Little Dream	Pickwick	3359		

DENNY DOHERTY

Wating for a Song	Ember	EMS–1036	'74

MICHELLE PHILLIPS

Victim of Romance	A&M	SP–4651	December '77

BARRY MANN/CYNTHIA WEIL. Another of the brilliant professional songwriting teams employed at New York's Brill Building during the Sixties, Barry Mann and Cynthia Weil wrote dozens of hit songs for a variety of acts. Among their songwriting credits are "On Broadway" (with Jerry Leiber and Mike Stoller) for The Drifters, "You've Lost That Lovin' Feelin'" (with Phil Spector) and "(You're My) Soul and Inspiration" for The Righteous Brothers, "Kicks" and "Hungry" for Paul Revere and The Raiders and, more recently, "Here You Come Again" for Dolly Parton.

Born in Brooklyn, New York, on February 9, 1939, Barry Mann abandoned his architecture studies to become a songwriter in 1958. Achieving his first hit in collaboration with Mike Anthony in early 1959 with "She Say (Oom Dooby Doom)" as performed by The Diamonds, he was employed as a staff songwriter by Al Nevins and Don Kirshner at New York's famed Brill Building from 1959 on. Teaming with several other writers on a number of early Sixties hits, Mann co-wrote "Footsteps," a near-smash for Steve Lawrence in 1960, "I Love How You Love Me," a smash hit for the Paris Sisters in 1961, and the maudlin "Patches," a smash hit for Dickey Lee in 1962. With Mike Anthony, he co-authored "I'll Never Dance Again" and "The Grass Is Greener," major hits for Bobby Rydell in 1962 and Brenda Lee in 1963, respectively. Encouraged by Don Kirshner, Mann recorded an album of his own for ABC Records that yielded a near-smash hit with the novelty song "Who Put the Bomp (in the Bomp, Bomp, Bomp)," co-written with Gerry Goffin.

Nonetheless, Barry Mann's greatest success came in collaboration with Cynthia Weil, whom he married in 1961. Their early hit compositions included "Bless You" for Tony Orlando in 1961, "Uptown" and "He's Sure the Boy I Love" for The Crystals, "Conscience" for James Darren, and "Johnny Loves Me" for Shelley Fabares, all from 1962. Hit Mann–Weil songs from 1963 included "My Dad" for Paul Petersen, "Blame It on the Bossa Nova" for Eydie Gorme, "I'll Take You Home" for The Drifters, and "Only in America" for Jay and The Americans. Other hit compositions by Mann–Weil in 1964–65 were "I'm Gonna Be Strong" for Gene Pitney, "Saturday Night at the Movies" for The Drifters, "We Gotta Get Out of This Place" for The Animals, and "Home of the Brave" for Jody Miller. In late 1964 the duo worked with producer–songwriter extraordinaire Phil Spector on "Walking in the Rain" for The Ronettes and the smash classic "You've Lost That Lovin' Feelin'" for The Righteous Brothers. During 1966 they provided The Righteous Brothers with "(You're My) Soul and Inspiration" and Paul Revere and The Raiders with "Kicks" and "Hungry," all smash hits. Other hit compositions with which they were associated through 1970 were Max Frost and The Troopers' "Shape of Things to Come," Cass Elliot's "It's Getting Better" and "Make Your Own Kind of Music," and B.J. Thomas' "I Just Can't Help Believing."

Around 1970 Barry Mann and Cynthia Weil moved to the West Coast, where Mann unsuccessfully attempted to launch a solo recording career with *Lay It All Out* on New Design Records. Another attempt in 1975 on RCA Records also fared dismally, although he did score a minor hit with "The Princess and the Punk" the following year on Arista. More recently, Barry Mann and/or Cynthia Weil have been associated with smash hits by Dolly Parton ("Here You Come Again") and Dan Hill ("Sometimes When We Touch"), both from 1977. Mann recorded yet another solo album in 1980.

BARRY MANN

Who Put the Bomp	ABC	399	November '61	
Lay It All Out	New Design	Z–30876	January '72	
Survivor	RCA	APL1– 0860	May '75	
Barry Mann	Casablanca	7228	September '80	A

MANFRED MANN. The third English group to achieve a top American hit (the rhythm-and-blues styled "Do Wah Diddy Diddy" in 1964), Manfred Mann scored more than a dozen British hits, though only four major American hits, before disbanding in 1969. Led by namesake Manfred Mann, the band included, at times, bassists Jack Bruce (Cream) and Klaus Voorman (The Plastic Ono Band) and guitarist Tom McGuinness, who later formed McGuinness–Flint. Subsequently forming the jazz-influenced Chapter Three and the "heavy-rock" Earth Band, Manfred Mann twice during his career recorded obscure classics by up-and-coming songwriters, hitting with probably the first released version of Bob Dylan's "The Mighty Quinn" in 1968 and Bruce Springsteen's "Blinded by the Light" in 1976.

MANFRED MANN

Manfred Mann Album	Ascot	ALS–16015	November '64
Five Faces of Manfred Mann	Ascot	ALS–16018	February '65
My Little Red Book of Winners	Ascot	ALS–16021	September '65
Mann Made	Ascot	ALS–16024	March '66
Pretty Flamingo	United Artists	UAS–6549	November '66
Up the Junction (soundtrack)	Mercury	SR–61159	May '68
The Mighty Quinn	Mercury	SR–61168	May '68

MANFRED MANN ANTHOLOGIES AND COMPILATIONS

Greatest Hits	United Artists	UAS–6551	December '66
The Best of Manfred Mann	Janus	3064	July '74
Greatest Hits	Capitol	M–11688 (M)	December '77
Best	Capitol	N–16073 (M)	

PAUL JONES

Sings Songs from *Privilege* and Others	Capitol	ST–2795	August '67
Crucifix in a Horseshoe	London	XPS–605	January '72

MANFRED MANN CHAPTER THREE

Manfred Mann Chapter Three	Polydor	244013	February '70

MANFRED MANN'S EARTH BAND

Manfred Mann's Earth Band	Polydor	PD–5015	February '72
Glorified, Magnified	Polydor	PD–5031	September '72
Get Your Rocks Off	Polydor	PD–5050	June '73
Solar Fire	Polydor	PD–6019	January '74

A

MICHAEL D'ABO

Down at Rachel's Place	A&M	SP–4346	August '72
Broken Rainbows	A&M	SP–3634	August '74

MANFRED MANN'S EARTH BAND

The Good Earth	Warner Brothers	BS–2826	October '74	
Nightingales and Bombers	Warner Brothers	BS–2877	August '75	
The Roaring Silence *	Warner Brothers	BS–2965 reissued as 3055	August '76	A
Watch	Warner Brothers	BSK–3157	February '78	
Angel Station	Warner Brothers	BSK–3302	March '79	A

MANFRED MANN

Chance	Warner Brothers	3498	January '81	A

NIGHT (WITH CHRIS THOMPSON)

Night	Planet	P–3	July '79	
Long Distance	Planet	10	January '81	A

BOB MARLEY AND THE WAILERS. The most important popularizers of authentic reggae music (Jimmy Cliff's music, though reggae-based, is essentially pop-oriented), Bob Marley and The Wailers were popular recording artists in Jamaica for years before securing a contract with the internationally distributed Island label in 1972. A quirky "scratch-guitar" music dominated by stop-beat bass and percussion accents and characterized thematically by lyrics largely concerned with Jamaican political and social repression and the tenets of the Rastafarian religion, reggae appeared to be the next major trend in contemporary music during the otherwise generally lackluster early and mid-Seventies, particularly as a result of the endorsement and incorporation of reggae by Eric Clapton, Mick Jagger, and Paul Simon. Save 1969's "Israelites" by Desmond Dekker and The Aces, the earliest reggae hit singles in the United States were compositions by Marley, "Stir It Up" by Johnny Nash and "I Shot the Sheriff" by Eric Clapton. Suffering the 1974 departures of founding members Peter Tosh and "Bunny" Livingston, Bob Marley and The Wailers' best-selling *Rastaman Vibration* album from 1976 revealed a decided rock orientation and, by 1978, the reggae craze was abating. The rise of reggae, touted internationally in the music press, may have failed to reach its promise due to a variety of factors: the heavy "patois" of the vocals, the minimalism of melodies, the ultimate sameness of the music's sound, or the preoccupation with religious and radical political themes which were of more interest to impoverished and oppressed Jamaicans than to pop music fans. Nonetheless, Bob Marley and The Wailers remained the most popular reggae group in the world, particularly in Jamaica, England, and certain African nations, whereas Peter Tosh is the only non-Rolling Stones act to record for Rolling Stones Records.

Born in St. Anne, Jamaica, on February 5 (or April 6), 1945, Bob Marley began recording in his native land in 1962. By 1964 he had joined fellow Jamaicans Peter Tosh (nee MacIntosh) and "Bunny" Livingston in the formation of The Wailing Rudeboys. Adding Junior Braithwaite and Beverley Kelso, the group soon became The Wailers and scored a series of Jamaican hits, yet suffered the departures of these additions in 1966. Extensive local success continued through the early Seventies, as The Wailers added drummer Carlton Barrett and his bass-playing brother Aston "Family Man" around 1970 and issued four Jamaican albums by 1972. Meeting Johnny Nash, Marley provided him with the 1972 British and 1973 American hit, "Stir It Up." Signed to Chris Blackwell's Island label in 1972, The Wailers' critically acclaimed debut album, *Catch a Fire*, was issued in the spring of 1973. It contained "Stir It Up" plus Tosh's militant "400 Years," yet it was largely ignored. Following quiet tours of Great Britain and the United States in 1973, The Wailers recorded *Burnin'*, which was also overlooked despite the inclusion of Tosh's "Get Up, Stand Up" and "One Foundation" and Marley's "I Shot the Sheriff." Eric Clapton scored a top hit with a tame version of the latter song in the summer of 1974, but, by then, both Tosh and Livingston had left The Wailers.

Natty Dread, credited to Bob Marley and The Wailers and recorded with lead guitarist Al Anderson and the Barrett brothers, became the group's first album chart entry. In addition to the title song, the album included "Them Belly Full (but We Hungry)," "Lively Up Yourself," and the touching "No Woman No Cry," regarded as one of Marley's finest personal songs. Successful tours of America and Britain in 1975 raised Marley to the status of a cult figure as the rock press declared reggae the up-and-coming music of the Seventies. That promise seemed to be kept with the release of the best-selling *Rastaman Vibration* in 1976. Yielding a minor hit with "Roots, Rock, Reggae," the album also contained "Positive Vibration" and "Who the Cap Fit." *Exodus*, which included the Marley favorites "Jamming" and "Exodus," also sold quite well, but 1978's *Kaya* apparently marked the beginning of diminishing American popularity for reggae in general and for Bob Marley in particular.

In the meantime, Peter Tosh had recorded two neglected albums for Columbia Records, *Legalize It* (the title song advocating the legalization of marijuana) and *Equal Rights*, before joining Rolling Stones Records as the only non-Rolling Stones act in 1978. Opening shows for the "superstar" group during the summer of 1978, Tosh's debut album for the label, produced by Mick Jagger, yielded a minor hit with "(You Got to Walk and) Don't Look Back," recorded with the vocal assistance of Jagger. However, neither that album nor Marley's double-record set *Babylon by Bus* fared particularly well. Nonetheless, Marley successfully toured America in late

1979 with the Barrett brothers, the female vocal trio The I-Threes, and guitarist Junior Marvin. Recent releases include Tosh's *Mystic Man* and *Wanted: Dread and Alive* and Marley's *Survival* and *Uprising* albums. One of the most revered third-world figures, Marley performed at the independence ceremony for Zimbabwe in 1980, but on May 11, 1981, he died of brain cancer in Miami, Florida.

BOB MARLEY AND THE WAILERS

Birth of a Legend	2-Calla	1240	October '76	
Birth of a Legend	Calla	ZX–34759	June '77	
Roots Music	Calla	ZX–34760	June '77	

THE WAILERS

Catch a Fire	Island	SW–9329	April '73	
		reissued as		
		ILPS–9241	October '75	A
Burnin'	Island	SMAS–9338	October '73	
		reissued as		
		ILPS–9256	December '74	A

BOB MARLEY AND THE WAILERS

Natty Dread	Island	ILPS–9281	March '75	A
Rastaman Vibration	Island	ILPS–9383	April '76	A
Live!	Island	ILPS–9376	October '76	A
Exodus	Island	ILPS–9498	May '77	A
Kaya	Island	ILPS–9517	March '78	A
Babylon by Bus	2-Island	11	December '78	A
Survival	Island	ILPS–9542	October '79	A
Uprising	Island	ILPS–9596	July '80	A

PETER TOSH

Legalize It	Columbia	PC–34253	July '76	A
Equal Rights	Columbia	PC–34670	May '77	A
Bush Doctor	Rolling Stones	39109	November '78	A
Mystic Man	Rolling Stones	39111	July '79	A
Wanted: Dread and Alive	EMI–America	SO–17055	July '81	A

BUNNY WAILER

Blackheart Man	Island/Mango	9415	September '76	A
Protest	Island/Mango	9512	October '77	A
Sings The Wailers	Mango	9629	February '81	A

BOB MARLEY

Chances Are	Atlantic	5228	October '81	A

THE MARSHALL TUCKER BAND. Another hard-working Southern rock band of the Seventies, The Marshall Tucker Band have established themselves as a popular live band through years of regular touring. Best known otherwise as an album band (their only major hit single has been "Heard It in a Love Song," while "Can't You See" is their acknowledged classic), The Marshall Tucker Band features the country-style songwriting of lead guitarist Toy Caldwell and the jazz-influenced reed instrument playing of Jerry Eubanks.

The later-day members of The Marshall Tucker Band were childhood friends in their hometown of Spartanburg, South Carolina; by 1966 all were working in local bands. Around 1970 Toy Caldwell, Doug Gray, and Jerry Eubanks formed The Toy Factory for local engagements, evolving into The Marshall Tucker Band by 1972. The members: Toy Caldwell (lead and pedal steel guitar, vocals, principal songwriter), brother Tommy Caldwell (bass, vocals), Doug Gray (lead vocals), Jerry Eubanks (saxophone, flute, vocals), George McCorkle (rhythm guitar), and Paul Riddle (drums). Spotted by Phil Walden in 1972, the group was quickly signed to Walden's newly formed Capricorn label. Touring in support of The Allman Brothers in 1973, The Marshall Tucker Band recorded their debut album at Capricorn's Macon, Georgia, studio. It contained Toy Caldwell's classic "Can't You See" and was eventually certified as the group's first gold-award album in 1975. Touring as a headline act by 1974, the band played 300 or more engagements a year to establish themselves as a popular live act. They managed their first minor hit single in the spring of 1975 with "This Ol' Cowboy," followed by the moderate hit "Fire on the Mountain" in the fall. Their *Searchin' for a Rainbow* album included the latter song, another version of "Can't You See," and Toy's title song. Whereas *Long Hard Ride* sold quite well without benefit of a hit single, 1977's *Carolina Dreams* produced the group's first and only major hit, "Heard It in a Love Song." The Marshall Tucker Band's final album of new material for Capricorn, *Together Forever*, recorded at Miami's Criteria Studios (rather than in Macon) under a new producer, yielded a minor hit with McCorkle and Eubanks' "Dream Lover." By 1979 they had switched to Warner Brothers Records for *Running like the Wind*, its moderate hit single "Last of the Singing Cowboys," and *Tenth*. On April 28, 1980, Tommy Caldwell, 30, died from injuries sustained in an auto accident on April 22, in Spartanburg. He was replaced on bass by Franklin Wilkie, a past member of The Toy Factory.

THE MARSHALL TUCKER BAND

The Marshall Tucker Band*	Capricorn reissued on Warner Brothers	CP–0112 3606	June '73 October '81	A
A New Life*	Capricorn	CP–0124	February '74	
Where We All Belong*	2-Capricorn reissued on Warner Brothers	2C–0145 2WB–3608	November '74 October '81	A

Searchin' for a	Capricorn	CP–0161	September '75	
Rainbow*	reissued on Warner Brothers	3609	October '81	A
Long Hard Ride	Capricorn	CP–0170	June '76	
Carolina Dreams**	Capricorn	K–0180	February '77	
	reissued on Warner Brothers	3610	October '81	A
Together Forever*	Capricorn	0205	April '78	
Greatest Hits*	Capricorn	0214	October '78	
	reissued on Warner Brothers	3611	October '81	A
Running like the Wind	Warner Brothers	BSK–3317	April '79	A
Tenth	Warner Brothers	HS–3410	March '80	A
Dedicated	Warner Brothers	HS–3525	February '81	A

MARTHA AND THE VANDELLAS. An early Motown female vocal trio, Martha and The Vandellas achieved two smash hits before the 1964 ascendancy of The Supremes, who came to be considered as Motown's most important female act. Scoring numerous hit singles with songs composed by Holland–Dozier–Holland between 1963 and 1967 that featured a raucous rhythm-and-blues style distinct from the less exuberant Supremes, Martha Reeves and The Vandellas endured a period of personnel changes and minor hits before disbanding around 1972. Martha Reeves subsequently pursued an inauspicious solo career, recording with little luck for three different labels.

In the early Sixties, Martha Reeves (born on July 18, 1941, in Detroit) was employed as a secretary at Motown Records. Recording the occasional demonstration tape as a part of her job, she first came to the attention of Berry Gordy, Jr., by substituting for an absent Motown artist at a recording session. With high school friends Rosalind Ashford (born on September 2, 1943, in Detroit) and Annette Sterling (also born in Detroit), she backed Marvin Gaye's recording of "Stubborn Kind of Fellow," his first, albeit minor, hit from 1962. Signed to the newly formed Gordy label as Martha and The Vandellas, the three scored their first hit in the spring of 1963 with the rather tame "Come and Get These Memories." Subsequently utilizing a harder-edged, brassy, rhythm-and-blues style propelled by Martha's dynamic vocals, they achieved a smash hit with Holland–Dozier–Holland's classic "Heat Wave" that summer. Annette Sterling soon quit, to be replaced by Betty Kelly (born on September 16, 1944), and the group continued scoring smash hits with the raw-sounding "Quicksand," "Dancing in the Street," and "Nowhere to Run" through early 1965. By then, Motown was concentrating on the career development of The Supremes, Gordy's favorite act, yet Martha and The Vandellas were able to achieve major hits with the less raunchy "My Baby Loves Me," "I'm Ready for Love," "Jimmy Mack," and "Honey Chile" through 1967.

However, Martha Reeves and The Vandellas, as they were billed beginning in 1967, never had another major hit. Martha's sister Lois replaced Betty Kelly in 1968, but Martha was out of commission during much of 1969 due to illness. With Martha and Lois Reeves and Sandra Tilley as members, the group resumed touring and recording in 1970, only to split up around 1972. Eventually securing her release from Motown, Martha Reeves recorded her solo debut album for MCA Records under producer Richard Perry. Although "Power of Love," a Joe Simon hit from 1972, became a minor hit for Reeves in early 1974, the album failed to make the charts. Switching to Arista Records, she recorded the mundane *Rest of My Life* album in 1976 and later moved to Fantasy Records for *We Meet Again* and 1980's *Gotta Keep Moving*.

MARTHA AND THE VANDELLAS

Come and Get These Memories	Gordy	902(M)	July '63	
Heat Wave	Gordy	907(M)	October '63	
Dance Party	Gordy	915	April '65	
Watch Out	Gordy	920	December '66	
Live!	Gordy	925	September '67	

MARTHA REEVES AND THE VANDELLAS

Ridin' High	Gordy	926	May '68	
Sugar and Spice	Gordy	944	April '70	
Natural Resources	Gordy	952	November '70	
Black Magic	Gordy	958	March '72	

MARTHA AND THE VANDELLAS ANTHOLOGIES AND COMPILATIONS

Greatest Hits	Gordy	917	May '66	
Anthology	2-Motown	7–778	October '74	A
Dancing in the Streets	Pickwick	3386	January '75	

MARTHA REEVES

Martha Reeves	MCA	414	June '74	
The Rest of My Life	Arista	4105	December '76	
We Meet Again	Fantasy	9549	April '78	A
Gotta Keep Moving	Fanasy	9591	March '80	A

DAVE MASON. A founding member of Traffic, having contributed the often recorded classic "Feelin' Alright?" to that group's second album, Dave Mason established himself on his own as an excellent songwriter and fluid lead guitarist with 1970's stunning *Alone Together* album. However that album, which featured a fold-out jacket and initially a multi-colored record, has overshadowed much of Mason's subsequent career, through a duet album with the late Cass Elliot and a series of solo albums for Columbia during the Seventies. Nonetheless, Dave Mason's recent *Let It Flow* (which yielded his only major hit single, "We Just Disagree") and *Mariposa de Oro* albums have been certified gold-award.

Born on May 10, 1946, in Worcester, England, Dave Mason took up guitar at the age of 14, playing in several Birmingham groups such as The Jaguars and The Hellians before forming Deep Feeling with drummer Jim Capaldi. Serving as a "roadie" for The Spencer Davis Group, Mason was a founding member of Traffic in 1967, along with Capaldi, Stevie Winwood, and Chris Wood. Traffic's first British hit, "Hole in My Shoe," was the first song Mason had ever written, but his tenure with the group was stormy; he departed in late 1967, returned in the spring of 1968, and left permanently that fall. During that time, he produced Family's Debut album and provided Traffic with the classic "Feelin' Alright?". Upon leaving Traffic for the second time, Mason moved to Los Angeles and toured with Delaney and Bonnie, appearing on their best-selling *On Tour* album with Eric Clapton. Mason's debut solo album, *Alone Together*, was issued in the summer of 1970 as he toured with Clapton's Derek and The Dominoes. Packaged in an unusual fold-out jacket that could be hung, the record was initially pressed on multi-colored vinyl, later becoming a valued collectors' item. Recorded with Capaldi, Delaney and Bonnie, Rita Coolidge, and Leon Russell, *Alone Together* contained seven excellent compositions by Mason, including "World in Changes," "Sad and Deep as You," "Shouldn't Have Took More Than You Gave," and "Only You Know and I Know" (a moderate hit), plus Capaldi and Mason's 7-minute-plus "Look at You Look at Me." Enthusiastically received by critics on both sides of the Atlantic, the album was eventually certified gold-award in 1974.

In late 1970 Dave Mason teamed with former Mamas and Papas member Cass Elliot, but the duo's sole album for Blue Thumb Records was quickly deleted from the label's catalog. After parting company with Elliot following a single American tour, Mason rejoined Traffic for touring and the resultant live set, *Welcome to the Canteen*. In early 1972, much to his chagrin, Blue Thumb issued *Headkeeper* without his approval. Comprised of one live side and one studio side, the album featured several noteworthy songs on the studio side, including the title song, "To Be Free" and "A Heartache, a Shadow, a Lifetime." Switching to Columbia Records, the disgruntled Mason recorded *It's Like You Never Left* with the assistance of Stevie Wonder and Graham Nash. Produced by Mason, the album included his "Every Woman," "Misty Morning Stranger," and "The Lonely One" and sold moderately without yielding a hit single. *Dave Mason*, which contained six new Mason compositions as well as Sam Cooke's "Bring It On Home to Me" and Bob Dylan's "All Along the Watchtower," became a best-seller, as did *Split Coconut*. Following a self-produced live double-record set, Mason recorded *Let It Flow*, which contained his only major hit single, "We Just Disagree" (written by guitarist Jim Krueger).

Mariposa de Oro, recorded with Krueger and long-time drummer Rick Jaeger, yielded a moderate hit with a reworked version of The Shirelles' hit "Will You Still Love Me Tomorrow," and was followed in 1980 by *Old Crest on a New Wave*.

DAVE MASON

Alone Together*	Blue Thumb	BTS–19	June '70	A

DAVE MASON AND CASS ELLIOT

Dave Mason and Cass Elliot	Blue Thumb	BTS–8825	March '71	

DAVE MASON

Headkeeper	Blue Thumb	BTS–34	February '72	A
Dave Mason Is Alive	Blue Thumb	BTS–54	April '73	A
It's Like You Never Left	Columbia	PC–31721	October '73	A
Dave Mason*	Columbia	PC–33096	October '74	A
Split Coconut	Columbia	PC–33698	October '75	A
Certified Live	2-Columbia	PG–34174	November '76	A
Let It Flow*	Columbia	PC–34680	April '77	A
Mariposa de Oro*	Columbia	PC–35285	June '78	A
Old Crest on a New Wave	Columbia	JC–36144	June '80	A

DAVE MASON ANTHOLOGIES AND COMPILATIONS

Best	Blue Thumb	BTS–6013	June '74	A
Very Best	Blue Thumb	BTS–6032	October '78	A
At His Best	ABC/MCA	AB–880	February '75	A
Best	Columbia	FC–37089	June '81	A

JOHN MAYALL. Often labeled the "grandfather" of English blues, John Mayall was instrumental in sparking the blues revival of the late Sixties. A staunch defender and champion of neglected and exploited black American bluesmen, Mayall might himself have remained overlooked (as were Alexis Korner and Graham Bond) had not later-day "superstar" guitarist Eric Clapton been an early member of his Bluesbreakers. Supplying a loose, noncommercial format within which his band members could explore their proclivities for the blues, John Mayall provided the training ground for many of Britain's leading instrumentalists. Among Mayall's former band members were lead guitarists Eric Clapton, Peter Green (founder of the original Fleetwood Mac), and Mick Taylor (later a member of The Rolling Stones), bassists John McVie (Fleetwood Mac) and Jack Bruce (Cream), and drummers Hughie Flint (McGuinness–Flint), Aynsley Dunbar (his own Retaliation, The Mothers of Invention, Journey and The Jefferson Starship), Mick Fleetwood (Fleetwood Mac), Keef Hartley, and

Jon Hiseman (Colosseum). Among Mayall's most successful and best-remembered albums are *Bluesbreakers with Eric Clapton* (sometimes considered the first classic British blues album), *A Hard Road, The Turning Point,* and *U.S.A. Union.* The *Turning Point,* Mayall's astounding acoustic, drummerless album and only certified gold-award album, and *Empty Rooms* featured guitarist Jon Mark and saxophone-flute player Johnny Almond, who subsequently achieved modest success on their own with jazz-oriented recordings such as "New York State of Mind" and the classic "The City." However, former members Keef Hartley and Jon Hiseman, with Colosseum, never broke through with their bands in the United States. Mayall's *U.S.A. Union,* recorded with American musicians such as violinist Don "Sugarcane" Harris, lead guitarist Harvey Mandel, and former Canned Heat bassist Larry Taylor, revealed an interesting fusion of jazz and blues that appealed to blues, jazz, and rock fans. A British expatriate to the United States since the late Sixties, John Mayall has recorded over 20 albums for London, Polydor, Blue Thumb, ABC/MCA, and, most recently, DJM Records.

Born in Manchester, England, on November 29, 1933, John Mayall became fascinated with the blues at the age of 13 and eventually learned to play guitar, keyboards, and harmonica. Forming his first group, The Powerhouse Four, while in college during the mid-Fifties, he assembled the semiprofessional Bluesbreakers in March 1962 and moved to London in 1963 at the encouragement of Alexis Korner. Turning professional in February 1963, The Bluesbreakers included bassist John McVie. By the time of Mayall's first British album, the band was comprised of Mayall, McVie, guitarist Roger Dean, and drummer Hughie Flint. During the spring of 1965, former Yardbird Eric Clapton replaced Dean, and McVie and Jack Bruce shared bass chores through June 1966. This aggregation recorded the classic *Bluesbreakers with Eric Clapton* album. When Hughie Flint left and Bruce and Clapton departed to form Cream, Mayall recruited guitarist Peter Green and drummers Aynsley Dunbar and Mick Fleetwood for *A Hard Road,* considered by some as Mayall's finest album to date.

By the spring of 1967 Peter Green had left The Bluesbreakers to form Fleetwood Mac in the fall. Mayall subsequently recorded *Crusade* with John McVie, guitarist Mick Taylor, drummer Keef Hartley, and two saxophonists and *The Blues Alone* as a solo album, accompanied only by Hartley. By August 1967, McVie had left to join Fleetwood Mac, and Mayall reconstituted The Bluesbreakers with Taylor, Hartley, saxophonists Chris Mercer and Dick Heckstall-Smith, and a new bassist for *Diary of a Band. Bare Wires,* the final Bluesbreakers' album, was recorded with Taylor, Mercer, Heckstall-Smith, drummer Jon Hiseman, bassist Tony Reeves, and a trumpeter–violinist and contained only Mayall compositions, a departure from the past. Mayall then moved to Los Angeles, where he recorded *Blues from Laurel Canyon* with Mick Taylor, who dropped out to join The Rolling Stones in 1969.

During 1968 drummer Keef Hartley formed The Keef Hartley Band with singer–songwriter–guitarist Miller Anderson and bassist Gary Thain, among others. The group developed a strong British following, but never made serious inroads in the United States, although the ballad "Just to Cry" was a brief underground favorite in 1969. The Keef Hartley Band dissolved during 1972 as Thain joined Uriah Heep and Anderson joined Savoy Brown for *Boogie Brothers.* Following *Seventy-Second Brave* and *Lancashire Hustler*, essentially solo albums, Hartley rejoined Anderson in late 1974 for the short-lived Dog Soldier.

Also in 1968 Jon Hiseman departed Mayall to form Colosseum with Dick Heckstall-Smith and Tony Reeves, among others. Again, the band was moderately successful in Great Britain but almost totally ignored in the United States and disbanded in the autumn of 1971. Later-day members included vocalist Chris Farlowe, later in Atomic Rooster with drummer Carl Palmer, and guitarist Dave Clempson, who subsequently joined Humble Pie. Heckstall-Smith recorded a solo album in 1972, whereas Hiseman eventually formed Colosseum II in 1975.

Following the departure of Mick Taylor, John Mayall decided to abandon the loud electric format in favor of a revolutionary, acoustic, drummerless aggregation with bassist Stephen Thompson, guitarist Jon Mark, and tenor saxophonist–flutist Johnny Almond. Both Mark and Almond had been professional sidemen for years, and Mark was a former accompanist to Marianne Faithfull. This grouping recorded the stunning *Turning Point* album for Mayall's new label, Polydor. Critically hailed and eventually certified gold-award in 1977, the album included the favorites "Room to Move," featuring Mayall's exciting harmonica solo, and the 9-minute-plus "California." *Empty Rooms*, recorded by the same lineup with the addition of former Canned Heat bassist Larry Taylor, even yielded a minor hit with "Don't Waste My Time."

Jon Mark and Johnny Almond then left Mayall, with Almond recording two solo albums for Deram before joining Mark for recordings on Blue Thumb Records. Featuring a format in which Mark's guitar and Almond's saxophone or flute alternated as lead instrument, they recorded extended pieces such as "The Ghetto," "Solitude," and the classic "The City," even scoring a minor hit in early 1972 with "One Way Sunday." Switching to Columbia Records where they recorded "New York State of Mind" and two more albums, Jon Mark and Johnny Almond reunited for *To the Heart* in 1976 after Mark had recorded a solo album; they eventually moved to Horizon Records for 1979's *Other People's Rooms*.

In 1970 John Mayall made yet another stylistic shift by employing American musicians Don "Sugarcane" Harris (violin), well-traveled Harvey Mandel (guitar), and Larry Taylor (bass) for the jazz-oriented *U.S.A. Union.* After recording *Back to the Roots* with various alumni (including Clapton, Green, Mick Taylor, Dunbar, Hartley, and Hiseman) and *Memories*, Mayall assembled an all-black band that included trumpeter Blue Mitchell and Stax guitarist Freddie Robinson for the appropriately titled *Jazz Blues Fusion* and, with some changes, *Moving On* and *Ten Years Are Gone.* Thereafter Mayall assembled yet another group for *The Latest Edition*, his final album for Polydor, before briefly switching to Blue Thumb Records for *New Year, New Band, New Company,* his last album chart entry. Subsequently moving to ABC (now MCA) Records, Mayall recorded *Notice to Appear* under New Orleans producer Allen Toussaint and three more albums before switching to DJM Records in 1979.

JOHN MAYALL'S BLUESBREAKERS

The Bluesbreakers with Eric Clapton	London	PS–492 reissued as 50009	February '67 February '78	A
A Hard Road	London	PS–502	August '67	A
Crusade	London	PS–529	February '68	A
Diary of a Band	London	PS–570	February '70	
Bare Wires	London	PS–537	September '68	A
Live in Europe	London	PS–589	April '71	

JOHN MAYALL

The Blues Alone	London	PS–534	June '68	A
Blues from Laurel Canyon	London	PS–545	February '69	A

KEEF HARTLEY (BAND)

Halfbreed	Deram	DES–18024	July '69
The Battle of Northwest Six	Deram	DES–18035	January '70
The Time Is Near	Deram	DES–18047	November '70
Overdog	Deram	DES–18057	July '71
The Seventy-Second Brave	Deram	XDES–18065	September '72
Lancashire Hustler	Deram	XDES–18070	May '73

DOG SOLDIER (WITH KEEF HARTLEY)

Dog Soldier	United Artists	LA405	March '75

COLOSSEUM (WITH JON HISEMAN)

Those Who Are about to Die, Salute You	Dunhill	DS–50062	April '70
Grass Is Green	Dunhill	DS–50079	April '70
Daughter of Time	Dunhill	DSX–50101	February '71
Live	2-Warner Brothers	XS–1942	November '71

COLOSSEUM II (WITH JON HISEMAN)

Electric Savage	MCA	2294	July '77

DICK HECKSTALL-SMITH

| A Story Ended | Warner Brothers | BS–2650 | November '72 | |

JOHN MAYALL

| The Turning Point * | Polydor | 244004 | September '69 | A |
| Empty Rooms | Polydor | 244010 | February '70 | |

JOHNNY ALMOND

| Music Machine | Deram | DES–18030 | October '69 | |
| Hollywood Blues | Deram | DES–18037 | April '70 | |

MARK–ALMOND

Mark–Almond	Blue Thumb	BTS–27	April '71	
Mark–Almond II	Blue Thumb	BTS–32	November '71	A
Best	Blue Thumb	BTS–50	May '73	A
Rising	Columbia	KC–31917	September '72	A
'73	Columbia	KC–32486	August '73	
'73/Rising	2-Columbia	CG–33648	October '75	

JON MARK

| Songs for a Friend | Columbia | PC–33339 | May '75 | |

MARK–ALMOND

To the Heart	ABC/MCA	AB–945	July '76	A
Other People's Rooms	Horizon	730	January '79	A
Best . . . Live	Pacific Arts	7–142	February '81	

JOHN MAYALL

U.S.A. Union	Polydor	244022	October '70	
Back to the Roots	2-Polydor	253002	April '71	
Memories	Polydor	PD–5012	November '71	
Jazz Blues Fusion	Polydor	PD–5027	June '72	
Moving On	Polydor	PD–5036	October '72	
Ten Years Are Gone	2-Polydor	PD2–3005	September '73	
The Latest Edition	Polydor	PD–6030	August '74	
New Year, New Band, New Company	Blue Thumb	BTSD–6019	February '75	
Notice to Appear	ABC	926	January '76	
A Banquet in Blues	ABC	958	July '76	
Lots of People	ABC	992	March '77	
Hard Core Package	ABC/MCA	AB–1039	November '77	A
Last of the British Blues	ABC/MCA	AA–1086	August '78	A
Bottom Line	DJM	23	May '79	

No More Interviews	DJM	29	December '79	A

JOHN MAYALL ANTHOLOGIES AND COMPILATIONS

Looking Back	London	PS–562	September '69	A
Through the Years	2-London	PS–600/1	November '71	
Down the Line	2-London	PS–618/9	January '73	
Primal Solos	London	50003	March '77	A
The Best of John Mayall	2-Polydor	PD2–3006	March '74	A

CURTIS MAYFIELD. Creative genius behind the success of The Impressions, one of the most popular non-Motown soul acts of the Sixties, Curtis Mayfield was one of the first black songwriters to combine gospel vocal stylizations with politically aware, socially conscious lyrics. Forming his own label, Curtom, in 1969 and leaving The Impressions for a solo career in 1970, Mayfield scored a smash success in 1972 with his soundtrack to *Superfly*. That album, often considered one of the finest examples of orchestral soul music, was hailed for its honest and compassionate treatment of the ghetto experience. However, by 1974 Curtis Mayfield's own albums began to suffer, as he put his creative energies into writing and producing the best-selling soundtracks to *Claudine*, *Let's Do It Again*, and *Sparkle*.

Chicago-born on June 3, 1942, Curtis Mayfield began writing songs before he became a teenager. He was 16 years old when his "For Your Precious Love" became a major hit, which was mistakenly credited to Jerry Butler and The Impressions. That success prompted Butler to leave The Impressions to pursue a solo career, and Mayfield served as his guitar player for two years, co-authoring Butler's first solo hit "He Will Break Your Heart" before re-establishing The Impressions with "Gypsy Woman" in 1961. Over the next nine years, Mayfield led The Impressions, writing virtually all their material, as the group scored at least ten major hits before his 1970 departure. Also, in 1963–64, he provided Major Lance with three major hits, "Monkey Time," "Hey Little Girl," and "Um, Um, Um, Um, Um, Um, Um." During the late Sixties, Mayfield wrote some of the earliest politically aware, socially conscious hit songs for The Impressions, including "We're a Winner," "This Is My Country," and "Choice of Colors." Around 1969 he formed his own record label Curtom, with manager Eddie Thomas, for subsequent recordings by The Impressions, whom he continued to record and produce after his 1970 departure.

Curtis Mayfield's debut solo album, *Curtis*, was a best-seller and yielded a major hit with "(Don't Worry) If There's a Hell Below We're All Going to Go," as well as his only British chart entry with "Move On Up." The follow-up, the double-record live set *Curtis Live!*, also proved a best-seller, and *Roots* was also well-received. Nonetheless, Mayfield's biggest success came in 1972 with the soundtrack to the black-oriented film *Superfly*. The album produced two smash hits with "Freddie's Dead" and "Superfly" and was certified as his first gold-award album before year's end. However, his subsequent singles were only moderate successes at best and, following the best-selling *Back to the World* album, Mayfield's albums fared only marginally. He then wrote and produced the film score to *Claudine*, performed by Gladys Knight and The Pips, and the soundtrack album yielded a smash hit with "On and On." Mayfield's own *There's No Place Like America Today* was critically acclaimed in 1975, but the album failed to sell in significant quantities. Later that year Curtom released the soundtrack to *Let's Do It Again*, scored and written by Mayfield and performed by The Staple Singers, and the album became a best-seller, producing a top hit with the title song. Mayfield's next soundtrack album, *Sparkle*, was performed by Aretha Franklin, yielding a major hit with "Something He Can Feel." Nonetheless, Mayfield's own albums were faring progressively less well and even the soundtrack to *A Piece of the Action*, which he wrote and produced with Mavis Staples performing the songs, failed to sell. Then, in 1979, he changed distribution of Curtom to RSO Records, and his own debut album for the label, *Heartbeat*, was issued in midyear. During 1980, Curtis Mayfield recorded the solo set *Something to Believe In*, and *The Right Combination* with Linda Clifford.

CURTIS MAYFIELD

His Early Years with The Impressions	2-ABC	ABCX–780	January '73
Curtis *	Curtom	CRS–8005	September '70
Curtis Live!	2-Curtom	CRS–8008	May '71
Roots	Curtom	CRS–8009	October '71
Superfly (soundtrack) *	Curtom	CRS–8014	August '72
Back to the World *	Curtom	CRS–8015	May '73
Curtis in Chicago Live	Curtom	CRS–8018	October '73
Sweet Exorcist	Curtom	CRS–8601	May '74
Got to Find a Way	Curtom	CRS–8604	October '74
There's No Place Like America Today	Curtom	CU–5001	May '75

CURTIS MAYFIELD/THE STAPLE SINGERS

Let's Do It Again (soundtrack)	Curtom	CU–5005	October '75

CURTIS MAYFIELD

Give, Get, Take, and Have	Curtom	CU–5007	June '76
Never Say You Can't Survive	Curtom	CU–5013	March '77
Short Eyes	Curtom	CU–5017	November '77
Do It All Night	Curtom	CU–5022	August '78

| Heartbeat | RSO | RS1–3053 | July '79 | |
| Something to Believe In | RSO | RS1–3077 | July '80 | A |

CURTIS MAYFIELD AND LINDA CLIFFORD

| The Right Combination | RSO | RS1–3084 | July '80 | A |

PAUL McCARTNEY/WINGS. Often considered the singular Beatle who stabilized the group's appeal with audiences of all ages, Paul McCartney was responsible for writing most of the group's original material in conjunction with John Lennon. The primary author of Beatles' hits such as "Michelle" and "Hey, Jude," McCartney also composed the classic "Yesterday," which has been recorded by more than 1,000 artists. Thought to be the prime instigator of The Beatles' 1970 breakup (a claim he disputes), Paul McCartney became the first former member to mount a major tour of his own in 1973. Initially pursuing a commercially successful but artistically suspect career based on his ability to produce highly melodic ditties, at first solo, then with wife Linda and finally with the group Wings, McCartney eventually established himself with the "Live and Let Die" single and *Band on the Run* album. This success was largely due to his astute understanding of the nature of the "pop" song and the legacy of the Tin Pan Alley tradition and his frequent and innovative use of reprises, codas, shifting time signatures and multiple musical themes within a single song. However, McCartney's songs have never seriously dealt with the personal and political themes once favored by John Lennon, or with the spiritual concerns voiced by George Harrison, since his compositions are grounded primarily in form, to the detriment of content. Paul McCartney's undisputed ongoing popularity has also been based on his ability to attract a new and young audience that is perhaps unaware of his achievements with The Beatles. The first former Beatle to tour the United States with unequivocal success, McCartney was credited by the 1980 edition of the *Guinness Book of World Records* with being the most successful composer of all time, the world's most successful recording artist, and the world's top-selling recipient of gold-award records.

Liverpool-born on June 18, 1942, Paul McCartney met John Lennon in June 1956 and subsequently joined Lennon's skiffle group, the Quarrymen. George Harrison joined the group in August 1958 and, by 1960, they had evolved into The Silver Beatles. The group's lineup was completed with the August 1962 addition of Ringo Starr and The Beatles burst onto the British musical scene in early 1963, subsequently establishing themselves in the United States in 1964. (The Beatles' full story is chronicled elsewhere.) Needless to say, Lennon and McCartney wrote many of the most successful songs of the Sixties, and The Beatles permanently changed the nature of contemporary popular music. In 1967 Paul McCartney recorded the soundtrack to the film *Family Way*, his first solo project. On March 12, 1969, he married American photographer Linda Eastman (born on September 24, 1942), of the Eastman–Kodak photography conglomerate. The film of The Beatles' final album release, *Let It Be*, aptly revealed McCartney's attempt to dominate the group. The four were soon embroiled in personal and business disputes as McCartney objected to the nearly simultaneous release of *Let It Be* and his first solo album, *McCartney*, and the others sought to employ Allen Klein as financial advisor while McCartney sought the appointment of his father-in-law, Lee Eastman. In April 1970 the breakup of The Beatles was announced and, on December 31, 1970, McCartney sued Klein and Apple Records for legal dissolution of the group's corporate empire.

McCartney, recorded with Linda providing harmonies and Paul playing all instruments and singing, was a decidedly homemade effort and was critically attacked by the rock press. The album contained ditties by Paul such as "Every Night," "That Would Be Something," "Man, We Was Lonely," and "Maybe I'm Amazed." Following the smash singles release "Another Day" in early 1971, Paul and Linda McCartney recorded *Ram* with New York sessions players; the album included "Heart of the Country" and yielded a top hit with "Uncle Albert/Admiral Halsey."

In August 1971 Paul McCartney formed his recording and touring band, Wings, with wife Linda, guitarist Denny Laine, and drummer Danny Seiwell. Sessions musician Seiwell had played on the *Ram* album, whereas Laine, born Brian Haynes on October 29, 1944, in Birmingham, England, had been an original member of The Moody Blues and lead vocalist on the group's first blues-inflected hit, "Go Now." *Wild Life*, credited to Paul McCartney and Wings, is generally considered McCartney's weakest effort, failing to yield even a minor hit. Joined in January 1972 by guitarist Henry McCullough, the band scored hits with the singles release "Give Ireland Back to the Irish," McCartney's feeble attempt at political consciousness, the inane "Mary Had a Little Lamb," and "Hi, Hi, Hi." *Red Rose Speedway* did little to establish his artistic credibility, although it did yield the top hit "My Love." In 1973 McCartney and Wings recorded the title song to the James Bond film *Live and Let Die* and the single became a smash hit which served as the prototype to the clever pop-style songs replete with reprises, codas, changing time signatures, and multiple musical themes that McCartney was to craft so successfully.

During 1973 Paul McCartney and Wings appeared in a British and American television special, successfully toured Europe, and scored a major hit with "Helen Wheels." However, by July Henry McCullough and Danny Seiwell had dropped out of Wings, McCullough later to record a solo album for George Harrison's Dark Horse label in 1975 before joining The Frankie Miller Band. The McCartneys and Laine traveled to Lagos, Nigeria, to record their next album, *Band on the Run*, at Ginger Baker's new ARC Studio. Often regarded as McCartney's finest post-Beatles work, it brought the group their first critical praise and yielded smash hits with "Jet" and "Band on the Run" while also containing "Let Me Roll It," "Helen Wheels," and another McCartney ditty, "Mamunia." Remaining on the album charts for more than two years and selling nearly five million copies, the album effectively established McCartney as a pop-style songwriter–arranger.

In May 1974 Wings added Scottish guitarist Jimmy McCulloch, a former member of Thunderclap Newman and Stone the Crows, and drummer Geoff Britton; this lineup went to Nashville, where they recorded the smash hit "Junior's Farm" and the moderate hit "Sally G." After replacing Britton with Joe English in February 1975, the group recorded *Venus and Mars Are Alright Tonight* as Wings, primarily at producer Allen Toussaint's Sea Saint Studio in New Orleans. The album produced the top hit "Listen to What the Man Said," the moderate hit "Letting Go," and the major hit "Venus and Mars Rock Show." Between the fall of 1975 and the summer of 1976, Wings successfully completed their first worldwide tour and *Wings at the Speed of Sound* was issued in the spring. Considered the band's first team effort, the album included McCulloch's "Wino Junko," Laine's "Time to Hide," and Linda McCartney's first effort as lead vocalist, "Cook of the House," as well as Paul's smash hit "Let 'em In" and top hit "Silly Love Songs," a gentle swipe at critics who had regularly attacked him for his inconsequential ditties.

The United States' segment of Wings' tour, called Wings Over America, was successfully conducted during the early summer of 1976; live recordings from the tour were released as a three-record set at the end of 1976 and yielded a major hit with "Maybe I'm Amazed." Otherwise generally inactive during 1977, Wings scored a smash British hit with the singles release "Mull of Kintyre" (the location of one of the McCartneys' estates), whereas the flip side, "Girls' School," became a moderate American hit. During this hiatus, Denny Laine recorded an entire album of Buddy Holly songs entitled *Holly Days* (Paul McCartney had earlier obtained the rights to all of Holly's songs). *London Town*, Wings' final release of new material for Capitol, was primarily recorded on a chartered yacht in the Virgin Islands and produced hits with "With a Little Luck," "I've Had Enough," and "London Town" during 1978. Following that album's completion, Jimmy McCulloch and Joe English left Wings, with McCulloch joining the re-formed Small Faces for a time and English joining Sea Level. On September 27, 1979, McCulloch, scheduled to debut the next night with his new band, The Dukes, was found dead in his London apartment at the age of 26.

In July 1978 sessions musicians Lawrence Juber (guitar) and Steve Holly (drums) joined Wings. By early 1979 Paul McCartney had signed a long-term contract with Columbia Records rumored to be the most lucrative ever in the history of popular music. Following the broadcast of an ABC television special taken from their 1976 Wings Over America tour on March 16, 1979, Wings scored their first smash hit for Columbia with the disco-styled "Goodnight Tonight." Their debut album for the label, *Back to the Egg*, yielded major hits with "Getting Closer" and "Arrow Through Me" during 1979. Scheduled to make his first appearance in Japan since playing there with The Beatles in 1966, McCartney was busted upon arrival on January 16, 1980, for possession of nearly a half-pound of marijuana. Perhaps the most highly publicized drug bust in pop music history, McCartney was deported after spending ten days in jail. He subsequently wrote, engineered, produced, played, and sang all parts of his second "solo" album, *McCartney II*, which included the top hit "Coming Up." In April 1981 Denny Laine left Wings.

PAUL McCARTNEY

Family Way (soundtrack)	London	MS–82007	June '67	
McCartney*	Apple/Capitol reissued on	SMAS– 3363	April '70	
	Columbia	JC–36478	June '80	A

PAUL AND LINDA McCARTNEY

Ram*	Apple/Capitol reissued on	SMAS– 3375	May '71	
	Columbia	JC–36479	June '80	A

PAUL McCARTNEY AND WINGS

Wild Life*	Apple/Capitol reissued on	SW–3386	December '71	
	Columbia	JC–36480	June '80	A
Red Rose Speedway*	Apple/Capitol reissued on	SMAL– 3409	May '73	
	Columbia	JC–36481	June '80	A
Band on the Run*	Apple/Capitol reissued on	SO–3415	December '73	
	Columbia	JC–36482	June '80	A

HENRY McCULLOUGH

Mind Your Own Business!	Dark Horse	SP–22005	October '75	

WINGS

Venus and Mars Are Alright Tonight*	Capitol reissued on	SMAS– 11419	May '75	
	Columbia	JC–36801		
Wings at the Speed of Sound**	Capitol reissued on	SW–11525	March '76	
	Columbia	FC–37409		
Wings Over America**	3-Capitol	SWCO– 11593	December '76	A
London Town**	Capitol	SW–11777	March '78	A
Greatest Hits**	Capitol	SOO– 11905	December '78	A
Back to the Egg**	Columbia	FC–36057	June '79	A

DENNY LAINE

Holly Days	Capitol	ST–11588	May '77	

PAUL McCARTNEY

McCartney II *   Columbia   FC–36511   June '80   A

JOHN McLAUGHLIN/THE MAHAVISHNU ORCHESTRA. Perhaps

the most important guitarist of the Seventies, John McLaughlin first came
to the attention of jazz fans by playing on jazz trumpeter Miles Davis'
seminal *In a Silent Way* and *Bitches' Brew* albums. The latter album
heralded the advent of so-called "fusion" music and ultimately became the
first jazz album since The Dave Brubeck Quartet's *Time Out* album to be
certified gold-award. Quickly recognized as a virtuoso guitarist for his
technically amazing, incredibly rapid, and harmonically intriguing guitar
stylizations, John formed The Mahavishnu Orchestra around 1971. Frequently utilizing the physically and technically demanding double-neck
guitar after 1971, McLaughlin was one of the first guitarists to use a guitar
synthesizer, a device which provided a synthesizer for each string of the instrument. One of the first bands to utilize multiple keyboards and electric
violin, The Mahavishnu Orchestra was one of the first "fusion" groups to
enjoy both critical and commercial success, particularly with the stunning
Birds of Fire album, regarded as one of the few masterpieces of the genre.
More recently McLaughlin has recorded albums which fused Eastern and
Western musical traditions from a decidedly Eastern point of view.

Born in Yorkshire, England, on January 4, 1942, into a musical family,
John McLaughlin started classical piano lessons at the age of nine and
took up guitar around the age of 12. Forming his first band at 15 while still
in school, he later was a member of The Graham Bond Organization with
Jack Bruce and Ginger Baker and also served brief tenures with Brian
Auger and Georgie Fame. McLaughlin's first solo album, *Extrapolation*,
from 1969 (though apparently not released in the United States till 1972),
had little commercial impact, yet brought him to the status of a near-
legend by means of his extraordinarily fast and technically dazzling guitar
playing. The album brought him to the attention of jazz drummer Tony
Williams; McLaughlin subsequently recorded *In a Silent Way* with
Williams and jazz great Miles Davis. McLaughlin then assisted in the
recording of Davis' pioneering *Bitches' Brew* album, the album that
launched so-called "fusion" music into international popularity and introduced McLaughlin to American audiences. Next McLaughlin recorded
Emergency and *Turn It Over* with the Tony Williams Lifetime before
traveling to France to record *Devotion*. Converting to the philosophy of
Bengal mystic Sri Chinmoy during 1970, he recorded *My Goal's Beyond*, a
meditation album of solo acoustic pieces and group improvisations, with
American violinist Jerry Goodman (a former member of The Flock) and
powerhouse drummer Billy Cobham.

During 1971 John McLaughlin formed The Mahavishnu Orchestra
with Goodman, Czechoslovakian keyboardist Jan Hammer, and bassist
Rick Laird. Their debut album, *The Inner Mounting Flame*, garnered excellent critical reviews for its technically adroit and emotionally moving

music, but the follow-up, *Birds of Fire* (with Hammer using the synthesizer for the first time) was the album that established McLaughlin among rock fans and became the group's best selling album. McLaughlin next recorded the "jam" album *Love, Devotion, Surrender* with Sri Chinmoy convert Carlos Santana, and the album sold quite well despite its spiritually obsessive nature. Following the live set *Between Nothingness and Eternity*, recorded at New York's Central Park in August 1973, McLaughlin disbanded the first edition of The Mahavishnu Orchestra in January 1974 and formed a new group under that name with French violinist Jean-Luc Ponty and small horn and string sections. This aggregation recorded the ambitious *Apocalypse* album with the London Symphony Orchestra under former Beatles producer George Martin. However, neither that album nor *Visions of the Emerald Beyond* reversed the critical tendency to dismiss The Mahavishnu Orchestra. In the summer of 1975 McLaughlin fired several members and eliminated the horn and string sections for the final Mahavishnu album, *Inner Worlds*, featuring keyboardist Stu Goldberg.

No longer a disciple of Sri Chinmoy by 1976, John McLaughlin and Indian violinist L. Shankar formed Shakti with tabla player Zakir Hussain and two other Indian musicians to pursue acoustically McLaughlin's interest in Indian musical forms. Although none of Shakti's albums sold particularly well, they did reveal an exciting mixture of Eastern and Western musical forms, with the Eastern forms dominating. During 1978 *John McLaughlin, Electric Guitarist*, recorded with various associates such as Chick Corea, Stanley Clark, Tony Williams, Billy Cobham, and Carlos Santana, was issued. That spring McLaughlin assembled a new touring and recording band, The One Truth Band, with violinist L. Shankar, keyboardist Stu Goldberg, and a three-piece rhythm section. Their debut album, *Electric Dreams*, was issued in 1979. In 1981 Columbia issued *Friday Night in San Francisco*, recorded the prior December with McLaughlin, Al DiMeola, and flamenco guitarist Paco DeLucia on acoustic instruments.

JOHN McLAUGHLIN

Extrapolation	Polydor	PD–5510 reissued as PD–6074	October '72 July '76	

MILES DAVIS (WITH JOHN McLAUGHLIN)

In a Silent Way	Columbia	PC–9875	August '69	A
Bitches' Brew *	2-Columbia	PG–26	May '70	A

TONY WILLIAMS LIFETIME (WITH JOHN McLAUGHLIN)

Emergency, Volumes 1 and 2	2-Polydor	244017/8 reissued as 253001	May '70	
Turn It Over	Polydor	244021	June '70	

JOHN McLAUGHLIN

Devotion	Douglas	4 reissued as KZ– 31568 and Z– 32446	August '70
My Goal's Beyond	Douglas	Z–30766 reissued as 6003	August '71 September '76

THE MAHAVISHNU ORCHESTRA

The Inner Mount- ing Flame	Columbia	PC–31067	November '71	A
Birds of Fire	Columbia	PC–31996	February '73	A
Between Nothing- ness and Eternity—Live	Columbia	C–32766	December '73	A
Apocalypse	Columbia	C–32957	May '74	A
Visions of the Emerald Beyond	Columbia	PC–33411	February '75	A
Inner Worlds	Columbia	PC–33908	January '76	
Best	Columbia	JC–36394	April '80	A

JOHN McLAUGHLIN AND CARLOS SANTANA

Love, Devotion, Surrender *	Columbia	PC–32034	June '73	A

SHAKTI

Shakti	Columbia	PC–34162	June '76	A
A Handful of Beauty	Columbia	PC–34372	March '77	A
Natural Elements	Columbia	PC–34980	December '77	A

JOHN McLAUGHLIN

John McLaughlin, Electric Guitar- ist	Columbia	JC–35326	May '78	
Best	Columbia	JC–36355	October '80	A
Belo Horizonte	Warner Brothers	3619	October '81	A

JOHN McLAUGHLIN AND THE ONE TRUTH BAND

Electric Dreams	Columbia	JC–35785	April '79

JOHN McLAUGHLIN/AL DiMEOLA/PACO DeLUCIA

Friday Night in San Francisco	Columbia	FC–37152	June '81	A

DON McLEAN. Catapulted into international stardom in late 1971 with his brilliant personal song "American Pie," which chronicled contemporary history in terms of rock music, Don McLean was subsequently unable to sustain widespread popularity. Far more popular in Great Britain than in the United States, Don McLean nonetheless retains a devoted, if limited, following for his folk-style songs in his native country.

DON McLEAN

Tapestry	Mediarts	41–4	December '70	
	reissued on			
	United	UAS–5522	February '72	
	Artists			
American Pie *	United Artists	UAS–5535	November '71	
		reissued as		A
		LN–		
		10037		
Don McLean	United Artists	UAS–5651	November '72	
Playin' Favorites	United Artists	LA161	October '73	
Homeless Brothers	United Artists	LA315	October '74	
Solo	2-United	LA652	February '77	
	Artists			
Prime Time	Arista	4149	December '77	
Chain Lightning	Casablanca	7173	May '80	
	reissued on	BXL1–	February '81	A
	Millenium	7756		
Believers	Millenium	BXL1–	October '81	A
		7762		

CLYDE McPHATTER/THE DRIFTERS. Probably the most important and influential vocalist of the rhythm-and-blues Fifties, Clyde McPhatter recorded dozens of hits as lead vocalist for Billy Ward's Dominoes and his own Drifters and as a solo act. His distinctive high tenor voice and gospel-style phrasing, supported by smooth harmonies, set the standard for vocalists throughout the Fifties and Sixties. Best remembered for the classic "Money Honey," recorded with his Drifters, and for his solo hits "A Lover's Question" and "Lover Please," Clyde McPhatter was reduced to the status of an "oldies" act by the late Sixties. The Drifters, with Johnny Moore as lead vocalist, scored a rhythm-and-blues hit with the classic "Ruby Baby" in 1956, but manager George Treadwell totally reconstituted the group in 1958 for subsequent hits such as "There Goes My Baby" and "Dance with Me" that represented early fusions of pop and gospel styles that became known as "soul" music. Clyde McPhatter, unable to stage a comeback with 1970's *Welcome Home* after several years in England, died on June 13, 1972.

Born in Durham, North Carolina, on November 15, 1933, to a Baptist preacher father, Clyde McPhatter began singing in his father's choir at the age of five; he later moved to the New York area with his family. Turning professional at age 14 with the gospel group The Mount Lebanon Singers, he met pianist–arranger Billy Ward in 1950. Joining Ward's Dominoes as lead tenor, McPhatter and the group scored their first rhythm-and-blues hit with "Do Something for Me" on Federal Records in early 1951. Within a few months, The Dominoes' lascivious "Sixty-Minute Man," featuring lead vocals by bass voice Bill Brown, was a smash rhythm-and-blues hit, followed by several other hits, including "Have Mercy Baby," with lead vocals by McPhatter. Early recordings by McPhatter with The Dominoes were released on King Records later in the Fifties and reissued in the late Seventies.

After training Jackie Wilson as his replacement, Clyde McPhatter dropped out of The Dominoes to form his own Drifters in May 1953. The lineup stabilized with McPhatter (lead tenor), Gerhart Thrasher (tenor), his brother Andrew "Bubba" Thrasher (baritone), and Bill Pinkney (bass) and The Drifters' first successful recording session for Atlantic Records was conducted in August 1953. It produced the smash rhythm-and-blues hit and instant classic, "Money Honey." Rhythm-and-blues hits continued with "Such a Night," "Honey Love," a stunning harmony version of "White Christmas" (with lead vocals by Pinkney and McPhatter), and "Watcha Gonna Do." However, in 1954, McPhatter was drafted into the air force and was replaced initially by David Baughn and later by Johnny Moore, who sang lead on the hits "Adorable" and "Ruby Baby" in 1955–56. Frequent personnel changes ensued and the original Drifters broke up in June 1958. Manager George Treadwell, owner of The Drifters' name, drafted all new members for subsequent pop hit recordings such as "There Goes My Baby" and "Dance with Me" which blended pop and gospel musical styles with sophisticated arrangements and orchestrations.

While on leave from the air force, Clyde McPhatter recorded "Seven Days" solo, and the single became a rhythm-and-blues hit in early 1956. Upon discharge later that year, he pursued a solo career on Atlantic Records, scoring a smash rhythm-and-blues and major pop hit with "Treasure of Love" that spring. Touring with Bill Haley in 1956 and the Fats Domino Caravan in 1957, McPhatter achieved rhythm-and-blues/pop hits with "Without Love (There Is Nothing)," "Just to Hold My Hand," and "Long, Lonely Nights." His biggest hit, a pop smash, came in late 1958 with Brook Benton's "A Lover's Question." Switching to MGM Records in 1959, McPhatter suffered through inappropriate nongospel arrangements with the label and subsequently signed with Mercury Records through producer Clyde Otis in 1960. That summer he achieved a major pop hit with "Ta Ta," but his next did not come until early 1962, when his version of Billy Swan's "Lover Please" became a smash hit. A remake of "Little Bitty Pretty One" soon became a major hit, but it proved to be his last; his final Mercury album was issued in 1965. After several unsuccessful singles for small labels, McPhatter went to England in 1968, where he performed in small clubs. Upon return, Clyde Otis was able to secure him a recording contract with Decca Records, but *Welcome Home* failed to endear him to the record-buying public. Subsequently relegated to small clubs and the "rock-and-roll revival" circuit, Clyde McPhatter died on

June 13, 1972, in New York at the age of 38 from complications arising from heart, liver, and kidney ailments.

CLYDE McPHATTER WITH BILLY WARD AND THE DOMINOES

Billy Ward with Clyde McPhatter	King	548(M)	July '58	
Clyde McPhatter with Billy Ward and The Dominoes	King	559(M)	July '58	
Billy Ward and The Dominoes Featuring Clyde McPhatter	King	733(M)	May '61	
18 Hits	King	5006(M)	December '77	A

BILLY WARD AND THE DOMINOES

14 Hits (1951–1965)	King	5005(M)	December '77	A
21 Hits	King	5008(M)	December '77	A

CLYDE McPHATTER AND THE DRIFTERS

Clyde McPhatter and The Drifters	Atlantic	8003(M)	August '57	
The Greatest Recordings/The Early Years	Atco	33–375(M)	November '71	A

CLYDE McPHATTER

Love Ballads	Atlantic	8024(M)	November '58
Clyde	Atlantic	8031(M)	October '59
Best	Atlantic	8077(M)	July '63
Let's Start Over Again	MGM	SE–3775	September '59
Greatest Hits	MGM	SE–3866	July '60
Ta Ta	Mercury	SR–60262	October '60
Golden Blues Hits	Mercury	SR–60655	December '61
Lover Please	Mercury	SR–60711	June '62
Rhythm and Soul	Mercury	SR–60750	January '63
Greatest Hits	Mercury	SR–60783	July '63
Songs of the Big City	Mercury	SR–60902	May '64
Live at the Apollo	Mercury	SR–60915	September '64
May I Sing for You	Mercury	SRW–16224	June '65
Welcome Home	Decca	DL–75231	October '70

HAROLD MELVIN AND THE BLUE NOTES/TEDDY PENDERGRASS.
Obscure Fifties rhythm-and-blues vocal group, Harold Melvin and The Blues Notes worked the so-called "chitlin" circuit for years before

graduating to the white supper club circuit in the mid-Sixties at the suggestion of Martha Reeves. Breaking up, re-forming and moving backup
drummer Teddy Pendergrass into the lead vocalist role in 1970, Harold
Melvin and The Blue Notes began receiving recognition after signing with
Kenny Gamble and Leon Huff's Philadelphia International Records in
1971. Following his final album with the group, *Wake Up Everybody*,
Teddy Pendergrass embarked on an enormously successful career as an
album artist and gained recognition as one of the finest soul singers and
most potent black sex symbols since Al Green; Harold Melvin's career has
faded since Pendergrass' departure.

The Blue Notes originated in Philadelphia around 1954 as a black
rhythm-and-blues street-corner vocal group with Harold Melvin and Bernard Wilson. Making their first unsuccessful recording in 1956 for Josie
Records, The Blue Notes developed a night club act for tours of the so-
called "chitlin" circuit, eventually scoring minor hits with "I Don't Know
What It Is" on Brooke Records and "My Hero" on Val-ue Records in 1960.
Returning to club work, the group later added John Atkins, with Melvin
assuming lead vocal chores. During the early and mid-Sixties, they left the
rhythm-and-blues circuit in favor of white supper clubs, adopting ties and
tails at the suggestion of Martha Reeves. In 1965, as Harold Melvin and
The Blue Notes, the group scored a minor rhythm-and-blues hit with "Get
Out" on Landa Records, but they soon found themselves relegated to club
work as singles for a variety of labels failed to sell.

During 1970 Harold Melvin and The Blue Notes broke up briefly but,
when they re-formed, backup drummer Teddy Pendergrass (born in King-
tree, South Carolina, on March 26, 1950) was brought forward as lead
vocalist. The other members were Melvin, Bernard Wilson, Lloyd Parkes,
and Lawrence Brown. Pendergrass had been singing since the age of two
and was drumming by age 13. He had joined The Cadillacs, The Blue
Notes' backup band, in 1969, the year Parkes had joined the vocal group.
Signed to songwriter–producers Kenny Gamble and Leon Huff's Philadelphia International Records in 1971, Harold Melvin and The Blue Notes
scored a smash hit with "If You Don't Know Me by Now" in late 1972.
Their second album, *Black and Blue*, yielded a near-smash with "The
Love I Lost" in 1973, but the followup, *To Be True*, was the album that
firmly established the group. That album and *Wake Up Everybody* were
both certified gold-award, and major hits in 1975 were "Bad Luck" and
"Wake Up Everybody." However, the latter album was the group's final
album with Teddy Pendergrass, who had apparently become dissatisfied
with his anonymous status in the group. Switching to ABC Records by
1977, Harold Melvin suffered the loss of the rest of the group's members
and diminishing popularity, as ironically indicated by his late 1978 solo
album, *The Trip Is Over*. Melvin's most recent albums were recorded with
a reconstituted Blue Notes.

Teddy Pendergrass wisely stayed with Philadelphia International
Records. Not performing for almost a year, he emerged in 1977 as his
debut solo album was becoming an instant best-seller, yielding a moderate
hit with "I Don't Love You Anymore." Quickly established as one of the

most engaging soul singers of the Seventies, Pendergrass was elevated to the status of a sex symbol by means of his husky, sensual baritone voice, his natural, passionate, and sexy stage demeanor, and a repertoire based on lovemaking. His *Life Is a Song Worth Singing* was another best-seller, producing a major hit with "Close the Door." During 1978 he successfully performed concerts across the United States billed as "For Women Only," and 1979's *Teddy* became his third consecutive certified platinum-award album. At year's end, live recordings by Teddy Pendergrass were issued in a double-record set, followed in 1980 by *T.P.* On March 18, 1982, Pendergrass was severely injured in an automobile accident in Philadelphia that left him partially paralyzed.

HAROLD MELVIN AND THE BLUE NOTES

I Miss You	Philadelphia International	KZ–31468	August '72	
Black and Blue	Philadelphia International	KZ–32407	November '73	
To Be True*	Philadelphia International	KZ–33148	February '75	
Wake Up Everybody*	Philadelphia International	ZX–33808	November '75	A
Collector's Item	Philadelphia International	PZ–34232	June '76	A
Reaching for the World	ABC	AB–969	January '77	
Now Is the Time	ABC	AA–1041	December '77	
The Blue Album	Source	3197	March '80	A
All Things Happen in Time	MCA	5261	November '81	A

HAROLD MELVIN

The Trip Is Over	ABC	AA–1093	October '78

TEDDY PENDERGRASS

Teddy Pendergrass**	Philadelphia International	PZ–34390	February '77	A
Life Is a Song Worth Singing**	Philadelphia International	PZ–35095	April '78	A
Teddy**	Philadelphia International	FZ–36003	March '79	A
Teddy Live! Coast to Coast*	2-Philadelphia International	KZ2–36294	December '79	A

| TP** | Philadelphia International | FZ–36745 | August '80 | A |
| It's Time for Love | Philadelphia International | TZ–37491 | September '81 | A |

BETTE MIDLER.   An artist of remarkably wide-ranging talents as song stylist, comedienne, and cabaret performer, Bette Midler burst into prominence in 1972–73 through television appearances, live performances, and two best-selling albums. Perfecting the persona of The Divine Miss M during a long-running engagement at New York's notorious Continental Baths club, Midler projected the image of a street-wise, all-around entertainer through her flamboyant and uninhibited use of gutter comics and her command of a variety of musical styles. Touring the United States extensively with music director and early producer Barry Manilow in 1973, Bette Midler found her popularity dissipating as a result of a year's layoff from performing and recording in 1974. Re-established as a cabaret performer with her 1975 cross-country tour and box office record-breaking *Clams on the Half-Shell Revue*, Midler has since fared only modestly as a recording artist. Nonetheless, as an actress, Bette Midler won near-unanimous praise and an Academy Award nomination for her riveting performance in the title role of 1979's *The Rose*, portraying a tough but vulnerable rock star unable to escape the vicious cycle of liquor, drugs, sex, and public adulation.

Born in Paterson, New Jersey, on December 1, 1945, Bette Midler was raised in Honolulu, Hawaii, where she majored in drama at college for one year before securing a minor role in the 1965 film, *Hawaii*. Enabled to travel to the mainland with earnings from the film role, she ended up in New York, where she worked a variety of mundane jobs while securing roles in several off-Broadway productions and singing in clubs and restaurants for experience. During 1966 she landed a part in the chorus of *Fiddler on the Roof* and stayed with the show for three years, eventually working her way up to the central role of Tzeitel. In 1970 Midler decided to concentrate on the singing aspect of her career by devising a cabaret-style show that proved enormously popular at New York's Continental Baths, a group-games club largely frequented by homosexuals and transvestites. Playing piano and performing widely eclectic material, she developed the persona of The Divine Miss M as a street-wise, foul-mouthed, flamboyant singer and comedienne, backed by the female vocal trio, The Harlettes (Sharon Redd, Ula Hedwig, and Charlotte Crossley). Her Saturday night performances became *the* cult attraction of New York and led to national notoriety. Introduced to a larger audience through regular television appearances in 1972, Midler was signed to Atlantic Records, where her debut album, naturally titled *The Divine Miss M*, became an instant best-seller and led to successful engagements at exclusive clubs across the country. The album yielded a major hit with a remake of "Do You Want to Dance?" and a near-smash with the old Andrews Sisters' song, "Boogie Woogie Bugle Boy," while also containing her theme, the bittersweet "Friends," John Prine's "Hello In There," and remakes of "Chapel of Love" and "Leader of the Pack." Headliner at lavish New Year's Eve shows at Philharmonic Hall in 1972 and 1973, Midler successfully toured throughout the United States in 1973, accompanied by The Harlettes and pianist–music director Barry Manilow. Co-produced by Manilow, as had been her debut album, *Bette Midler* became a best-seller despite yielding no major hit single and containing such diverse material as "I Shall Be Released," "In the Mood," and "Uptown/Da Doo Run Run."

Bette Midler took 1974 off and Barry Manilow left to pursue his highly successful solo career early in the year. During 1975 she returned to live performance with a cross-country tour which concluded with her box office record-breaking *Clams on the Half-Shell Revue* on Broadway. However, 1976's *Songs for the New Depression* was greeted by negative critical reviews, sold much less well than prior releases, and failed to yield even a minor hit single. Midler's next album, the double-record *Live at Last*, fared even less well and, by the end of 1977, her *Broken Blossom* had been issued and she had appeared in her first television special on NBC, "Ol' Red Hair Is Back." In early 1978 The Harlettes left her and soon recorded an album for Columbia. Spending much of 1978 working on her first feature film for 20th Century-Fox, Midler eventually recorded *Thighs and Whispers* for 1979 release. The film, *The Rose*, won Midler excellent critical reviews and an Academy Award nomination for her intense and sensitive portrayal of a tough but vulnerable rock star seemingly unable to escape a maelstrom of liquor, drugs, and sex that leads to her self-destruction. The soundtrack album, which featured "When a Man Loves a Woman," "Stay with Me," and the smash hit "The Rose," was issued before year's end. In 1980 Simon and Schuster released the Bette Midler book, *A View from a Broad*, which chronicled her world tour; the R-rated film *Divine Madness*, released in the fall, recreated her bawdy one-woman Broadway show for the cinema. During 1981, Midler completed yet another film, *Jinxed*, under director Don Siegel.

BETTE MIDLER

The Divine Miss M*	Atlantic	SD–7238	November '72	A
Bette Midler*	Atlantic	SD–7270	November '73	A
Songs for the New Depression	Atlantic	SD–18155	January '76	A
Live at Last	2-Atlantic	SD2–9000	April '77	A
Broken Blossom	Atlantic	SD–19151	November '77	

REDD, HEDWIG, AND CROSSLEY

Formerly of The Harlettes	Columbia	JC–35250	January '78

BETTE MIDLER

Thighs and Whispers	Atlantic	SD–16004	August '79	A
The Rose (soundtrack) **	Atlantic	SD–16010	December '79	A
Divine Madness (soundtrack)	Atlantic	16022	November '80	A

THE STEVE MILLER BAND. Mistakenly identified with the "psyche-delic" movement emerging from San Francisco in the late Sixties, The Steve Miller Band signed with Capitol Records for a virtually un-precedented $60,000 advance and recorded two albums, often regarded as classics of the era, featuring sophisticated production, elaborate sound ef-fects, and the singing, guitar playing, and songwriting of William "Boz" Scaggs. The Steve Miller Band retained their reputation as an album band after Scaggs' departure and a variety of personnel changes to emerge as a widely popular commercial success with their 1973 *Joker* album and its top hit title single. Judiciously waiting over two years to release the follow-up, *Fly like an Eagle*, Miller achieved platinum-award level sales with that album and *Book of Dreams* based on his ability to manufacture consum-mate but inconsequential recordings, given his average voice and guitar playing and adequate but unexceptional songwriting.

Born in Milwaukee, Wisconsin, on October 5, 1943, Steve Miller moved with his family to Dallas, Texas, as an infant. He took up guitar at the age of five and formed his first blues band, The Marksmen Combo, at age 12 with friend William "Boz" Scaggs, born in Ohio on June 8, 1944. Enrolling at the University of Wisconsin in 1961, Miller assembled The Ardells, a white "soul" group, again with Scaggs, and played locally for more than three years. After college, Miller traveled to Chicago where he jammed with black bluesmen such as Muddy Waters and Buddy Guy and white blues players such as Paul Butterfield, Mike Bloomfield, and Barry Goldberg; Scaggs went to Europe and played around Scandinavia as a folksinger. The Miller–Goldberg Band was formed and signed to Epic, but Miller soon quit and returned to Texas before moving to San Francisco in 1966. There he formed The Steve Miller Blues Band with guitarist Curly Cooke, bassist Lonnie Turner, drummer Tim Davis, and later, with organist Jim Peterman. This group backed Chuck Berry on his *Live at the Fillmore* album; Miller, beseiged by contract offers, carefully and slowly conducted negotiations and eventually signed with Capitol Records for highly favorable terms, which included a $60,000 advance.

In September 1967 Curly Cooke dropped out of the group, by then known simply as The Steve Miller Band, and Miller summoned Boz Scaggs from Europe. This grouping (Miller, Scaggs, Peterman, Turner, and Davis) went to England to record their debut album. *Children of the Future*, issued in early 1968, was well-received critically although it was only minimally associated with "progressive" rock and "acid-rock" as claimed by some reviewers. Slickly produced, the album also bore little resemblance to the highly touted "San Francisco Sound" then emerging. The Steve Miller Band quickly recorded the follow-up, *Sailor*, employing carefully produced sound effects throughout. The album contained Miller's "Song for Our Ancestors," "Living in the U.S.A." (a minor hit), and "Quicksilver Girls" and Scaggs' "Overdrive," as well as one of Miller's theme songs, "Gangster of Love." Selling quite well, the album established the group as an album band, but Scaggs left in August 1968 and was soon followed by Jim Peterman. Subsequently featuring himself more on stage and in recordings, Miller recruited a new keyboardist–vocalist for the band's next two moderately selling albums but, by 1970, both he and Lonnie Turner had departed. Augmented by a new bassist, the remaining two originals, Miller and Tim Davis, traveled to Nashville to finish *Number Five*, after which Davis also left.

Enlisting bassist Ross Vallory (later a member of Journey) for the poorly selling *Rock Love* album, Steve Miller retained only his drummer for the even worse selling *Recall the Beginning*. Miller was subsequently laid up by illness for six months; when he reconvened the group with a returned Lonnie Turner, they recorded the band's first certified gold-award album, *The Joker*, which yielded a top hit with its trite and self-indulgent title song. Between the spring of 1974 and the summer of 1975, The Steve Miller Band did not perform live. New recording sessions by Miller with guitarist David Denny, Lonnie Turner, drummer Gary Mallaber, and others, produced *Fly like an Eagle* and *Book of Dreams*. *Fly like an Eagle*, considered Miller's strongest work since *Sailor*, yielded the near-smash hit "Take the Money and Run" and the smash hits "Rock'n Me" and "Fly like an Eagle." The album was certified platinum-award in September, and The Steve Miller Band's personnel stabilized with Miller, Denny, guitarist Greg Douglas, Mallaber, Turner, and keyboardist Byron Alfred by early 1977. *Book of Dreams*, certified platinum-award within a month of its release, also produced three major hit singles with "Jet Airliner," "Jungle Love," and "Swingtown" before year's end. The Steve Miller Band was thereafter relatively inactive, yet 1978's *Greatest Hits* became an instant best-seller. Finally, in late 1981, the group re-emerged with *Circle of Love*, which included the trite, side-long "Macho City."

THE STEVE MILLER BAND

Children of the Future	Capitol	SKAO–2920	May '68	A
Sailor	Capitol	ST–2984	October '68	A
Brave New World	Capitol	SKAO–184 reissued as SN–16078	June '69	A
Your Saving Grace	Capitol	SKAO–331 reissued as SN–16079	September '69	A
Number Five	Capitol	SKAO–436	July '70	A

Children of the Future/Living in the U.S.A.	2-Capitol	STBB–717	April '71	
Rock Love	Capitol	SW–748	September '71	A
Recall the Beginning . . . A Journey from Eden	Capitol	SMAS–11022	March '72	A
Anthology*	2-Capitol	SVBB–11114	November '72	A
The Joker*	Capitol	SMAS–11235	September '73	A
Fly like an Eagle**	Capitol	SW–11497	May '76	A
Book of Dreams**	Capitol	SO–11630	May '77	A
Greatest Hits 1974–1978**	Capitol	SOO–11872	November '78	A
Circle of Love	Capitol	12121	November '81	A

JONI MITCHELL. Gaining her first recognition as the composer of the classics "Circle Game" and "Both Sides Now" as recorded by Tom Rush and Judy Collins, respectively, in the late Sixties, Joni Mitchell developed an increasing following with her first two folk-style albums, based on her intensely personal, often confessional style of songwriting, her distinctive dulcimer and guitar playing, and her expressive, clear, and full-bodied soprano voice. Often using obscure yet sophisticated tunings on her stringed instruments, Mitchell employed a sense of harmony that went beyond the limits extant in both the rock and pop fields, whereas her songwriting—more accurately described as "song-poetry"—explored themes of romantic love, the independence achieved through love's loss, and the guarded optimism of the youthful humanitarian ethic in such fiercely personal and ruthlessly honest terms as to be embarassing were it not for their underlying poignancy. Introducing piano-based songs with 1970's *Ladies of the Canyon* album, Joni Mitchell was established in the forefront of the female singer–songwriter movement, along with Carole King, with the certified gold-award success of that album. Mitchell's *Blue* album marked a turning point, revealing an ever-growing poetic sensibility, more refined musicianship, and a willingness to experiment. Scoring her first major hit with "You Turn Me On, I'm a Radio" from the adventuresome *For the Roses* album, Joni Mitchell achieved her greatest commercial success with *Court and Spark*.

Constantly evolving poetically and musically (leading to comparisons with Bob Dylan), Joni Mitchell daringly left behind the lucrative and restrictive stereotype of pop-style singer–songwriter with *Hissing of Summer Lawns*, a frequently exotic album featuring complex, imaginative melodies, highly expressive singing, and less of her confessional style of songwriting. However, the album was almost unanimously denigrated by critics unable or unwilling to grant the artistic license she obviously sought. Regularly using jazz musicians beginning with *Hejira*, Mitchell had fully broken away from pop music with the ambitious *Don Juan's Reckless Daughter*, which included the side-long "Paprika Plains," recorded with full symphony orchestra. Thereby impressing ailing legendary jazz acoustic-bassist and composer Charles Mingus, Joni Mitchell collaborated with him on *Mingus* (completed after his death), which was received by critics as a bold if erratic episode in her constantly evolving career. Well known for her reclusiveness, Joni Mitchell emerged in 1979 with her first in-depth interview in more than ten years (published in *Rolling Stone*) and her first major tour in four years.

Born Roberta Joan Anderson on November 7, 1943, in McLeod, Alberta, Canada, Joni Mitchell was raised in Saskatoon, Saskatchewan, where she took up informal singing at age nine and developed an interest in painting and art. Taking up ukelele during her teens and later learning guitar, she performed in Calgary, Alberta's, best known coffeehouse, The Depression, while attending Alberta College of Art in pursuit of a career in commercial art. After a year, she decided to pursue folk-style music professionally and moved to Toronto, where she frequently played at clubs in that city's famed Yorktown district. There she met folksinger Chuck Mitchell, whom she soon married. They moved to Detroit in 1966 and later toured the East Coast folk circuit; but in less than two years, the marriage foundered. She subsequently moved to New York City, where she played folk clubs and struck up friendships with Judy Collins and Tom Rush among others. Signed to Reprise Records in 1967, Joni Mitchell gained her first recognition as a songwriter by means of Tom Rush's recording of her "Circle Game" and "Urge for Going" on his 1968 *Circle Game* album and Judy Collins' near-smash hit recording of her "Both Sides Now" late that year. Mitchell's debut album, sometimes referred to as *Song to a Seagull*, was produced in a thin and understated manner by David Crosby, who was then experiencing a career hiatus between The Byrds and Crosby, Stills, and Nash. Although the album sold minimally, it featured her own cover art and was entirely comprised of her own song compositions, including the poignant and brilliantly sung "Michael from Mountains," "I Had a King," and "Cactus Tree."

Joni Mitchell's second album, *Clouds*, included her colorful self-portrait and effectively established her in the forefront of the female singer–songwriter movement of the Seventies. The album contained her celebratory "Chelsea Morning," the ominous "The Fiddle and the Drum," and her own version of "Both Sides Now," as well as several movingly personal songs such as "I Don't Know Where I Stand," "Songs to Aging Children Come," and "I Think I Understand." Her next album, *Ladies of the Canyon*, again with her own cover art, became a best-seller and was certified as her first gold-award album by year's end. Bolstered commercially by the success of Crosby, Stills, Nash, and Young's version of her classic "Woodstock," the album introduced her use of the piano and included her own electrifying version of "Woodstock" (far and away superior to CSNY's rock version), the often recorded "Circle Game," and her first minor hit, the wry ecology song "Big Yellow Taxi." Containing wide-ranging music and varied emotional nuances, the album also included "For Free," a joyous look back at her pre-commercial days, the gentle autobiographical "Ladies of the Canyon," and "Willy," written about former lover Graham Nash. Joni Mitchell's final album for Reprise, *Blue*, showed her flowering as an arranger and continued her string of best-selling, highly personal, and exquisitely performed releases. Among the song inclusions were "All I Want," "California," "This Flight Tonight," "A Case of You" (her second minor hit), "Carey," and the disturbing "The Last Time I Saw Richard."

Switching to Asylum Records, Joni Mitchell recorded *For the Roses* as her debut for the label. The album, revealing jazz influences, included her first major hit, "You Turn Me On, I'm a Radio," as well as "Cold Blue Steel and Sweet Fire," "See You Sometime," and "Blonde in the Bleachers." *Court and Spark*, recorded with members of Tom Scott's jazz-style L.A. Express in addition to David Crosby, Graham Nash, and The Band's Robbie Robertson, became one of her most popular albums and yielded three hits with "Raised on Robbery," "Help Me" (a near-smash), and "Free Man in Paris." The album also included "People's Parties," the romantic title song, and a version of Lambert, Hendricks, and Ross' "Twisted," featuring background vocals by Cheech and Chong. Touring for the first time in several years during 1974 with Tom Scott and The L.A. Express, Joni Mitchell's live double-record set *Miles of Aisles* compiled much of her finest material and produced a major hit with "Big Yellow Taxi."

With 1975's *Hissing of Summer Lawns*, Joni Mitchell began to move beyond the restrictive role of female pop-style singer–songwriter. Eschewing the confessional style of songwriting in favor of songs both musically and lyrically ambitious and complex, Mitchell suffered near-unanimous critical disparagement for the album in the rock and pop press. Maintaining an even more reduced personal profile, she recorded *Hejira* with jazz bassist Jaco Pastorius, guitarist Larry Carlton, and L.A. Express drummer John Guerin. Regarded by some jazz critics as a masterpiece, this album included no piano songs yet encompassed a variety of musical textures and nuances on songs such as "Coyote," "Black Crow," and "Furry Sings the Blues." With 1977's double-record *Don Juan's Reckless Daughter*, Mitchell firmly broke with her pop music past, recording the album with Pastorius, Guerin, Latin percussionist Airto, and several members of the "fusion" group Weather Report. Inspiring critics to coin yet another hyphenated label, "folk-jazz," to describe the music, the album featured the side-long "Paprika Plains," recorded with full symphony orchestra.

"Paprika Plains," heard by ailing jazz bassist and composer Charles Mingus, so fascinated him that in the spring of 1978 he contacted Ms. Mitchell regarding the possibility of working together. She consented and Mingus soon turned over to her six tunes to which she was to supply lyrics, in addition to the Mingus standard, "Goodbye Pork Pie Hat." Mitchell worked on the collaboration for more than 18 months, but the project was not completed until after Mingus' death in January 1979. Recorded with

Wayne Shorter, Jaco Pastorius and drummer Peter Erskine of Weather Report, and popular "fusion" keyboardist Herbie Hancock, the album was greeted by equivocal reviews upon release. Mitchell's own guitar provided the most exceptional instrumental work on the album, and Mingus' difficult, elusive melodies seemed to overshadow her lyrics. The album contained "Goodbye Pork Pie Hat," three of the six specially written tunes, and Mitchell's own tribute to Mingus, "God Must Be a Boogie Man." The album also featured four paintings by Mitchell which were inspired by Mingus, including the back cover's touching *Charlie down in Mexico*. After the release of *Mingus*, Joni Mitchell assembled an ad hoc group with Pastorius, percussionist Don Alias, guitarist Pat Metheny, and others for her first public performances in four years. With Mitchell playing electric guitar, recordings from the tour were issued as *Shadows and Light* in the fall of 1980. That year, she worked on a 14-minute segment of the Canadian film, *Love*, writing and starring in her own mini-screenplay.

JONI MITCHELL

Joni Mitchell	Reprise	RS–6293	April '68	A
Clouds	Reprise	RS–6341	May '69	A
Ladies of the Canyon*	Reprise	RS–6376	April '70	A
Blue*	Reprise	MS–2038	June '71	A
For the Roses*	Asylum	SD–5057	November '72	A
Court and Spark*	Asylum	7E–1001	January '74	A
Miles of Aisles*	2-Asylum	AB–202	November '74	A
Hissing of Summer Lawns*	Asylum	7E–1051	November '75	A
Hejira*	Asylum	7E–1087	November '76	A
Don Juan's Reckless Daughter*	2-Asylum	BB–701	December '77	A
Mingus	Asylum	5E–505	June '79	A
Shadows and Light	Asylum	704	September '80	A

MOBY GRAPE. Sometimes labeled as legendary, Moby Grape was another of the groups to emerge from San Francisco in the late Sixties. Featuring a three-guitar lineup and interesting vocal harmonies, Moby Grape has even been called one of the earliest purveyors of "country-rock." The group's debut album is often considered a minor masterpiece, but their record label's massive promotional campaign (which included the simultaneous release of the album's content as singles) virtually destroyed the group's credibility with fans. Recording the early "jam" album *Grape Jam* before re-forming a number of times since their initial breakup in 1968, one of the latest incarnations of the group, now known simply as The Grape, issued *Live Grape* on their own label in 1978 in an attempt to stage a comeback.

MOBY GRAPE

Moby Grape	Columbia	CS–9498	June '67
Wow/Grape Jam	2-Columbia	CXS–3 also issued as CS– 9613	April '68
Wow	Columbia	CS–9613	
Grape Jam	Columbia	MGS–1	

SKIP SPENCE

Oar	Columbia	CS–9831	July '69

MOBY GRAPE

'69	Columbia	CS–9696	February '69
Truly Fine Citizen	Columbia	CS–9912	September '69
Omaha	Harmony	KH–30392	March '71
20 Granite Creek	Reprise	RS–6460	August '71
Great Grape	Columbia	31098	March '72

BOB MOSLEY

Bob Mosley	Reprise	MS–2068	May '72

THE GRAPE

Live Grape	Escape		April '78

THE MONKEES/ MIKE NESMITH. Crassly manufactured group of the late Sixties, The Monkees were essentially actors hired to portray musicians for an NBC–TV situation comedy series modeled on The Beatles' *A Hard Day's Night.* Don Kirshner, mastermind of the Brill Building professional songwriting "factory," was the show's musical director and his staff provided many of The Monkees' hits. Eventually allowed to actually play their own instruments on their albums (they only sang on their first two) and to tour the country, The Monkees appealed to pubescent and pre-pubescent fans, making them the first "teenybopper" group and opening the way for The Partridge Family, The Osmonds, and The Jackson Five during the Seventies. Since the group's 1969 breakup, only Michael Nesmith has been able to establish himself as a solo artist. Having provided Linda Ronstadt and The Stone Poneys with their first major hit, "Different Drum," Nesmith produced an instrumental album of his own songs, *The Wichita Train Whistle Sings,* and scored a major hit with "Joanne" in 1970. After forming the short-lived Countryside label in 1972, Mike Nesmith eventually established his own independent label, Pacific Arts, in the mid-Seventies.

The Monkees were created by NBC television in the spring of 1966 to portray musicians for the network's situation comedy series blatantly based on the zany antics performed by The Beatles in the movies *A Hard Day's Night* and *Help*. Chosen from auditions, The Monkees were: Michael Nesmith (guitar, vocals), Davy Jones (tambourine, vocals), Peter Tork (bass, vocals), and Mickey Dolenz (drums, vocals). Born in Los Angeles on March 8, 1946, Dolenz had been a child actor, whereas Jones, born in Manchester, England, on December 30, 1945, had played the role of Artful Dodger in the Broadway production of the musical *Oliver*. Dolenz had also been the lead singer of The Missing Links, and Jones had already unsuccessfully attempted a solo singing career before joining The Monkees. Both Tork, born in Washington, D.C., on February 13, 1946, and Nesmith, born in Houston, Texas, on December 30, 1943, had been performing music professionally before joining, Tork in Greenwich Village coffeehouses, Nesmith in California. "The Monkees" television series debuted in September 1966, with Don Kirshner as musical director. His songwriting staff provided the group with many of their hits, starting with Tommy Boyce and Bobby Hart's "Last Train to Clarksville." The series proved enormously successful and subsequent hits (on which the group *did not* play instruments) included the smashes "I'm a Believer" and "A Little Bit Me, a Little Bit You," both written by Neil Diamond. The Monkees' albums were instant best-sellers and quickly certified gold-award, as the members, led by Nesmith, were finally allowed to play their own instruments beginning with *Headquarters*. Touring the United States, briefly with Jimi Hendrix as the opening act, The Monkees' fourth album yielded a smash hit with Carole King and Gerry Goffin's "Pleasant Valley Sunday," whereas *The Birds, The Bees, and The Monkees* produced the smash hits "Daydream Believer" (by John Stewart) and "Valleri" (by Boyce and Hart). However, after scoring with Jerry Leiber and Mike Stoller's "D.W. Washburn," The Monkees never achieved another major hit. Peter Tork quit The Monkees following the film and soundtrack album *Head*, and *Instant Replay* was recorded by the remaining trio. By the end of 1969, The Monkees had disbanded. Davy Jones subsequently recorded an unsuccessful solo album for Bell Records in 1971 and later reunited with Mickey Dolenz and songwriters Tommy Boyce and Bobby Hart for an American tour and one album in 1975–76.

Only Michael Nesmith was able to establish himself as a solo artist. Earlier, he had provided Linda Ronstadt and The Stone Poneys with their first major hit, "Different Drum," and produced and conducted an instrumental album of his own songs, *The Wichita Train Whistle Sings*. Signed to RCA Records, he formed The First National Band, often regarded as among the finest "country-rock" bands to emerge from Los Angeles, with pedal steel guitarist Orville "Red" Rhodes; they recorded two albums and scored a major hit in the fall of 1970 with Nesmith's "Joanne." With The First National Band falling into disarray during the recording of *Nevada Fighter*, the album was completed with legendary guitarist James Burton (sessions guitarist for Rick Nelson and Elvis Presley) and keyboardist Glen D. Hardin, both later members of Emmylou Harris' Hot Band. Nesmith formed The Second National Band, again with Rhodes, for *Tantamount to Treason*, but this group also broke up, leaving just the two, Nesmith and Rhodes, to record *And the Hits Just Keep On Coming*, generally regarded as Nesmith's finest work to date.

During 1972 Michael Nesmith founded his own label, Countryside, in conjunction with Elektra Records, and formed The Countryside Band, again with Red Rhodes, for his final recording for RCA, *Pretty Much Your Standard Ranch Trash*. Countryside was later abandoned when David Geffen succeeded to the presidency of Elektra. Nesmith allowed his RCA contract to expire, purchased his old masters, and formed Pacific Arts Records in the mid-Seventies. The label's first release, *The Prison*, was initially distributed through mail orders, and Pacific Arts has since reissued some of Nesmith's RCA material in addition to his more recent material. Becoming somewhat of a cult figure, Michael Nesmith continues to run Pacific Arts, records for the label, and independently distributes albums by himself, Kaleidoscope, Chris Darrow, Charles Lloyd, and others.

DAVID JONES

David Jones	Colpix	CP–493	October '65	

THE MONKEES

The Monkees*	Colgems	COS–101	September '66	
More of The Monkees*	Colgems	COS–102	January '67	
Monkees' Head-quarters*	Colgems	COS–103	May '67	
Pisces, Aquarius, Capricorn, and Jones, Ltd.*	Colgems	COS–104	November '67	
The Birds, The Bees, and The Monkees*	Colgems	COS–109	May '68	
Head (soundtrack)	Colgems	COSO–5008	November '68	
Instant Replay	Colgems	COS–113	February '69	
The Monkees Present	Colgems	COS–117	October '69	

THE MONKEES ANTHOLOGIES AND COMPILATIONS

Greatest Hits	Colgems	COS–115	June '69	
Changes	Colgems	COS–119	July '70	
Barrel Full	2-Colgems	SCOS–1001	March '71	
Greatest Hits	Arista	AL–4089	July '76	A

DAVY JONES

Davy Jones	Bell	6067	January '72	

DOLENZ, JONES, BOYCE, AND HART

Dolenz, Jones, Boyce, and Hart	Capitol	ST–11513	June '76	

MIKE NESMITH

The Wichita Train Whistle Sings	Dot reissued on	25861	July '68	
	Pacific Arts	7–113		A

MIKE NESMITH AND THE FIRST NATIONAL BAND

Magnetic South	RCA	LSP–4371	May '70
Loose Salute	RCA	LSP–4415	November '70
Nevada Fighter	RCA	LSP–4497	May '71

MIKE NESMITH AND THE SECOND NATIONAL BAND

Tantamount to Treason	RCA	LSP–4563	February '72

MIKE NESMITH

And the Hits Just Keep On Comin'	RCA reissued on	LSP–4695	August '72	
	Pacific Arts	9439 reissued as	May '77	
		7–116		A
Pretty Much Your Standard Ranch Trash	RCA reissued on	APL1– 0164	December '73	
	Pacific Arts	9440 reissued as	May '77	
		7–117		A
The Prison	Pacific Arts	9428 reissued as		
		11–101		A
Compilation	Pacific Arts	9425 reissued as	February '77	
		7–106		A
From a Radio Engine to a Photon Wing	Pacific Arts	9486 reissued as	March '77	
		7–107	April '79	A
Live at the Palais	Pacific Arts		August '78	
		reissued as 7–118	June '79	A
Infinite Rider on the Big Dogma	Pacific Arts	7–130	June '79	A

THE MOODY BLUES. Initially formed as a British rhythm-and-blues band in 1964, The Moody Blues suffered the departures of two founding members after breaking through in the United States with "Go Now!" in early 1965. Regrouping, they recorded the landmark *Days of Future Passed* album which established the precedent for their subsequent recording career. Recorded with The London Symphony Orchestra, the album was hailed for its fusion of rock and classical musics, leading to the invention of the term "progressive" to describe subsequent experimentation by rock groups with classical instrumentation and/or compositions. Thereby paving the way for groups such as Yes, Genesis, and The Electric Light Orchestra and serving to encourage other groups such as Deep Purple to record with full orchestras, the album's success also prompted the proliferation of "concept" albums, of which *Days of Future Passed* was ostensibly one of the first. The album is also noteworthy for its use and popularization of the mellotron, an advanced keyboard-synthesizer instrument that enables its player to produce prerecorded sounds of non-keyboards. Without using an orchestra, *In Search of the Lost Chord* retained this lush and sumptuous sound, as the members played more than 30 instruments on the album. Moreover, Tony Clarke's immaculate production, coupled with the recurrence of conceptual themes and vaguely philosophical and often poetic lyrics, resulted in a formula that The Moody Blues pursued through 1972's *Seventh Sojourn*. Forming their own record label Threshold in 1969, the group also managed themselves and promoted their own tours, unlike most acts. The members worked on a variety of solo and duo projects after 1973, eventually reuniting in 1978 for the certified platinum-award *Octave* album and a sell-out worldwide tour.

Formed around 1964 in Birmingham, England, by vocalist–guitarist Denny Laine (born Brian Haynes in Birmingham on October 29, 1944), keyboardist–vocalist Mike Pinder (born in Birmingham on December 27, 1941), flutist–vocalist Ray Thomas (born in Stourport-on-Severn, England, on December 29, 1942), bassist–vocalist Clint Warwick (born in Birmingham on June 25, 1949), and drummer Graeme Edge (born in Rochester, England, on March 30, 1944), The Moody Blues debuted at London's famed Marquee club and quickly signed with British Decca (London/Deram in the United States). Only Laine was a well-known musician, having led Denny Laine and The Diplomats between 1962 and 1964. The Moody Blues' second single, the blues-style "Go Now!," became a smash British and major American hit in early 1965, but the initial lineup never again achieved even a moderate hit. In 1966 both Laine and Warwick left, Laine to front the short-lived Electric String Band in 1967, to form Balls with Trevor Burton (formerly with The Move) in 1969, and eventually to join Paul McCartney's Wings in 1971.

Suffering declining popularity, The Moody Blues added vocalist–multi-instrumentalists Justin Hayward (born in Swindon, Wiltshire, England on October 14, 1946) and John Lodge (born in Birmingham on July 20, 1945), with Hayward usually playing guitar and Lodge bass. Nearly disbanding, the group obtained a mellotron and embarked on a totally new musical direction. The new lineup's debut album, *Days of Future Passed*, eschewed the members' blues backgrounds and was hailed as both a "concept" album and for its adventurous fusion of rock and classical musics. Recorded with The London Symphony Orchestra and produced by Tony Clarke, the album yielded a major hit with "Tuesday Afternoon" and included the classic "Nights in White Satin," a smash hit upon re-release in 1972. For their next album, *In Search of the Lost Chord*, The Moody Blues made extensive use of the mellotron and played more than 30 different instruments to produce their characteristic lush, sumptuous sound without an orchestra. The album included the favorites "Legend of a Mind" and "Om" and produced a minor hit with "Ride My See-Saw." In 1969 *On the Threshold of a Dream* was issued, yielding another minor hit with "Never Comes the Day" and remaining on the album charts for more than two years. However, the group's songs had become so intricate that they were not able to replicate them live, onstage. During that same year they formed Threshold Records and the label's first album release, *To Our Children's Children's Children*, containing band favorites such as "Higher and Higher" and "I Never Thought I'd Live to Be a Hundred/Million," became an instant best-seller.

The year 1970 was probably The Moody Blues' most successful, as all of the group's albums with their second lineup were certified gold-award during the year, including that fall's *A Question of Balance*. This album yielded a major hit with "Question" and was followed by "The Story in Your Eyes" from *Every Good Boy Deserves Favour*. *Seventh Sojourn* produced two major hits, "Isn't Life Strange" and "I'm Just a Singer (in a Rock and Roll Band)," but after a worldwide tour in 1973, the members of The Moody Blues settled down for a variety of outside projects. The first and most successful of these, Justin Hayward and John Lodge's *Blue Jays*, yielded two minor hits with "I Dreamed Last Night" and "Blue Guitar" and was accompanied by a sell-out European tour. Other projects through 1977 included two solo albums by Ray Thomas, two albums by Graeme Edge with Adrian Gurvitz, and solo sets by Michael Pinder, Justin Hayward, and John Lodge.

Earlier The Moody Blues had issued the double-record compilation set *This Is The Moody Blues* and, in mid-1977, *Caught Live + 5*, which contained a live recording from 1969 and five previously unreleased songs from the *In Search of the Lost Chord* period. Then, in July 1977, the five announced their intention to reunite for yet another album. Issued in mid-1978, *Octave* became an instant best-seller and even yielded two minor hits with "Steppin' in a Slide Zone" and "Driftwood." After the album's release, The Moody Blues conducted a successful worldwide tour with Patrick Moraz, formerly of Yes, substituting for Michael Pinder. A 30-city U.S. tour in November and December proved successful, and Moraz joined The Moody Blues permanently, although Pinder would still join the band for recording sessions. In 1980 Justin Hayward recorded the solo set, *Night Flight*, for Deram Records. In 1981, The Moody Blues issued *Long Distance Voyager*, scoring hits with "The Voice" and "Meanwhile."

THE MOODY BLUES

Number 1	London	428	August '65
In the Beginning	Deram	DES–18051	February '71
Days of Future Passed*	Deram	DES–18012	April '68
In Search of the Lost Chord*	Deram	DES–18017	September '68

On the Threshold of a Dream*	Deram	DES– 18025	May '69	
To Our Children's Children's Children*	Threshold	THS–1	January '70	A
A Question of Balance*	Threshold	THS–3	September '70	A
Every Good Boy Deserves Favour*	Threshold	THS–5	July '71	
Seventh Sojourn*	Threshold	THS–7	October '72	

JUSTIN HAYWARD AND JOHN LODGE

Blue Jays	Threshold	THS–14	March '75

GRAEME EDGE BAND WITH ADRIAN GURVITZ

Kick Off Your Muddy Boots	Threshold	THS–15	August '75
Paradise Ballroom	London	686	June '77

RAY THOMAS

From Mighty Oaks	Threshold	THS–16	August '75
Hopes, Wishes, and Dreams	Threshold	THS–17	July '76

MICHAEL PINDER

The Promise	Threshold	THS–18	April '76

JUSTIN HAYWARD

Songwriter	Deram	DES– 18073	February '77
Night Flight	Deram	4801	July '80	A

JOHN LODGE

Natural Avenue	London	PS–683	April '77

THE MOODY BLUES

This Is The Moody Blues*	2-Threshold	THS–12/13	November '74	
Caught Live + 5	2-London	2PS–690/1	May '77	
Octave**	London	PS–708	June '78	
Long Distance Voyager**	Threshold	2901	June '81	A

VAN MORRISON/THEM. Founding member and lead vocalist of the rhythm-and-blues style group Them, perhaps the first Irish group to gain international popularity, Van Morrison wrote and recorded the rock classic "Gloria" with the group in early 1966. With Them recruiting a new

lead vocalist for several obscure albums following his subsequent departure, Morrison moved to the United States and scored his first solo hit with
"Brown-Eyed Girl." Changing labels, Van Morrison recorded the compel-
lingly evocative *Astral Weeks* album, often regarded as one of the ten
essential albums of rock music. Impossible to classify, the album was a subtle and fragile, intensely personal admixture of songs at once emotionally
accessible, subtly romantic, and intellectually stimulating, as evidenced
by the album's two extended cuts, "Cyprus Avenue" and "Madame
George." Quickly developing a limited yet fanatical following, Morrison
established himself as an album artist with 1970's *Moondance*. Containing
up-tempo dance songs, joyous love songs, and subtle songs of mystery and
longing, the album set the precedent for his subsequent recordings. He
continued to record best-selling albums through 1974 featuring his stunning vocal stylizations, replete with melismas, repeated words or phrases,
and jazz-style "scat" singing that occasionally drew the attention of even
jazz fans. Certainly one of the most enigmatic and private figures of Seventies rock, a reputation bolstered by Morrison's hostility to the music industry, his erratic and retiring stage manner, and his reluctance to indulge
the rock press with regular interviews, he retired from recording and performing after a grueling round of tours in 1973-74. Van Morrison re-
established himself in the hearts of fans as a compelling vocalist,
songwriter, and performer in 1978 with another round of tours and his
Wavelength album.

Born George Ivan in Belfast, Northern Ireland, on August 13, 1945,
into a musical family, Van Morrison began singing at the age of 12 and attained proficiency on guitar, harmonica, and saxophone by age 13. In
1960, at the age of 15, he dropped out of high school to pursue a musical
career. He initially played and sang with Deanie Sands and The Javelins
and joined the rhythm-and-blues band The Monarchs in 1961 for engagements throughout Great Britain and Europe. Around 1964 Morrison
formed Them in Belfast, and the group soon secured a regular engagement
at a local rhythm-and-blues club and attracted a following. Morrison
served as the mainstay of the group, as personnel changes occurred
regularly. Signed to British Decca (Parrot in the United States), Them
traveled to London to record that winter and scored their first major
British and American hit with producer–songwriter Bert Berns' "Here
Comes the Night" in early 1965. The group's debut album also included
their second hit "Mystic Eyes" and the rock classic "Gloria," twice a minor
hit, the second time backed with "Baby, Please Don't Go," which featured
lead guitarist Jimmy Page. *Them Again* was issued in the spring of 1966
and the group was soon completing their first and only tour of the United
States. However, upon returning to Britain in June 1966, Van Morrison
quit the band. The group recruited Keith McDowell as lead vocalist, but
neither their singles nor albums for Tower sold well.

Invited to the United States by record producer Bert Berns, Van Morrison initially settled in Boston and began recording for Berns' Bang
Records. In the summer of 1967 Morrison scored his first solo hit with his
own composition of "Brown-Eyed Girl" and, by the fall, Bang had as-

sembled *Blowin' Your Mind* from songs originally recorded as singles, much to Morrison's chagrin. Nonetheless, the album did contain two songs that served as precursors to his landmark *Astral Weeks* album, "T.B. Sheets" and "Who Drove the Red Sports Car." Berns died at the end of 1967 and Morrison played East Coast clubs as a member of a trio for six months, until his recording contract was bought up by Warner Brothers Records. His debut solo album for the label, *Astral Weeks*, recorded in 48 hours with a veteran jazz rhythm section, was issued before the end of 1968. Greeted by critical acclaim but poor sales, the album featured an impressionistic kind of lyricism that was at once evocative, intelligent, and undeniably compelling. Propelled by Morrison's unique vocal style and distinctive stream-of-consciousness lyrics, the album showcased his stirring "Cypress Avenue" and "Madame George" while also containing "Ballerina" and "Slim Slo Slider."

Van Morrison's next album, *Moondance*, did not appear until more than a year after *Astral Weeks*. Produced by Morrison, the album was recorded with saxophonist Jack Schroer, guitarist John Platania, and bassist John Klingberg, and sported a diversity of mature material. It yielded a moderate hit with "Come Running" and included a number of Morrison favorites such as "These Dreams of You," "Stoned Me," "Moondance," "Crazy Love," "Caravan," and "Into the Mystic," the last often regarded as one of the most finely crafted songs in rock history. Thereby established as an album artist, Morrison then moved to Woodstock, New York, and quickly recorded *His Band and Street Choir*, again with Schroer, Platania, and Klingberg, among others. The album produced two major hits with "Domino" and "Blue Money" while also containing "I've Been Working," "Gypsy Queen," and "Call Me Up in Dreamland." In the spring of 1971 Morrison moved to northern California's Marin County and later dismissed his Band and Street Choir, recording the countrified *Tupelo Honey* in San Francisco with Schroer, bassist Bill Church, keyboardist Mark Jordan, and guitarist Ronnie Montrose. Co-produced by Morrison, the album yielded a major hit with "Wild Night" and included more favorites such as "Old Woodstock," "I Wanna Roo You," and "Moonshine Whiskey."

Saint Dominic's Preview, ostensibly the first album over which Van Morrison exercised total artistic control, continued his best-selling ways, although it produced only two minor hits with "Jackie Wilson Said" and "Redwood Tree," yet included the stunning "Listen to the Lion." *Hard Nose the Highway* sold quite well without yielding even a minor hit, and Morrison soon embarked on his first full-scale tour of Europe and America with the Caledonia Soul Orchestra, which resulted in the live double-record set, *It's Too Late to Stop Now*. However, in 1974, he disbanded his group and recorded *Veedon Fleece* before "retiring" for nearly three years, including more than a year's exile in England. Eventually re-emerging in 1977 with *A Period of Transition*, Morrison took on rock impressario Bill Graham as his manager in 1978. He staged a dramatic comeback with *Wavelength*, thought to be his finest album in years, and conducted his first American tour in over four years. In 1979 Van Morrison recorded *Into the Music* and again toured, recording *Common One* the following year.

THEM

Here Comes the Night	Parrot	PAS–71005	July '65
Them Again	Parrot	PAS–71008	April '66
Now and Them	Tower	ST–5104	March '68
Time Out! Time In! For Them	Tower	ST–5116	October '68

THEM ANTHOLOGIES AND COMPILATIONS

Them	Happy Tiger	HT–1004		
Them in Reality	Happy Tiger	HT–1012	October '70	
Them Featuring Van Morrison	2-Parrot	BP–71053/ 4	July '72	
Backtracking	London	639	October '74	
Story of Them	London	50001	March '77	A

VAN MORRISON

Blowin' Your Mind	Bang	BLPS–218	September '67	
The Best of Van Morrison	Bang	BLPS–222	November '70	A
T.B. Sheets	Bang	BLPS–400	January '74	
Astral Weeks	Warner Brothers	WS–1768	November '68	A
Moondance*	Warner Brothers	WS–1835 reissued as BSK– 3103	March '70	A
His Band and Street Choir	Warner Brothers	WS–1884	December '70	A
Tupelo Honey*	Warner Brothers	WS–1950	October '71	A
Saint Dominic's Preview	Warner Brothers	BS–2633	July '72	A
Hard Nose the Highway	Warner Brothers	BS–2712	July '73	
It's Too Late to Stop Now	2-Warner Brothers	2BS–2760	February '74	A
Veedon Fleece	Warner Brothers	BS–2805	October '74	A
A Period of Transition	Warner Brothers	BS–2987	April '77	A
Wavelength	Warner Brothers	BSK–3212	September '78	A
Into the Music	Warner Brothers	HS–3390	August '79	A
Common One	Warner Brothers	HS–3462	August '80	A

MOTT (THE HOOPLE)/IAN HUNTER/MICK RONSON. Seminal English rock band of the early Seventies, Mott the Hoople featured the songwriting and singing of Ian Hunter through four poorly received albums for Atlantic Records. Briefly disbanding, Mott the Hoople reassembled at the prompting of David Bowie, who provided the group with their only major hit, "All the Young Dudes." Successfully touring the United States as headliners in 1973 during the rise of so-called "glitter-rock," Mott the Hoople later added guitar virtuoso Mick Ronson, from Bowie's Spiders From Mars band, but the relationship lasted a scant six months, and Hunter and Ronson left to pursue marginally successful solo careers, initially together as The Hunter–Ronson Band. Ian Hunter eventually broke through with 1979's *You're Never Alone with a Schizophrenic*, on which he was assisted by Ronson.

In the mid-Sixties, Silence was formed by Overend Pete Watts (born in Birmingham, England, on May 13, 1947) and Dale "Buffin" Griffin (born in Leeds, England, on October 24, 1948) in Herefordshire, later adding Mick Ralphs (born in Hereford, England, on May 31, 1944) and Verden Allen (born in Hereford on May 26, 1944). Recruiting vocalist Ian Hunter (born in Shrewsbury, England, on June 3, 1946) in London in 1969, the band changed their name to Mott the Hoople in June at the suggestion of manager Guy Stevens, who secured the group a recording contract with Island Records (Atlantic in the United States). The members: Ian Hunter (piano, guitar, lead vocals), Mick Ralphs (guitar, vocals), Verden Allen (organ), Overend Pete Watts (bass, vocals), and Dale Griffin (drums, vocals). With Hunter serving as primary songwriter as well as visual and aural focus of the group, Mott the Hoople recorded their debut album later in 1969, but it barely made the album charts when issued in 1970. *Mad Shadows* showcased Hunter's rather forceful style on a collection of gloomy songs, whereas *Wildlife* featured Ralphs' lighter style. However, neither of those albums nor *Brain Capers*, which included "Sweet Angeline," registered much impact. Disbanding in March 1972, Mott the Hoople re-formed at the encouragement of "glitter-rock" star David Bowie, who produced the band's debut album for Columbia and wrote the group's only major American hit, "All the Young Dudes." With Hunter assuming leadership of the group, Verden Allen quit in January 1973, followed in July by Mick Ralphs, who subsequently joined the enormously successful Bad Company. Allen was later permanently replaced by keyboardist Morgan Fisher, and former Spooky Tooth guitarist Luther Grosvenor (using the name Ariel Bender) took over for Ralphs on Mott the Hoople's August 1973 headlining "glitter-rock" tour of the United States. *Mott* had been critically well received, at least in the United States, and yielded major British hits with "Honaloochie Boogie" and "All the Way from Memphis," while also containing "Ballad of Mott the Hoople." *The Hoople* included the group's final, albeit minor, American hit, "The Golden Age of Rock 'n' Roll," as well as "Roll Away the Stone."

However, in August 1974, Luther Grosvenor left Mott the Hoople, and was replaced by guitarist Mick Ronson. Ronson, who had taken piano lessons as a child and experimented with violin and recorder before taking up guitar at age 17, had been instrumental in forming David Bowie's Spiders From Mars band, providing the major musical force behind Bowie's *Man Who Sold the World* and *Hunky Dory* albums. Ronson had pursued a solo career following Bowie's "retirement" from performing in 1973, recorded the solo set *Slaughter on Tenth Avenue*, and toured during the spring of 1974. Perhaps Mott the Hoople's best-selling album, *Live*, was issued near the end of 1974, but in December, both Ronson and Hunter left amid unbecoming rumors and public recriminations. Ronson soon issued his second solo album, *Play, Don't Worry*, and, after six months, the group reassembled as simply Mott, with Watts, Griffin, and Fisher plus guitarist–vocalist Ray Major and lead vocalist Nigel Benjamin. Mott recorded their final album, *Shouting and Pointing*, in 1976, before disbanding in November. With John Fiddler of Medicine Head replacing Benjamin, the other four re-emerged as The British Lion in 1977.

Ian Hunter subsequently moved to New York and began working with Mick Ronson, recording *Ian Hunter with Mick Ronson* and touring as The Hunter–Ronson Show during 1975. The two later separated, as Ronson joined Bob Dylan's late 1975 Rolling Thunder Revue and Hunter recorded the poorly selling *All-American Alien Boy*. Hunter's third solo album, *Overnight Angels*, was only issued briefly in the United States, after which Columbia dropped him from their roster. Ronson produced Roger McGuinn's *Cardiff Rose* album and later assisted Hunter in the production and arrangement of *You're Never Alone with a Schizophrenic*, on which Ronson also played guitar. The well-received album became Ian Hunter's best-selling solo album ever, yielding a minor hit with "Just Another Night." Shortly after the release of the anthology set *Shades of Ian Hunter*, Barry Manilow scored a major hit with his "Ships." Recorded at the Roxy in Los Angeles in the fall of 1979 with Ronson, 1980's *Welcome to the Club* included several Mott favorites as well as Ronson's instrumental "FBI" and Hunter's "Once Bitten, Twice Shy."

MOTT THE HOOPLE

Mott the Hoople	Atlantic	SD–8258	May '70	
Mad Shadows	Atlantic	SD–8272	November '70	
Wildlife	Atlantic	SD–8284	April '71	
Brain Capers	Atlantic	SD–8304	February '72	
Rock and Roll Queen	Atlantic	SD–7297	June '74	
All the Young Dudes	Columbia	PC–31750	October '72	A
Mott	Columbia	PC–32425	August '73	A
The Hoople	Columbia	PC–32871	April '74	
Live	Columbia	PC–33282	November '74	A
Greatest Hits	Columbia	PC–34368	November '76	A

MOTT

Drive On	Columbia	PC–33705	October '75
Shouting and Pointing	Columbia	PC–34236	July '76

MICK RONSON

Slaughter on Tenth Avenue	RCA	APL1– 0353	March '74

| Play, Don't Worry | RCA | APL1–0681 | January '75 | |

IAN HUNTER

Ian Hunter with Mick Ronson	Columbia	PC–33480	April '75	A
All-American Alien Boy	Columbia	PC–34142	April '76	A
Overnight Angels	Columbia	PC–34721	June '77	
Shades of Ian Hunter: The Ballad of Ian Hunter and Mott the Hoople	2-Columbia	C2–36251	October '79	A
You're Never Alone with a Schizophrenic	Chrysalis	CHR–1214	April '79	A
Live: Welcome to the Club	2-Chrysalis	CHR–1269	April '80	A
Short Back 'n' Sides	Chrysalis	CHR–1326	October '81	A

MUDDY WATERS. One of the few black blues artists to achieve widespread recognition and admiration from white audiences, Muddy Waters was instrumental in establishing the sound and style known as "Chicago blues" that influenced a whole generation of black blues musicians in the late Forties and Fifties and the entire white blues "revival" of the late Sixties. His first release on Chess, "Rollin' Stone," was later adopted as the name of both the heavily rhythm-and-blues–influenced English "superstar" group and the underground rock music–oriented periodical. Fully established as a rhythm-and-blues recording star by 1952 on the strength of his powerful and intricate vocal style and distinctive, hard-driving bottleneck guitar playing, Muddy Waters' early Fifties band was one of the first electric blues bands in the world, with Little Walter Jacobs' amplification of his harmonica being probably the first such instance in music history. During the Fifties and Sixties, virtually every practitioner of the Chicago-style blues populated his bands at one time or another, including Willie Dixon, James Cotton, Otis Spann, Buddy Guy, and Junior Wells, making Waters' band the proving ground for young blues musicians. His recordings during the Fifties reads like a compendium of the greatest blues songs, as they included "Hoochie Coochie Man," "I Just Want to Make Love to You," "I Got My Mojo Working," and others. Bringing Chuck Berry to Chess Records in 1955, Muddy Waters was overwhelmed by the rise of rock-and-roll in the late Fifties. Nonetheless, he became one of the few black blues artists to benefit from both the folk boom of the early Sixties and the British blues revival of the late Sixties. Subjected to unsympathetic treatment by Chess Records during the Seventies, Muddy Waters finally found a compatible setting in the late Seventies with Blue Sky Records, where he was produced and joined by Johnny Winter for the most successful albums of his 30-year-plus career.

Born McKinley Morganfield in Rolling Forks, Mississippi, on April 4, 1915, Muddy Waters moved at an early age to Clarksdale, where he grew up on the Stovall plantation. He started playing harmonica at the age of seven and switched to guitar at age 17. Strongly influenced by blues guitarists Son House and Robert Johnson, Waters developed a distinctive style of acoustic guitar playing using a bottleneck that produced a remarkable biting, stinging sound. Becoming the area's best known and most popular blues artist through engagements at picnics, dances, and small clubs, he was sought out by folklorist Alan Lomax, who first recorded Waters during the summers of 1941 and 1942. These classic recordings are still available on Testament Records. In May 1943 Waters permanently left Mississippi for Chicago, where he played local clubs and obtained his first electric guitar in 1945. Around 1946 he made his first commercial recordings for Columbia Records, but they were not released until years later, on Testament Records. Signing with Aristocrat Records (which became Chess in 1949) in 1947, Waters recorded the blues classics "I Can't Be Satisfied" and "I Feel Like Going Home" in early 1948, and the record became Aristocrat's biggest seller. He began playing larger clubs and scored another rhythm-and blues hit with "Rollin' Stone," his first release on Chess.

Around 1950 Muddy Waters began recording with harmonica players Little Walter (Jacobs) and Walter Horton. Waters soon scored the rhythm-and-blues hits "Louisiana Blues" with Jacobs and "Long Distance Call" with Horton in 1951. Forming his own band with Jacobs and second guitarist Jimmy Rogers, Waters hit with "She Moves Me" in early 1952. Augmented by pianist Otis Spann, this legendary blues band, the prototype of all subsequent Chicago blues bands, defined the style of modern blues. Jacobs left the band in 1952 and later recordings featured Horton or Jacobs sitting in. Rhythm-and-blues hits continued with "Mad Love," the Willie Dixon-composed classics "I'm Your Hoochie Coochie Man," "(I) Just (Want to) Make Love to You" and "I'm Ready," plus "Mannish Boy," "Sugar Sweet," "Forty Days and Forty Nights" and "Don't Go No Farther" through 1956. Jimmy Rogers left the band around 1956, but Spann stayed on until his death in 1968.

In 1955 Muddy Waters brought Chuck Berry to Chess Records, where he was quickly signed. However, by 1956 Waters was being overwhelmed by the rise of so-called "rock-and-roll" as practiced by Berry, Bill Haley, Elvis Presley, and others. Waters' last rhythm-and-blues hit came in 1958 with "Close to You," recorded with harmonica player James Cotton, bassist Willie Dixon, and of course, Otis Spann. Muddy Waters' first album, initially issued as *The Best of Muddy Waters* (reissued as *Sail On*) was released in 1958 and contained most of his best-remembered recordings, including "I Can't Be Satisfied," "Rollin' Stone," "Long Distance Call," "Honey Bee," "Mad Love," "Hoochie Coochie Man," and "Just Make Love to You." However, the album failed to sell in significant quantities as rock-and-roll had become *the* music of young blacks and whites.

Nonetheless, Muddy Waters was able to maintain some of his popularity in conjunction with the folk movement of the late Fifties and early Sixties. He played the 1960 Newport Festival, live recordings of which were released as an album, and recorded infrequent albums with the word "folk" in the title. Waters played unamplified guitar on *Folk Singer*, which included "Feel Like Going Home" and the Sonny Boy Williamson classic "Good Morning, Little School Girl." *Brass and the Blues* found him struggling with a brass section, and other late Sixties albums included odd couplings with Bo Diddley and Little Walter and with Howlin' Wolf and Bo Diddley. In 1968 the Chess subsidiary Cadet issued the deplorable *Electric Mud*, Waters' first album chart entry, followed by *After the Rain* and, on Chess, *Fathers and Sons*, recorded with Otis Spann and white blues players such as Mike Bloomfield and Paul Butterfield. At this time he was receiving the praise of a number of British and American artists strongly influenced by his work, including Bloomfield, Eric Clapton, and Mick Jagger. However, when Leonard Chess died in October 1969, the Chess organization was bought out by GRT, and Waters no longer received the personal treatment to which he had become accustomed. A variety of albums were issued by Chess/GRT for Muddy Waters through 1975, including the ubiquitous *London Sessions*, but none served to truly encourage sales.

Finally, in 1976, Muddy Waters moved to Blue Sky Records. With white blues artists Johnny and Edgar Winter and guitarist Rick Derringer on the label's roster, Waters was finally again in the position of receiving sympathetic treatment from his record company. His debut for Blue Sky, *Hard Again*, was produced by Johnny Winter, who also played on the album, as did James Cotton. Greeted by excellent critical reviews, the album became Waters' second album chart entry. Shortly after the album's release, Waters successfully toured with Winter and Cotton. *I'm Ready*, again produced by Johnny Winter, featured as players Winter and old associates Walter Horton and Jimmy Rogers. Waters again toured the country in 1978, concluding the year as opening act to none other than Eric Clapton in Europe. *Live*, again produced by Winter, compiled recordings made during the 1977 and 1978 tours.

MUDDY WATERS

Down on Stovall's Plantation (recorded 1941–42)	Testament	T–2210(M)	June '69	A
Chicago Blues: The Beginning (recorded 1946)	Testament	T–2207(M)		A
The Best of Muddy Waters	Chess	LP–1427 (M)	September '58	
reissued as Sail On	Chess	LP–1539 (E)	December '69	
Sings "Big Bill" Broonzy	Chess	LP–1444 (M)		
At Newport 1960	Chess	LP–1449 (M)	January '61	

Muddy Waters, Folk Singer	Chess	LP–1483 (M)	April '64
The Real Folk Blues	Chess	LP–1501 (M)	March '66
Muddy, Brass, and the Blues	Chess	LP–1507	December '66
More Real Folk Blues	Chess	LP–1511	March '67

MUDDY WATERS, BO DIDDLEY, AND LITTLE WALTER

| Super Blues | Checker | LPS–3008 | July '67 |

MUDDY WATERS, HOWLIN' WOLF, AND BO DIDDLEY

| Super Super Blues Band | Checker | LPS–3010 | March '68 |

MUDDY WATERS

Electric Mud	Cadet	CS–314	October '68
After the Rain	Cadet	CS–320	August '69
Fathers and Sons	2-Chess	LPS–127 reissued as 2CH– 50033	September '69
They Call Me Muddy Waters	Chess	LP–1553	May '71
AKA McKinley Morganfield	2-Chess	2CH– 60006	August '71
Live at Mr. Kelly's	Chess	CH–50012	November '71
London Sessions	Chess	CH–60013	May '72
Mud in Your Ears	Muse	5008	July '73
Can't Get No Grindin'	Chess	CH–50023	September '73
"Unk" in Funk	Chess	CH–60031	April '74
At Woodstock	Chess	CH–60035	April '75
Muddy Waters	2-Chess	203(M)	January '77

MUDDY WATERS AND HOWLIN' WOLF

| London Revisited | Chess | CH–60026 | June '74 |

MUDDY WATERS

Hard Again	Blue Sky	PZ–34449	February '77	A
I'm Ready	Blue Sky	JZ–34928	January '78	A
Muddy "Missis- sippi" Waters Live	Blue Sky	JZ–35712	February '79	A
King Bee	Blue Sky	JZ–37064	June '81	A

GEOFF AND MARIA MULDAUR. Members of the Jim Kweskin Jug Band during most of the Sixties, Geoff and Maria Muldaur pursued a neglected career during the early Seventies. Separating legally and professionally in 1973, Geoff Muldaur joined Paul Butterfield's Better Days band as Maria scored the near-smash hit "Midnight at the Oasis" from her certified gold-award solo debut album, *Maria Muldaur*. Attracting jazz as well as rock fans and sustaining her success with *Waitress in a Donut Shop* and its staunchly feminist statement of self-reliance, "I'm a Woman," Maria Muldaur has fared less well in her subsequent career, whereas Geoff Muldaur has achieved little success on his own.

THE EVEN DOZEN JUG BAND (WITH MARIA MULDAUR)

The Even Dozen Jug Band	Elektra	EKS–7246	January '64	

GEOFF MULDAUR

Geoff Muldaur reissued as Sleepy Man Blues	Prestige	14004(M)	February '64	
	Prestige	7727	April '70	

GEOFF AND MARIA MULDAUR

Pottery Pie	Reprise	RS–6350	January '70	
Sweet Potatoes	Reprise	MS–2073	August '72	

MARIA MULDAUR

Maria Muldaur *	Reprise	MS–2148	August '73	A
Waitress in a Donut Shop	Reprise	MS–2194	October '74	A
Sweet Harmony	Reprise	MS–2235	February '76	
Southern Winds	Warner Brothers	BSK–3162	March '78	
Open Your Eyes	Warner Brothers	BSK–3305	June '79	
Gospel Nights	Takoma	7084	August '81	A

GEOFF MULDAUR

Geoff Muldaur Is Having a Wonderful Time	Reprise	MS–2220	August '75	
Motion	Reprise	MS–2255	October '76	
Geoff Muldaur and Amos Garrett	Flying Fish	061	October '78	A
Blues Boy	Flying Fish	201	January '80	A

AMOS GARRETT

Go, Cat, Go	Flying Fish	226	October '80	A

GEOFF MULDAUR AND THE NITE LITES

I Ain't Drunk	Antilles	1304	September '81	A

RICK(Y) NELSON. One of the most popular rock-and-roll artists of the late Fifties and early Sixties, Ricky Nelson scored over 40 singles chart entries between 1957 and 1963. The first artist to benefit from regular television exposure of his recordings (on his parents' long-running series "The Adventures of Ozzie and Harriet"), Ricky Nelson developed a clean-cut image and gentle, clearly sung vocal style (a marked contrast to Elvis Presley's early image and singing style) that led to his acceptance by parents as well as by their teenage children. Nonetheless, much of Nelson's success was due to the definitive guitar playing of accompanist James Burton, who later toured and recorded with Presley and manned Emmylou Harris' excellent Hot Band. Overwhelmed by the so-called "English invasion" of the Sixties, Rick Nelson began exploring country music, recording the classic *Bright Lights and Country Music* and *Country Fever* albums that some credit as laying the foundation for the rise of Los Angeles "country-rock." Quitting the night club circuit which had presented him as an "oldies" act by the late Sixties, Rick Nelson formed The Stone Canyon Band (whose members included Randy Meisner) in 1969 and scored a surprise hit in 1972 with the autobiographical "Garden Party." However, his subsequent recordings have not fared well, and virtually none of his 30-plus albums are currently available, although Rick Nelson and The Stone Canyon Band continue to tour 100 days a year, performing at fairs, night clubs, colleges, and concerts.

Born in Teaneck, New Jersey, on May 8, 1940, into a show business family, Ricky Nelson joined the cast of his parents' "Adventures of Ozzie and Harriet" radio show in 1948 at the age of eight. The show moved to television in 1952, where it ran for a remarkable 14 years. Signed to Verve Records in 1956, Ricky Nelson soon scored the two-sided hit "A Teenager's Romance/I'm Walking" the next year, followed by "You're My One and Only Love." The songs were introduced on the television show, as were virtually all of his subsequent singles. Around August 1957 Nelson switched to Imperial Records, where he began a string of hits featuring his understated yet distinctive voice with "Be Bop Baby" and "Stood Up/Waitin' in School." By 1958 he was being accompanied by talented guitarist James Burton, who had played the solo on Dale Hawkins' 1957 hit "Susie Q," and bassist Joe Osborne. Sparked by these exceptional musicians, Nelson's singles regularly became hits, often two-sided hits. Successes in 1958 included Johnny and Dorsey Burnette's "Believe What You Say" backed with Hank Williams' "My Bucket's Got a Hole in It," the smash "Poor Little Fool" (written by Eddie Cochran's girlfriend Sharon Sheeley), and "Lonesome Town/I Got a Feeling." In 1959 Nelson scored with "Never Be Anyone Else but You/It's Late," "Sweeter Than You/Just a Little Too Much" and "I Wanna Be Loved," followed in 1960 by "Young Emotions." After 1961's "You Are the Only One" and the double-sided smash "Travelin' Man/Hello Mary Lou," Nelson began using the name Rick, as initiated on *Rick Is 21* and "A Wonder Like You/Everlovin'." In 1962 Rick Nelson achieved smash hits with "Young World," the quasi-autobiographical "Teen Age Idol," and "It's Up to You," but in 1963, he switched to Decca Records, where he scored his last major hits for years with "String Along," "Fools Rush In/For You," and "The Very Thought of You."

Overwhelmed by the myriad British groups who dominated rock music in the mid-Sixties, Rick Nelson found himself relegated to the night club circuit, playing his old hits. He began exploring country music, as evidenced by *Bright Lights and Country Music* and *Country Fever* (reissued in 1973 as the double-record *Rick Nelson Country*), and even scored a moderate hit in 1969 with Bob Dylan's "She Belongs to Me." Nelson then quit the nightclub circuit, as James Burton joined Elvis Presley for his return to live performing. Forming The Stone Canyon Band with bassist Randy Meisner and pedal steel guitarist Tom Brumley, Nelson began playing the rock concert circuit, recorded an entire album of his own songs, *Rick Sings Nelson*, and scored a near-smash in 1972 with the autobiographical "Garden Party." Personnel changes in The Stone Canyon Band were frequent, Meisner's departure to join The Eagles being one example, but Brumley remained, thus providing excellent accompaniment for Nelson's "country-rock" sound. However, further albums by Nelson and the band fared poorly, and he was released from his 20-year contract with MCA/Decca. Eventually signed to Epic Records, Rick Nelson and The Stone Canyon Band have yet to re-establish themselves as a contemporary recording act, yet they continue to tour fairs, colleges and night clubs regularly. He finally re-emerged in 1981 with *Playing to Win*, produced by Jack Nitzche, on Capitol Records.

RICKY NELSON

Ricky	Imperial	LP–9048 (M) reissued as LP–12392 (E)	October '57
Ricky Nelson	Imperial	LP–9050 (M) reissued as LP–12393 (E)	July '58

reissued as Ricky	United Artists	LM–1004 (E)	April '80	A
Ricky Sings Again	Imperial	LP–9061 (M) reissued as LP–12090 (E)	January '59	
	reissued on Liberty	LN–10134	November '81	A
Songs by Ricky	Imperial	LP–12030	September '59	
More Songs by Ricky	Imperial	LP–12059	August '60	

RICK NELSON

Rick Is 21	Imperial	LP–12071	May '61
Album 7 by Rick	Imperial	LP–12082	April '62
For Your Sweet Love	Decca	DL–74419	June '63
Sings "For You"	Decca	DL–74479	December '63
The Very Thought of You	Decca	DL–74559	September '64
Spotlight on Rick	Decca	DL–74608	December '64
Best Always	Decca	DL–74660	May '65
Love and Kisses	Decca	DL–74678	December '65
Bright Lights and Country Music	Decca	DL–74779	June '66
Country Fever	Decca	DL–74837	May '67
Another Side of Rick	Decca	DL–74944	December '67
Perspective	Decca	DL–75014	October '68
In Concert	Decca reissued on MCA	DL–75162 MCA–3	February '70 June '73
Rick Sings Nelson	Decca reissued on MCA	DL–75236 MCA–20	November '70
Rudy the Fifth	Decca reissued on MCA	DL–75297 MCA–37	October '71
Garden Party	Decca reissued on MCA	DL–75391 MCA–62	December '72
Windfall	MCA	383	January '74
Intakes	Epic	PE–34420	October '77
Playing to Win	Capitol	SOO–12109	February '81 A

RICK NELSON ANTHOLOGIES AND COMPILATIONS

Best Sellers	Imperial	LP–9218 (M) reissued as LP–12218 (E)	February '63

It's Up to You	Imperial	LP–9223 (M) reissued as LP–12223 (E)	April '63
Million Sellers By Rick Nelson	Imperial	LP–9232 (M) reissued as LP–12232 (E)	'63
A Long Vacation	Imperial	LP–9244 reissued as LP–12244 (E)	'63
Ricky Nelson Sings for You	Imperial	LP–9251 (M) reissued as LP–12251 (E)	January '64
Rick Nelson	Sunset	SUS–5118	May '66
I Need You	Sunset	SUS–5205	August '69
Legendary Masters	2-United Artists	UAS–9960	February '72
Rick Nelson Country	2-MCA	2–4004	June '73
The Very Best of Ricky Nelson	United Artists	LA330	March '75

WILLIE NELSON. Prolific country music songwriter of the Sixties, having written over 800 songs, Willie Nelson composed the classics "Hello Walls" and "Crazy," major pop as well as top country hits in 1961 for Faron Young and Patsy Cline, respectively. While those songs have been recorded by over 70 artists from virtually every musical field, Nelson has also written such outstanding songs as "Funny How Time Slips Away" and "Night Life." Signed to Liberty Records and then RCA Records on the strength of his songwriting, Willie Nelson languished in his own recording career throughout the Sixties, as his jazz-style vocal phrasing, complex melodies, sophisticated chord changes, and profound thematic concerns served to brand him as noncommercial in Nashville. At great personal risk, Nelson launched the career of Charley Pride, the only important black country singer, in the late Sixties. Constantly thwarted and frustrated by the slick, predictable productions and inane image fabrications used during his Nashville career, Willie Nelson moved to Austin, Texas, at the end of 1969, where he wrote the material for *Yesterday's Wine*, his final yet most personal Nashville album, generally regarded as Nashville's first fully conceived "concept" album.

Switching to Atlantic Records by 1973, thus becoming the first prominent country artist to sign with a non-Nashville label, Willie Nelson's debut album for the label, *Shotgun Willie*, was his first album to reflect his exciting yet personal on-stage sound. Following another rather conceptual album, *Phases and Stages*, Willie Nelson, for the first time, was allowed to produce and arrange *Red-Headed Stranger* on Columbia, his first certified gold-award album. It yielded perhaps the first country hit of the Seventies to "crossover" into the pop field, "Blue Eyes Crying in the Rain," which initiated and defined so-called "progressive" country music and proved that country music could appeal to fans outside the genre. Bolstered by the success of his July 4th "picnics" held near Austin since 1973, Willie Nelson showed that country music could attract rock and pop fans as well, thus making him the "leader" of country music's so-called "outlaw" movement and opening the way to success for a number of fresh, exciting country songwriters and performers, as well as encouraging the burgeoning popularity of country music during the Seventies. The anthology set, *The Outlaws*, recorded with Waylon Jennings and others, became the first country album to be certified platinum-award in 1976. That success enabled Nelson to pursue a variety of projects, including popular duet albums with Waylon Jennings and Leon Russell, and 1978's collection of Tin Pan Alley standards, *Stardust*.

Born in Abbott, Texas, on April 30, 1933, Willie Nelson had his first guitar lesson at the age of six and played his first dance-hall engagement at age 10. He joined the air force in 1950 and worked a variety of jobs around Waco upon discharge; he later moved to Fort Worth, where he worked as a radio announcer by day and as a honky-tonk performer at night. A prolific songwriter, Nelson wrote the classic "Night Life" in 1959. His earliest songwriting successes, "Wake Me When It's Over" and "Family Bible," were a minor pop hit for Andy Williams and major country hit for Claude Gray, respectively, in early 1960. Moving to Nashville in 1961, Nelson was signed to a songwriting contract by Hank Cochran and obtained a job as bass guitarist with country star Ray Price's band. During that year a number of his songs became major pop hits for other artists, including "Hello, Walls" by Faron Young and "Crazy" by Patsy Cline (both smash country hits), and "Funny How Time Slips Away" by Jimmy Elledge. Signed to Liberty Records on the strength of his songwriting in 1962, Willie Nelson scored a major country hit with "Touch Me" during that year. During the later part of 1963, Ray Price and Rusty Draper scored a moderate country hit and a minor pop hit, respectively, with Nelson's "Night Life," whereas Roy Orbison hit in the pop field with his "Pretty Paper" at year's end. Switching to RCA Records in 1965, Nelson had a number of moderate country hits over the next five years, including "The Party's Over," "Little Things," "Bring Me Sunshine," and "Once More, with Feeling." In 1967, at no small personal and professional risk, he introduced black country singer Charley Pride on his tours of honky-tonks.

Nashville's Sixties "countrypolitan" sound, replete with strings, horns, and vocal choruses, subjugated artists to depersonalized predictable music. Thereby thwarted and frustrated in the studio, Willie Nelson retreated to Austin after his Nashville home burned in late 1969, there to write the material that appeared on his last Nashville album, *Yesterday's Wine*. Regarded as his most personal album and as Nashville's first "concept" album, the album yielded only a minor country hit with "Yesterday's Wine/Me and Paul," the latter song concerning the travails of Nelson and his longtime drummer, Paul English. Around 1972 Willie Nelson permanently moved to Austin, Texas, and switched to Atlantic Records. Working with veteran producer Jerry Wexler, he recorded *Shotgun Willie* and *Phases and Stages*, sometimes considered his finest albums. In 1973 Nelson initiated his celebrated Fourth of July "picnics" that drew tens of thousands of fans and proved to be the origin of the so-called "outlaw" or "progressive country" music, as Waylon Jennings, Kris Kristofferson, and Leon Russell performed to a curiously diverse audience of rednecks and hippies.

Switching to Columbia Records, Willie Nelson finally was allowed to produce and arrange his own albums, beginning with his Columbia debut, *Red-Headed Stranger*. The album yielded a major pop hit with "Blue Eyes Crying in the Rain," which led to a succession of "crossover" hits by other country artists and encouraged rising interest in country music. RCA Records' 1976 anthology set, *The Outlaws*, provided this developing, more personalized, and less artificial music movement with its label and became the first country album to be certified platinum-award. Containing songs performed by Nelson, Waylon Jennings, Jessi Colter, and Tompall Glaser, the album included Nelson's "Me and Paul" and "Yesterday's Wine" and the Nelson–Jennings duet on the pair's "Good-Hearted Woman." Nelson's *Sound in Your Mind* album showcased the distinctive harmonica playing of Mickey Raphael and contained a medley of "Funny How Time Slips Away/Crazy/Night Life," Steve Fromholtz' touching "I'd Have to Be Crazy" and the country hit, "If You've Got the Money, I've Got the Time," written by Fifties country artist Lefty Frizzell.

The title song to Willie Nelson's *The Troublemaker* depicted Jesus as a rejected hippie type, whereas *To Lefty from Willie* contained Nelson's recordings of the songs of Lefty Frizzell. Having scored a major pop hit with "Luckenbach, Texas (Back to the Basics of Love)" in collaboration with Waylon Jennings during 1977, Nelson recorded a duo album with Jennings that yielded a moderate pop and major country hit with "Mamas, Don't Let Your Babies Grow Up to Be Cowboys" and was certified platinum-award within three months. Nelson had opened his own Austin Opry House in October 1977 and his next album, *Stardust*, produced by Booker T. Jones, broke all country music conventions by containing only Tin Pan Alley standards, of which "Georgia on My Mind," "Blue Skies," and "All of Me" became smash country hits. The live double-record set *Willie and Family Live* was issued at the end of 1978, and the Lone Star subsidiary of Mercury Records, United Artists (heir to his Liberty recordings), and RCA released albums comprised of his older material. In 1979 Nelson recorded the double-record set *One for the Road* with old friend Leon Russell, and the album, soon certified gold-award, yielded a country hit with "Heartbreak Hotel." Near the end of the year, Columbia issued Nelson's *Sings Kristofferson* and *Pretty Paper*, followed in early 1980 by the soundtrack to *The Electric Horseman*. The album produced a country hit with "My Heroes Have Always Been Cowboys" and the film featured Nelson along with stars Jane Fonda and Robert Redford. Subsequent 1980 albums by Nelson included sets with trumpeter Danny Davis and his Nashville Brass and old boss Ray Price (which provided a country hit with Bob Wills' "Faded Love"), as well as the soundtrack to the film *Honeysuckle Rose*, in which he starred, opposite Dyan Cannon, as a traveling Texas country musician not unlike himself in the late Sixties. The soundtrack album included four new songs and a guest appearance by Emmylou Harris and yielded a top country and major pop hit with "On the Road Again."

WILLIE NELSON

And Then I Wrote	Liberty	LST–7239	November '62	
Here's Willie Nelson	Liberty	LST–7308	August '63	
His Own Songs	RCA	LSP–3418	October '65	
Country Favorites	RCA	LSP–3528	May '66	
Country Music Concert	RCA	LSP–3659	November '66	
Make Way	RCA	LSP–3748	April '67	
The Party's Over	RCA	LSP–3858	October '67	
Texas in My Soul	RCA	LSP–3937	April '68	
Good Times	RCA	LSP–4057	October '68	
My Own Peculiar Way	RCA	LSP–4111	March '69	
Both Sides Now	RCA	LSP–4294	May '70	
Laying My Burdens Down	RCA	LSP–4404	October '70	
Willie Nelson with Family	RCA	LSP–4489	May '71	
Yesterday's Wine	RCA	LSP–4568 reissued as ANL1–1102 reissued as AYL1–3800	September '71 September '75	A
The Words Don't Fit the Picture	RCA	LSP–4653	'72	
The Willie Way	RCA	LSP–4760	August '72	
Live (I Gotta Get Drunk)	RCA	AFL1–1487 reissued as AYL1–4165	April '76 November '81	A
Sweet Memories	RCA	AAL1–3243	February '79	A
Minstrel Man	RCA	AHL1–4045	June '81	A
Shotgun Willie	Atlantic	SD–7262	July '73	A

The Troublemaker	Atlantic	SD–7275	January '74	
Phases and Stages	Atlantic	SD–7291	March '74	A
Red-Headed Stranger*	Columbia	PC–33482	July '75	A

WILLIE NELSON, WAYLON JENNINGS, JESSI COLTER, AND TOMPALL GLASER

The Outlaws**	RCA	AFL1–1321	February '76	A

WILLIE NELSON

The Sound in Your Mind*	Columbia	PC–34092	March '76	A
The Troublemaker	Columbia	PC–34112	September '76	A
To Lefty from Willie	Columbia	PC–34695	July '77	A
Stardust**	Columbia	JC–35305	May '78	A
Willie and Family Live**	2-Columbia	KC2–35642	November '78	A
Sings Kristofferson*	Columbia	JC–36188	November '79	A
Pretty Paper	Columbia	JC–36189	November '79	A
The Electric Horseman (soundtrack)*	Columbia	JS–36327	January '80	A
Honeysuckle Rose (soundtrack)**	Columbia	S2–36752	August '80	A
Somewhere over the Rainbow**	Columbia	FC–36883	April '81	A
Greatest Hits (and Some That Will Be)*	2-Columbia	KC2–37542	September '81	A
Family Bible	Song Bird	3258	October '80	A

WILLIE NELSON ANTHOLOGIES AND COMPILATIONS

Hello, Walls	Sunset	SUS–5138	October '66	
	reissued on Pickwick	3584	April '78	A
Columbus Stackade Blues	Camden	2444	December '70	
Country Winners	Camden	ACL–0326	December '73	A
Spotlight	Camden	ACL–0705	December '74	A
What Can You Do to Me Now	RCA	AFL1–1234	November '75	
		reissued as AYL1–3958		A
Before His Time	RCA	AFL1–2210	May '77	
		reissued as AYL1–3671	June '80	A

Country Willie	United Artists	LA410 reissued as LN–10013	January '76	A
Best of Willie Nelson	United Artists	LA086 reissued as LN–10118	June '76	A
There'll Be No Teardrops Tonight	United Artists	LA930	December '78	A
Face of a Fighter	Lone Star	4602	October '78	

WILLIE NELSON AND VARIOUS ARTISTS

| Willie Nelson and Friends | Plantation | 24 | September '76 | A |
| Honky-Tonkin' | RCA | AHL1–3422 | July '79 | |

WILLIE NELSON AND WAYLON JENNINGS

| Waylon and Willie** | RCA | AAL1–2686 | January '78 | A |

WILLIE NELSON AND LEON RUSSELL

| One for the Road* | 2-Columbia | KC2–36064 | June '79 | A |

WILLIE NELSON AND DANNY DAVIS

| With the Nashville Brass | RCA | AHL1–3549 | February '80 | A |

WILLIE NELSON AND RAY PRICE

| San Antonio Rose | Columbia | JC–36476 | June '80 | A |

NEW RIDERS OF THE PURPLE SAGE. First attracting attention through the presence of Grateful Dead members Jerry Garcia, Phil Lesh, and Mickey Hart, The New Riders of the Purple Sage featured on their debut album the guitar playing of mainstay David Nelson, the pedal steel guitar and banjo playing of Garcia, and the excellent songwriting of guitarist John Dawson. Persevering without Garcia, The New Riders of the Purple Sage mixed Fifties rock-and-roll and country-style originals in achieving their reputation as a performing band. Scoring their biggest success with *The Adventures of Panama Red* and its classic title song, The New Riders of the Purple Sage have since experienced frequent personnel changes that have seemingly diluted the group's popularity.

THE NEW RIDERS OF THE PURPLE SAGE

N.R.P.S.	Columbia	PC–30888	August '71	A
Powerglide	Columbia	C–31284	April '72	A
Gypsy Cowboy	Columbia	PC–31930	December '72	A
The Adventures of Panama Red*	Columbia	PC–32450	September '73	A
Home, Home on the Road	Columbia	PC–32870	April '74	A

KINGFISH

Kingfish	Round	LA564	February '76	
Live 'n' Kickin'	Jet/United Artists	LA732	April '77	
Trident	Jet/Columbia	JZ–35479	August '78	
Live at the Roxy	Townhouse	SN–7128	November '81	A

THE NEW RIDERS OF THE PURPLE SAGE

Brujo	Columbia	PC–33145	October '74	
Oh, What a Mighty Time	Columbia	PC–33688	October '75	A
Best	Columbia	PC–34367	December '76	A
New Riders	MCA	2196	July '76	
Who Are These Guys?	MCA	2248	February '77	
Marin County Line	MCA	2307 reissued as 632	November '77	A
Feelin' All Right	A&M	4818	April '81	A

THE NEW YORK DOLLS. Generally regarded as the first "punk-rock" band and thus an inspiration to the late Seventies movement, The New York Dolls found their popularity largely restricted to the New York area despite international publicity received through an article in England's *Melody Maker* tabloid. Playing a crude, raw form of rock with lyrics preoccupied with the seamier side of New York life, The New York Dolls quickly fell from fashion with the ascendancy of Patti Smith, The Ramones, and English "punk" groups such as The Damned and The Sex Pistols and disbanded around 1975.

Formed at the beginning of 1972, The New York Dolls were initially comprised of David Johansen (lead vocals), Johnny Thunders (guitar, vocals), Arthur Kane (bass), Billy Murcia (drums), and Rick Rivets (guitar), who was soon replaced by Sylvain Sylvain (guitar, vocals). Johansen had been vocalist for several Staten Island groups, whereas Thunders, Murcia, and Sylvain had constituted the trio Actress. Attracting attention in cheap, trashy New York clubs with their brutal style of rock, their sexually ambiguous costumes, and their songs centered on drugs and low-life concerns, The New York Dolls failed to extend their popularity beyond New York despite attempts at national touring and international publicity from a *Melody Maker* article that some suggest destroyed the group's credibility. In November 1972 drummer Murcia died of a drug overdose and was replaced by Jerry Nolan, and the group subsequently signed with Mercury Records. Their debut album, produced by Todd Rundgren, included "punk" classics such as "Bad Girls," "Personality Crisis," and "Looking for a Kiss," yet sold minimally. Their second, *Too Much, Too Soon*, was produced by veteran George "Shadow" Morton and sold even less well; by the summer of 1974, The New York Dolls were relegated to the New York circuit of small clubs. Persevering through April 1975, the group broke up, although Johansen amd Sylvain continued to work together until the beginning of 1977. Thereafter Sylvain played with The Criminals, and Johansen eventually signed with Blue Sky Records, for whom he has recorded three solo albums. Sylvain left Johansen in December 1978 and signed with RCA Records, who issued his debut solo album a year later.

THE NEW YORK DOLLS

The New York Dolls	Mercury	SRM1–675	August '73	
Too Much, Too Soon	Mercury	SRM1–1001	May '74	

DAVID JOHANSEN

David Johansen	Blue Sky	JZ–34926	May '78	
In Style	Blue Sky	JZ–36082	August '79	A
Here Comes the Night	Blue Sky	FZ–36589	June '81	A

SYLVAIN SYLVAIN

Sylvain Sylvain	RCA	AFL1–3475	November '79	

SYL SYLVAIN AND THE TEARDROPS

Syl Sylvain and The Teardrops	RCA	AFL1–3913	June '81	A

THE NEW YORK ROCK AND ROLL ENSEMBLE. Sorely neglected outside the American East Coast and Europe, The New York Rock and Roll Ensemble may have been the only truly "progressive" rock band of the late Sixties and early Seventies. Whereas British "progressive" rock groups of the era utilized banks of keyboards and synthesizers to record classical compositions, three of the five members of The New York Rock and Roll Ensemble could easily switch from standard rock instrumentation to classical instruments such as French and English horns, oboes, and cellos during a performance. However, despite excellent critical reviews, successful European tours, and the development of a following among college students, The New York Rock and Roll Ensemble was discounted as a "novelty" act. By 1973 the group was reduced to two original members, after which they apparently disbanded, although Michael Kamen resurfaced in 1977 with the soundtrack to *Next Man*.

THE NEW YORK ROCK AND ROLL ENSEMBLE

The New York Rock and Roll Ensemble	Atco	SD33–240	July '68
Faithful Friends. . .	Atco	SD33–294	August '69
Reflections	Atco	SD33–312	April '70

THE NEW YORK ROCK ENSEMBLE

Roll Over	Columbia	C–30033	October '70
Freedomburger	Columbia	KC–31317	June '72
New York Rock	Atco	SD–7020	'73

MICHAEL KAMEN

Next Man (soundtrack)	Buddah	BDS–5685	March '77

RANDY NEWMAN. One of the most fascinating and distinctive songwriters of the late Sixties and Seventies, Randy Newman first became known after his "I Think It's Gonna Rain Today" was recorded by Judy Collins on her 1966 *In My Life* album. Recording his first album in 1968, Newman attracted the attention of musicians and developed a cult following with his songs alternately cynical, ironic, whimsical, and sarcastic that nonetheless retained a deep-seated sense of humanity. Writing and recording such classic songs as "Living without You," "Mama Told Me Not to Come," "Lonely at the Top," "Political Science," and "Sail Away," Randy Newman eventually broke through to a larger audience with 1974's *Good Old Boys*, a vaguely conceptual work revolving around the American South. Sparking his first controversy with the repeated use of the word "nigger" in "Rednecks" from that album, Newman achieved his largest success with 1977's *Little Criminals*, primarily on the basis of the popularity and attendant publicity surrounding his satirical ditty, "Short People."

Born in New Orleans on November 28, 1943, Randy Newman moved to southern California with his family at the age of five. Highly influenced by several uncles who composed film scores, he began playing piano at age six and studied music theory by age 12. By the age of 16, while still attending high school, he worked as a songwriter at Metric Music, a subsidiary of Liberty Records, whose board chairman was the father of his boyhood friend Lenny Waronker. In the early Sixties, Newman cut demonstration tapes with sessions players such as Glen Campbell and Leon Russell, as he attended UCLA as a music major and wrote songs for Schroeder Music and, later, for January Music. His first commercial success as a songwriter came at the end of 1966, when Judy Collins recorded his tender "I Think It's Gonna Rain Today" on her gold-award *In My Life* album. In 1967 Newman began working as a sessions arranger at Warner Brothers and signed his own record contract with the label's Reprise subsidiary by 1968. Recorded with an orchestra playing his arrangements, his debut album featured "I Think It's Gonna Rain Today" and the touching "Living without You," as well as the American profile "Beehive State" and the satirical "Davy, the Fat Boy." However, despite critical acclaim, the album sold so poorly that the record company later gave away copies as a promotional gimmick. Never a prolific writer, Newman's second album, *12 Songs*, was issued 18 months later; it also enjoyed critical success but commercial failure. Recorded with guitarists Ry Cooder and Clarence White and produced by Lenny Waronker, the album included the wry "Yellow Man" and "Mama Told Me Not to Come," a top hit for Three Dog Night in the spring of 1970. That year Newman began performing live occasionally, usually unaccompanied; an engagement at New York's Bitter End resulted in 1971's *Live*, which compiled many of his earlier songs while also containing "Tickle Me," "Last Night I Had a Dream," and his wry look at his lack of success, "Lonely at the Top."

In 1972 Randy Newman debuted *Sail Away* with the New York Philharmonic in Philharmonic Hall. The album included the melodic "Sail Away," his satirical solution to the world's problems, "Political Science," the sexual spoof "You Can Leave Your Hat On" and the sarcastic "God's Song (That's Why I Love Mankind)." Newman's first major album success came with *Good Old Boys* which was debuted with the Atlanta Symphony Orchestra and supported by a 20-city tour. Concerned in a vaguely conceptual way with the American South, the album contained "Birmingham" and "Louisiana 1927" as well as his sly attack on Southern lower-class morality, "Rednecks," and "Naked Man" and "Back on My Feet Again." The song "Rednecks" sparked a minor controversy with its repeated use of the word "nigger."

Generally inactive for more than two years, Randy Newman eventually re-emerged in 1977 with *Little Criminals*. The album yielded a smash hit with "Short People," his satirical assault on prejudice that some myopic listeners misconstrued as an affront to small-statured people, resulting in the song's banishment by several radio stations. The album also featured the countrified "Rider in the Rain," recorded with members of The Eagles, and became Newman's first certified gold-award album. The success of *Little Criminals* was probably due more to the controversy than anything else, as 1979's *Born Again* sold only moderately, despite the inclusion of songs such as "It's the Money I Love," "Mr. Sheep," and "The Story of a Rock & Roll Band." In late 1981, the film *Ragtime*, based on E.L. Doctorow's novel and featuring a score composed and performed by Randy Newman, was released.

THE RANDY NEWMAN ORCHESTRA

Original Music from "Peyton Place"	Epic	BN–26147	June '65

RANDY NEWMAN

Randy Newman	Reprise	RS–6286	May '68	A
12 Songs	Reprise	RS–6373	February '70	A
Live	Reprise	RS–6459	June '71	A
Sail Away	Reprise	MS–2064	May '72	A
Good Old Boys	Reprise	MS–2193	September '74	A
Little Criminals*	Warner Brothers	BSK–3079	September '77	A
Born Again	Warner Brothers	HS–3346	August '79	A

NILSSON. Although he started as a songwriter, Nilsson is best remembered for his recordings of Fred Neil's "Everybody's Talkin'" and Badfinger's "Without You." Becoming somewhat of a cult figure through his association with Beatles John Lennon and Ringo Starr during the late Sixties, Nilsson scored his biggest successes in 1971–72 with the Richard Perry-produced *Nilsson Schmilsson* and *Son of Schmilsson* albums while retaining the curiously unique distinction of never having performed in public.

NILSSON

Spotlight	Tower	5095	June '69	
Early Tymes	Musicor	2505	August '77	
Pandemonium Shadow Show	RCA	LSP–3874	November '67	
Aerial Ballet	RCA	LSP–3956	July '68	
Skidoo (soundtrack)	RCA	LSO–1152	November '68	
Harry	RCA	LSP–4197	August '69	
Nilsson Sings Newman	RCA	LSP–4289 reissued as APL1– 0203	March '70 May '73	
The Point (TV soundtrack)	RCA	LSPX– 1003 reissued as AYL1– 3811	March '71	A
Aerial Pandemonium Ballet	RCA	LSP–4543	July '71	
Nilsson Schmilsson*	RCA	LSP–4515 reissued as ANL1– 3464	November '71	A

Son of Schmilsson*	RCA	AFL1–4717	July '72	
		reissued as AYL1–3812		A
A Little Touch of Schmilsson in the Night	RCA	AFL1–0197	June '73	
		reissued as AYL1–3761		A
Son of Dracula (soundtrack)	Rapple/RCA	ABL1–0220	March '74	
Pussycats	RCA	CPL1–0570	August '74	
Duit on Mon Dei	RCA	APL1–0817	March '75	
Sandman	RCA	APL1–1031	January '76	
. . . That's the Way It Is	RCA	APL1–1119	June '76	
Knnillssonn	RCA	AFL1–2276	July '77	
World's Greatest Lover (sound-track)	RCA	ABL1–2709	March '78	
Popeye (soundtrack)	Boardwalk	SW–36880	November '80	A

NILSSON ANTHOLOGIES AND COMPILATIONS

Rock 'n' Roll	Pickwick	3321		
Best of Nilsson	RCA	AFL1–2257	May '77	A
Greatest Hits	RCA	AFL1–2798	May '78	

THE NITTY GRITTY DIRT BAND. A zany, country-styled American rock band of the late Sixties and Seventies, The Nitty Gritty Dirt Band performed an eclectic melange of bluegrass, country, rock, and jug band musics while displaying remarkable instrumental virtuousity. Although they scored their first major hit with Jerry Jeff Walker's "Mr. Bojangles" and first recorded Kenny Loggins' "House at Pooh Corners," The Nitty Gritty Dirt Band is best remembered for 1972's certified gold-award *Will the Circle Be Unbroken* album, recorded with country music legends such as Maybelle Carter, Roy Acuff, and Earl Scruggs. The triple-record album served to enhance the reputations of the older country stars and that of The Nitty Gritty Dirt Band and sparked a revival of interest in such traditional American music. Becoming the first American rock-style band to tour Russia in May 1977, The Dirt Band have recently scored surprise hits with "An American Dream" and "Make a Little Magic."

THE NITTY GRITTY DIRT BAND

The Nitty Gritty Dirt Band	Liberty	LST–7501	April '67	
Ricochet	Liberty	LST–7516	September '67	
Rare Junk	Liberty	LST–7540	May '68	
Alive	Liberty	LST–7611	March '69	
Uncle Charlie and His Dog Teddy	Liberty	LST–7642	September '70	
All the Good Times	United Artists	UAS–5553	January '72	A
Will the Circle Be Unbroken*	3-United Artists	UAS–9801	November '72	A
Stars and Stripes Forever	2-United Artists	LA184	June '74	A
Dream	United Artists	LA469	September '75	A
Dirt, Silver, and Gold	3-United Artists	LA670	December '76	A

THE DIRT BAND

The Dirt Band	United Artists	LA854	June '78	
An American Dream	United Artists	LA974	September '79	A
Make a Little Magic	United Artists	LT–1042	July '80	A
Jealousy	Liberty	LW–1106	September '81	A

JIMMY IBBOTSON

Nitty Gritty	First American	7718	June '80	A

TED NUGENT/THE AMBOY DUKES. Scoring his first national hit with the "psychedelic" "Journey to the Center of the Mind" in 1968 as lead guitarist for The Amboy Dukes, Ted Nugent established himself in the American Midwest through years of heavy touring (150–200 engagements a year) despite numerous personnel changes. Failing to follow up the single, The Amboy Dukes recorded unsuccessfully for three different labels before Nugent went solo in 1975. Recording for Epic Records, Ted Nugent quickly established himself as an album artist and performing act based on his bombastic, feedback-based, high-decibel lead playing and blatantly sexist lyrics, replete with frequent scatalogical references. Well known for his on-stage acrobatics and appeal to an audience composed primarily of adolescent males, Ted Nugent has recorded repetitious but best-selling albums grounded in the style he developed with *Free-For-All* and *Cat Scratch Fever*.

Born in 1949 and raised in Detroit, Ted Nugent obtained his first guitar at the age of nine, started lessons at 11, and formed his first rock band by age 12. He played for a while in The Lourds, but the group dissolved when he moved to Chicago with his family in 1965. He later formed The Amboy Dukes and returned to Detroit, securing a contract with Mainstream

Records. In the summer of 1968, the band scored a major hit with "Journey to the Center of the Mind," but neither albums nor subsequent singles served to sustain that success. Nonetheless established in the Midwest through rigorous touring, The Amboy Dukes endured over 30 personnel changes during its history. Switching to Polydor Records, the group recorded two marginally successful albums, including the live set *Survival of the Fittest*, before moving to DiscReet for two almost totally ignored 1974 albums recorded as Ted Nugent and The Amboy Dukes.

During 1975 Ted Nugent dissolved The Amboy Dukes in favor of a solo career but retained Dukes bassist Rob Grange and added Detroit vocalist–guitarist Derek St. Holmes and English drummer Cliff Davies. Signing with Epic Records, Nugent co-produced his albums with Davies. His debut album, featuring his ear-shattering, feedback-laden guitar playing, included characteristically violent songs such as "Stranglehold," "Storm-troopin'," "Motor City Madhouse," and the minor hit "Hey, Baby." The album was certified gold-award in 1976, the year Nugent performed 250 engagements, thereby establishing a reputation nationally for his gross sexist lyrics, frequent scatalogical references, and bombastic guitar playing. *Free-For-All* yielded a minor hit with "Dog Eat Dog" and was certified platinum-award in September 1977, simultaneously with *Cat Scratch Fever*. That album included Nugent's only major hit single, "Cat Scratch Fever," as well as "Wang Dang Sweet Poontang" and "Death by Misadventure." The double-record live set, *Double Live Gonzo*, and *Weekend Warriors*, both from 1978, followed suit. By the beginning of 1979 Nugent's band consisted of himself, drummer Davies, bassist John Sauter, and vocalist–guitarist Charlie Huhn. Both *State of Shock* and *Scream Dream*, which featured the parodic "Wango Tango," have since become best-sellers.

THE AMBOY DUKES

The Amboy Dukes	Mainstream	6104	January '68	
Journey to the Center of the Mind	Mainstream	6112	June '68	
Migration	Mainstream	6118	October '69	
The Best of the Original Amboy Dukes	Mainstream	6125	June '71	
Journeys and Migrations	2-Mainstream	2–801		
Dr. Slingshot	Mainstream	414		
Marriage on the Rocks/Rock Bottom	Polydor	244012 reissued as	February '70	
		PD– 6073	August '76	A

TED NUGENT AND THE AMBOY DUKES

Survival of the Fittest/Live	Polydor	244035	March '71	A

| Call of the Wild | DiscReet | DS–2181 | March '74 | A |
| Tooth, Fang, and Claw | DiscReet | DS–2203 | September '74 | A |

TED NUGENT

Ted Nugent *	Epic	PE–33692	October '75	A
Free-For-All **	Epic	PE–34121	September '76	A
Cat Scratch Fever **	Epic	JE–34700	June '77	A
Double Live Gonzo **	2-Epic	KE2–35069	January '78	A
Weekend War-riors **	Epic	FE–35551	October '78	A
State of Shock *	Epic	FE–36000	May '79	A
Scream Dream *	Epic	FE–36404	May '80	A
Intensities in Ten Cities	Epic	FE–37084	March '81	A
Great Gonzos— The Best of Ted Nugent	Epic	FE–37667	November '81	A

LAURA NYRO. At the forefront of the female singer–songwriter movement during the late Sixties, Laura Nyro received widespread critical acclaim for *Eli and the Thirteenth Confession* and its modestly selling followup, *New York Tendaberry*. Nonetheless she remained an elusive cult figure, as artists such as The Fifth Dimension, Blood, Sweat and Tears, Three Dog Night, and Barbra Streisand scored smash hits with her early compositions in pop-style renditions. Never a prolific songwriter, Laura Nyro retreated from the exigencies of the music business during the early Seventies, eventually re-emerging in 1976, but she has yet to extend her reputation and popularity beyond her devoted, yet limited, following.

Born in New York in 1947, Laura Nyro began playing music at a very early age, ostensibly writing her first songs at the age of eight. At 18 she made her first extended professional appearance at San Francisco's hungry i and, by 1966, she had signed with Verve Records. Her debut album, *More Than a New Discovery* (reissued by Columbia as *The First Songs*), included "Wedding Bell Blues," "And When I Die," "Stoney End," and "Blowin' Away," yet was sorely overlooked by the record-buying public. At 1967's celebrated Monterey Pop Festival, she played as a soul revue with a trio of black female backup singers, but the experiment proved less than successful, and she was nearly booed off the stage. Switching to Columbia Records that year, her debut for the label, *Eli and the Thirteenth Confession*, was greeted by highly favorable critical reviews but barely sold, despite the inclusion of "Sweet Blindness," "Eli's Coming," "Stoned Soul Picnic," and the neglected "Woman's Blues." Although the public seemingly failed to take note of her exceptional songwriting, her dynamic delivery, and fine piano accompaniment, a number of acts, most notably

The Fifth Dimension, began covering her songs with astounding success. In 1968 that group scored a smash hit with "Stoned Soul Picnic" followed by "Sweet Blindness," the top hit "Wedding Bell Blues" in 1969, and the major hits "Blowing Away" and "Save the Country" in 1970. Blood, Sweat and Tears had a smash hit with "And When I Die" in 1969, at the same time that Three Dog Night was hitting with "Eli's Coming." In late 1970 Barbra Streisand scored a near-smash with "Stoney End."

Laura Nyro's second Columbia album, *New York Tendaberry*, was probably her best selling album and included the aforementioned "Save the Country." *Christmas and the Beads of Sweat* sold somewhat less well, yet yielded her only (minor) hit with Carole King and Gerry Goffin's "Up on the Roof." In 1971 Nyro recorded an album of soul/rhythm-and-blues classics with Labelle but, by the beginning of 1973, she had dropped out of public view and music for a quiet married life. The marriage later failed and, in early 1976, she re-emerged with the modestly selling jazz-style *Smile*. She returned to performing that year and the four-month tour resulted in the 1977 live set, *Season of Lights*. During 1978 her *Nested* album was issued, yet it failed to re-establish Laura Nyro in the singer–songwriter genre.

LAURA NYRO

More Than a New Discovery	Verve	FTS–3020	February '67	
reissued as The First Songs	Columbia	C–31410	October '72	A
Eli and the Thirteenth Confession	Columbia	PC–9626	March '68	A
New York Tendaberry	Columbia	PC–9737	August '69	A
Christmas and the Beads of Sweat	Columbia	PC–30259	November '70	A
It's Gonna Take a Miracle	Columbia	PC–30987	November '71	A
Smile	Columbia	C–33912	February '76	A
Season of Lights	Columbia	PC–34331	June '77	
Nested	Columbia	PC–35449	June '78	A

PHIL OCHS. Author of some of the most potent and clever, topical and satirical socially conscious songs of American folk music's "protest" era and at one time considered Bob Dylan's only major rival, Phil Ochs is probably best remembered for the songs "I Ain't Marching Anymore," "There but for Fortune," and "Outside a Small Circle of Friends." Never truly able to progress beyond topical "protest" music, Phil Ochs never achieved any major album or singles successes and, after 1970, he never recorded again and performed only occasionally, ultimately committing suicide in 1976.

PHIL OCHS

All the News That's Fit to Sing	Elektra	EKS–7269	May '64	A
I Ain't Marching Anymore	Elektra	EKS–7287	March '65	A
In Concert	Elektra	EKS–7310	May '66	A
Pleasures of the Harbor	A&M	SP–4133	November '67	A
Tape from California	A&M	SP–4148	July '68	A
Rehearsals for Retirement	A&M	SP–4181	March '69	
Greatest Hits	A&M	SP–4253	March '70	
Chords of Fame	2-A&M	SP–4599	February '77	A
Greatest Hits	A&M	3125	April '81	A
Songs for Broadside (Broadside #10)	Folkways	5320(M)	August '76	A
Broadside Tapes 1 (Broadside #14)	Folkways	FD–5362	November '80	A

THE O'JAYS. Long-lived American black vocal group, The O'Jays eventually achieved enormous success during the Seventies as the first major act on producer–songwriters Kenny Gamble and Leon Huff's Philadelphia International Records. They quickly became established with their debut for the label, *Backstabbers*, and its smash hit title song, often thought to be a pioneering "crossover" hit (from soul to pop) of the Seventies. The O'Jays' landmark *Ship Ahoy* album featured sophisticated production and socially conscious lyrics, as evidenced by the 9-minute-plus title cut. Repeating that formula through consecutive gold-award albums, The O'Jays' first platinum-award album, *So Full of Love*, was their first album in years to contain purely romantic material.

The O'Jays initially formed in Canton, Ohio, during 1958 as the five-piece vocal group, The Mascots. The members: Eddie Levert, Walter Williams, William Powell, Bobby Massey, and Bill Isles. Touring the so-called "chitlin'" circuit, the group changed their name to The O'Jays and recorded several unsuccessful singles for King Records before signing with Imperial. They scored their first minor pop hit with "Lonely Drifter" in 1963, but their next (moderate) hit did not come until two years later with "Lipstick Traces." Bill Isles departed while the O'Jays were working sessions for Phil Spector in 1965; the group continued as a four-piece and switched to Bell Records, where they achieved a major rhythm-and-blues hit with "I'll Be Sweeter Tomorrow" in late 1967. Subsequently recording for independent producer–songwriters Kenny Gamble and Leon Huff's short-lived Neptune label, The O'Jays scored moderate rhythm-and-blues hits with the duo's "One Night Affair," "Deeper (in Love with You)" and "Looky Looky (Look at Me, Girl)" in 1969–70, but the label later folded.

In late 1971 Kenny Gamble and Leon Huff resurfaced with their newly formed Philadelphia International label under the auspices of Columbia Records. Serving as the label's first major act, The O'Jays, now without Bobby Massey, recorded *Backstabbers*, and Gamble and Huff's sophisticated production and socially aware lyrics helped make the album a best-seller, yielding smash pop hits with the title song and "Love Train" and the moderate hit "Time to Get Down." After the poorly selling *In Philadelphia* album, the group recorded the landmark *Ship Ahoy* album, which contained the political-social "message" songs of Gamble and Huff, including the 9-minute-plus title cut and the major hits "Put Your Hands Together" and "For the Love of Money." A European tour in the winter of 1973 resulted in *Live in London*, and the group's next album, *Survival*, became a best-seller without producing a hit single. *Family Reunion* yielded the smash hit "I Love Music" and the major hit "Livin' for the Weekend"; but in early 1976 William Powell was replaced by Sam Strain, a veteran of Little Anthony and The Imperials. Powell subsequently died of cancer on May 26, 1977. Although regarded as their weakest albums, *Message in the Music* and *Travelin' at the Speed of Thought* became best-sellers without benefit of a major hit single. In 1978 Philadelphia International issued *So Full of Love* for The O'Jays, and the album contained romantic pop-style songs rather than political or religiously oriented material. Certified as the group's first platinum-award album within two months of its release, the album contained the smash hit "Use Ta Be My Girl." The instant best-seller *Identify Yourself* included the major hit "Forever Mine" and was followed in 1980 by *The Year 2000*.

THE O'JAYS

| Comin' Through | Imperial | LP–12290 | October '65 |
| Soul Sounds | Minit | 24008 | April '67 |

Back on Top	Bell	6014	July '68	
reissued as The O'Jays		6082	February '75	
Full of Soul	Sunset	SUS–5222	August '68	
Greatest Hits	United Artists	UAS–5655	November '72	
	reissued on Liberty	LN–10119		A
Back Stabbers*	Philadelphia International	ZX–31712	August '72	A
In Philadelphia	Philadelphia International	ZX–32120	April '73	A
Ship Ahoy*	Philadelphia International	KZ–32408	October '73	A
Live in London*	Philadelphia International	KZ–32953	May '74	A
The O'Jays Meet the Moments	Stang	1024	January '75	
Survival*	Philadelphia International	KZ–33150	April '75	
Family Reunion*	Philadelphia International	PZ–33807	November '75	A
Message in the Music*	Philadelphia International	PZ–34245	September '76	A
Travelin' at the Speed of Thought	Philadelphia International	PZ–34684	May '77	A
Collectors' Items	2-Philadelphia International	PZG–35024	November '77	A
So Full of Love**	Philadelphia International	PZ–35355	March '78	A
Identify Yourself**	Philadelphia International	FZ–36027	August '79	A
The Year 2000	TSOP	FZ–36416	August '80	A

ROY ORBISON. Starting out as a rockabilly singer in the mid-Fifties, Roy Orbison achieved his greatest success as a singles artist between 1960 and 1965 with his dramatic and emotional renditions of his own ballads delivered in almost operatic fashion. Possessing a stunning tenor voice of extraordinary range and depth, perhaps the most distinctive voice of the early Sixties, Roy Orbison scored more than 15 major hits, including "Running Scared" and the classic "Pretty Woman," the latter virtually his signature song. Little heard from after switching to MGM Records in

1965, Roy Orbison endured personal tragedies and diminishing American popularity, while maintaining his British "superstar" status by means of regular tours. Rarely performing in the United States between the late Sixties and late Seventies, Roy Orbison eventually re-emerged with new albums on three different labels between 1975 and 1979 and with the 1980 country hit single in duet with Emmylou Harris, "That Loving You Feeling Again."

Born in Wink, Texas, on April 23, 1936, Roy Orbison started playing guitar at age six and formed the "rockabilly" group The Wink Westerners as a teenager. That group evolved into The Teen Kings, whose first unsuccessful recordings were made under Norman Petty, Buddy Holly's producer. Signed to the Memphis-based Sun label in 1956, Orbison's soaring voice was hardly suited to the "rockabilly" material he recorded, yet "Ooby Dooby" became a minor hit that year. Making his final recording for Sun in 1957, he moved to Nashville to concentrate on songwriting after The Everly Brothers scored a major hit with his "Claudette" as the flip side of "All I Have to Do Is Dream." Briefly recording for RCA Records, Orbison switched to the newly formed Monument label in late 1959. His second release for the company, "Only the Lonely," became a smash hit in 1960 and initiated a string of powerful, almost operatic ballad hits. After the hits "Blue Angel" and "I'm Hurtin'," Orbison achieved a top hit with "Running Scared," which was recorded complete with a string section, male backing voices and a driving bolero-like crescendo. The smash hit "Crying" was backed by the major hit "Candy Man," written by Fred Neil, and Orbison's success continued with "Dream Baby," "Leah," "In Dreams," "Falling," and the two-sided hit "Mean Woman Blues/Blue Bayou." In 1962 he first toured Great Britain, where he quickly became a "superstar" and, in 1963, he toured that country as headline act to The Beatles and Gerry and The Pacemakers. Orbison's 1962 *Greatest Hits* album remained on the charts nearly three years, and the hits continued with "Pretty Paper," "It's Over," and the top hit classic, "Pretty Woman."

After a major hit with "Goodnight" in 1965, Roy Orbison switched to MGM Records; but only "Ride Away" proved to be a major hit on the label and, by 1968, he had dropped out of the charts. Dogged by personal misfortune (his wife was killed in a motorcycle accident in June 1966; two of his children died when his Nashville home burned while he was touring Britain in September 1968), Orbison appeared in the silly 1966 film *The Fastest Guitar Alive* and recorded country-style material, such as entire albums of songs by Don Gibson and Hank Williams and a duet effort with Hank Williams, Jr. Seldom touring the United States after the late Sixties and refusing to join rock-and-roll "revival" shows, Roy Orbison eventually recorded a new album for Mercury in 1975, after which he returned to Monument for 1977's *Regeneration*. During that year, he resumed American touring and saw Linda Ronstadt score a smash hit with his "Blue Bayou." In 1979 Roy Orbison recorded *Laminar Flow* for Elektra, later opened several shows for The Eagles in early 1980, and scored a major country hit in duet with Emmylou Harris with "That Loving You Feeling Again," which he co-wrote.

ROY ORBISON

At the Rock House reissued as The Original Sound	Sun	LP-1260 (M) 113(E)	March '70	A
Sun Story, Volume 4	Sunnyvale	904(M)	November '77	
Orbiting with Roy Orbison	Design	DLP-164 (M)		
Early Orbison	Monument	18023	October '64	
Lonely and Blue	Monument	14002	'61	
Crying	Monument	14007	March '62	
In Dreams	Monument	18003 reissued as 6620	August '63 October '77	A
Orbisongs	Monument	18035	October '65	
There Is Only One Roy Orbison	MGM	SE-4308	August '65	
The Orbison Way	MGM	SE-4322	January '66	
Classic Roy Orbison	MGM	SE-4379	July '66	
Roy Orbison Sings Don Gibson	MGM	SE-4424	December '66	
Fastest Guitar Alive (soundtrack)	MGM	SE-4475	June '67	
Cry Softly, Lonely One	MGM	SE-4514	October '67	
Many Moods	MGM	SE-4636	May '69	
Great Songs	MGM	SE-4659	May '70	
Roy Orbison and Hank Williams, Junior	MGM	SE-4683	October '70	
Hank Williams The Orbison Way	MGM	SE-4835	August '72	
Memphis	MGM	SE-4867	March '73	
Milestones	MGM	SE-4934	December '73	
I'm Still in Love with You	Mercury	SRM1-1045	October '75	
Regeneration	Monument	7600	October '77	A
Laminar Flow	Elektra	198	June '79	
Ooby Dooby	Accord	SN-7150	December '81	A

ROY ORBISON ANTHOLOGIES AND COMPILATIONS

Greatest Hits	Monument	14009 reissued as 6619	August '62 October '77	A
More of Roy Orbison's Greatest Hits	Monument	SLP-18024 reissued as 6621	August '64 October '77	A
The Very Best of Roy Orbison	Monument	SLP-18045 reissued as 6622	July '66 October '77	A

The All-Time Greatest Hits of Roy Orbison	2-Monument	KZG– 31484 reissued as 8600	October '72	
			October '77	A

JOHNNY OTIS. A pioneering figure in the development of rhythm-and-blues following the demise of big bands during the late Forties, Johnny Otis made his mark as a bandleader, songwriter, and discoverer of talented black acts. His Barrelhouse Club, opened in Los Angeles in 1948, is regarded as the first night club exclusively to feature rhythm-and-blues music. After assembling one of the first rhythm-and-blues combos to play at the club, Johnny Otis, following extensive recording success in 1950, organized perhaps the first and most enduring large rhythm-and-blues revues to tour America. The revues, at times, featured such legendary performers as Little Esther (Phillips), Willie Mae "Big Mama" Thornton, Johnny Ace, and "Big" Joe Turner. Among Otis' "discoveries" were Phillips, The Robins (several members of which went on to become The Coasters), Hank Ballard, Little Willie John, and Jackie Wilson. In addition to the early Fifties rhythm-and-blues hits, Johnny Otis composed the hits "Wallflower (Dance with Me, Henry)" for Etta James, "Every Beat of My Heart" (a near-smash hit for Gladys Knight and The Pips in 1961), and his own 1958 novelty hit, "Willie and the Hand Jive." Working behind the scenes in the music business during much of the Sixties, Otis re-emerged with the critically acclaimed *Cold Shot* album and reassembled his revue for the 1970 Monterey Jazz Festival and subsequent engagements at clubs, auditoriums and colleges.

JOHNNY OTIS

The Original Johnny Otis Show (1945–1951)	2-Savoy	SJL–2230 (M)	August '78	A
The Original Johnny Otis Show, Volume II (1949–1951)	2-Savoy	SJL–2252 (M)	November '80	A
The Johnny Otis Show—Rock and Roll Hit Parade Volume One	Dig	LP–104(M)		
The Johnny Otis Show	Capitol	T–490(M)	February '58	
Cold Shot	Kent	KST–534		
Cuttin' Up	Epic	BN–26524	April '70	
The Johnny Otis Show Live at Monterey	2-Epic	EG–30473	June '71	

GRAHAM PARKER. Accompanied by one of the finest rock bands involved in London's early Seventies pub scene, The Rumour, which included Brinsley Schwarz (one of Britain's most exceptional guitarists who had led his own namesake "cult" band during the Seventies), Graham Parker has been regarded, along with Elvis Costello, as one of the most compelling singer–songwriters of the British "new wave" scene. By writing songs with a unique personalized vision that dealt with anger, frustration, and defiance in a variety of contemporary styles from rockabilly to reggae, Graham Parker and The Rumour registered critical praise for their early albums, *Howlin' Wind* in particular. Though they failed to sell, their albums presaged "punk" music's rebellion against the pomposity of "progressive" rock and slick, bland, complacent commercialism of many Seventies groups. Switching labels by 1979, Graham Parker and The Rumour have begun to achieve some commercial recognition for their highly original brand of contemporary rock, as Parker has been gaining a reputation as one of the most passionate performers since Bruce Springsteen.

Born in London, Graham Parker was raised in nearby Surrey and formed his first band, The Deepcut Three, at the age of 13. After a stint with the rhythm-and-blues styled Blackrockers band, he dropped out of high school at age 17 to travel around Europe by working a variety of mundane jobs and manning several bands. Years later, in 1975, Parker recorded a demonstration tape that led to a connection with The Rumour, an excellent band comprised of veterans of England's declining "pub rock" scene. The members: Brinsley Schwarz (guitar), Bob Andrews (keyboards), Martin Belmont (guitar), Andrew Bodnar (bass), and Stephen Goulding (drums). Andrews and Schwarz had been members of the "cult" band Brinsley Schwarz, whereas Belmont had been with Ducks Deluxe and Goulding and Bodnar with Bontemps Roulez. Signed to Mercury Records, Graham Parker and The Rumour recorded two well-received but poorly selling albums released in 1976. With Parker's songs and his gruff, raspy voice singing lead, *Howlin' Wind* featured such powerful and vituperative songs as "Between You and Me," "Back to Schooldays" and "Don't Ask Me Questions." *Heat Treatment*, which included "That's What They All Say," the excellent "Pourin' It All Out," and "Fool's Gold," became their first American album chart entry, sparked by two American tours.

Scoring a minor hit with "Hold Back the Night" in the spring of 1977, Graham Parker and The Rumour recorded *Stick to Me* under producer Nick Lowe, another veteran of Brinsley Schwarz. However, the album was not particularly well received, as Lowe's use of complex arrangements and a horn section was criticized. Nonetheless, it sold somewhat better than had the earlier albums as it contained such outstanding songs as "Soul on Ice," the ominous "Thunder and Rain," and the title song. Earlier, The Rumour had recorded their own *Max* album and, in 1978, they and Parker released the equivocal double-record live set, *The Parkerilla*. Switching to Arista Records, Parker and the group recorded *Squeezing Out Sparks* under veteran producer Jack Nitzche, projecting a simpler guitar-dominated sound unmuddled by horns. Critically lauded as containing Parker's best compositions and vocal performances to date, the album included "Nobody Hurts You," the passionate "You Can't Be Too Strong," and the potent "Passion Is No Ordinary Word," plus "Mercury Poisoning" and "No Protection." Supported by a three-month American tour, the album sold far better than had previous releases and was followed by The Rumour's *Frogs, Sprouts, Clogs, and Krauts* and Graham Parker and The Rumour's *The Up Escalator*. The latter album, recorded with guest keyboardists Nicky Hopkins and Danny Federici in place of Bob Andrews (who left Parker to front The Rumour as a separate act), featured "Stupefaction," "No Holding Back," "Love without Greed," and, with Bruce Springsteen singing vocal harmony, "Endless Night." During 1981, Graham Parker and The Rumour ended their association.

GRAHAM PARKER AND THE RUMOUR

Howlin' Wind	Mercury	SRM1–1095	June '76	A
Heat Treatment	Mercury	SRM1–1117	November '76	A
Stick to Me	Mercury	SRM1–3706	October '77	A
The Parkerilla	2-Mercury	SRM2–100	May '78	
Squeezing Out Sparks	Arista	AB–4223	April '79	A
The Up Escalator	Arista	9517	May '80	A

THE RUMOUR

Max	Mercury	SRM1–1174	August '77	
Frogs, Sprouts, Clogs, and Krauts	Arista	4235	July '79	

PARLIAMENT/FUNKADELIC. Masterminded by George Clinton, The Parliaments/Parliament weathered years of relative failure as a rhythm-and-blues vocal group for a variety of labels, only to lose the right to the name during the early Seventies. Regrouping as the rock-oriented Funkadelic and incorporating the innovations of Sly Stone and Jimi Hendrix, the group continued to record for a separate label even after Clinton had regained the use of the Parliament name. Augmented by a bassist and two horn players from James Brown's band, Parliament recorded a series of bizarre, oddly conceptual albums of so-called "funk" music, perhaps the last vestiges of rhythm-and-blues music not obliterated by the rise of mindless disco music. Appealing primarily to ghetto teenagers and promoting humanitarian values such as equality and self-determination through an off-the-wall synthesis of ghetto jargon, science fiction fantasies, parodied psychedelic and spiritual values, and just plain nonsense, Parliament finally broke through with 1976's *Mothership Connection* album and tour. Subsequently scoring consecutive certified gold-award albums as Parliament, George Clinton later concentrated on the Funkadelic side of the group, achieving platinum-level success with 1978's *One Nation under a Groove*. Bolstered by those successes, George Clinton attained an almost unprecedented degree of control over and independence of his music, as evidenced by the recording of various subgroups of the Parliament/Funkadelic amalgam and the establishment of his own label, Uncle Jam Records.

Born in Kannapolis, North Carolina, on July 22, 1940, George Clinton also lived in the Washington, D.C., area before his family settled in New Jersey when he was nine. In 1955, as a teenager, he formed the five-man rhythm-and-blues vocal group The Parliaments, recording unsuccessfully for ABC–Paramount during the late Fifties and drifting from label to label until signing with Motown in 1964. The group's Motown recordings were never issued and they eventually achieved a major rhythm-and-blues and pop hit with "(I Wanna) Testify" on the Revilot label in 1967. However, the company folded the next year, as Motown claimed the rights to the Parliament name; yet the group did manage to record *Osmium* for Holland–Dozier–Holland's Invictus label before losing the rights to the name.

George Clinton, assuming the persona of Dr. Funkenstein, augmented and regrouped Parliament as the instrument-dominated Funkadelic aggregation, with guitarists Eddie Hazel and Lucius Ross, keyboardist Bernard Worrell, drummer Ramon Fullwood, and vocalist Ray Davis. Signed to the Detroit-based Westbound label, Funkadelic recorded a series of poorly selling "funk" albums with such engaging titles as *Maggot Brain*, *America Eats Its Young*, and *Cosmic Slop*, their first album chart entry. With Clinton regaining the right to use the Parliament name by 1974, the group signed with Casablanca Records, recording bizarre yet entertaining albums backed by Funkadelic that culminated in the astounding success of the classic "Tear the Roof Off the Sucker (Give Up the Funk)" single and the certified platinum-award *Mothership Connection* album. By then, the members of Parliament/Funkadelic included horn players Maceo Parker and Fred Wesley (who had previously recorded as Maceo and The King's Men and together as The JB's) and bassist William "Bootsy" Collins, all former members of the James Brown band, veterans Worrell, Hazel, and

Davis, plus guitarists Gary Shider and Mike Hampton and former Ohio Players keyboardist Walter Morrison. A weird conceptual album blending brilliant if erratic music and Clinton's funk monologues regarding science fiction and psychedelic and spiritual fantasies, *Mothership Connection* was supported by a successful sell-out tour that incorporated odd costumes and massive stage props, including a spaceship dubbed The Mothership.

The success of *Mothership Connection* paved the way for subsequent best-selling albums by Parliament, including late 1977's platinum-award *Funkentelechy vs. The Placebo Syndrome* and its hit single, "Flash Light." Also in 1976, the first of many spinoff groups from the Parliament/Funka-delic aggregation, Bootsy's Rubber Band, headed by "Bootsy" Collins, began recording for Warner Brothers Records. That group's *Ahh . . . The Name Is Bootsy, Baby!* and *Bootsy? Player of the Year* albums were both certified gold-award during the year of release. Furthermore, Funkadelic switched to Warner Brothers during 1976 and, as George Clinton began to concentrate on that group, they established themselves with 1978's *One Nation under a Groove* hit single and platinum-award album. In the meantime, horn players Fred Wesley and Maceo Parker had begun record-ing for Atlantic as Fred Wesley and The Horny Horns, whereas guitarist Eddie Hazel had recorded a solo album for Warner Brothers. In 1978 the five-person female backup group to Parliament/Funkadelic split into the two-member Brides of Funkenstein and three-member Parlet for record-ings on Atlantic and Casablanca, respectively. Releases in 1979 included Bootsy's Rubber Band's *This Boot Is Made for Funkin'*, Funkadelic's *Uncle Jam Wants You*, Parliament's *Gloryhallastoopid (Pin the Tale on the Funky)* and Bernie "Woo" Worrell's solo debut on Arista, *All the Woo in the World*. Subsequent albums included sets by Junie (Walter) Morrison, Parlet, Bootsy Collins, Zapp (fronted by Collins), and The Sweat Band (former members of Bootsy's Rubber Band), as well as Funkadelic's *The Electric Spanking of War Babies*, and *Connections and Disconnections*, by former members of Funkadelic.

PARLIAMENT

Osmium	Invictus	ST–7302	August '70

GEORGE CLINTON

The George Clinton Band Arrives	ABC	831	August '74

FUNKADELIC

Funkadelic	Westbound	2000 reissued as 216	December '75
Free Your Mind and Your Ass Will Follow	Westbound	2001 reissued as 217	November '70 December '75

Maggot Brain	Westbound	2007 reissued as 218	November '71 December '75	
America Eats Its Young	2-Westbound	2020 reissued as 221	September '72 December '75	
Cosmic Slop	Westbound	2022(M) reissued as 223	July '73	
Standing on the Verge of Getting It On	Westbound	1001 reissued as 208	June '74 April '75	
Greatest Hits	Westbound	1004	March '75	
Let's Take It to the Stage	Westbound	215	July '75	
Tales of Kidd Funkadelic	Westbound	227	September '76	
Best of the Early Years, Volume 1	Westbound	303	June '77	

PARLIAMENT

Up for the Down Stroke	Casablanca	9003 reissued as 7002	August '74	A
Chocolate City	Casablanca	7014	April '75	A
Mothership Connection**	Casablanca	7022	January '76	A

MACEO AND THE KING'S MEN

Doin' Their Own Thing	House	1	May '71

MACEO AND THE MACKS

Maceo	People	6601	May '74

THE JB'S

Food for Thought	People	5601	July '72
Doing It to Death	People	5603	July '73
Damn Right I Am Somebody	People	6602	May '74
Breakin' Bread	People	6604	January '75
Hustle with Speed	People	6606	September '75

JUNIE (WALTER) MORRISON

When We Do	Westbound	200	April '75	
Freeze	Westbound	214	January '76	
Suzie Super Groupie	Westbound	228	August '76	
Bread Alone	Columbia	JC–36585	October '80	A
Junie 5	Columbia	ARC– 37133	June '81	A

FRED WESLEY AND THE HORNY HORNS

| A Blow for Me, A Toot for You | Atlantic | 18214 | April '77 | |

BOOTSY'S RUBBER BAND

Stretchin' Out in Bootsy's Rubber Band	Warner Brothers	2920	April '76	
Ahh . . . The Name Is Bootsy, Baby! *	Warner Brothers	2972	February '77	
Bootsy? Player of the Year *	Warner Brothers	BSK–3093	January '78	
This Boot Is Made for Funkin'	Warner Brothers	BSK–3295	June '79	

BOOTSY

| Ultra Wave | Warner Brothers | 3433 | November '80 | A |

PARLIAMENT

The Clones of Dr. Funkenstein *	Casablanca	7034	September '76	A
Parliament Live-P-Funk Earth Tour *	2-Casablanca	7053	May '77	A
Funkentelechy vs. The Placebo Syndrome **	Casablanca	7084	December '77	A
Motor Booty Affair *	Casablanca	7125	December '78	
Gloryhallastoopid (Pin the Tale on the Funky) *	Casablanca	7195	December '79	A

FUNKADELIC

Hardcore Jollies	Warner Brothers	2973	November '76	
One Nation under a Groove **	Warner Brothers	3209	August '78	A
Uncle Jam Wants You *	Warner Brothers	HS–3371	September '79	A
The Electric Spanking of War Babies	Warner Brothers	3482	April '81	A

EDDIE HAZEL

| Games, Dames, and Other Thangs | Warner Brothers | 3058 | August '77 | |

PARLET

Pleasure	Casablanca	7094	September '78	A
Invasion of the Body Snatchers	Casablanca	7146		A
Play Me or Trade Me	Casablanca	7224		A

BRIDES OF FUNKENSTEIN

Funk or Walk	Atlantic	SD–19201	October '78
Never Buy Texas from a Cowboy	Atlantic	SD–19261	January '80

BERNIE WORRELL

All the Woo in the World	Arista	4209	October '79

ZAPP

Zapp *	Warner Brothers	3463	September '80	A

THE SWEAT BAND

The Sweat Band	Uncle Jam	JZ–36857	November'80	A

FUNKADELIC (FORMER MEMBERS)

Connections and Disconnections	Lax	JW–37087	May '81	A

PEARLS BEFORE SWINE. Obscure and sorely neglected American group of the late Sixties and early Seventies, Pearls Before Swine recorded two abstract, poorly produced albums for the avant garde label ESP before switching to Reprise Records for more conventional-sounding albums pervaded by brilliantly arranged and poignantly effective songs written by leader Tom Rapp. In particular, *These Things, Too* and *The Use of Ashes* were stunningly profound and moving albums, yet Pearls Before Swine were never able to attract more than a cult following and disbanded by 1972, as Rapp recorded solo for a time before totally disappearing by 1974.

PEARLS BEFORE SWINE

One Nation Underground	ESP	1054	September '67	
Balaklava	ESP	1075	November '68	
reissued as Best	2-Adelphi	4111	October '80	A
These Things, Too	Reprise	RS–6364	September '69	
The Use of Ashes	Reprise	RS–6405	November '70	
City of Gold	Reprise	RS–6442	June '71	

TOM RAPP/PEARLS BEFORE SWINE

. . . Beautiful Lies You Could Live In	Reprise	RS–6467	December '71	A

TOM RAPP

Familiar Songs	Reprise	MS–2069	September '72
Stardancer	Blue Thumb	BTS–44	November '72
Sunforest	Blue Thumb	BTS–56	September '73

PENTANGLE.   Probably the first British "folk-rock" band, Pentangle continued to record and perform their eclectic music on primarily acoustic instruments even after other British groups of the genre, such as Fairport Convention, were utilizing electric instruments. Sparked by the outstanding soprano voice of Jacqui McShee and the virtuoso guitar playing of Bert Jansch and John Renbourn, Pentangle mixed traditional British folk songs, jazz instrumentals, blues songs, and occasional contemporary original songs into their repertoire. One of the most popular folk-style British bands between 1968 and 1971, Pentangle attracted only a limited following in the United States, as virtually no British folk-oriented group achieved massive popularity in this country at that time. Both Jansch and Renbourn recorded solo and duet albums during the existence of Pentangle but, following the group's demise in 1973, neither recorded albums for American release until 1978, when they both began recording for the small Kicking Mule label.

BERT JANSCH

Lucky Thirteen	Vanguard	VSD– 79212	May '66

PENTANGLE

Pentangle	Reprise	RS–6315	September '68
Sweet Child	2-Reprise	2RS–6334	January '69
Basket of Light	Reprise	RS–6372	January '70
Cruel Sister	Reprise	RS–6430	March '71
Reflection	Reprise	RS–6463	October '71

BERT JANSCH AND JOHN RENBOURN

Stepping Stones	Vanguard	VSD–6506	March '69	A
Jack Orion	Vanguard	VSD–6544	February '71	A

JOHN RENBOURN

Sir John Alot	Reprise	RS–6344	July '69	
The Lady and the Unicorn	Reprise	RS–6407	February '71	A
John Renbourn	2-Reprise	2RS–6482		
Faro Annie	Reprise	MS–2082	August '72	

Maid in Bedlam	Shanachie	79004	February '79	A
The Black Balloon	Kicking Mule	163	November '79	A
Hermit	Transatlantic	336	August '80	A
Enchanted Group	Kicking Mule	312	December '81	A

JOHN RENBOURN AND STEFAN GROSSMAN

Stefan Grossman and John Renbourn	Kicking Mule	152	August '78	A
Under the Volcano	Kicking Mule	162	January '80	A

BERT JANSCH

Birthday Blues	Reprise	RS–6343	November '69	
Rosemary Lane	Reprise	RS–6455	November '71	
Moonshine	Reprise	MS–2129	March '73	
A Rare Conumdrum	Kicking Mule	302	November '78	A
The Best of Bert Jansch	Kicking Mule	334	November '79	A
Thirteen Down	Kicking Mule	309	May '80	A

CARL PERKINS. With his smash hit classic from early 1956, "Blue Suede Shoes," one of the earliest singles to become a smash hit in the pop, country-and-western *and* rhythm-and-blues fields, Carl Perkins helped create and establish the "rockabilly" sound and brought Sun Records into national prominence. As with Chuck Berry, Perkins was one of the artists of the early "rock-and-roll" era to both write many of his own songs and play lead guitar while singing in performances and recordings, unlike Elvis Presley. The first "rockabilly" artist to be booked on a network television show, Carl Perkins was unable to make the engagement due to a serious automobile accident that resulted in a long period of recuperation which impeded his career's momentum. Enjoying renewed public interest in 1964–65 when The Beatles covered three of his songs, Perkins later toured as part of Johnny Cash's road show for nearly a decade before forming his own touring unit with two of his sons in 1976.

CARL PERKINS ON SUN

Dance Album	Sun	LP–1225 (M)	'58	
reissued as Teen Beat				
Original Golden Hits	Sun	111(M) reissued as 111(E)	April '70	A
Blue Suede Shoes	Sun	112(M) reissued as 112(E)		A
The Sun Story, Volume 3	Sunnyvale	903(M)	November '77	

Carl Perkins, Jerry Lee Lewis, Charlie Rich, and Friends	Sun	1018	January '80	A

CARL PERKINS

Whole Lotta Shakin'	Columbia	CL–1234 (M)	November '58
Country Boy's Dream	Dollie	4001	'66
On Top	Columbia	CS–9931	November '69
Boppin' the Blues	Columbia	CS–9981	March '70
My Kind of Country	Mercury	SRM1–691	January '74
Ol' Blue Suede's Back	Jet	JZ–35604	October '78

CARL PERKINS ANTHOLOGIES AND COMPILATIONS

Greatest Hits	Columbia	CS–9833	July '69
Carl Perkins	Harmony	HS–11385	April '70
Brown-Eyed, Handsome Man	Harmony	KH–31179	April '72
Greatest Hits	Harmony	KH–31792	January '73

CARL PERKINS/THE SHANGRI–LAS

Supercharged Rock Originals	Pickwick	3316

PETER AND GORDON/PETER ASHER. Perhaps the most popular British vocal duo of the so-called "English invasion," Peter and Gordon, like rivals Chad and Jeremy, experienced greater success in the United States than in Great Britain. Aided by Beatles John Lennon and Paul McCartney, who contributed two previously unrecorded compositions that became the duo's first two hits, Peter and Gordon later hit with several novelty songs before splitting up in late 1967. Peter Asher subsequently became staff producer and, later, head of the A&R (artists and repertoire) department for Apple Records, where he contracted James Taylor as the company's first signing. Abandoning Apple, Asher negotiated Taylor's contract with Warner Brothers Records, produced his first three albums for the label, including *Sweet Baby James*, and became Taylor's manager. Assisting in the completion of Linda Ronstadt's *Don't Cry Now* album, Asher has since produced all of her albums, including *Heart like a Wheel*, the album that established her. Today one of the most important producer–managers in rock music through his continuing association with Taylor and Ronstadt, Peter Asher could be given the bulk of the credit for Ronstadt's enormous success inasmuch as his astute song selection and sympathetic production are more significant therein than her powerful yet overrated and emotionless voice.

Peter Asher (born June 22, 1944, in London, England) was raised in London and became a child star in films along with his sister Jane. As a teenager he took piano lessons and attempted to learn both oboe and double bass before briefly joining a skiffle group at the age of 15. At 13 he had met Gordon Waller (born June 4, 1945, in Braemaer, Scotland) in public school, and the two teamed up in 1962 and played the coffeehouse circuit for nearly two years before signing with EMI (Capitol in the United States) near the beginning of 1964. At that time Jane Asher was Paul McCartney's girlfriend, and the relationship resulted in Lennon and McCartney contributing their previously unrecorded "World Without Love" to Peter and Gordon. The single became a top American hit and helped make their debut album a best-seller. Soon touring regularly in the United States, where they achieved their greatest success, Peter and Gordon subsequently hit with Lennon and McCartney's "Nobody I Know," "I Don't Want to See You Again," Del Shannon's "I Go to Pieces," Buddy Holly's "True Love Ways," and "To Know You Is to Love You," through the summer of 1965. Their early 1966 hit, "Woman," credited to Bernard Webb, was in fact written by Paul McCartney; they subsequently scored their final major hits in 1966–67 with the novelty songs "Lady Godiva" and "Knight in Rusty Armour."

Near the end of 1967 Peter and Gordon split up; Gordon eventually resurfaced with an unsuccessful solo album on ABC in 1972. After producing three singles for former Manfred Mann vocalist Paul Jones, Peter Asher was asked by Paul McCartney to join Apple Records as a producer, and he was soon elevated to head of A&R for the label. Asher signed James Taylor, who was then visiting London, to Apple and produced his neglected debut album. In 1969 Asher resigned his position with Apple, moved to Los Angeles, and negotiated a new contract for Taylor with Warner Brothers Records. He subsequently produced Taylor's first three albums for the label, including *Sweet Baby James*, the certified gold-award album that established Taylor. Asher also produced albums by Tony Joe White and John Stewart and functioned for a while as Cat Stevens' co-manager, while also serving as Kate Taylor's producer–manager. In 1973 Peter Asher agreed to help Linda Ronstadt complete her *Don't Cry Now* album, and he later limited himself to managing James Taylor and producing and managing Linda Ronstadt. After years of relative obscurity Ronstadt quickly became established with *Heart like a Wheel*, largely on the strength of Asher's production, arrangements, and astute song selections. He has since produced all of her albums as well as James Taylor's *JT* and *Flag* albums and Bonnie Raitt's *The Glow*.

PETER AND GORDON

A World Without Love	Capitol	ST-2115	June '64
I Don't Want to See You Again	Capitol	ST-2220	December '64
Peter and Gordon—I Go to Pieces	Capitol	ST-2324	May '65

True Love Ways	Capitol	ST–2368	August '65	
Sing and Play the Hits of Nashville, Tennessee	Capitol	ST–2430	October '65	
Woman	Capitol	ST–2477	March '66	
The Best of Peter and Gordon	Capitol	SM–2549 reissued as SN–16084	June '66	A
Lady Godiva	Capitol	ST–2664	January '67	
Knight in Rusty Armour	Capitol	ST–2729	April '67	
In London for Tea	Capitol	ST–2747	July '67	
Hot, Cold, and Custard	Capitol	ST–2882	July '68	

GORDON WALLER

And Gordon	ABC	ABCX–749	April '72

PETER, PAUL, AND MARY. One of the two most popular and successful folk groups of the Sixties (the other being The Kingston Trio), Peter, Paul, and Mary scored a series of major hits between 1962 and 1969 as seven of their first eight albums achieved gold-award certification by 1970. Perhaps the quintessential folk group, Peter, Paul, and Mary were key figures in the early Sixties ascension of folk music, while introducing and popularizing the compositions of songwriters Bob Dylan, Gordon Lightfoot, and John Denver. The trio's huge commercial success exposed both the folk and protest movements to a mass audience and opened the way for the later successes of Bob Dylan and "folk-rock" music. Going their separate ways in 1970, the members of Peter, Paul, and Mary encountered difficulty in establishing themselves as solo performers during the Seventies. In 1978 the three reunited for touring and recording, while continuing to pursue individual projects.

Peter, Paul, and Mary were brought together by manager Albert Grossman in New York's Greenwich Village during 1961. Peter Yarrow (born May 31, 1938, in New York) was a Cornell University graduate in psychology who had worked for a time as a solo artist and appeared at the 1960 Newport Folk Festival. (Noel) Paul Stookey (born November 30, 1937, in Birmingham, Michigan) had led a high school rock band before pursuing a career around Greenwich Village as a stand-up comic. He encouraged former folk group member Mary Travers (born November 7, 1937, in Louisville, Kentucky) to return to singing after her appearance in the flop Broadway show, *The Next President.* Conducting intensive rehearsals for seven months, Peter, Paul, and Mary signed with Warner Brothers Records and their debut album became a top album hit, remaining on the charts for more than three years. The album included standard folk-style material such as Reverend Gary Davis' "If I Had My Way,"

Hedy West's "500 Miles," and Pete Seeger's "Where Have All the Flowers Gone," and original compositions by Yarrow and Stookey, yielding a moderate hit with "If I Had a Hammer," co-authored by Pete Seeger. Quickly thrust into the forefront of the folk movement, Peter, Paul, and Mary became favorites on the college circuit and frequently performed at political rallies and protest marches, unlike many other popular folk acts.

As with their debut album, Peter, Paul, and Mary's second, *(Moving)*, was quickly certified gold-award; it produced a smash hit with "Puff, the Magic Dragon," written by Yarrow and Leonard Lipton, and moderate hits with "Stewball" and "Tell It on the Mountain," and contained Woody Guthrie's "This Land Is Your Land." With *In the Wind*, the trio began featuring songs by then-unknown contemporary songwriters, and the smash successes of "Blowin' in the Wind" and "Don't Think Twice, It's All Right" introduced Bob Dylan and bolstered the burgeoning "folk-protest" movement. Following the live double-record set *In Concert*, Peter, Paul, and Mary recorded *Song Will Rise*, which contained the first hit version of Gordon Lightfoot's "For Lovin' Me," and *See What Tomorrow Brings*, which included Lightfoot's "Early Morning Rain" and Tom Paxton's "Last Thing on My Mind." *Peter, Paul, and Mary Album* became a best-seller without yielding a major hit and was followed by perhaps their finest albums, *Album 1700* and *Late Again*. *Album 1700* produced a near-smash with Stookey's collaborative tongue-in-cheek "I Dig Rock and Roll Music" while also containing John Denver's "Leaving on a Jet Plane" (a top hit when released as a single two years later) and some of the group's finest compositions, including the touching "The House Song" (Stookey, et al.), Yarrow's anti-war "The Great Mandella (The Wheel of Life)," and the collaborative classic "The Song Is Love." "Hymn" and "Rich Man, Poor Man," co-authored by Stookey and Yarrow, respectively, "Tramp on the Street," and Tim Hardin's "Reason to Believe" were included on *Late Again*, which yielded a moderate hit with Bob Dylan's "Too Much of Nothing."

Following *Peter, Paul, and Mommy*, Peter Yarrow, Paul Stookey, and Mary Travers went their separate ways in 1970. Stookey fared best of the three as a solo artist, scoring a major hit with "Wedding Song (There Is Love)" in 1971 from the excellent *Paul And*. Thereafter albums by each of the three fared poorly. By the mid-Seventies Paul Stookey had retreated to Maine and Peter Yarrow had become involved in television and record production work, leaving Mary Travers as the only former member to perform extensively. In 1976 Yarrow produced Mary MacGregor's best-selling *Torn Between Two Lovers* album; the title song, which he co-authored, became a top hit. An animated television special, "Puff, the Magic Dragon," co-produced by Yarrow and based on the song, was aired in the fall of 1978 on the CBS network and featured two other Yarrow compositions, "Weave Me the Sunshine" and "Build Me a Boat," and garnered an Emmy nomination. By then Peter, Paul, and Mary had regrouped for *Reunion* and another round of touring, while continuing to pursue individual projects. The trio toured again in early 1980.

PETER, PAUL, AND MARY

Peter, Paul, and Mary*	Warner Brothers	WS–1449	April '62	A
(Moving)*	Warner Brothers	WS–1473	January '63	
In the Wind*	Warner Brothers	WS–1507	October '63	
In Concert*	2-Warner Brothers	2WS–1555	August '64	A
Song Will Rise*	Warner Brothers	WS–1589	April '65	
See What Tomor-row Brings*	Warner Brothers	WS–1615	October '65	
Album	Warner Brothers	WS–1648	August '66	
Album 1700*	Warner Brothers	WS–1700	August '67	A
Late Again	Warner Brothers	WS–1751	August '68	
Peter, Paul, and Mommy	Warner Brothers	WS–1785	May '69	A
Best (10 Years Together)	Warner Brothers	BS–2552 reissued as BSK–3105	May '70	A

MARY TRAVERS

Mary	Warner Brothers	WS–1907	April '71	
Morning Glory	Warner Brothers	BS–2609	April '72	
All My Choices	Warner Brothers	BS–2677	February '73	
Circles	Warner Brothers	BS–2795	June '74	
It's in Every One of Us	Chrysalis	CHR–1168	February '78	A

PAUL STOOKEY

Paul And	Warner Brothers	WS–1912	August '71	
Noel—One Night Stand	Warner Brothers	BS–2674	January '73	

PETER YARROW

Peter	Warner Brothers	BS–2599	February '72	
That's Enough for Me	Warner Brothers	BS–2730	November '73	
Hard Times	Warner Brothers	BS–2860	May '75	
Love Songs	Warner Brothers	BS–2891	December '75	

SAM PHILLIPS/SUN RECORDS. Probably best remembered as the man who "discovered" and first recorded Elvis Presley, Sam Phillips was instrumental in the development of so-called "rockabilly" music that fused elements of black rhythm-and-blues and white country-and-western music in a unique and original way. Having previously made the initial recordings of famous bluesmen such as B.B. King, Howlin' Wolf, and Junior Parker, Phillips switched his attention to white Southern singers after the initial success and departure of Presley and signed and recorded the initial work of Johnny Cash, Carl Perkins, Roy Orbison, and Jerry Lee Lewis on his Sun label. Sun Records and the Chicago-based Chess Records were the labels that pioneered "rock-and-roll" and challenged the complacency of established major record labels during the Fifties. Encouraging other producers and record companies to treat other young singers more sympathetically as a consequence of its own success, Sun Records eventually lost all of its major acts to larger labels. Although the influence of Sun Records was in decline by the end of the Fifties, the label was the training ground for producers Billy Sherill and Jack Clement, and the subsidiary Phillips International label managed major hits for Bill Justis, Carl Mann, and Charlie Rich.

Born in Florence, Alabama, in 1923, Sam Phillips was working as a disc jockey at Memphis' WRAC when he realized that few facilities existed to record local black performers. In 1950 he established the Sun studio and made early recordings by B.B. King, Howlin' Wolf, and others and leased them to established independent companies such as Modern/RPM and Chess/Checker. Forming the Sun label in late 1952, Phillips scored his first rhythm-and-blues hits the next year with Little Junior Parker's "Mystery Train" and Rufus Thomas' "Bear Cat." Searching for a white singer who sounded black (his actual words were purportedly far less delicate), he found his man in Elvis Presley, who had first come to the Sun studio in July 1953 ostensibly to make a private recording for his mother. Teamed with guitarist Scotty Moore and standup bassist Bill Black, Presley made his first recordings for Sun, "Blue Moon of Kentucky" backed with Arthur "Big Boy" Crudup's "That's All Right (Mama)," in July 1954. With some help from a local disc jockey, "That's All Right (Mama)" became a regional hit and Phillips subsequently recorded Presley's versions of songs written by black writers, such as "Good Rockin' Tonight," "Baby, Let's Play House" (a country hit), and "Mystery Train" (a top country hit), backed by country-and-western standards. In November 1955 Phillips sold Presley's Sun contract as well as his master recordings to RCA-Victor for an unprecedented $35,000.

With Presley's departure, Sam Phillips began working with other white Southern singers such as Johnny Cash and Carl Perkins. Perkins soon scored a smash country-and-western, rhythm-and-blues, *and* pop hit with his own "Blue Suede Shoes" in early 1956, followed by several country hits, whereas Cash achieved his first major pop hit for Sun (after two country hits) with "I Walk the Line" in the fall of 1956, followed by the pop-style hits "Ballad of a Teenage Queen," "Guess Things Happen That Way," and "The Ways of a Woman in Love," recorded under arranger–producer Bill Justis. Issuing the early recordings of Roy Orbison in 1956 (including the minor pop hit "Ooby Dooby"), Sun Records next achieved smash country-and-western, rhythm-and-blues, and pop hits with Jerry Lee Lewis' "Whole Lotta Shakin' Going On," "Great Balls of Fire," and "Breathless" in 1957–58. During 1957 Phillips formed the subsidiary label Phillips International, and hits on the label included Bill Justis' 1957 instrumental "Raunchy," Carl Mann's 1959 "Mona Lisa," and Charlie Rich's 1960 "Lonely Weekends." However, by 1958, Johnny Cash, Carl Perkins, and Roy Orbison had all left Sun for major established labels, and Jerry Lee Lewis also departed in 1962. Sun Records continued operations in the Sixties, but the label failed to produce any more significant hits or discover any important new acts. In 1968 Sam Phillips retired and sold the Sun masters to Nashville's Shelby Singleton. Original Sun recordings have since been issued on Singleton's Sun label and the Sunnyvale subsidiary of GRT Records.

WILSON PICKETT.   One of the most popular rhythm-and-blues/soul singles artists of the Sixties, Wilson Pickett was helped immeasurably in achieving his success by the excellent studio bands backing him in Memphis, Tennessee, and Muscle Shoals, Alabama. Projecting a tough, aggressive, hard-driving emotionalism in his recordings, Wilson Pickett scored at least 11 major pop and five top rhythm-and-blues/soul hits between 1965 and 1971, including the classics "In the Midnight Hour" and "Funky Broadway." Achieving his last major hits under producers Kenny Gamble and Leon Huff, purveyors of the so-called "Philadelphia sound," Wilson Pickett has endured limited popularity in the Seventies due to an ill-advised label switch away from Atlantic Records, the recording of less-than-appropriate material, and the rise of black vocal groups and disco music.

WILSON PICKETT

It's Too Late	Double L	8300	January '64
In the Midnight Hour	Atlantic	SD–8114 (M)	October '65
Exciting Wilson Pickett	Atlantic	SD–8129	August '66
Wicked Pickett	Atlantic	SD–8138	January '67
The Sound of Wilson Pickett	Atlantic	SD–8145	August '67
I'm in Love	Atlantic	SD–8175	February '68
Midnight Mover	Atlantic	SD–8183	July '68

Hey, Jude	Atlantic	SD–8215	February '69	
Right On	Atlantic	SD–8250	March '70	
In Philadelphia	Atlantic	SD–8270	September '70	
Don't Knock My Love	Atlantic	SD–8300	December '71	
Mr. Magic Man	RCA	LSP–4858	March '73	
Miz Lena's Boy	RCA	APL1–0312	October '73	
Pickett in the Pocket	RCA	APL1–0495	July '74	
Join Me and Let's Be Free	RCA	APL1–0856	June '75	
		reissued as ANL1–2149	May '77	
Chocolate Mountain	Wicked	9001	June '76	
A Funky Situation	Big Tree	76011	September '78	
I Want You	EMI-America	SW–17019	November '79	A
Right Track	EMI-America	SW–17043	March '81	A

WILSON PICKETT ANTHOLOGIES AND COMPILATIONS

Great Wilson Pickett Hits	Wand	WDS–672	December '66	
The Best of Wilson Pickett	Atlantic	SD–8151	November '67	
The Best of Wilson Pickett, Volume 2	Atlantic	SD–8290	May '71	
Greatest Hits	2-Atlantic	SD2–501	January '73	A
Wickedness	Trip	8010	November '71	

PINK FLOYD. Generally regarded as the first "underground" group to emerge from the London music scene, Pink Floyd was probably the first British "psychedelic" band, due in large part to founder Syd Barrett's lead guitar playing and surrealistic, mystically obsessed lyrics. The first British rock group to utilize a light show in performance, Pink Floyd began expanding their cult following with their excellent debut album. After recording only one album with Pink Floyd, Syd Barrett dropped out of the group in 1968, apparently due to psychological problems and/or psychedelic drug abuse, after which he became a mysterious and inscrutable cult idol whose following persists to this day. Having replaced him with lead guitarist Dave Gilmour while bassist Roger Waters assumed the role of chief songwriter, Pink Floyd subsequently used progressively sophisticated lighting systems in performance and invested huge sums in amassing one of the most elaborate and advanced sound systems in rock music. After winning a reputation as one of the first "intellectual" rock bands, Pink Floyd remained a cult band during the early Seventies and their performances became increasingly theatrical, complete with massive stage props. With keyboardist Rick Wright utilizing advanced synthesizer instruments, Pink

Floyd became regarded as one of the many so-called "progressive" groups of the era.

Pink Floyd eventually broke through with 1973's *Dark Side of the Moon*, a monumental album concerned with lunacy and alienation as wrought by contemporary society. The album established the group as "superstars," selling 13 million copies worldwide and remaining on the album charts over seven years, thus eclipsing Carole King's pop music chart longevity record established with *Tapestry*. Tours continued to be staged with elaborate and massive stage props and sophisticated musical equipment, as evidenced by the eleven semitrailers used to haul materials for their 1977 tour in support of *Animals*. This trend culminated in the 1980 tour in support of *The Wall*, an ambitious and personal album again concerned with alienation and repression, that incorporated a 30-foot high, stage-wide wall of blocks so massive that Pink Floyd performed the album in only three cities, Los Angeles, New York, and London.

Roger "Syd" Barrett (born January 6, 1946, in Cambridge, England) attended school with Roger Waters (born September 6, 1944, in Great Bookham, England) and Dave Gilmour (born March 6, 1944, in Cambridge). Barrett moved to London after school where he took up guitar and played with several groups, including a folk duo with Gilmour. Waters moved to London to study architecture, and met Rick Wright (born July 28, 1945, in London) and Nick Mason (born January 27, 1945, in Birmingham, England) in an architecture course. Waters, Mason, and Wright formed Sigma 6, which later became The T-Set and The Abdabs, and played rhythm-and-blues style music. Around 1965 The Abdabs broke up; Mason, Wright, and Waters recruited guitarists Bob Close and Syd Barrett and adopted the name Pink Floyd. Close remained with the group only briefly. The members of the first stable lineup of Pink Floyd were: Syd Barrett (lead guitar, vocals), Rick Wright (keyboards, vocals), Roger Waters (bass, piano, vocals), and Nick Mason (drums). By February 1966 Pink Floyd had obtained their first regular engagement at The Marquee and built their first small following. In October they moved to London's Sound/Light Workshop, where they were accompanied by a light show, the first of its kind in Great Britain. Becoming the house band at the UFO Club by year's end, Pink Floyd signed with EMI Records (the small, experimental Tower label in the United States). Their first single, Barrett's "Arnold Layne," concerned a perverted transvestite and proved so controversial that even "underground" Radio London banned the song, yet it became a moderate British hit. Barrett's "See Emily Play" became a smash British hit in the spring and Pink Floyd's debut album was released in the United States near the end of 1967. Critically acclaimed, *The Piper at the Gates of Dawn* was dominated by Barrett's surreal, mystical songwriting. However, the group's next three British singles fared poorly as Pink Floyd toured America for the first time in October 1967. Barrett's behavior, erratic as it was, began to deteriorate by early 1968 and Dave Gilmour joined the group as second guitarist in February. By April Barrett had left amid rumors of drug abuse and bizarre stories of his unpredictable behavior. He inspired a devoted cult following that persists to this day, and recordings made by him with Gilmour and Wright during 1970 were eventually released in the United States in 1974. Syd Barrett remains a mysterious and enigmatic figure, seldom appearing in public.

With Barrett's departure, Roger Waters began assuming the role of chief songwriter, and the acclaimed *Saucerful of Secrets* contained his "Let There Be More Light" and "Set the Controls for the Heart of the Sun," songs that earned Pink Floyd the label of "space-rock" band. The band's soundtrack to the film *More* was released in the summer of 1969, during which time they first toured with a custom-built quadraphonic sound system. At the beginning of 1970, Pink Floyd's double-record set *Ummagumma* was issued on EMI's new "underground" label, Harvest. Their first modestly successful album in the United States, it consisted of one live album and a studio album divided equally among the four. *Atom Heart Mother* was debuted at the Bath Festival in England during June; it featured choirs, orchestras, and remarkably diverse sounds under the influence of electronics wizard Ron Geesin. Pink Floyd's stage show became ever more elaborate and, in the summer of 1971, an outdoor concert in London utilized a 60-foot inflatable octopus. *Relics* was comprised of early recordings by the group, and the group-produced *Meddle*, though not well received, did contain the side-long "Echoes," one of their most popular songs.

Following the soundtrack to the film *Le Vallee* entitled *Obscured by Clouds*, Pink Floyd spent nine months recording their next album. Released in the spring of 1973, *The Dark Side of the Moon* was entirely comprised of songs written by Roger Waters and became an instant best-seller, quickly achieving gold-award certification and establishing the group as "superstars." Dealing with alienation and madness as caused by the pressures of contemporary society, the album yielded Pink Floyd's first major American hit, "Money," and remained on the album charts for a record-breaking seven years-plus. Before the end of 1973 Pink Floyd's first two albums were reissued as *A Nice Pair* and their next set of new material was not issued until the fall of 1975. *Wish You Were Here* was generally regarded as disappointing, yet it became an immediate best-seller on the group's new label, Columbia. Continuing to explore the themes of repression, alienation, and loneliness, *Animals* became Pink Floyd's first certified platinum-award album. Depicting society as divided into three castes, dogs, pigs, and sheep, the album was supported by a massive tour that featured tons of musical and lighting equipment and, in performance, a huge flying pig. During 1978 Dave Gilmour recorded his self-produced debut solo album with bassist Rick Wills and drummer Willie Wilson. Finally, near the end of 1979, Pink Floyd's newest album, *The Wall*, was released. Another bleak and gloomy view of modern society, the album was considered their most ambitious and personal work in years and yielded a smash hit with the controversial "Another Brick in the Wall." The 1980 tour in support of the album was so massive that it was performed in only three cities, Los Angeles, New York, and London. It was one of the most elaborate rock productions ever mounted, utilizing a

30-foot high, stage-wide wall of cardboard blocks that was toppled just before the end of the show. Backed by four male singers and bolstered by an additional musician for each of the group's instruments, the production featured films, elaborate lighting, and gigantic plastic inflatables in one of the most awesome and spectacular performances in rock history.

PINK FLOYD

The Piper at the Gates of Dawn	Tower	ST–5093	November '67	

SYD BARRETT

The Madcap Laughs and "Barrett"	2-Harvest	SABB–11314	July '74	A

PINK FLOYD

A Saucerful of Secrets	Tower	ST–5131	August '68	
A Nice Pair	2-Harvest	SABB–11257	December '73	A
Relics	Harvest	SW–759	June '71	A
More (soundtrack)	Tower	ST–5169	July '69	
	reissued on Harvest	SW–11198	August '73	A
Ummagumma*	2-Harvest	SKBB–388	December '69	A
Atom Heart Mother	Harvest	SMAS–382	October '70	A
Meddle*	Harvest	SMAS–832	October '71	A
Obscured by Clouds	Harvest	SW–11078	June '72	A
The Dark Side of the Moon*	Harvest	SMAS–11163	March '73	A
Wish You Were Here*	Columbia	JC–33453	September '75	A
Animals**	Columbia	JC–34474	January '77	A
The Wall**	2-Columbia	PC2–36183	December '79	A
A Collection of Great Dance Songs	Columbia	TC–37680	December '81	A

DAVID GILMOUR

David Gilmour	Columbia	JC–35388	June '78	A

NICK MASON

Fictitious Sports	Columbia	FC–37307	May '81	A

THE PLATTERS. Featuring a smooth sophisticated sound and the superb lead tenor voice of Tony Williams, The Platters were likely the most popular black vocal group of the Fifties. Masterminded by manager, producer, arranger, and chief songwriter Buck Ram, The Platters scored a series of smash hits, including the classics "Only You," "The Great Pretender," and "The Magic Touch" (all written by Ram), between 1955 and 1960 that led to successful appearances on television and the cabaret circuit as well as with rock-and-roll package shows. Virtually unchanged stylistically over the course of their career, The Platters suffered declining popularity after the 1960 hit "Harbor Lights" and the departure of Williams that June and later enduring other personnel changes before re-emerging as a contemporary soul group during the late Sixties.

During 1953, lead tenor Tony Williams (born April 5, 1928, in Elizabeth, New Jersey), second tenor David Lynch, baritone Alex Hodge, and bass Herb Reed (born in Kansas City, Missouri) formed The Platters under the auspices of Buck Ram, a former writer and arranger for the big bands of the Thirties. Contracted to the Cincinnati-based Federal/King label, The Platters were unsuccessful with their initial recordings (eventually released in album form in the late Fifties). Ram subsequently replaced Hodge with Paul Robi (born in New Orleans), recruited female vocalist Zola Taylor (born in Los Angeles), and placed the group with Mercury Records. In the fall of 1955, The Platters scored a top rhythm-and-blues and smash pop hit with Ram's "Only You." During 1956 they achieved smash rhythm-and-blues and pop hits with the classics "The Great Pretender," "The Magic Touch" (both by Ram), and "My Prayer," as well as the major two-sided hit, "You'll Never Never Know/It Isn't Right." After the 1957 hits "I'm Sorry/He's Mine" and "My Dream," The Platters had top hits with the classics "Twilight Time" (co-authored by Ram) and "Smoke Gets in Your Eyes." Developing a widely based audience among television viewers, rock-and-roll fans, and the larger pop audience, The Platters performed both at rock-and-roll shows and on the lucrative supper club circuit. They subsequently hit with "Enchanted" and "Harbor Lights" in 1959 and 1960, respectively, but thereafter endured declining popularity. In June 1960 Tony Williams left the group to pursue a dismally unsuccessful solo recording career and was replaced by Sonny Turner. The Platters managed several moderate hits with "To Each His Own," "If I Didn't Care," and "I'll Never Smile Again" during the early Sixties, before the departure of Zola Taylor around 1964. By 1966, after four hitless years, The Platters re-emerged as a contemporary soul act on Musicor Records and scored a major rhythm-and-blues hit with "I Love You 1,000 Times" and a major pop hit with "With This Ring" before totally dropping out of the charts at the end of 1967. Several groupings continued to tour in the Seventies, including Tony Williams and The Platters and The Five Platters. On January 2, 1981, in Long Beach, California, original member David Lynch died of cancer at the age of 51.

THE PLATTERS

The Platters	King	LP–549(M)	July '58
The Platters	King	LP–651(M)	October '59
The Platters	Mercury	MG–20146 (M)	July '56

The Platters— Volume 2	Mercury	MG–20216 (M)	January '57
Rock All Night	Mercury	MG–20293 (M)	June '57
The Flying Platters	Mercury	MG–20298 (M)	August '57
Around the World with The Flying Platters	Mercury	MG–20366 (M) reissued as SR– 60043	March '58 July '59
Remember When	Mercury	SR–60087	March '59
Reflections	Mercury	SR–60160	May '60

TONY WILLIAMS

A Girl Is a Girl Is a Girl	Mercury	SR–60138	December '59
Tony Williams Sings His Greatest Hits	Reprise	9–6006	November '61
Magic Touch of Tony	Philips	PHS– 60051	

THE PLATTERS

Life Is Just a Bowl of Cherries	Mercury	SR–60245	June '61
Song for the Lonely	Mercury	SR–60669	February '62
Encore of Broad- way Golden Hits	Mercury	SR–60613	August '62
Moonlight Memories	Mercury	SR–60759	March '63
The Platters Sing All-Time Movie Hits	Mercury	SR–60782	July '63
The Platters Sing Latino	Mercury	SR–60808	October '63
Christmas with The Platters	Mercury	SR–60841	December '63
Golden Hits of the Groups	Mercury	SR–60893	May '64
10th Anniversary Album	Mercury	SR–60933	October '64
New Soul Campus Style of The Platters	Mercury	SR–60983	February '65
I Love You 1,000 Times	Musicor	MS–3091	July '66
Have the Magic Touch	Musicor	MS–3111	
Going Back to Detroit	Musicor	MS–3125	
Sweet, Sweet Lovin'	Musicor	MS–3156	

I Get the Sweetest Feeling	Musicor	MS–3171	November '68	

THE PLATTERS REISSUES, ANTHOLOGIES, AND COMPILATIONS

19 Hits	King	5002(M)	December '77	A
Encore of Golden Hits	Mercury	MG–20472 (M)	January '60	A
		reissued as SR–60243	June '61	A
More Encore of Golden Hits	Mercury	MG–20591 (M)	September '60	
		reissued as SR–60252	June '61	
		reissued as ML–8002	October '79	A
Encores	Mercury	12112(M)	February '60	
The Flying Platters	Mercury	SRW–16226	September '62	
10th Anniversary Album	Mercury	SRW–16346	September '67	
New Golden Hits	Musicor	MS–3141		
Golden Hour	Musicor	MS–3231	August '72	
In the Still of the Night	Pickwick	3120	January '69	
Super Hits	Pickwick	3236		
Only You	2-Pickwick	2083(M)	April '76	A
Only You	Musico	1002	December '70	
The Platters	Springboard International	4059(M)	October '76	

POCO.   Seminal West Coast "country-rock" band of the late Sixties and Seventies, Poco did not attain the popularity of The Eagles, the first commercially successful band of the genre, until the late Seventies, if then. By the mid-Seventies, founders Jim Messina and Richie Furay had moved on to Loggins and Messina and The Souther–Hillman–Furay Band, respectively, whereas original member Randy Meisner had joined and departed The Eagles and was replaced by later-day Poco member Tim Schmit. Nonetheless Poco maintained a remarkably consistent sound, featuring group vocal harmonies and country and rock instrumentation, and recorded several outstanding albums, including 1973's *Crazy Eyes*. With Rusty Young as the only original member, Poco finally broke through in 1979 with *Legend* and its hit singles "Crazy Love" and "Heart of the Night."

Producer, engineer, guitarist, bassist, and singer–songwriter Jim Messina (born December 5, 1947, in Maywood, California) and guitarist–singer–songwriter Richie Furay (born May 9, 1944, in Dayton, Ohio), both former members of The Buffalo Springfield, formed Poco in August 1968 with pedal steel guitarist and dobro player Rusty Young (born February 23, 1946, in Long Beach, California), bassist–vocalist Randy Meisner (born March 8, 1946, in Scottsbluff, Nebraska), and vocalist–drummer George Grantham (born January 20, 1947, in Cordell, Oklahoma). Debuting at The Troubadour in Los Angeles in November, Poco auditioned for Apple Records but signed with Epic. Given the remarkably chaotic career of The Buffalo Springfield, Poco's debut album was appropriately titled *Pickin' Up the Pieces*. Though Poco was touted as the "next big thing," the album sold modestly at best, failing to yield even a minor hit single. By the time of the album's release, Meisner had already left the group to join Rick Nelson's Stone Canyon Band, later to help form the highly successful Eagles. Poco remained a quartet until February 1970, when bassist–vocalist Tim Schmit (born October 30, 1947, in Sacramento, California) joined the band. *Poco* produced a minor hit with Messina's "You Better Think Twice," and the live set *Deliverin'* nearly became a best-seller as it contained re-recordings of several Buffalo Springfield songs and yielded a minor hit with Furay's "C'mon."

However, in November 1970, Jim Messina departed Poco to form the successful Loggins and Messina duo with Kenny Loggins. He was replaced by Paul Cotton (guitar, vocals, songwriting), a former member of The Illinois Speed Press. This lineup—Furay, Young, Cotton, Schmit, and Grantham—recorded three albums and toured extensively, usually as a support act. They expected Furay's title song to *Good Feelin' to Know* to become their first major hit, but it failed even to make the charts. *Crazy Eyes*, possibly their finest album, sold moderately well and included Furay's title song and excellent versions of Gram Parsons' "Brass Buttons" and J. J. Cale's "Magnolia." Nonetheless, Furay left Poco in September 1973 to form the ill-fated "superstar" group, The Souther–Hillman–Furay Band. Poco continued as a four-piece, with Cotton taking over as lead singer and Cotton and Young composing most of the material. They recorded the disappointing *Seven* and *Cantamos* albums before switching to ABC Records in 1975. For ABC they managed minor hits with "Keep On Tryin'" from *Head Over Heels* and the title songs to *Rose of Cimarron* and *Indian Summer*. However, by March 1978, Tim Schmit had departed to join The Eagles and George Grantham had left, eventually to join The Doobie Brothers. Rusty Young, the only remaining original member, and Paul Cotton recruited two Englishmen, bassist Charlie Harrison and drummer Steve Chapman, and later, former Crosby, Stills, and Nash keyboardist Kim Bullard, for yet another edition of Poco. Finally, after more than a decade of existence, Poco scored major hits with "Crazy Love" and "Heart of the Night" from *Legend*, their first certified gold-award album.

POCO

Pickin' Up the Pieces	Epic	BXN–26460	June '69	A
Poco	Epic	PE–26522	May '70	A

Deliverin'	Epic	PE–30209	January '71	A
From the Inside	Epic	PE–30753	September '71	A
A Good Feelin' to Know	Epic	PE–31601	November '72	A
Crazy Eyes	Epic	PE–32354	September '73	A
Seven	Epic	KE–32895	April '74	
Cantamos	Epic	PE–33192	November '74	A
Live	Epic	PE–33336	February '76	A
Head Over Heels	ABC/MCA	AB–890	July '75	
	reissued on MCA	37009		A
Rose of Cimarron	ABC/MCA	AB–946	May '76	
	reissued on MCA	37010		A
Indian Summer	ABC/MCA	AB–989	April '77	
	reissued on MCA	37011		A
Legend*	ABC/MCA	AA–1099	October '78	A
Under the Gun	MCA	5132	July '80	A

POCO ANTHOLOGIES AND COMPILATIONS

The Very Best of Poco	2-Epic	PEG–33537	July '75	A
The Songs of Paul Cotton	Epic	JE–36210	November '79	A
The Songs of Richie Furay	Epic	JE–36211	November '79	A

THE POINTER SISTERS. Rapidly emerging in 1973–74, The Pointer Sisters, under manager–producer David Rubinson, created a unique distillation of improvisatory jazz-style vocals, song material and dress from the Forties, and "camp" burlesque-style, on-stage demeanor that produced two certified gold-award albums, yet earned them the limiting label as a "nostalgia" and "novelty" act. Initially established as entertainers more than as recording artists, The Pointer Sisters performed a highly eclectic repertoire, from contemporary rhythm-and-blues to jazz classics and original compositions that demonstrated a remarkable degree of vocal versatility. They even scored a major country hit with their own "Fairytale," an unusual feat for any black vocal group. Languishing in their recording career after 1975, The Pointer Sisters discarded their prior image and re-established themselves as rock-and-roll artists under producer Richard Perry with their *Energy* album and smash hit version of Bruce Springsteen's "Fire," as departed sister Bonnie Pointer began to establish herself as a soul artist on Motown Records.

The Pointer sisters Ruth, Anita, Bonnie, and June were born in 1946, 1948, 1950 and 1954, respectively, in Oakland, California, where both of their parents were preachers in the Church of God. All four started singing in church and later discovered secular material during high school.

Around 1968–69, Bonnie Pointer began singing professionally in the area and was joined by June for local performances as The Pointers—A Pair. Later they were members of Dorothy Morrison's Northern California State Youth Choir before being joined by Anita in December 1969 for the formation of The Pointer Sisters. Stranded in Houston by their first manager, the three contacted San Francisco producer David Rubinson, who arranged for their return to the area. He subsequently became their manager and found them sessions work with Cold Blood, Elvin Bishop, and later, with Taj Mahal, Boz Scaggs, and Dave Mason. During 1972 The Pointer Sisters recorded two singles for Atlantic Records, but they proved unsuccessful. Joined by sister Ruth in September 1972, The Pointer Sisters signed with Blue Thumb Records under Rubinson, who produced their early albums. Their debut album displayed a striking versatility of vocal talents and diversity of musical styles and contained original compositions such as "Sugar," "Jada," and the Lambert, Hendricks, and Ross classic "Cloudburst," and yielded a major hit with Allen Toussaint's "Yes, We Can-Can" and a minor hit with Willie Dixon's "Wang Dang Doodle." Substituting for a canceled act at The Troubadour in Los Angeles in May 1973, The Pointer Sisters were ecstatically received for their unique blend of camp on-stage patter, exciting vocals and harmonies, and distinctive, if dated, material. The successful performance led to frequent appearances on the television shows of Helen Reddy and Flip Wilson, and the debut album was certified gold-award in February 1974.

The Pointer Sisters' second album, *That's a Plenty*, was even more jazz-oriented than was their debut, containing vocal renditions of Thelonius Monk's "Straight No Chaser" and "Round Midnight" and "Salt Peanuts," a jazz standard popularized by Dizzie Gillespie. The certified gold-award album was followed by the double-record set, *Live at the Opera House*, recorded in San Francisco in April 1974. Compiling much of their early material, the album yielded a major pop hit with Anita and Bonnie's "Fairytale," which later became a smash country-and-western hit. *Steppin'* produced a major hit with "How Long" while containing Stevie Wonder's "Sleeping Alone" and "Easy Days," co-authored by Isaac Hayes. However, subsequent releases on Blue Thumb fared poorly and, by 1977, The Pointer Sisters were without a recording contract. During the year Bonnie Pointer left the other three to pursue her own solo career at Motown Records. She scored a minor hit with "Free Me from My Freedom" in late 1978, followed by a major hit with Holland–Dozier–Holland's "Heaven Must Have Sent You" and a moderate hit with a remake of the Motown classic "I Can't Help Myself (Sugar Pie, Honey Bunch)." In August 1978 the three remaining Pointer Sisters signed with producer Richard Perry's Planet label. Recording contemporary Seventies material rather than jazz standards, their debut for the label, *Energy*, yielded a smash hit with Bruce Springsteen's "Fire" and a moderate hit with "Happiness." Late 1979's *Priority* album again contained contemporary rock material by writers such as Springsteen, Bob Seger, and Graham Parker. In 1980 The Pointer Sisters hit again with "He's So Shy," followed in 1981 with the sensual yet liberated top hit, "Slow Hand."

THE POINTER SISTERS

The Pointer Sisters*	Blue Thumb	BTS–48	April '73	
That's a Plenty*	Blue Thumb	BTS–6009	February '74	
Live at the Opera House	2-Blue Thumb	BTS–8002	August '74	
Steppin'	Blue Thumb	BTSD–6021	May '75	
The Best of The Pointer Sisters	2-Blue Thumb	BTSY–6026	November '76	
Having a Party	Blue Thumb	BTS–6023	October '77	
Retrospect	MCA	3275	November '81	A
Energy*	Planet	P–1	November '78	A
Priority	Planet	P–9003	September '79	A
Special Things	Planet	P–9	August '80	A
Black and White*	Planet	18	June '81	A

BONNIE POINTER

Bonnie Pointer	Motown	7–911	December '78	A
Bonnie Pointer	Motown	7–929	December '79	A

ELVIS PRESLEY.   The biggest single attraction in the history of popular music, Elvis Presley legitimated black rhythm-and-blues music as "rock-and-roll." One of the first white performers of the mid-Fifties to exude passionate, sexually charged emotionalism in performance and to sing in the guttural mumbling style of black rhythm-and-blues vocalists without stripping the songs of their vitality, Elvis Presley's music was initially decried by parents, clergy, and fearful record company executives as a danger to the proper morals of youthful fans. However, their protestations were subsequently stilled as Presley's smash hit classics "Heartbreak Hotel" and "Hound Dog" became immensely popular in the country-and-western, rhythm-and-blues, *and* pop fields and introduced "rock-and-roll" to an entire generation of white teenagers who were accustomed to passionless banal ditties and unfamiliar with the fervent and intense black rhythm-and-blues music that had existed since the beginning of the Fifties. Following his move to RCA Records from the small Memphis-based Sun Records, the label that launched so-called "rockabilly" music, Elvis Presley quickly and totally revolutionized the recording industry. Never again would contemporary popular music be dominated by movie stars, crooning male singers like Bing Crosby and Perry Como, and cabaret entertainers such as Frank Sinatra and Andy Williams. In identifying a form of music and life-style totally distinct from that of his fans' parents, Elvis Presley became the most important symbol of and idol within late Fifties rock-and-roll, enhancing its attendant aura of teenage rebellion.

However, not all credit for Elvis Presley's virtually unprecedented success can be attributed to the open sexuality of his late Fifties performances and recordings. His voice, regularly enhanced through the use of reverb, and his guitar playing were, in fact, only technically adequate. These factors notwithstanding, national television appearances did much to spread Presley's fame and notoriety, and much of his success was due to the stunning and compelling lead guitar playing of Scotty Moore, the vocal accompaniment of The Jordanaires, and the crass yet skillful merchandising of manager "Colonel" Tom Parker. Indeed, the astute marketing of the "Colonel," combined with the quality of Presley's music as performed by Moore and The Jordanaires, resulted in no lessening of his popularity and appeal during his two year absence while serving in the Army between 1958 and 1960.

Although he retained the title of the "King of Rock-and-Roll" and remained this music's most widely recognized figure until his death, Elvis Presley's primacy as a rock-and-roll artist quickly evaporated after his army discharge. To his credit, Presley did record two excellent gospel albums (a facet of his career usually neglected by biographers) that were certified gold-award, a seldom-attained feat. At the Colonel's behest, he began recording inferior material featuring a bigger sound and embarked on a dismal but lucrative career of inane movies and vacuous soundtrack albums that saw him fall into disfavor with country-and-western, rhythm-and-blues, and, for a time, even easy-listening audiences. Dropping live performances after 1961, Elvis Presley was carefully "rationed" by Parker, ironically leading to Presley's elevation from the status of mere "superstar" to that of "living legend." His virtual absence unfortunately also led to the emergence of a number of passionless young male singers cut in his mold, such as Frankie Avalon, Fabian, and Bobby Rydell.

Despite the fact that all of his movies were commercial successes, Elvis Presley's singles and album sales were diminishing by the late Sixties. With the advent of the rock-and-roll "revival" of the era, Presley unexpectedly and unequivocally staged a successful come-back with a December 1968 television special that revealed him as continuing to be a passionate, compelling, and unique performer. He returned to live appearances in 1969; the initial engagement and many of those subsequent occurred in Las Vegas, where he quickly established himself as one of the most popular and highly paid cabaret artists in the world. However, Presley was not able to re-establish his popularity with the kind of youthful audience that had so ardently followed him during the late Fifties and, in a sense, he developed into a "nostalgia" act as his weight increased, health problems developed, and performances became sloppier and more perfunctory. Yet in 1973 his "Aloha from Hawaii" television show, the first television show to be transmitted internationally by satellite, was viewed by an estimated audience of *one billion people* and the album from the show became an instant top-seller.

Elvis Presley's success was virtually unparalleled. More than 480,000,000 copies of his records had been sold by the time of his August 1977 death, and the record industry records he set were simply phenomenal. Though he was surpassed in several album and singles categories by The Beatles, Bing Crosby, and Frank Sinatra, Elvis Presley holds the records for the most charted albums, the most top-ten records, the most consecutive top-ten records, the most two-sided hit records, and the most consecutive years on the charts, 24.

Elvis Presley was born January 8, 1935, in East Tupelo, Mississippi. He began singing with his parents at the First Assembly of God Church as a child and later accompanied his parents to camp meetings and revivals. He obtained his first guitar for his eleventh birthday and moved with his family to Memphis, Tennessee, in September 1948. Presley sang at a high school variety show late in 1952 and became a truck driver after graduation in June 1953. The next month, in the often told (and now disputed) story, he went to the small local Sun Records studio to make a private recording of "My Happiness" for his mother. Noticed by secretary Marion Keisker, Presley was later teamed with guitarist Scotty Moore (born in Humbolt, Tennessee, on December 27, 1931) and standup bassist Bill Black (born in Memphis on September 18, 1926; died in Memphis on October 21, 1965) by Sun Records president Sam Phillips, and the three rehearsed for several months. Returning to Sun studios in July 1954, the three recorded the country standard "Blue Moon of Kentucky" and Arthur "Big Boy" Crudup's "That's All Right (Mama)," among others. Local disc jockey Dewey Phillips (unrelated to Sam Phillips) played the latter song on his radio show and the single became a regional hit. Presley made his professional performing debut at Memphis' Overton Park on August 10, 1954, and was greeted ecstatically by an audience enthralled with his rough emotional vocals and sexually charged persona. Presley soon began touring the South with Moore and Black, billed as "The Hillbilly Cat," as his second and third Sun singles were becoming regional hits. In late 1954 they performed on Shreveport's "Louisiana Hayride" radio show and performed on the show's television version the following March. By July "Baby, Let's Play House" had become Presley's first national chart entry, followed in September by "Mystery Train," a top country-and-western hit. Observed by former carnival barker and one-time country-and-western manager "Colonel" Tom Parker, Elvis Presley left his prior manager to sign up with Parker. Presley's potent style had created a stir among record companies, and RCA-Victor finally won the bidding war in November for $35,000, an astoundingly high figure for 1955.

In January 1956 Elvis Presley, backed by guitarists Scotty Moore and Chet Atkins, bassist Bill Black, and drummer D. J. Fontana, among others, completed his first recording session in Nashville. Presley made his national television debut on the CBS network "Dorsey Brothers Show" on January 28, 1956, and shortly thereafter his first RCA release, "Heartbreak Hotel," became a smash country-and-western, rhythm-and-blues, *and* pop hit. The subject of both controversy and adulation for his openly sexual television and concert performances, Presley scored smash hits with the ballad "I Want You, I Need You, I Love You" and the two-sided classic "Don't Be Cruel/Hound Dog" (his first recording with The Jordanaires) before appearing on television's "Ed Sullivan Show" on September 9th, on which he was shown from the waist up only. Presley's success was phenomenal, and the smash hits continued with "Love Me Tender," "Love Me,"

"Too Much," and "All Shook Up." During 1956 his first movie, *Love Me Tender*, was released, followed in 1957 by *Loving You* and *Jailhouse Rock*. In late 1956, Presley had returned to the Sun studio informally to join Sun stalwarts Carl Perkins, Jerry Lee Lewis, and Johnny Cash in singing and playing a number of gospel songs. Unknown to them, the performance was recorded, and record collectors still anticipate the American release of the recordings of the so-called "Million Dollar Quartet" 25 years later. Presley's hits for RCA continued with "Teddy Bear," "Jailhouse Rock," and "Don't," as all of his first four albums, including a Christmas album, went to the top of the charts. He was allowed a two-month deferment to complete the film *King Creole*, but, in March 1958, he was drafted into the army. Although he was to record only once during the next two years, the hits did not stop; during his absence, he scored with "Wear My Ring Around Your Neck," "Hard-Headed Woman," the two-sided "One Night/I Got Stung," and "(Now and Then There's) A Fool such as I/I Need Your Love Tonight," and "A Big Hunk o' Love."

Returning to civilian life in March 1960, Presley subsequently assembled the so-called "Memphis Mafia" entourage that served to protect and insulate him from the public until July 1976, and began recording with additional musicians to produce a fuller recorded sound. The material was far less exuberant and exciting than previously, yet the smash hits resumed with "Stuck on You," "It's Now or Never," and "Are You Lonesome Tonight." Aired on ABC–TV May 12, 1960, "Welcome Home, Elvis" featured six minutes of Presley, for which he was paid $125,000. The television show, Elvis' last for eight years, was hosted by Frank Sinatra, a man who had previously denounced rock-and-roll as "the most brutal, ugly, desperate, vicious form of expression," and into whose footsteps Presley would later move. Appearing at his last live performance for eight years in 1961, Presley made several worthwhile films, including *Flaming Star*, *Wild in the Country*, and *Follow That Dream*, while also starring in a series of lucrative but mindless movies usually staged at exotic locations and featuring numerous fleshy but virginal women and only the bare semblance of a plot. Presley's only redeeming albums over the next seven years were the gospel albums *His Hand in Mine* and *How Great Thou Art*, as his hits continued with "Surrender," "I Feel So Bad," "(Marie's the Name of) His Latest Flame/Little Sister," "Can't Help Falling in Love," "Good Luck Charm," "She's Not You," and "Return to Sender." After 1962 the hits devolved into pedestrian fluff with "(You're the) Devil in Disguise," "Bossa Nova Baby," "Kissin' Cousins," "Viva Las Vegas," and the totally forgettable "Do the Clam."

In 1968, with the first inkling of a revival of interest in Fifties rock-and-roll, Elvis Presley returned to television for an attempted come-back. Less than a week before the airing of his special, "If I Can Dream," one of his finer later-day singles, became a major hit. The special, televised on NBC December 3, 1968, featured large-scale production numbers and Presley performing in front of a selected audience with old associates Scotty Moore and D. J. Fontana. The special was one of the five highest-rated shows of the television year and represented, to some, the peak of his career. Presley's first album thereafter, *From Elvis in Memphis*, was his first in 14 years to be recorded in Memphis and is generally regarded as one of his finest later-day albums; it included one of his few attempts at a socially conscious song with Mac Davis' "In the Ghetto," a smash hit. During the summer of 1969 Presley returned to live performance at the International Hotel in Las Vegas, backed by a 30-piece orchestra, chorus, and a five-man combo led by guitarist James Burton and keyboardist Glen D. Hardin, two of the finest instrumentalists in the country. In September he scored a top hit with "Suspicious Minds" before again recording inconsequential top songs such as "Don't Cry, Daddy" and "The Wonder of You." After two month-long appearances at the International Hotel in February and August 1970, he again toured selected venues across the United States, a practice he was to follow through 1975, after which he only infrequently appeared in Las Vegas. Exceptional recordings of the era included 1971's *Elvis Country* album and 1972's "Burning Love" smash hit single. In January 1973 Presley performed a Honolulu benefit which was beamed to 36 countries around the world and aired on NBC–TV in April. The show was viewed by an estimated one billion people and recordings of the show became his last major hit album before his death. After his divorce was finalized in October 1973, Presley's live performances became sloppier and more perfunctory, as rumors of drug abuse and erratic private behavior began to circulate. He managed important hits with "Promised Land" in 1974 and "Way Down" in 1977, and his earliest recordings were released as *The Sun Sessions* in 1976. On August 16, 1977, he died of heart-related problems in Memphis at the age of 42. Hitting posthumously with "My Way," Frank Sinatra's theme song, Presley's albums had not been selling at all well prior to his death, yet fans staged an enormous buying spree of his albums following his death. Television specials and expanded merchandising ensued in the wake of the death of the "King of Rock-and-Roll," detracting from the legend of rock-and-roll's most widely known performer. The year 1981 saw the releases of the film "docu-drama" *This is Elvis* and the rather contemptuous Albert Goldman biography *Elvis*.

EARLY ALBUMS OF ELVIS PRESLEY

The Sun Sessions	RCA	APM1–1675(M)	April '76	
		reissued as AYM1–3893(M)		A
Elvis Presley *	RCA	LPM–1254(M)	March '56	
		reissued as LSP–1254(E)	January '62	A
Elvis *	RCA	LPM–1382(M)	October '56	
		reissued as LSP–1382(E)	January '62	A
Loving You *	RCA	LPM–1515(M)	July '57	

		reissued as LSP–1515(E)	January '62	A
Elvis' Christmas Album	RCA	LOC–1035(M)	November '57	
		reissued as LPM–1951(M)	December '58	
	reissued on Camden	CAL–2428(M)	November '70	
		reissued as CAS–2428(E)		A
For LP Fans Only	RCA	LPM–1990(M)	February '59	
		reissued as LSP–1990(E)		A
A Date with Elvis	RCA	LPM–2011(M)	July '59	
		reissued as LSP–2011(E)		A
Elvis Is Back	RCA	AFL1–2231	April '60	A

SCOTTY MOORE

The Guitar That Changed the World	Epic	BN–26103	September '64	

ELVIS PRESLEY SOUNDTRACKS

King Creole	RCA	LPM–1884(M)	August '58	
		reissued as LSP–1884(E)	January '62	A
		reissued as AYL1–3733		A
G.I. Blues	RCA	AFL1–2256	September '60	
		reissued as AYL1–3735		A
Blue Hawaii*	RCA	LSP-2426	September '61	
		reissued as AYL1–3683		A
Girls! Girls! Girls!*	RCA	AFL1–2621	November '62	A
It Happened at the World's Fair	RCA	LSP-2697	March '63	
		reissued as AFL1–2568	October '77	A

Fun in Acapulco	RCA	AFL1–2756	November '63	
Kissin' Cousins	RCA	AFL1–2894	March '64	A
Roustabout	RCA	AFL1–2999	October '64	
Girl Happy	RCA	AFL1–3338	March '65	A
Harum Scarum	RCA	LSP–3468 reissued as AFL1–2558	October '65 October '77	
		reissued as AYL1–3734		A
Frankie and Johnny	RCA	LSP–3553 reissued as APL1–2559	April '66 October '77	
Paradise, Hawaiian Style	RCA	AFL1–3643	June '66	A
Spinout	RCA	LSP–3702 reissued as APL1–2560	October '66 October '77	
		reissued as AYL1–3676	June '80	
		reissued as AYL1–3684		A
Double Trouble	RCA	LSP–3787 reissued as AFL1–2564	May '67 October '77	
Clambake	RCA	LSP–3893 reissued as AFL1–2565	October '67 October '77	
Speedway	RCA	AFL1–3989	June '68	

OTHER ELVIS PRESLEY ALBUMS

His Hand in Mine*	RCA	LSP–2328 reissued as ANL1–1319	November '60 April '76	
		reissued as AYL1–3935		A
Something for Everybody	RCA	AFL1–2370	May '61	
Pot Luck	RCA	AFL1–2523	May '62	A

Elvis for Everyone!	RCA	AFL1–3450 reissued as AYL1– 4232	July '65 January '82	 A
How Great Thou Art *	RCA	AQL1– 3758	February '67	A
Elvis (TV Special) *	RCA	AFM1– 4088(M)	December '68	A
From Elvis in Memphis *	RCA	AFL1– 4155	May '69	A
From Memphis to Vegas/From Vegas to Memphis *	2-RCA	LSP–6020	November '69	A
On Stage—February 1970 *	RCA	AQL1– 4362	May '70	A
Elvis in Person at the International Hotel	RCA	AFL1– 4428	November '70	
Elvis Back in Memphis	RCA	AFL1– 4429	November '70	
That's the Way It Is (soundtrack) *	RCA	AFL1– 4445	December '70	A
Elvis Country *	RCA	AFL1– 4460 reissued as AYL1– 3956	January '71	 A
Love Letters from Elvis	RCA	AFL1– 4530	June '71	
Elvis Sings the Wonderful World of Christmas	RCA	LSP–4579 reissued as ANL1– 1936	November '71 November '76	 A
Elvis Now	RCA	AFL1– 4671	February '72	A
He Touched Me	RCA	AFL1– 4690	April '72	A
Elvis as Recorded at Madison Square Garden *	RCA	AFL1– 4776	July '72	A
Elvis—Aloha from Hawaii via Satellite *	2-RCA	VPSX– 6089	February '73	
Elvis	RCA	APL1– 0283	July '73	
Raised on Rock	RCA	AFL1– 0388	November '73	
Good Times	RCA	AFL1– 0475	March '74	
Elvis—Recorded Live on Stage in Memphis	RCA	AFL1– 0606	July '74	A
Having Fun with Elvis on Stage	RCA	AFM1– 0818(M)	October '74	A

Promised Land	RCA	AFL1–0873	January '75	A
Today	RCA	AFL1–1039	May '75	
From Elvis Presley Boulevard, Memphis, Tennessee*	RCA	AFL1–1506	May '76	A
Welcome to My World*	RCA	APL1–2274	April '77	A
Moody Blue*	RCA	AQL1–2428	July '77	A

ELVIS PRESLEY ANTHOLOGIES AND COMPILATIONS

Elvis' Golden Records*	RCA	LPM–1707(M)	March '58	
		reissued as LSP–1707(E)	January '62	A
50,000,000 Elvis Fans Can't Be Wrong—Elvis' Golden Records, Volume 2*	RCA	LPM–2075(M)	November '59	
		reissued as LSP–2075(E)	January '62	A
Elvis' Golden Records, Volume 3*	RCA	AFL1–2765	August '63	A
Elvis' Golden Records, Volume 4	RCA	AFL1–3921	January '68	A
Elvis' Worldwide 50 Gold Award Hits, Volume 1*	4-RCA	LPM–6401(M)	August '70	A
Elvis—The Other Sides—Worldwide Gold Award Hits, Volume 2	4-RCA	LPM–6402(M)	August '71	
Elvis—A Legendary Performer, Volume 1*	RCA	CPL1–0341	January '74	A
Pure Gold*	RCA	ANL1–0971(E)	June '75	
		reissued as AYL1–3732		A
Elvis—A Legendary Performer, Volume 2*	RCA	CPL1–1349	January '76	A

ELVIS PRESLEY BUDGET ALBUMS

| Elvis Sings Flaming Star and Others | Camden | CAS–2304 | April '69 | A |

Let's Be Friends	Camden	CAS–2408	April '70	A
Almost in Love	Camden	CAS–2440	November '70	A
You'll Never Walk Alone	Camden	CAS–2472(M)	March '71	A
C'mon Everybody	Camden	CAL–2518(M)	July '71	A
I Got Lucky	Camden	CAL–2533(M)	November '71	A
Elvis Sings Hits from His Movies	Camden	CAS–2567	June '72	A
Burning Love and Hits from His Movies	Camden	CAS–2595	November '72	A
Separate Ways	Camden	CAS–2611	January '73	A
Double Dynamite	2-Camden	DL2–5001		A
Mahalo	Camden	CAS–7064		A

POSTHUMOUS ELVIS PRESLEY ALBUMS

Elvis Concert (TV) **	2-RCA	APL2–2587	October '77	
He Walks Beside Me: Favorite Songs of Faith and Inspiration	RCA	AFL1–2772	March '78	A
Elvis Sings for Children and Grownups, Too	RCA	AFL1–2901	July '78	
A Canadian Tribute	RCA	KKL1–7065	October '78	
Elvis—A Legendary Performer, Volume 3 *	RCA	CPL1–3082	December '78	A
Our Memories of Elvis	RCA	AQL1–3279	March '79	A
Our Memories of Elvis, Volume II	RCA	AQL1–3448	August '79	A
Elvis Aron Presley: 1955–80	8-RCA	CPL8–3699	August '80	A
Guitar Man	RCA	AAL1–3917	March '81	A
This Is Elvis (selections from the soundtrack)	2-RCA	CPL2–4031	May '81	A
Greatest Hits, Volume 1	RCA	AHL1–2347	October '81	A

JOHN PRINE. Along with Steve Goodman, John Prine was one of the singer–songwriters to emerge from the Chicago folk scene during the Seventies, sharing a predilection for clever and compassionate yet eccentric songwriting with Goodman and Loudon Wainwright, III. Although his outstanding debut album contained the classic post-Vietnam war epic "Sam Stone" and the often covered "Angel from Montgomery" and "Hello in There," John Prine has been unable to expand his following beyond a small devoted cult over the years, despite a change of label by 1978.

JOHN PRINE

John Prine	Atlantic	SD–8296 reissued as SD–19156	October '71	A
Diamonds in the Rough	Atlantic	SD–7240	September '72	A
Sweet Revenge	Atlantic	SD–7274	November '73	A
Common Sense	Atlantic	SD–18127	March '75	A
Prime Prine/The Best of John Prine	Atlantic	SD–18202	December '76	A
Bruised Orange	Asylum	6E–139	May '78	A
Pink Cadillac	Asylum	6E–222	August '79	A
Storm Windows	Asylum	286	July '80	A

PROCOL HARUM/ROBIN TROWER. One of the first groups to feature regularly and prominently two keyboard instruments (piano and organ) as well as guitars in their recordings and performances, Procol Harum burst into popular music with 1967's smash hit, "A Whiter Shade of Pale," certainly one of the classic singles of the entire decade. Quickly suffering the loss of two members, Procol Harum maintained a remarkably sophisticated and distinct sound based on the stirring organ, dynamic piano, and stunning lead guitar playing of Matthew Fisher, Gary Brooker, and Robin Trower, respectively, and the scholarly lyrics of the group's virtually unseen sixth member, Keith Reid. Also noteworthy was the amazingly innovative free-form drumming of B. J. Wilson, one of the most overlooked drummers of the Sixties and Seventies. With melodist Brooker favoring minor key tunes profoundly influenced by classical composers such as Bach, and Reid contributing stark and majestic lyrics alternately surreal, melancholic, mythic, and ominous, Procol Harum's first three albums were in the forefront of rock as literate and thoughtful music and encouraged the development of so-called "progressive" rock music.

Later emphasizing the outstanding lead guitar playing of Robin Trower, Procol Harum frequently toured the United States, where they became far more popular than they were in their native England. Trower subsequently left the group and enjoyed consistent success in America as leader of a power trio that performed music clearly derived from that of Jimi Hendrix, while remaining curiously suspect and ignored in his native country. Regrouping, Procol Harum enjoyed heightened popularity with the unexpected critical and commercial success of *Live*, recorded with The Edmonton Symphony Orchestra. *Grand Hotel* seemed to solidify Procol Harum's reputation, but later albums fared less well and, by 1978, Procol Harum had disbanded.

Procol Harum began their evolution as The Paramounts, a rhythm-and-blues group formed in southern England in 1962. The members were vocalist–pianist Gary Brooker (born May 29, 1945, in London), guitarist Robin Trower (born March 9, 1945, in London), bassist Chris Copping (born August 29, 1945), and drummer B. J. Wilson (born March 18, 1947, in Middlesex, England). Having recorded a series of unsuccessful British rhythm-and-blues singles, The Paramounts persevered until 1966, when Brooker left to form a group to record the songs he and lyricist Keith Reid (born October 10, 1946, in London) had written. Thus was formed Procol Harum, with Brooker as lead vocalist, organist Matthew Fisher (born March 7, 1946, in London), guitarist Ray Rowyer (born October 8, 1945), bassist David Knights (born June 28, 1945, in London), and drummer Bobby Harrison (born June 28, 1943, in London). Featuring mythic and surreal lyrics and the ominous organ playing of Fisher, their debut single, "A Whiter Shade of Pale," became a smash British and American hit and launched Procol Harum into international prominence. However, both Rowyer and Harrison soon quit, threatening at least the British credibility of the group, and former Paramounts Robin Trower and B. J. Wilson were recruited for completion of their debut album. Released in monaural and electronically reprocessed stereo sound only, *Procol Harum* served as an excellent first release, containing 9 Brooker–Reid collaborations including "A Whiter Shade of Pale," the foreboding "Something Following Me," the raunchy "Mabel," "Conquistador," "Kaleidoscope/Salad Days," and the powerful five-minute tour de force, "(Outside the Gates of) Cerdes." Intellectually as well as emotionally stimulating, the album produced music unlike any other heard to that time.

Touring the United States with moderate success for the first time in the fall of 1967 and again in early 1968 as "Homburg" was becoming a moderate hit single, Procol Harum next recorded *Shine On Brightly*. Issued in the United States on A&M Records, the album included songs such as "Skip Softly (My Moonbeams)," "Rambling On," and the title song, but showcased the 18-minute classic "In Held Twas in I," which depicted a stunning musical and lyrical journey from the depths of self-pity and depression to regal reaffirmation and faith. For their next album, *A Salty Dog*, Brooker played celeste, harmonica, and recorder as well as piano, Fisher added guitar and marimba, and Trower and Fisher contributed vocals. Exploring a number of musical avenues enhanced by various dubbed-in sounds, the album was filled with excellent songs, all with lyrics by Reid, including the title song, "The Milk of Human Kindness," "Too Much Between Us," "All This and More," "Pilgrim's Progress," and the amusing but fateful "Boredom."

However, after producing *A Salty Dog*, Matthew Fisher left Procol Harum to become a producer and to pursue a neglected solo career that eventually saw the release of albums on RCA Records in 1973 and 1974. David Knights also soon left, and he and Fisher were replaced by a single new member, bassist–organist Chris Copping, another former member of The Paramounts. Reduced to a quartet, Procol Harum featured the dynamic lead guitar playing of Robin Trower on *Home* and *Broken Bar-*

ricades. Home included at least two Trower–Reid collaborations, "Whisky Train" and "About to Die," as well as Brooker–Reid compositions such as "Still There'll Be More" and "Your Own Choice." *Broken Barricades* contained three more melodies supplied by Trower, most significantly the tribute to Jimi Hendrix, "Song for a Dreamer," in addition to Brooker and Reid's "Simple Sister," "Power Failure," and the lurid "Luskus Delph."

In July 1971 Robin Trower departed Procol Harum, initially to form the short-lived Jude with Scottish vocalist Frankie Miller, former Stone The Crows bassist Jim Dewar, and former Jethro Tull drummer Clive Bunker. Procol Harum realigned one more time, with Gary Brooker, Chris Copping (who switched to organ), guitarist Dave Ball (born March 30, 1950), bassist Alan Cartwright (born October 10, 1945, in North London) and B. J. Wilson. While touring North America in late 1971, Procol Harum was invited to record with The Edmonton Symphony Orchestra in Canada. Live recordings of the concert, issued during the spring of 1972, became an instant surprise success, garnering the group critical acclaim, an expanded audience, and the group's only certified gold-award album. The album, which compiled several of the group's early songs and the "In Held Twas in I" suite in full orchestral and choral context, yielded the group's third hit single, "Conquistador," originally included on their debut album. Bolstered by the album's enormous success, the group switched to Chrysalis Records and completed their debut for the label, *Grand Hotel*, with guitarist Mick Grabham after Dave Ball had left. Within months, A&M issued a "best of" set that included "Homburg," the previously unissued "Long-Gone Geek," and "In the Wee Small Hours." However, Procol Harum's fortunes began to fade with *Exotic Birds and Fruit*, a decidedly "hard-rock" effort, in contrast to prior classically influenced albums. The group's decline was briefly halted by *Procol's Ninth*, produced by legendary producers Jerry Leiber and Mike Stoller, and its underground favorite, "Pandora's Box"; but *Something Magic*, recorded with organ and synthesizer player Pete Solley, fared poorly, leading to the demise of Procol Harum.

Following the unsuccessful Jude grouping, Robin Trower formed his own powerhouse trio with vocalist–bassist Jim Dewar (a veteran of Jude) and drummer Reg Isidore. Their debut album for Chrysalis, *Twice Removed from Yesterday*, featured Trower's Hendrix-derived lead guitar playing on songs such as "Hannah" and "Man of the World" yet sold only marginally. However, *Bridge of Sighs* became an instant best-seller, at least in the United States (where Trower consciously concentrated his efforts), and was certified gold-award the year of its release. In the summer of 1974 former Sly and The Family Stone drummer Bill Lordan replaced Isidore, and the group's next album, *For Earth Below*, was certified gold-award in 1976. *Live!* failed to sell at the requisite level, but *Long Misty Days* and *In City Dreams* were both certified gold-award the years of release. *Long Misty Days* included Trower's only (minor) hit, "Caledonia," wheras *In City Dreams* featured new bassist Rustee Allen and Jim Dewar as full-time vocalist. Robin Trower has since recorded *Caravan to Midnight* and *Victims of the Fury*, whereas Brooker recorded the solo set *No More Fear of Flying* in 1979, and Matthew Fisher re-emerged with another solo album on A&M Records in 1980. Lyricist Keith Reid now manages Frankie Miller.

PROCOL HARUM

Procol Harum	Deram	DES–18008 (E)	September '67	
reissued as A Whiter Shade of Pale	A&M	SP–4373 reissued as 3136	January '73 April '81	A
Shine On Brightly	A&M	SP–4151	October '68	A
A Salty Dog	A&M	SP–4179 reissued as 3123	April '69	A

MATTHEW FISHER

Journey's End	RCA	APL1–0195	September '73
I'll Be There	RCA	APL1–0325	June '74
Matthew Fisher	A&M	SP–4801	March '80

PROCOL HARUM

Home	A&M	SP–4261	July '70	A
Broken Barricades	A&M	SP–4294	April '71	A
Live (with the Edmonton Symphony Orchestra and De Camera Singers) *	A&M	SP–4335	May '72	A
The Best of Procol Harum ·	A&M	SP–4401	October '73	A
Grand Hotel	Chrysalis	CHR–1037	March '73	A
Exotic Birds and Fruit	Chrysalis	CHR–1058	March '74	A
Procol's Ninth	Chrysalis	CHR–1080	June '75	A
Something Magic	Chrysalis	CHR–1130	March '77	

ROBIN TROWER

Twice Removed from Yesterday	Chrysalis	CHR–1039	April '73	A
Bridge of Sighs*	Chrysalis	CHR–1057	March '74	A
For Earth Below *	Chrysalis	CHR–1073	February '75	A
Live!	Chrysalis	CHR–1089	March '76	A
Long Misty Days*	Chrysalis	CHR–1107	September '76	
In City Dreams*	Chrysalis	CHR–1148	September '77	A
Caravan to Midnight	Chrysalis	CHR–1189	August '78	A
Victims of the Fury	Chrysalis	CHR–1215	February '80	A

| B. L. T. (with Jack Bruce and Bill Lordan) | Chrysalis | 1324 | April '81 | A |

ROBIN TROWER AND JACK BRUCE

| Truce | Chrysalis | 1352 | January '82 | A |

GARY BROOKER

| No More Fear of Flying | Chrysalis | CHR–1224 | June '79 | A |

PURE PRAIRIE LEAGUE/AMERICAN FLYER/CRAIG FULLER AND ERIC KAZ.

Exceptional Midwestern "country-rock" band of the Seventies, Pure Prairie League recorded two outstanding albums, often considered classics of the genre, before suffering the departure of co-founder Craig Fuller and almost disbanding. Bolstered by the belated success of "Amie" from their second 1972 album, Pure Prairie League regrouped for a modestly successful career, whereas Fuller joined songwriter Eric Kaz and rock veterans Doug Yule (The Velvet Underground) and Steve Katz (The Blues Project; Blood, Sweat and Tears) in American Flyer for a brief recording career that failed to achieve the success the members' credentials would warrant. Kaz, best known as the author of the often recorded "I'm Blowin' Away" and co-author of the classic "Love Has No Pride," subsequently teamed with Fuller for 1978's *Craig Fuller/Eric Kaz.*

PURE PRAIRIE LEAGUE

Pure Prairie League	RCA	AFL1–4650	March '72	
		reissued as AYL1–3719		A
Bustin' Out *	RCA	AFL1–4769	September '72	A
Two Lane Highway	RCA	APL1–0933	May '75	
		reissued as AYL1–3669	June '80	A
If the Shoe Fits	RCA	AFL1–1247	January '76	
		reissued as AYL1–3717		A
Dance	RCA	APL1–1924	November '76	
		reissued as AYL1–3723		A

Live! Takin' the Stage	2-RCA	CPL2–2404	August '77	A
Just Fly	RCA	AFL1–2590	May '78	
		reissued as AYL1–3718		A
Can't Hold Back	RCA	AFL1–3335	June '79	
Firin' Up	Casablanca	7212	May '80	A
Something in the Night	Casablanca	7255	May '81	A

ERIC KAZ

| If You're Lonely | Atlantic | SD–7246 | December '72 |
| Cul-de-Sac | Atlantic | SD–7290 | March '74 |

AMERICAN FLYER

| American Flyer | United Artists | LA650 | August '76 |
| Spirit of a Woman | United Artists | LA720 | June '77 |

CRAIG FULLER AND ERIC KAZ

| Craig Fuller/Eric Kaz | Columbia | JC–35324 | September '78 |

QUICKSILVER (MESSENGER SERVICE).

QUICKSILVER (MESSENGER SERVICE). Although one of the original bands to emerge from San Francisco in the mid-Sixties, Quicksilver Messenger Service played locally for more than two years before signing a recording contract in 1968, thus becoming one of the last important San Francisco bands to secure a contract. Sparked by the "psychedelic" guitar ruminations of John Cipollina, Quicksilver recorded two excellent Capitol albums before enduring several personnel changes. Originally set to join the initial grouping, folksinger Dino Valenti, author of perhaps the most popular "hippie" anthem of the era, "Let's Get Together," eventually joined Quicksilver in 1970 and briefly revitalized the group with songs such as "Fresh Air" and "What About Me." However, after the departure of Cipollina in late 1970, Quicksilver was unable to re-establish itself, though the group remained nominally intact until the dismal 1975 reunion album. Original member David Freiberg, later with the Jefferson Starship, was the only former member to retain a position of musical prominence.

QUICKSILVER MESSENGER SERVICE

Quicksilver Messenger Service	Capitol	ST–2904 reissued as SN–16089	June '68	A
Happy Trails	Capitol	ST–120 reissued as SN–16090	March '69	A

DINO VALENTI

Dino	Epic	BN–26335	September '68

QUICKSILVER

Shady Grove	Capitol	SM–391 reissued as SN–16094	January '70	A

Just for Love	Capitol	SMAS–498 reissued as SN–16093	August '70	A
What About Me	Capitol	SMAS–630 reissued as SN–16092	December '70	A
Quicksilver	Capitol	SW–819 reissued as SN–16091	November '71	A
Comin' Thru	Capitol	SMAS–11002	April '72	
Anthology	2-Capitol	SVBB–11165	May '73	A
Solid Silver	Capitol	ST–11462 reissued as SM–11820	November '75 September '78	A

BONNIE RAITT. One of the most talented female song interpreters and bottleneck acoustic guitar stylists of the Seventies, Bonnie Raitt is as well known for her dedication to black country blues and its originators as she is for her renditions of songs by obscure contemporary songwriters such as Eric Kaz, John Prine, and Karla Bonoff. Recording the definitive versions of Kaz and Libby Titus' moving "Love Has No Pride" and Prine's "Angel from Montgomery," Raitt has achieved moderate success with FM radio listeners, while more frequently utilizing electric guitar during the late Seventies to attain a decidedly "hard rock" sound, as evidenced by *The Glow*. A Quaker by birth, Bonnie Raitt has regularly appeared at colleges and benefit concerts in support of various feminist and political causes and, during 1979, she became a founding board member of MUSE (Musicians United for Safe Energy) with John Hall, Jackson Browne, and Graham Nash.

BONNIE RAITT

Bonnie Raitt	Warner Brothers	WS–1953	October '71	A
Give It Up	Warner Brothers	BS–2643	September '72	A
Takin' My Time	Warner Brothers	BS–2729	October '73	A
Streetlights	Warner Brothers	BS–2818	September '74	A
Home Plate	Warner Brothers	BS–2864	September '75	A
Sweet Forgiveness *	Warner Brothers	BS–2990	March '77	A
The Glow	Warner Brothers	HS–3369	September '79	A

THE (YOUNG) RASCALS. American singles band that achieved their biggest success between 1966 and 1968, The Young Rascals, as they were initially known, started out as a white rhythm-and-blues band that appealed to both black and white audiences and ostensibly influenced rhythm-and-blues oriented New York-based and British groups. One of the first white rock groups to record for Atlantic Records, The Young Rascals shifted to pop-oriented material and a smoother sound as evidenced by their smash 1967 single "Groovin'." Continuing to have hits through 1969 as simply The Rascals, the group was subsequently reconstituted with only two original members and then disbanded by 1972, as both Felix Cavaliere and Eddie Brigati pursued separate, inauspicious solo careers.

The Young Rascals were formed in early 1965 in the New York area by three former members of Joey Dee's Starlighters, organist–vocalist Felix Cavaliere (born November 29, 1944, in Pelham, New York), guitarist Gene Cornish (born May 14, 1945, in Ottawa, Canada) and vocalist Eddie Brigati (born October 22, 1946, in Garfield, New Jersey), whose brother David was an original member of The Starlighters. Augmented by drummer Dino Danelli (born July 23, 1945, in Jersey City, New Jersey), The Young Rascals started playing together at The Choo Choo Club in Garfield, New Jersey, in February 1965; they graduated to Long Island's The Barge discotheque and then to Manhattan clubs by the fall of 1965. Playing primarily rhythm-and-blues–oriented music centered around Cavaliere's organ playing, the group quickly developed a reputation as an exciting live act and were signed to Atlantic Records by Ahmet Ertegun. Their second single, "Good Lovin'," became a top hit in early 1966 and was followed by the major hits "You Better Run," co-authored by Cavaliere and Brigati, and "I've Been Lonely Too Long," written by Cavaliere. Their first two rhythm-and-blues styled albums became best-sellers, but for *Groovin'* they adopted a lighter sound and utilized largely their own pop-oriented material. The album yielded a top hit with the title song and major hits with "A Girl Like You" and "How Can I Be Sure," all three co-written by Cavaliere and Brigati. After another major hit with "It's Wonderful," the group became simply The Rascals and scored smash hits with "A Beautiful Morning" and "People Got to Be Free," and moderate successes with "A Ray of Hope," "See," and "Carry Me Back" through 1969. However, The Rascals achieved no other major hits thereafter and, by the time of the group's 1971 switch to Columbia, only Cavaliere and Danelli remained in the group. They disbanded after two unsuccessful albums for the label, as Gene Cornish and Dino Danelli formed Bulldog, who scored a moderate hit with "No" in late 1972 on Decca. In 1974 Cavaliere surfaced as a solo artist, but neither his debut album nor its single, "A High Price to Pay," made the charts. Eddie Brigati joined his brother David for Brigati in 1976, but their album also failed to sell. During 1977 Felix Cavaliere was a member of Treasure; he subsequently returned to a solo career on Epic Records with 1980's *Castles in the Air* and the moderate hit "Only a Lonely Heart Sees."

THE YOUNG RASCALS

| The Young Rascals * | Atlantic | SD–8123 | April '66 |

Collections*	Atlantic	SD–8134	January '67	
Groovin'*	Atlantic	SD–8148	August '67	

THE RASCALS

Once Upon A Time	Atlantic	SD–8169	February '68	
Time Peace—The Rascals' Greatest Hits*	Atlantic	SD–8190	July '68	A
Freedom Suite*	Atlantic	SD2–901	March '69	
See	Atlantic	SD–8246	January '70	
Search and Nearness	Atlantic	SD–8276	March '71	
Peaceful World	2-Columbia	G–30462	May '71	
The Island of Real	Columbia	KC–31103	May '72	

BULLDOG

Bulldog	Decca	75370	November '72
Smasher	Buddah	BDS–5600	March '74

FELIX CAVALIERE

Felix Cavaliere	Bearsville	BR–6955	September '74
Destiny	Bearsville	BR–6958	July '75

BRIGATI

Lost in the Wilderness	Elektra	7E–1074	September '76

TREASURE

Treasure	Epic	PE–34890	November '77

FELIX CAVALIERE

Castles in the Air	Epic	JE–35990	January '80

OTIS REDDING. Regarded by many as the single most important male rhythm-and-blues/soul artist of the Sixties, Otis Redding was one of the first black artists to extend his appeal to white audiences with raw and spontaneous music that bore a stark contrast to the smooth, sophisticated music of Motown. Possessing an intensely expressive yet gruff baritone voice that exuded both gentleness and assertiveness, that was alternately seductive and agonized, Otis Redding was aided immeasurably by Booker T. and The MGs and the Memphis Horns in creating a unique mixture of "funk" and gospel musics. Helping establish Stax-Volt Records, Redding opened the way for black singers such as Sam and Dave and Arthur Conley. Moreover, his modest early pop success encouraged black artists such as Aretha Franklin and Wilson Pickett to record some of their biggest hits with the same Memphis backing group. Generally unrecognized as a song-writer, Redding authored or co-authored most of his own hits such as "I've

Been Loving You Too Long (to Stop Now)," "I Can't Turn You Loose," and "Fa-Fa-Fa-Fa-Fa (Sad Song)," as well as "Respect" (a top hit for Aretha Franklin in 1967) and "Sweet Soul Music" (a smash hit for Arthur Conley the same year). The only soul artist to perform at the legendary Monterey Pop Festival in June 1967, Otis Redding's popularity was beginning to take on immense proportions when he was killed in an airplane crash on December 10, 1967, at the age of 26. His biggest hit, the posthumous classic "(Sittin' on) The Dock of the Bay," revealed a more personal and introspective direction in his songwriting.

Otis Redding was born in Dawson, Georgia, on September 9, 1941, and grew up in nearby Macon, where he first sang in a church choir. Through high school friend Phil Walden (who later became his manager), he met and joined Johnny Jenkins and The Pinetoppers for tours of the South, making his first recording with them in 1959 as Otis and The Shooters and subsequently recording, in a "shout" style reminiscent of Little Richard, "Shout Bamalama," which was released nationally on the Bethlehem label. In 1962 Redding was allowed to record his own "These Arms of Mine" at a Jenkins Memphis session that was completed early. Immediately signed to the newly formed subsidiary of Stax Records, Volt, Redding's song became a moderate rhythm-and-blues and minor pop hit in early 1963. Recording with the Stax house bands of Booker T. and the MGs and The Memphis Horns, and frequently augmented by keyboardist Isaac Hayes, Redding toured regularly between 1964 and 1967, accompanied by either Booker T. and The MGs or The Bar-Kays. Headlining the Stax-Volt European tour of 1965, he developed a greater initial following in Europe than at home for his raw, powerful music.

During 1965 Otis Redding managed to score his first moderate pop hit with the up-tempo "Mr. Pitiful," followed by major hits with the classics "I've Been Loving You Too Long (to Stop Now)," co-written with Jerry Butler, and his own boldly sexual "Respect." His *Otis Blue* album, generally considered to be his finest album (some favor *Dictionary of Soul*), included both the later hits plus Sam Cooke's "Shake" and "A Change Is Gonna Come" and The Rolling Stones' "Satisfaction." The last song helped begin to establish Redding with white fans, whereas the Cooke songs musically affirmed the influence and legacy of Redding's acknowledged idol. Major pop hits in 1966–67 included "Fa-Fa-Fa-Fa-Fa (Sad Song)," co-written with Booker T. and The MGs' guitarist Steve Cropper, and the classic "Try a Little Tenderness." In early 1967 Arthur Conley scored a smash pop hit with the Conley–Redding composition "Sweet Soul Music" and Aretha Franklin had a top pop hit with Redding's "Respect." Redding subsequently achieved major pop hits with "Tramp" and "Knock on Wood," recorded in duet with Carla Thomas. Performing as the only soul act at June 1967's Monterey Pop Festival, Redding attained widespread recognition with his performance and began firmly establishing himself with pop audiences. However, while touring, Redding's airplane crashed near Madison, Wisconsin, on December 10, 1967, killing him and four members of the Bar-Kays, James King, Ronald Caldwell, Phalon Jones, and Carl Cunningham. In early 1968 Redding's recording of "(Sittin' on) The Dock of the Bay," co-written with Steve Cropper, became a top pop and rhythm-and-blues/soul hit, revealing a more personal and introspective development in his songwriting. Through 1969, posthumous hits for Otis Redding continued with "The Happy Song (Dum Dum)," "Amen," "I've Got Dreams to Remember," and "Papa's Got a Brand New Bag."

OTIS REDDING

Pain in My Heart	Atco	SD33–161(M)	March '64	
The Great Otis Redding Sings Soul Ballads	Volt reissued on Atco	411 SD33–248	April '65	
Otis Blue	Volt reissued on Atco	412 SD33–284	October '65	
The Soul Album	Volt reissued on Atco	413 SD33–285	April '66	
Dictionary of Soul	Volt reissued on Atco	415 SD33–249	November '66	

OTIS REDDING AND CARLA THOMAS

King and Queen	Stax	(7)716	April '67	

OTIS REDDING/JIMI HENDRIX EXPERIENCE

Historic Performances at the Monterey International Pop Festival*	Reprise	MS–2029	August '70	A

OTIS REDDING

Live in Europe	Volt reissued on Atco	416 SD33–286	August '67	A
History	Volt reissued on Atco	418 SD33–261(E)	November '67	A
Here Comes Some Soul from Otis Redding and Little Joe Curtis	Stereo Fidelity	SF–29200	February '68	
Dock of the Bay	Volt reissued on Atco	419 SD33–288	March '68	
The Immortal Otis Redding	Atco	SD33–252	July '68	
In Person at the Whiskey A-Go-Go	Atco	SD33–265	November '68	

Love Man	Atco	SD33–289	July '69	
Tell the Truth	Atco	SD33–333	July '70	
Best	2-Atco	SD2–801	August '72	A

PAUL REVERE AND THE RAIDERS. Popular Pacific Northwest rock group that utilized Revolutionary War costumes and a humorous stage act complete with precise choreography, Paul Revere and The Raiders scored a number of smash hit singles and best-selling albums in 1966 and 1967. One of the first rock groups to sign with Columbia Records and the first rock group to achieve a gold award for Columbia (*Just Like Us*), Paul Revere and The Raiders directed their attention toward very young fans, although their early Seventies recordings were more pop-oriented. Lead vocalist Mark Lindsay pursued a parallel solo career beginning in 1969 but, by 1973, both he and the group were out of the charts.

PAUL REVERE AND THE RAIDERS

Like, Long Hair	Gardena	1000	
Paul Revere and The Raiders	Sande	1001	
In the Beginning	Jerden	7004	March '66
Here They Come	Columbia	CS–9107	June '65
Just Like Us*	Columbia	CS–9251	January '66
Midnight Rider*	Columbia	CS–9308	June '66

THE BROTHERHOOD

The Brotherhood	RCA	LSP–4092	December '68
The Brotherhood	RCA	LSP–4228	November '69

PAUL REVERE AND THE RAIDERS

The Spirit of '67*	Columbia	CS–9395	December '66
Revolution!	Columbia	CS–9521	August '67
Christmas Present . . . and Past	Columbia	CS–9555	December '67
Goin' to Memphis	Columbia	CS–9605	February '68
Something Happening	Columbia	CS–9665	August '68
Hard 'n' Heavy	Columbia	CS–9753	March '69
Alias Pink Puzz	Columbia	CS–9905	August '69

PAUL REVERE AND THE RAIDERS ANTHOLOGIES AND COMPILATIONS

Greatest Hits*	Columbia	CS–9462	May '67	
		reissued as C–35593	February '79	A
Two All-Time Great Selling LPs	2-Columbia	GP–12	November '69	
Greatest Hits, Volume II	Columbia	C–30386	February '71	

All-Time Greatest Hits	2-Columbia	CG–31464 (E)	July '72	A
Paul Revere and The Raiders Featuring Mark Lindsay	Harmony	KH–30089	December '70	
Good Thing	Harmony	KH–30975		
Movin' On	Harmony	KH–31183	April '72	
Paul Revere and The Raiders	Pickwick	3176		A

MARK LINDSAY

Arizona	Columbia	CS–9986	March '70	
Silverbird	Columbia	C–30111	August '70	
You've Got a Friend	Columbia	C–30735	October '71	

THE RAIDERS

Collage	Columbia	CS–9964	April '70	
Indian Reservation	Columbia	C–30768	June '71	A
Country Wine	Columbia	KC–31106	April '72	

THE RIGHTEOUS BROTHERS. Among the first to capitalize on what became known (disparagingly to some) as "blue-eyed soul" (one of the more offensive terms coined to describe a genre of rock music), The Righteous Brothers achieved their biggest success in the mid-Sixties under producer extraordinaire Phil Spector, whose so-called "wall-of-sound" technique, coupled with Bill Medley's booming bass voice and Bobby Hatfield's soaring gospel-style vocal, yielded one of the greatest rock singles of all time, "You've Lost That Lovin' Feelin'." Following up with the similarly styled "Just Once in My Life" and "Ebb Tide," The Righteous Brothers managed a soundalike hit in 1966 away from Spector with "(You're My) Soul and Inspiration" on Verve, but were unable to sustain the impetus of that recording and broke up in 1968. Medley subsequently pursued a prolific if neglected solo career, reuniting with Hatfield in the mid-Seventies for the surprise necrological hit, "Rock and Roll Heaven."

THE RIGHTEOUS BROTHERS

Right Now!	Moonglow	1001	November '63
Some Blue-Eyed Soul	Moonglow	1002	January '65
This Is New	Moonglow	1003	June '65
You've Lost That Lovin' Feelin'	Philles	PHLP–4007	January '65
Just Once in My Life	Philles	PHLP–4008	May '65
Back to Back	Philles	PHLP–4009	December '65

Soul and Inspiration*	Verve	V–65001	April '66	
Go Ahead and Cry	Verve	V–65004	August '66	
Sayin' Somethin'	Verve	V–65010	February '67	
Souled Out	Verve	V–65031	October '67	
Standards	Verve	V–65051	February '68	
One for the Road	Verve	V–65058	July '68	

RIGHTEOUS BROTHERS ANTHOLOGIES AND COMPILATIONS

Best	Moonglow	1004	May '66	
Greatest Hits*	Verve	V–65020	September '67	A
Greatest Hits, Volume 2	Verve	V–65071	March '69	
The Righteous Brothers	MGM	GAS–102	November '70	
History	MGM	SE–4885	April '73	

JIMMY WALKER AND BOBBY HATFIELD AS THE RIGHTEOUS BROTHERS

Re-birth	Verve	V–65076	February '70

BOBBY HATFIELD

Messin' in Muscle	MGM	SE–4727	April '71

BILL MEDLEY

100%	MGM	SE–4583	June '68
Soft and Soulful	MGM	SE–4603	March '69
Someone Is Standing Outside	MGM	SE–4640	January '70
Nobody Knows	MGM	SE–4702	September '70
Gone	MGM	SE–4741	January '71
A Song for You	A&M	SP–3505	November '71
Smile	A&M	SP–3517	May '73

THE RIGHTEOUS BROTHERS

Give It to the People	Haven	ST–9201	August '74
The Sons of Mrs. Righteous	Haven	ST–9203	April '75

BILL MEDLEY

Lay a Little Lovin' on Me	United Artists	LA929	December '78	
Sweet Thunder	United Artists reissued on Liberty	LT–1024 LT–1097	May '80 May '81	A

JOHNNY RIVERS. Popularizer of the mid-Sixties discotheque trend through his live recordings of rock favorites at Los Angeles' Whiskey A-Go-Go, Johnny Rivers later recorded hits such as "Secret Agent Man" and his own "Poor Side of Town." Founder of his own record company, Soul City Records, in 1966, Rivers signed The Fifth Dimension to the label and the group scored at least nine major hit singles between 1967 and 1970, as well as three certified gold-award albums. Important in advancing the career of songwriter Jimmy Webb, Johnny Rivers was also on the Board of Directors of the Monterey Pop Festival in 1967. His *Realization* album, certified gold-award a year after its release, ostensibly helped herald the singer–songwriter trend, whereas his 1965 hit, "Midnight Special," became the theme song to the late-night television music show of the same name in 1972. Recording for four different labels during the Seventies, Johnny Rivers hit in 1977 with "Swayin' to the Music (Slow Dancin')."

Born John Ramistella in New York City on November 7, 1942, Johnny Rivers at the age of three moved with his family to Baton Rouge, Louisiana, where he grew up. Taking up guitar at an early age, he formed his first music group at age 14 while in junior high school. While playing on demonstration records in Nashville and New York, he received the "Rivers" surname from disc jockey Alan Freed. After moving to Los Angeles around 1960, he started playing regularly in local discotheques in 1962 and obtained a regular engagement at the newly opened Whiskey A-Go-Go that resulted in several live albums and the hits "Memphis," "Maybelline," "Mountain of Love," "Midnight Special," and "Seventh Son" in 1964 and 1965. Having scored moderate hits in late 1965 with Pete Seeger's "Where Have All the Flowers Gone" and Buck Owens' "Under Your Spell Again," Rivers subsequently had smash hits with P. F. Sloan and Steve Barri's television theme "Secret Agent Man," the first single which he wrote, "Poor Side of Town," in 1966, as well as the major hit " (I Washed My Hands in) Muddy Waters."

During 1966 Johnny Rivers formed his own record label, Soul City Records, which utilized the songwriting talents of discovery Jimmy Webb for the initial hits of The Fifth Dimension, who eventually hit with at least nine major hit singles and three certified gold-award albums for the label. In 1968 Al Wilson had a major hit on Soul City with "The Snake." In the meantime, Rivers scored major hits with remakes of the Motown classics "Baby, I Need Your Lovin' " and "The Tracks of My Tears," as well as James Hendricks' "Summer Rain," his last hit for nearly five years. In 1967 he had been on the Board of Directors of the famed Monterey Pop Festival, and his 1968 album, *Realization*, was certified gold-award the following year. By then, he was no longer making personal appearances; he divested himself of Soul City Records by the end of 1969. Rivers helped promote several then-unknown singer–songwriters with minor hit recordings, such as Van Morrison's "Into the Mystic" and James Taylor's "Fire and Rain" in 1970, before switching from Imperial to United Artists Records. Beginning in August 1972, Rivers' version of "Midnight Special" was used as the theme song to the late-night television program of the same name, although he re-recorded the song for subsequent use in 1974. Huey "Piano" Smith's classic "Rockin' Pneumonia—Boogie-Woogie Flu" became a near-smash for Rivers in late 1972 and, after unsuccessfully recording for Atlantic Records, he managed a major hit with "Help Me, Rhonda," recorded with the vocal assistance of Brian Wilson, in 1975 on Epic. Reactivating the Soul City label by 1977, Johnny Rivers scored a major hit at mid-year with "Swayin' to the Music (Slow Dancin')," released on the Big Tree subsidiary of Atlantic Records.

JOHNNY RIVERS

Discotheque Au Go Go	Design	DLP–194(M)		
The Sensational Johnny Rivers	Capitol	ST–2161	September '64	
Go, Johnny, Go!	United Artists	UAS–6386	October '64	
Johnny Rivers at the Whiskey A-Go-Go	Imperial	LP–12264	June '64	
Here We A-Go-Go Again!	Imperial	LP–12274	October '64	
Johnny Rivers in Action!	Imperial	LP–12280	February '65	
Meanwhile, Back at the Whiskey A-Go-Go	Imperial	LP–12284	June '65	
Rivers Rocks the Folk	Imperial	LP–12293	September '65	
And I Know You Wanna Dance	Imperial	LP–12307	April '66	
Changes	Imperial reissued on Liberty	LP–12334 LN–10121	December '66	A
Rewind	Imperial	LP–12341	June '67	
Realization *	Imperial	LP–12372	June '68	
A Touch of Gold	Imperial	LP–12427	June '69	A
Slim Slo Slider	Imperial	LP–16001	August '70	
Home Grown	United Artists	UAS–5532	September '71	
L.A. Reggae	United Artists	UAS–5650	October '72	
Blue Suede Shoes	United Artists	LA075	December '73	A
Wild Night	United Artists	LA486	September '76	
Road	Atlantic	SD–7301	April '74	
New Lovers and Old Friends	Epic	PE–33681	September '75	
Outside Help	Big Tree	76004	December '77	
Borrowed Time	RSO	3082	August '81	A

JOHNNY RIVERS ANTHOLOGIES AND COMPILATIONS

Johnny Rivers	Pickwick	3022	June '65	
If You Want It, I Got It	Pickwick	3191		
Golden Hits *	Imperial	LP–12324	September '66	A
Johnny Rivers— Whiskey A-Go-Go Revisited	Sunset	SUS–5157	October '67	
Early Years	Sunset	SUS–5251	August '69	
Superpak	2-United Artists	UXS–93	October '72	

| Very Best | United Artists | LA253 reissued as LA444 | August '74 September '75 | |
| Best | Liberty | LN–10120 | April '81 | A |

SMOKEY ROBINSON AND THE MIRACLES. Along with the Brian Holland–Lamont Dozier–Eddie Holland team, William "Smokey" Robinson was the songwriting and production mainstay of Berry Gordy, Jr.'s, Detroit-based Tamla-Motown organization during the Sixties. In fact, "Shop Around," written by Gordy and Robinson and recorded by Robinson's Miracles, effectively launched the record company into national prominence. Through the Sixties, with much credit due to Smokey Robinson, the Motown family of record labels became the most important independent record company in the country *and* the largest black-owned and operated business in the United States. While providing such classic songs as "My Guy" to Mary Wells, "My Girl" to The Temptations, and "Ain't That Peculiar" to Marvin Gaye, Robinson wrote and sang lead on classics by The Miracles such as "You've Really Got a Hold on Me," "The Tracks of My Tears" (usually regarded as his single most important song), and "I Second That Emotion." His emotion-laden vocals, sung in a characteristic falsetto with impeccable phrasing and exquisite timing, were arguably the most expressive of any of the Motown singers, and some might even say of any vocalist of the Sixties. A prolific songwriter, having written over 4,000 songs during his career, Smokey Robinson was appointed to an executive position at Motown Records in 1967, after which his songs seemed less exuberant. Around the same time, the group became Smokey Robinson and The Miracles in an effort to focus attention on the front line lead singer, and the group continued to tour and record till mid-1972, when Robinson, road-weary, assumed his duties as Motown vice-president full-time. He later also pursued a solo recording career as The Miracles persisted with a new lead vocalist, but The Miracles encountered only modest success until late 1975's top hit, "Love Machine (Part 1)." They subsequently languished for several years before switching to Columbia Records, where their fortunes were little improved. Robinson, returning to at least intermittent touring in 1975, re-emerged in late 1979 with a surprise smash hit single, "Cruisin'."

Born in Detroit on February 19, 1940, William "Smokey" Robinson started writing songs as a child. Around 1955 he formed The Matadors with neighborhood friends Bobby (born in 1940) and Emerson Rogers, Ronnie White (born in 1939), and Warren "Pete" Moore (born in 1939), while still in high school. When Bobby Rogers' sister Claudette (born in 1942) replaced Emerson Rogers, the group became The Miracles around 1957. The lineup: Smokey Robinson (lead vocals), Claudette and Bobby Rogers (first and second tenors), Ronnie White (baritone,) and Pete Moore (bass vocals), with guitarist Marvin Tarplin. The Miracles unsuccessfully auditioned for Berry Gordy, Jr., but Gordy was impressed by the songs of Robinson. The group made their first recording in early 1958 with "Got a Job," released on End Records, followed by Gordy and Robinson's "Bad Girl," a minor hit from late 1959, which was distributed nationally by Chess. Finally signed to Tamla Records that year, the group's first nationally distributed release on the label, "Shop Around," written by Robinson and Gordy, became a smash hit and effectively launched the entire Motown organization. Moderate pop hits for The Miracles continued into 1962, when Mary Wells scored three near-smash hits with songs composed by Robinson, "The One Who Really Loves You," "You Beat Me to the Punch" (co-authored by Ronnie White), and "Two Lovers." In 1962–63 The Miracles had a near-smash hit with Robinson's "You've Really Got a Hold on Me," hitting with Holland–Dozier–Holland's "Mickey's Monkey" in the fall of 1963. Thereafter The Miracles regularly placed singles in the middle level of the pop charts through 1964, as Robinson completed his first production with "The Way You Do the Things You Do" for The Temptations. Claudette Rogers, Smokey's wife since 1959, retired from touring in 1964, although she continued to record with The Miracles until Smokey's departure.

In early 1965 Smokey Robinson provided top hits to Mary Wells ("My Guy") and The Temptations ("My Girl"), and between 1965 and late 1966, The Miracles achieved a series of major hits with "Ooo, Baby, Baby," the classic "The Tracks of My Tears," "My Girl Has Gone," and "(Come 'Round Here) I'm the One You Need," all co-authored by Robinson. During that time, he also supplied Marvin Gaye with "I'll Be Doggone" and "Ain't That Peculiar," The Temptations with "My Baby," and The Marvelettes with "Don't Mess with Bill." His group became Smokey Robinson and The Miracles in early 1967, the year Robinson was appointed vice-president in charge of "artist development," and they continued their hits with "The Love I Saw in You Was Just a Mirage," "More Love," the smash classic "I Second That Emotion," "If You Can Want," and "Baby, Baby Don't Cry," through early 1969. Thereafter, however, the group had difficulty scoring major hits, perhaps due to the creative exhaustion of Robinson. "The Tears of a Clown," co-written by Stevie Wonder, became a top hit at the end of 1970, followed by the major hit "I Don't Blame You at All," but again the big hits ceased. In January 1972 Motown announced the impending "retirement" of Smokey Robinson, and the group completed a six-month "farewell tour," performing their final concert in Washington, D.C., on July 16. Robinson subsequently assumed full-time duties as Motown vice-president, as the other Miracles sought out a new lead vocalist. They eventually recruited William Griffin and *Renaissance*, produced by Robinson and released in the fall of 1973, fared poorly. Smokey Robinson's solo debut, *Smokey*, fared somewhat better, yielding a moderate hit with "Baby, Come Close." In the fall of 1974 The Miracles rebounded with "Do It, Baby," a major hit, whereas Robinson scored his next major hit with "Baby, That's Backatcha" in the spring of 1975. Robinson resumed intermittent touring that year as he apparently tired of his executive duties, but he achieved no major recorded successes. At the end of 1975 The Miracles had a top hit with "Love Machine (Part

1),'' but faltering thereafter, the group switched to Columbia Records in 1977. The big surprise came in late 1979 when Smokey Robinson's seductive "Cruisin'," from *Where's the Smoke*, became a smash hit, thrusting him back into the public eye in a way he had not experienced in nearly a decade. Robinson subsequently provided Kim Carnes with the near-smash hit "More Love" and scored a smash hit with "Being with You."

THE MIRACLES

From the Beginning	Bell	1063(M)	
Hi, We're The Miracles	Tamla	220(M)	
Cookin' with The Miracles	Tamla	223(M)	
Shop Around	Tamla	224(M)	
I'll Try Something New	Tamla	230(M)	
Christmas with The Miracles	Tamla	236(M)	
The Fabulous Miracles	Tamla	238(M)	May '63
Miracles "Live" on Stage	Tamla	241(M)	September '63
Doin' Mickey's Monkey	Tamla	245(M)	December '63
Tribute to the Great Nat King Cole	Tamla	261	
Going to A Go-Go	Tamla	267	November '65
Away We A Go-Go	Tamla	271	December '66

SMOKEY ROBINSON AND THE MIRACLES

Make It Happen	Tamla	276	September '67
reissued as Tears of a Clown	Tamla	276	December '70
Special Occasion	Tamla	290	September '68
Live!	Tamla	289	February '69
Time Out	Tamla	295	August '69
Four in Blue	Tamla	297	November '69
What Love Has Joined Together	Tamla	301	May '70
A Pocket Full of Miracles	Tamla	306	October '70
The Season for Miracles	Tamla	307	
One Dozen Roses	Tamla	312	September '71
Flying High Together	Tamla	318	August '72

THE MIRACLES/SMOKEY ROBINSON AND THE MIRACLES
ANTHOLOGIES AND COMPILATIONS

Greatest Hits from the Beginning	2-Tamla	7–254	April '65	A

Greatest Hits, Volume 2	Tamla	7–280	January '68	A
1957–1972	2-Tamla	320	December '72	
Anthology	3-Motown	7–793	February '74	A
Tears of a Clown	Pickwick	3389	January '75	

SMOKEY ROBINSON

Smokey	Tamla	328	July '73	
Pure Smokey	Tamla	331	March '74	
A Quiet Storm	Tamla	7–337	March '75	A
Smokey's Family Robinson	Tamla	341	February '76	
Deep in My Soul	Tamla	350	February '77	
Love Breeze	Tamla	7–359	March '78	A
Smokin'	Tamla	7–363	January '79	A
Where There's Smoke	Tamla	7–366	June '79	A
Warm Thoughts	Tamla	8–367	March '80	A
Being with You*	Motown	8–375	March '81	A

THE MIRACLES

Renaissance	Tamla	325	May '73	
Do It Baby	Tamla	334	August '74	
Don't Cha Love It	Tamla	336	January '75	
City of Angels	Tamla	339	October '75	
The Power of Music	Tamla	344	October '76	
Greatest Hits	Tamla	7–357	September '77	A
Love Crazy	Columbia	PC–34460	March '77	
The Miracles	Columbia	JC–34910	February '78	

THE ROLLING STONES. The first London-area rhythm-and-blues group to emerge in the wake of the more rock-and-roll oriented Beatles, during their first few years The Rolling Stones interpreted American black rhythm-and-blues more sympathetically than had perhaps any other group of white musicians. Vocalist Mick Jagger demonstrated a remarkable understanding of rhythm-and-blues vocal styles, complete with his poorly enunciated singing, and adopted the blatant sexuality of black artists as had Elvis Presley years before, yet later modified the image into androgyny. Cultivating an arrogant, rebellious, outrageous, and irreverent image, The Rolling Stones quickly became one of the most identifiable of British groups and established themselves as personalities at a time when the emergence of a plethora of groups tended to make most groups' members anonymous. Developing their reputation as a live act, sparked by Jagger's flamboyant, boisterous, and ostentatious stage persona and Keith Richard's powerful lead guitar playing, The Rolling Stones became the only genuine competition to The Beatles, particularly after the 1965 smash hit classic, "Satisfaction." Writing their own songs by 1964, Jagger and Richard developed into a potent songwriting team that provided a number of classic Sixties singles such as "Get Off My Cloud," "As Tears Go By," and "19th Nervous Breakdown."

Polarizing fans and attracting substantial media attention inasmuch as the group's image contrasted with that of The Beatles, The Rolling Stones ceased touring between 1966 and 1969. Sparked by the singular versatility of Brian Jones, the group's initial leader and most talented instrumentalist, The Rolling Stones' *Aftermath* album became a classic of the era, initiating their penchant for producing songs ominous and demonic ("Paint It Black") and openly sexist ("Stupid Girl," "Under My Thumb"), while also containing the early extended cut, "Going Home." Ably demonstrating the ability to record songs in a country-and-western style while injecting gentle ballads, The Rolling Stones revealed their debt to the innovations of The Beatles with the unfortunate *Their Satanic Majesties Request* album, a pale, fatuous, and trendy imitation of *Sgt. Pepper's Lonely Hearts Club Band*. Nonetheless, The Rolling Stones re-established their independent credibility with 1968's "Jumping Jack Flash" single, sometimes regarded as their finest single since "Satisfaction," and *Beggar's Banquet* album, generally acknowledged as their most cohesive and fully realized album, which contained the classics "Street Fighting Man" and "Sympathy for the Devil."

However, Brian Jones' status in The Rolling Stones had become problematic by 1969, given his well-publicized drug and health problems and an apparent divergence of musical aspirations from Jagger and Richard, leading to his departure in June. His ambitions were never realized; he was found dead less than a month later. He was replaced by guitarist Mick Taylor from John Mayall's band but, before year's end, The Rolling Stones had participated in the debacle at Altamont, a tragically vicious event that brought into question the group's credibility and sincerity, led to horrendous criticism, and demonstrated the group's remoteness from their audience. Abandoning touring for several years, The Rolling Stones nonetheless sustained their popularity with *Let It Bleed*, which included the classic "You Can't Always Get What You Want," plus "Gimme Shelter" (which paradoxically equated rape, murder, and love in its choruses) and "Midnight Rambler," the first of their violent sexist songs also to be racist.

With the loss of their most innovative musician (Brian Jones) and the breakup of their primary musical challenge (The Beatles), The Rolling Stones ascended to the self-ascribed position of "the world's greatest rock-and-roll band," as Mick Jagger became the world's best known rock performer. After forming their Rolling Stones record label in 1971, The Stones experimented with various forms of music other than rhythm-and-blues during the Seventies and issued as the label's first album release *Sticky Fingers*, which included the country-styled "Wild Horses" and "Dead Flowers," "Sister Morphine," and the racist-sexist "Brown Sugar," usually considered the group's last classic single. With Jagger's 1971 marriage to Bianca de Macias, he was inducted into the so-called "jet set," as the press chronicled his every movement. Returning to touring in 1972 with immense success (by then, their concerts had become more cultural than musical events), The Rolling Stones issued *Exile on Main Street*, usually regarded as their last significant work. Subsequent albums seemed to be mere collections of second-rate songs, which often reflected contemporary trends such as reggae and disco, as their penchant for satanic songs became restricted with *Goat's Head Soup*, which nonetheless included the notorious "Star, Star (Starfucker)." Mick Taylor left The Rolling Stones in December 1974 and was replaced for their massive 1975 tour by former Faces guitarist Ron Wood, thought by some to be an inadequate substitute for Brian Jones and Taylor. Although their popularity remained essentially undiminished, The Rolling Stones' reputation was brought into question with Keith Richard's 1977 heroin bust in Toronto, and the release of Robert Frank's legally suppressed film *Cocksucker Blues* and former associate Tony Sanchez' 1979 *Up and Down with The Rolling Stones* book, both of which sensationalistically depicted the untoward behavior of the group's most celebrated members. *Some Girls* became the group's best seller to date in 1978–79, bolstered by the top-hit success of the disco-styled "Miss You" single, and the much-delayed *Emotional Rescue* album, released in 1980, did little to counter the allegation that The Rolling Stones' most memorable work was over a decade behind them. Nonetheless, The Rolling Stones re-established themselves with critics and fans alike with *Tattoo You* and their 1981 tour, which reportedly was the highest-grossing and best-attended tour in American rock history.

Michael "Mick" Jagger and Keith Richard (born Richards) were both born in Dartford, Kent, in 1943, Jagger on July 26 and Richard on December 18. They first met at the age of six and encountered each other again around 1960. Jagger, a student at the London School of Economics, was playing with mutual friend Dick Taylor (guitar) in Little Blue and The Blue Boys, who subsequently added Richard. Brian Jones, born Lewis Brian Hopkins-Jones in Cheltenham on February 28, 1942, had been playing as a jazz saxophonist before briefly joining The Ramrods and subsequently moving to London, where he played with Alexis Korner's Blues Incorporated. Wanting to form his own rhythm-and-blues band, Jones recruited pianist Ian Stewart and guitarist Jeff Bradford, among others, first meeting Jagger, Richard, and Taylor at the Ealing Club, where Blues Incorporated held residency. Jagger and Richard were soon jamming there with harmonica player Cyril Davies and Charlie Watts (born Islington, London, on June 2, 1941), Korner's drummer. By 1961 Jagger was rehearsing with Jones, Bradford, and Stewart and was soon joined by Richard and Taylor as Bradford became the first departure. Jagger began singing with Blues Incorporated in late 1961, joining as permanent singer in early 1962, by which time the band had graduated to the London Marquee Club. Jagger, Jones, and Richard began sharing an apartment and cut a demonstration tape that was rejected by EMI Records; Taylor became the next departure, later to form The Pretty Things. After debuting at the Marquee Club in the spring of 1962 as Brian Jones and Mick Jagger and The Rolling Stones, the group added bassist Bill Wyman (born William Perks, October 24, variously reported as 1936 and 1941) through auditions in December 1962 and attempted to persuade drummer Charlie Watts also to join. He eventually did join in January 1963 and the group (Jagger, Richard, Jones, Stewart, Watts, and Wyman) subsequently played the rhythm-and-blues club circuit and secured an eight-months' residency at the Crawdaddy Club in Richmond, where they attracted a burgeoning cult following. In April, Andrew Oldham became their manager and signed the group with Decca Records (London in the United States).

The Rolling Stones' first single, Chuck Berry's "Come On," became a minor British hit in June 1963, and Oldham began cultivating a rebellious image for the group; Ian Stewart was ousted from the group, though he continued to record and occasionally to play with them and eventually became their tour manager. After performing in a support role to The Everly Brothers and Little Richard in September, The Rolling Stones scored their first major British hit with "I Wanna Be Your Man," provided by Beatles songwriters John Lennon and Paul McCartney, in December. They scored a smash British hit with the Buddy Holly song "Not Fade Away" in April 1964, and the single soon became the group's first American chart entry. Their debut American album, pervaded by American rhythm-and-blues songs such as "Walking the Dog," "I Just Want to Make Love to You," "Can I Get a Witness," and "Tell Me" (their first major American hit), sold quite well, and the group first toured the United States in June. Before year's end, *12 x 5* had yielded a major hit with "It's All Over Now" and a near-smash with "Time Is on My Side," but the group nonetheless remained a cult band during the early "English invasion." By *Now!* Jagger and Richard were writing some of the group's songs, and the album produced a major American hit with "Heart of Stone" in early 1965.

Out of Our Heads, recorded primarily in Chicago, finally established The Rolling Stones in the United States. The album yielded a near-smash hit with Jagger and Richard's "The Last Time" (backed with "Play with Fire") and a top hit with their classic "(I Can't Get No) Satisfaction" and included the satirical "The Under Assistant West Coast Promotion Man," becoming the first of 23 consecutive certified gold-award albums for the group. The Rolling Stones toured the United States twice in 1965, achieving a top hit with "Get Off My Cloud" and a smash hit with the ballad "As Tears Go By," from *December's Children*, by early 1966. "19th Nervous Breakdown" soon became a smash hit and in July, shortly after the release of *Aftermath*, the group completed their last tour of America for over three years. That album, the first Rolling Stones' album comprised entirely of Jagger–Richard songs, was an instant best-seller and yielded a top hit with the ominous "Paint It Black" (on which Brian Jones played sitar) and a major hit with "Lady Jane" (Jones on dulcimer), while containing the chauvinistic "Stupid Girl" and "Under My Thumb," and the 11-minute-plus "Going Home." During July "Mother's Little Helper" (the flip side of "Lady Jane") became a near-smash hit, as did "Have You Seen Your Mother, Baby, Standing in the Shadows" in November.

Shortly after the live set, *Got LIVE, If You Want It*, The Rolling Stones issued *Between the Buttons*, which included the top hit "Ruby Tuesday" (backed by "Let's Spend the Night Together") and the overlooked "Yesterday's Papers." Appearing on television's "Ed Sullivan Show" in January 1967, the group performed "Let's Spend the Night Together" as "Let's Spend Some Time Together." Later Jagger and Richard, and then Jones, were charged in the first big drug busts in English rock, in response to which the stately *London Times* came to the group's defense. Following *Flowers*, The Rolling Stones attempted to capitalize on the so-called "psychedelic" trend initiated by San Francisco bands and bolstered by The Beatles' *Sgt. Pepper's Lonely Hearts Club Band* with *Their Satanic Majesties Request*, but the album was not well received critically. It did yield a minor hit with "We Love You" (fronted by the single "Dandelion," a major hit) and a major hit with "She's a Rainbow." During 1967 Brian had ostensibly played very little on the group's recordings, became estranged from the rest of the members, and even required hospitalization in December. He was busted again in May 1968, shortly before "Jumpin' Jack Flash," often regarded as the group's most potent single since "Satisfaction," started the re-establishment of The Rolling Stones that culminated in *Beggar's Banquet*. That much-delayed album, undoubtedly the finest and most coherent of the group's works, included the classic "Sympathy for the Devil," the overlooked countrified "No Expectations," and "Stray Cat Blues," as well as "Street-Fighting Man," oddly enough only a minor hit as a single. After participating in the legendary never-to-be-seen television special "Rock and Roll Circus," Brian Jones quit the group in early June 1969 and was replaced in less than a week by guitarist Mick Taylor (born January 17, 1948, in Hertfordshire), who had quit John Mayall's group to join The Stones. On July 3 Jones was found dead in a swimming pool at the age of 25; two days later Taylor publicly debuted with the group at a free concert in London's Hyde Park, attended by 250,000, which launched King Crimson and Family. Mick Jagger soon left for Australia to perform the title role in the film *Ned Kelly*, released in 1970.

During the summer of 1969 another Rolling Stones classic single, "Honky-Tonk Women," recorded with Mick Taylor, became a top hit, and the group subsequently embarked on an American tour in October. Concluding the tour, the group announced plans for a free concert in northern California, but the concert site was changed several times and eventually took place at Altamont Speedway. Held on December 6, the concert was a highly publicized tragedy. With the Hells Angels providing security in exchange for beer, the concert was staged without adequate food services and health facilities and The Stones, demonstrating their aloofness from the audience, delayed more than an hour before appearing on the stage. Once they took the stage, the group worked the crowd into hysteria with unfortunate results. During "Sympathy for the Devil," a fan near the front was stabbed to death, as graphically captured on film, and the concert devolved into ugly chaos. Charges and counter-charges by participants were later aired, and the leftist press denounced the event as the "death" of rock-and-roll and the "Woodstock spirit." The Rolling Stones did not perform "Sympathy for the Devil" for six years. A film recording of the 1969 tour and Altamont concert, *Gimme Shelter*, was premiered in late 1970.

Also in late 1969 The Rolling Stones released *Let It Bleed*, their last album of new material for one and one-half years, and the album became an instant best-seller; it contained "Gimme Shelter" (ironic in the light of Altamont), the classic "You Can't Always Get What You Want," the sexist and racist "Midnight Rambler," "Country Honk," and the title song. A period of inactivity for the group followed, as Jagger appeared as the ambisexual star of Nicholas Roeg's *Performance* film, released during 1970. The soundtrack album included a Jagger solo single, "Memo from Turner." In March 1971 The Rolling Stones announced they were leaving England for tax purposes, yet they conducted their first English tour in five years, augmented by keyboardist Nicky Hopkins, trumpeter Jim Price, and saxophonist Bobby Keyes. In April they issued what is usually regarded as their last classic single, the sexist and racist "Brown Sugar" (a top hit), on their newly formed record label, Rolling Stones Records, distributed by Atlantic in the United States. Their debut album for the label, *Sticky Fingers*, included "Brown Sugar," the countrified "Wild Horses" (a moderate hit), the jam-style "Can't You Hear Me Knocking," plus "Dead Flowers" and "Sister Morphine," the latter co-authored without credit by Marianne Faithfull. By now, Rolling Stones' concerts were being attended more as cultural events than as musical performances, and Jagger, in particular, was adopted by the so-called "jet set," especially following his much-publicized marriage to Bianca de Macias in May 1971. The double-record set, *Exile on Main Street*, released to coincide with their massive 1972 American tour accompanied by Hopkins, Price, and Keyes, was greeted by equivocal reviews and produced major hits with "Tumbling Dice" and "Happy." The following January The Rolling Stones performed a benefit concert in Los Angeles with Cheech and Chong and Santana for victims of the recent Nicaraguan earthquake, raising more than $350,000 in relief funds. Conducting immensely successful tours of America and Europe in 1973 yet not touring in 1974, the group's next two albums, *Goat's Head Soup* and *It's Only Rock 'n Roll*, were considered minor works compared to previous albums, yet each contained a few exceptional songs. *Goat's Head Soup* yielded a top hit with the ballad "Angie" and a minor hit with "Doo Doo Doo Doo Doo (Heartbreaker)," while containing the notorious "Star Star" (perhaps better known as "Starfucker"), whereas *It's Only Rock 'n Roll* produced major hits with the title song and "Ain't Too Proud to Beg" (originally recorded by The Temptations), while including "Time Waits for No One." In 1974 the in-concert film *Ladies and Gentlemen: The Rolling Stones*, filmed in Texas during the 1972 tour, was released.

During 1975 The Rolling Stones again mounted a huge, lavishly staged and lucrative American tour augmented by Billy Preston, yet the group did not release an album of new material until the following spring. Bill Wyman had issued his first solo album in the spring of 1974; Mick Taylor had quit the group the following December and was replaced by "guest artist" Ron Wood (born June 1, 1947, in London), guitarist for The Faces, for the grandiose 1975 tour and subsequent recordings. Taylor briefly joined the Jack Bruce Band and eventually resurfaced in 1979 with a solo album on Columbia Records. The Stones' *Black and Blue*, another much-delayed album, met with critical disapproval and later inspired a boycott by the Woman Against Violence Against Women (WAVAW) against the entire organization responsible for distribution of Rolling Stones Records, Warner Communications, due to the sexist nature of the promotional campaign. The album yielded only one major hit, "Fool to Cry," and Ron Wood finally became an official member of the group in June 1977. After the release of the live double-record set *Love You Live*, The Rolling Stones again toured the United States during 1978, this time without the elaborate staging and massive props of the 1975 tour, accompanied by keyboardists Ian McLagan (formerly of The Faces) and Ian Stewart. Performing at small and medium-sized venues as well as at huge outdoor concerts, The Rolling Stones broke the rock concert attendance record in July at the New Orleans Superdome, where over 80,000 fans were present. In mid-year *Some Girls* was issued by The Rolling Stones and the album ultimately became the group's best seller (4 million-plus copies), sparked by a top hit with the disco-style "Miss You," a near-smash with "Beast of Burden" and the moderate hit "Shattered"; it stirred controversy with the racist and sexist lyrics to the title song.

In February 1977, Keith Richard was busted in Toronto on serious drug charges (possession of heroin for sale), yet he got off lightly in October 1978, being required to continue drug rehabilitation and to perform a benefit concert. For the concert, performed in April 1979, Richard and Ron Wood assembled The New Barbarians with keyboardist Ian Mc-Lagan, saxophonist Bobby Keyes, jazz bassist Stanley Clarke, and Meters drummer Joe Modeliste, with Mick Jagger making a guest appearance. The concert and the subsequent 14-city American tour by The New Barbarians neatly coincided with the release of Wood's third solo album, *Gimme Some Neck*, which included eight originals by Wood and Bob Dylan's "Seven Days." During 1979 The Rolling Stones became the subject of controversy as the result of former associate Tony Sanchez' ghastly and lurid account of his eight-year tenure with The Rolling Stones, *Up and Down with The Rolling Stones*. Their reputation had also been damaged by a film made by Robert Franks during the group's 1972 tour, *Cocksucker Blues*. The film, completed in 1973 and shown several times during 1975 and 1976, was legally suppressed by the group and, apparently, can be shown only four times a year. Finally, in 1980, another much delayed Rolling Stones album, *Emotional Rescue*, was issued, but it did little to dispel the allegation that the group was no longer the "world's greatest rock-and-roll band." In early 1981 the anthology album *Sucking in the Seventies* was released by the group, as was the rhythm-and-blues styled *Rocket 88*, fronted by Stones associate Ian Stewart. Later in the year The Rolling Stones redeemed themselves in the United States with the unaffected *Tattoo You* album, its two smash singles, "Start Me Up" and "Waiting for a Friend," and a massively successful tour conducted between September and December.

THE ROLLING STONES

The Rolling Stones	London	PS–375	June '64	A
12 x 5	London	PS–402	November '64	A
Now!	London	PS–420	March '65	A

Out of Our Heads*	London	PS–429	July '65	A
December's Children (and Everybody's)*	London	PS–451	November '65	A
Aftermath*	London	PS–476	June '66	A
Got LIVE, If You Want It*	London	PS–493	December '66	A
Between the Buttons*	London	PS–499	February '67	A
Flowers*	London	PS–509	July '67	A
Their Satanic Majesties Request*	London	NPS–2	December '67	A
Beggar's Banquet*	London	PS–539	December '68	A

BRIAN JONES

| Brian Jones Presents The Pipes of Pan at Joujouke | Rolling Stones | 49100 | November '71 | |

THE ROLLING STONES

Let It Bleed*	London	NPS–4	December '69	A
Get Yer Ya-Ya's Out*	London	NPS–5	September '70	A
Sticky Fingers*	Rolling Stones	COC–59100	May '71	A
Exile on Main Street*	2-Rolling Stones	COC2–2900	May '72	A
Goat's Head Soup*	Rolling Stones	COC–59101	September '73	
		reissued as 39106		A
It's Only Rock 'n Roll*	Rolling Stones	COC–79101	October '74	A

WYMAN, WATTS, JAGGER, RY COODER, AND NICKY HOPKINS

| Jammin' with Edward | Rolling Stones | COC–39100 | February '72 | |

BILL WYMAN

| Monkey Grip | Rolling Stones | COC–79100 | May '74 | A |
| Stone Alone | Rolling Stones | COC–79103 | February '76 | |

MICK TAYLOR

| Mick Taylor | Columbia | JC–35076 | June '79 | |

THE ROLLING STONES

| Made in the Shade* | Rolling Stones | COC–79102 | June '75 | A |

Black and Blue**	Rolling Stones	COC–79104	April '76	A
Love You Live*	2-Rolling Stones	COC2–9001	September '77	A
Some Girls**	Rolling Stones	COC–39108	June '78	A
Emotional Rescue**	Rolling Stones	16015	July '80	A
Tattoo You**	Rolling Stones	16052	August '81	A

RON WOOD

| Gimme Some Neck | Columbia | PC–35702 | May '79 | A |

ROCKET 88 (WITH IAN STEWART)

| Rocket 88 | Atlantic | 19293 | February '81 | |

ROLLING STONES ANTHOLOGIES AND COMPILATIONS

Big Hits (High Tides and Green Grass)*	London	NPS–1	April '66	A
Through the Past Darkly (Big Hits, Volume 2)*	London	NPS–3	September '69	A
Hot Rocks*	2-London	2PS–606/7	January '72	A
More Hot Rocks (Big Hits and Fazed Cookies)*	2-London	2PS–626/7	December '72	A
Metamorphosis	ABKCO	ANA–1	May '75	
Sucking in the Seventies (Greatest Hits)*	Rolling Stones	16028	February '81	A

THE RONETTES. Perhaps the best-remembered of the so-called "girl groups" launched into stardom during the early Sixties by legendary producer Phil Spector, The Ronettes scored a smash hit in the fall of 1963 with "Be My Baby," followed by two major and two moderate hits through early 1965, all featuring Spector's revolutionary "wall-of-sound" production technique. The group quickly faded from popularity with Spector's withdrawal from the music business in 1966 and the demise of his Philles label in 1967, and lead singer Ronnie Bennett subsequently married Spector. He unsuccessfully attempted to revive The Ronettes' career on A&M Records in 1969, and Ronnie Spector attempted several come-backs on her own during the Seventies, eventually reemerging in 1980 with *Siren* on Genya Ravan's Polish Records label.

Starting as Ronnie and The Ronettes around 1959, this vocal group consisted of sisters Estelle and Veronica "Ronnie" Bennett and cousin Nedra Talley. Debuting professionally as dancers at the opening of the

Peppermint Lounge in New York City in 1961, the group was signed to Don Kirshner's Colpix label, for whom they recorded five unsuccessful singles. Signed to Philles Records by Phil Spector in 1963, The Ronettes soon scored a smash hit with Spector, Jeff Barry, and Ellie Greenwich's "Be My Baby," featuring Spector's patented "wall-of-sound" production-arrangement technique, that fall. At year's end, they achieved a major hit with "Baby, I Love You," again written by Spector, Barry, and Greenwich, following up with the moderate hits "(The Best Part of) Breaking Up" and "Do I Love You." They scored their last major hit in late 1964 with the classic "Walking in the Rain," authored by Spector with Barry Mann and Cynthia Weil, yet they continued to record on Philles through 1966. In 1968 Ronnie Bennett married Phil Spector, who attempted unsuccessfully to revive the group's career on A&M Records in 1969 with "You Came, You Saw, You Conquered." In 1971 Ronnie Spector achieved a minor hit with George Harrison's "Try Some, Buy Some" on Apple Records; she recruited two new members the following year for an unsuccessful come-back try as The Ronettes on Buddah Records, without the assistance of Spector. During 1976 "Paradise," produced by Spector, written by Spector and Harry Nilsson, and originally intended as the follow-up to "Walking in the Rain," was released on the Spector-Warner label as recorded by Ronnie Spector, but the single failed to make the charts. Divorced from Phil Spector in 1974, Ronnie Spector recorded "Say Goodbye to Hollywood," written for her by Billy Joel and produced by "Miami" Steve Van Zandt of Bruce Springsteen's E Street Band, in 1978, but it too proved unsuccessful. During 1980 Ronnie Spector once more re-emerged with "Darlin" from the soundtrack to the film *Urban Cowboy* and *Siren* on former Ten Wheel Drive vocalist Genya Ravan's New York-based independent label, Polish Records. Recorded with members of Mink DeVille and The Dead Boys, the album included The Troggs' "Any Way That You Want Me," The Ramones' "Here Today, Gone Tomorrow," and "Happy Birthday, Rock and Roll," dedicated to Phil Spector.

THE RONETTES

The Ronettes Featuring Veronica	Colpix	CP–486	
The Ronettes	Philles	4006(M)	December '64

RONNIE SPECTOR

Siren	Polish	PRG–808	October '80	A

LINDA RONSTADT. By 1975 the single most popular female vocalist in rock music, Linda Ronstadt first came to public attention with the folk-style Stone Poneys by means of their late Sixties "Different Drum" hit and subsequently pursued an inauspicious solo recording career of reworked country-and-western and contemporary songs marred by lackluster production and a constantly shifting retinue of backing musicians. Eventually securing her first stellar group of accompanying musicians in 1971 in the persons of Glen Frey, Don Henley, Bernie Leadon, and Randy Meisner (who, within four months, departed to form The Eagles), Ronstadt finally found sympathetic production under Peter Asher of the English duo Peter and Gordon. His first full production effort for her, *Heart like a Wheel*, yielded two smash hits and became the first in a continuing series of certified gold-award albums. An interpretive singer rather than a singer–songwriter, Linda Ronstadt has regularly used the compositions of up-and-coming songwriters such as J. D. Souther, Lowell George, Karla Bonoff, Warren Zevon, and Elvis Costello during her career, while simultaneously establishing herself with country-and-western audiences with country-style material. Ronstadt's distinctive, strong, and resonant voice disguises her inability to infuse emotional nuance and meaning into her recordings. Having regularly scored smash hits with Fifties material and reworked Motown classics, Linda Ronstadt's enormous success is due more to astute song selection, Asher's sympathetic production, the excellence of her supporting musicians, and the careful marketing of Asylum Records than to any innate talent.

Linda Ronstadt was born on July 15, 1946, in Tucson, Arizona, where she was raised and inspired to sing by a musically talented father. By the age of 14 she was singing with brother Pete and sister Suzi in local pizza parlors and clubs, occasionally accompanied by bassist–guitarist Bob Kimmel. After one semester at the University of Arizona, Ronstadt acceded to Kimmel's entreaties to join him in Los Angeles, where the two formed The Stone Poneys with local guitarist Kenny Edwards. Playing the region's club circuit, the group signed with Capitol Records in 1966 and recorded two albums comprised primarily of Kimmel–Edwards compositions before the departure of Edwards, then of Kimmel. The second album, *Evergreen—Volume 2*, produced a major hit with former Monkee Mike Nesmith's "Different Drum," whereas the third album, credited to Linda Ronstadt, The Stone Poneys, and Friends, was recorded with sessions musicians and contained three Tim Buckley compositions. Subsequently pursuing a solo career with Capitol Records, Ronstadt developed a formula of reworking country-and-western songs augmented by the compositions of contemporary songwriters such as Bob Dylan, Randy Newman, and Jackson Browne. In 1970 she scored a major hit with "Long, Long Time"; she later achieved a minor hit with Browne's "Rock Me on the Water" in early 1972 from *Linda Ronstadt*, on which she was accompanied by later-day Eagles Glen Frey, Don Henley, Randy Meisner, and Bernie Leadon.

Touring with Neil Young in early 1973 and then switching to Asylum Records (although she remained obligated to provide Capitol with one more album), Linda Ronstadt re-enlisted Kenny Edwards, who recruited songwriter–guitarist Andrew Gold, for her new backup band. *Don't Cry Now*, completed with three different producers, yielded minor hits with Eric Kaz and Libby Titus' "Love Has No Pride" and "Silver Threads and Golden Needles," while containing three songs by John David Souther (one of the producers)—the title song, "I Can Almost See It" and "The Fast

One." Peter Asher, another of the producers and the producer of James Taylor's hits, became her producer and manager by 1974 and was the sole producer of the landmark *Heart like a Wheel* album (her final album for Capitol) and subsequent Asylum albums. The album was an instant smash success and was certified gold-award within three months of its release, furnishing two small hits with "You're No Good" (a minor hit for Betty Everett in 1963) and Phil Everly's classic "When Will I Be Loved." The album also included Souther's "Faithless Love," Anna McGarrigle's title song, the Lowell George favorite "Willin'," as well as Hank Williams' "I Can't Help It If I'm Still in Love with You," a major country hit. Augmented by pedal steel guitarist Dan Dugmore, Ronstadt's *Prisoner in Disguise* yielded a smash hit with the Holland–Dozier–Holland classic "Heat Wave" (backed by Neil Young's "Love Is a Rose") and a major hit with the Smokey Robinson classic "Tracks of My Tears." Other album inclusions were Souther's "Silver Blue" and title song, Lowell George's "Roll Um Easy," and Dolly Parton's "I Will Always Love You." *Hasten down the Wind*, Ronstadt's first certified platinum-award album, contained a major hit with the Buddy Holly classic "That'll Be the Day," as well as Willie Nelson's "Crazy," Warren Zevon's title song, and three compositions by Karla Bonoff, including "Someone to Lay Down Beside Me," a moderate hit.

After completing a six-month tour of Europe and America in December 1976 and singing at President Carter's inaugural the following January, Linda Ronstadt next recorded *Simple Dreams*, which sold three and one-half million copies in less than a year. It produced an astounding four hit singles, two smashes with Roy Orbison's "Blue Bayou" and Buddy Holly's "It's So Easy," and two moderate hits with Warren Zevon's "Poor, Poor, Pitiful Me" and The Rolling Stones' "Tumbling Dice." "I Never Will Marry" became the country hit from the album. During 1978 Ronstadt attempted to record a female "superstar" album with Emmylou Harris and Dolly Parton, but the hastily made recordings apparently proved unsatisfactory for release. By then sessions veteran Waddy Wachtel had replaced Andrew Gold on guitar in Ronstadt's backup band, and the hit-making formula continued with Chuck Berry's "Back in the U.S.A.," Smokey Robinson's "Ooh, Baby, Baby," and "Just One Look" (a major hit for Doris Troy in 1963) from *Living in the U.S.A.*, which also contained J. D. Souther's "White Rhythm and Blues," and Elvis Costello's "Alison," Ronstadt's concession to the burgeoning "new wave." With the departure of Kenny Edwards, the replacement of Waddy Wachtel by Danny Kortchmar, and the addition of former Little Feat keyboardist Bill Payne, Ronstadt's 1980 *Mad Love* may very well have been her first challenging album. However, despite the inclusion of three songs by Elvis Costello— "Girls Talk," "Party Girl," and "Talking in the Dark"—and three songs by Mark Goldenberg of the Los Angeles-based Cretones—"Justine," "Mad Love," and "Cost of Love"—the album's singles releases were the aggressive staccato "How Do I Make You" and the oldies "Hurt So Bad," a major hit for Little Anthony and The Imperials in 1965, and "I Can't Let Go," a moderate hit for The Hollies in 1966. During the latter half of 1980,

Linda Ronstadt performed in the 100th anniversary New York stage production of Gilbert and Sullivan's *Pirates of Penzance* in the role of Mabel.

THE STONE PONEYS

The Stone Poneys	Capitol	ST–2666	February '67	
reissued as Beginnings		ST–11383 reissued as SN–16133	April '75	A
Evergreen— Volume 2	Capitol	ST–2763	July '67	
Volume 3	Capitol	ST–2863	March '68	
Different Drum	Capitol	ST–11269	January '74	A
Stoney End	Pickwick	3298	June '72	A

LINDA RONSTADT AND THE STONE PONEYS/DAVID CLAYTON–THOMAS

Back on the Street Again	Pickwick	3245

LINDA RONSTADT

Hand Sown . . . Home Grown	Capitol	ST–208 reissued as SN–16130	March '69	A
Silk Purse	Capitol	ST–407 reissued as SN–16131	April '70	A
Linda Ronstadt	Capitol	SMAS–635 reissued as SN–16132	December '71	A
Heart like a Wheel*	Capitol	SW–11358	November '74	A
Retrospective*	2-Capitol	SKBB–11629	May '77	A
Don't Cry Now*	Asylum	SD–5064	September '73	A
Prisoner in Disguise*	Asylum	7E–1045	September '75	A
Hasten down the Wind**	Asylum	7E–1072	August '76	A
Greatest Hits**	Asylum	7E–1092 reissued as 6E–106	December '76	A
Simple Dreams**	Asylum	6E–104	September '77	A
Living in the U.S.A.**	Asylum	155	September '78	A
Mad Love**	Asylum	510	February '80	A
Greatest Hits, Volume 2*	Elektra	516	October '80	A
Keeping Out of Mischief	Asylum	540	September '81	A

PIRATES OF PENZANCE (ORIGINAL CAST, WITH LINDA RONSTADT)

Broadway Cast   2-Elektra   VE–601   July '81   A
Album

DIANA ROSS AND THE SUPREMES. Undoubtedly Motown's most successful group, scoring ten top hits between 1964 and 1967, The Supremes were prime purveyors of the sophisticated, highly commercial, and sometimes bland black vocal group sound that found acceptance with white audiences as well as with black. Certainly much of their popularity was based on the production and songwriting of the Holland–Dozier–Holland team, who seemingly reserved much of their finest material for the group. Their hit compositions for The Supremes included the classics "Where Did Our Love Go," "Come See About Me," "Stop! In the Name of Love," "Back in My Arms Again," "You Can't Hurry Love," and "You Keep Me Hangin' On." With a change of billing to Diana Ross and The Supremes, the Motown organization and Berry Gordy, Jr., in particular, keyed on developing Ross as a multimedia star. Though challenged by the popularity of the grittier, rougher, and more openly erotic sound of Stax Records artists after 1966 and suffering the loss of the Holland–Dozier–Holland team in 1968, Diana Ross and The Supremes nonetheless retained their status as the most widely recognized black group with hits such as "Love Child," one of Motown's earliest attempts at social consciousness, and "Someday We'll Be Together." "Discoverer" of The Jackson Five, one of Motown's most successful groups of the Seventies, Diana Ross subsequently embarked on a solo career, sparked by the chart-topping success of 1970's "Ain't No Mountain High Enough" classic, that saw her appearing on Broadway and in Las Vegas as well as on television, as the reconstituted Supremes managed major hits only through 1972. With her well-received portrayal of Billie Holiday in the film *Lady Sings the Blues*, which depicted the lives of black people more realistically than did the flood of early Seventies black exploitation films, Diana Ross was launched as a movie star and earned the first Academy Award nomination for a black woman in a starring role. After another top hit with "Touch Me in the Morning" and a duet album with Marvin Gaye, she reaffirmed her status as both actress and singer with the film *Mahogany* and its theme song, also known as "Do You Know Where You're Going To." Late 1978's musical extravaganza, *The Wiz*, proved a conspicuous failure for Diana Ross, yet her first album in nearly two years, *The Boss*, and its followup, *Diana*, saw her back in fine form.

Diana Ross (born on March 26, 1944, in Detroit), Florence Ballard (born June 30, 1944, in Detroit), and Mary Wilson (born March 4, 1944, in Mississippi) began singing together while still in high school, around 1960, as The Primettes, companion group to The Primes, whose members Otis Williams and Eddie Kendricks later formed The Temptations. After winning a high school talent contest, the group auditioned for Berry Gordy,

Jr., but he insisted they finish high school. Signed to Motown in 1962, the group performed background vocals and recorded as The Supremes, scoring their first chart entry with "Your Heart Belongs to Me." Their first major hit eventually came in 1963–64 with "When the Lovelight Starts Shining Through His Eyes," but mid-1964's "Where Did Our Love Go" was the first of five consecutive top hits written for the group by Brian Holland, Lamont Dozier, and Eddie Holland. The string of top H–D–H hits ("Baby Love," "Come See About Me," "Stop! In the Name of Love," and "Back in My Arms Again") was broken in mid-1965 with "Nothing But Heartaches," after which The Supremes achieved another run of consecutive top hits with "You Can't Hurry Love," "You Keep Me Hangin' On," and "Love Is Here and Now You're Gone," all by Holland–Dozier–Holland, and the "psychedelic" sounding "The Happening." During 1967 Florence Ballard quit or was forced out of the group, briefly attempted a solo career, and eventually died impoverished on February 22, 1976, at the age of 31. She was replaced by Cindy Birdsong (born December 15, 1939, in Camden, New Jersey) of Patti Labelle and The Bluebelles, yet neither the group's light pop sound nor their polished, sophisticated image changed appreciably.

In an effort to emphasize the primacy of lead singer Diana Ross, the group's billing was changed to Diana Ross and The Supremes for the 1967 "psychedelic soul" hit "Reflections," another H–D–H song. After their final near-smash hit written by the team, "In and Out of Love," the group scored top hits with "Love Child," one of Motown's few attempts at socially conscious lyrics, and "Someday We'll Be Together," in late 1968 and late 1969, respectively. During that time, Ross and The Supremes also successfully teamed with The Temptations to record the best-selling albums *The Supremes Join The Temptations* and *TCB* and hit with "I'm Gonna Make You Love Me."

At the end of 1969 Diana Ross left the group, and The Supremes continued with original Mary Wilson, Cindy Birdsong, and new member Jean Terrell, although personnel shifts occurred regularly through the Seventies. They managed major hits into 1972 with "Up the Ladder to the Roof," "Stoned Love," "Nathan Jones," and "Floy Joy," yet their teaming with The Four Tops proved remarkably unsuccessful, except for a remake of the Phil Spector–Ellie Greenwich–Jeff Barry classic, "River Deep—Mountain High." By 1977 The Supremes were comprised of original Mary Wilson, Scherrie Payne (the younger sister of Freda Payne), and Susaye Greene; but by late 1979, Wilson had recorded a solo album, and Scherrie Payne and Susaye Greene a duet album, both for Motown.

Solo, Diana Ross had her first major hit with the anti-drug song "Reach Out and Touch (Somebody's Hand)," soon followed by the top hit classic, "Ain't No Mountain High Enough," by songwriter–producers Nicholas Ashford and Valerie Simpson. However, after "Remember Me," Ross' recording career began to fade; she began appearing regularly on television, including a 1971 special. Her seeming slip from popularity was arrested by her praiseworthy performance as Billie Holiday in the 1972 film

Lady Sings the Blues, and the movie's soundtrack album became a best-seller. Ross' "Touch Me in the Morning" was another top hit in 1973, after which she teamed with Marvin Gaye for an album and the major hits "You're a Special Part of Me" and "My Mistake (Was to Love You)," with her solo hit, "Last Time I Saw Him," intervening. In 1975 Diana Ross appeared as the star of another successful film, *Mahogany*, and scored another chart-topping hit with the movie's theme song, also known as "Do You Know Where You're Going To?" She subsequently achieved a top hit with the disco-sounding "Love Hangover" in 1976, followed by the moderate hits "One Love in My Lifetime" and "Gettin' Ready for Love." In June 1976 she brought her *Evening with Diana Ross* stage show to Broadway; she later toured the country with the show and appeared in the first one-woman, prime-time, 90-minute television special the following March. Released in late 1978, the film version of the hit play *The Wiz*, an all-black version of L. Frank Baum's book *The Wizard of Oz*, starred Ross with Michael Jackson, Nipsey Russell, Lena Horne, and Richard Pryor. Probably the most expensive all-black film ever made, *The Wiz* was accompanied by a $6,000,000 promotional budget. Although the film was visually spectacular, utilizing stunning costuming, elaborate special effects, and massive production numbers, it proved a relative failure and has yet to recoup its $20,000,000 expenses. Nonetheless, the soundtrack album provided a near-smash hit with the Ross–Jackson duet, "Ease on Down the Road." In 1979 Diana Ross scored her first major hit in nearly two years with Nicholas Ashford and Valerie Simpson's "The Boss," the title song to her Ashford–Simpson-produced album and followed it in 1980 with the top pop, soul, and disco hit "Upside Down" from *Diana*. Her subsequent 1980 smash hits were "I'm Coming Out" and "It's My Turn," followed in 1981 by the top hit duet with Lionel Richie of The Commodores, "Endless Love," and a remake of Frankie Lymon and The Teenagers' 1956 smash hit "Why Do Fools Fall in Love" on her new label, RCA.

THE SUPREMES

Meet The Supremes	Motown	606(M)	April '63
Where Did Our Love Go	Motown	621	September '64
A Bit of Liverpool	Motown	623	November '64
Country, Western, and Pop	Motown	625	March '65
We Remember Sam Cooke	Motown	629	April '65
More Hits	Motown	627	August '65
Live at the Copa	Motown	636	November '65
Merry Christmas	Motown	638	December '65
I Hear a Symphony	Motown	643	March '66
Supremes A Go-Go	Motown	649	September '66
Sing Holland–Dozier–Holland	Motown	650	February '67
Sing Rodgers and Hart	Motown	659	June '67

DIANA ROSS AND THE SUPREMES

Reflections	Motown	665	April '68	
Funny Girl	Motown	672	September '68	
Live at London's Talk of the Town	Motown	676	September '68	
Love Child	Motown	670	December '68	
Let the Sunshine In	Motown	689	June '69	
Cream of the Crop	Motown	694	November '69	
Farewell	Motown	708	May '70	

ANTHOLOGIES AND COMPILATIONS BY THE SUPREMES WITH DIANA ROSS

Greatest Hits	2-Motown	7–663	September '67	A
Greatest Hits, Volume 3	Motown	702	January '70	
Anthology	3-Motown	9–794	June '74	A
Baby Love	Pickwick	3383	January '75	A
Motown Superstar Series, Volume 1	Motown	5–101		A

THE SUPREMES AND THE TEMPTATIONS

The Supremes Join The Temptations	Motown	679	November '68
TCB	Motown	682	December '68
Together	Motown	692	October '69
On Broadway	Motown	699	November '69

THE SUPREMES (WITHOUT DIANA ROSS)

Right On	Motown	705	May '70
New Ways, but Love Stays	Motown	720	October '70
Touch	Motown	737	June '71
Floy Joy	Motown	751	May '72

THE SUPREMES AND THE FOUR TOPS

The Magnificent Seven	Motown	717	October '70
The Return of The Magnificent Seven	Motown	736	June '71
Dynamite	Motown	745	December '71

THE SUPREMES (WITHOUT DIANA ROSS)

The Supremes	Motown	756	November '72
The Supremes	Motown	828	June '75
High Energy	Motown	863	May '76
Mary, Scherrie, and Susaye	Motown	873	January '77
At Their Best (1973–1978)	Motown	904	July '78

MARY WILSON

Mary Wilson	Motown	927	October '79	

SCHERRIE PAYNE AND SUSAYE GREENE

Partners	Motown	920	November '79	A

DIANA ROSS

Diana Ross	Motown	711	July '70	
Diana! (TV)	Motown	719	April '71	
Everything Is Everything	Motown	724	November '70	
Surrender	Motown	723	August '71	
Lady Sings the Blues (soundtrack)	2-Motown	758	November '72	A
Touch Me in the Morning	Motown	772	July '73	

DIANA ROSS AND MARVIN GAYE

Diana and Marvin/ Ross and Gaye	Motown	7–803	October '73	A

DIANA ROSS

The Last Time I Saw Him	Motown	812	December '73	
Live at Caesar's Palace	Motown	6–801	June '74	
Mahogany (soundtrack)	Motown	6–858	November '75	
Diana Ross	Motown	6–861	February '76	
Greatest Hits	Motown	7–869	July '76	A
An Evening with Diana Ross	2-Motown	7–877	February '77	
Baby, It's Me	Motown	7–890	October '77	
Ross	Motown	7–907	October '78	A

DIANA ROSS AND OTHERS

The Wiz (soundtrack	2-MCA	2–14000 reissued as 6010	October '78	A

DIANA ROSS

The Boss*	Motown	7–923	June '79	A
Diana**	Motown	8–936	June '80	A
To Love Again	Motown	8–951	March '81	A
All the Greatest Hits	2-Motown	13–960	November '81	A
Why Do Fools Fall in Love	RCA	AFL1– 4153	October '81	A

ROXY MUSIC. One of the most intelligent and provocative bands to emerge from the early Seventies British school of "art-rock," Roxy Music has also been considered one of the genre's most influential, given the decadent, romantically nostalgic, and vaguely existentialist lyrics of lead vocalist and chief songwriter Bryan Ferry and the "avant garde" ruminations of saxophone and oboe player Andy Mackay and early synthesizer player Brian Eno. Winning immediate public acceptance in Great Britain and Europe, yet not in the United States, Roxy Music moved through a variety of eccentric images based in part on their dress, dropped their initial "glitter-rock" stance, and adopted a more musical approach with the departure of Eno, who subsequently achieved critical acclaim and a limited following for his experimental other-worldly music in collaboration with King Crimson's Robert Fripp and on his own, as capped by his 1976 album, *Another Green World*. Ferry adopted white tuxedo and bow tie gear (and later Nazi-style paramilitary outfits) with Roxy Music and also pursued a parallel solo career that failed in America, while guitarist Phil Manzanera recorded the excellent, if overlooked, *Diamond Head* album. Eventually established in the United States with *Country Life* and *Siren*, the latter considered one of the most important albums of Seventies "art-rock," Roxy Music was thought to have opened the way for bizarre late Seventies bands such as Devo and Talking Heads before disbanding in 1976 and reuniting in 1978.

Bryan Ferry, born on September 26, 1945, in Washington, County Durham, England, manned his first band, The Banshees, in the summer of 1964 and subsequently attended Newcastle University, from which he obtained a fine-arts degree in 1968. During college he was a member of the white soul band Gas Board with bassist Graham Simpson. In November 1970 Ferry and Simpson formed Roxy Music with guitarist Roger Bunn, added Andy Mackay (born July 23, 1946) the following January, and subsequently enlisted Brian Eno (born May 15, 1948) and drummer Dexter Lloyd. Eno had studied "avant garde" music in England and Italy prior to his induction into the group through Mackay. Drummer Paul Thompson (born May 13, 1951), a former member of Newcastle's Smokestack, replaced Lloyd in June 1971 and, with the September departure of Bunn, former Nice guitarist David O'List manned Roxy Music through February 1972. Playing their first engagement in late 1971, Roxy Music added guitarist Phil Manzanera (born January 31, 1951), a previous member of Quiet Sun, when O'List left. The first stable lineup of Roxy Music was Bryan Ferry (lead vocals, piano, songwriting), Phil Manzanera (guitar), Brian Eno (synthesizer), Andy Mackay (saxophone, oboe), Graham Simpson (bass), and Paul Thompson (drums). Signed to Island Records (Warner Brothers/Reprise in the United States) and given early British exposure through a "Melody Maker" article, Roxy Music recorded their debut album in the spring of 1972 with King Crimson lyricist Peter Sinfield as producer before their first tour of Great Britain that August. The album sold quite well in Britain and yielded a major hit with "Virginia Plain," but in June Simpson dropped out, to be replaced by a succession of bassists, including Rik Kenton, John Porter, John Wetton, and John Gustafson. First touring America in late 1972 and Europe in the spring of 1973, Roxy Music also hit in Britain with "Pyjamarama." *For Your Pleasure*, which included the dance parody "Do the Strand" and "In Every Dream Home a Heartache," became a British best-seller; Brian Eno departed in July and was replaced by Eddie Jobson (violin, keyboards, synthesizer). Brian Eno subsequently recorded two albums for Island Records before collaborating with Robert Fripp of King Crimson on two "avant garde" albums. He later recorded *Another Green World*, thought to be his finest work, assisted on albums by Phil Manzanera, John Cale, and David Bowie, and subsequently formed his own Obscure label in conjunction with Island in late 1975 and produced Talking Heads' second, third, and fourth albums and Devo's first.

Dropping his "glitter" garb in favor of white tuxedo and bow tie, and adopting a more traditionally musical approach, Bryan Ferry and Roxy Music next recorded for their new label Atco *Stranded*, which included the British hit "Street Life" and the ballad "A Song for Europe." By touring America several times between the spring of 1974 and early 1976, the group began to establish themselves in the United States with *Country Life*, which contained "The Thrill of It All," and *Siren*, often regarded as their masterpiece, which included the moderate American hit "Love Is the Drug" as well as "She Sells" and "Sentimental Fool." By then Ferry had initiated a solo recording career that never took off in the United States, and Manzanera had recorded the excellent yet neglected *Diamond Head* before rejoining Quiet Sun for *Mainstream*. Though well established in Great Britain and Europe, Roxy Music disbanded in June 1976, with Manzanera joining 801 and Ferry touring and recording with his own band, which included drummer Paul Thompson and guitarist Chris Spedding. Manzanera joined The Bryan Ferry Band in 1977, but the group subsequently folded; Eddie Jobson joined UK with one-time Roxy Music bassist John Wetton and well-traveled drummer Bill Bruford. In August 1978 Roxy Music re-formed with Bryan Ferry, Phil Manzanera, Andy Mackay, and Paul Thompson, plus keyboardist Paul Carrack (replaced by David Skinner) and bassist Gary Tibbs. *Manifesto* yielded a moderate hit with "Dance Away" and the reunited group toured America in the spring of 1979 and recorded *Flesh and Blood* the following year with originals Ferry, Manzanera, and Mackay. In early 1981, *My Life in the Bush of Ghosts*, an unusual experimental collaboration between Brian Eno and Talking Heads' leader David Byrne, was issued on Sire Records.

ROXY MUSIC

Roxy Music	Reprise	MS–2114	November '72	
	reissued on Atco	SD36–133	June '76	A
For Your Pleasure	Warner Brothers	BS–2696	July '73	
	reissued on Atco	SD36–134	June '76	A

BRIAN ENO

Here Come the Warm Jets	Island	9268	July '74	
Taking Tiger Mountain by Strategy	Island	9309	February '75	

BRIAN ENO AND ROBERT FRIPP

No Pussyfooting	Island reissued on Antilles	16 7001	November '75	
Evening Star	Antilles reissued on Editions E. G.	7018 103	June '76	A

BRIAN ENO

Another Green World	Island	9351	March '76	
Discreet Music	Antilles	7030	February '77	
Before and After Science	Island	9478	March '78	
Music for Films	Antilles reissued on Editions E. G.	7070 105	January '79 July '81	A
Music For Airports	PVC	7908		A

BRIAN ENO AND DAVID BYRNE

My Life in the Bush of Ghosts	Sire	6093	March '81	A

ROXY MUSIC

Stranded	Atco	SD-7045	April '74	A
Country Life	Atco	SD36-106	December '74	A
Siren	Atco	SD36-127	November '75	A
Viva! Roxy Music	Atco	SD36-139	July '76	A
Greatest Hits	Atco	38-103	November '77	A

BRYAN FERRY

These Foolish Things	Atlantic	SD-7304	July '74	A
Another Time, Another Place	Atlantic	SD-18113	November '74	
Let's Stick Together	Atlantic	SD-18187	September '76	A
In Your Mind	Atlantic	SD-18216	April '77	
The Bride Stripped Bare	Atlantic	SD-19205	October '78	

PHIL MANZANERA

Diamond Head	Atco	SD36–113	May '75	
K-Scope	Polydor	PD1–6178	January '79	A

QUIET SUN

Mainstream	Antilles	7008	January '76

ROXY MUSIC

Manifesto	Atco	38–114	March '79	A
Flesh and Blood	Atco	32–102	June '80	A

TODD RUNDGREN. First coming to public attention as the leader of the late Sixties Philadelphia group The Nazz, whose decidedly English-looking appearance and careful blend of lead guitar work and vocal harmonies contrasted markedly with the burgeoning wave of "psychedelia," Todd Rundgren quickly established himself as one of America's most sought-after recording engineers and producers after engineering The Band's certified gold-award *Stage Fright* album and recording virtually single-handedly his own *Runt* album. Managing major early Seventies hits with the melodic pop-style songs "We Gotta Get You a Woman" and "I Saw the Light," Rundgren was able to sustain a modest recording career while reaping financial success as producer of albums such as Grand Funk Railroad's certified gold-award *We're an American Band*. Enabled to form his own synthesizer-dominated esoteric band Utopia with the smash success of 1973's "Hello, It's Me," Todd Rundgren experimented with new electronic musical devices and advanced technology with the group, while continuing to record solo and producing Meatloaf's gold-award debut album *Bat out of Hell*, The Tubes' *Remote Control*, and The Patti Smith Group's *Wave*.

THE NAZZ

Introducing The Nazz	Screen Gems-Columbia	SD–5001	October '68
Nazz Nazz	Screen Gems-Columbia	SD–5002	April '69
Nazz III	Screen Gems-Columbia	SD–5004	July '71

TODD RUNDGREN

Runt	Ampex reissued on Bearsville	10105 BR–2046	September '70	
The Ballad of Todd Rundgren	Ampex reissued on Bearsville	10116 BR–2047	June '71	
Something/Any-thing?*	2-Bearsville	2BX–2066	March '72	A

A Wizard/A True Star	Bearsville	BR–2133	March '73	A
Todd	2-Bearsville	2BR–2169 reissued as 2BR– 6952	December '73	A

TODD RUNDGREN'S UTOPIA

Todd Rundgren's Utopia	Bearsville	BR–6954	October '74	A
Another Live	Bearsville	BR–6961	October '75	A

ROGER POWELL

Cosmic Furnace	Atlantic	SD–7251	February '73	
Air Pocket	Bearsville	BRK–6994	February '80	A

UTOPIA

Ra	Bearsville	BR–6965	February '77	A
Oops! Wrong Planet	Bearsville	BR–6970	September '77	A
Adventures in Utopia	Bearsville	BRK–6991	January '80	A
Deface the Music	Bearsville	3487	October '80	A

TODD RUNDGREN

Initiation	Bearsville	BR–6957	May '75	A
Faithful	Bearsville	BR–6963	April '76	A
Hermit of Mink Hollow	Bearsville	BSK–6981	April '78	A
Back to the Bars	2-Bearsville	2BRX– 6986	November '78	A
Healing	Bearsville	3522	February '81	A

LEON RUSSELL. One of the most active sessions musicians around Los Angeles during the first half of the Sixties, having played on most of Phil Spector's classic recordings as well as with The Byrds, Herb Alpert, Frank Sinatra, and others, Leon Russell first came to the public's attention with The Asylum Choir, in collaboration with songwriter–guitarist Marc Benno. Benno subsequently recorded three solo albums during the early Seventies, yet faded into obscurity despite the fact that Rita Coolidge recorded two of his songs on each of her first three albums, including the excellent "Second Story Window" and "Nice Feelin'." Leon Russell subsequently came to prominence as tour organizer and mastermind of Joe Cocker's 1970 Mad Dogs and Englishmen tour and frequently stole the show from Cocker. After embarking on a solo career highlighted by his gospel-style piano playing, raspy vocals, and excellent songwriting, Russell established himself as a potent album artist with *Leon Russell and The Shelter People* and *Carney* and helped to restore piano as a rock instrument and to revive the horn section as an integral part of rock music. One of the stars of George Harrison's 1971 Concert for Bangla Desh, Leon Russell's popularity began to slip after *Leon Live* and the cessation of his touring. Re-established with 1975's *Will o' the Wisp* and its hit single "Lady Blue," Russell later left the label he helped to found, Shelter, for poorly received solo and duet sets with his wife Mary McCreary. Nonetheless, Leon Russell's 1979 duet set with Willie Nelson proved a best-seller and successfully confirmed his talent for country-and-western music, an interest first revealed with 1973's *Hank Wilson's Back*.

Leon Russell was born in Lawton, Oklahoma, on April 2, 1941, and initiated ten years of classical piano studies at the age of three. At age 14 he took up trumpet, and formed his own band; he briefly played with Ronnie Hawkins and The Hawks and later toured with Jerry Lee Lewis for six months. After moving to Los Angeles in 1959, Russell learned guitar from James Burton and became a regular sessions musician, playing on most of Phil Spector's hit productions through 1966. He also played on isolated hits by The Byrds ("Mr. Tambourine Man"), Herb Alpert ("A Taste of Honey"), and Bob Lind ("Elusive Butterfly"), while recording with an incredible variety of artists, from Frank Sinatra to Gary Lewis and The Playboys, and from Bobby Darin to Paul Revere and The Raiders. In 1966 Russell met songwriter–guitarist Marc Benno (born July 1, 1947, in Dallas, Texas), who had written his first song and formed his first group as a teenager. By 1967 Russell had basically retired from the studio scene to build his own elaborate home studio, although he occasionally appeared with friends Delaney and Bonnie and played on infrequent sessions. Playing with the Bramletts, vocalist Don Nix, guitarist Don Preston, bassist Carl Radle, and others, in The New Electric Horn Band, Russell formed The Asylum Choir with Benno in 1968 and signed with the Smash subsidiary of Mercury Records for their well-received but poorly selling debut album. The two recorded another set in 1969 which was ultimately released on Shelter Records in late 1971, and the album included Russell's "Hello, Little Friend" and the collaborative "Sweet Home Chicago" and "Tryin' to Stay Alive." Benno subsequently returned to Texas and then back to Los Angeles, where he signed with A&M Records as a solo act. By 1972 he had recorded three albums, but none of them sold particularly well despite the inclusions of excellent songs such as "Family Full of Soul," "Don't Let the Sun Go Down," "Share," and "Either Way It Happens." Benno did travel with Rita Coolidge's Dixie Flyers during her 1971 European tour, and she included two of his songs on each of her first three albums—*Rita Coolidge* with "(I Always Called Them) Mountains" and the outstanding "Second Story Window"; *Nice Feelin'* with "Family Full of Soul" and the title song; and *The Lady's Not for Sale* with "Donut Man" and the collaborative "Inside of Me." He was subsequently off the concert and recording scene for years and ultimately resurfaced in 1979 with *Lost in Austin*, ably assisted by Eric Clapton.

During 1969 Leon Russell assisted with Delaney and Bonnie's *Original—Accept No Substitute* album, along with organist Bobby

Whitlock, bassist Carl Radle, and vocalist Rita Coolidge. Later in the year Russell worked on Joe Cocker's second album, which included Russell's "Delta Lady," written for Rita Coolidge. By the beginning of 1970 Russell and English producer Denny Cordell had formed Shelter Records, which soon released Russell's debut solo album. Recorded with Eric Clapton, George Harrison, Ringo Starr, Stevie Winwood, and others, the moderately selling album contained three classic Russell compositions, "Delta Lady," "Hummingbird," and "A Song for You," plus two excellent collaborations, "Prince of Peace" and "Roll Away the Stone." In a single day that March, Russell assembled the nucleus of the Mad Dogs and Englishmen aggregation for a two-month tour behind Joe Cocker, whose Grease Band had apparently broken up. Consisting of more than 40 people, the entourage included Carl Radle, guitarists Chris Stainton and Don Preston, and back-up singers Rita Coolidge and Claudia Lennear. The tour proved enormously successful, as did the subsequent live album but, much to Cocker's chagrin, the spotlight frequently fell on Russell or Coolidge, who was regularly featured performing Russell and Bonnie Bramlett's "Superstar" (a smash hit for The Carpenters in 1971). Shortly after the tour's conclusion in May, Russell assisted Eric Clapton with his solo debut album and co-authored "Blues Power" from the best-selling album.

Leon Russell's next album, *Leon Russell and The Shelter People*, was recorded with four sets of accompanying musicians, The Shelter People, The Tulsa Tops, The Muscle Shoals Swampers, and Friends From England. Without the benefit of a hit single, the album became Russell's first certified gold-award album in 1972 and included two Bob Dylan songs, excellent originals such as "Sweet Emily" and "She Smiles like a River," plus Russell and Don Preston's "Stranger in a Strange Land" and his own "The Ballad of Mad Dogs and Englishmen" from the soundtrack to the tour's popular film. During 1971 Russell produced the Dylan singles, "Watching the River Flow" and "George Jackson," and appeared at George Harrison's August Concert for Bangla Desh. Finally, in 1972, Russell scored his first major hit with "Tight Rope" from *Carney*. The album also contained his own "If the Shoe Fits . . . ," "Magic Mirror," the minor hit "Queen of the Roller Derby," and the excellent "This Masquerade," a near-smash hit for George Benson in 1976. Following the best-selling triple-record set *Leon Live*, Russell confounded critics with an unexpected album of country-and-western standards, *Hank Wilson's Back, Volume 1*, which yielded a minor hit with "Roll in My Sweet Baby's Arms/I'm So Lonesome I Could Cry." He ceased touring in 1974, appeared that year in the film biography *A Poem Is a Naked Person*, and issued the equivocal *Stop All That Jazz* album. After scoring his second major hit with "Lady Blue" from *Will o' the Wisp*, which also incuded the minor hit "Back to the Island," Russell severed his relationship with Shelter Records in 1976, switching to Warner Brothers, where he recorded for his own label, Paradise. In the spring of 1976 he announced his secret marriage the previous June to vocalist Mary McCreary, who had already recorded two solo albums and contributed background vocals to Russell's *Will o' the Wisp*. The couple initiated the Paradise label with their appropriately titled *Wedding Album*, which yielded the minor hit "Rainbow in Your Eyes." Another duet set, *Make Love to the Music*, fared poorly, as did Leon Russell's *Americana* and *Life and Love*, despite resumed touring. Nonetheless, Leon Russell scored a certified gold-award album in tandem with country "superstar" Willie Nelson on *One for the Road*, which produced a top country-and-western hit with a remake of Elvis Presley's "Heartbreak Hotel." In 1980 Russell began touring occasionally with the bluegrass-style New Grass Revival group, with whom he recorded *Live Album*.

LEON RUSSELL

Looking Back	Olympic G. M.	7112	February '74	

THE ASYLUM CHOIR

Look Inside the Asylum Choir	Smash	SRS–67107	October '68	
Asylum Choir II	Shelter	SW–8910 reissued as SW– 2120 reissued as 52010	November '71 October '74	A

MARC BENNO

Marc Benno	A&M	SP–4273	December '70	A
Minnows	A&M	SP–4303	October '71	A
Ambush	A&M	SP–4364	August '72	A
Lost in Austin	A&M	SP–4767	July '79	A

LEON RUSSELL

Leon Russell	Shelter	SHE–1001 reissued as SW– 8901 reissued as 2118 reissued as 52007	February '70 October '74	A
Leon Russell and The Shelter People*	Shelter	SW–8903 reissued as 2119 reissued as 52008	May '71 October '74	A
Carney*	Shelter	SW–8911 reissued as 2121 reissued as 52011	June '72 October '74	A
Leon Live*	3-Shelter	STCO– 8917	June '73	

Hank Wilson's Back, Volume 1	Shelter	SW–8923 reissued as 2131 reissued as 52014	August '73 May '75	A
Stop All That Jazz	Shelter	SR–2108 reissued as 52016	May '74	A
Will o' the Wisp	Shelter	SR–2138 reissued as 52020	April '75	A
Best of Leon*	Shelter	52004	September '76	A

MARY McCREARY

Butterflies in Heaven	MCA	347	July '73
Jezebel	Shelter	2110 reissued as 52027	October '74 February '77

LEON AND MARY RUSSELL

Wedding Album	Paradise	2943	April '76
Make Love to the Music	Paradise	K–3066	June '77

LEON RUSSELL

Americana	Paradise	3172	July '78
Live and Love	Paradise	3341	May '79

MARY (McCREARY) RUSSELL

Heart of Fire	Paradise	3292	March '79

WILLIE (NELSON) AND LEON (RUSSELL)

One for the Road*	2-Columbia	KC2– 36064	June '79	A

LEON RUSSELL AND THE NEW GRASS REVIVAL

Live Album	Paradise	3532	March '81	A

DOUG SAHM/THE SIR DOUGLAS QUINTET. In another of the stranger odysseys in the history of rock music, Doug Sahm started his musical career as a country music prodigy at the age of six, switched to rock-and-roll and rhythm-and-blues during the mid-Fifties with the Texas group The Knights, and eventually scored a major mid-Sixties hit as leader of The Sir Douglas Quintet with "She's about a Mover," featuring the simple "vamping" organ of Augie Meyers. Subsequently relocated in San Francisco, the band managed another major hit with "Mendocino" in early 1969, again with Meyers, since which time Sahm has recorded curious albums mixing country and so-called "Tex-Mex" musics with blues and rock. Returning to Texas and embarking on an erratic and unsuccessful solo recording career in 1971, Doug Sahm recorded an album on Meyers' small independent Texas Re-Cord Company label before switching to John Fahey's Takoma label; he recently re-formed The Sir Douglas Quintet with Meyers.

THE SIR DOUGLAS QUINTET

The Best of the Sir Douglas Quintet	Tribe	TRS– 47001	July '66
Honkey Blues	Smash	SRS–67108	August '68
Mendocino	Smash	SRS–67115	March '69
Together After Five	Smash	SRS–67130	January '70
1 + 1 + 1 = 4	Philips	PHS– 600344	August '70
Rough Edges	Mercury	SRM1–655	March '73

DOUG SAHM

The Return of Doug Saldana	Philips	PHS– 600383	August '71
Doug Sahm and His Band	Atlantic	SD–7254	January '73
Groover's Paradise	Warner Brothers	BS–2810	August '74

SIR DOUGLAS BAND

Texas Tornado	Atlantic	SD–7287	December '73

SIR DOUG AND THE TEXAS TORNADO

Texas Rock for Country Rollers	Dot	DOSD– 2057	July '76	

THE SIR DOUGLAS QUINTET

Live Love	Texas Re-Cord	TRC–1007	February '78	
Best	Takoma	7086		A
Border Wave	Takoma	7088	February '81	A

DOUG SAHM

Hell of a Spell	Takoma	7075	January '80	A

SAM AND DAVE. One of the most exciting live soul acts of the mid-and late Sixties, Sam and Dave scored hits with the soul classics, "Hold On, I'm Comin' " and "Soul Man," written by songwriter–producer Isaac Hayes and Dave Porter, backed by Hayes, Booker T. and the MGs, and the potent and raunchy Memphis Horns. Exemplifying the raw sound of Stax Records that contrasted so remarkably with that of Motown, Sam and Dave switched to Atlantic Records before disbanding in 1969; they reunited during the mid-Seventies on United Artists Records, but with little success.

SAM AND DAVE

Sam and Dave	Roulette	SR–25323	February '67	
Hold On! I'm Comin'	Stax	STS–708	July '66	
Double Dynamite	Stax	STS–712	January '67	
Soul Men	Stax	STS–725	November '67	
I Thank You	Atlantic	SD–8205	November '68	
The Best of Sam and Dave	Atlantic	SD–8218	February '69	A
Back at 'Cha	United Artists	LA524	September '75	

SANTANA. One of the few unknown acts to appear at 1969's Woodstock Festival, Santana was quickly launched into international prominence by their 12-minute segment in the *Woodstock* film and their landmark debut album as the first group successfully to blend Latin and African rhythms with rock instrumentation. Propelled by the stunning lead guitar playing of leader Carlos Santana, who was generally recognized as one of contemporary music's most intensely emotional and technically disciplined lead guitarists, Santana spawned a number of less successful (and generally less aggressive) imitators and encouraged the adoption of Latin, African, and exotic percussion instrumentation by soul, rock, and jazz groups. After producing probably their most cohesive album with *Abraxas*, Santana suffered internal disputes in 1971 that led to regular personnal changes, leaving Carlos Santana the only remaining original member by 1973. Touring more extensively than perhaps any other band in the history of rock music, Santana became the most popular American band in the world by playing engagements on virtually every continent. Beginning in 1972, Carlos Santana recorded albums away from the group, first a jam-style album with drummer Buddy Miles, followed by decidedly jazz-oriented albums with fellow devotees of guru Sri Chinmoy, "Mahavishnu" John McLaughlin and "Turiya" Alice Coltrane. Re-established with the mainstream rock audience as prime purveyors of Latin-style rock music with 1976's *Amigos* album, Santana was enhanced by the unheralded contribution of co-leader, song collaborator, and interim keyboardist Tom Coster. As 1977's *Moonflower* became the group's best selling album since *Abraxas*, Carlos assembled yet another edition of the group, while continuing his spiritual jazz-style extrapolations solo; former drummer Michael Shrieve joined Japanese avant garde percussionist Stomu Yamashta for his "Go" series of albums.

Born in Autlan, in the Mexican state of Jalisco, on July 20, 1947, Carlos Santana began studying music at the age of nine, switched from clarinet to violin, and eventually took up guitar in 1961. His family moved to San Francisco in 1962; after high school graduation he traveled to Tijuana to play bars and clubs and returned to San Francisco in 1966. Around the beginning of 1967, he formed The Santana Blues Band to play local engagements and attained headline status before they had even recorded. First recognized as a guitarist for his guest appearance on *The Live Adventures of Mike Bloomfield and Al Kooper*, Carlos Santana began exploring Latin and African rhythms in his music with the addition of percussionists Mike Carabello and Jose "Chepito" Areas and shortened the group's name simply to Santana. One of the few unknown groups to appear at August 1969's legendary Woodstock Festival, Santana electrified the hundreds of thousands attending with a stunning 12-minute performance of the band's "Soul Sacrifice." When signed to Columbia Records, the group's members were Carlos Santana (lead guitar, vocals), Gregg Rolie (keyboards, vocals), Dave Brown (bass), Mike Carabello (congas, percussion), Jose Areas (timbales, congas, percussion), and Mike Shrieve (drums).

Santana's debut album, featuring layers of exotic percussion and Carlos Santana's passionate lead guitar playing (replete with his signature sustained note style), became an instant success, quickly achieving gold-award certification and remaining on the charts more than two years. The album included "Soul Sacrifice," a minor hit version of Olatunji's "Jingo," and the near-smash hit "Evil Ways." Santana's second album, *Abraxas*, generally recognized as their most cohesive work, yielded a smash hit with Peter Green's "Black Magic Woman" and a major hit with Tito Puente's "Oye Como Va," while containing Carlos' own "Samba Pa Ti." For their third album, variously referred to as *New Album* and *Santana III*, the group added guitarist Neal Schon and recorded with percussionist Pete "Coke" Escovedo, trumpeter Luis Gasca, and the Tower of Power horns.

The album produced a major hit with "Everybody's Everything" and a moderate hit with "No One to Depend On," their last hit for years. During 1971, internal disputes became rife and led to the group's disbandment by 1972.

Carlos Santana subsequently recorded a best-selling live album with powerhouse drummer Buddy Miles and formed a new edition of Santana in the fall of 1972, by which time he had embraced the teachings of guru Sri Chinmoy and taken on the spiritual name "Devadip." The new group's lineup: Santana, holdovers Chepito Areas, Mike Shrieve, Neal Schon, and Gregg Rolie, plus bassist Doug Rauch, conga player James Mingo Lewis, and percussionist Armando Peraza. This aggregation recorded Santana's first departure from Latin-style rock, *Caravanserai*, which revealed a decided orientation toward jazz. Although a best-seller, the album's new sound proved disconcerting to some fans. Gregg Rolie and Neal Schon subsequently departed Santana to form Journey and, during 1973, Carlos recorded *Love, Devotion, Surrender* and toured with "Mahavishnu" John McLaughlin, the man who had introduced him to the philosophy of Sri Chinmoy. He later recorded *Illuminations* with fellow devotee "Turiya" Alice Coltrane, saxophonist John Coltrane's keyboardist widow. Both Carlos Santana's spiritual bent and jazz orientation were revealed on Santana's *Welcome* album, recorded with keyboardists Tom Coster and Richard Kermode and jazz vocalist Leon Thomas. Yet another edition of the band, with vocalist Leon Pattilo and drummers Michael Shrieve and Leon "Ndugu" Chancler (Shrieve's subsequent replacement), recorded the disappointing and relatively unsuccessful *Borboletta* album. During 1975 Santana, rejoined by original bassist Dave Brown, toured the United States co-billed with Eric Clapton and, at mid-year, impressario Bill Graham became the group's manager.

Eventually, in 1976, Santana returned to their Latin-style sound with the highly acclaimed *Amigos* album, which featured "Europa," "Dance, Sister, Dance," and "Gitaro" and had Tom Coster utilizing synthesizer for the first time. By now the members were Santana, Coster (who was co-writing most of the group's songs with Carlos), Leon "Ndugu" Chancler, Armando Peraza, bassist Byron Miller, and vocalist Greg Walker. However, before the release of *Festival*, Chancler, Peraza, Miller, and Walker departed, and subsequent additions were conga player Raul Rekow and bassist Pablo Tellez, both former members of Malo (best known for 1972's "Suavecito"), which had been formed by Carlos' brother, Jorge Santana. Chepito Areas and Greg Walker returned and drummer Graham Lear was added for 1977's double-record *Moonflower* set, which consisted of one live record of Santana classics and one record of Coster–Santana studio originals. The album yielded the group's first major hit in more than five years with "She's Not There," originally a smash hit for The Zombies in late 1964, and became the group's best selling album since *Abraxas*. David Margen subsequently replaced Tellez on bass, and keyboardist Chris Ryne was featured on *Inner Secrets*, which provided a minor hit with Buddy Holly's "That's All Right" and a moderate hit with "Stormy," a smash hit for The Classics IV in late 1968. During 1979 Carlos Santana recorded the solo set *Oneness—Silver Dreams—Golden Reality*, as vocalist Greg Walker and keyboardists Chris Ryne and Tom Coster departed the group. *Marathon*, produced by Keith Olsen (*Fleetwood Mac*), featured new keyboardist Alan Pasqua, new vocalist Alexander Ligertwood, and new rhythm guitarist Chris Solberg and yielded a moderate hit with "You Know That I Love You." By early 1980 Santana consisted of Carlos Santana, Pasqua, Ligertwood, Solberg, Armando Peraza, David Margen, Graham Lear, and Raul Rekow. During the year Carlos Santana recorded *Swing of Delight* with recognized jazz musicians such as keyboardist Herbie Hancock, saxophonist Wayne Shorter, bassist Ron Carter, and drummer Tony Williams.

Drummer Michael Shrieve, who had left Santana in 1974, joined the multi-talented Japanese artist Stomu Yamashta for his "Go" series of albums. Yamashta, a percussionist with the Osaka Philharmonic during the early Sixties and composer of the score for Akira Kurosawa's *Yojimbo* film, had led the extraordinary Red Buddha Theater troup and the "jazz-rock" group East Wind and was acclaimed as the finest concert percussionist in the world. For the first set of his trilogy, *Go*, he assembled Shrieve, Stevie Winwood, and electronics and synthesizer wizard Klaus Schulze to perform his original compositions. In 1977 *Go Too* was issued and, during 1978, *Go Live from Paris*, with Shrieve, Winwood, and Schulze among others, was issued on Island as a double-record set. All of Yamashta's "Go" albums were astounding in their synthesis of rock, jazz, electronic and Eastern musics. In 1981 Santana managed a hit with Russ Ballard's "Winning" from *Zebop!* and Tom Coster recorded his first solo album for Fantasy.

SANTANA

Santana*	Columbia	PC–9781	September '69	A
Abraxas*	Columbia	JC–30130	October '70	A
New Album*	Columbia	PC–30595	October '71	A
Caravanserai*	Columbia	PC–31610	October '72	A
Welcome*	Columbia	PC–32445	November '73	A
Greatest Hits*	Columbia	JC–33050	July '74	A

CARLOS SANTANA AND BUDDY MILES

Live!*	Columbia	PC–31308	June '72	A

CARLOS SANTANA AND MAHAVISHNU JOHN McLAUGHLIN

Love, Devotion, Surrender*	Columbia	PC–32034	June '73	A

DEVADIP CARLOS SANTANA AND TURIYA ALICE COLTRANE

Illuminations	Columbia	C–32900	October '74	A

SANTANA

Borboletta	Columbia	PC–33135	October '74	A
Amigos*	Columbia	PC–33576	March '76	A

Festival*	Columbia	PC–34423	December '76	
Moonflower*	2-Columbia	C2–34914	October '77	A
Inner Secrets*	Columbia	FC–35600	October '78	A
Marathon	Columbia	FC–36154	October '79	A
Zebop!*	Columbia	FC–37158	April '81	A

CARLOS SANTANA

Oneness—Silver Dreams— Golden Reality	Columbia	JC–35686	March '79	A
Swing of Delight	2-Columbia	C2–36590	August '80	A

STOMU YAMASHTA'S GO

Go	Island	9358 reissued as 9387	July '76	A
Go Too	Arista	4138	September '77	
Go Live from Paris	2-Island	10	April '78	A

TOM COSTER

T.C.	Fantasy	9612	October '81	A

LEO SAYER. Initially coming to prominence as the chief lyricist for Roger Daltrey's excellent 1973 debut solo album (arguably the finest solo album by a member of The Who), Leo Sayer broke through on his own in America with 1975's "Long, Tall Glasses." Achieving his biggest success with 1976's *Endless Flight* and its top hits "You Make Me Feel Like Dancing" and "When I Need You," Sayer's popularity began to slip, yet he scored another major hit in 1980 with the ballad "More Than I Can Say."

LEO SAYER

Silverbird	Warner Brothers	BS–2738	December '73	
Just a Boy	Warner Brothers	BS–2836	January '75	A
Another Year	Warner Brothers	BS–2885	October '75	
Endless Flight**	Warner Brothers	BS–2962 reissued as BSK– 3101	November '76	A
Thunder in My Heart	Warner Brothers	BSK–3089	October '77	
Leo Sayer	Warner Brothers	BSK–3200	May '78	
Here	Warner Brothers	BSK–3374	September '79	A
Living in a Fantasy	Warner Brothers	3483	October '80	A

BOZ SCAGGS. An unexceptional musician and singer, William "Boz" Scaggs participated in the recording of The Steve Miller Band's best-remembered early albums, *Children of the Future* and *Sailor*, before departing for a solo career that for years generated little popular interest outside the San Francisco Bay area, his adopted home. Nonetheless, Scaggs' solo debut album *Boz Scaggs*, recorded with lead guitarist Duane Allman, is often regarded as one of the finest albums of the Sixties and, despite its lack of commercial success, included at least two classic songs, "I'll Be Long Gone" and "Loan Me a Dime." Subsequently recording in a pop-oriented style that produced no major national hits, Boz Scaggs nonetheless became a major star in the Bay area, initiating a completely new type of concert presentation with his "black tie optional" shows staged at Oakland's Paramount Theatre in March 1974 that featured a substantial symphonic-style orchestra. At that show Scaggs debuted his *Slow Dancer* album, which marked his abdication from rock music in favor of sophisticated soul-style music. Finally established nationally with 1976's *Silk Degrees* and its four singles, Boz Scaggs later scored two hits from 1980's *Middle Man*.

Born on June 8, 1944, in Ohio, William Royce Scaggs grew up in Oklahoma and Texas. Having acquired the nickname "Boz," he met Steve Miller at age 15 while in a Dallas area high school and soon accepted an offer to join Miller's band, The Marksmen, as vocalist and tambourine player. Scaggs learned rhythm guitar from Miller, who moved to Wisconsin to attend the University of Madison a year before Scaggs' graduation. He followed Miller to the university the following year and joined Miller's band, The Ardells, before returning to Texas, where he formed his own band, The Wigs. In 1964 Scaggs and several companions traveled to England and, while his friends returned to the United States, he stayed on, singing in the streets of European cities and eventually establishing Stockholm as his base. Around 1966 he recorded a folk and blues-style album, *Boz*, on Polydor Records, which was issued in Europe only. Summoned by Steve Miller in 1967, Scaggs moved to San Francisco, where he joined Miller's band during the heyday of "psychedelia" and recorded *Children of the Future* and *Sailor*, two of Miller's most highly regarded albums, before departing in August 1968.

Signed to Atlantic Records, Boz Scaggs' self-titled solo debut was arguably his finest work, yet it failed to sell outside the San Francisco Bay area. Recorded in Muscle Shoals, Alabama, with *Rolling Stone* editor Jann Wenner as producer and ably assisted by guitarist Duane Allman, the album featured the 13-minute "Loan Me a Dime," Scaggs' theme song for years, and the classic "I'll Be Long Gone" plus "Sweet Release" and early country artist Jimmy Rodgers' "Waiting for a Train." After returning to San Francisco permanently in 1970, Scaggs switched to Columbia for recordings in a less bluesy, more pop-oriented style. *Moments*, recorded in San Francisco, yielded two minor hits with "We Were Always Sweethearts" and "Near You," but *Boz Scaggs and Band*, recorded mainly in London, failed to produce a hit, though it did contain the favorite, "Runnin' Blue." For his three-month, late 1971 national tour, Scaggs recruited guitarist Ronnie Montrose; the troupe disbanded after the tour's conclusion. *My Time*, partially recorded in Muscle Shoals, included another minor hit, "Dinah Flo," but Scaggs did not achieve another chart entry for more than three years. Employing veteran Motown producer Johnny Bristol and utilizing studio musicians exclusively, he recorded *Slow Dancer* in an orchestrated "soul" style, and the album became his best seller to date and came to be regarded as his finest latter-day effort; it included "Angel Lady," "You Make It So Hard (to Say No)," and Bristol's "I've Got Your Number." Retaining a devoted Bay area following, Scaggs debuted the album in March 1974 at Oakland's Paramount Theatre in a first-of-its-kind "black tie optional" setting, lavishly staging the performance with 27-piece orchestra and formally attired rock band, which included guitarist Les Dudek, who remained a regular feature of Scaggs' touring band into 1976. Scaggs repeated the concert formula, which became a regular format for concert staging, to ecstatic and well-dressed audiences at year's end in 1974, 1975, and 1976.

With the release of *Silk Degrees*, Boz Scaggs fully embraced a sophisticated soul and disco-tinged style to the detriment of rock. The album finally established him nationally and yielded a moderate hit with "It's Over"; the smash hit "Lowdown" followed, as did another moderate hit with "What Can I Say" and finally the near-smash hit "Lido Shuffle" in early 1977. The album also included Scaggs' "We're All Alone," a near-smash hit for Rita Coolidge later in the year. However, the album's phenomenal success has overshadowed most of Scaggs' subsequent work. The equivocal *Down Two, Then Left* was certified platinum-award within weeks of its release, yet produced only minor hits with "Hard Times" and "Hollywood." Issued more than two years later, *Middle Man* featured David Foster (co-author of the Earth, Wind, and Fire smash "After the Love Is Gone") as co-writer of six of the album's nine songs. The album produced two hits during 1980 with "Breakdown Dead Ahead" and "Jojo." Also in 1980 Scaggs hit with "Look What You've Done to Me" (from the *Urban Cowboy* soundtrack) and "Miss Sun" (from *Hits!*). At the end of 1981 he debuted in the Nevada casino showroom milieu.

BOZ SCAGGS

Boz Scaggs	Atlantic	SD–8239	September '69	
		reissued as 19166	March '78	A
Moments	Columbia	PC–30454	March '71	A
Boz Scaggs and Band	Columbia	PC–30796	November '71	A
My Time	Columbia	PC–31384	September '72	A
Slow Dancer	Columbia	PC–32760	March '74	A
Silk Degrees **	Columbia	JC–33920	February '76	A
Two Down, Then Left **	Columbia	JC–34729	November '77	A
Middle Man **	Columbia	FC–36106	April '80	A
Hits! *	Columbia	FC–36841	November '80	A

BRINSLEY SCHWARZ/NICK LOWE/IAN GOMM.

The British group Brinsley Schwarz, almost ruined by one of the most outlandishly premeditated promotional campaigns in rock that saw a planeload of British journalists flown to New York for their debut, subsequently maintained a low profile as one of the pioneering bands on London's early to mid-Seventies "pub rock" scene that served as a precursor to the late Seventies "punk" and "new wave" movements. Developing a small but devoted following in both Great Britain and the United States, Brinsley Schwarz was never able to translate their lively and exuberant stage act effectively to recordings, although both *Silver Pistol* and *Nervous on the Road* were critically well received and have become valued collector's items. With the group's demise in 1975, former member Nick Lowe initiated collaborative efforts with producer–musician Dave Edmunds, including the energetic Rockpile aggregation, and later produced albums for Elvis Costello and Graham Parker and The Rumour, two of the most exciting and compelling British "new wave" acts to emerge during the late Seventies. Former group leader Brinsley Schwarz and former member Bob Andrews, in fact, became members of The Rumour, whereas both Nick Lowe and later-day Brinsley Schwarz member Ian Gomm launched solo careers that resulted in major hits in late 1979.

BRINSLEY SCHWARZ

Brinsley Schwarz	Capitol	ST–589	November '70	
Despite It All	Capitol	ST–744	March '71	
Silver Pistol	United Artists	UAS–5566	February '72	
	reissued on Liberty	LN–10145	November '81	A
Nervous on the Road	United Artists	UAS–5647	October '72	
	reissued on Liberty	LN–10146	November '81	A
Brinsley Schwarz	2-Capitol	SWBC–11869	October '78	A

THE RUMOUR

Max	Mercury	SRM1–1174	August '77	
Frogs, Sprouts, Clogs, and Krauts	Arista	4235	August '79	

NICK LOWE

Pure Pop for Now People	Columbia	JC–35329	March '78	A
Labour of Lust	Columbia	JC–36087	June '79	A

IAN GOMM

Gomm with the Wind	Stiff/Epic	JE–36103	August '79	A
What a Blow	Stiff/Epic	JE–36433	July '80	A

ROCKPILE

| Seconds of Pleasure | Columbia | JC–36886 | November '80 | A |

SEALS AND CROFTS. Seven-year members of The Champs (1958's "Tequila"), Jim Seals and Dash Crofts emerged in 1972 as a "soft-rock" duo with their classic "Summer Breeze" that appealed to both pop and "easy listening" fans. Sustaining themselves with the near-smash hits "Diamond Girl" and "Get Closer," Seals and Crofts also became successful album artists, scoring five consecutive certified gold-award albums through 1976.

SEALS AND CROFTS

Seals and Crofts	Talent Associates	5001	June '70	
Down Home	Talent Associates	5004	October '74	
I and II	2-Warner Brothers	2WS–2809	July '74	
Year of Sunday	Warner Brothers	BS–2568	November '71	
Summer Breeze*	Warner Brothers	BS–2629	July '72	A
Diamond Girl*	Warner Brothers	BS–2699	March '73	A
Unborn Child*	Warner Brothers	BS–2761	February '74	
I'll Play for You*	Warner Brothers	BS–2848	March '75	
Greatest Hits*	Warner Brothers	BS–2886 reissued as BSK–3109	October '75	A
Get Closer*	Warner Brothers	BS–2907	April '76	
Sudan Village	Warner Brothers	BS–2976	November '76	
One on One (soundtrack)	Warner Brothers	BS–3076	August '77	
Takin' It Easy	Warner Brothers	BSK–3163	April '78	
The Longest Road	Warner Brothers	3365	July '80	A

NEIL SEDAKA. A prolific music writer, Neil Sedaka scored a continuous string of pop-style hit singles between 1959 and 1963 with songs co-authored by Howard Greenfield, Sedaka's lyricist until 1973. The hits included "Oh! Carol," written for Carole King while working as a songwriter at New York's famed Brill Building under Don Kirshner, and "Breaking Up Is Hard to Do," perhaps his finest composition. By 1963 Sedaka and Greenfield had written over 500 songs which had sold over 20,000,000 records but, with his own waning popularity and the advent of the so-called "English invasion," Sedaka ceased live appearances although continuing to write songs. In the early Seventies, encouraged by the enormous success of Carole King's *Tapestry*, he attempted a come-back, succeeding first in Great Britain and later in the United States on Elton John's Rocket label with the top hits "Laughter in the Rain" and "Bad Blood." Though his careful mixture of early and recent material works well on television and the cabaret circuit, Neil Sedaka has not fared well since switching to Elektra Records in 1977.

Born in Brooklyn, New York, on March 13, 1939, Neil Sedaka was initially trained as a concert pianist and studied at the Juilliard School of Music. Having written his first song at the age of 13, he later joined lyricist Howard Greenfield, a Brooklyn friend, and they became professional songwriters at Al Nevins and Don Kirshner's Aldon Publishing Company, housed at New York's Brill Building, where Carole King, Gerry Goffin, Barry Mann, and Cynthia Weil also worked. Sedaka and Greenfield's first songwriting success came in the summer of 1958 with "Stupid Cupid" as recorded by Connie Francis. Signed to his own recording contract with RCA Records, Sedaka quickly achieved his first hit with "The Diary" at the end of 1958. Over the next four years, he regularly scored major hits with Greenfield collaborations such as "Oh! Carol" in 1959, "Stairway to Heaven" in 1960, "Calendar Girl," "Little Devil" and "Happy Birthday, Sweet Sixteen" in 1961, and the classic "Breaking Up Is Hard to Do" (a top hit) and "Next Door to an Angel" in 1962. Sedaka managed moderate hits with "Alice in Wonderland," "Let's Go Steady Again," and "Bad Girl" in 1963, but his next major American hit did not come for more than ten years. He subsequently ceased live performances while continuing to write songs with Greenfield such as "Workin' on a Groovy Thing" (a major hit for The Fifth Dimension in 1969) and "Puppet Man" (a moderate hit for Tom Jones in 1971).

In 1971, buoyed by the success of Carole King's *Tapestry*, Neil Sedaka attempted a come-back on mentor Don Kirshner's Kirshner label. Although the albums failed to sell in the United States, he encountered success in Great Britain, where he concentrated his activities and returned to live performance at London's Albert Hall. The second Kirshner album, *Solitaire*, and the British *The Tra-La Days Are Over* were recorded with a group called Hot Legs, who later became better known as 10 cc. A second British album, *Laughter in the Rain*, yielded a British hit single with the title song. Unsigned to an American record company at the time, Sedaka was immediately signed by Elton John to his Rocket Records label. His debut American release for Rocket, *Sedaka's Back*, compiled material from *Solitaire* and the two British albums and yielded a top hit in late 1974 with "Laughter in the Rain," followed by the major hits "The Immigrant" and "That's Where the Music Takes Me." During 1975 The Captain and Tenille scored a top hit with his "Love Will Keep Us Together," and The

Carpenters hit with his "Solitaire." Sedaka's *The Hungry Years*, another compilation of the prior British material, was certified gold-award by year's end, as was its predecessor. The album yielded a top hit with "Bad Blood," co-authored by Sedaka's new lyricist, Phil Cody, and produced a near-smash with a new version of "Breaking Up Is Hard to Do." *Steppin' Out*, issued in identical form in America and Great Britain, produced a major hit with "Love in the Shadows" and a moderate hit with the title song. After performing his first television special on NBC–TV in 1976, Sedaka switched to Elektra Records and recorded *A Song* under former Beatles producer George Martin. However, neither that album, nor its follow-up, *All You Need Is the Music*, yielded any major hits. 1980's *In the Pocket*, recorded with his teenage daughter Dara, produced a hit with "Should Have Never Let You Go," and Neil Sedaka performed another television special that summer as he continued to tour the cabaret circuit.

NEIL SEDAKA

Neil Sedaka	RCA	LSP–2035	July '59	
Circulate	RCA	LSP–2317	January '61	
Little Devil and Other Hits	RCA	LSP–2421	June '61	
Italiano	RCA	10140	January '64	
Live in Australia	RCA	VPL1– 1540	June '76	
Emergence	Kirshner	111	October '71	
	reissued on RCA	APL1– 1789	August '76	
Solitaire	Kirshner	117	November '72	
	reissued on RCA	APL1– 1790	August '76	
Sedaka's Back*	MCA/Rocket	463	November '74	
	reissued on Rocket	BXL1– 3046	November '78	
The Hungry Years*	Rocket	2157	October '75	
Steppin' Out	Rocket	2195	April '76	
	reissued as BXL1– 3049		November '78	
A Song	Elektra	6E–102	May '77	A
All You Need Is the Music	Elektra	161	October '78	A
In the Pocket	Elektra	259	April '80	A
Now	Elektra	348	June '81	A

NEIL SEDAKA ANTHOLOGIES AND COMPILATIONS

Neil Sedaka Sings His Greatest Hits	RCA	LSP–2627	December '62	
	reissued as APL1– 0928		April '75	
	reissued as ANL1– 3465			A

Oh, Carol and Other Hits	RCA	ANL1–0879	July '75	
Pure Gold	RCA	ANL1–1314	May '76	
'50s and '60s	RCA	APL1–2254(E)	May '77	
Many Sides	RCA	AFL1–2524	March '78	
Singer, Songwriter, Melody Maker	Accord	SN–7152	December '81	A

BOB SEGER. Little known nationally except for his 1968–69 hit "Ramblin' Gamblin' Man," Bob Seger was a major star of the Midwest for nearly ten years before finally breaking through nationally with *Night Moves*, generally regarded as one of the finest albums of 1976–77, and its three hit singles. For years seemingly destined to remain a minor cult figure, Seger's first widespread recognition came with 1976's live double-record set *Live Bullet*, which compiled many of his dozen Detroit region hits and achieved gold-award certification largely on its selling strength in that area. *Night Moves*, and its platinum-award follow-up, *Stranger in Town*, succeeded in their careful mix of original high-energy songs in the classic rock-and-roll mold and poignant, intelligent and personal ballads written by Seger.

Born in Detroit, Michigan, as variously reported on May 6, 1945, or on June 6, 1946, Bob Seger was playing ukelele at the age of five and moved the following year with his family to Ann Arbor, where he grew up. Having taken up guitar and piano, he was playing local lounges and teen clubs with the three-piece band The Decibels while still in high school. Later joining The Town Criers after high school, Seger met Eddie Andrews, on whose Hideout label Seger recorded his first single, "East Side Story," a local hit. Subsequent local successes with "Persecution Smith" and "Heavy Music" led to a Capitol Records recording contract in 1968. He assembled The Bob Seger System and scored a major national hit with the title song to the group's debut album, *Ramblin' Gamblin' Man*, which also included the powerful "hard rock" anti-war "2 + 2 = ?" However, neither *Noah* nor *Mongrel* sold well or produced another hit outside the Detroit region, so he disbanded the group and recorded the all-acoustic *Brand New Morning* solo. Subsequently recording for Eddie Andrews' Palladium label (distributed nationally by Reprise), Seger recorded *Smokin' O.P.'s* and *Back in '72* before assembling the nucleus of what became The Silver Bullet Band in Detroit with guitarist Andrew "Drew" Abbott, keyboardist Rick Manasa, bassist Chris Campbell, and drummer Charlie Martin. With Abbott taking over lead guitar, Seger was able to concentrate on his characteristic, raspy style of singing; *Seven* revealed his developing talent as a songwriter and even yielded a minor hit with the hard-driving "Get Out of Denver." Returning to Capitol Records, he toured the nation extensively in 1974 and 1975 and recorded the critically acclaimed *Beautiful*

Loser album, which included the powerful title song, the ballad "Jody Girl," and the moderate rock-style hit "Katmandu." Recorded in Muscle Shoals, Alabama, the album sold more copies than the combined total sales of his first seven albums.

After adding saxophonist Alto Reed and replacing Rick Manasa with Robyn Robbins, Bob Seger and The Silver Bullet Band recorded the live set *Live Bullet* in Detroit and, surprisingly, the album was certified gold-award before the end of 1976, largely on its regional selling strength. The album included many of his local hits, including "Heavy Music," "Ramblin' Gamblin' Man," "Lookin' Back," "Get Out of Denver," and "Katmandu," and featured the medley "Beautiful Loser/Jody Girl/Travelin' Man." Finally, after ten years of at-best moderate recording success, Bob Seger became nationally established with *Night Moves*, hailed as one of the finest albums of the era. Yielding a smash hit with the near-autobiographical title song, a major hit with the ballad "Mainstreet," and a moderate hit with the hard-charging "Rock and Roll Never Forgets," the album also included "The Fire Down Below." In 1977 Charlie Martin was replaced by David Teegarden, an associate of Seger's from the early Seventies and a one-time member of Teegarden and Van Winkle (best remembered for 1970's "God, Love, and Rock and Roll"). Eight months in the making, *Stranger in Town*, recorded with the Muscle Shoals Rhythm Section plus Eagles Glenn Frey and Don Felder, repeated the formula of balancing poignant personal ballads with high-energy rock songs and yielded a smash hit with "Still the Same" and major hits with "Hollywood Nights" and "We've Got Tonight," while also containing "Old Time Rock and Roll" and "Feel like a Number." Before work was begun on the group's next album, Robyn Robbins departed and was replaced by former Grand Funk Railroad keyboardist Craig Frost. Seger co-authored The Eagles' top hit "Heartache Tonight" with Don Henley, Glen Frey, and John David Souther, and Henley, Frey, and Tim Schmit subsequently added background vocals to his hit "Fire Lake" from 1980's *Against the Wind*, which also yielded hits with the title song and "You'll Accomp'ny Me." In late 1981 the double-record set *Nine Tonight*, featuring the hit "Tryin' to Live Without You," was issued for Bob Seger and The Silver Bullet Band.

THE BOB SEGER SYSTEM

Ramblin' Gamblin' Man	Capitol	ST–172 reissued as SN–16105	February '69	A
Noah	Capitol	ST–236	October '69	
Mongrel	Capitol	ST–499 reissued as SN–16106	October '70	A

BOB SEGER

Brand New Morning	Capitol	ST–731	November '71

Smokin' O.P.'s	Palladium	1006	July '72	
	reissued on Reprise/ Palladium	MS–2109		
	reissued on Reprise	MS–2262	April '77	
	reissued on Capitol	ST–11746 reissued as SN– 16107	February '78	A
Back in '72	Reprise/ Palladium	MS–2126	February '73	
	reissued on Reprise	MS–2263	April '77	
Seven	Reprise/ Palladium	MS–2184	April '74	
	reissued on Reprise	MS–2264	April '77	
	reissued on Capitol	ST–11748 reissued as SN– 16108	February '78	A
Beautiful Loser	Capitol	ST–11378	March '75	A

BOB SEGER AND THE SILVER BULLET BAND

Live Bullet**	2-Capitol	SKBB– 11523	April '76	A
Night Moves**	Capitol	ST–11557	November '76	A
Stranger in Town**	Capitol	SW–11698	May '78	A
Against the Wind**	Capitol	SOO– 12041	March '80	A
Nine Tonight	Capitol	STBX– 12182	October '81	A

THE SEX PISTOLS.   The prototypical "punk rock" band, The Sex Pistols quickly developed a notorious reputation in Great Britain based on their cynical, irreverent anticommercial songs and deliberate onstage vulgarity. Reacting to the complacency of established popular musicians, their bland music, and the policies of the music industry in general, The Sex Pistols intentionally sought to shock and agitate fans out of their musical apathy with tasteless acts of outrage, antagonism, and hostility. Thus lending an aura of disrepute to rock music (as previously had some Fifties rock-and-rollers, the early Rolling Stones and Who, Iggy Pop and The Stooges, and Alice Cooper), The Sex Pistols quickly became transformed from unknowns to the most publicized and discussed rock band in the world in less than a year, without having even released an album, as other similarly-styled bands were signed and recorded. Most likely the direct inspiration for much of the "punk rock" movement, The Sex Pistols scored their first recorded successes in Great Britain with "Anarchy in the U.K." and the controversial "God Save the Queen" in 1976–77 and were roundly banned from performing in that country. They produced little of interest after the firing of Johnny Rotten following their much overpublicized debut American tour of early 1978, although Sid Vicious retained massive media attention for the alleged murder of his girlfriend in October 1978 and his apparent drug overdose death in February 1979.

The Sex Pistols were initially formed in England in August 1975 with vocalist Johnny Rotten (born John Lydon) and three former members of The Swankers, guitarist–vocalist Steve Jones, bassist Glen Matlock, and drummer Paul Cook, among others. Stabilizing with those four members by November, The Sex Pistols played their first engagement that month and quickly caused outrage and havoc with their cynical and nihilistic songs and tastelessly hostile and abusive performances. Widely banned in London and the subject of rapidly spreading notoriety, The Sex Pistols eventually signed with EMI Records in October 1976 and soon scored a minor British hit with the widely banned "Anarchy in the U.K." However, they were dropped by EMI in January after swearing on television's "Today Show" at the beginning of December, an incident that won them front-page news coverage. Disputes between Matlock and Rotten led to Matlock's departure in February and he was replaced on bass by Sid Vicious (born John Ritchie), a former member of Siouxsie and The Banshees and Flowers of Romance. Picked up by A&M Records in March, The Sex Pistols were dumped by the label within one week and subsequently moved to Virgin Records in May. Their first release for the label, the sarcastic "God Save the Queen," became a major British hit despite its banishment. Their debut album, *Never Mind the Bollocks, Here's The Sex Pistols*, was issued in late 1977 (on Warner Brothers in the United States) and included the above two songs as well as "Pretty Vacant," "No Feelings," and the vitriolic "tribute" to their first label, "EMI." In January 1978 The Sex Pistols made their first American tour accompanied by media coverage unseen since the advent of The Beatles and The Rolling Stones. However, with the tour's completion, Johnny Rotten was fired, and the remaining three, Cook, Jones, and Vicious, later recorded a crude version of Frank Sinatra's theme song, "My Way." By April Johnny Rotten (now using the name Johnny Lydon) had formed Public Image Ltd. with former Clash and Flowers of Romance guitarist Keith Levene and bassist Jah Wobble (real name: John Wardle) and they recorded their debut British album that year and subsequently recorded for Warner Brothers and Island. Charged with the October slaying of his girlfriend, Nancy Spungeon, at Manhattan's Chelsea Hotel, Sid Vicious was found dead in a Greenwich Village apartment at the age of 21 on February 2, 1979, a day after his release on bail; he was apparently the victim of a drug overdose.

THE SEX PISTOLS

Never Mind The Bollocks, Here's The Sex Pistols	Warner Brothers	BSK–3147	November '77	A

PUBLIC IMAGE LTD.

Public Image Ltd.	Warner Brothers	3288	May '79	
Second Edition	2-Island	2WX–3288	March '80	A
The Flowers of Romance	Warner Brothers	3536	April '81	A

SHA NA NA. Performing amusing and lively recreations of the music, dress, and choreography of Fifties rock-and-roll, Sha Na Na were launched into international prominence by a brief appearance in the *Woodstock* film in 1970. Retaining a remarkably stable lineup other than guitarists, Sha Na Na frequently upstaged more contemporary acts in concert during the early Seventies. Totally specializing in the various rock-and-roll styles of the Fifties and early Sixties, Sha Na Na managed a certified gold-award album of "oldies" in 1973 with *The Golden Age of Rock 'n' Roll* and later moved on to their popular television series in 1977, while continuing to perform for the "nostalgia" audience. Former guitarist Henry Gross pursued a solo career after leaving the group and eventually scored a near-smash hit with "Shannon" in early 1976, since which time he has been relatively unsuccessful.

SHA NA NA

Rock 'n' Roll Is Here to Stay!	Kama Sutra	KSBS–2010 reissued as KSBS–2077	December '69 January '74	
Sha Na Na	Kama Sutra	KSBS–2034	August '71	
The Night Is Still Young	Kama Sutra	KSBS–2050	June '72	
The Golden Age of Rock 'n' Roll *	2-Kama Sutra	KSBS–2073	April '73	
From the Streets of New York	Kama Sutra	KSBS–2075	November '73	
Hot Sox	Kama Sutra	KSBS–2600	May '74	
Sha Na Na	Kama Sutra	KSBS–2605	August '75	
The Best	2-Kama Sutra	KSBS–2609	November '76	
Sha Na Na Is Here to Stay	Buddah	BDS–5692	'78	A
Remember Then	Accord	SN–7115	April '81	A
Sh-Boom	Accord	SN–7146	December '81	A

HENRY GROSS

Henry Gross	ABC	747	April '72	
Henry Gross	A&M	SP–4416	January '74	
Plug Me into Something	A&M	SP–4502	January '75	A
Release	Lifesong	LS–6002 reissued as PZ–34995	February '76	

Show Me to the Stage	Lifesong	LS–6010	March '77	
Love Is the Stuff	Lifesong	JZ–35280	April '78	
What's in a Name	Capitol	ST–12113	February '81	A

"SCREAMIN' " SCOTT SIMON

Transmissions from Space	Rolling Rock	026	January '82	A

THE SHIRELLES. One of the most popular "girl groups" of the early Sixties, The Shirelles recorded excellent material provided by such creators as Carole King and Gerry Goffin, Luther Dixon, and Burt Bacharach and Hal David and scored smash hits with "Will You Love Me Tomorrow," "Dedicated to the One I Love," "Soldier Boy," and "Foolish Little Girl." Achieving their last major hit in 1963, The Shirelles continued to have releases on Scepter Records through 1967, unsuccessfully attempting a come-back at RCA Records in the early Seventies.

All New Jersey-born, the members of The Shirelles attended school together in Passaic. Lead vocalist Shirley Alston was born on June 10, 1941, and the other three members, Addie "Micki" Harris, Doris Kenner, and Beverly Lee were born on January 22, 1940, and August 2 and 3, 1941, respectively. "Discovered" performing at a New Jersey high school talent show in 1957, the four were signed to Florence Greenberg's small Tiara label. They achieved their first minor success with their own composition "I Met Him on a Sunday," as distributed by Decca, in 1958. Florence Greenberg subsequently formed Scepter Records, and The Shirelles soon scored a minor hit with "Dedicated to the One I Love" in 1959, followed by the moderate hit "Tonight's the Night," co-written by Alston and Luther Dixon, in 1960. Later that year they scored a top hit with Carole King and Gerry Goffin's "Will You Love Me Tomorrow," followed by the smash hits "Dedicated to the One I Love" (upon re-release) and "Mama Said," co-authored by Luther Dixon. After the major hit "Big John (Ain't You Gonna Marry Me)" in late 1961, the group achieved a near-smash hit with the Burt Bacharach–Hal David–Barney Williams collaboration, "Baby It's You," and a top hit with "Soldier Boy," co-written by Luther Dixon and Florence Greenberg. After the major hits "Welcome Home, Baby" and "Everybody Loves a Lover," The Shirelles had another smash hit with "Foolish Little Girl," co-authored by Howard Greenfield, and their final major hit with "Don't Say Goodnight and Mean Goodbye" in 1963. Releases for The Shirelles continued on Scepter Records through 1967 (including the title song to the film *It's a Mad, Mad, Mad, Mad World*) with little success. They performed at several of Richard Nader's rock-and-roll "revival" shows during the early Seventies and unsuccessfully attempted a come-back on RCA Records. Now comprised of Micki Harris, Beverly Lee, and a new member, The Shirelles are still active on the club circuit.

THE SHIRELLES

Tonight's the Night	Scepter	501(M)	
Baby, It's You	Scepter	504(M)	April '62
Foolish Little Girl	Scepter	511(M)	June '63
The Shirelles Sing Their Songs in the Great Movie It's a Mad, Mad, Mad, Mad World and Others	Scepter	514(M)	
The Shirelles Sing The Golden Oldies	Scepter	516(M)	
Spontaneous Combustion	Scepter	562	December '67
Happy and in Love	RCA	LSP–4581	October '71
The Shirelles	RCA	LSP–4698	June '72

THE SHIRELLES AND KING CURTIS

Give a Twist Party	Scepter	505(M)	
Eternally Soul	Scepter	569	June '70

SHIRELLES ANTHOLOGIES AND COMPILATIONS

Great Hits	Scepter	507(M)	January '63
Greatest Hits, Volume 2	Scepter	560	August '67
Remember When	2-Scepter	599	March '72
Sing Their Very Best	Springboard International	4006	May '73
Very Best	United Artists	LA340	March '75

CARLY SIMON. Best known for her top hit of 1972–73, "You're So Vain," and her marriage to singer–songwriter James Taylor, Carly Simon achieved her biggest album success with *No Secrets* under producer Richard Perry. Co-writing many of her own songs, Simon's slick, sophisticated style and image strongly contrasted with that of most other Seventies female singer–songwriters.

Born in New York City on June 25, 1945, Carly Simon was raised in affluence in Greenwich Village and Riverdale as the daughter of the co-founder of the Simon and Schuster publishing firm. While attending the exclusive Sarah Lawrence College, she began singing folk-style material with her sister Lucy as The Simon Sisters. After performing in area folk clubs during the early Sixties, they signed with Kapp Records in 1963 and scored a minor hit the following year with "Winkin', Blinkin', and Nod." With Lucy's marriage, The Simon Sisters broke up and Carly later met manager Albert Grossman in 1966. He envisioned her as a female Bob Dylan, but recordings with The Band's Rick Danko and Richard Manuel, Al Kooper, and Mike Bloomfield were never issued. While serving as co-lead singer for six months in 1969 with Elephant's Memory (before John Lennon brought the group into notoriety), Simon also wrote commercial jingles during 1969 and 1970. In 1970 she began co-writing songs with film critic and writer Jacob Brackman and signed with Elektra Records late in the year. Possessing a powerful contralto voice and playing guitar and piano, she scored a major hit with "That's the Way I've Always Heard It Should Be," co-authored by Brackman, from her debut album. Her debut as a solo performer in support of Cat Stevens occurred at Los Angeles' Troubadour club in April of 1971; Simon met James Taylor that month and ultimately married him in November 1972. *Anticipation*, produced by former Yardbirds and Cat Stevens producer Paul Samwell-Smith, included the hit title song and the minor hit "Legend in Your Own Time."

Carly Simon conducted her first headlining tour in 1972, then recorded her next three albums under producer Richard Perry. The first, *No Secrets*, became her first certified gold-award album and yielded a top pop and "easy listening" hit with her own "You're So Vain" (spurred into popularity by speculation as to whom the ambiguous reference concerned), which featured Mick Jagger as back-up vocalist, and a major hit with "The Right Thing to Do," while also containing "We Have No Secrets." Simon abandoned touring in 1973 as a result of her notorious stage fright and retained a low public profile after the birth of her daughter in January 1974. Nonetheless, *Hotcakes* yielded a smash hit with a horrendous remake of the Charles and Inez Foxx 1963 hit "Mockingbird," recorded in tandem with husband James Taylor, and a major hit with "Haven't Got Time for the Pain," co-authored by Jacob Brackman. *Playing Possum*, Simon's final album under Richard Perry, included a major hit with "Attitude Dancing" (featuring Carole King on background vocals) and the minor hits "Waterfall" and "More and More." Appearing with Taylor on his summer 1975 tour and singing backup on sister Lucy Simon's debut solo album, Carly Simon recorded *Another Passenger* under producer Ted Templeman. The album, her poorest selling in years, only yielded a minor hit with The Doobie Brothers' "It Keeps You Runnin'." In the summer of 1977 she scored a smash hit with the Carole Bayer Sager–Marvin Hamlisch composition "Nobody Does It Better," used as the theme song to the James Bond film *The Spy Who Loved Me*, and briefly toured later that year and again in 1978 in support of *Boys in the Trees*. That album, her first and only certified platinum-award album, included the near-smash hit "You Belong to Me," co-written by Simon and Doobie Brother Mike McDonald; later in the year, she had a moderate hit with The Everly Brothers' "Devoted to You," again with James Taylor. *Spy* was Carly Simon's final album for Elektra, as she switched to Warner Brothers for 1980's *Come Upstairs*, produced by new song collaborator Mike Mainieri. During the year, she had a major hit with "Jesse," subsequently recording *Torch*, largely comprised of Tin Pan Alley standards.

THE SIMON SISTERS

Winkin', Blinkin', and Nod	Kapp	3359
Cuddlebug	Kapp	3397

CARLY SIMON

Carly Simon	Elektra	EKS–74082	January '71	A
Anticipation*	Elektra	EKS–75016	November '71	A
No Secrets*	Elektra	EKS–75049	November '72	A
Hot Cakes*	Elektra	7E–1002	January '74	A
Playing Possum	Elektra	7E–1033	April '75	A
Best*	Elektra	7E–1048	November '75	
		reissued as 6E–109		A
Another Passenger	Elektra	7E–1064	June '76	A
Boys in the Trees**	Elektra	6E–128	March '78	A
Spy	Elektra	5E–506	June '79	A
Come Upstairs	Warner Brothers	3443	June '80	A
Torch	Warner Brothers	3592	September '81	A

LUCY SIMON

Lucy Simon	RCA	APL1–1074	November '75
Stolen Time	RCA	APL1–1745	June '77

(PAUL) SIMON AND (ART) GARFUNKEL. Probably the most successful American vocal duo since The Everly Brothers, Paul Simon and Art Garfunkel, who in late 1957 achieved a minor rock hit with "Hey, Schoolgirl" as Tom and Jerry, established themselves in 1965–66 with Simon's classic "Sounds of Silence," to which producer Tom Wilson had added rock instrumentation in their absence. Thus thrust into the forefront of so-called "folk-rock," Simon and Garfunkel helped open the way for so-called "soft rock" with their beautiful overdubbed harmony performances and the use of strings on Simon's exquisitely melodic early songs of isolation and alienation. Simon's songs later became more diversified and personal, yet were occasionally criticized as self-consciously poetic; his compositions were, in fact, some of the most literate, honest, and finely crafted songs of the second half of the Sixties, which led to their use and study in English literature classes all over the world. While all of their albums were certified gold-award, the duo's classic hit singles included "Sounds of Silence," "Mrs. Robinson" (from the soundtrack to *The*

Graduate), and "The Boxer" and culminated in "Bridge over Troubled Water" from their final album, ostensibly Columbia's biggest selling album ever.

Simon and Garfunkel parted company in 1970 and, by the time of Art Garfunkel's first solo album in the fall of 1973, Paul Simon had already established himself solo as one of the most astute, tasteful, and stimulating, if eclectic, pop song craftsmen of the Seventies with hits such as "Mother and Child Reunion," "Kodachrome," and "Love Me like a Rock." Having recorded albums for release every two years since his debut *Angel Claire*, Garfunkel has pursued an "easy listening" recorded sound with hits such as Jimmy Webb's "All I Know," whereas Simon has continued to record poignant, personal, and clever hits such as "50 Ways to Leave Your Lover," "My Little Town" (a reunion duet with Garfunkel), and "Slip-Slidin' Away," eschewing an easy listening sound in favor of straightforward yet sophisticated rock. A switch to Warner Brothers in early 1978 led to a flurry of legal suits and countersuits for Paul Simon; he has recently released his first feature film, *One-Trick Pony*, on Warner Brothers Films, in which he portrays a faded rock star seeking to re-establish himself. Reuniting for a benefit concert in September 1981, Simon and Garfunkel may again record together.

Born in Newark, New Jersey, on October 13, 1941, Paul Simon grew up in Queens, New York, where at the age of 11 he met and attended public school with Art Garfunkel, born in Forest Hills, New York, on November 5, 1941. Simon began singing with Garfunkel around the age of 13 and took up guitar while in high school. In late 1957, the two scored a moderate hit with their "Hey, Schoolgirl" as Tom and Jerry on Big Records, which led to an appearance on Dick Clark's "American Bandstand"; but subsequent singles failed, and the two split up after high school to attend college. They attended separate area colleges, as Simon began writing songs and working as a song promoter for E. B. Marks Publishing, recording demonstration tapes (including one with Carole King, "Just to Be with You," a minor hit for The Passions in 1959) and, in the early Sixties, working as a writer–producer at Amy Records. There he recorded under a variety of pseudonyms, including Tico and The Triumphs ("Motorcycle"). Jerry Landis ("The Lone Teen Ranger") and, for Tribute, Paul Kane ("He Was My Brother"). Around the same time, Garfunkel was recording as Arty Garr on Octavia and Warwick Records.

After renewing his friendship with Art Garfunkel in 1962, Paul Simon attempted a career as a folk singer around Greenwich Village and eventually won an audition with Tom Wilson of Columbia Records that led to the duo's debut album, *Wednesday Morning, 3 A.M.* Simon subsequently left for England, where he played folk clubs and recorded the British release, *Paul Simon Song Book*. During summers he was joined by vacationing Art Garfunkel and, in their absence, Wilson overdubbed rock instrumentation onto "Sounds of Silence." With the advent of "folk-rock" with Bob Dylan and The Byrds, the song became a top hit at the end of 1965. After returning to New York, the two began touring the college circuit and recorded *Sounds of Silence* for release in early 1966. The album, pervaded by Paul Simon's compositions and the duo's precise, overdubbed close-harmony singing, was bolstered by the smash hit "Homeward Bound" (included on their next album) and yielded a smash hit with the alienated "I Am a Rock." Strings were utilized for *Parsley, Sage, Rosemary, and Thyme*, which included the self-consciously poetic hit "The Dangling Conversation," plus the ditty "The 59th Street Bridge Song (Feelin' Groovy)," the satiric "A Simple Desultory Philippic," and the depressing yet moving "7 O'Clock News/Silent Night." The album became Simon and Garfunkel's first certified gold-award album in 1968.

Paul Simon and Art Garfunkel subsequently scored major hits with "A Hazy Shade of Winter," "At the Zoo," and "Fakin' It" before working on the soundtrack to the popular Mike Nichols' film, *The Graduate*, which included the hit "Scarborough Fair/Canticle," one of the few songs co-authored by Garfunkel, and the smash classic "Mrs. Robinson." *Bookends*, their first self-produced album, contained all the above hits (save "Scarborough Fair") plus "Save the Life of the Child." During 1969 the duo achieved a near-smash hit with the classic "The Boxer," followed in 1970 by smash hits with the dirge-like "Bridge over Troubled Water" (with lead vocal by Garfunkel) and the rollicking "Cecilia" and their final major hit, "El Condor Pasa," recorded with the Peruvian group Los Incas. *Bridge over Troubled Water*, possibly their finest album, also included "Keep the Customer Satisfied," "So Long, Frank Lloyd Wright," and "Baby Driver."

Earlier, Art Garfunkel had worked in the Mike Nichols films *Catch-22* (1969) and *Carnal Knowledge* (1970) and, during 1970, the Simon and Garfunkel team separated. Both were out of the public eye in 1971 but, by early 1972, Paul Simon was back with his debut solo album on Columbia Records. Co-produced by Simon and engineer Roy Halee, *Paul Simon* confirmed his reputation as one of the consummate craftsmen of Seventies rock with compositions such as "Duncan" and "Run That Body Down" and the hits "Mother and Child Reunion" (a smash recorded in Jamaica) and "Me and Julio Down By the Schoolyard." *There Goes Rhymin' Simon*, largely recorded in Muscle Shoals, Alabama (with co-production credits to Phil Ramone, Roy Halee, and former Yardbird Paul Samwell-Smith), included the smash hits "Kodachrome" and "Loves Me like a Rock" (featuring The Dixie Hummingbirds), and a major hit with the poignant "American Tune," as well as "Something So Right" and "Take Me to the Mardi Gras." Touring America and Europe with the Jessy Dixon Singers and the South American band Urubamba in 1973, Simon recorded his next album on the tour. In the meantime Art Garfunkel had recorded his debut solo album, *Angel Claire*, which featured lush orchestration and "easy listening" material such as Jimmy Webb's "All I Know" (a near-smash hit) and Van Morrison's "I Shall Sing" (a moderate hit). Garfunkel also scored a moderate hit in 1974 with "Second Avenue."

During 1975 both Paul Simon and Art Garfunkel recorded solo albums. Co-produced by Simon and Phil Ramone, Simon's *Still Crazy After All These Years* yielded the top hit "50 Ways to Leave Your Lover" and, disappointingly, only a moderate hit with the title song, while including "I Do It for Your Love" and "Have a Good Time." The album additionally contained Simon's hit duet with Phoebe Snow, "Gone at Last," and the near-smash hit reunion with Garfunkel, "My Little Town," which was also included on Garfunkel's *Breakaway*. That album, produced by Richard Perry, yielded a major hit with a remake of "I Only Have Eyes for You" (a hit for The Flamingos in 1959) and a moderate hit with Benny Gallagher and Graham Lyle's title song. Paul Simon toured again in 1975 with the Jessy Dixon Singers, saxophonist Dave Sanborn, keyboardist Richard Tee, guitarist Hugh McCracken, and drummer Steve Gadd, plus jazz harmonica player Toots Thielmans, all of whom had assisted on *Still Crazy After All These Years*. That October Simon appeared on NBC–TV's "Saturday Night Live," with Art Garfunkel as his guest.

Paul Simon appeared in Woody Allen's Academy Award-winning 1977 film *Annie Hall* and issued *Greatest Hits, Etc.* near year's end. In addition to compiling many of his prior hits, the album also included two new songs, the smash hit classic "Slip-Slidin' Away" and "Stranded in a Limousine." Art Garfunkel's *Watermark*, largely self-produced, was recorded at Muscle Shoals and featured material written by Jimmy Webb; yet its only hit, a remake of Sam Cooke's 1960 hit "(What a) Wonderful World," was recorded with James Taylor and Paul Simon. Garfunkel conducted his only tour in early 1978, as Simon switched to Warner Brothers Records while still owing Columbia one last album. By year's end, Simon had sued CBS to sever their relationship permanently and to recover allegedly unpaid funds. In the meantime he worked on his first feature film for Warners, *One-Trick Pony*, which he wrote, scored, and starred in as a musician seeking another hit record after years on the road. Released in October 1980, the movie featured performances by The B–52's, Sam and Dave, and a reunited Lovin' Spoonful, with Lou Reed appearing as Simon's unsympathetic record producer. As his "Late in the Evening" was becoming a hit, Paul Simon toured for the first time in five years in support of the movie and its soundtrack album with his movie band: keyboardist–vocalist Richard Tee, guitarist Eric Gale, bassist Tony Levin and drummer Steve Gadd, augmented by a four-piece horn section and the Jessy Dixon Singers. Earlier Art Garfunkel had scored a minor hit with "Since I Don't Have You" (a near-smash hit for the Skyliners in 1959) from 1979's *Fate for Breakfast* and subsequently co-starred in the disconcerting and explicit Nicholas Roeg film *Bad Timing/A Sensual Obsession* as a psychiatrist haunted by his love for a young woman. In September 1981 Simon and Garfunkel reunited for a benefit concert in New York's Central Park, and recordings of the show were issued on Warner Brothers early the next year.

SIMON AND GARFUNKEL

Simon and Garfunkel	Pickwick	3059	October '67	
Wednesday Morning, 3 A.M.	Columbia	PC–9049	December '64	A
Sounds of Silence*	Columbia	JC–9269	February '66	A

Parsley, Sage, Rosemary, and Thyme*	Columbia	PC–9363	November '66	A
The Graduate (soundtrack)*	Columbia	JS–3180	March '68	A
Bookends*	Columbia	PC–9529	April '68	A
Bridge over Troubled Water*	Columbia	JC–9914	February '70	A
Greatest Hits*	Columbia	JC–31350	June '72	A
Collected Works	5-Columbia	C5X–37587	December '81	A

PAUL SIMON

Paul Simon*	Columbia	KC–30750	February '72	
There Goes Rhymin' Simon*	Columbia	KC–32280	May '73	
Live Rhymin'*	Columbia	PC–32855	March '74	
Still Crazy After All These Years*	Columbia	PC–33540	October '75	
Greatest Hits, Etc.**	Columbia	JC–35032	November '77	A
Collected Works	5-Columbia	C5X–37581	December '81	A
One-Trick Pony*	Warner Brothers	HS–3472	August '80	A

ART GARFUNKEL

Angel Claire*	Columbia	PC–31474	September '73	A
Breakaway*	Columbia	PC–33700	October '75	A
Watermark*	Columbia	PC–34975	November '77	A
Fate for Breakfast	Columbia	JC–35780	April '79	A
Scissors Cut	Columbia	FC–37392	September '81	A

SIMON AND GARFUNKEL

The Concert in Central Park	2-Warner Brothers	2BSK–3654	February '82	A

SLY AND THE FAMILY STONE. Sylvester Stewart, later-day leader of Sly and The Family Stone, first came to prominence as producer of the earliest rock hits to come out of San Francisco during the mid-Sixties, Bobby Freeman's "The Swim" and the initial hits by The Beau Brummels. Under Stewart's directorship, Sly and The Family Stone became the first group successfully to combine rhythm-and-blues style rhythms and vocals with "psychedelic" guitar work, jazz-style horn arrangements, and lyrics reflecting the themes of social optimism and self-awareness. Thus initiating a new kind of rock music, "psychedelic soul," later much imitated (most obviously by The Temptations under producer Norman Whitfield), Sly and The Family Stone were uniquely characterized by a vocal style that featured the juxtaposition of a woman's high and man's bass voice and the sharing of lead vocals by as many as three members on a single song. Benefiting from both AM and FM "underground" radio airplay, the group appealed to both black and white audiences and performed an exciting stage act that was at once colorful, energetic, and spontaneous, in contrast to the carefully planned and executed routines of various Motown acts. With Stewart providing classics such as "Dance to the Music," "(I Want to Take You) Higher," and "Everyday People," and with the group launched with their stunning appearance in the *Woodstock* film and their excellent *Stand!* album, Sly and The Family Stone were one of the most popular bands of the early Seventies; yet their career faded as they became involved in concert cancellations and legal disputes, usually centered around Stewart. After utilizing a softer and more personal style for their final smash hit, "Family Affair," Sylvester Stewart has not re-established himself.

Born in Dallas, Texas, on March 15, 1944, Sylvester Stewart as a child moved to northern California's Vallejo, where he sang with his siblings in a family gospel group, The Stewart Four, who recorded "On the Battlefield of My Lord" when Sylvester was four. By then he was already playing drums and guitar and he eventually learned a number of other instruments, including piano and organ. Scoring a local hit at age 16 with "Long Time Ago," he later manned The Stewart Brothers (with brother Fred) and The Viscanes, who had a local hit with "Yellow River" when he was a high school senior. Thereafter he attended junior college and radio broadcasting school and secured disc jockey positions on San Francisco Bay area black radio stations KSOL and KDIA. In 1964 Stewart met disc jockey Tom Donahue, and he soon became staff producer for Donahue's Autumn label. There he wrote and produced Bobby Freeman's smash dance hit "C'mon and Swim" and produced the early hits of The Beau Brummels ("Laugh, Laugh," "Just a Little"), while recording local groups such as The Vejtables, The Mojo Men, and Great Society (with Grace Slick). With the formation of The Stoners in 1966, Stewart began a long-time association with trumpeter Cynthia Robinson.

During 1967 Sylvester Stewart formed Sly and The Family Stone and took the name Sly Stone. The members: Sly Stone (organ, guitar, vocals), pianist–soprano vocalist Rose "Stone" Stewart (born March 21, 1945, in Vallejo, California), guitarist–vocalist Fred "Stone" Stewart (born June 5, 1946, in Dallas, Texas), bassist–bass vocalist Larry Graham, Jr. (born August 14, 1946, in Beaumont, Texas), saxophonist–clarinetist–pianist–accordionist Jerry Martini (born October 1, 1946, in Boulder, Colorado), trumpeter–vocalist Cynthia Robinson (born January 12, 1946, in Sacramento, California), and drummer Greg Errico (born September 1, 1946, in San Francisco). Developing a regional reputation as a live act, Sly and The Family Stone signed with Epic Records, where their debut album, *A Whole New Thing*, featured shared and contrasted lead vocals, "psychedelic" guitar work, complex horn arrangements, and a "funky" rhythm sound rooted in Graham's bass playing. The album fared miserably, yet the title song to their second album, *Dance to the Music*, became a near-smash hit and was later acknowledged as a rock classic. The experimental *Life* also did poorly, but early 1969's *Stand!* firmly established the group with both black and white audiences. Sometimes disputedly labeled as soul music's first "concept" album, *Stand!* included the classic "(I Want to take You) Higher," "Don't Call Me Nigger, Whitey," the ominous "Somebody's Watching You," and "You Can Make It if You Try," and yielded a top hit with "Hot Fun in the Summertime."

One of the most dynamic acts at August 1969's Woodstock Festival, Sly and The Family Stone enjoyed even greater popularity with the release of the film and top hit single "Thank You (Falletinme Be Mice Elf Again)." However, the group, and Sylvester Stewart in particular, became mired in legal and drug-related problems and, by 1971, the group had developed a negative reputation for failing to show up at scheduled concerts, a circumstance which occasionally led to riots as it did in Chicago. The group's next album of new material, the ironically titled *There's a Riot Goin' On*, came more than two years after *Stand!* and revealed a softer and more personal feel to the music. The album yielded the top hit "Family Affair" and the major hit "Runnin' Away," yet the group's next album did not come for nearly two years. During this time Rusty Allen replaced Larry Graham (who formed Graham Central Station), Andy Newmark took over for drummer Greg Errico, and saxophonist Pat Rizzo was added. *Fresh* included one major hit, "If You Want Me to Stay," but it proved to be the group's last. Sylvester Stewart married Kathy Silva in concert at Madison Square Garden in 1974 and, following *Small Talk* (which yielded the moderate hit "Time for Livin'"), he recorded *High on You* solo. The next year Sly and The Family Stone issued the poorly selling *Heard Ya Missed Me, Well, I'm Back*, but they were little heard until 1979's *Back on the Right Track* on Warner Brothers Records. At the same time Epic issued *Ten Years Too Soon*, a compilation of the group's early hits with new disco-style backing, in a belated effort to capitalize on the declining disco trend.

SLY AND THE FAMILY STONE

A Whole New Thing	Epic	BN–26324 reissued as E–30335	November '67 February '71	
Dance to the Music	Epic	BN–26371 reissued as E–30334	March '68 February '71	A
Life	Epic	BN–26397 reissued as E–30333	July '68 February '71	A
Stand! *	Epic	BN–26456	April '69	A
Greatest Hits *	Epic	PE–30325	November '70	A
There's a Riot Goin' On *	Epic	E–30986	October '71	A

Fresh*	Epic	KE–32134	June '73	
Small Talk*	Epic	PE–32930	July '74	
High Energy	2-Epic	KEG–33462	May '75	

SLY STONE

High on You	Epic	PE–33835	October '75	

SLY AND THE FAMILY STONE

Heard Ya Missed Me, Well, I'm Back	Epic	PE–34348	December '76	
Ten Years Too Soon	Epic	JE–35974	October '79	A
Back on the Right Track	Warner Brothers	BSK–3303	October '79	A
Anthology	2-Epic	E2–37071	August '81	A

PATTI SMITH. A unique late Seventies female singer–songwriter, Patti Smith has self-consciously attempted to establish her literate and somewhat bizzare poetry as a rock art form by utilizing minimalist yet hard-driving rock backing. By 1975 Smith had become the darling of the "avant garde" set that followed New York's emerging underground rock scene, a scene that was also producing numerous so-called "punk rock" bands. Winning a cult following on both American coasts for her volatile and personal lyrics, erratic vocal style, and unusual stage antics, Patti Smith finally broke through nationally in 1978 with her hit single "Because the Night," co-authored by Bruce Springsteen. However, her 1979 tour in support of *Wave* showed her as arrogant and openly hostile to bemused audiences.

PATTI SMITH

Horses	Arista	AL–4066	November '75	A

THE PATTI SMITH GROUP

Radio Ethiopia	Arista	AL–4097	November '76	A
Easter	Arista	AB–4171	March '78	A
Wave	Arista	AB–4221	May '79	A

SONNY AND CHER. Sonny and Cher were one of the most successful couples of the mid-Sixties and probably the most famous couple in rock music. Established as a popular duet act with "I Got You, Babe," composed by Sonny, Sonny and Cher each attempted tandem solo careers, with Cher's proving the more successful, often with songs written by Sonny. Erroneously identified with the burgeoning "folk-rock" movement, whether by regional association, through Cher's hit recording of Bob Dylan's "All I Really Want to Do," or by their hippie-style attire (more affected than authentic), Sonny and Cher, and Cher solo, scored a string of pop-style hits through 1967. Later re-established with an older, more staid audience through appearances at Las Vegas clubs and "easy listening" hits such as "Gypsys, Tramps, and Thieves," "Half-Breed" and "Dark Lady" (Cher) and "All I Ever Need Is You" (Sonny and Cher), Sonny and Cher reinforced their popularity with their successful television series. The television exposure resulted in Cher becoming one of this country's leading fashion queens, but the breakup of their marriage and the cancellation of their TV show in 1974 led to another hitless period. Sonny pursued acting, as Cher attained her own television series and recorded unsuccessfully for Warner Brothers, including the dismal *Two the Hard Way* with on-again, off-again husband Gregg Allman. After severing that relationship and switching to Casablanca, Cher scored her first major hit in years in 1979 with "Take Me Home," since which time she has formed and dissolved the "new wave" band Black Rose.

"Sonny" Bono, born Salvatore Bono in Detroit on February 16, 1935, began writing songs during the early Fifties while he manned a succession of different jobs to support his family. In 1957 Larry Williams recorded his "High School Dance" as the flip side of the near-smash hit "Short, Fat Fannie" on Specialty Records and, as a consequence, Bono became an apprentice producer for the label while recording unsuccessfully as Don Christy. With the demise of Specialty in 1959, he continued to write and to record unsuccessfully, although his "Needles and Pins" did become a major hit for The Searchers in 1964.

Cher, born Cherilyn Sarkisian in El Centro, California, on May 20, 1946, to Armenian and Cherokee Indian parents, moved to Hollywood as a teenager to pursue acting and supplemented her income by singing background vocals on sessions for Phil Spector's Philles Records. There she met Sonny, who was working as Spector's assistant, in 1963, and the couple married the following year. They recorded as Caesar and Cleo for Reprise Records (three songs on 1965's *Baby, Don't Go*) and as Sonny and Cher for Vault and switched to Atco Records in 1965. Their debut album for Atco, *Look at Us*, yielded a top hit with Sonny's "I Got You, Babe," which he also arranged and produced, and a major hit with Sonny's "Just You" and attained gold-award certification before year's end. Moreover, Cher scored solo hits with Bob Dylan's "All I Really Want to Do" and "Where Do You Go" on Imperial; Sonny hit with his own mildly protesting "Laugh at Me," and "Baby, Don't Go," issued as performed by Sonny and Cher on Reprise, became a near-smash, all before the end of 1965.

Having become prominent members of Los Angeles' elite hippie set, Sonny and Cher achieved major hits with "But You're Mine," "What Now, My Love," and "Little Man" through 1966, whereas Cher scored a smash hit with Sonny's "Bang-Bang" and a moderate hit with "Alfie." In early 1967 the duo had a near-smash hit with Sonny's classic "The Beat Goes On" and issued their first soundtrack album, *Good Times*, in the spring.

Cher achieved another near-smash with "You Better Sit Down, Kids" late that year, but the hit proved to be the last for Sonny and/or Cher for nearly four years. By 1969 Cher had switched to Atco Records for two albums, including the soundtrack to the unsuccessful film, *Chastity*, which they financed themselves. In 1970 she began modeling for *Vogue* and became a fashion queen, an international celebrity, and the object of regular gossip column publicity. Around the same time, Sonny and Cher moved onto the Las Vegas club circuit and hosted a successful summer replacement television show in 1971 that led to their own CBS–TV series in 1972. Thus proving successful with older "easy listening" audiences rather than with rock fans, Sonny and Cher scored two consecutive gold-award albums with *Live* and *All I Ever Need Is You* and achieved major pop and easy listening hits with "All I Ever Need Is You" and "A Cowboy's Work Is Never Done"; Cher had a top hit with "Gypsys, Tramps, and Thieves" and a near-smash with "The Way of Love," both from the certified gold-award *Cher* album, in 1971–72, on Kapp Records. Sonny and Cher also scored a major easy listening hit with "When You Say Love," while Cher had major easy listening hits with "Living in a House Divided" and "I Saw a Man and He Danced with His Wife" and top pop hits with "Half-Breed" and "Dark Lady," the last three on MCA Records (which had absorbed Kapp). However, in 1974 their television series was canceled and they sued each other for divorce. Each subsequently had a television series, Sonny's on ABC and Cher's on CBS, but Sonny's quickly proved unsuccessful.

By 1975 Cher had switched to Warner Brothers Records and recorded *Stars* under producer–songwriter Jimmy Webb; but none of her albums for the label, including *Two the Hard Way*, recorded with Gregg Allman, fared well with the public. She had married Allman in the summer of 1975, but the relationship was a stormy one, with Cher filing for divorce after nine days, withdrawing that action several weeks later, and ultimately separating from him at the end of 1978. In the meantime, Sonny was pursuing an acting career on television and in the movies, whereas Cher continued to appear successfully on television and in Nevada cabarets. By 1979 she had moved to Casablanca Records, where her debut gold-award album, *Take Me Home*, produced a major hit with the discofied title song, her first substantial hit in five years. That winter, Cher began putting together a new-wave style band, Black Rose, with guitarist Les Dudek (formerly with Steve Miller and Boz Scaggs), second guitarist Ron Ritchotte, and drummer Gary Ferguson, among others. The group's debut album appeared on Casablanca Records in late 1980, but by 1981 Black Rose had dissolved. In February 1982 Cher debuted on Broadway in a straight dramatic role in *Come Back to the Five and Dime Jimmy Dean, Jimmy Dean*.

SONNY AND CHER

Baby, Don't Go	Reprise	RS–6177	October '65
Look at Us *	Atco	SD33–177	August '65
The Wondrous World of Sonny and Cher	Atco	SD33–183	April '66

In Case You're in Love	Atco	SD33–203	March '67
Good Times (soundtrack)	Atco	SD33–214	May '67

CHER

All I Really Want to Do	Imperial	LP–12292	September '65
The Sonny Side of Cher	Imperial	LP–12301	April '66
Cher	Imperial	LP–12320	September '66
With Love	Imperial	LP–12358	November '67
Backstage	Imperial	LP–12373	July '68

SONNY

Inner Views	Atco	SD33–229	November '67

CHER

3614 Jackson Highway	Atco	SD33–298	August '69
Chastity (soundtrack)	Atco	SD33–302	September '69
Cher *	Kapp	3649	September '71
		reissued as 5549	September '72
	reissued on MCA	2020	
		reissued as 624	A
Foxy Lady	Kapp	5514	July '72

SONNY AND CHER

Sonny and Cher Live *	Kapp	3654	September '71
		reissued as 5554	September '72
	reissued on MCA	2009	
All I Ever Need Is You *	Kapp	3660	February '72
		reissued as 5560	September '72
	reissued on MCA	2021	
Mama Was a Rock 'n' Roll Singer, Papa Used to Write All Her Songs	MCA	2102	June '73
Live in Las Vegas, Volume 2	2-MCA	2–8004	December '73

SONNY AND CHER ANTHOLOGIES AND COMPILATIONS

The Best of Sonny and Cher	Atco	SD33–219	August '67
The Two of Us	2-Atco	SD2–804	September '72

The Beat Goes On	Atco	SD–11000	January '76
Greatest Hits	MCA	2117	September '74

CHER

Bittersweet White Light	MCA	2101	April '73
Half-Breed*	MCA	2104	September '73
Dark Lady	MCA	2113	May '74
Stars	Warner Brothers	BS–2850	March '75
I'd Rather Believe In You	Warner Brothers	BS–2898	September '76
Cherished	Warner Brothers	BS–3046	September '77

GREGG ALLMAN AND CHER (ALLMAN AND WOMAN)

Two the Hard Way	Warner Brothers	BSK–3120	December '77

CHER

Take Me Home*	Casablanca	NBLP–7133	February '79	A
Prisoner	Casablanca	NBLP–7184	December '79	A

BLACK ROSE

Black Rose	Casablanca	NBLP–7234	September '80	A

CHER ANTHOLOGIES AND COMPILATIONS

Cher's Golden Greats	Imperial	LP–12406	November '68	
This Is Cher	Sunset	5276	April '70	
Superpak	2-United Artists	UXS–88	January '72	
Superpak, Volume 2	2-United Artists	UXS–94	October '72	
The Very Best of Cher	United Artists	LA237 reissued as LA377	August '74 March '75	
The Very Best of Cher, Volume 2	United Artists	LA435	September '75	
Greatest Hits	MCA	2127 reissued as 37028	November '74	A
Cher Sings the Hits	Springboard International	4029	June '75	
Best, Volume 1	Liberty	LN–10110	April '81	A
Best, Volume 2	Liberty	LN–10111	April '81	A

JOHN DAVID SOUTHER/THE SOUTHER–HILLMAN–FURAY BAND/RICHIE FURAY.

Later recognized as a songwriter through hit songs co-authored with and recorded by The Eagles ("The Best of My Love," "New Kid in Town," and "Heartache Tonight") and compositions recorded by Linda Ronstadt ("The Fast One," "Faithless Love," and "White Rhythm and Blues"), John David Souther helped form a prospective "supergroup" with Chris Hillman (The Byrds, The Flying Burrito Brothers) and Richie Furay (Buffalo Springfield, Poco) at the behest of David Geffen, head of Asylum Records, in 1973. With their credibility suffering due to the massive "hype" campaign mounted by the label, The Souther–Hillman–Furay Band did manage one hit single, "Fallin' in Love," and one certified gold-award album before disintegrating in late 1975. Although Richie Furay has been unable to establish himself as a solo artist subsequently, John David Souther did break through in 1979 with the hits, "You're Only Lonely" and "White Rhythm and Blues."

Born around 1946 in Texas, John David Souther grew up in Amarillo, took up guitar and violin as a child, and scored a local hit, "Good Lovin' Is Hard to Find," with John David and The Cinders while still in high school. In the late Sixties he moved to Los Angeles, where he met Jackson Browne and Glenn Frey, formed the acoustic duo Longbranch Pennywhistle with Frey, and recorded one album for the small Amos label. Frey, for a time a member of Linda Ronstadt's back-up group, later helped form The Eagles in 1971. Souther signed with the same label as did The Eagles, Asylum, and his self-produced debut solo album, recorded with Frey's assistance, revealed him to be an exceptional songwriter with compositions such as "The Fast One," "Run Like a Thief," and "Out to Sea." The album failed to sell, however, and Souther later co-authored "Doolin' Dalton" with Jackson Browne, Glenn Frey, and Don Henley from The Eagles' *Desperado* album. Souther subsequently served as one of the producers of Linda Ronstadt's *Don't Cry Now* album, contributing three of his songs, "The Fast One," "I Can Almost See It," and the title song, to the album, and collaborated on three of the songs from The Eagles' *On the Border* album, "You Never Cry like a Lover," "James Dean," and the top hit "The Best of My Love."

At the behest of Asylum Records head David Geffen, John David Souther helped form The Souther–Hillman–Furay Band, a prospective "supergroup" in the tradition of Crosby, Stills, Nash, and Young. Chris Hillman (guitar, bass, mandolin, vocals), born in Los Angeles on December 4, 1942, had been a member of The Byrds, The Flying Burrito Brothers, and Steve Stills' Manassas, whereas guitarist–vocalist Richie Furay (born May 9, 1944, in Yellow Springs, Ohio) had been part of both The Buffalo Springfield and Poco. The other members of the group were steel guitarist Al Perkins (a veteran of both The Flying Burrito Brothers and Manassas), two other former members of Manassas, keyboardist Paul Harris and percussionist Joe Lala, and drummer Jim Gordon. Their debut album yielded a major hit with "Fallin in Love" and was certified gold-award before year's end. The group toured nationally only once, replacing

Gordon with Ron Grinel for *Trouble in Paradise*, which fared less well, perhaps due to resentment that developed to Asylum's "hype" campaign, perhaps due to persistent rumors that the group was breaking up. The Souther–Hillman–Furay Band did break up in late 1975.

All three namesake members recorded solo for Asylum in 1976; John David Souther's release appeared first. *Black Rose*, produced by Peter Asher, included "Faithless Love" and "Silver Blue," both already recorded by Linda Ronstadt. Although the album sold only modestly, it fared much better than did either Hillman's *Slippin' Away* or Furay's *I've Got a Reason*, recorded with the short-lived Richie Furay Band. Hillman later recorded another poorly selling solo album for Asylum before rejoining former Byrds Roger McGuinn and Gene Clark for *McGuinn, Clark, and Hillman* and *City* on Capitol Records. Richie Furay continued to record for Asylum Records, but neither 1978's *Dance a Little Light* nor 1979's *I Still Have Dreams* sparked the public's buying impulse.

In the meantime, John David Souther had collaborated on The Eagles' "New Kid in Town" (a top hit) and "Victim of Love" from *Hotel California*, and Linda Ronstadt had recorded his "Simple Man, Simple Dream" and "White Rhythm and Blues." The Eagles' late 1979 *The Long Run* included three Souther collaborations, the hit "Heartache Tonight," "Teenage Jail," and "The Sad Cafe." Souther's first solo album in over three years, *You're Only Lonely*, on Columbia Records, finally established him with a national audience and yielded the major hit title song and the moderate hit "White Rhythm and Blues" (with background vocals by Linda Ronstadt), while also containing "Last in Love" (recorded by Nicolette Larson), "If You Don't Want My Love," and "Trouble in Paradise."

LONGBRANCH PENNYWHISTLE

Longbranch Pennywhistle	Amos	7007

JOHN DAVID SOUTHER

John David Souther	Asylum	SD–5055	August '72

THE SOUTHER–HILLMAN–FURAY BAND

The Souther–Hillman–Furay Band*	Asylum	7E–1006	July '74
Trouble in Paradise	Asylum	7E–1036	June '75

RICHIE FURAY

I've Got a Reason	Asylum	7E–1067	July '76	A
Dance a Little Light	Asylum	6E–115	February '78	A

| I Still Have Dreams | Asylum | 231 | November '79 | A |
| I've Got a Reason | Myrrh | 6672 | May '81 | A |

JOHN DAVID SOUTHER

| Black Rose | Asylum | 7E-1059 | April '76 | A |
| You're Only Lonely | Columbia | JC-36093 | September '79 | A |

PHIL SPECTOR. Undoubtedly the single most important and influential producer in the entire history of rock music, Phil Spector devised his trademark "wall-of-sound" technique for a series of smash hit records between 1962 and 1966 for The Crystals, Bob B. Soxx, The Ronettes, and The Righteous Brothers, on his own label, Philles. Integrating numerous guitars, massive string and horn sections, and dozens of background voices to produce a dense, murky sound that emphasized no particular voices or set of instruments (save the drums) in favor of an overwhelming all-encompassing sound that showcased the lead vocals, Spector's "wall-of-sound" technique brought an unprecedented level of sophistication and complexity to record production. The youngest-ever head of a record label at the age of 21 with Philles Records, Spector produced smash hit classics on the label such as "He's a Rebel," "Da Doo Ron Ron," and "Then He Kissed Me" for The Crystals, "Zip-A-Dee Doo-Dah" for Bob B. Soxx and The Blue Jeans, "Be My Baby" for The Ronettes, and, for The Righteous Brothers, "You've Lost That Lovin' Feelin'," usually regarded as one of the ten classic singles of the entire history of rock.

Utilizing the services of some of the best songwriting teams of the day (Jeff Barry and Ellie Greenwich, Barry Mann and Cynthia Weil, Carole King and Gerry Goffin) and many of Los Angeles' finest sessions musicians and technicians (pianist Leon Russell, guitarists Barney Kessel, Glen Campbell, Herb Ellis and Joe Pass, arranger Jack Nitzche, and engineer Larry Levine), Phil Spector was the most successful independent producer in rock music when, in 1966, the dismal showing of Ike and Tina Turner's "River Deep—Mountain High" led to his withdrawal from the music business for several years and the closure of Philles Records. One of rock music's most enigmatic and perplexing figures, Spector eventually re-emerged with productions for The Beatles, John Lennon, and George Harrison in the early Seventies, but these efforts paled in comparison to his earlier work, still acknowledged as classics 15 years after their initial releases. Phil Spector's later work, including a late Sixties stint with A&M Records and that on his own Warner-Spector label, as well as recent independent productions for Leonard Cohen and The Ramones, has produced little of lasting value. Nonetheless, the 1977 compilation set *Phil Spector's Greatest Hits* forms an essential foundation for contemporary rock that has influenced everyone from Brian Wilson to The Electric Light Orchestra, from Elton John to The Carpenters, and contemporary producers such as Richard Perry, Keith Olsen, and Dave Edmunds.

Born in the Bronx, New York, on December 26, 1940, Phil Spector moved to Los Angeles at the age of 13 with his mother and sister. Having taken guitar and piano in high school, he formed The Teddy Bears in 1958 with Annette Kleinbard and Marshall Lieb. Signed to Dore Records, they soon had a top hit with Spector's own "To Know Him Is to Love Him," but subsequent recordings for Imperial proved unsuccessful and the group disbanded in 1959. He later worked on the West Coast under Lester Sill and Lee Hazlewood and subsequently served as understudy to Jerry Leiber and Mike Stoller in New York. Co-authoring Ben E. King's solo debut hit "Spanish Harlem" with Leiber, Spector had already scored his first hit as a producer with Ray Peterson's "Corinna, Corinna." His hit productions during 1961 included Curtis Lee's "Pretty Little Angel Eyes" and The Paris Sisters' "I Know How You Love Me."

Phil Spector then returned to the West Coast, where he formed Philles Records with Lester Sill in late 1961. The Crystals were the label's first signing and they soon had major hits with "There's No Other" and "Uptown." The so-called "wall-of-sound" technique devised by Spector was launched into international prominence with The Crystals' top 1962 hit "He's a Rebel." Following "He's Sure the Boy I Love," The Crystals had smash hit classics in 1963 with "Da Doo Ron Ron" and "Then He Kissed Me," both co-authored by Spector, Jeff Barry, and Ellie Greenwich. In late 1962 Spector bought out Lester Sill and thus assumed total control of Philles Records. Bob B. Soxx and The Blue Jeans followed their near-smash hit "Zip-A-Dee Doo-Dah" with the moderate hit "Why Do Lovers Break Each Other's Hearts," whereas Darlene Love scored moderate hits with "(Today I Met) The Boy I'm Gonna Marry" and "Wait 'Til My Bobby Gets Home," all produced by Spector. In mid 1963 Spector signed The Ronettes to Philles Records and they soon had a smash hit with "Be My Baby" (by Spector, Barry, and Greenwich), followed by the moderate-to-major hits "Baby, I Love You," "(The Best Part of) Breakin' Up," "Do I Love You," and "Walking in the Rain" through 1964. In late 1963 Philles had issued the celebrated Christmas album *A Christmas Gift for You* featuring Philles artists performing seasonal standards, and the album has since been repackaged several times.

During 1964 Phil Spector signed The Righteous Brothers and, at year's end, the duo scored a top hit with "You've Lost That Lovin' Feelin' " (co-written by Spector, Barry Mann, and Cynthia Weil), generally regarded as one of rock's all-time classic singles. The Righteous Brothers subsequently achieved smash hits with "Just Once in My Life" (by Spector, Carole King, and Gerry Goffin), "Unchained Melody," and "Ebb Tide" and switched to Verve Records where their first top hit record, "(You're My) Soul and Inspiration," mimicked Phil Spector's production style. In the spring of 1966 Philles issued the Spector–Barry–Greenwich epic "River Deep—Mountain High" as recorded by Ike and Tina Turner, but the single failed to become anything more than a minor hit (although it was a smash hit in Britain) much to Spector's chagrin, as he ostensibly considered it his consummate production effort. Thus rebuffed by the American public, Spector withdrew from the record business and soon closed Philles Records, ending a stellar chapter in the history of rock music.

During the rest of the Sixties, Phil Spector was generally inactive, though he did make a cameo appearance in the *Easy Rider* film and worked for a year and one-half at A&M Records beginning in the summer of 1968, producing one album for The Checkmates. He later salvaged The Beatles' *Let It Be* album (much to the chagrin of Paul McCartney) and produced George Harrison's *All Things Must Pass* and four albums for John Lennon, including *Imagine*. Leaving Apple Records in 1973, Spector formed Warner-Spector Records under the aegis of Warner Brothers Records, but productions for Cher ("A Woman's Story") and Cher and Nilsson ("A Love Like Yours Don't Come Knocking Every Day") fared dismally. Forming Phil Spector International in Great Britain in conjunction with Polydor Records, Spector produced Dion's *Born to Be with You* for the label (unreleased in the United States), and the label issued a whole series of *Rare Masters* taken from the old Philles recordings. During 1977 Warner-Spector released the excellent compilation set, *Phil Spector's Greatest Hits*, but Spector's production of Leonard Cohen's *Death of a Ladies' Man* was denounced by the artist. Phil Spector's recent production of The Ramones' *End of the Century* has failed to elevate him back to the status and renown he enjoyed at Philles Records. During 1981 Spector assisted Yoko Ono with her *Season of Glass* album.

THE TEDDY BEARS

The Teddy Bears	Imperial	LP–9067(M)	

PHIL SPECTOR

A Christmas Gift for You	Philles	PHLP–4005(M)	November '63	
reissued as Phil Spector's Christmas Album	Apple	SW–3400(M)	December '72	
	reissued on Warner-Spector	SP–9103	December '75	
	reissued on Pavillion	PZ–37686		A
Phil Spector's Greatest Hits	2-Warner-Spector	2SP–9104	February '77	

THE SPINNERS. Long-lived Detroit-based black harmony vocal group, The Spinners initially recorded during the early Sixties on Harvey Fuqua's Tri-Phi label until the company was absorbed by the Motown empire, where the group languished for eight years with only one hit, "It's a Shame," produced by Stevie Wonder. Having switched to Atlantic Records in 1972 at the urging of Aretha Franklin, The Spinners were teamed with Philadelphia songwriter–producer Thom Bell, with whom they scored a succession of smooth soul ballad hits such as "I'll Be Around," "Could It Be I'm Falling in Love," and "One of a Kind (Love Affair)," featuring the distinctive lead vocals of Phillipe Wynne. Thereby established with both white and black audiences, The Spinners were introduced to the Nevada cabaret circuit by Dionne Warwick, with whom they achieved the top 1974 hit "Then Came You." Maintaining their chart popularity through 1976, The Spinners fared poorly after the departure of Wynne and eventually re-established themselves in 1979–80 with remakes of The Four Seasons' "Working My Way Back to You" and Sam Cooke's "Cupid."

THE SPINNERS

The Original Spinners	Motown	639	January '68	
Best	Motown	769	May '73	
Motown Superstar Series, Volume 9	Motown	5–109		A
Second Time Around	V.I.P.	405	November '70	
The Spinners*	Atlantic	SD–7256	April '73	
Mighty Love*	Atlantic	SD–7296	March '74	A
New and Improved*	Atlantic	SD–18118	December '74	
Pick of the Litter*	Atlantic	SD–18141	July '75	
Live	2-Atlantic	SD2–910	November '75	
Happiness Is Being With The Spinners*	Atlantic	SD–18181	July '76	
Yesterday, Today, and Tomorrow	Atlantic	SD–19100	March '77	
8	Atlantic	SD–19146	December '77	
The Best of The Spinners	Atlantic	SD–19179	May '78	A
From Here to Eternally	Atlantic	SD–19219	May '79	
Dancin' and Lovin'	Atlantic	SD–19256	October '79	A
Love Trippin'	Atlantic	SD–19270	June '80	A
Can't Shake This Feelin'	Atlantic	19318	December '81	A

JOHN EDWARDS

Life, Love and Living	Cotillion	9909	November '76

PHILLIPE WYNNE

Starting All Over	Cotillion	9920	October '77	
Drums and Wires	Virgin	13134		A
Jammin'	Uncle Jam	JX–36843		A

SPIRIT/JO JO GUNNE/JAY FERGUSON. Acclaimed as one of America's finest groups of the late Sixties, Spirit never progressed beyond a cult group with their jazz-style improvisations on songs primarily written by Jay Ferguson, despite recording such classics as "Mechanical World" and "Nature's Way" and hitting with "I've Got a Line on You" in 1969. The group fragmented after *12 Dreams of Dr. Sardonicus* and members Mark Andes and Jay Ferguson formed the "hard-rock" band Jo Jo Gunne, but that group scored only one hit with "Run Run Run" during their four years of existence. Spirit re-formed during the mid-Seventies with little success, but Ferguson began to establish himself solo with the pop-style 1977 near-smash, "Thunder Island."

Born in Los Angeles on May 10, 1947, Jay Ferguson took piano lessons between the ages of 7 and 12 and played music during high school with bassist Mark Andes (born in Los Angeles on February 19, 1948). The two later formed The Red Roosters with guitarist Randy California, and that group evolved into Spirit in the summer of 1967 with the additions of keyboardist John Locke (born September 25, 1943, in Los Angeles) and drummer Ed Cassidy (born May 4, 1931, in Chicago). Cassidy, a veteran jazz drummer, had previously worked with Cannonball Adderley and Thelonius Monk. After developing a respectable following through engagements in West Coast clubs, Spirit was signed to Lou Adler's Ode label. Their debut album featured Andes and Ferguson's neglected classic, "Mechanical World," Ferguson's "Fresh-Garbage," and Locke's instrumental "Elijah" but failed to yield a hit single. Their second album produced their only major hit with "I Got a Line on You" and, following *Clear*, the group switched to Epic Records for *12 Dreams of Dr. Sardonicus*, eventually certified as their only gold-award album in 1976, which included Ferguson's "Mr. Skin" and another neglected classic, "Nature's Way."

By 1971 Jay Ferguson and Mark Andes had left Spirit to form the "hard-rock" Jo Jo Gunne with drummer Curley Smith and Andes' guitarist brother, Matthew Andes. One of the first signings to the newly formed Asylum label, Jo Jo Gunne achieved their only real success with "Run Run Run" from their debut album. John Locke and Ed Cassidy recruited brothers Al (bass, vocals) and Christian Staehly (guitar, vocals) for Spirit's *Feedback*; by 1973, no original members remained in the group. After convalescing from accident injuries, Randy California eventually re-emerged in 1972 with the poorly received experimental *Kaptain Kopter and The Fabulous Twirly Birds* and subsequently recorded *Spirit of '76* and *Son of Spirit* with Cassidy and bassist Barry Keene. By 1976 Jo Jo Gunne had broken up and Spirit was revived with all original members save Ferguson. After two poorly selling albums for Mercury, Spirit was reduced to issuing a live set on the small Potato label in late 1978. In 1976 Mark Andes left to join Firefall; Jay Ferguson initiated a solo career on Asylum Records aided by Joe Walsh and eventually scored a near-smash hit with the pop-style "Thunder Island" at the end of 1977. During 1979 Ferguson had a moderate hit with "Shakedown Cruise."

SPIRIT

Spirit	Ode	Z–1244004	March '68	
The Family That Plays Together	Ode reissued on Epic	Z–1244014 KE–31461	January '69 July '72	
Clear	Ode	Z–1244016	August '69	
12 Dreams of Dr. Sardonicus*	Epic	PE–30267	December '70	A
Feedback	Epic	E–31175	March '72	A
Fresh-Garbage	2-Epic	PEG–31457	February '73	A
The Best of Spirit	Epic	PE–32271	July '73	A
The Family That Plays Together/ Feedback	2-Epic	BG–33761	October '75	A

JO JO GUNNE

Jo Jo Gunne	Asylum	SD–5053	February '72
Bite Down Hard	Asylum	SD–5063	March '73
Jumpin' the Gunne	Asylum	SD–5071	December '73
So . . . Where's the Show?	Asylum	7E–1022	November '74

RANDY CALIFORNIA

Kaptain Kopter and The Fabulous Twirly Birds	Epic	E–31755	November '72

RANDY CALIFORNIA AND ED CASSIDY

Spirit of '76	2-Mercury	SRM2–804	May '75
Son of Spirit	Mercury	SRM1–1053	October '75

SPIRIT

Farther Along	Mercury	SRM1–1094	July '76	
Future Games	Mercury	SRM1–1133	February '77	
Live Spirit	Potato	2001	November '78	A
Potatoland	Rhino	303	November '81	A

JAY FERGUSON

All Alone in the End Zone	Asylum	7E–1063	June '76	
Thunder Island	Asylum	7E–1115	August '77	
Real Life Ain't This Way	Asylum	6E–158	January '79	
Terms and Conditions	Capitol	ST–12083	August '80	A

SPOOKY TOOTH/GARY WRIGHT. A part of the British underground rock scene during the late Sixties "progressive rock" and "heavy metal" movements, Spooky Tooth was co-led by keyboardists Gary Wright and Mike Harrison, whose writing and singing styles contrasted drastically. One of the few British groups to include an American (Wright), Spooky Tooth never had a British or American hit, yet may well have become more popular in the United States than in their native country. After the group disbanded in 1970, Wright and Harrison both pursued inauspicious solo careers (as did original guitarist Luther Grosvenor) before re-forming Spooky Tooth in 1973. Original bassist Greg Ridley joined Humble Pie, whereas Grosvenor joined Mott the Hoople before forming Widowmaker in 1975. Both Harrison and Wright pursued solo careers after Spooky Tooth's final breakup in late 1974, but only Wright's proved successful, particularly with his keyboard-dominated *Dream Weaver* album and its two smash singles, "Love Is Alive" and the title song.

SPOOKY TOOTH

Tobacco Road	A&M	SP–4300	May '71	A
Spooky Two	A&M	SP–4194	July '69	
		reissued as 3124		A
Ceremony	A&M	SP–4225	March '70	
The Last Puff	A&M	SP–4266	August '70	A

GARY WRIGHT

Extraction	A&M	SP–4277	January '71
Footprint	A&M	SP–4296	October '71

MIKE HARRISON

Mike Harrison	Island	SMAS–9313	March '72
Smokestack Lightning	Island	SW–9321	November '72
Rainbow Rider	Island	9359	January '76

LUTHER GROSVENOR

Under Open Skies	Island	SMAS–9312	February '72

WIDOWMAKER

Widowmaker	United Artists	LA642	July '76
Too Late to Cry	United Artists	LA723	June '77

SPOOKY TOOTH

You Broke My Heart . . . So I Busted Your Jaw	A&M	SP–4385	May '73	A
Witness	Island	SW–9337	October '73	

The Mirror	Island reissued on Antilles	ILPS–9292 7046	August '74	A

GARY WRIGHT AND SPOOKY TOOTH

That Was Only Yesterday	2-A&M	3528	April '76

GARY WRIGHT

The Dream Weaver *	Warner Brothers	BS–2868	July '75	A
The Light of Smiles	Warner Brothers	BS–2951	January '77	
Touch and Gone	Warner Brothers	BSK–3137	November '77	
Headin' Home	Warner Brothers	3244	February '79	
The Right Place	Warner Brothers	3511	June '81	A

BRUCE SPRINGSTEEN.   Virtually unknown save to adulatory critics and ardent fans from the Northeast until 1975, Bruce Springsteen burst upon the rock scene with his outstanding *Born to Run* album accompanied by a massive publicity campaign financed by Columbia Records that made him the most talked-about new rock performer since Elton John. Although the album was certified gold-award within six weeks of its release, Springsteen's credibility was severely damaged by simultaneous cover stories which appeared in the news magazines *Time* and *Newsweek* in late October 1975. Nonetheless, the urgency of his songs of street life and youthful concerns, the power of his vocal delivery, the vitality of his guitar playing, the excellence of his back-up band, and the ferocity of his live performances sustained Springsteen through a turbulent period during which he was able to live down such bombastic hyperbole as "the savior of rock and roll" and "the next Bob Dylan." However, within a year, he was embroiled in legal disputes with his former manager that prevented subsequent recording, a situation that could have easily ruined an artist with less talent and dynamism than had Springsteen. Eschewing the glamorous aspects of rock music and developing a reputation as a "peoples'" band with marathon two- to four-hour performances, Springsteen ultimately settled his legal problems during the spring of 1977; his first album thereafter, *Darkness at the Edge of Town*, was greeted with equivocal reviews, yet became an instant best-seller. However, 1980's *The River*, hailed by some as the best rock album of the year and certainly one of the most anticipated since Fleetwood Mac's *Tusk*, solidified his reputation as one of the most creative and exciting rock artists to emerge in the last decade.

Born in Freehold, New Jersey, on September 23, 1949, Bruce Springsteen joined his first band at age 14 and subsequently commuted to New

York's Greenwich Village in 1965 to perform with The Castiles at the Cafe Wha. Later forming a succession of bands such as Steel Mill and Doctor Zoom and The Sonic Boom, he played engagements around New Jersey for years and unsuccessfully auditioned for a West Coast record label during the early Seventies before returning East and meeting his future manager Mike Appel in the fall of 1971. Signed with Appel's management firm the following March, Springsteen successfully auditioned for A&R (artists-and-repertoire) man John Hammond and signed with Columbia Records in June 1972. His debut album, *Greetings from Asbury Park, New Jersey*, was produced by Appel and Springsteen and included "Blinded by the Light," "Spirit in the Night," and "It's Hard to Be a Saint in the City" but was largely ignored by the public other than rock critics and his cult following based in the Northeast. The album received little radio airplay, perhaps because of Columbia's absurd claim that Springsteen was "the next Bob Dylan"; following an unfortunate tour in June 1973 opening for Chicago, he and his band would only perform as a headlining act. *The Wild, the Innocent and the E-Street Shuffle* suffered a similarly neglected fate, although it included such excellent songs as "4th of July, Asbury Park (Sandy)"—a minor hit for The Hollies in the spring of 1975—"Rosalita (Come Out Tonight)," and "New York City Serenade."

Rigorously touring primarily on the East Coast during 1974, Bruce Springsteen had formed his permanent backup group, The E-Street Band, with keyboardists Roy Bittan and Danny Federeci, saxophonist Clarence Clemons, bassist Gary Tallent, and drummer Max Weinberg. Later joined by guitarist "Miami" Steve Van Zandt, Springsteen burst onto the music scene in the fall of 1975 with *Born to Run.* A massive "hype" campaign, estimated to cost in excess of $200,000, was launched in August with a national advertising program and a five-day, 10-show run at New York's Bottom Line, for which nearly one-fourth of the tickets were reserved for so-called "media tastemakers." The album, co-produced by Appel, Springsteen, and one-time rock critic Jon Landau (whom Springsteen had met in April 1974), quickly yielded a major hit with the title song and was soon certified gold-award, but nearly identical cover stories in the October 27, 1975, issues of *Newsweek* and *Time* brought Springsteen's credibility into question. The album also featured "Tenth Avenue Freeze-Out" (a minor hit), "Thunder Road," and "She's the One," and its rapid sales helped advance the sales of the first two albums, both certified gold-award by 1978. Scheduled to begin recording his next album in the spring of 1976, Springsteen became enmeshed in legal disputes with manager Mike Appel that prevented him from recording for a year. Nonetheless touring in the fall of 1976 and early 1977, Springsteen resolved his legal problems in May and quickly went into the studio to record a new album under mentor–producer Jon Landau. Issued in mid-1978, *Darkness on the Edge of Town* started to reveal a growing maturity to Springsteen's songwriting and aptly showcased The E-Street Band, yet yielded only moderate hits with "Prove It All Night" and "Badlands," while also containing "Racing in the Streets," "Streets of Fire," and the title song. Touring tirelessly from July to September 1978 and again beginning in November, Bruce Springsteen performed at the September 1979 benefit concerts in New York for MUSE (Musicians United for Safe Energy), and his segment came to be regarded as the highlight of the resulting movie and triple-record album. He spent more than a year recording his next album, ostensibly recording over 50 songs and, upon release, *The River* was acclaimed as not only the best album of the year, but of the past several years. Pervaded by songs using the automobile as the primary metaphor (such as "Stolen Car," "Drive All Night," "Wreck on the Highway," and "Cadillac Ranch"), the double-record set also included "Hungry Heart" (a smash hit), "I'm a Rocker," "Independence Day," and "The Price You Pay," and was accompanied by a three-month nationwide tour, the first for Bruce Springsteen and The E-Street Band in two years. During 1980–81, Springsteen completed a year-long tour and produced Gary "U.S." Bonds' *Dedication* album.

BRUCE SPRINGSTEEN

Greetings from Asbury Park, New Jersey*	Columbia	JC–31903	February '73	A
The Wild, the Innocent and the E-Street Shuffle*	Columbia	PC–32432	December '73	A
Born to Run*	Columbia	JC–33795	August '75	A
Darkness on the Edge of Town*	Columbia	JC–35318	June '78	A
The River**	2-Columbia	PC2–36854	October '80	A

THE STAPLE SINGERS/THE STAPLES. Most likely the only American gospel group to achieve international popularity and widespread American recognition, The Staple Singers first developed a national reputation as a straightforward family gospel group during the Fifties, later endured attempts to transform them into a folk group during the Sixties, and eventually emerged as a successful "soul" group in the Seventies, with hits on Stax Records such as "Respect Yourself," "I'll Take You There," and "If You're Ready (Come, Go with Me)" and the best-selling album, *Bealtitude*. Featuring the blues-style guitar playing of leader Roebuck Staples and the frankly astonishing contralto voice of Mavis Staples, The Staple Singers never abandoned gospel music, but rather expanded its boundaries to include pop-style songs of joyous optimism, international brotherhood, and interpersonal love. Scoring a top hit with the title song to the film *Let's Do It Again* under Curtis Mayfield in 1975, The Staples (as they now call themselves) now record for Warner Brothers, as does Mavis Staples as a solo act.

THE STAPLE SINGERS

Uncloudy Day	VeeJay	5000(M)	May '61
Will the Circle Be Unbroken	VeeJay	5008(M)	

Swing Low	VeeJay	5014(M)	January '62	
Gospel Program	Gospel	3001(M)	January '62	
Hammers and Nails	Riverside	93501	June '62	
The Twenty-Fifth Day of December	Riverside	93513		
This Land	Riverside	93524		
This Little Light	Riverside	93527	January '66	
Amen	Epic	BN–26132	February '65	
Freedom Highway	Epic	BN–26163	October '65	
Why	Epic	BN–26196	May '66	
Pray On	Epic	BN–26237		
For What It's Worth	Epic	BN–26332	November '67	
What the World Needs Now	Epic	BN–26373		
Heavy Makes You Happy	2-Epic	KEG–30635	June '71	
Soul Folk in Action	Stax	STS–2004		
We'll Get Over	Stax	STS–2016		
The Staple Singers	Stax	STS–2034	October '68	
Bealtitude: Respect Yourself	Stax	STS–3002 reissued as 4116	February '72 October '78	A
Be What You Are	Stax	STS–3015	August '73	
City in the Sky	Stax	5515	August '74	
This Time Around	Stax	8511	July '81	A

MAVIS STAPLES

Only for the Lonely	Volt	VOS–6010	September '70	
Mavis Staples	Volt reissued on Stax	VOS–6007 4118	September '71 October '78	A
A Piece of the Action (soundtrack)	Curtom	5017	November '77	
Oh, What a Feeling	Warner Brothers	3319	May '79	

THE STAPLE SINGERS/CURTIS MAYFIELD

Let's Do It Again (soundtrack)	Curtom	5005	October '75	

THE STAPLES

Pass It On	Warner Brothers	2945	September '76	
Family Tree	Warner Brothers	3064	September '77	A
Unlock Your Mind	Warner Brothers	3192	August '78	A
Hold On to Your Dream	20th Century-Fox	636	August '81	A

STAPLE SINGERS REISSUES, COMPILATIONS, AND ANTHOLOGIES

The Staple Singers	Archive of Gospel Music	62(E)		
The Staple Singers, Volume 2	Archive of Gospel Music	72(E)		
Best	VeeJay	5014(M)	January '62	
Best	Buddah	2009	May '69	
Will the Circle Be Unbroken	Buddah	7508	November '70	
Uncloudy Day	Trip	7000		
Swing Low	Trip	7014		
Best	Trip	7019		
Other Side	Trip	8014	November '71	
Tell It Like It Is	Harmony	KH–31775	November '72	
Use What You Got	Fantasy	9423	May '73	A
The Twenty-Fifth Day of December	Fantasy	9442	December '73	A
Great Day	2-Milestone	47028	July '75	A
Pray On/Tell It Like It Is	2-Epic	BG–33764	October '75	
Best	Stax	5523	September '75	
Chronicle	Stax	4119	February '79	A

RINGO STARR. With his adequate drumming and undistinguished voice, little was expected of Ringo Starr after the breakup of The Beatles, yet he managed a string of smash singles between 1971 and 1975 with his own compositions "It Don't Come Easy," "Back-Off Boogaloo," and "Photograph," two Sixties remakes, and Hoyt Axton's "No-No Song." Pursuing a parallel film career, Starr enjoyed his greatest album successes with *Ringo* and *Goodnight, Vienna* under producer Richard Perry, but subsequent releases on Atlantic and Portrait Records have fared poorly.

Born Richard Starkey in Liverpool, England, on July 7, 1940, Ringo Starr did not take up drums until completing high school; he eventually joined Rory Storm and The Hurricanes. In 1961 he met Brian Epstein and subsequently joined The Beatles as Pete Best's replacement in August 1962. During the career of The Beatles, Starr was constantly overshadowed by the group's more talented members; he developed the image of a cheerful, self-effacing buffoon in concerts and movies. He occasionally sang lead vocals on songs such as "I Wanna Be Your Man," "Matchbox," "Honey, Don't," "Boys," and the minor hits "Act Naturally" and "What Goes On" and achieved his biggest successes as a lead singer with the smash hit "Yellow Submarine" in 1966 and the classic "With a Little Help from My Friends," perhaps the crowning glory of his career with The Beatles, from *Sgt. Pepper's Lonely Hearts Club Band*.

After appearing in a cameo role in the 1968 film *Candy*, Ringo Starr performed a major role with Peter Sellers in *The Magic Christian*, which opened in London around the time of his first solo album, *Sentimental Journey*. Largely comprised of Tin Pan Alley standards, the album failed to yield even a minor hit single. His next, *Beaucoups of Blues*, was recorded in Nashville and featured country-and-western-style material. During 1971 Starr scored a smash hit with his own "It Don't Come Easy," performed at George Harrison's August Concert for Bangla Desh, and appeared in the role of Frank Zappa in Zappa's outlandish movie *200 Motels*. In 1972 he had a near-smash hit with his own "Back-Off Boogaloo" and later appeared in the films *Son of Dracula* (with Harry Nilsson), the highly acclaimed *That'll Be the Day*, and the western *Blindman*. He also directed the film documentary concerning Marc Bolan, *Born to Boogie*.

Recording under producer Richard Perry, Ringo Starr's first album in three years, *Ringo*, yielded top hits with "Photograph" (co-written by Starr and George Harrison) and the rock classic "You're Sixteen" (originally a hit for Johnny Burnette), plus the smash "Oh, My, My," while containing one song written by each of the former Beatles. The album was quickly certified gold-award, as was *Goodnight Vienna*, also produced by Perry. That album included two smash hits, a remake of The Platters' "Only You" and Hoyt Axton's humorous anti-drug "No-No Song" (backed as a single by Elton John and Bernie Taupin's "Snookero"), and the moderate hit title song by John Lennon. *Blast from Your Past* assembled Starr's hit singles plus "Early 1970," his song about the breakup of The Beatles. He then switched to Atlantic Records, where he scored his last major hit with "A Dose of Rock 'n' Roll" from *Ringo's Rotogravure*. Following *Ringo the Fourth*, Ringo Starr switched to Portrait Records for *Bad Boy*, but neither proved particularly successful. In 1981 he co-starred opposite Barbara Bach in the inane *Caveman* movie and moved to Boardwalk Records for *Stop and Smell the Roses* and "Wrack My Brain."

RINGO STARR

Sentimental Journey	Apple/Capitol	SW–3365	April '70	
	reissued on Capitol	SN–16218		A
Beaucoups of Blues	Apple/Capitol	SMAS–3368	September '70	
	reissued on Capitol	SN–16235	November '81	A
Ringo *	Apple/Capitol	SWAL–3413	October '73	
	reissued on Capitol	SN–16114		A
Goodnight Vienna *	Apple/Capitol	SW–3417	November '74	
	reissued on Capitol	SN–16219		A
Blast from Your Past	Apple/Capitol	SW–3422	November '75	A
Ringo's Rotogravure	Atlantic	SD–18193	September '76	
Ringo the Fourth	Atlantic	SD–19108	September '77	

Bad Boy	Portrait	JR–35378	May '78	
Stop and Smell the Roses	Boardwalk	NB1–33246	November '81	A

STEELY DAN. Having worked nearly two years as members of Jay and The Americans' back-up group, songwriter–instrumentalists Walter Becker and Donald Fagen formed Steely Dan as a vehicle for their musically sophisticated, lyrically erudite, and oblique songs and scored two major hits with "Do It Again" and "Reeling in the Years" from their excellent debut album. Admittedly more influenced by jazz than by rock, Becker and Fagen essentially constituted Steely Dan themselves after *Pretzel Logic* and their final 1974 tour. Languishing for more than three years without a major hit, Steely Dan revived its career with the esoteric *Aja* album and its three hits yet switched record companies in 1976 while still owing their prior label one album.

Walter Becker, born February 20, 1950, in New York City, and Donald Fagen, born January 10, 1948, in Passaic, New Jersey, met while attending Bard College in upstate New York in 1967. Becker played guitar, whereas Fagen had studied jazz piano in high school, and the two decided to form a composing team. Following Fagen's graduation and Becker's dismissal, they unsuccessfully attempted to sell their songs around New York and formed a short-lived group on Long Island with guitarist Denny Dias. After composing the score to the obscure underground film *You Gotta Walk It Like You Talk It* (eventually issued in 1972 as an album), Fagen and Becker joined the back-up group to Jay and The Americans and toured with them in 1970 and 1971. Through that group's producer, Gary Katz, the team was hired as staff songwriters for ABC-Dunhill in Los Angeles, but their failure to write hit songs led them to form Steely Dan as a vehicle for their songwriting.

Formed in 1972, Steely Dan was initially comprised of Walter Becker (bass, vocals), Donald Fagen (keyboards, vocals), Denny Dias (guitar), Jeff "Skunk" Baxter (guitar and pedal steel guitar), David Palmer (lead vocals), and Jim Hodder (drums, vocals). Their exceptional debut album for ABC, *Can't Buy a Thrill*, included the disdainful "Dirty Work" and the vaguely political "Change of the Guard" and yielded near-smash hits with "Do It Again" and "Reeling in the Years." Touring infrequently, Steely Dan recorded its second jazz-inflected album without Palmer, as Fagen assumed the role of lead vocalist. The album failed to produce a major hit, but their next, *Pretzel Logic*, contained the smash hit "Rikki, Don't Lose That Number." Dismissing their band following their 1974 tour (with Baxter ultimately joining The Doobie Brothers), Fagen and Becker retained Denny Dias while recording subsequent albums with sessions musicians. Neither *Katy Lied* nor *The Royal Scam*, however, yielded a major hit and, during 1976, the two ostensibly signed with Warner Brothers Records while still apparently owing ABC two albums. The first, *Aja*, produced three major hits by the end of 1978, "Peg," "Deacon Blues," and "Josie," with the hit title song to the film *FM* intervening. By 1980, Steely Dan had completed its first album in three years, but its release was legally delayed by MCA Records, which bought ABC Records in 1979. Finally released at the end of 1980, *Gaucho* produced a major hit with "Hey, Nineteen."

FAGEN, BECKER, DIAS

You Gotta Walk It Like You Talk It (soundtrack)	Spark	02	March '72	

STEELY DAN

Can't Buy a Thrill*	ABC/MCA reissued on MCA	AB–758 37040	September '72	A
Countdown to Ecstasy*	ABC/MCA reissued on MCA	AB–779 37041	July '73	A
Pretzel Logic*	ABC/MCA reissued on MCA	AB–808 37042	March '74	A
Katy Lied*	ABC/MCA reissued on MCA	AB–846 37043	April '75	A
The Royal Scam*	ABC/MCA reissued on MCA	AB–931 37044	April '76	A
Aja**	ABC reissued on MCA	AB–1004 AA–1004	September '77	A
Greatest Hits**	2-ABC/MCA	AK–1107	October '78	A
Gaucho**	MCA	6102	December '80	A

STEPPENWOLF. Led by one-time folk singer John Kay, Steppenwolf scored two smash hits with the classics "Born to Be Wild" and "Magic Carpet Ride" during the late Sixties while recording Kay's decidedly existential and politically oriented compositions such as "Desperation," "The Ostrich," and "Don't Step on the Grass, Sam." After experiencing declining popularity following 1970's *Seven* album, Steppenwolf announced their disbandment in February 1972, and Kay went on to an inauspicious solo career; Steppenwolf re-formed in 1974 only to break up in 1976.

THE SPARROW

The Sparrow	Columbia	CS–9758	March '69

MARS BONFIRE

Faster Than the Speed of Life	Columbia	CS–9834	June '69

STEPPENWOLF

Early Steppenwolf	Dunhill	DS–50060	June '69	
Steppenwolf*	Dunhill	DS–50029	February '68	
	reissued on MCA	37045		A
The Second*	Dunhill	DS–50037	September '68	
	reissued on MCA	37046		A
At Your Birthday Party	Dunhill	DSX–50053	March '69	
Monster*	Dunhill	DS–50066	November '69	

T.I.M.E. (WITH LARRY BYROM AND NICK ST. NICHOLAS)

12 Originals	Liberty	LST–7558	May '68
Smooth Ball	Liberty	LST–7605	February '69

STEPPENWOLF

Live*	2-Dunhill	DSD–50075	April '70	A
Seven*	Dunhill	DSX–50090	October '70	
	reissued on MCA	37047		A
For Ladies Only	Dunhill	DSX–50110	September '71	

JOHN KAY

Forgotten Songs and Unsung Heroes	Dunhill	DSX–50120	April '72
My Sportin' Life	Dunhill	DSX–50147	May '73
All in Good Time	Mercury	3715	April '78

STEPPENWOLF

Slow Flux	Mums	PZ–33093	August '74
Hour of the Wolf	Epic	PE–33583	August '75
Skullduggery	Epic	PE–34120	April '76

STEPPENWOLF ANTHOLOGIES AND COMPILATIONS

Steppenwolf Gold*	Dunhill	DSX–50099	February '71	
Rest in Peace	Dunhill	DSX–50124	June '72	
16 Greatest Hits	Dunhill	DSX–50135	February '73	
	reissued on MCA	37049		A
16 Great Performances	ABC	4011	February '75	
	reissued on Pickwick	3603	April '78	A
Reborn to Be Wild	Epic	PE–34382	December '76	

CAT STEVENS. A popular English singer–songwriter, Cat Stevens utilized a distinctive acoustic guitar sound for his simple songs, backed by infectious rhythms, to produce a series of early Seventies hits before modifying his sound and writing rather mediocre songs without experiencing a lessening of his popularity. More recently, however, Cat Stevens has ceased performing and recording to become a practicing Moslem.

Born in London, England, on July 21, 1948, to Greek parents as Steve Georgiou, Cat Stevens began writing songs in the mid-Sixties while at Hammersmith College of Art. Signed to Deram Records on the strength of a demonstration tape, he hit the British charts with "I Love My Dog" and "Matthew and Son." Restricting his touring to England, Belgium, and France, Stevens nonetheless worked tirelessly and neglected his health to the point of requiring hospitalization in September 1968 for a long treatment for tuberculosis. Emerging in the spring of 1970, he returned to the studio with lead guitarist Alun Davies and a handful of recent compositions. The resulting album for A&M Records, *Mona Bone Jakon*, was critically hailed and led to his first recognition in the United States. His next album, *Tea for the Tillerman*, became his first certified gold-award album and included a number of exciting acoustic guitar songs such as "Where Do the Children Play," "Hard-Headed Woman," "Longer Boats," and "On the Road to Find Out," as well as the major hit "Wild World." The follow-up, *Teaser and the Firecat*, was similarly intriguing and contained "Bitterblue" plus the hits "Moon Shadow," "Peace Train," and "Morning Has Broken." In late 1971, *Very Young and Early Songs*, an album of Sixties material, was issued on Deram; *Catch Bull at Four* yielded only one hit, "Sitting." Alun Davies recorded a solo album in 1972, and Stevens subsequently abandoned his guitar-dominated sound in favor of the piano. Hitting with "Oh Very Young" and Sam Cooke's "Another Saturday Night" in 1974, Cat Stevens managed only moderate hits with "Ready," "Two Fine People," "Banapple Gas," and "(Remember the Days of the) Old School Yard" through 1977. Around 1977 Cat Stevens became a Moslem, adopted the name Yusef Islam, and subsequently dropped entirely out of music after 1978's *Back to the Earth*.

CAT STEVENS

Matthew and Son	Deram	18005	May '67	
New Masters	Deram	18010	February '68	
Very Young and Early Songs	Deram	DES–18061	December '71	
Cat's Cradle	London	50010	February '78	A
Mona Bone Jakon *	A&M	4260	August '70	A
Tea for the Tillerman *	A&M	SP–4280	December '70	A
Teaser and the Firecat *	A&M	SP–4313	October '71	A
Catch Bull at Four *	A&M	SP–4365	October '72	A
Foreigner *	A&M	SP–4391	July '73	A
Buddah and the Chocolate Box *	A&M	SP–3623	March '74	A

Greatest Hits*	A&M	4519	July '75	
Numbers*	A&M	SP-4555	November '75	A
Izitso*	A&M	SP-4702	May '77	A
Back to the Earth	A&M	4735	December '78	A

ALUN DAVIES

| Daydo | Columbia | KC–31469 | October '72 |

AL STEWART. An English folk-style artist of the late Sixties, Al Stewart saw only one of his first four albums ever released in the United States. That album, *Love Chronicles*, featured the 18-minute title song which recounted his personal travails with love from childhood to adulthood. Adopting an electric back-up band and composing narrative-style songs self-consciously drawn from historical and literary sources, Al Stewart broke through in the United States with late 1976's "Year of the Cat," although his American popularity has not been matched in England.

AL STEWART

Love Chronicles	Epic	BN–26564	July '70	
Early Years	2-Janus	7026	April '79	
Past, Present, and Future	Janus	JLS–3063	March '74	
	reissued on Arista	9524		A
Modern Times	Janus	7012	February '75	
	reissued on Arista	9525		A
The Year of the Cat**	Janus	7022	September '76	
	reissued on Arista	9503		A
Time Passages**	Arista	4190	September '78	A
Live: Indian Summer	2-Arista	8607	November '81	A

AL STEWART AND SHOT IN THE DARK

| 24 PCarrots | Arista | 9520 | September '80 | A |

JOHN STEWART. Until recently best remembered as a former member of The Kingston Trio and as the author of The Monkees' 1967–68 top hit "Daydream Believer," John Stewart combined the themes of love for a woman and fascination with rural America for his own recordings on several different labels, including his acknowledged classic *California Bloodlines* and the sorely neglected *Lonesome Picker Rides Again*. Without a major hit or best-selling album through a decade of solo recording, Stewart finally took up electric guitar, abandoned his preoccupation with Americana, and scored a smash hit with 1979's somewhat cynical "(Turning Music into) Gold."

THE CUMBERLAND THREE

Folk Scene	Roulette	SR–25121	June '60
Civil War Almanac—Volume 1 (Yankees)	Roulette	SR–25132	October '60
Civil War Almanac—Volume 2 (Rebels)	Roulette	SR–25133	October '60

JOHN STEWART AND SCOTT ENGEL

I Only Came to Dance with You	Tower	5026(M)	June '66

JOHN STEWART AND BUFFY FORD

John Stewart and Buffy Ford	Capitol	ST–2975	September '68	
reissued as Signals through the Glass	Capitol	SM–2975 reissued as SN–11988 reissued as SN–16152	November '75 October '79	A

JOHN STEWART

California Bloodlines	Capitol	ST–203 reissued as SN–11987 reissued as SN–16150	June '69 October '79	A
Willard	Capitol	ST–540 reissued as SN–11989 reissued as SN–16151	July '70 October '79	A
The Lonesome Picker Rides Again	Warner Brothers	WS–1948	November '71	
Sunstorm	Warner Brothers	BS–2611	May '72	
Cannons in the Rain	RCA	AFL1–4827 reissued as AYL1–3731	March '73	A
The Phoenix Concerts	2-RCA	CPL2–0265	May '74	
Wingless Angels	RCA	APL1–0816	April '75	

In Concert	RCA	AFL1–3513	February '80	
Fire in the Wind	Polydor	3027	October '77	
Bombs Away, Dream Babies	RSO	3051	May '79	A
Dream Babies Go Hollywood	RSO	3074	April '80	A

ROD STEWART. A one-time member of many of the seminal British rhythm-and-blues style bands of 1963–66, Rod Stewart first gained recognition as the vocalist with The Jeff Beck Group during the late Sixties. Pursuing a solo recording career while performing and recording with The Faces, one of Britain's best rock bands of the Seventies, Stewart quickly eclipsed the group's popularity with his *Gasoline Alley* album, arguably his finest, and became a "superstar" with *Every Picture Tells a Story* and its classic top hit single, "Maggie May." An excellent songwriter as evidenced by "Lady Day," "Mandolin Wind," and "Maggie May," Stewart developed a flamboyant, athletic, and spectacular stage act with The Faces that, along with his raspy vocal style, remained his trademark after his split from The Faces at the end of 1975. Without a major hit for four years after "You Wear It Well," Rod Stewart nonetheless became an international celebrity and regained popular if not critical acclaim with *A Night on the Town* and its mildly controversial top hit, "Tonight's the Night." After scoring a smash hit with "You're in My Heart" from his next album, Stewart seemed to have lost much of his musical and lyrical vitality as evidenced by *Blondes Have More Fun* and its silly disco-style top hit, "Do Ya Think I'm Sexy?"

Born in north London, England, on January 10, 1945, to Scottish parents, Rod Stewart attended the same secondary school as did Ray and Dave Davies (later of The Kinks) and worked a variety of jobs after school. He subsequently hitchhiked around Europe for two years and learned guitar, then returned to England, where he joined Jimmy Powell and The Five Dimensions as harmonica player and manned the group for part of 1963 and 1964. Stewart recorded "Good Morning Little Schoolgirl" for Decca solo in 1964, joined the rhythm-and-blues band The Hoochie Coochie Men during the year, and shared lead vocals with leader "Long" John Baldry; he stayed with the group until it disbanded in the autumn of 1965. He then joined Baldry's Steampacket, which also included Julie Driscoll and Brian Auger, for a year before joining the short-lived aggregation Shotgun Express, whose members included guitarist Peter Green and drummer Mick Fleetwood, who later formed Fleetwood Mac. In early 1967 Stewart helped form The Jeff Beck Group with former Yardbirds lead guitarist Jeff Beck and bassist–guitarist Ron Wood. That group became widely popular in the United States by means of numerous tours over the next two years, and Stewart became recognized as a distinctive and potent vocalist. However, The Jeff Beck Group's career was notably unstable and the band fragmented in mid-1969.

Already signed as a solo artist to Mercury Records, Rod Stewart pursued a parallel career with the Faces, which evolved out of The Small Faces, whose leader Steve Marriott had quit the group to form Humble Pie with Peter Frampton. In addition to Stewart, The Faces were Ron Wood, keyboardist Ian McLagan, bassist Ronnie Lane, and drummer Kenney Jones. Even before The Faces had recorded their debut album for Warner Brothers, Mercury issued *The Rod Stewart Album*, which sold poorly despite the inclusion of Mike D'Abo's "Handbags and Gladrags" and The Rolling Stones' "Street-Fighting Man." Recording his solo albums with Wood, McLagan, guitarist Martin Quittenton, and drummer Mick Waller (previously with Steampacket and The Jeff Beck Group), Stewart overshadowed the career of The Faces beginning with his second solo album, *Gasoline Alley*. Though the album failed to yield a hit single, it sold respectably, particularly in the United States, and included Elton John and Bernie Taupin's "Country Comforts," Stewart's own "Lady Day," and the title song written by Stewart and Wood. Developing an energetic and flamboyant stage act through successful American tours with The Faces beginning in 1970, Stewart became an internationally recognized star with *Every Picture Tells a Story* and its classic hit single, "Maggie May," written by Stewart and Quittenton. The album also contained Stewart's beautiful "Mandolin Wind" and the major hit " (I Know) I'm Losing You," a near-smash hit for The Temptations in 1966–67. After achieving a major hit with Wood and Stewart's "Stay with Me" by The Faces, Stewart's *Never a Dull Moment* yielded a major hit with "You Wear It Well" and a moderate hit with "Angel," while including "I'd Rather Go Blind." Subsequently involved with contractual disputes between Mercury and Warner Brothers, Stewart saw his next album, *Smiler*, delayed nearly a year and, upon release, it sold poorly compared to prior albums, producing no major hit single. Ron Wood toured America with The Rolling Stones during 1975 and, following The Faces' subsequent U.S. tour, Rod Stewart announced his departure from the group in December.

Having signed with Warner Brothers in the spring of 1975, Rod Stewart recorded *Atlantic Crossing* without the assistance of The Faces in Muscle Shoals, Alabama. Seemingly marking a deterioration of his songwriting, the album included no major hit singles, yet became a best-seller. Stewart formed his own road band during 1976 with three guitarists and drummer Carmine Appice (of Vanilla Fudge and Beck, Bogert, and Appice), among others. His next album, *A Night on the Town*, became his first certified platinum-award album, yielding the top hit "Tonight's the Night (Gonna Be Alright)" and the major hits "The First Cut Is the Deepest" (by Cat Stevens) and "The Killing of Georgie." Conducting a massive worldwide tour between mid-1976 and late 1977, Stewart's *Foot-Loose and Fancy Free* produced the smash hit "You're in My Heart (The Final Acclaim)" and major hits with the disco style "Hot Legs" and "I Was Only Joking." By this time a recognized international celebrity, Rod Stewart again mounted a marathon world tour in support of *Blondes Have More Fun*, which included the trivial top hit "Do Ya Think I'm Sexy" and the major hit "Ain't Love a Bitch." After scoring a smash hit with

"Passion" in late 1980, Stewart conducted another American tour in 1981–1982, and his December 19 show at the L. A. Forum was watched by an estimated 35 million viewers on independent television stations in the U.S and 23 foreign countries.

ROD STEWART AND STEAMPACKET

Rod Stewart and Steampacket	Springboard International	4063	November '76	

ROD STEWART

The Rod Stewart Album	Mercury	SR–61237 reissued as ML–8001	December '69	A
Gasoline Alley	Mercury	SR–61264	June '70	A
Every Picture Tells a Story*	Mercury	SRM1–609	May '71	A
Never a Dull Moment*	Mercury	SRM1–646	July '72	A
Smiler	Mercury	SRM1–1017	October '74	
Atlantic Crossing*	Warner Brothers	BS–2875 reissued as BSK–3108	August '75	A
A Night on the Town**	Warner Brothers	BS–2938 reissued as BSK–3316	July '76	A
Foot-Loose and Fancy Free**	Warner Brothers	BSK–3092	October '77	A
Blondes Have More Fun**	Warner Brothers	3261	December '78	A
Foolish Behaviour**	Warner Brothers	HS–3485	November '80	A
Tonight I'm Yours	Warner Brothers	3602	October '81	A

ROD STEWART ANTHOLOGIES AND COMPILATIONS

A Shot of Rhythm and Blues	Private Stock	PS–2021	December '76	
Rod the Mod	Accord	SN–7142	December '81	A
Sing It Again, Rod*	Mercury	SRM1–680	July '73	A
The Best of Rod Stewart*	2-Mercury	SRM2–7507	May '76	A
The Best of Rod Stewart, Volume 2	2-Mercury	SRM2–7509	January '77	
Greatest Hits, Volume 1**	Warner Brothers	HS–3373	October '79	A

STEPHEN STILLS. Probably best remembered for his *Supersessions* album with Al Kooper, his involvement in the "folk-rock" Buffalo Springfield, and the on-again, off-again Crosby, Stills, Nash (and Young) aggregation, Stephen Stills has regularly recorded solo and ensemble albums since 1970, highlighted by his solo debut, *Stephen Stills*. Having built a reputation as one of America's finest guitarists, Stills recorded with Manassas in the early Seventies, later introduced guitarist Donnie Dacus (later with Chicago), and recorded the best-selling *Long May You Run* album with former associate Neil Young and *CSN* with Crosby and Nash.

Born in Dallas, Texas, on January 3, 1945, Stephen Stills was well-traveled as a youth and mastered piano, drums, and guitar by the time he was a teenager. Associated with Florida high school bands such as The Radars, he played folk music around New Orleans after graduation and traveled to New York around 1964, where he manned the large vocal group The Au Go Go Singers with Richie Furay. After moving to California, Stills helped form The Buffalo Springfield and wrote that group's first hit, the classic "For What It's Worth." Remaining with the group through three albums until May 1968, he was featured guitarist on one side of the certified gold-award *Supersession* album with Al Kooper. In December 1968 Stills, ex-Byrd David Crosby, and ex-Hollie Graham Nash announced the formation of their "supergroup," and their debut album contained four Stills songs, including "Helplessly Hoping" and the hit "Suite: Judy Blue Eyes." Joined by Neil Young in the summer of 1969, the group appeared at the Woodstock Festival and conducted a world-wide tour that concluded in London in early 1970, shortly after which the quartet's first album, *Deja Vu*, featuring Stills' "Carry On" and "4 & 20," was issued.

Stephen Stills' debut solo album, recorded in London and Los Angeles with the assistance of vocalists Rita Coolidge, John Sebastian, Crosby, and Nash, yielded his only major hit with "Love the One You're With." Comprised entirely of Stills songs, the album also contained the moderate hit "Sit Yourself Down," the inebriated "Black Queen," and "We Are Not Helpless," plus the instrumental "Old Times, Good Times" (featuring Jimi Hendrix) and "Go Back Home" (with Eric Clapton on second lead guitar). After touring again with Crosby, Nash, and Young during the summer of 1970, Stills released his second solo album, which included "Sugar Babe" and "Singin' Call" and yielded moderate hits with "Change Partners" and "Marianne." Launching his first major solo tour in July 1971 with keyboardist Paul Harris, bassist Calvin "Fuzzy" Samuels, and drummer Dallas Taylor, Stills subsequently formed Manassas in October with those three plus former Flying Burrito Brother Chris Hillman and pedal steel guitarist Al Perkins. Although accompanied by extensive touring, Manassas' debut album produced no major hits, yet contained Stills' "So Begins the Task" and "Johnny's Garden." Following a second less well-received album, Manassas disintegrated in September 1973 when Hillman, Perkins, and Harris left to form The Souther–Hillman–Furay Band. Stills formed a new band with guitarist Donnie Dacus and keyboardist Jerry Aiello, but he reunited with Crosby, Nash, and Young in May 1974 and concluded another world tour in London in early 1975. After a switch to Columbia Records, Stills' debut album for the label featured Dacus and Aiello and yielded his last minor hit with "Turn Back the Pages," co-authored by Dacus. Stills assembled yet another band for 1976's *Illegal Stills* and subsequently formed The Stills–Young Band with Neil Young, Jerry Aiello, bassist George Perry, percussionist Joe Lala, and drummer Joe Vitale. Having recorded only one album, highlighted by Young's title song, "Long May You Run," the group dissolved during their 1976 tour due to Young's recurring throat problem. Stephen Stills next reunited with David Crosby and Graham Nash for *CSN*, which featured Still's "Dark Star," before recording his poorly received *Thoroughfare Gap*.

BLOOMFIELD, KOOPER, AND STILLS

Supersession*	Columbia	PC–9701	August '68	A

STEPHEN STILLS

Stephen Stills*	Atlantic	SD–7202	November '70	A
Stephen Stills 2*	Atlantic	SD–7206	June '71	A
Manassas*	2-Atlantic	SD2–903	April '72	A
Down the Road (with Manassas)	Atlantic	SD–7250	May '73	A
Live	Atlantic	SD–18156	December '75	A
Still Stills—The Best of Stephen Stills	Atlantic	SD–18201	January '77	
Stills	Columbia	PC–33575	June '75	A
Illegal Stills	Columbia	PC–34148	April '76	A
Thoroughfare Gap	Columbia	PC–35380	October '78	A

THE STILLS–YOUNG BAND

Long May You Run*	Reprise	MS–2253	September '76	A

THE STOOGES/IGGY POP. Now generally considered the chief forerunner to many of the so-called "punk" groups of the late Seventies with their minimalist music and vituperative and insolent lyrics, The Stooges were led by Iggy Pop, whose spontaneously outrageous and sadomasochistic onstage behavior served as a precursor to the calculated theatrical excesses of Alice Cooper and Kiss. While The Stooges' first two albums became prized collectors' items, their third, *Raw Power*, was viewed by some as the quintessential "heavy metal" album of the early Seventies. That album was produced by mentor David Bowie, and the professional association with Bowie helped Iggy Pop gain an air of respectability and a degree of mainstream acknowledgement he might not have otherwise attained. Following a chaotic period of drug and psychological problems, Iggy Pop re-emerged in 1977 with two uneven albums for RCA Records that strengthened the ardent cult following for his bizarre and frankly disconcerting public persona.

Born James Osterberg in Ann Arbor, Michigan, around 1947, Iggy Stooge first played drums and sang lead with the Detroit-area high school band The Iguanas and later manned The Prime Movers. After traveling to Chicago to drum for a blues band, he returned to Detroit where he formed The Stooges with Asheton brothers Ron and Scott (guitar and drums, respectively) and Dave Alexander (bass). Debuting in Ann Arbor on Halloween in 1967, The Stooges performed loud, three-chord rock music fronted by the vocals and disturbing onstage antics of Iggy. Over the years, his notoriety grew with deeds such as threatening and vilifying audiences, cutting himself with broken bottles, pouring hot wax over his body, intentionally smashing out his teeth, and throwing up, even urinating on audiences and allowing ardent fans to perform fellatio on him. Signed to Elektra Records, The Stooges recorded their debut album under producer John Cale of The Velvet Underground. It featured Stooges' favorites such as "No Fun" and "I Wanna Be Your Dog" and sold marginally, but the follow-up, *Funhouse*, failed even to make the album charts and the group experienced a period of disintegration. Taken to England by mentor David Bowie in 1972, Osterberg and new guitarist James Williamson were joined by the Asheton brothers for the Bowie-produced *Raw Power* on Columbia, one of the classics of so-called "heavy metal" music. Featured songs included "Search and Destroy," "Gimme Danger," "Death Trip," and "Your Pretty Face Is Going to Hell." The Stooges eventually broke up in early 1974 and Osterberg ended up in Los Angeles, where he became addicted to heroin, later kicked his habit, and entered a mental hospital in 1975. After moving to West Berlin in the spring of 1976, he again encountered Bowie, who managed to secure for him a recording contract with RCA Records. His two 1977 albums for the label, *The Idiot* and *Lust for Life*, were critically hailed, and Osterberg, using the name Iggy Pop, returned to live performance, often accompanied by Bowie on keyboards. Following a live album for RCA, Iggy Pop switched to Arista Records for 1979's *New Values* and another round of disturbing, if not outrageous, live performances late that year with former Sex Pistols bassist Glen Matlock and guitarist–keyboardist Ivan Kral from The Patti Smith Group. In 1980 Arista issued *Soldier* for Iggy Pop, followed in 1981 by *Party*.

THE STOOGES

The Stooges	Elektra	EKS–74051	August '69
Funhouse	Elektra	EKS–74071	September '70
Raw Power	Columbia	PC–32111	February '73

IGGY POP

The Idiot	RCA	APL1–2275	March '77
Lust for Life	RCA	APL1–2488	September '77

TV Eye—1977 Live	RCA	AFL1– 2796	May '78	
New Values	Arista	4237	August '79	
Soldier	Arista	4259	March '80	A
Party	Arista	9572	September '81	A

THE SWEET. Although achieving enormous British success during the early Seventies with "bubblegum" songs written by the songwriting-management team of Nicky Chinn and Mike Chapman, The Sweet were regularly castigated critically for their live performances and recordings. After adopting a "glitter-rock" pose in 1972, The Sweet became European stars by the time of the release of Chinn and Chapman's "Little Willy," their first American smash hit. Having left the directorship of Chinn and Chapman in late 1974, the group later scored smash hits with their own "Fox on the Run" and "Love Is like Oxygen"; they have experienced diminished popularity since the departure of lead vocalist Brian Connolly. In the meantime, Mike Chapman achieved widespread success as the producer of smash hits for Nick Gilder ("Hot Child in the City"), Exile ("Kiss You All Over"), and Suzi Quatro ("Stumblin' In") and as producer of certified platinum-award albums for Blondie (*Parallel Lines*) and The Knack (*Get The Knack*); he and Nicky Chinn formed their own record label, Dreamland Records, distributed by RSO, in 1980.

THE SWEET

The Sweet	Bell	1125	July '73	
Desolation Boule-vard*	Capitol	ST–11395	May '75	A
Give Us a Wink!	Capitol	ST–11496 reissued as SN–16115	February '76	A
Off the Record	Capitol	STAO–11636 reissued as SN–16116	May '77	A
Level-Headed	Capitol	SKAO–11744 reissued as SN–16117	February '78	A
Cut Above the Rest	Capitol	SO–11929 reissued as SN–16118	May '79	A
Sweet VI	Capitol	ST–12106	September '80	A

JAMES, LIVINGSTON, KATE, AND ALEX TAYLOR.   One of the first non-British acts signed to The Beatles' Apple label, James Taylor switched to Warner Brothers with the assistance of manager–producer Peter Asher (of Peter and Gordon fame) and soon established himself in the forefront of the Seventies singer–songwriter movement with the desperately personal smash hit "Fire and Rain" and his *Sweet Baby James* album. Finding a mass audience among both pop and easy listening fans, Taylor toured and recorded with Carole King in early 1971, scored a top hit with her "You've Got a Friend," and subsequently formed the excellent touring and recording group The Section, who eventually recorded several albums of their own. James' siblings Livingston, Kate, and Alex Taylor also initiated recording careers during 1970–71, but all three became stalled after 1974, by which time James Taylor's songs reflected less personal anguish and more gentle compassion, probably due to the domesticity of married life with Carly Simon. Without a major hit between 1973 and the spring of 1975, James Taylor most recently hit with remakes of early Sixties classics. Both Kate and Livingston Taylor re-emerged with new albums in 1978, but only Livingston achieved a major hit single.

Alex, James, and Kate Taylor were all born in Boston, Massachusetts, Alex in 1947, James on March 12, 1948, and Kate on August 15, 1949, whereas Livingston was born in nearby Weston in 1951. Raised in affluence, the Taylor children moved with their parents to Chapel Hill, North Carolina, after Livingston's birth and subsequently spent summers on exclusive Martha's Vineyard beginning in 1953. From an early age, Alex studied violin, Livingston and Kate learned piano, and James took cello lessons. After meeting guitarist Danny "Kootch" Kortchmar on Martha's Vineyard in 1963, James Taylor formed The Fabulous Corsairs with brother Alex and three friends in North Carolina in 1964. While later attending boarding school near Boston, James began to suffer bouts of depression, which led him to commit himself voluntarily to a psychiatric hospital in 1965, where he began to write songs. After discharging himself nine months later, he went to New York City in the summer of 1966, where he formed The Flying Machine with Kortchmar, drummer Joel O'Brien, and bassist Zach Weisner. The group debuted at the Cafe Bizarre that fall and later moved up to The Night Owl, where they played regularly for nearly seven months. They also made some recordings, before disintegrating in the spring of 1967, which were issued after the success of *Sweet Baby James*.

James Taylor next moved to London, where he made a demonstration tape that so impressed Paul McCartney and Apple A&R chief Peter Asher that he was signed to The Beatles' record label. Taylor's debut solo album, which contained odd orchestral segues between songs, featured "Knocking 'round the Zoo" (which recollected his stay in the mental hospital), "Something in the Way She Moves," the excellent "Carolina on My Mind" and "Rainy-Day Man," and the ominous "The Blues Is Just a Bad Dream." However, the album went generally unnoticed; with affairs in disarray at Apple, Peter Asher negotiated a contract for Taylor with Warner Brothers Records, as the artist again entered a mental institution. After debuting at Los Angeles' Troubadour in the summer of 1969, James Taylor recorded his next album in California with Asher, now his manager, producing. *Sweet Baby James* became a best-selling album and established him at the forefront of the emerging singer–songwriter movement with its anguished smash hit single, "Fire and Rain." Recorded with Danny Kortchmar, Carole King, and drummer Russ Kunkel, among others, the album also featured the moderate hit "Country Road" and the gentle "Sunny Skies" and "Blossom." In early 1971 Taylor recorded *Mud Slide Slim* with King, Kortchmar, Kunkel, and bassist Leland Sklar under producer Asher and subsequently toured with Carole King, backed by the same musicians. The album yielded a top hit with King's "You've Got a Friend" and a moderate hit with "Long Ago and Far Away" and contained the classic "Hey Mister, That's Me up on the Jukebox."

Livingston Taylor, who had played Boston folk clubs during 1968, was the first of James Taylor's siblings to secure a recording contract. His debut album sold modestly and even produced a minor hit with "Carolina Day," but his next two albums for Capricorn Records fared dismally. Kate Taylor, also managed by Peter Asher, recorded her debut album for Cotillion Records with brother James, Carole King, and Linda Ronstadt, and it sold modestly without yielding a hit single. Alex Taylor fared least well of the three with only his debut Capricorn album making the charts; he persevered through two more albums, the last for Dunhill Records in 1974. Earlier, The Section, with keyboardist Craig Doerge, guitarist Danny Kortchmar, bassist Leland Sklar, and drummer Russ Kunkel, formed to back and tour with James Taylor, and recorded two albums of their own for Warner Brothers Records. During 1973 Kortchmar also recorded a solo album for Warner Brothers. The Section subsequently served as Peter Asher's "house band" and later toured with Jackson Browne on his *Running on Empty* tour.

In November 1972 James Taylor married Carly Simon; his next album release, *One-Man Dog*, backed by The Section and recorded on Martha's Vineyard with the vocal assistance of Carole King, Linda Ronstadt, and Simon, yielded a major hit with "Don't Let Me Be Lonely Tonight." In 1973 he co-starred with Beach Boy Dennis Wilson in the film *Two-Lane Blacktop* and scored a smash hit with Carly Simon on a deplorable off-key remake of "Mockingbird" (originally a near-smash for Charlie and Inez Foxx in 1963). Taylor's next album, *Walking Man*, his first not produced by Peter Asher, broke his string of gold-award albums and failed to furnish a hit single. However, 1975's *Gorilla* produced a smash hit with Holland–Dozier–Holland's "How Sweet It Is (to Be Loved by You)" (a smash hit for Marvin Gaye in 1964–65) and the minor hit "Mexico." After touring again in 1975, Taylor recorded his final album for Warner Brothers, *In the Pocket*, which yielded a major hit with "Shower the People"; he then switched to Columbia Records. His debut for the label, *JT*, produced by Peter Asher, furnished a smash hit with a remake of "Handyman" (a smash hit for Jimmy Jones in 1960), a major hit with "Your Smiling Face," and also included "Bartender's Blues," a major country-and-western hit for George Jones in 1978. During that year, Taylor had a major hit with Art Garfunkel and Paul Simon on a remake of Sam Cooke's "(What a) Wonderful World" and a moderate hit with The Everly Brothers' "Devoted to You" in conjunction with Carly Simon. His next album, *Flag*, produced a moderate hit with Carole King and Gerry Goffin's classic, "Up on the Roof."

During 1977 The Section recorded another album, *Fork It Over*, for Capitol Records, and the following year both Kate and Livingston Taylor re-emerged with new albums. Kate had spent the last six years on Martha's Vineyard, whereas Livingston had continued to play in clubs and at colleges during the interim. He managed a moderate hit with "I Will Be in Love with You" and a minor hit with "I'll Come Running" in 1978–79, but Kate's second Columbia album fared poorly. During 1980 Dany Kortchmar and Livingston Taylor both had solo albums issued by Asylum and Epic Records, respectively, and Livingston scored a moderate hit with "First-Time Love." During 1981 James Taylor managed a hit with "Her Town Too" in duet with J. D. Souther.

JAMES TAYLOR

James Taylor and The Original Flying Machine—1967	Euphoria reissued on Springboard International	EST–2 4023	January '71 June '75	
James Taylor	Apple	SKAO–3352	December '68	
Sweet Baby James *	Warner Brothers	WS–1843	February '70	A
Mud Slide Slim and the Blue Horizon *	Warner Brothers	BS–2561	March '71	A

LIVINGSTON TAYLOR

Livingston Taylor	Atco	SD33–334	July '70
Liv	Capricorn	SD–863	November '71
Over the Rainbow	Capricorn	CP–0114	October '73

3-Way Mirror	Epic	JE–35540	August '78	A
Man's Best Friend	Epic	JE–36153	May '80	A

KATE TAYLOR

Sister Kate	Cotillion	SD–9045	February '71
Kate Taylor	Columbia	JC–35089	May '78
It's in There and It's Got to Come Out	Columbia	JC–36034	July '79

ALEX TAYLOR

With Friends and Neighbors	Capricorn	SD–860	March '71
Dinnertime	Capricorn	CP–0101	March '72
The Third Time's for Music	Dunhill	50151	April '74

JO MAMA (WITH DANNY KORTCHMAR)

Jo Mama	Atlantic	8269	December '70
J Is for Jump	Atlantic	8288	September '71

DANNY KORTCHMAR

Kootch	Warner Brothers	BS–2711	August '73	
Innuendo	Asylum	250	January '80	A

THE SECTION

The Section	Warner Brothers	BS–2661	October '72
Forward Motion	Warner Brothers	BS–2714	September '73
Fork It Over	Capitol	ST–11656	June '77

JAMES TAYLOR

One-Man Dog*	Warner Brothers	BS–2660	October '72	A
Walking Man	Warner Brothers	W–2794	June '74	A
Gorilla*	Warner Brothers	BS–2866	May '75	A
In the Pocket*	Warner Brothers	BS–2912	June '76	A
Greatest Hits**	Warner Brothers	BS–2979 reissued as 3113	October '76	A
JT**	Columbia	JC–34811	June '77	A
Flag*	Columbia	FC–36058	May '79	A
Dad Loves His Work*	Columbia	TC–37009	April '81	A

THE TEMPTATIONS/JIMMY AND DAVID RUFFIN/EDDIE KENDRICKS.

Motown's longest enduring and most popular male vocal group, The Temptations achieved their earliest success under the aegis of songwriter–producer Smokey Robinson, who co-wrote their first major hit, "The Way You Do the Things You Do" and the classic "My Girl." Working primarily under producer–songwriter Norman Whitfield after early 1966, The Temptations scored a dozen major hits featuring the brilliant combination of David Ruffin's rich, earthy voice and Eddie Kendricks' plaintive near-falsetto voice, including the classics "(I Know) I'm Losing You" and "I Wish It Would Rain." With the departure of Ruffin in 1968, Whitfield capitalized on the musical advances of Sly and the Family Stone and the developing social-consciousness of lyrics in black music by experimenting with so-called "psychedelic soul" for The Temptations with song collaborator Barrett Strong during the late Sixties and early Seventies. They provided the group with the smash hits "Cloud Nine," "Psychedelic Shack," "Ball of Confusion," and the classic, "Papa Was a Rolling Stone," with the more traditionally styled "Just My Imagination" intervening. Suffering several personnel changes during their career, The Temptations lost Kendricks to a solo career in 1971. Although David Ruffin (with 1969's "My Whole World Ended") and Kendricks (with "Keep On Truckin'" and "Boogie Down" from 1973–74) both enjoyed periods of widespread popularity and The Temptations rebounded with the 1973 near-smash "Masterpiece," none have retained the enormous public adulation received by The Temptations during the Sixties. Moreover, during 1979 neither Kendricks, Ruffin, nor The Temptations were recording for the Motown organization, although The Temptations did return to the fold in 1980.

The evolution of The Temptations began during the late Fifties with two Detroit-based groups, The Primes and The Distants. The Distants, which included baritone Otis Williams (born Otis Miles on October 30, 1941, in Texarkana, Texas), bass vocalist Melvin Franklin (born David English on October 12, 1942, in Montgomery, Alabama), Richard Street (born October 5, 1942, in Detroit) and Elbridge Bryant, had evolved out of The Questions and The Elegants. The Distants had managed a local hit for Northern Records around 1959. The Primes (whose companion group The Primettes later became The Supremes) included tenor vocalist Eddie Kendricks (born December 17, 1939, in Birmingham, Alabama) and Paul Williams (born July 2, 1939, in Birmingham). In 1960 Kendricks and Paul Williams joined Bryant, Franklin, and Otis Williams to become The Elgins and signed with Berry Gordy, Jr.'s Miracle label. After switching to Motown's Gordy label and adopting the name The Temptations, the group scored a minor rhythm-and-blues hit in 1962 with "Dream Come True," but in late 1963 Bryant quit the group and was replaced by baritone David Ruffin (born January 18, 1941, in Meridian, Mississippi).

In early 1964 The Temptations achieved their first major pop hit with "The Way You Do the Things You Do," co-written and produced by

William "Smokey" Robinson and featuring the lead vocals of Eddie Kendricks, who shared lead vocal chores with David Ruffin throughout their association. After two moderate hits, the group scored a top pop hit with the classic "My Girl," written and produced by Robinson and Ronald White, with Ruffin on lead vocals. Subsequent hits for The Temptations produced and co-written by Robinson included "It's Growing," "Since I Lost My Baby," "My Baby," and "Get Ready," but thereafter the group recorded primarily under songwriter–producer Norman Whitfield. Through mid-1968 he produced and co-authored the smash and near-smash hits "Ain't Too Proud to Beg," "Beauty Is Only Skin Deep," "(I Know) I'm Losing You," "You're My Everything," "(Loneliness Made Me Realize) It's You that I Need," the classic "I Wish It Would Rain," and "I Could Never Love Another (after Loving You)" for The Temptations, with "All I Need," produced by Frank Wilson, intervening in 1967. In July 1968 David Ruffin left the group for a solo career, and was replaced by Dennis Edwards (born February 3, 1943, in Birmingham, Alabama) of The Contours. By then, former Distant and Monitor member Richard Street had begun filling in for an ailing Paul Williams.

David Ruffin's brother Jimmy, born May 7, 1939, in Collinsville, Mississippi, had been recording for Berry Gordy's Soul label since 1966. He had scored a near-smash pop hit that year with "What Becomes of the Broken Hearted," followed by the major hits "I've Passed This Way Before" and "Gonna Give Her All the Love I've Got," but thereafter his singles became only minor hits. David Ruffin had a near-smash solo hit in early 1969 with "My Whole World Ended (the Moment You Left Me)," but his subsequent releases also fared poorly. A 1970 duet album by the brothers failed to arrest their slip from popularity and, by 1972, Jimmy Ruffin had left the Motown organization. David Ruffin stayed on, eventually achieved a near-smash hit in late 1975 with "Walk Away from Love," and switched to Warner Brothers for 1979's *So Soon We Change*.

The reconstituted Temptations were teamed with The Supremes during 1968 and 1969 and scored a smash hit with "I'm Gonna Make You Love Me." Beginning in late 1968 Norman Whitfield began experimenting with the musical advances of Sly and The Family Stone and writing songs alternately "psychedelic" and socially conscious for The Temptations. With this new sound, dubbed "psychedelic soul," the group achieved a series of smash and near-smash hits into 1970 with "Cloud Nine," "Run-Away Child, Running Wild," the classic "I Can't Get Next to You," "Psychedelic Shack," and "Ball of Confusion," all co-written by Whitfield and Barrett Strong. The Temptations returned to their mellow ballad style in 1971 for the classic top hit "Just My Imagination (Running Away with Me)" with Eddie Kendricks on lead vocals, but that summer Kendricks left the group for a solo career and was permanently replaced by Damon Harris (born July 3, 1950, in Baltimore). Around the same time, Paul Williams retired from touring due to illness and was replaced by stand-in Richard Street. On August 17, 1973, Paul Williams was found dead in his car in Detroit, an apparent suicide at the age of 34.

In late 1971 The Temptations scored a major hit with "Superstar (Remember How You Got Where You Are)," followed by the classic top hit "Papa was a Rollin' Stone" in late 1972 and the near-smash "Masterpiece" in early 1973. Subsequent releases proved only moderate pop hits; Damon Harris was asked to leave the group in 1975 and was replaced by tenor Glenn Leonard (born 1948 in Washington, D.C.), a former member of True Reflection. Harris returned to his prior group, The Vandals, who later became Impact, and recorded two albums before his solo bid in late 1978. Following the largely self-produced *The Temptations Do The Temptations*, Dennis Edwards left the group, was replaced by lead vocalist Louis Price (born 1953 in Chicago), and The Temptations signed with Atlantic Records in May 1977. Having achieved no hits for Atlantic, not even from the Brian and Eddie Holland-produced *Bare Back*, The Temptations moved back to Motown's Gordy label and replaced Louis Price with the returned Dennis Edwards. The title song to 1980's *Power*, written by Berry Gordy, Jr., became a moderate hit.

In the meantime, Eddie Kendricks' solo career had taken off slowly. He eventually achieved smash hits in 1973–74 with the up-tempo disco-oriented songs, "Keep on Truckin'" and "Boogie Down," but since the follow-up hit "Son of Sagittarius," Kendricks has scored only one other major pop hit, 1975's "Shoeshine Boy." During 1977 Eddie Kendricks switched to Arista Records, where he has not yet hit. Surprisingly, Jimmy Ruffin scored a near-smash hit in 1980 with "Hold On to My Love."

THE TEMPTATIONS

Meet The Temptations	Gordy	911	April '64	
Sing Smokey	Gordy	912	February '65	
Temptin'	Gordy	914	November '65	
Gettin' Ready	Gordy	918	July '66	
Live!	Gordy	921	March '67	
With a Lot o' Soul	Gordy	922	August '67	
In a Mellow Mood	Gordy	924	December '67	
I Wish It Would Rain	Gordy	927	April '68	

JIMMY RUFFIN

Sings Top 10	Soul	704	May '67	
Ruff 'n Ready	Soul	708	April '69	
Groove Governor	Soul	727	November '70	
Sunrise	RSO	3078	May '80	A

DAVID AND JIMMY RUFFIN

I Am My Brother's Keeper	Soul	728	October '70	
Motown Superstar Series, Volume 8	Motown	5–108		A

DAVID RUFFIN

My Whole World Ended	Motown	685	June '69	
Doin' His Thing— Feelin' Good	Motown	696	December '69	
David Ruffin	Motown	762	February '73	
Me 'n Rock 'n Roll Are Here to Stay	Motown	818	November '74	
Who I Am	Motown	849	November '75	
Everything's Coming, Love	Motown	866	June '76	
In My Stride	Motown	885	July '77	
At His Best	Motown	7–895	February '78	A
So Soon We Change	Warner Brothers	3306	September '79	
Gentleman Ruffin	Warner Brothers	3416	August '80	A

THE TEMPTATIONS AND THE SUPREMES

The Supremes Join The Temptations	Motown	679	November '68
T.C.B.	Motown	682	December '68
Together	Motown	692	October '69
On Broadway	Motown	699	December '69

THE MONITORS (WITH RICHARD STREET)

Greetings! We're The Monitors	Soul	714	May '69

THE TEMPTATIONS

Live at the Copa	Gordy	938	December '68
Cloud Nine	Gordy	939	March '69
TV Show	Gordy	933	August '69
Puzzle People	Gordy	949	October '69
Christmas Card	Gordy	951	December '69
Psychedelic Shack	Gordy	947	March '70
At London's Talk of the Town	Gordy	953	August '70
Sky's the Limit	Gordy	957	May '71
Solid Rock	Gordy	961	January '72
All Directions	Gordy	962	August '72
Masterpiece	Gordy	965	March '73
1990	Gordy	966	December '73
The Temptations	Gordy	967	November '74
A Song for You	Gordy	969	January '75

TRUE REFLECTION (WITH GLENN LEONARD)

Where I'm Coming From	Atco	7031	November '73

IMPACT (WITH DAMON HARRIS)

Impact	Atco	SD36–135	June '76	
The 'Pac Is Back	Fantasy	9359	October '77	A

DAMON HARRIS

Damon	Fantasy/ WMOT	9567	December '78	A

THE TEMPTATIONS

House Party	Gordy	973	November '75	
Wings of Love	Gordy	971	March '76	
The Temptations Do The Temptations	Gordy	975	August '76	
Hear to Tempt You	Atlantic	19143	November '77	
Bare Back	Atlantic	19188	October '78	
Power	Gordy	8–994	May '80	A
The Temptations	Gordy	8–1006	September '81	A

TEMPTATIONS ANTHOLOGIES AND COMPILATIONS

Greatest Hits	Gordy	7–919	December '66	A
Greatest Hits, Volume 2	Gordy	7–954	September '70	A
Anthology	3-Motown	9–782	September '73	A
Puzzle People	Pickwick	3396		

EDDIE KENDRICKS

All By Myself	Tamla	309	May '71	
People . . . Hold On	Tamla	315	May '72	
Eddie Kendricks	Tamla	327	May '73	
Boogie Down	Tamla	330	March '74	
For You	Tamla	335	November '74	
The Hit Man	Tamla	338	July '75	
He's a Friend	Tamla	343	December '75	
Goin' Up in Smoke	Tamla	346	September '76	
Slick	Tamla	7–356	October '77	A
At His Best	Tamla	7–354	February '78	
Vintage '78	Arista	4170	March '78	
Something More	Arista	4250	December '79	
Love Keys	Atlantic	SD–19294	August '81	A

10 cc/GRAHAM GOULDMAN. Starting out with the English group Wayne Fontana and The Mindbenders, Eric Gouldman and Eric Stewart scored a smash hit with The Mindbenders in 1966 with "A Groovy Kind of Love." Gouldman, an excellent writer of pop-style songs, provided a number of hits to English groups during the mid-Sixties, including "For

Your Love" and "Heart Full of Soul" for The Yardbirds, "Listen People" for Herman's Hermits, and "Bus Stop" and "Stop, Stop, Stop" for The Hollies. He later joined Stewart in a group called Hotlegs, who backed Neil Sedaka's first two Seventies come-back albums. Becoming 10 cc in 1972, the group quickly established themselves as purveyors of witty and intelligent singles in Great Britain, yet their American popularity has remained limited despite smash successes with the sophisticated pop-style hits "I'm Not in Love" and "The Things We Do for Love."

WAYNE FONTANA AND THE MINDBENDERS

Game of Love	Fontana	SRF–67542	April '65	

THE MINDBENDERS

A Groovy Kind of Love	Fontana	SRF–67554	July '66	

WAYNE FONTANA

Wayne Fontana	MGM	SE–4459	April '67	

GRAHAM GOULDMAN

The Graham Gouldman Thing	RCA	LSP–3954	April '68	

HOTLEGS

Thinks School Stinks	Capitol	ST–587	February '71	

10 CC

10 cc	UK	53105	July '73	A
Sheet Music	UK	53107	May '74	A
100 cc	UK	53110	September '75	A
The Original Soundtrack	Mercury	SRM1–1029	March '75	
How Dare You!	Mercury	SRM1–1061	February '76	
Deceptive Bends	Mercury	3702	March '77	
Live and Let Live	2-Mercury	8600	November '77	
Bloody Tourists	Polydor	PD1–6161	September '78	
Greatest Hits, 1972–78	Polydor	PD1–6244	December '79	A
Look, Hear?	Warner Brothers	3442	May '80	A
Ten out of Ten	Warner Brothers	3575	January '82	A

LOL CREME AND KEVIN GODLEY

Consequences	3-Mercury	SRM3–1700	November '77	

| L | Polydor | PD1–6177 | December '78 | |
| Freeze Frame | Polydor | PD1–6257 | February '80 | A |

GRAHAM GOULDMAN

| Animalympics | A&M | 4810 | August '80 | |

TEN YEARS AFTER/ALVIN LEE. Among the wave of late Sixties British blues bands, the members of Ten Years After became established as international stars without a hit single on the strength of their appearance in the 1970 *Woodstock* film, in which lead guitarist Alvin Lee performed stunning lightning-quick solos in a ten-minute version of "Goin' Home." Unfortunately lumped with Grand Funk Railroad stylistically, Ten Years After endured the alternating attacks on and praises of Lee as the "world's fastest guitarist" while recording several best-selling albums, including 1971's certified gold-award *A Space in Time*, before disintegrating during the mid-Seventies. Alvin Lee has since pursued an inauspicious solo career.

TEN YEARS AFTER

Ten Years After	Deram	DES–18009	February '68	A
Undead	Deram	DES–18016	August '68	A
Stonedhenge	Deram	DES–18021	February '69	
Ssssh	Deram reissued on Chrysalis	DES–18029 CHR–1083	August '69	A
Cricklewood Green	Deram reissued on Chrysalis	DES–18038 CHR–1084	April '70	A
Watt	Deram reissued on Chrysalis	XDES–18050 CHR–1085	December '70	A
Alvin Lee and Company	Deram reissued on London	DES–18064 50013	March '72 September '78	
A Space in Time*	Columbia	PC–30801	August '71	A
Rock and Roll Music to the World	Columbia	C–31779	September '72	A
Recorded Live	2-Columbia	C2X–32288	May '73	A
Positive Vibration	Columbia	C–32851	April '74	A

TEN YEARS AFTER ANTHOLOGIES AND COMPILATIONS

| Goin' Home! Their Greatest Hits | Deram | DES–18072 | July '75 | |
| Greatest Hits | London | 50008 | September '77 | A |

Classic Perfor- mances	Columbia	PC–34366		A

ALVIN LEE AND MYLON LeFEVRE

On the Road to Freedom	Columbia	C–32729	December '73	A

CHICK CHURCHILL

You and Me	Chrysalis	CHR–1051	January '74	

ALVIN LEE

In Flight	2-Columbia	PG–33187	December '74	
Pump Iron	Columbia	C–33796	August '75	A
Rocket Fuel	RSO	3033	May '78	
Ten Years Later/ Ride On	RSO	3049	May '79	
Free Fall	Atlantic	19287	November '80	A
RX5	Atlantic	19306	October '81	A

THREE DOG NIGHT. One of the most commercially successful American rock acts between 1969 and 1974 as a performing and singles band, Three Dog Night attained twelve consecutive certified gold-award albums. Featuring three lead vocalists who also provided tight vocal harmonies, Three Dog Night was responsible for exposing to widespread attention the compositions of once-neglected songwriters such as Harry Nilsson ("One"), Laura Nyro ("Eli's Coming"), Randy Newman ("Mama Told Me Not to Come"), Hoyt Axton ("Joy to the World" and "Never Been to Spain"), Paul Williams ("An Old-Fashioned Love Song"), and Leo Sayer and David Cortney ("The Show Must Go On").

Danny Hutton, born September 10, 1942, in Buncrana, Ireland, was raised in the United States and initiated his musical career at age 19 as a producer, songwriter, and, eventually, vocalist. In 1965 he had a minor hit on the Hanna-Barbera label with "Roses and Rainbows." Devising the concept of a group fronted by three singers who would share lead vocal chores and contribute three-part harmonies, Hutton recruited Cory Wells (born February 5, 1942, in Buffalo, New York) from a group he was producing, The Enemies, and Chuck Negron (born June 8, 1942, in the Bronx, New York) in 1968. Wells had led a high school vocal group and manned a Texas band called The Satellites before moving to Los Angeles with The Enemies, whereas Negron was a solo artist on Columbia Records. The three subsequently rounded out their lineup with keyboardist Jimmy Greenspoon (born February 7, 1948, in Los Angeles), lead guitarist Mike Allsup (born March 8, 1947, in Modesto, California), bassist Joe Schermie (born February 12, 1948, in Madison, Wisconsin), and drummer Floyd Sneed (born November 22, 1943, in Calgary, Alberta, Canada) and took the name Three Dog Night. After successful engagements in West Coast clubs and a long-term stand at Los Angeles' Whiskey A-Go-Go, the group signed with Dunhill Records.

Three Dog Night's debut album initiated a phenomenal career of smash hit singles and certified gold-award albums; it yielded a moderate hit with the Otis Redding classic "Try a Little Tenderness" and a smash hit with Harry Nilsson's "One." Quickly becoming an enormously popular live act, Three Dog Night issued their second album, *Suitable for Framing*, which produced three major hits with "Easy to Be Hard" (from the play *Hair*), Laura Nyro's "Eli's Coming," and "Celebrate," while it also included Elton John and Bernie Taupin's obscure "Lady Samantha." *It Ain't Easy* contained the top hit "Mama Told Me Not to Come," written by Randy Newman, and the major hit "Out in the Country," whereas *Naturally* included the major hit "One-Man Band," the top hit classic "Joy to the World" by Hoyt Axton, and the near-smash "Liar," written by Russ Ballard of Argent. Paul Williams' "An Old-Fashioned Love Song" and Axton's "Never Been to Spain" were smash hits from *Harmony* (which also yielded a major hit with "The Family of Man"), and *Seven Separate Fools* contained the top hit "Black and White" and the major hit "Pieces of April." *Cyan* included the hits "Shambala" and "Let Me Serenade You," whereas *Hard Labor* produced hits with Leo Sayer and David Courtney's "The Show Must Go On" and John Hiatt's "Sure As I'm Sitting Here." Personnel changes had by then affected the group, as Jack Ryland replaced Joe Schermie in 1973. Three Dog Night added second keyboardist Skip Konte in 1974 and, during 1975, James "Smitty" Smith replaced Mike Allsup, Dennis Belfield supplanted Jack Ryland, and Mickey McMeel took over for Floyd Sneed. After a final moderate hit for Dunhill with Allen Toussaint's "Play Something Sweet (Brickyard Blues)" in 1974, Three Dog Night recorded two more albums and one moderate hit, "Till the World Ends," for ABC Records before disbanding in 1976. Cory Wells subsequently initiated a solo career on A&M Records in 1978 with little success.

DANNY HUTTON

Pre-Dog Night	MGM	SE–4664	May '70	

THREE DOG NIGHT

Three Dog Night*	Dunhill	50048	January '69	A
Suitable for Framing*	Dunhill	50058	July '69	
Captured Live at the Forum*	Dunhill	50068	November '69	A
It Ain't Easy*	Dunhill	50078	April '70	
Naturally*	Dunhill	DSX–50088	December '70	
Golden Biscuits*	Dunhill	DSX–50098	February '71	
Harmony*	Dunhill	DSX–50108	September '71	
Seven Separate Fools*	Dunhill	DSD–50118	July '72	

Recorded Live in Concert*	2-Dunhill	DSY–50138	March '73	
Cyan*	Dunhill	DSX–50158	September '73	
Hard Labor*	Dunhill	DSD–50168	March '74	
Joy to the World—Their Greatest Hits*	Dunhill	DSD–50178	December '74	A
Dog Style	Dunhill	50198	October '74	
Coming Down Your Way	ABC	888	May '75	
American Pastime	ABC	928	April '76	

CORY WELLS

Touch Me	A&M	4673	March '78

TRAFFIC/STEVIE WINWOOD. The driving force behind The Spencer Davis Group as a teenager, Stevie Winwood achieved his first recognition as organist, singer, and songwriter with the hits "Gimme Some Lovin'" and "I'm a Man." Coupled with songwriting collaborator Jim Capaldi, reed player Chris Wood (one of the first horn players to be an integral part of a major British rock band), and intermittent member Dave Mason, Winwood recorded three fascinating albums with Traffic characterized by surreal lyrics, a jazz-style sound, and Winwood's unique voice. After enduring a chaotic history of breakups, re-formations and personnel changes, Traffic regrouped following Winwood's brief experience with the ready-made "supergroup" Blind Faith for the best-selling folk-style *John Barleycorn Must Die* album. Never achieving a major hit single and becoming more popular in the United States than in their native country, Traffic could not always effectively translate their recorded successes into live performances, which were often pervaded by meandering instrumental interludes that belied their jazz orientation. After recording three more gold-award albums, including the classic *The Low Spark of High-Heeled Boys*, Traffic broke up at the end of 1974, since which time Capaldi has pursued a modest solo career; Winwood has recently staged a remarkable come-back with *Arc of a Diver*.

Born in Birmingham, England, on May 12, 1948, Stevie Winwood gained his first musical experience with a skiffle band at the age of 11. An accomplished singer and multi-instrumentalist (keyboards, guitar, bass), he was a member of The Spencer Davis Group by his fifteenth birthday and co-authored the group's two near-smash hits, "Gimme Some Lovin'" and "I'm a Man," from 1967. Wanting to form his own group, Winwood left Davis that spring and retreated to a Berkshire cottage for six months of rehearsal with multi-talented instrumentalists Dave Mason, Chris Wood, and Jim Capaldi. Capaldi (drums, vocals, lyric writing), born August 2, 1944, in Evesham, Worcestershire, had played in the Birmingham-based group Deep Feeling, as had Dave Mason (guitar, bass, vocals, songwriting), born May 10, 1945, in Worcester. Chris Wood (flute, saxophone, keyboards, vocals), born June 24, 1944, in Birmingham, and the other three had jammed together in Birmingham clubs before Winwood's departure from Spencer Davis. Winwood and Capaldi's "Paper Sun," featuring Mason on sitar, and Mason's "Hole in My Shoe" became major British hits in 1967 and were included along with "Coloured Rain," "Dear Mr. Fantasy," and "Smiling Phases" on Traffic's remarkably diverse and experimental debut album.

Dave Mason's penchant for pop-style melodies conflicted with the jazz orientation of the others and led to his departure in December 1967, yet he was back for *Traffic*, which included his classic "Feelin' Alright?" plus "Pearly Queen" and Winwood and Capaldi's surreal "Forty Thousand Headman." First touring America in 1968, Traffic then again suffered the loss of Mason that October and, following *Last Exit*, which contained a live side and a studio side that featured "Shanghai Noodle Factory" and "Medicated Goo," Traffic fell into disarray. Winwood joined Ginger Baker, Eric Clapton, and bassist Rick Grech in Blind Faith for one American tour and one gold-award album which included Winwood's "Can't Find My Way Home" and "Sea of Joy"; he subsequently manned Ginger Baker's Air Force. Winwood, Wood, and Capaldi regrouped in January 1970 for Traffic's first certified gold-award album, *John Barleycorn Must Die*, which combined elements of jazz, rock, and folk music and served as a fitting tribute to Winwood's versatility. In addition to the title song, the album included Winwood and Capaldi's "Freedom Rider" and "Stranger to Himself." The group toured again in 1970, augmented by Rick Grech (who subsequently joined the band); during the summer of 1971 they conducted a brief British tour with Dave Mason and others that resulted in the live set *Welcome to the Canteen*. Mason returned to his solo career as the others recorded *The Low Spark of High-Heeled Boys*. In addition to the title song, the album contained "Many a Mile to Freedom," Grech and drummer Jim Gordon's "Rock and Roll Stew," and Capaldi's "Light Up or Leave Me Alone."

Jim Capaldi recorded his debut solo album for Island Records at Muscle Shoals, Alabama, with Stevie Winwood, Dave Mason, and studio veterans David Hood (bass) and Roger Hawkins (drums), who joined Traffic for *Shoot-Out at the Fantasy Factory*, recorded in Jamaica and featuring Winwood and Capaldi's "Sometimes I Feel So Uninspired." Joined by Muscle Shoals' associate Barry Beckett (keyboards), the aggregation conducted a 1973 world tour and recorded the live *On the Road* album. The Muscle Shoals recruits left after the tour and bassist Rosko Gee joined for Traffic's 1974 British tour, their final keyboard-dominated *When the Eagle Flies* album, and their final American tour in late 1974. Traffic then disbanded, and Capaldi resumed his solo recording career for Island and later for RSO Records. Stevie Winwood recorded a "jam" album for Antilles Records before joining Japanese percussionist–keyboardist Stomu Yamashta in the ambitious "Go" aggregation, with his solo debut album intervening in 1977. In 1981 Winwood re-emerged with the platinum-award *Arc of a Diver* and the smash hit "While You See a Chance."

TRAFFIC

Mr. Fantasy	United Artists	UAS–6651	April '68	A
Traffic	United Artists	UAS–6676	November '68	
Last Exit	United Artists	UAS–6702	May '69	
Best	United Artists	UAS–5500	December '69	

BLIND FAITH

Blind Faith *	Atco	SD33–304	August '69	
	reissued on			
	RSO	3016	February '77	A

TRAFFIC

John Barleycorn Must Die *	United Artists	UAS–5504	July '70	
Welcome to the Canteen	United Artists	UAS–5550	September '71	
Heavy Traffic	United Artists	LA421	April '75	
More Heavy Traffic	United Artists	LA526	September '75	
The Low Spark of High-Heeled Boys *	Island	SW–9306	November '71	
		reissued as 9180		A
Shoot-Out at the Fantasy Factory*	Island	SW–9323 reissued as 9224	January '73	A
On the Road	Island	SMAS–9336 reissued as 2	October '73	A
When the Eagle Flies *	Island	7E–1020	August '74	

JIM CAPALDI

Oh, How We Danced	Island	SW–9314 reissued as 9187	February '72	
Whale Meat Again	Island	ILPS–9254	July '74	
Short Cut Draw Blood	Island reissued on Antilles	ILPS–9336 7050	January '76	A
Daughter of the Night	RSO	3037	September '78	
Electric Nights	RSO		June '79	

STEVIE WINWOOD

Winwood	2-United Artists	UAS–9950 reissued as UAS–9964	May '71 November '72	
Stevie Winwood	Island	ILPS–9494	June '77	A
Arc of a Diver **	Island	ILPS–9576	January '81	A

STEVIE WINWOOD, REMI KABAKA, AND ABDUL LASISI AMAO

Mdash-Aiye-Keta	Antilles	7005	February '76	

STOMU YAMASHTA'S GO (WITH STEVIE WINWOOD)

Go	Island	ILPS–9358 reissued as 9387	July '76	A
Go Live from Paris	2-Island	10	April '78	A

THE TUBES. A Seventies rock satire band, The Tubes achieved notoriety and a cult following in the San Francisco Bay area with their outlandish blend of rock music and irreverent lyrics, costume changes and characters, choreography and theatrical presentation in live performances. Eschewing the ill-humor of Iggy Pop and the calculated exploitation of Alice Cooper, The Tubes' satirical and iconoclastic bent often resulted in humorous self-parody. Although their debut album showed great promise with songs such as "What Do You Want from Life" and "White Punks on Dope," The Tubes remained most effective in performance. By the time of their first "concept" album, *Remote Control* (which concerned television), The Tubes had dropped many of the elaborate features of their stage show in an effort to reduce expenses and to expand their still limited audience as a straightforward Eighties rock band.

THE TUBES

The Tubes	A&M	SP–4534	July '75	A
Young and Rich	A&M	SP–4580	April '76	A
Now	A&M	SP–4632	May '77	A
What Do You Want from Live	2-A&M	6003	February '78	A
Remote Control	A&M	SP–4751	March '79	A
T.R.A.S.H. (Tubes Rarities and Smash Hits)	A&M	4870	August '81	A
The Completion Backward Principle	Capitol	SOO– 12151	May '81	A

IKE AND TINA TURNER. Bandleader, songwriter, arranger, and multi-instrumentalist Ike Turner achieved his first success in 1951 with vocalist Jackie Brenston on the top rhythm-and-blues hit "Rocket 88," regarded by some as the first "rock-and-roll" record. Ostensibly having discovered B. B. King and Howlin' Wolf during the Fifties while a talent scout, Turner adopted a revue format for his band in St. Louis during the mid-Fifties and added vocalist and wife-to-be Tina Turner in 1957. Touring the so-called "chitlin" circuit for virtually ten years, Ike and Tina

Turner developed a gutsy and ribald stage act, with Tina, the show's focal point, performing in a flauntingly sexual manner, complete with feigned orgasms and provocative verbal exchanges between Ike and Tina, backed by the miniskirted Ikettes, whose stage routines were blatantly suggestive. Perhaps on the strength of their smash British hit "River Deep—Mountain High," produced by Phil Spector and usually acknowledged as one of the finest singles ever made, Ike and Tina Turner became more popular in Great Britain than in America. They eventually achieved the first massive exposure of their stage act during The Rolling Stones' 1969 tour and subsequently looked to the world of rock music for an expanded audience and material performed in an overtly sexual manner, such as the smash pop hit, "Proud Mary." Thereafter playing both exclusive supper clubs such as those in Las Vegas and rock venues such as the Fillmores, the Turners' first and only certified gold-award album came with 1971's *What You Hear Is What You Get*. Touring with virtually the same show for years, the excitement of which was seldom captured even on live albums, Ike and Tina Turner divorced in 1977, since which time Tina solo and the pair have recorded albums.

Ike Turner, born in Clarksdale, Mississippi, on November 5, 1931, started playing piano at the age of six, initiated his professional career at age 11 as accompanist to Robert Nighthawk, and subsequently mastered guitar. Upon high school graduation, he formed The Rhythm Kings, who recorded the top rhythm-and-blues hit "Rocket 88," perhaps the first "rock-and-roll" record, with vocalist Jackie Brenston in 1951. During the Fifties, Turner backed a number of blues artists, worked as a songwriter and talent scout for Kent/Modern Records, authored B. B. King's "Sweet Little Angel," and allegedly "discovered" King and Howlin' Wolf. Around 1954 he moved to St. Louis, where he developed a revue format for The Rhythm Kings.

Annie Mae "Tina" Bullock, born in Brownsville, Tennessee, on November 26, 1938 (or 1939), grew up in Knoxville and sang in a local church choir. Around 1954 she moved to St. Louis, attempted to join Ike Turner's revue at age 17, and eventually succeeded in 1957. The couple married in 1958 and recorded for the Midwestern rhythm-and-blues label Sue, scoring a smash rhythm-and-blues and moderate pop hit in 1960 with "A Fool in Love." Thus enabled to recruit a trio of female backup singers, The Ikettes (which would include P. P. Arnold, Bonnie Bramlett, and Merry Clayton over the years), Ike and Tina Turner began nearly a decade of tours on the "chitlin" circuit with their raunchy and overtly sexual stage act. Through 1962, they scored smash rhythm-and-blues hits with "I Idolize You," Ike's "It's Gonna Work Out Fine" (a major pop hit), "Poor Fool," and "Tra La La La," but subsequent hits eluded them. The Ikettes managed a major hit in early 1962 with "I'm Blue" on Atco Records and a moderate hit in 1965 with "Peaches and Cream" on Modern. The Turners subsequently recorded for a variety of labels, including Kent, Modern, Warner Brothers, and its rhythm-and-blues subsidiary Loma, before meeting producer–songwriter Phil Spector while working on the film *The TNT Show*. For them he co-authored and produced "River Deep—

Mountain High," regarded as one of the finest singles of all time; but although the song became a smash British hit, it fared dismally in the United States, resulting in Spector's withdrawal from the music business. The album of the same name (not all produced by Spector) was eventually reissued in 1969 on A&M Records.

During the latter half of the Sixties, Ike and Tina Turner recorded for several more labels, including Atlantic's Pompeii subsidiary, Blue Thumb (on which they achieved a minor hit with Otis Redding's "I've Been Loving You Too Long," which became a centerpiece of their stage show) and Minit Records, with little success. They finally broke through to a mass audience in late 1969 as support act for The Rolling Stones' American tour, by which time they had begun recording raunchy versions of rock standards. Signed to Liberty Records at the beginning of 1970, the duo scored a smash rhythm-and-blues and pop hit in early 1971 with a reworking of Creedence Clearwater Revival's "Proud Mary." Subsequently graduating to both Las Vegas supper clubs and the Fillmores, Ike and Tina Turner recorded albums for Capitol and Ray Charles' Tangerine label before moving to United Artists for their first and only certified gold-award album, *What You Hear Is What You Get*, recorded live at Carnegie Hall. They had another major pop hit in 1973 with Tina's "Nutbush City Limits," but subsequent releases fared poorly. Ike Turner, who had recorded a solo album for Pompeii in 1969, recorded two more solo sets, *Blues Roots* and *Confined to Soul* (with their newly named backing group, The Family Vibes) in 1972–73. Tina Turner appeared as The Acid Queen in Ken Russell's 1975 *Tommy* film, and the pair endured until 1976, when they separated; they divorced the following year. Tina Turner, who had recorded her first solo album for 1972 release, continued to record solo albums and to pursue a solo career and reunited with Ike for 1978's *Airwaves* album.

IKE AND TINA TURNER

The Soul of Ike and Tina Turner	Sue	LP–2001 (M)	
Dance	Sue	LP–2003 (M)	
Dynamite	Sue	LP–2004 (M)	
Don't Play Me Cheap	Sue	LP–2005 (M)	
It's Gonna Work Out Fine	Sue	LP–2007 (M)	
Revue Live	Kent	5014	
The Soul of Ike and Tina Turner	Kent	5019	
Festival of Live Performances	Kent	538	
Please, Please, Please	Kent	550	November '70
The Ike and Tina Show Live	Warner Brothers	WS–1579	January '65

Show—Volume 2	Loma	5904	January '67	
River Deep— Mountain High	Philles reissued on	4011(M)	'66	
	A&M	SP–4178	March '69	
So Fine	Pompeii	6000	July '68	
Cussin', Cryin', and Carryin' On	Pompeii	6004	September '69	
The Hunter	Blue Thumb	BTS–11	January '69	
Outta Season	Blue Thumb	BTS–5	March '69	
In Person	Minit	24018	July '69	
Come Together	Liberty	LST–7637	April '70	
Workin' Together	Liberty	LST–7650	November '70	
Her Man . . . His Woman	Capitol	ST–571	November '70	
Souled Out	Tangerine	TRCS– 1511	November '71	
What You Hear Is What You Get*	2-United Artists	UAS–9953	June '71	
'Nuff Said	United Artists	UAS–5530	October '71	
Feel Good	United Artists	UAS–5598	July '72	
Nutbush City Limits	United Artists	LA180	December '73	
The Gospel According to Ike and Tina Turner	United Artists	LA203	April '74	
Airwaves	United Artists	LA917	October '78	A

IKE AND TINA TURNER ANTHOLOGIES AND COMPILATIONS

The Greatest Hits of Ike and Tina Turner	Sue	1038		
Greatest Hits	Warner Brothers	WS–1810	September '69	
Best	Blue Thumb	BTS–49		
Fantastic	Sunset	5265	November '69	
Greatest Hits	Sunset	5285	September '70	
Ooh Poo Pah Doo	Harmony	H–30400	May '70	
Something's Got a Hold on Me	Harmony	H–30567	July '71	
Greatest Hits	United Artists	UAS–5667	January '73	
World of Ike and Tina Turner	2-United Artists	LA064	December '73	
Greatest Hits	United Artists	LA592	April '76	
16 Great Performances	ABC	4014	January '75	
Too Hot to Hold	Springboard International	4011		
Workin' Together	Pickwick	3032 reissued as 3606	April '78 September '79	A
Too Hot to Hold	Pickwick	3284		
Get It—Get It!	Pickwick	3328		
Hot 'n' Sassy	Accord	SN–7147	December '81	A

IKE TURNER

Ike Turner Rocks the Blues	Crown	CST–367		
Black Man's Soul	Pompeii	6003	June '69	
Blues Roots	United Artists	UAS–5576	June '72	
Confined to Soul	United Artists	LA051	March '73	
The Edge	Fantasy	9597	August '80	A

TINA TURNER

Let Me Touch Your Mind	United Artists	UAS–5660	November '72	
Turns the Country On	United Artists	LA200	September '74	
Acid Queen	United Artists	LA495	August '75	
Rough	United Artists	LA919	October '78	A

THE TURTLES/FLO AND EDDIE. Mistakenly identified with the "folk-rock" movement with their near-smash hit version of Bob Dylan's "It Ain't Me, Babe" in 1965, The Turtles evolved from a surf band and favored pop-style arrangements and productions on smash hits such as "Happy Together," "She'd Rather Be with Me," and "Elenore," the last from their satirical pastiche *Battle of the Bands* album, now a valued collectors' item. Turtles vocalists and masterminds Mark Volman and Howard Kaylan subsequently joined Frank Zappa's Mothers of Invention as Phlorescent Leech and Eddie. With Zappa, they toured extensively, performed their own feature spot, and recorded four albums, including the movie soundtrack *200 Motels*, in which they actually overshadowed Zappa. Also recording with Marc Bolan/T. Rex, the two recorded four brilliant but overlooked albums of rock satire and parody as Flo and Eddie through 1976, since which time they have worked as producers and television writers.

Mark Volman, born in Los Angeles on April 19, 1944, and Howard Kaylan, born in New York City on June 22, 1945, met in a southern California high school in 1961 and manned the surf groups The Nightriders and The Crossfires with Al Nichol (born March 31, 1946, in Winston-Salem, North Carolina) and Chuck Portz (born March 28, 1945) between 1962 and 1965. Adopting the name The Turtles under a new manager and signing with White Whale Records, the group was initially comprised of Volman (guitar, vocals), Kaylan (vocals), guitarist–vocalists Nichol and Jim Tucker (born October 17, 1946), Portz (bass), and drummer Don Murray (born November 8, 1945). During the burgeoning days of "folk-rock," The Turtles scored a near-smash hit with Bob Dylan's "It Ain't Me, Babe," followed by the moderate hit "Let Me Be" from their debut folk-oriented album. After the major hit "You, Baby" in early 1966, John Barbata replaced Murray on drums, and The Turtles subsequently achieved their most successful year in 1967 with the top hit "Happy Together," the smash hit "She'd Rather Be with Me," and the major hits

"You Know What I Mean" and "She's My Girl." In 1968–69 "Elenore" and "You Showed Me" became near-smash hits from *Battle of the Bands*, on which the band recorded under a number of different names in different styles and showcased a developing satirical bent with songs such as "Surfer Dan," "I'm Chief Kamanananalea (We're the Royal Macadamia Nuts)," and "Chicken Little Was Right." However, The Turtles never had another major hit and, before their breakup in 1970, Tucker, Portz, and Barbata had been replaced by bassist–vocalist Jim Pons and drummer John Seiter.

As John Barbata pursued sessions work (later recording and touring with Crosby, Stills, Nash, and Young and eventually joining The Jefferson Airplane/Starship), Mark Volman and Howard Kaylan joined Frank Zappa's Mothers of Invention (as did Jim Pons) as Phlorescent Leech and Eddie. Touring Europe and the United States extensively with Zappa, Flo and Eddie (as they became known) performed their own feature spot in concert and recorded four albums with the group, including the soundtrack to *200 Motels*. Also appearing in that film, Volman and Kaylan easily eclipsed the performances of Zappa and Ringo Starr. Recording as background vocalists for Marc Bolan/T. Rex in 1971–72 (including the major hit "Bang a Gong"), Flo and Eddie left The Mothers in 1972. They then recorded two outstanding, if neglected, albums of rock satire for Reprise Records and toured in 1973 in support of Alice Cooper on his Billion Dollar Babies tour. The two subsequently scored and wrote the screenplay to the X-rated animated movie *Cheap*, wrote satirical articles for the American rock press, and hosted their own successful syndicated radio show originating from Los Angeles' KROQ. Signed to Columbia Records in 1975, Flo and Eddie recorded two more excellent but poorly selling albums of rock satire and parody before moving into production work and writing scripts for prospective television movies and comedy shows. During 1981 Rhino Records released vintage material by The Crossfires, and Epiphany Records issued an album of reggae songs, including a reworked version of "Happy Together," for Flo and Eddie.

THE CROSSFIRES

Out of Control	Rhino	RNLP–019	May '81	A

THE TURTLES

It Ain't Me, Babe	White Whale	WWS–7111	October '65
You, Baby	White Whale	WWS–7112	April '66
Happy Together	White Whale	WWS–7114	April '67
The Turtles Present The Battle of the Bands	White Whale	WWS–7118	November '68
Turtle Soup	White Whale	WWS–7124	October '69
Woodenhead	White Whale	WWS–7133	October '70

TURTLES ANTHOLOGIES AND COMPILATIONS

Golden Hits*	White Whale	WWS–7115	November '67	
More Golden Hits	White Whale	WWS–7127	April '70	
Happy Together Again	2-Sire	3703	November '74	

FLO AND EDDIE

The Phlorescent Leech and Eddie	Reprise	MS–2099	September '72	
Flo and Eddie	Reprise	MS–2141	March '73	
Illegal, Immoral, and Fattening	Columbia	PC–33554	August '75	
Moving Targets	Columbia	PC–34262	August '76	
Rock Steady with Flo and Eddie	Epiphany	4010	October '81	A

VANILLA FUDGE/CACTUS. Best remembered for their bombastic, dirge-like near-smash hit version of The Supremes' "You Keep Me Hangin' On" from 1968, Vanilla Fudge was one of the first "heavy" American bands, blending gospel-style harmonies with loud organ and guitar interplay on slowed-down renditions of then-current hits. Thwarted in their effort to join Jeff Beck in late 1969, leaders Carmine Appice and Tim Bogert formed the similarly styled Cactus and eventually united with Beck for 1973's best-selling *Beck, Bogert, and Appice* album. Reconstituted without any original members, The New Cactus Band featured one of America's most popular guitarists of the early Seventies, Mike Pinera (Blues Image, Iron Butterfly), who later formed Thee Image and has since recorded solo.

VANILLA FUDGE

Vanilla Fudge*	Atco	SD33–224	September '67	A
The Beat Goes On	Atco	SD33–237	February '68	
Renaissance	Atco	SD33–244	July '68	
Near the Beginning	Atco	SD33–278	February '69	
Rock and Roll	Atco	SD33–303	July '69	
While the Whole World Was Eating	Wand	687	May '70	

BOOMERANG (WITH MARK STEIN)

Boomerang	RCA	LSP–4577	August '71

CACTUS

Cactus	Atco	SD33–340	July '70
One Way . . . or Another	Atco	SD33–356	March '71
Restrictions	Atco	SD33–377	November '71
'Ot and Sweaty	Atco	SD–7011	October '72

BECK, BOGERT, AND APPICE

Beck, Bogert, and Appice	Epic	PE–32140	March '73	A

THE NEW CACTUS BAND

Son of Cactus	Atco	SD–7017	May '73	

THEE IMAGE

Thee Image	Manticore	MA6–504	February '75	A
Inside Thee Image	Manticore	MA6–506	November '75	A

MIKE PINERA

Isla	Capricorn	0202	July '78	A
Forever	Spector Interna- tional	SW–00001	September '79	

TIM BOGERT

Progressions	Accord	ST–7004	December '81	A

CARMINE APPICE

Carmine Appice	Pasha	ARZ– 37676	January '82	A

THE VELVET UNDERGROUND/JOHN CALE/LOU REED. Seminal late Sixties New York band whose enormous influence was not recognized until years after their disbandment, The Velvet Underground featured the stark, sinister, and lurid real-life songs of Lou Reed (although some of his compositions revealed a decided pop sensibility), the "avant garde" musical innovations of John Cale, the thin but sensual voice of Nico, and the drumming of Maureen Tucker, one of the few female drummers in rock music. Launched in association with artist Andy Warhol (he provided the famous banana cover of their debut album) and his touring "total environment" show, The Exploding Plastic Inevitable (perhaps the first multimedia show complete with music, dancers, films, lights, and projections), The Velvet Underground recorded overpowering, desperate songs of sadomasochism and drug addiction (the classic "Heroin") and bizarre fantasy tales on their debut album, subjects rarely explored in popular music to that time. Thus an inspiration to performers of outrageous, menacing, and blatantly graphic material up through the late Seventies "punk" movement, The Velvet Underground became the vehicle for Reed's eerie visions of life in the streets after the departures of Nico (after the first album) and Cale (after the second album), yet the group was essentially defunct after 1970. Whereas Nico's solo career remained relatively undistinguished (save early recordings of Jackson Browne's "These Days" and Bob Dylan's "I'll Keep It with Mine") and Cale retained a following only among critics and avant garde fans, Lou Reed became the most successful, if erratic, of the former members as a solo artist. As Cale produced The Stooges' debut album, all of Nico's albums, and Patti Smith's stunning 1975 debut album *Horses*, Reed scored astounding suc-

cesses with his major pop hit, "Walk on the Wild Side," in 1973, the certified gold-award live *Rock 'n' Roll Animal* album, and the best-selling
Sally Can't Dance album, vitiated by the critically derided album of electronic music, *Metal Music Machine*. Having previously exploited the image of a beleaguered victim of life and developed a reputation for obnoxious
onstage behavior, Lou Reed's recent work and performances seem to indicate that he is becoming a mellowed mainstream rock artist.

Born in New York City on March 2, 1944, Lou Reed initiated five years
of classical piano training at the age of five and first played professionally
while in his early teens with Long Island bands such as Pasha and The
Prophets and The Jades. Working as a songwriter for Pickwick Records, a
journalist, and a published poet, he met John Cale in 1964. Cale, born in
Garnant, South Wales, on December 5, 1942, had studied classical viola
and piano in London, and his compositions had been broadcast on the
BBC when he was eight years old. He came to the United States on a
Leonard Bernstein fellowship but abandoned his classical studies to pursue
his interest in "avant garde" music, joining LaMonte Young's experimental
group on electric viola. In the meantime, Reed formed various groups such
as The Primitives and The Warlocks and recruited classically trained Sterling Morrison and female drummer Maureen Tucker. Around 1966 Cale
joined the group; they became The Velvet Underground, debuted at Cafe
Bizarre in Greenwich Village that winter, and immediately sparked local
controversy for their unorthodox music and stage demeanor. The band
came to the attention of artist Andy Warhol, who was looking for a rock
group to add to his multimedia outfit, The Factory. Among the members
of The Factory was German-born Nico, who had been a European model
and actress before unsuccessfully attempting a career as a singer in London
in 1965 and before appearing in Warhol's *Chelsea Girls* film. Augmented
by Nico, The Velvet Underground joined Warhol's "total environment"
show, The Exploding Plastic Inevitable, which opened in New York and
subsequently toured Canada and the United States. The members: Lou
Reed (lead guitar, vocals), John Cale (electric viola, keyboards, bass),
Nico (vocals), Sterling Morrison (rhythm guitar, bass), and Maureen
Tucker (drums).

Signed to MGM/Verve Records, The Velvet Underground recorded
their debut album with Andy Warhol as nominal producer. Packaged in a
jacket that featured Warhol's famous banana cover, *The Velvet Underground and Nico* was comprised of music and lyrics the likes of which had
not yet appeared in rock music. Propelled by Cale's innovative avant garde
musical experimentation and Reed's disarmingly realistic and sinister
lyrics, the album included the startling "Heroin," with its screeching, electronic drugged-out crescendo, the sadomasochistic "Venus in Furs," the
gritty "I'm Waiting for the Man," "There She Goes Again," and the gentle
"Sunday Morning" and "I'll Be Your Mirror," sung by Nico. Enjoying virtually no radio airplay, the album failed to sell in mass quantities, yet it
was eventually recognized as one of the most influential albums of the late

Sixties. Nico subsequently left The Velvet Underground to pursue a solo career and, with an attendant loss of interest by Warhol and the press, the group's *White Light/White Heat* was largely ignored by the public, yet it contained the lurid 17-minute classic "Sister Ray." The group toured to diminishing audiences; Cale departed before their next album and was replaced by multi-instrumentalist Doug Yule. After *The Velvet Underground*, which featured the ballad "Pale Blue Eyes," Maureen Tucker was replaced by Billy Yule (Doug's brother) and the group switched to Cotillion Records for their final studio album, *Loaded*, which included "Rock and Roll" and "Sweet Jane." Following a summer's residency at Max's Kansas City in New York, Reed left The Velvet Underground in August 1970, after which the Yule brothers attempted to keep the group going with new members through 1972.

Nico was the first former member to record a solo album, but *Chelsea Girl* failed to sell despite the production and accompaniment of John Cale and the inclusion of Jackson Browne's "These Days" and Bob Dylan's "I'll Keep It with Mine." *The Marble Index*, for Elektra, featured her own songs and the sparse instrumentation and production of Cale and fared no better; after *Desertshore* for Reprise, again under Cale, Nico fled to France. During that time, Cale had produced The Stooges' debut album, launched his solo career with *Vintage Violence*, and recorded *Church of Anthrax* with experimental musician Terry Riley. Cale switched to Reprise for *The Academy in Peril* and the critically acclaimed *Paris 1919*; but by 1974, he had returned to England.

In the meantime, Lou Reed had signed a solo contract with RCA Records and recorded his debut album in London. His second, *Transformer*, produced by David Bowie, sold quite well, perhaps on the strength of its pop-style major hit single "Walk on the Wild Side." However, its follow-up, *Berlin*, was attacked by critics and sold poorly despite the assistance of Jack Bruce and Stevie Winwood, after which Cale assembled a touring band which recorded *Rock 'n' Roll Animal* (eventually certified gold-award in 1978) at New York's Academy of Music. Reed's next, *Sally Can't Dance*, surprisingly became a best-seller despite its air of parody, and his career subsequently reached its nadir with 1975's *Metal Music Machine*, which consisted of little other than electronic beeps and tape hiss.

In 1974 Nico and John Cale performed a concert at London's Rainbow Theatre with guitarist Kevin Ayers (of Soft Machine) and synthesizer player Brian Eno (of Roxy Music) and, after a live album of the show on Island Records, each recorded solo albums for the label, Nico's produced by Cale and Cale's featuring Eno and guitarist Phil Manzanera, another veteran of Roxy Music. Cale toured Europe in the spring of 1975, recorded *Slow Dazzle* with Eno and Manzanera, and subsequently produced Patti Smith's stunning debut album. After a final American album for Island, *Guts*, Cale switched to A&M Records for 1979's *Sabotage* album and later formed the small independent label Spy Records with manager Jane Friedman. Following Lou Reed's final album for RCA, *Coney Island Baby*, he switched to Arista Records. Although none of his recordings for the label sold particularly well (*Take No Prisoners* was a live double-record set recorded in binaural and *The Bells* featured three songs co-written with Nils Lofgren), Reed's recent performances and *Growing Up in Public* have revealed an almost good-natured mainstream direction in his career.

THE VELVET UNDERGROUND

The Velvet Under- ground and Nico	Verve	V–65008	February '67	
White Light/White Heat	Verve	V–65046	February '68	
The Velvet Under- ground	MGM	SE–4617	March '69	
1969 Velvet Under- ground Live	2-Mercury	SRM2– 7504	March '74	A
Loaded	Cotillion	SD–9034	November '70	A
Live at Max's Kansas City	Cotillion	SD–9500	June '72	A

VELVET UNDERGROUND ANTHOLOGIES AND COMPILATIONS

The Velvet Under- ground	MGM	GAS–131	January '71
Archetype	MGM	SE–4950	August '74
Lou Reed with The Velvet Under- ground	Pride	PRD–0022	June '73

NICO

Chelsea Girl	Verve	V–65032	September '67
The Marble Index	Elektra	EKS– 74029	September '68
Desertshore	Reprise	RS–6424	April '72
The End	Island	9311	January '75

JOHN CALE

Vintage Violence	Columbia	CS–1037	July '70	A
The Academy in Peril	Reprise	MS–2079	August '72	
Paris 1919	Reprise	MS–2131	March '73	

JOHN CALE AND TERRY RILEY

Church of Anthrax	Columbia	C–30131	March '71

JOHN CALE, KEVIN AYERS, BRIAN ENO, AND NICO

June 1, 1974	Island	9291	September '74

JOHN CALE

Fear	Island	9301	January '75
Slow Dazzle	Island	9317	August '75

Guts	Island	9459	April '77	
	reissued on			
	Antilles	7063		A
Sabotage	A&M	SP–004	November '79	A
Honi Soit	A&M	4849	March '81	A

LOU REED

Lou Reed	RCA	LSP–4701	April '72	
Transformer	RCA	AFL1–4807	November '72	
	reissued as	AYL1–3806		A
Berlin	RCA	APL1–0207	October '73	
Rock 'n' Roll Animal*	RCA	APL1–0472	February '74	
	reissued as	AYL1–3664	June '80	A
Sally Can't Dance	RCA	CPL1–0611	September '74	
Live	RCA	AFL1–0959	March '75	
	reissued as	AYL1–3752		A
Metal Music Machine: The Amine Beta Ring	2-RCA	CPL2–1101	July '75	
Coney Island Baby	RCA	APL1–0915	January '76	
	reissued as	ANL1–2480	November '77	
Walk on the Wild Side—The Best of Lou Reed	RCA	AFL1–2001	April '77	
	reissued as	AYL1–3753		A
Rock and Roll Heart	Arista	AL–4100	November '76	
Street Hassle	Arista	AB–4169	March '78	A
Live . . . Take No Prisoners	2-Arista	8502	November '78	
The Bells	Arista	4229	May '79	A
Growing Up in Public	Arista	9522	May '80	A
Rock and Roll Diary 1967–1980	2-Arista	8603	December '80	A
Blue Mask	RCA	AFL1–4221	January '82	A

THE VENTURES. Best remembered for their 1960 smash instrumental hit "Walk—Don't Run" and, more recently, "Hawaii Five–O," The Ventures bolstered the exploding popularity of the guitar that was initiated by Chuck Berry and Elvis Presley. Noted for their cleanness of sound and use of tremolo, The Ventures endured longer than did any other instrumental group of the late Fifties and early Sixties on a formula based on simple recreations of other artist's hits. Placing over 30 albums in the charts (including three certified gold-award albums), The Ventures turned their attentions to the Far East during the mid-Sixties, where they became the area's best-selling recording artists.

THE VENTURES

Walk Don't Run	Dolton	BST–8003	October '60
The Ventures	Dolton	BST–8004	January '61
Another Smash!	Dolton	BST–8006	May '61
The Colorful Ventures	Dolton	BST–8008	September '61
Twist with The Ventures	Dolton	BST–8010	January '62
The Ventures' Twist Party, Volume 2	Dolton	BST–8014	May '62
Mashed Potatoes and Gravy	Dolton	BST–8016	August '62
Going to The Ventures' Dance Party!	Dolton	BST–8017	November '62
Play Telstar, the Lonely Bull, and Others*	Dolton	BST–8019	January '63
Surfing	Dolton	BST–8022	April '63
The Country Classics	Dolton	BST–8023	June '63
Let's Go!	Dolton	BST–8024	August '63
Ventures in Space	Dolton reissued on Pickwick	BST–8027 3604	January '64 April '78
The Fabulous Ventures	Dolton	BST–8029	July '64
Walk, Don't Run—Volume 2	Dolton	BST–8031	October '64
The Ventures Knock Me Out!	Dolton	BST–8033	February '65
The Ventures on Stage	Dolton	BST–8035	June '65

THE VENTURES' INSTRUCTIONAL ALBUMS

Play Guitar with The Ventures	Dolton	17501	July '65
Volume 2	Dolton	17502	July '66

Volume 3	Dolton	17503	July '66	
Play Electric Bass with The Ventures	Dolton	17504	July '66	

THE VENTURES

The Ventures A Go-Go	Dolton	BST–8037	September '65	
Christmas Album	Dolton	BST–8038	December '65	
	reissued on United Artists	LM–1069		A
Where the Action Is!	Dolton	BST–8040	February '66	
Batman Theme	Dolton	BST–8042	March '66	
Go with The Ventures!	Dolton	BST–8045	June '66	
Wild Things!	Dolton	BST–8047	September '66	
Guitar Freakout	Dolton	BST–8050	February '67	
Super Psychedelics	Liberty	LST–8052	May '67	
$1,000,000 Weekend	Liberty	LST–8054	December '67	
Flights of Fantasy	Liberty	LST–8055	May '68	
The Horse	Liberty	LST–8057	August '68	
Underground Fire	Liberty	LST–8059	January '69	
Hawaii Five–O *	Liberty	LST–8061	May '69	
Swamp Rock	Liberty	LST–8062	December '69	
New Testament	United Artists	UAS–6796	June '71	
Theme from Shaft	United Artists	UAS–5547	November '71	
Joy—The Ventures Play the Classics	United Artists	UAS–5575	March '72	
Rock and Roll Forever	United Artists	UAS–5649	October '72	
	reissued on Pickwick	3589	April '78	
Jim Croce Song Book	United Artists	LA217	August '74	

THE NEW VENTURES

Rocky Road	United Artists	LA586	June '76	

VENTURES ANTHOLOGIES AND COMPILATIONS

Runnin' Strong	Sunset	5116	May '66	
Genius	Sunset	5160	June '67	
Supergroup	Sunset	5271	February '70	
Decade	Sunset	5317	April '71	
Golden Greats by The Ventures*	Liberty	LST–8053	August '67	
More Golden Greats	Liberty	LST–8060	March '70	
The Ventures' 10th Anniversary Album	2-Liberty	35000	October '70	A
Very Best	Liberty	LN–10122	April '81	A

Superpak	2-United Artists	UXS–80	October '71
The Very Best of The Ventures	United Artists	LA331	March '75

GENE VINCENT.

GENE VINCENT. In one of the most tragic and depressing episodes in the history of rock, Gene Vincent rose to widespread popularity with 1956's near-smash hit "Be-Bop-a-Lula," only to be discounted as a major artist in the United States by mid-1958. Lacking Elvis Presley's magnetism and sporting a lower-class image that contrasted with rising stars such as Ricky Nelson and Fabian, Vincent withdrew to England at the end of 1959, where he became more popular than he did in his native country. After an unsuccessful attempt at an American come-back at the beginning of the Seventies, Gene Vincent died destitute and neglected in 1971.

GENE VINCENT AND THE BLUE CAPS

Blue Jean Bop	Capitol	T–764(M)	September '56	
Gene Vincent and The Blue Caps	Capitol	T–811(M)	March '57	
Gene Vincent Rocks and The Blue Caps Roll	Capitol	T–970(M)	March '58	
A Gene Vincent Record Date	Capitol	T–1059(M)	September '58	
The Bop That Just Won't Stop	Capitol	ST–11287 reissued as SM– 11826 reissued as N–16209 (M)	June '74 September '78	A

GENE VINCENT

Sounds Like Gene Vincent	Capitol	T–1207(M)	June '59	
Crazy Times	Capitol	ST–1342	March '60	
Gene Vincent's Greatest	Capitol	SM–380(E) reissued as N–16208 (M)	November '69	A
I'm Back and I'm Proud	Dandelion	D9–102	March '70	
Slow Times Comin'/Sunshine	Kama Sutra	KSBS–2019	October '70	
The Day the World Turned Blue	Kama Sutra	KSBS–2027	May '71	
Forever	Rolling Rock	022	January '82	A

TOM WAITS. One of the authentic characters of rock music in the Seventies, Tom Waits has written compassionate songs concerned with the tawdry side of urban life performed in an incisive stream-of-consciousness manner reminiscent of the "beat" poets of the Fifties. Interspersing his repertoire with humorous and often bawdy monologues and projecting the image of an inebriated yet intelligent denizen of the streets, Tom Waits is best remembered for his compositions "Ol' 55" (popularized by The Eagles) and the often recorded "(Looking for) The Heart of Saturday Night."

TOM WAITS

Closing Time	Asylum	SD–5061	March '73	A
The Heart of Saturday Night	Asylum	7E–1015	October '74	A
Nighthawks at the Diner	2-Asylum	2008	October '75	A
Small Change	Asylum	7E–1078	September '76	A
Foreign Affairs	Asylum	7E–1117	September '77	A
Blue Valentine	Asylum	6E–162	September '78	A
Heartattack and Vine	Asylum	295	September '80	A

JERRY JEFF WALKER. In a diverse Sixties career, Jerry Jeff Walker started as a folk-style artist, manned a rock band called Circus Maximus, and recorded several neglected solo albums before scoring his most conspicuous success as the author of the classic "Mr. Bojangles," a near-smash hit when covered by The Nitty Gritty Dirt Band in late 1970. Moving to Austin, Texas, in 1972 and signing with MCA Records (which granted him artistic control over his recordings), Walker became intimately involved with the area's burgeoning country music scene, later labeled the "outlaw" movement. Although he has yet to attain the popularity of fellow "outlaws" Waylon Jennings and Willie Nelson, Jerry Jeff Walker has regularly recorded the compositions of Texas songwriters such as Guy Clark and Rodney Crowell and even achieved a certified gold-award album with 1973's *Viva Terlingua*, now acknowledged as a landmark in the rise of Texas "country-rock" music.

CIRCUS MAXIMUS

Circus Maximus	Vanguard	VSD–79260	October '67	A
Neverland Revisited	Vanguard	VSD–79274	June '68	A

JERRY JEFF WALKER

Driftin' Way of Life	Vanguard	VSD–6521	May '69	A
Mr. Bojangles	Atco	SD33–259	October '68	
Five Years Gone	Atco	SD33–297	September '69	
Bein' Free	Atco	SD33–336	September '70	
Jerry Jeff Walker	MCA	DL–75384 reissued as 510 reissued as 2358 reissued as 37004	February '73	A
Viva Terlingua *	MCA	382 reissued as 2350 reissued as 37005	November '73	A
Walker's Collectibles	MCA	450 reissued as 2355	October '74	A
Ridin' High	MCA	2156 reissued as 37006	September '75	A
It's a Good Night for Singin'	MCA	2202	June '76	A
A Man Must Carry On	2-MCA	2–6003 reissued as 8013	May '77	A
Contrary to Ordinary	MCA	3041	June '78	A
The Best of Jerry Jeff Walker	MCA	5128	July '80	A
Jerry Jeff	Elektra	163	November '78	A
Too Old to Change	Elektra	239	October '79	A
Reunion	MCA	5199	June '81	A

THE LOST GONZO BAND

The Lost Gonzo Band	MCA	487	June '75	A
Thrills	MCA	2232	October '76	
Signs of Life	Capitol	SW–11788	July '78	

JUNIOR WALKER AND THE ALL STARS. As leader of Motown's most successful instrumental group, Junior Walker was perhaps the only musician in rock and rhythm-and-blues/soul music during the latter half of the Sixties to achieve popularity as a saxophone soloist. Scoring at least a half dozen smash rhythm-and-blues and major pop hits between 1965 and 1970, including "Shotgun," "(I'm a) Road Runner," and "What Does It Take (to Win Your Love)," Junior Walker and The All Stars' hits were mainly rollicking dance tunes, although several later hits were ballads.

JUNIOR WALKER AND THE ALL STARS

Shotgun	Soul	701	July '65	
Soul Session	Soul	702	April '66	
Road Runner	Soul	703	August '66	
Live!	Soul	705	September '67	
Home Cookin'	Soul	710	February '69	
What Does It Take to Win Your Love	Soul	721	January '70	
Live	Soul	725	September '70	
A Gasssss	Soul	726	September '70	
Rainbow Funk	Soul	732	July '71	
Moody Jr.	Soul	733	January '72	
Hot Shot	Soul	745	January '76	

JUNIOR WALKER AND THE ALL STARS ANTHOLOGIES AND COMPILATIONS

Greatest Hits	Soul	7–718	June '69	A
Anthology	2-Motown	7–786	July '74	A
Shotgun	Pickwick	3391	January '75	
Motown Superstar Series, Volume 5	Motown	5–105		A

JUNIOR WALKER

Sax Appeal	Soul	6–747	June '76
Whopper Bopper Show Stopper	Soul	6–748	November '76
Smooth	Soul	7–750	May '78
Back Street Boogie	Whitfield	3331	May '79

JOE WALSH. Acknowledged as one of the finest lead guitar players in rock, as attested to by Jimmy Page, Eric Clapton, and Pete Townshend, Joe Walsh manned The James Gang during their most successful period before forming his own band and scoring a major hit with "Rocky Mountain Way" from his certified gold-award *The Smoker You Drink, The Player You Get* album. Subsequently achieving another gold-award album solo, Walsh then joined The Eagles at the end of 1975 and brought them a much-needed instrumental bite, as evidenced by "Life in the Fast Lane" from *Hotel California*. Composing memorable melodies featuring excellent guitar and synthesizer work and textured production, Joe Walsh bolstered his intermittent solo career with 1978's certified platinum-award *"But Seriously, Folks . . ."* and its pointed hit single, "Life's Been Good."

Born in New York in 1947, Joe Walsh was raised in New Jersey, took up clarinet and oboe in junior high school, and later switched to rhythm guitar with the duo The G-Clefs. After playing bass for The Nomads during his senior year of high school, he enrolled at Kent State (Ohio) in the fall of 1965 and subsequently joined The Measles on lead guitar for three years. Recruited as Glenn Schwartz' replacement in The James Gang in April 1969, Walsh sang and played lead guitar with the power trio through their most successful period. Authoring their hits "Walk Away" and "Midnight Man" and co-authoring "Funk #49," he recorded four albums with the group, three of which were certified gold-award, before leaving in November 1971. After moving to Boulder, Colorado, resting for six months, and rejecting an offer to join Humble Pie, he assembled Barnstorm with bassist Kenny Passarelli and drummer Joe Vitale for *Barnstorm*, which featured the ballad "Turn to Stone." Adding keyboardists Rocko Grace and Tom Stephenson, Barnstorm toured extensively and scored a certified gold-award album with *The Smoker You Drink, The Player You Get*, which included the major hit "Rocky Mountain Way." By the end of 1973 Barnstorm had dissolved, so Walsh moved to Los Angeles and co-produced his own *So What* album with the assistance of several of The Eagles, J. D. Souther, and Dan Fogelberg. Featuring a re-worked version of "Turn to Stone," the album was certified gold-award in 1975 without benefit of a major hit single. Having produced Dan Fogelberg's first gold-award album, *Souvenirs*, and Joe Vitale's *Roller Coaster Weekend*, Walsh assembled another band for touring in 1975 which produced the live set *You Can't Argue with a Sick Mind*. At the end of 1975 he joined The Eagles as Bernie Leadon's replacement and added a much-needed instrumental punch to the group, as evidenced most particularly on their 1977 hit, "Life in the Fast Lane," co-authored by Walsh. By 1978 he had joined The Eagles' label, Asylum; *"But Seriously, Folks . . .,"* which prominently featured his singing, yielded a major hit with his sardonic view of stardom, "Life's Been Good," and was certified platinum-award within three months of its release. One of the most consistently popular guitar heroes of the Seventies, Joe Walsh continues to enjoy success as a solo artist and as a member of The Eagles. In 1980 he scored a major hit with "All Night Long"; he toured solo again in 1981.

JOE WALSH

Barnstorm	Dunhill	DSX–50130	September '72	
	reissued on MCA	37053		A
The Smoker You Drink, The Player You Get *	Dunhill	DSX–50140	June '73	
	reissued on MCA	37054		A

So What*	Dunhill	DSD–50171	November '74	
	reissued on MCA	37055		A
You Can't Argue with a Sick Mind	ABC/MCA reissued on MCA	AB–932 37051	March '76	A
The Best of Joe Walsh	ABC/MCA reissued on MCA	AA–1083 37052	October '78	A
"But Seriously, Folks . . ."**	Asylum	6E–141	May '78	A
There Goes the Neighborhood	Elektra	523	May '81	A

WAR. An all-black southern California band of ten years experience with varying personnel, War took their name and stabilized their membership with the addition of Danish-born white harmonica player Lee Oskar under former Animals vocalist Eric Burdon, with whom they had a smash hit in 1970 with "Spill the Wine." Initiating their own career in 1971, War became popular with white AM radio listeners while retaining an avid black following as a "progressive soul" band with smash hits such as "The World Is a Ghetto," "The Cisco Kid," and "Gypsy Man." Thus opening the door to the crossover successes of other black groups by the mid-Seventies, War was alternately mellow and percussive in their sound, distinctively fusing elements of jazz and "funk" with Latin rhythms and harmonius singing on songs with catchy melodies and obvious "hooks." Aided by three near-smash hit singles in 1975 and 1976, War has scored seven consecutive gold-award albums since *All Day Music; The Music Band—2*, with some personnel changes, broke that string.

Ostensibly started as a group by drummer Harold Brown (born March 17, 1946, in Long Beach, California), reed player Charles Miller (born June 2, 1939, in Olathe, Kansas), and guitarist Howard Scott (born March 15, 1946, in San Pedro, California) around 1959, the three were joined by bassist Morris "B. B." Dickerson (born August 3, 1949, in Torrance, California) and keyboardist Leroy "Lonnie" Jordan (born November 21, 1948, in San Diego) in the formation of The Creators during the early Sixties. Enduring regular personnel shifts, the departure of Dickerson, and the drafting into the army of several members, the group persevered on the southern California club circuit under a variety of names. Around 1966 Brown, Miller, and Scott got together with Jordan, percussionist Thomas "Papa Dee" Allen (born July 18, 1931, in Wilmington, Delaware), and a returned Dickerson as Night Shift. Introduced to former Animals vocalist Eric Burdon and his harmonica-playing friend Lee Oskar (born March 24, 1948, in Copenhagen, Denmark), Night Shift began working with the two as War. The members: Howard Scott (guitar, percussion, vocals), Lonnie Jordan (keyboards, percussion, vocals), Charles Miller (flute, clarinet, saxophone, vocals), Lee Oskar (harmonica, percussion, vocals), B. B. Dickerson (bass, percussion, vocals), Dee Allen (congas, percussion, vocals), and Harold Brown (drums, percussion).

Having recorded two albums of excellent material with Eric Burdon, War and the English vocalist scored a smash hit with "Spill the Wine" in 1970. While conducting tours of Europe in 1970 and again in 1971, War completed the latter tour without Burdon, as he left the tour exhausted and road-weary. After signing with United Artists as an act in their own right, War's debut album was largely overlooked, but their second, *All Day Music*, yielded a moderate hit with the title song and a major hit with "Slippin' into Darkness" and became their first certified gold-award album in 1972. That album and *The World Is a Ghetto*, which included the near-smash hit title song and the smash "The Cisco Kid," established War as a "progressive soul" outfit with both black and white audiences. After *Deliver the Word*, which produced major hits with "Gypsy Man" and "Me and Baby Brother," War became entangled in disputes with United Artists that resulted in only one album release, a mediocre live set which yielded only a moderate hit with the Spanish-language "Ballero," in the next two years. In the summer of 1975, they returned with *Why Can't We Be Friends?*, which produced smash hits with the title song and "Low Rider." During 1976 United Artists released Lee Oskar's first solo album, which yielded a minor hit with "BLT," and War achieved another smash hit with "Summer." Following *Platinum Jazz* on United Artists' Blue Note label, War switched to MCA Records for *Galaxy*, which was certified gold-award despite producing only a moderate hit with the title song. In 1978 releases included Lonnie Jordan's first solo album on MCA, Oskar's second on Elektra, and the soundtrack to *Youngblood*, composed and performed by War, on United Artists. For *The Music Band*, certified gold-award without benefit of even a minor hit single, Luther Rabb replaced B. B. Dickerson on bass and War added a female vocalist–percussionist in the person of Alice Smith. Before the recording of the surprisingly modestly selling *Music Band—2*, Charles Miller departed and horn player Pat Rizzo and a second drummer, Ron Hammon, were added to the lineup of War.

ERIC BURDON AND WAR

Eric Burdon Declares "War"	MGM	SE–4663	March '70	
reissued as Spill the Wine	Lax	PW–37109	April '81	A
Black Man's Burdon	2-MGM	SE–4710	November '70	
Love Is All Around	ABC	966	December '76	

WAR

War	United Artists	UAS–5508	January '71	
All Day Music*	United Artists	UAS–5546	October '71	
	reissued on Lax	PW–37111	April '81	A

The World Is a Ghetto*	United Artists reissued on Lax	UAS–5652 PW–37112	October '72 April '81	A
Deliver the Word*	United Artists	LA128	August '73	
War Live*	2-United Artists	LA193	March '74	
Why Can't We Be Friends?*	United Artists reissued on Lax	LA441 PW–37113	June '75 April '81	A
Greatest Hits**	United Artists	LA648	August '76	
Youngblood (soundtrack)	United Artists	LA904	July '78	A
Platinum Jazz*	Blue Note	LA690	July '77	
Galaxy*	MCA	3030	November '77	A
The Music Band*	MCA	3085	April '79	A
The Music Band— 2	MCA	3193	December '79	A
The Music Band Live	MCA	5156	December '80	A

LEE OSKAR

Lee Oskar	United Artists reissued on Lax	LA594 PW–37114	March '76 April '81	A
Before the Rain	Elektra	150	August '78	
My Road, Our Road	Elektra	526	July '81	A

LONNIE JORDAN

Different Moods of Me	MCA	2329	February '78	

DIONNE WARWICK(E). In perhaps the most successful hit-making partnership of the Sixties, singer Dionne Warwick, lyricist Hal David, and arranger–producer–writer Burt Bacharach achieved more than 35 singles chart entries, a number of them smash hits, between late 1962 and 1971 beginning with "Don't Make Me Over." Featuring Warwick's svelte, light, and perfectly phrased vocals, Bacharach's carefully arranged orchestral backdrop complete with masses of strings, and David's pop-style lyrics, their songs brought a new level of sophistication to soul music with hits such as "Anyone Who Had a Heart," "Walk On By," and "Message to Michael." However, by 1967, Bacharach and David's material had become geared to easy listening and cabaret-style audiences and, although her recordings continued to be popular in the pop and rhythm-and-blues/soul fields, her most consistent later success was in the easy listening arena. Scoring her last smash pop hit with "I'll Never Fall in Love Again" at the end of 1969, Dionne Warwick maintained her in-concert popularity with the easy listening audience, despite a change of labels in 1971 and the loss of the Bacharach–David team in 1972. After achieving a top pop hit in

1974 with the Thom Bell-produced "Then Came You" in collaboration with The Spinners, Warwick scored her first solo smash hit in nearly a decade with "I'll Never Love This Way Again," produced by Barry Manilow, in 1979.

Born in East Orange, New Jersey, on December 12, 1941, as Marie Dionne Warrick, Dionne Warwick started singing in church choirs and local gospel groups at the age of six. After studying at the Hart College of Music in Connecticut and singing at recording sessions in New York in the early Sixties with sister Dee Dee and cousin Cissy Houston, Dionne came to the attention of songwriter–producer–arranger Burt Bacharach, who arranged a recording contract for her with Scepter Records. With Bacharach arranging and providing the music and collaborator Hal David supplying the lyrics, she scored a major pop and rhythm-and-blues hit at the end of 1962 with "Don't Make Me Over." "Anyone Who Had a Heart" and the classic "Walk On By" became smash pop and easy listening hits in 1963–64, followed by the moderate pop hit "You'll Never Get to Heaven" and the major pop hit "Reach Out for Me." During 1965 Warwick's singles fared less well, but in 1966 she achieved a near-smash pop and major rhythm-and-blues *and* easy listening hit with "Message to Michael" plus the major pop hits "Trains and Boats and Planes" and "I Just Don't Know What to Do with Myself." Fully established as an international recording artist and cabaret performer, Warwick began recording less dynamic Bacharach–David songs as the team started working on movie scores and stage musicals. Both "Alfie" (from the film of the same name) and "I Say a Little Prayer" were big hits in 1967 and, beginning with "(Theme from) The Valley of the Dolls," her most consistent success was in the easy listening field. Virtually all of her recordings through 1971 were smash easy listening hits, with "Do You Know the Way to San José" and "Promises, Promises" also becoming major pop hits, whereas "This Girl's in Love with You" was a smash hit in the pop, easy listening, and rhythm-and-blues fields. After "You've Lost That Lovin' Feeling" and the smash "I'll Never Fall in Love Again," Warwick's singles through 1971 were moderate pop hits at best.

In 1971 Dionne Warwick legally changed her surname to Warwicke and switched to Warner Brothers Records, taking the Bacharach–David team with her; but after a single album with them, the two split up. She utilized material supplied by Lamont Dozier and Brian Holland for *Just Being Myself* and her next album, coming a full two years later, featured the top pop hit "Then Came You," recorded with The Spinners and produced by Thom Bell. The album of the same name, otherwise produced by Jerry Ragavoy, fared poorly, as did *Track of the Cat*, which was written, produced, and arranged by Bell. Dropping the "e" from her surname, Warwick recorded a double-record set with Isaac Hayes and a final album for Warner Brothers before switching to Arista Records for 1979's *Dionne*. The album, produced by Barry Manilow, yielded her first smash hit in nearly a decade with "I'll Never Love This Way Again" and the major hit "Deja Vu" and was certified gold-award in September. She scored a major hit in 1980 with "No Night So Long." Dionne Warwick hosted the syndicated music/variety TV show "Solid Gold" for several years until being replaced by Andy Gibb in 1981.

DIONNE WARWICK

Presenting Dionne Warwick	Scepter	508(M)		
Anyone Who Had a Heart	Scepter	517(M)		
Make Way for Dionne Warwick	Scepter	523	September '64	
The Sensitive Sound of Dionne Warwick	Scepter	528	February '65	
Here I Am	Scepter	531	December '65	
In Paris	Scepter	534	April '66	
Here, Where There Is Love*	Scepter	555	December '66	
On Stage and at the Movies	Scepter	559	May '67	
The Windows of the World	Scepter	563	August '67	
Magic of Believing	Scepter	567		
Valley of the Dolls*	Scepter	568	March '68	
Promises, Promises	Scepter	571	December '68	
Soulful	Scepter	573	March '69	
Greatest Motion Picture Hits	Scepter	575	August '69	
I'll Never Fall in Love Again	Scepter	581	April '70	
Very Dionne	Scepter	587	December '70	
Dionne	Warner Brothers	BS–2585	December '71	
Just Being Myself	Warner Brothers	BS–2658	January '73	
Then Came You	Warner Brothers	BS–2846	February '75	
Track of the Cat	Warner Brothers	BS–2893	November '75	
Love at First Sight	Warner Brothers	3119	November '77	
Dionne**	Arista	AB–4230 reissued as 9512	June '79	
No Night So Long	Arista	9526	August '80	A
Hot! Live and Otherwise	2-Arista	8605	June '81	A

DIONNE WARWICK AND ISAAC HAYES

A Man and a Woman	2-ABC reissued on	996	February '77	
	MCA	10012		A

DIONNE WARWICK ANTHOLOGIES AND COMPILATIONS

Golden Hits, Volume 1	Scepter	565	November '67	
Golden Hits, Volume 2	Scepter	577	October '69	
The Dionne Warwick Story —A Decade of Gold*	2-Scepter	596	October '71	
From Within	2-Scepter	598	April '72	
Golden Voice	Springboard International	4001	January '73	
Sings Her Very Best	Springboard International	4002	January '73	
One Hit After Another	Springboard International	4003	January '73	
Greatest Hits, Volume 2	Springboard International	4032	November '75	
Dionne Warwicke	2-Pickwick	2056	October '73	A
Make It Easy on Yourself	Pickwick	3326		
Alfie	Pickwick	3338		
The Very Best of Dionne Warwicke	United Artists	LA337 reissued as LA388	January '75 March '75	
Only Love Can Break a Heart	Musicor	2501	June '77	

JANN WENNER/*ROLLING STONE* MAGAZINE. With *Rolling Stone* magazine, editor and mastermind Jann Wenner created a viable alternative to trade magazines and fan magazines in the coverage of contemporary popular music. Concerned with aspects of the so-called "youth culture" as well as with music while initially remaining decidedly nonpolitical, *Rolling Stone* became identified with what was termed the "counterculture," much to the chagrin of Wenner, who sought to establish the periodical as a professional, journalistic mainstream publication. Quickly becoming a financial success and recognized as an authority within the music industry, *Rolling Stone* established a high standard of writing that others have since sought to achieve; it employed some of the finest music writers in the business, notably Jon Landau, probably the first rock critic to gain a legitimate reputation. Largely supported by the advertising revenues of record companies and stereo equipment manufacturers, *Rolling Stone* endured a period of ill-advised investments by Wenner and a large-scale purge of personnel in 1970 finally to attain respectability with the "straight" press through award-winning articles on the Altamont debacle of The Rolling Stones and the Charles Manson family. Subsequently consolidating its gains and professionalizing its staff, *Rolling Stone* drew widespread attention with "Doctor" Hunter S. Thompson, the "inventor" of the so-called "Gonzo" style of journalism, through his highly acclaimed two-part article, "Fear and Loathing in Las Vegas," and his astute coverage of the 1972 presidential campaign. Probably then at the height of its editorial power and influence, *Rolling Stone* later began emphasizing investigative reporting and coverage of aspects of "pop culture" to the detriment of rock music coverage and focused on established acts in its record review section; the magazine obtained advertising from "straight" sponsors such as cigarette, liquor, and automobile manufacturers and increased its circulation. The magazine's enormous success served to encourage the proliferation of rock magazines such as *Circus*, *Zoo World*, *Creem*, and a revived *Crawdaddy;* by the mid-Seventies, *Rolling Stone* was only nominally a music magazine. Suffering the departures of Thompson and Landau, Jann Wenner and *Rolling Stone* moved from San Francisco to New York in early 1977.

Born in New York in 1946, Jann Wenner was raised in suburban Marin County, north of San Francisco. He attended the University of California at Berkeley during the Free Speech Movement, which he covered for the *Daily Californian*, and met *San Francisco Chronicle* music critic Ralph Gleason in 1965. By 1967 Wenner had dropped out of college to pursue freelance music writing and to work as arts editor for the local radical magazine, *Sunday Ramparts*. That year Wenner and Gleason formulated a plan to publish a professional, journalistic periodical that would serve as an alternative to music trade magazines, fan magazines, and "underground" journals in its coverage of contemporary popular music and the "youth culture." By borrowing $7,500 from friends and relatives, persuading a printer to provide credit and free office space, and employing a part-time volunteer staff, Wenner published the first issue of *Rolling Stone* with a cover date of November 9, 1967. Although most of the issue's press run was returned, the publication was remarkably professional; but Wenner's management soon led to the departures of early staff members and the recruitment of Jon Landau. Eschewing "psychedelic" art and obtaining newsstand distribution (rather than having it sold on the streets by vendors), *Rolling Stone* was a financial success by 1969, and increased revenues allowed Wenner to expand and professionalize his staff. Supported by record company advertising since its eighth issue, *Rolling Stone* moved to a new, expensive location in 1970, opened offices in Los Angeles and New York, and unsuccessfully attempted to launch a British edition in conjunction with Mick Jagger. As *Rolling Stone* expanded rapidly, Wenner spent money extravagantly and failed at establishing two magazines, *New York Scenes* and the environmental-minded *Earth Times*. On the verge of financial collapse, the magazine was ostensibly bailed out by record companies; but a 1970 cover article on American politics, published in Wenner's absence, led to the dismissal of many staff members (including managing editor John Burks, who was largely responsible for much of the magazine's success) and the end of political coverage. Nonetheless, award-winning articles on Altamont and the Charles Manson family brought *Rolling Stone* respectability with the "straight" press and the publication's heretofore chaotic front-office operation was stabilized by self-made millionaire–investor Max Palevsky.

With *Rolling Stone* at perhaps the height of its fame in 1970, Jann Wenner employed writer "Doctor" Hunter S. Thompson, a cult figure largely on the basis of his book, *The Hell's Angels*. Practicing a style of writing that became known as "Gonzo" journalism, a careful and precise if rambling stream-of-consciousness style complete with his accounts of fortifying drug use, Thompson quickly made an impact with the critically acclaimed two-part article, "Fear and Loathing in Las Vegas." He subsequently produced perhaps the most discerning coverage of the 1972 presidential campaign, which encouraged Wenner to increase the magazine's political coverage, hire first-rate reporters such as Joe Klein and Richard Goodwin, and to expand the provinces of cultural critic Jonathon Cott and investigative reporter Joe Eszterhas. During 1975 *Rolling Stone* eliminated such possibly offensive items as four-letter words and nude pictures and actively sought "straight" advertisers of autos, cameras, liquors, and cigarettes; but the decline of Thompson's writing and the death of Ralph Gleason in June marked a difficult period for the magazine. The book-publishing wing of *Rolling Stone*, Straight Arrow Press, was abandoned, and celebrities such as Truman Capote, Andy Warhol, and John Dean were hired to write articles. Jon Landau departed to become a producer and the quality of the magazine's music coverage began to diminish as the record review section presented longer, more in-depth articles primarily concerned with established artists. Although the magazine gained notoriety for its investigative reporting, as evidenced by articles on Patty Hearst and Karen Silkwood, *Rolling Stone* was "scooped" by the "straight" press on reports of music industry "payola" and "drugola" and endured a lessened reputation for less-than-astute coverage of then-current music. In September 1976 Wenner announced he was moving the magazine to New York, where he has sought to shake the periodical's "counterculture" image and to establish a new legitimacy as a general interest magazine with cover stories on personalities such as Jane Fonda, Johnny Carson, and Robert Redford. By 1979 another of Jann Wenner's pet projects, the magazine *Outside*, had been sold as *Rolling Stone's* circulation reached 600,000 and a film deal was struck with Paramount Pictures. With the February 5, 1981, issue, *Rolling Stone* expanded its coverage of motion pictures and introduced sections featuring "hard news" analysis and contemporary fiction. In November, Wenner launched yet another magazine, *The Record*, which was concerned solely with contemporary rock music.

THE WHO. Hugely popular in their native England by 1966 on the basis of a series of major hit singles and, more importantly, their reputation as a wildly exciting and visually arresting in-concert band, The Who, like The Beatles and perhaps The Rolling Stones (but unlike virtually every other early Sixties British rock group), was comprised of four distinct and immediately recognizable personalities. Pete Townshend, primary author of the group's material and one of rock music's all-time greatest showmen, provided the group's powerful guitar riffs that served as the band's initial trademark, as well as characteristic onstage feats such as his rapid windmill guitar strokes, acrobatic leaps and knee drops, plus his legendary guitar smashing. Keith Moon, one of rock music's most flamboyant and maniacally colorful figures, performed on drums in an incredibly energetic and melodic style that influenced an entire generation of rock drummers. Roger Daltrey, one of rock music's most distinctive singers whose voice retained its melodiousness even at high volume, added his own touches by madly twirling his microphone and vigorously prancing on stage; bassist John Entwhistle, whose rapid virtuoso technique has been largely overlooked, remained unmoved and stock-still as the group's apparent center of gravity.

By means of Townshend's guitar smashing and Moon's drum kit wrecking, The Who became established as rock music's first self-destructive group; they retained this expensive practice through 1969 or so. As a three-piece instrumental group with lead vocalist, The Who were the first successful band to utilize the now popular format. Moreover, Pete Townshend was one of the first guitarists to popularize the creative use of feedback, although rock scholars still dispute whether Townshend or The Yardbird's Jeff Beck was the first to utilize the technique. Townshend's use of feedback, coupled with Moon's vigorous drumming, led to the The Who's identification as one of the earliest "heavy metal" bands (along with Led Zeppelin) and, on the basis of songs such as "My Generation" (usually regarded as one of the greatest rock singles of the Sixties), The Who were also considered one of the first "punk" groups years before a burgeoning scene developed in the latter half of the Seventies.

Becoming the musical representatives of the "mod" movement (along with The Small Faces) on the basis of "My Generation" and their flashy pop-art stage apparel, The Who eventually broke through in the United States with the major hit "Happy Jack" and their celebrated performance at the Monterey Pop Festival in June 1967. Their Sell Out album is recognized as one of the first fully realized "concept" albums and its hit single, "I Can See for Miles," is regarded as an early example of "psychedelic" music. Moreover, by 1968, Pete Townshend had become one of the most often quoted, respected, and articulate spokesmen for rock music and its role in contemporary culture, as evidenced by a two-part interview published in Rolling Stone that September.

Nonetheless, The Who's best remembered claim to fame and eternal recognition came with 1969's Tommy album. Although arguably not the first "rock opera," it was the first successful one and brought fortune, international fame, and artistic respectability to The Who. Drawing the favorable attention of "serious" drama, opera, and classical music critics, the album and its artistic success finally led to the recognition of rock music as something more than trivial, cacaphonous, and youth-oriented music and to the legitimization of rock as a valid art form. As a consequence of *Tommy's* success, The Who became the first rock band to appear at New York's prestigious Metropolitan Opera House; they started to vie with The Rolling Stones for the honor of being called "The Best Rock Band in the World."

Their fans' preoccupation with *Tommy* notwithstanding, The Who recorded one of the finest live albums in the history of rock, *Live at Leeds*, and the innovative *Who's Next* album before the members began pursuing a variety of solo projects. John Entwhistle became the first member to release a solo album and to tour with his own band, whereas Roger Daltrey's debut was a moving and profound work that helped launch songwriter Leo Sayer's recording career. Although equivocally reviewed by critics, The Who's 1973 *Quadrophenia* album was every bit the work *Tommy* was and, in fact, revealed a growing maturity to Pete Townshend's work. The mid- to late Seventies proved to be a fallow period for the group, and they retained the distinction of being rock music's longest-lived intact band until Keith Moon's death in September 1978. Bouncing back with *Who Are You*, renewed touring, and the 1979 films *The Kids Are Alright* and *Quadrophenia*, The Who are arguably the greatest rock band in the world.

Around 1959 Pete Townshend (born May 19, 1945, in Chiswick, London, England) and classically trained John Entwhistle (born October 9, 1946, also in Chiswick) were members of a Dixieland jazz group, with Townshend on banjo and Entwhistle on trumpet. By the early Sixties, the two had helped form The Detours with Roger Daltrey (born March 1, 1944, in Hammersmith, London) and drummer Doug Sanden. Daltrey functioned as leader, lead guitarist, and lead singer with the group but, by the time they first used the name The Who, he had assumed the sole role of vocalist. Under manager Peter Meaden, they adopted a colorful mod image, became The High Numbers, and issued their first single, "I'm the Face," in mid-1964. By October 1964, they had replaced their original drummer with Keith Moon (born August 23, 1947, in Wembley, London) from the surf band The Beachcombers and again become The Who under new managers Kit Lambert and Chris Stamp. The members: Roger Daltrey (lead vocals), Pete Townshend (lead and rhythm guitar), John Entwhistle (bass), and Keith Moon (drums). Lambert and Stamp encouraged Townshend to develop his writing and urged the group to display open aggression on stage; they cultivated the group's mod image with flashy clothes, including Townshend's renowned Union Jack jacket. Signed to American Decca (Brunswick and later Reaction and Track in Great Britain) on the recommendation of Shel Talmy, The Who scored four consecutive top-ten singles in Britain under producer Talmy by the spring of 1966, bolstered by appearances on the British television show "Ready, Steady, Go." These hits were "I Can't Explain," the archetypal "heavy metal" "Anyway, Anyhow, Anywhere," the classic "My Generation," and "Substitute."

In 1965, during a performance at the Railway Tavern, Pete Townshend inadvertently broke the neck of his guitar on a low ceiling; this led to the first incident of Townshend and Keith Moon's destruction of their instruments, an expensive practice which the group reenacted at virtually every performance for the next four years and which brought the group widespread notoriety. Their debut album, released in early 1966, contained "My Generation," "The Kids Are Alright," and the satiric "A Legal Matter," all by Townshend, plus the manic instrumental "The Ox," but it failed to make the American charts. Their second album, *Happy Jack*, produced their first major American hit with the title song; it also included Entwhistle's "Boris the Spider" and "Whiskey Man," and Townshend's first attempt at a multi-thematic extended piece (which he called a "mini-opera"), "A Quick One While He's Away." Launched in America with their frenetic appearance at the Monterey Pop Festival in June 1967 (later chronicled in the D.A. Pennebaker film) and subsequent late summer tour in support of Herman's Hermits, The Who issued one of the earliest "concept" albums, *The Who Sell Out*, at year's end. Featuring a bizarre album cover and satiric radio station commercials between songs, the album contained the archetypal "psychedelic" near-smash hit, "I Can See for Miles," plus "Armenia City in the Sky" and the gentler "Rael." By now a major concert attraction in the United States as well as in Great Britain, The Who next released the anthology set *Magic Bus*, which included Townshend's "Call Me Lightning," "Magic Bus" (a major American hit), and "Pictures of Lily," and a remake of the surf song "Bucket T.," featuring Entwhistle's humorous French horn solo.

The Who's next album was the highly influential "rock opera," *Tommy*. Although not the first work of its kind, the album proved hugely successful, became the group's first certified gold-award album, remained on the album charts for more than two years, and yielded the major hit "Pinball Wizard." A bizarre and elaborate tale of lost innocence, redemption, and contrition, *Tommy* featured a number of innovative instrumental interludes, Sonny Boy Williamson's "Eyesight to the Blind," the psychedelic "Acid Queen," the inspiring "Sensation," the liberating "I'm Free," and Tommy's final rejection/plea for acceptance, "We're Not Gonna Take It/See Me, Feel Me." Performed in its entirety only twice—once in London and once in New York—*Tommy* drew the favorable praise of "serious" drama, opera, and classical music critics as well as rock fans and critics and may ultimately be judged as one of the most fully realized and important musical productions of the entire 20th century. Certainly not without its flaws ("Sally Simpson" for example), *Tommy* was performed by The Who in excerpted form for nearly two years and inspired both an all-star London stage production and an excessive, and frankly unfortunate, film by Ken Russell. The stage production, released in slightly different form as an album in late 1973, featured the London Symphony Orchestra and Chamber Choir and performances by Rod Stewart ("Pinball Wizard"), Merry Clayton ("Acid Queen"), Stevie Winwood, Sandy Denny, Richie Havens, Ringo Starr, and The Who. Director, screenplay writer, and co-producer Russell's 1975 film version, an extravagant and bizarre production replete with repulsive, inane, and tedious scenes, featured Roger Daltrey as the protagonist and performances by Eric Clapton ("Eyesight to the Blind"), Tina Turner ("Acid Queen"), Elton John ("Pinball Wizard"), and the members of The Who, plus decidedly shallow acting and poor musical performances by Ann-Margaret, Oliver Reed, and Jack Nicholson.

Seriously challenging The Rolling Stones' claim to being "The World's Greatest Rock-and-Roll Band," particularly after their celebrated appearance at the Woodstock Festival and the subsequent movie, The Who next released *Live at Leeds*, an excellent album that effectively represented the aural if not visual excitement of The Who in concert. The album produced a major hit with Eddie Cochran's "Summertime Blues" and contained extended versions of both "My Generation" and "The Magic Bus," while providing a number of documents and photographs from the history of The Who. Their first studio album in two years, *Who's Next*, was another milestone in the history of rock, showcasing Townshend's outstanding and innovative use of synthesizers. The album included several finely constructed and brilliantly performed extended pieces originally intended for Townshend's abandoned science fiction *Lifehouse* followup to *Tommy*, "Baba O'Riley," "Song Is Over," and the disillusioned "Won't Get Fooled Again" (a major hit), as well as the menacing "Behind Blue Eyes" (a moderate hit) and Entwhistle's "My Wife." Reviewed by Townshend in *Rolling Stone*, the anthology set *Meaty, Beaty, Big, and Bouncy* successfully encapsulated the singles of The Who through "Pinball Wizard" and "The Magic Bus" and included Townshend's overlooked "The Seeker." Scoring a major hit in the summer of 1972 with "Join Together," the group's next album of new material, released more than two years after *Who's Next*, was the double-record set *Quadrophenia*. Although greeted by equivocal reviews, the album was perhaps even more ambitious and personal than was *Tommy* and every bit its equal in musical and dramatic terms. Concerned with the early history of The Who and the mod movement through its protagonist Jimmy, *Quadrophenia's* title referred to Jimmy's double schizophrenia, the four members of The Who as representatives of the four sides of his personality, and the four recurrent musical themes of the album. Oddly criticized for its lack of unity, the album was heavily orchestrated and lavishly produced; it included "I'm One," "5:15," "Is It in My Head," and "Drowned" plus the minor hits "Love, Reign O'er Me" and "The Real Me." For the first time in two years, The Who toured, this time in support of *Quadrophenia*.

In the meantime, the members of The Who had pursued individual projects. John Entwhistle was the first to release a solo album, *Smash Your Head Against the Wall*, followed by *Whistle Rhymes* in 1972 and *Rigor Mortis Sets In* in 1973. Pete Townshend, a convert to the philosophy of Meher Baba, originally recorded his solo debut album for devotees of the guru, but it proved so popular that it was issued as a regular commercial release in 1972. With Townshend handling virtually every musical instrument and engineering chore, *Who Came First* included "Pure and Easy," "Nothing Is Everything (Let's See Action)," and an adaptation of Meher Baba's Universal Prayer, "Parvardigar." Roger Daltrey's debut solo album, *Daltrey*, was probably the most artistically and commercially successful of the group members' early releases. Produced by Dave Courtney and former pop star Adam Faith and featuring the collaboratively written songs of Faith, Courtney, and Leo Sayer, the album yielded a minor hit with "Giving It All Away" and contained outstanding existential songs such as "The Way of the World," "You Are Yourself" and "Hard Life," plus "One-Man Band." During 1974 John Entwhistle assembled a remarkable collection of primarily unreleased Who material issued as *Odds and Sods*. An excellent summation of the career of The Who, the album included their first single release, "I'm the Face," a dynamic and superior version of "Pure and Easy," "Too Much of Anything" from the abandoned *Lifehouse* project, the menacing and moving "Naked Eye," and the neglected rock anthem, "Long Live Rock." Also during this time, Keith Moon initiated his acting career through appearances in Frank Zappa's *200 Motels* (1971) and the David Essex films *That'll Be the Day* (1973, with Ringo Starr) and *Stardust* (1974, with Adam Faith and Dave Edmunds), as well as in *Tommy*.

Following the release of The Who's first four albums as double-record sets, John Entwhistle issued *Mad Dog*, recorded with the band Ox, with whom he toured in 1975. Keith Moon soon released his debut solo album and Roger Daltrey followed with *Ride a Rock Horse*, which included "Oceans Away" and Rufus Thomas' "Walking the Dog" and yielded a minor hit with Russ Ballard's "Come and Get Your Love." Although it was critically hailed and produced a major hit with "Squeeze Box," *The Who by Numbers* was probably the group's weakest effort, recorded during a relatively inactive period which lasted until 1977 and was interrupted only by a major American tour in 1975–76. Townshend, suffering a permanent hearing loss and desirous of spending more time with his family, remained out of the public eye; Daltrey appeared in Ken Russell's equivocal *Lisztomania* movie as composer Franz Liszt in 1975; and Moon moved to Los Angeles in 1976. During 1977 Daltrey recorded his third solo album and Townshend re-emerged triumphantly with *Rough Mix*, recorded with Ronnie Lane.

In 1978 The Who participated in a flurry of activity. Their first album in nearly three years, *Who Are You*, became an instant best-seller and produced a major hit with the title song; but on September 7, 1978, Keith Moon was found dead in his London flat at the age of 31, the victim of a sedative overdose. By the beginning of 1979 former Small Faces and Faces drummer Kenney Jones (born September 16, 1948, in Stepney, East London) had replaced Moon and The Who resumed touring that summer, augmented by keyboardist John "Rabbit" Bundrick, a former member of Free. During the year The Who released two feature-length films and double-record soundtrack albums, the excellent documentary-style *The Kids Are Alright* and the fictional *Quadrophenia*, based on the 1973 album. Although both films lasted only briefly in their first runs, they may very well become cult favorites at midnight showings. *The Kids Are Alright* included the first official release from the legendary unreleased 1968 television special "The Rolling Stones Rock and Roll Circus," and its soundtrack

album yielded a minor hit with "Long Live Rock" and was quickly certified platinum-award. Perhaps failing at the box office due to the un-
familiarity of American audiences with the mod movement, *Quadrophenia* and its soundtrack album featured remixes from the original album,
three new songs, and an entire side of "oldies" such as The Kingsmen's
"Louie, Louie" and The Crystals' "Da Doo Ron Ron." The Who toured
America again in late 1979 but, at a performance at Cincinnati's River-
front Stadium on December 3, 11 people were killed in the crush of callous
fans outside the stadium, an unfortunate legacy to the career of one of rock
music's most talented and exciting acts. By early 1980 The Who had
switched to Warner Brothers for their American releases and Pete
Townshend, contracted as a solo artist to Atco Records since 1979, made
his recording debut for the label that spring with *Empty Glass* and its hit
single "Let My Love Open the Door." Also that year, Roger Daltrey
starred in the title role of the film *McVicar*, based on the autobiography of
John McVicar, a contemporary bank robber widely known in Great Britain for his repeated escapes from prison. The soundtrack album, co-
credited to Daltrey and Russ Ballard, was issued in the fall. During 1981,
The Who issued *Face Dances*, which included the hit "You Better, You
Bet," and John Entwhistle released his first solo album in six years, *Too
Late the Hero*, recorded with Joe Walsh.

THE WHO

The Who Sings My Generation	Decca reissued on MCA	DL–74664 2044	April '66	
Happy Jack	Decca reissued on MCA	DL–74892 2045	April '67	
The Who Sell Out	Decca reissued on MCA	DL–74950 2046	December '67	
Magic Bus—The Who on Tour	Decca reissued on MCA	DL–75064 2047	September '68	

TOMMY

Tommy *	2-Decca reissued on MCA	DXSW– 7205 10005	May '69	A
Tommy with The London Sym- phony Orchestra and Chamber Choir *	2-Ode	SP–99001	November '72	
Tommy (sound- track) *	2-Polydor	PD2–9502	March '75	
Tommy—Studio Cast (excerpts)	Pickwick	3339		A

THE WHO

Live at Leeds*	Decca	DL–79175	May '70	
	reissued on			
	MCA	2022		
		reissued as 3023		
		reissued as 37000		A
Who's Next*	Decca	DL–79182	August '71	
	reissued on			
	MCA	2023		
		reissued as 3024		A
Meaty, Beaty, Big, and Bouncy*	Decca	DL–79184	November '71	
	reissued on			
	MCA	2025		
		reissued as 3025		
		reissued as 37001		A
Quadrophenia*	2-MCA	2–10004	October '73	A

JOHN ENTWHISTLE

Smash Your Head Against the Wall	Decca	DL–79183	October '71	
	reissued on			
	MCA	2024		A
Whistle Rhymes	Decca	DL–79190	October '72	
	reissued on			
	MCA	2027		
Rigor Mortis Sets In	MCA	321	May '73	
Mad Dog (with Ox)	MCA	2129	February '75	
Too Late the Hero	Atco	SD38–142	October '81	A

PETE TOWNSHEND

Who Came First	Decca	DL–79189	October '72	
	reissued on			
	MCA	2026		

ROGER DALTREY

Daltrey	MCA	328	May '73	
		reissued as 2349		
		reissued as 37032		A
Ride a Rock Horse	MCA	2147	July '75	
		reissued as 37030		A
One of the Boys	MCA	2271	June '77	
		reissued as 37031		A

ROGER DALTREY/RICK WAKEMAN

Lisztomania (soundtrack)	A&M	SP–4546	October '75	

KEITH MOON

Two Sides of the Moon	MCA	2136	March '75	

THE WHO

Odds and Sods*	MCA	2126	October '74	
Magic Bus/Sing My Generation	2-MCA	4068	November '74	A
A Quick One/Sell Out	2-MCA	4067	November '74	A
The Who by Numbers*	MCA	2161 reissued as 3026 reissued as 37002	October '75	A

PETE TOWNSHEND AND RONNIE LANE

Rough Mix	MCA	2295	September '77	A

THE WHO

Who Are You**	MCA	3050	August '78	
The Kids Are Alright (soundtrack)**	2-MCA	2–11005	June '79	A
Hooligans	2-MCA	12001	November '81	A
Face Dances**	Warner Brothers	HS–3516	April '81	A

THE WHO AND VARIOUS ARTISTS

Quadrophenia (soundtrack)	2-Polydor	PD2–6235	September '79	A

PETE TOWNSHEND

Empty Glass*	Atco	32–100	May '80	A

ROGER DALTREY/RUSS BALLARD

McVicar (soundtrack)	Polydor	PD–6284	August '80	A

JACKIE WILSON. Clyde McPhatter's 1953 replacement in The Dominoes, Jackie Wilson launched his own solo career in 1957 and became one of the first rhythm-and-blues vocalists to be successful in the early rock-and-roll era. Scoring a dozen major pop hits between 1958 and 1961, including the smash "Lonely Teardrops," Wilson was a masterful in-concert performer, passionately singing both rockers and ballads with his astonishingly wide-ranging voice. Overwhelmed by the emergence of soul music in the early Sixties, he managed a smash hit with the classic "(Your Love Keeps Lifting Me) Higher and Higher" in 1967, but found himself relegated to the "oldies" circuit. In September 1975, while appearing on a package show in New Jersey, Jackie Wilson suffered a massive heart attack that has since left him in a coma.

BILLY WARD AND THE DOMINOES

14 Hits (1951– 1965)	King	5005(M)	December '77	A
21 Hits	King	5008(M)	December '77	A

JACKIE WILSON AND THE DOMINOES

14 Hits	King	5007(M)	December '77	A

JACKIE WILSON

He's So Fine	Brunswick	BL–54042 (M)	May '58	
Lonely Teardrops	Brunswick	BL–54045 (M)	April '59	
So Much	Brunswick	754050	January '60	
Jackie Sings the Blues	Brunswick	754055	June '60	A
A Woman, a Lover, a Friend	Brunswick	754059	December '60	
You Ain't Heard Nothin' Yet	Brunswick	754100	March '61	
By Special Request	Brunswick	754101	November '61	
Body and Soul	Brunswick	754105	May '62	A
At the Copa	Brunswick	754108	September '62	A
Sings the World's Greatest Melodies	Brunswick	754106	February '63	A
Baby Workout	Brunswick	754110	April '63	A

JACKIE WILSON AND LINDA HOPKINS

Shake a Hand	Brunswick	754113	August '63	

JACKIE WILSON

Merry Christmas from Jackie Wilson	Brunswick	754112	December '63	
Somethin' Else	Brunswick	754117	September '64	
Soul Time	Brunswick	754118	May '65	
Spotlight on Jackie Wilson	Brunswick	754119	October '65	
Soul Galore	Brunswick	754120	March '66	
Whispers	Brunswick	754122	January '67	A
Higher and Higher	Brunswick	74130	November '67	

JACKIE WILSON AND COUNT BASIE

Manufacturers of Soul	Brunswick	754134	May '68	A

JACKIE WILSON

I Get the Sweetest Feelings	Brunswick	754138	November '68	
Do Your Thing	Brunswick	754154	November '69	
It's All a Part of Love	Brunswick	754158	April '70	A
This Love Is Real	Brunswick	754167	November '73	A
Nowstalgia	Brunswick	754199	August '74	A

JACKIE WILSON ANTHOLOGIES AND COMPILATIONS

My Golden Favorites	Brunswick	754058	September '60	A
My Golden Favorites, Volume 2	Brunswick	754115 reissued as 754155	February '64	A
Greatest Hits	Brunswick	754140	June '69	A

EDGAR WINTER. First coming to prominence as a keyboard and alto saxophone player on brother Johnny Winter's first two Columbia albums and early tours, Edgar Winter recorded a solo album before forming the rhythm-and-blues styled White Trash. Later assembling The Edgar Winter Group, whose guitarists would include Ronnie Montrose and Rick Derringer, Winter scored a top hit with the synthesizer-based instrumental "Frankenstein," a major hit with "Free Ride," and his first certified gold-award album with *They Only Come Out at Night*, all in 1973. However, after *Shock Treatment*, Edgar Winter has experienced declining popularity with recordings made solo, with brother Johnny, and with the re-formed Edgar Winter Group.

EDGAR WINTER

Entrance	Epic	BN–26503	June '70

EDGAR WINTER'S WHITE TRASH

White Trash	Epic	E–30512	April '71	A
Road Work*	2-Epic	PEG–31249	March '72	A
Recycled	Blue Sky	PZ–34858	October '77	

THE EDGAR WINTER GROUP

They Only Come Out at Night*	Epic	PE–31584	November '72	A
Shock Treatment*	Epic	PE–32461	May '74	

The Edgar Winter Group with Rick Derringer	Blue Sky	PZ–33798	October '75	

EDGAR WINTER

Jasmine Night- dreams	Blue Sky	PZ–33483	May '75	
Entrance/White Trash	2-Epic	BG–33770	October '75	A
The Edgar Winter Album	Blue Sky	JZ–35989	September '79	
Standing on Rock	Blue Sky	JZ–36494	March '81	A

EDGAR AND JOHNNY WINTER

Together Live	Blue Sky	PZ–34033	June '76	

DAN HARTMAN

Relight My Fire	Blue Sky	JZ–36302	March '80	A
It Hurts to Be in Love	Blue Sky	JZ–37045	July '81	A

JOHNNY WINTER. Signed to the largest recording contract ever offered a new artist by Columbia Records (reportedly between $300,000 and $600,000) in 1969 on the strength of a favorable mention in *Rolling Stone* magazine and the persistence of manager Steve Paul, blues guitarist Johnny Winter was initially hailed as rock music's next "superstar." Having gained a reputation as a fine guitarist by means of early recordings that owed as much to "hard rock" as to the blues, Winter never achieved the predicted career heights, possibly due to the waning of the blues revival and the rise of so-called "heavy metal" music. Never scoring a major hit single, Johnny Winter nonetheless gained widespread popularity under producer–guitarist Rick Derringer during the early Seventies, only to withdraw with psychological and drug problems for two years and to re-emerge triumphant with *Still Alive and Well*, generally regarded as his last important work. Emphasizing his blues roots with subsequent albums, Winter has helped renew interest in Muddy Waters through production of the legendary bluesman's late Seventies albums on Steve Paul's Blue Sky label.

JOHNNY WINTER

Austin, Texas	United Artists	LA139	
About Blues	Jansco/Janus	3008	
Early Times	Jansco	3023	December '70
Before the Storm	2-Janus	3056	
First Winter	Buddah	BDS–7513	June '70
The Johnny Winter Story	GRT	10010	September '69

The Progressive Blues Experiment	Imperial	LR–12431	March '69	
Johnny Winter	Columbia	CS–9826	April '69	A
Second Winter	2-Columbia	PC–9947	October '69	A
Johnny Winter And	Columbia	PC–30221	July '70	A
Johnny Winter And Live*	Columbia	PC–30475	February '71	A
Still Alive and Well	Columbia	KC–32188	March '73	A
Saints and Sinners	Columbia	PC–32715	February '74	A
Johnny Winter And/Live	2-Columbia	CG–33651		A
Ready for Winter	Accord	SN–7135	November '81	A
John Dawson Winter, III	Blue Sky	PZ–33292	November '74	
Captured Live	Blue Sky	PZ–33944	February '76	A
Johnny and Edgar Winter Together Live	Blue Sky	PZ–34033	June '76	

JOHNNY WINTER

Nothin' but the Blues	Blue Sky	PZ–34813	June '77	A
White, Hot, and Blue	Blue Sky	JZ–35475	July '78	
Raisin' Cain	Blue Sky	JZ–36343	March '80	A

STEVIE WONDER. Having achieved his first fame as a child prodigy with the top-hit instrumental "Fingertips" in 1963, Stevie Wonder recorded inappropriate material and languished for several years before establishing himself as a singles artist in 1965–66 with "Up-Tight (Everything's Alright)." After recording perhaps the first rhythm-and-blues/soul hit version of a Bob Dylan song ("Blowin' in the Wind"), Wonder regularly scored smash rhythm-and-blues/soul and major pop hits through 1970 with pop-style songs written in conjunction with lyricist Sylvia Moy and producer Henry Cosby or provided by Ron Miller and Bryan Wells, such as "A Place in the Sun," "I Was Made to Love Her," "Shoo-Be-Doo-Be-Doo-Da-Day," "For Once in My Life," "My Cherie Amour," and "Yester-Me, Yester-You, Yesterday." A multi-talented musician who had mastered harmonica, drums, and keyboards as a child, Stevie Wonder's first self-production, *Signed, Sealed, and Delivered*, yielded the smash hit title song plus a major hit with "We Can Work It Out," one of the first hit soul versions of a Beatles song. Wonder subsequently experimented with synthesizers and other electronic keyboard instruments on *Where I'm Coming From* (thereby establishing himself in the forefront of the "progressive soul" movement along with Sly Stone) and negotiated a new contract with the Motown organization that granted him artistic control of his recordings (thus making him, along with Marvin

Gaye, one of the first Motown artists to achieve independence); it allowed him to form his own publishing and production companies, an unprecedented move in the history of Motown Records.

Established as a serious composer with his first album after securing the new contract, *Music of My Mind*, Stevie Wonder broke through to a mass white rock audience without abandoning his black fans with his summer 1972 tour with The Rolling Stones and best-selling *Talking Book* album. Containing two top-hit classics, "Superstition" and "You Are the Sunshine of My Life," as well as the outstanding songs "You've Got It Bad, Girl," "Blame It on the Sun," and "I Believe (When I Fall in Love It Will Be Forever)," the album made Wonder, along with Marvin Gaye, one of the first black artists to become recognized as an album artist. With *Innervisions*, Stevie Wonder added songs of pointed social commentary to his repertoire ("Living for the City" and the classic "Higher Ground") while retaining up-tempo pop-style songs ("Don't Worry 'Bout a Thing") and romantic ballads ("All in Love Is Fair"), and *Fulfillingness' First Finale*, with the smash hit classic "Boogie On, Reggae Woman," completed a remarkable quartet of excellent albums. In August 1975 Wonder signed a new contract with Motown that was the biggest single artist deal in record industry history, guaranteeing him $13,000,000 over seven years. His first album thereafter, *Songs in the Key of Life*, amazingly became the first album by an American artist to *enter* the album charts in the top position; it also yielded two top-hit singles. Years in the works, Stevie Wonder's *Journey Through the Secret Life of Plants* was regarded as esoteric and relatively inaccessible, yet its follow-up, *Hotter Than July*, confirmed his reputation as one of the most consummate recording artists of the era and may lead to his recognition as the most important black artist since Duke Ellington.

Born blind in Saginaw, Michigan, on May 13, 1950, as Steveland Morris (although during his career he also used his father's name, Judkins, and his mother's remarried name, Hardaway), Stevie Wonder moved with his family to Detroit as an infant. Playing harmonica at the age of five, he initiated piano lessons at age six and started drums at eight. After writing his first song at age ten, Wonder was brought by Ronnie White, a member of The Miracles, to Brian Holland, who arranged an audition with Berry Gordy, Jr. Signed immediately to the Tamla label and given the name "Little" Stevie Wonder, he scored a surprising top hit in 1963 with a raucous harmonica instrumental, "Fingertips—Part 2," recorded live complete with mistakes, musical puns, and a shouting stage manager. During the next year he enrolled in the Michigan School for the Blind, studied classical piano, and managed moderate hits with the harmonica-based songs, "Workout, Stevie, Workout" and "Harmonica Man." Dropping the "Little" appellation, he finally emerged in 1965–66 with the energetic dance-style smash hit "Up-Tight (Everything's Alright)," co-written by Wonder, Sylvia Moy, and co-producer Henry Cosby, the major hit "Nothing's Too Good for My Baby," and a near-smash hit version of Bob Dylan's "Blowin' in the Wind" from *Up-Tight*. While covering a variety of material on his albums, Wonder quickly established himself as a popular singles artist with romantic ballads and up-tempo pop-style songs such as "A Place in the Sun," "Travlin' Man," the smash "I Was Made to Love Her," and "I'm Wondering." Following an album of Christmas material and an instrumental album featuring his harmonica playing (issued as performed by Eivets Rednow), Wonder's *For Once in My Life* included the near-smash hits, "Shoo-Be-Doo-Be-Doo-Da-Day" and the title song, from 1968, whereas *My Cherie Amour* contained the near-smashes, "Yester-Me, Yester-You, Yesterday" and the title song. Unjustly criticized for his allegedly easy listening material (actually his only smash easy listening hit until 1973 was "My Cherie Amour"), his songs were more pop-style and evinced a flexible vocal style unlike other Motown artists.

Stevie Wonder's first self-produced album, *Signed, Sealed, and Delivered*, produced four hits, the moderate hit "Never Had a Dream Come True" and the smash "Signed, Sealed, Delivered I'm Yours" (both of which he co-wrote), the near-smash "Heaven Help Us All," and a major hit version of Lennon and McCartney's "We Can Work It Out." He subsequently began experimenting with various rhythmic and musical textures and different electric keyboard instruments, including synthesizer, on *Where I'm Coming From*, which included the near-smash "If You Really Love Me" and the sorely neglected ballad "Never Dreamed You'd Leave in Summer," both written by Wonder and then-wife Syreeta Wright. During 1971, Wonder, then 21, negotiated a new contract with Motown that gained him artistic control of his recordings and allowed the unprecedented formation of his own music publishing company, Black Bull Music, and production company, Taurus Productions. For his first album under the new contract, *Music of My Mind*, he played every instrument and co-authored the songs with Syreeta. The album sold better than had any of those previously, yet yielded only one moderate hit with "Superwoman (Where Were You When I Needed You)." It began to establish him as an album artist and, as a consequence of a well-received summer 1972 tour (which introduced his back-up group, Wonderlove) with The Rolling Stones, Wonder attracted a huge following among the white rock audience while retaining his black fans. This growing popularity and recognition was immeasurably bolstered by the exceptional *Talking Book* album, one of the finest albums of the Seventies. In addition to producing *top* hits with the mellow pop-style "You Are the Sunshine of My Life" and the seminal "Superstition," the album contained at least three other excellent songs, "You've Got It Bad, Girl" and "Blame It on the Sun" (both co-written with Syreeta Wright) and "I Believe (When I Fall in Love It Will Be Forever)."

Performing virtually all the instrumental chores and solely composing all the songs, as well as arranging and producing, Stevie Wonder next recorded *Innervisions*. Another monumental work, the album yielded near-smash hits with the socially conscious "Higher Ground" and "Living for the City," plus a major hit with "Don't You Worry 'Bout a Thing," while including favorites such as "Too High," "Golden Lady," and "All in Love Is Fair." Having already produced The Spinners' 1970 hit "It's a Shame" and Syreeta Wright's debut album, Wonder later produced her second and Minnie Ripperton's *Perfect Angel* album. However, on August

6, 1973, he was involved in a serious auto accident near Durham, North Carolina, that left him in a coma for several days, yet he staged a remarkable recovery. In 1974, Wonder's *Fulfillingness' First Finale* entered the album charts in the top position (the first time for an American artist) and produced the top hit "You Haven't Done Nothin'" (ostensibly an indictment of Richard Nixon) and the seminal smash hit "Boogie On, Reggae Woman," while including the religious, almost spiritual song, "Heaven Is 10 Zillion Light-Years Away." Following a tour in the winter of 1974, Wonder essentially retired from the road to work on his epic, *Songs in the Key of Life.* Eventually issued in the fall of 1976 and containing a four-song EP record (necessitating the "½" notation) in addition to two full-length records, the album again included two top hits, "I Wish" and the tribute to Duke Ellington, "Sir Duke"; two moderate hits, "Another Star" and "As"; plus "Isn't She Lovely" and a wide variety of material, some moving, some didactic, and almost all captivating. Subsequently approached by film producer Michael Braun to compose a song for a documentary on plant life, Stevie Wonder ultimately composed and performed an entire score. Wonder later returned to the studio to add more songs and lyrics and to overdub the sounds of nature, and the recordings were eventually issued in late 1979 as *Stevie Wonder's Journey Through the Secret Life of Plants.* Though criticized as esoteric, inaccessible, and tedious, the album nonetheless quickly produced a smash hit with "Send One Your Love." In 1980 Stevie Wonder toured again and recorded yet another outstanding album of richly melodic and rhythmically powerful songs, *Hotter Than July.* Quickly yielding a smash hit with "Master Blaster (Jammin')," the album contained his tribute to Martin Luther King, "Happy Birthday," the ballad "Lately," and up-tempo songs such as "Let's Get Serious" and "Always," as well as the major hit "I Ain't Gonna Stand for It."

STEVIE WONDER

Tribute to Uncle Ray	Tamla	232(M)		
The Jazz Soul of Little Stevie	Tamla	233(M)		
The 12-Year-Old Genius	Tamla	240(M)	July '63	
Workout, Stevie, Workout	Tamla	248(M)		
With a Song in My Heart	Tamla	250(M)		
Stevie at the Beach	Tamla	255(M)		
Up-Tight, Everything's Alright	Tamla	268	May '66	
Down to Earth	Tamla	272	December '66	
I Was Made to Love Her	Tamla	279	May '67	
Someday at Christmas	Tamla	281 reissued as 7–362	December '67 November '78	A
Eivets Rednow	Gordy	932	November '68	

For Once in My Life	Tamla	291	January '69	
My Cherie Amour	Tamla	296	October '69	
Live	Tamla	298	April '70	
Signed, Sealed, and Delivered	Tamla	304	August '70	
Where I'm Coming From	Tamla	308	May '71	
Music of My Mind	Tamla	7–314	March '72	A
Talking Book	Tamla	7–319	November '72	A
Innervisions	Tamla	7–326	August '73	A
Fulfillingness' First Finale	Tamla	7–332	July '74	A
Songs in the Key of Life	2½-Tamla	13–340	September '76	A
Stevie Wonder's Journey Through the Secret Life of Plants	2-Tamla	13–371	November '79	A
Hotter Than July**	Tamla	373	November '80	A

STEVIE WONDER ANTHOLOGIES AND COMPILATIONS

Greatest Hits	Tamla	7–282	March '68	A
Greatest Hits, Volume 2	Tamla	7–313	November '71	A
Looking Back	3–Motown	804	December '77	

THE YARDBIRDS. Although best remembered as the group with which three of rock music's most outstanding lead guitar players (Eric Clapton, Jeff Beck, and Jimmy Page) achieved their first recognition, The Yardbirds were one of England's most influential groups, comparable in significance (but not popularity) to The Beatles, The Rolling Stones, and The Who. Since they were more proficient and innovative musicians than were The Rolling Stones, The Yardbirds' failure to become "superstars" has been attributed to the facts that The Stones were better performers, that lead vocalist Keith Relf lacked Mick Jagger's charisma, and that Beatles John Lennon and Paul McCartney were better songwriters, although their chaotic career of personnel and managerial hassles certainly did not help.

Under Eric Clapton, The Yardbirds developed what they termed the "rave-up," an extended instrumental passage which could last 30 minutes, which was later called "psychedelic" when employed by emerging San Francisco bands. One of the finest British rhythm-and-blues style bands with Clapton, The Yardbirds adopted a more innovative yet commercial pop style under Jeff Beck. Beck, along with The Who's Pete Townshend, was one of the first electric guitarists effectively and creatively to use feedback in his playing, thus reinforcing the group's "psychedelic" reputation and presaging the development of so-called "heavy metal" music. Scoring five major hits between the spring of 1965 and the summer of 1966, The Yardbirds added sessions guitarist Jimmy Page on bass around June 1966, and the group briefly featured Beck and Page as twin lead guitarists in one of the earliest uses of the format later popularized by The Allman Brothers and others. Although Page's arrival marked the beginning of the end for The Yardbirds, the group did record one prototypical "heavy metal" hit with Beck and Page on lead guitars, "Happenings Ten Years' Time Ago," which was nonetheless predated by The Who's "Anyway, Anyhow, Anywhere." With Beck's departure in November 1966, The Yardbirds survived a dismal period under producer Mickie Most and evolved into Led Zeppelin, the first group specifically described as "heavy metal," in October 1968.

Formed in 1962 or 1963 as The Metropolis Blues Quartet, the group was comprised of vocalist–harmonica player Keith Relf (born March 22, 1943, in Richmond, Surrey, England), rhythm guitarist Chris Dreja (born

November 11, 1946, in Surbiton, Surrey), bassist Paul Samwell-Smith (born May 8, 1943, in London), and drummer Jim McCarty (born July 25, 1943, in Liverpool, England). Playing Chicago-style blues, they became The Yardbirds in June 1963 with the addition of lead guitarist Anthony "Top" Topham, who was replaced by Eric Clapton, a former member of The Roosters and Casey Jones and The Engineers, that October. After developing a devoted following on the London-area rhythm-and-blues club circuit with their dynamic "rave-ups" (extended instrumental breaks) of blues material, The Yardbirds took over The Rolling Stones' residency at the Crawdaddy Club in Richmond and first recorded behind bluesman Sonny Boy Williamson an album eventually released on Mercury in 1966. The group later moved to London's Marquee Club, where they recorded their debut album, *Five Live Yardbirds*, for Britain's Columbia Records. Recorded for Epic in the United States, their debut American album, *For Your Love*, produced a near-smash hit with Graham Gouldman's title song. However, Clapton, disillusioned by the seemingly commercial and "pop" direction the group was taking, had already left in March 1965 in favor of John Mayall's Bluesbreakers and was replaced by Jeff Beck (born June 24, 1944, in Surrey, England).

The Yardbirds enjoyed their most creative and successful period during the tenure of Jeff Beck. Their second American album, *Having a Rave Up with The Yardbirds*, contained one live side of blues-style material, such as Howlin' Wolf's "Smokestack Lightning" and Bo Diddley's "I'm a Man" recorded with Eric Clapton, and a studio side featuring Beck. The studio side was comprised of two Graham Gouldman songs, "Heart Full of Soul" (a near-smash hit) and "Evil-Hearted You," the socially conscious "You're a Better Man than I," the Gregorian chant-like "Still I'm Sad," the group favorite "The Train Kept A-Rollin'," and the hit version of "I'm a Man." While gaining an enhanced reputation through their experimentation with exotic instruments and Beck's creative use of feedback, The Yardbirds scored another major hit with "Shapes of Things," which was followed by the title song to *Over Under Sideways Down*. The album also included the strange-sounding "Hot-House of Omagarashid" and "Ever Since the World Began," as well as the favorites "Lost Woman" and "Jeff's Boogie."

During 1966 Keith Relf recorded two unsuccessful solo singles; that June, Paul Samwell-Smith departed The Yardbirds to become a producer, primarily for Cat Stevens after 1969. Sessions guitarist Jimmy Page (born January 8 or 9, 1944, in Heston, Middlesex) was recruited to take up bass but switched to lead guitar when Jeff Beck became ill in September. With Chris Dreja moving to bass and Beck's return, Beck and Page played twin lead guitars until November, when Beck quit the group. This lineup had recorded only two songs, "Happenings Ten Years' Time Ago" (a moderate hit) and "Stroll On," featured and performed in the movie *Blow Up*. With Beck's departure, the remaining four continued to perform and to record as The Yardbirds through July 1968 under producer Mickie Most. Achieving minor hits with "Little Games," "Ha, Ha, Said the Clown" and Nilsson's "Ten Little Indians," the aggregation recorded one dismal American album, *Little Games*. During the summer of 1968, Keith Relf and Jim McCarty dropped out to form the short-lived duo Together, and Page and Dreja unsuccessfully attempted to recruit guitarist Terry Reid for The New Yardbirds. With Dreja's departure to become a photographer, Page enlisted three new members in order to meet their final obligations that fall and, in October, the group changed its name to Led Zeppelin. Relf and McCarty subsequently formed the "progressive" group Renaissance with Relf's vocalist–sister Jane, former Nashville Teens keyboardist John Hawken, and bassist Louis Cennamo in 1969, but after one album produced by Paul Samwell-Smith, Relf and McCarty left. Relf later played with Medicine Head and eventually formed Armageddon around 1975 with occasional Rod Stewart-guitarist Martin Pugh, former Johnny Winter drummer Bobby Caldwell, and ex-Renaissance bassist Cennamo. The group recorded one album for A&M Records but, on May 14, 1976, Keith Relf was found dead in his West London house at the age of 33, apparently electrocuted while playing guitar. Whereas Paul Samwell-Smith had become Cat Stevens' producer, Jim McCarty was a member of Shoot in 1973 and later formed Illusion with Jane Relf.

THE YARDBIRDS

Live with Sonny Boy Williamson	Mercury	SR–61071	April '66	
For Your Love	Epic reissued on Accord	BN–26167 SN–7143	July '65 December '81	A
Having a Rave Up with The Yardbirds	Epic	BN–26177	December '65	
Over Under Sideways Down	Epic	BN–26210	August '66	
Little Games	Epic	BN–26313	August '67	
The Yardbirds with Jimmy Page— Live!	Epic	E–30615	October '71	

YARDBIRDS ANTHOLOGIES AND COMPILATIONS

Greatest Hits	Epic	BN–26246	April '67
The Yardbirds Featuring Performances by Beck, Clapton, and Page	2-Epic	EG–30135	September '70
Favorites	Epic	E–34490	May '77
Great Hits	Epic	PE–34491	May '77
Eric Clapton and The Yardbirds	Springboard International	4036	November '75
Jeff Beck and The Yardbirds	Springboard International	4039	November '75

ERIC CLAPTON, JEFF BECK, AND JIMMY PAGE

Guitar Boogie	RCA	LSP–4624 reissued as AYL1– 3768(E)	January '72	A

RENAISSANCE (WITH KEITH RELF AND JIM McCARTY)

Renaissance	Elektra	EKS– 74068	January '70

ARMAGEDDON (WITH KEITH RELF)

Armageddon	A&M	SP–4513	May '75	A

SHOOT (WITH JIM McCARTY)

On the Frontier	EMI	SMAS– 11229	November '73

ILLUSION (WITH JIM McCARTY)

Out of the Mist	Island	9489	May '77
Illusion	Island	9519	May '78

YES/RICK WAKEMAN.   Along with The Moody Blues and Nice/Emerson, Lake, and Palmer, Yes was an early rock-derived "progressive" band to prominently feature keyboards, orchestral-style arrangements, and classical-style material. Gaining their first recognition as the opening act at Cream's farewell London performance in late 1968, Yes' success has been largely based on their characteristic thick vocal harmonies, their astounding but uninspired instrumental technique, and their regular use of sophisticated and advanced electronic gear. Propelled into American popularity with *The Yes Album*, which introduced the synthesizer to the group sound and featured all original material, Yes was fronted by songwriter–vocalist Jon Anderson, whose work has frequently been criticized as obtuse, pretentious, and inaccessible. After scoring their first album and single success ("Roundabout") under classically trained multi-keyboardist Rick Wakeman, Yes recorded several classics hailed for their textural and melodic richness, *Fragile* and *Close to the Edge*. American headliners on tour by 1972, Yes explored Eastern philosophy with *Tales from the Topographic Oceans* but subsequently suffered the departure of keyboard wizard Wakeman. Following the science fiction-oriented *Relayer*, Yes attained a level of popularity that allowed each of the members to record solo albums in 1975–76, whereas Wakeman quickly established himself as a purveyor of orchestrated rock-instrumental versions of classic tales such as Jules Verne's *Journey to the Centre of the Earth*, *The Six Wives of Henry VIII*, and *The Myths and Legends of King Arthur*. With Wakeman rejoining in late 1976, Yes recorded two inevitably certified gold-award albums before enduring the departures of both Wakeman and Anderson in 1980.

Yes was formed in 1968 after the meeting of vocalist Jon Anderson (born October 25, 1944, in Accrington, Lancashire, England) and bassist Chris Squire (born March 4, 1948, in London). Anderson had been performing and touring with various bands such as The Warriors for a decade, whereas the classically trained Squire had formed his own band at age 16 and joined Syn (whose guitarist was Peter Banks) in 1965 for two years of engagements. Seeking to form a group that emphasized vocal harmonies backed by dense, structured music, Anderson and Squire recruited Banks, keyboardist Tony Kaye, and drummer Bill Bruford. After substituting for an absent Sly and The Family Stone at The Speakeasy Club in October 1968, Yes soon secured a residency at the Marquee Club and subsequently opened for Cream's farewell concerts at Royal Albert Hall in December. Signed to Atlantic Records, Yes' classically influenced debut album and *Time and a Word*, recorded with full orchestra, began to establish the group's reputation as a technically proficient "progressive" rock band in England. During 1970 Banks departed to form his own band, Flash, and was replaced by classically trained Steve Howe (born April 8, 1947, in London), a veteran of bands such as The Syndicate, Bodast, and Tomorrow, whose instrumental talents extended from standard guitar to pedal steel guitar and later to guitar synthesizer. With Anderson primarily providing the group's material and Kaye introducing the synthesizer to the group sound, Yes broke through in the United States with *The Yes Album* and its moderate hit, "Your Move." Containing six pieces, three of which approximated nine minutes in length, the instrumentally complex album was hailed as an early example of "symphonic rock" and was eventually certified gold-award in 1973.

First touring the United States in a support role in 1971, Yes endured the departure of Tony Kaye for his own group, Badger, during the year and replaced him in August with former Strawb Rick Wakeman (born May 18, 1949, in West London). Wakeman had entered the prestigious Royal Academy of Music at age 16 for one and one-half years' study of piano and clarinet before leaving to teach music and to participate in recording sessions for T. Rex, Cat Stevens, and David Bowie (*Hunky Dory*). To Yes Wakeman introduced multiple keyboards, such as mellotron, clavinet, and harpsichord, in addition to the standard pianos and organs, and became the focal point of the group in concert. The next Yes album, *Fragile*, with cover art by Roger Dean, featured four group pieces and five individual works and yielded the group's only major hit with an edited version of "Roundabout." After touring the United States as a headline act in 1972, Yes next recorded *Close to the Edge*, which featured only three songs, the side-long title track plus "And You and I" (a moderate hit) and "Siberian Khatru." However, shortly after the album was recorded, Bill Bruford left to join King Crimson and was replaced in July by classically trained Alan White (born June 14, 1949, in Pelton, County Durham, England), a sessions player for Gary Wright, George Harrison, and Joe Cocker and a former member of John Lennon's Plastic Ono Band. Following the live triple-record set *Yessongs*, Jon Anderson and Steve Howe composed the lyrics to *Tales from the Topographic Oceans*, based on guru Paramhansa Yogananda's Shastric Scriptures. An elaborately experimental work, the album explored a variety of musical textures, themes, and instrumentation and received mixed reviews.

In June 1974 Rick Wakeman departed Yes to pursue his solo career, which was already launched on A&M Records with the instrumental *Six Wives of Henry VIII* album. His *Journey to the Centre of the Earth* album, based on the Jules Verne story and narrated by actor David Hemmings, was recorded live with 45-piece orchestra and 48-person choir at the London Royal Festival Hall in January 1974. The production was later performed in July at the Crystal Palace Garden Party, complete with orchestra and choir. The album was certified as Wakeman's first gold-award album within three months and led to Wakeman's recognition as a purveyor of contemporary light orchestral music. Wakeman next recorded the ambitious *Myths and Legends of King Arthur and the Knights of the Round Table* and premiered the work as a pageant on ice at the London Empire Pool in May 1975 with massive orchestral and choral support, plus his own group, The English Rock Ensemble. Having toured the United States in early 1975 with a 100-person-plus entourage of singers and musicians, Wakeman toured America in late 1975 with a trimmed-down English Rock Ensemble. He subsequently wrote the score to the Ken Russell film *Lisztomania*, recorded the poorly selling *No Earthly Connection* with The English Rock Ensemble, and performed the soundtrack to *White Rock*.

In the meantime, classically trained keyboardist Patrick Moraz (born June 24, 1948, in Morges, Switzerland), a former member of Refugee and the composer of numerous film scores, had joined Yes in August 1974. Containing only three pieces and including the side-long "Gates of Delirium," *Relayer* evidenced no diminution of Yes' popularity, and the members began recording solo albums for Atlantic in 1975, none of which fared particularly well. In early 1975 both the compilation set of early material, *Yesterdays*, and the in-concert film, *Yessongs*, were released, and Yes later mounted its most massive American tour in the summer of 1976. Late that year, Rick Wakeman rejoined Yes, with Moraz leaving to pursue a solo career. Yes' first album with the returned Wakeman, the group-produced *Going for the One*, featured songs of varying lengths, from the under-four-minute "Wonderous Stories" to the 15-minute "Awaken," and became an instant best-seller. After embarking on a massive 1977 world tour, the group continued their trend towards shorter songs with *Tormato*, another self-produced and best-selling work. By then, Wakeman had recorded the solo set *Criminal Record*, followed in 1979 by the double-record set *Rhapsodies*, and Moraz and Howe later recorded new solo albums. In the summer of 1980 both Jon Anderson and Rick Wakeman left Yes to pursue solo projects. They were replaced by vocalist Trevor Horn and keyboardist Geoff Downes, who had had a moderate hit in 1979–80 with "Video Killed the Radio Star" as The Buggles. By the fall, the new edition of Yes was touring in support of their first album with Horn and Downes, *Drama*. During 1980 Jon Anderson recorded an album with Greek keyboardist Vangelis that yielded a minor hit with "I Hear You Now."

YES

Yes	Atlantic	SD–8243	October '69	A
Time and a Word	Atlantic	SD–8273	November '70	A
The Yes Album *	Atlantic	SD–8283	March '71	
		reissued as		
		19131		A
Fragile *	Atlantic	SD–7211	January '72	
		reissued as		
		19132		A
Close to the Edge *	Atlantic	SD–7244	September '72	
		reissued as		
		19133		A
Yessongs *	3-Atlantic	SD3–100	May '73	A
Tales from the Topographic Oceans *	2-Atlantic	SD2–908	January '74	A

PETER BANKS

The Two Sides of Peter Banks	Capitol/Sovereign	SMAS–11217	September '73

RICK WAKEMAN

The Six Wives of Henry VIII *	A&M	SP–4361	March '73	A
Journey to the Centre of the Earth *	A&M	SP–3621	June '74	A
The Myths and Legends of King Arthur	A&M	SP–4515	April '75	A
No Earthly Connection	A&M	SP–4583	May '76	A
White Rock (soundtrack)	A&M	SP–4614	February '77	
Criminal Record	A&M	SP–4660	November '77	A
Rhapsodies	2-A&M	SP–6501	July '79	A

RICK WAKEMAN/ROGER DALTREY

Lisztomania (soundtrack)	A&M	SP–4546	October '75

REFUGEE (WITH PATRICK MORAZ)

Refugee	Charisma	6066	July '74

YES

Relayer *	Atlantic	SD–18122	December '74	
		reissued as		
		19135		A
Yesterdays	Atlantic	SD–18103	February '75	
		reissued as		
		19134		A

STEVE HOWE

Beginnings	Atlantic	SD–18154	November '75	A
The Steve Howe Album	Atlantic	SD–19243	January '80	A

CHRIS SQUIRE

Fish out of Water	Atlantic	SD–18159	December '75	A

ALAN WHITE

Ramshackled	Atlantic	SD–18167	April '76

PATRICK MORAZ

"i"	Atlantic	SD–18175	April '76
Patrick Moraz	Charisma	2201	January '79

JON ANDERSON

Olias of Sunhollow	Atlantic	SD–18180	June '76	
Song of Seven	Atlantic	16021	November '80	A

JON AND VANGELIS

Short Stories	Polydor	6272	May '80	A
Friends of Mr. Cairo	Polydor	6326	August '81	A

YES

Going for the One*	Atlantic	SD–19106	July '77	A
Tormato**	Atlantic	SD–19202	September '78	A
Drama	Atlantic	16019	September '80	A
Yesshows	2-Atlantic	2–510	December '80	A
Best	Atlantic	19320	December '81	A

THE BUGGLES

The Age of Plastic	Island	9585	February '80	A

NEIL YOUNG/CRAZY HORSE. Having achieved his first recognition as songwriter, vocalist, and guitaring duelist with Stephen Stills in The Buffalo Springfield, the seminal West Coast band of the "folk-rock" era, Neil Young established himself with his second "solo" album, *Everybody Knows This Is Nowhere*, recorded with Crazy Horse. Sparked by the intense guitar interplay between Young and Danny Whitten, the album featured the classics "Down by the River" and "Cowgirl in the Sand." While Neil Young was launched into international prominence through his association with Crosby, Stills, and Nash, to whom he brought a much-needed instrumental punch that facilitated their touring, Crazy Horse recorded an excellent debut album with guitarist Nils Lofgren that unfortunately failed to establish them as a separate act. An exceptional songwriter, the author of lyrically beautiful love songs, hard-edged rockers, potent sociopolitical pieces, and evocative songs sometimes reflectively melancholic, sometimes brooding and desperate, Young scored his biggest success with the *Harvest* album, from which "Heart of Gold" became his only major (in fact, top) hit. Recognized as a potent lead guitar player, Neil Young subsequently embarked on an erratic career marred by the poorly received film soundtrack, *Journey Through the Past,* and two equivocal albums that gained him a reputation as the most enigmatic and elusive former member of The Buffalo Springfield and of Crosby, Stills, Nash, and Young, perhaps of the entire Seventies singer–songwriter movement. Reunited with Crosby, Stills, and Nash for extensive touring in 1974–75, for nearly two years Neil Young delayed the release of *Tonight's the Night,* a dark, almost depressing album, recorded with Crazy Horse, which was preoccupied with the drug overdose deaths of Danny Whitten and road crew member Bruce Berry, as revealed in the title song and as counterpointed by Whitten's "Come On Baby, Let's Go Downtown." Involved again with Stephen Stills for *Long May You Run* and an abortive tour in 1976, Young finally re-established himself with 1978's *Comes a Time* album and subsequent American tour, which produced the odd in-concert film *Rust Never Sleeps* and *Live Rust* album, both of which featured the ominous rock anthem, "My My, Hey Hey (Out of the Blue)/ Hey Hey, My My (Into the Black)."

Born in Toronto, Ontario, Canada, on November 12, 1945, Neil Young grew up in Winnipeg, Manitoba, where he formed Neil Young and The Squires while in high school. He later returned to Toronto to play folk music at clubs in the city's Yorkville district, where he met Stephen Stills, Richie Furay, and Joni Mitchell. After joining The Mynah Birds, which included bassist Bruce Palmer and later-day disco star Rick James (1978's "You and I"), Young traveled with Palmer to Los Angeles, where he again encountered Furay and Stills and subsequently formed The Buffalo Springfield in March 1966. The group became known for exciting lead guitar duels between Stills and Young in concert and for their involvement in the developing "folk-rock" movement. Although the group disbanded in May 1968, Young contributed some of their best-remembered songs, including "Flying on the Ground Is Wrong," the gentle "Do I Have to Come Right Out and Say It," the "psychedelic" "Mr. Soul," the major production effort "Broken Arrow," and the lyrical "On the Way Home" and "I Am a Child."

Subsequently pursuing a solo career on Reprise Records following the demise of The Buffalo Springfield, Neil Young recorded his debut album, largely overlooked, which contained two of his typical brooding songs, "The Loner" and "I've Been Waiting for You," as well as the poignant "Old Laughing Lady" and the bizarre "Last Trip to Tulsa." His second album, *Everybody Knows This Is Nowhere,* was recorded with the long-lived group Crazy Horse, whom Young had met in 1968. Previously known as The Rockets, Crazy Horse was comprised of guitarist Danny Whitten, bassist Billy Talbot, and drummer Ralph Molina. During the mid-Sixties, the three had been members of the vocal group Danny and The Memories in the Los Angeles area before they moved to San Francisco in 1966 and took up their instruments. After returning to Los Angeles and adding violinist Bobby Notkoff and guitarists Leon and George Whitsell, they became The Rockets for local engagements and one album on White Whale Records. Young's *Everybody Knows This Is Nowhere*, often regarded as his finest album, yielded a minor hit with "Cinnamon Girl" and included the title song, "The Losing End," and the classics "Cowgirl in the Sand" and "Down by the River," the latter a nine-minute-plus song that featured extensive guitar interplay between Young and Whitten.

In June 1969 Neil Young joined David Crosby, Stephen Stills, and Graham Nash for touring and was included in their celebrated appearance at the Woodstock Festival and the recording of *Deja Vu*. Adding cohesion and an instrumental vitality to the otherwise remarkably subdued group, Young contributed "Helpless" and the three-part "Country Girl" to the best-selling album. Having fired Crazy Horse because of Danny Whitten's increasing dependence on heroin, Young reluctantly rehired the band in early 1970 for *After the Goldrush,* which featured Crazy Horse's newest member, guitarist Nils Lofgren, and producer–keyboardist Jack Nitzche. The album produced a moderate hit with "Only Love Can Break Your Heart" and contained the potent classic "Southern Man," "Tell Me Why," the title song favorite, "When You Dance I Can Really Love," and the Young obscurities "Birds" and "I Believe in You." Between May and August 1970 Young rejoined Crosby, Stills, and Nash on tour, and Young's quickly released response to the murder of four students at Kent State University by National Guardsmen, "Ohio," became a major hit at the end of June. The subsequent best-selling album from the tour, *Four-Way Street*, included a number of Young favorites and, after an American tour, Young was largely inactive, afflicted with a slipped disc, as rumors proliferated regarding the "true" story.

Having secured their own record deal with Reprise Records, Crazy Horse's debut 1971 album was hailed as one of the year's finest, yet it failed to sell in significant quantities. Recorded by Whitten, Talbot, Molina, Nils Lofgren, and Jack Nitzche, the album contained the original version of Lofgren's "Beggar's Day," Neil Young's "Dance, Dance, Dance," and Whitten's "I Don't Want to Talk About It" (a moderate hit for Rod Stewart in 1979–80) and the drug-oriented "Come On Baby, Let's Go Downtown." However, by the end of 1971, Lofgren had returned to his group, Grin, and Whitten had become useless to the group. With Molina and Talbot as mainstays, neither *Loose*, recorded with former Rocket George Whitsell, nor *At Crooked Lake*, recorded with Curtis brothers Mike and Rick and released on Epic, fared well. Inactive during much of 1972 and 1973, Crazy Horse was reassembled by Neil Young in August 1973 for his *Tonight's the Night* tour. However, Danny Whitten died of a heroin overdose on November 29, 1972, in Los Angeles; and that event, coupled with the overdose death of road crew member Bruce Berry, severely affected Neil Young.

Neil Young's next album, *Harvest*, released in early 1972, featured a new back-up group, The Stray Gators, with pedal steel guitarist Ben Keith, pianist Jack Nitzche, bassist Tim Drummond, and drummer Ken Buttrey, plus the vocal assistance of Crosby, Stills, Nash, James Taylor, and Linda Ronstadt. Perhaps Young's best selling album, *Harvest* emphasized vocals rather than Young's rough-hewn guitar playing and yielded a top hit, "Heart of Gold," and a moderate hit with the reflective "Old Man." Other inclusions were the resigned "Out on the Weekend," the favorite "Alabama," "A Man Needs a Maid" (recorded with the London Symphony Orchestra), and the ironically prophetic "The Needle and the Damage Done." After touring again in the fall of 1972 with The Stray Gators, Young issued *Journey Through the Past* as the soundtrack to the film which strangely was not premiered until five months later. The album—an odd collection of performances by The Buffalo Springfield and Crosby, Stills, Nash, and Young, a side-long "Words," and a bizarre fourth side which included the Brian Wilson instrumental "Let's Go Away for a While"—and the frankly incoherent movie were not well received.

Mounting a massive American tour in early 1973 with Stray Gators Jack Nitzche, Ben Keith, Tim Drummond, and veteran CSNY drummer John Barbata, Neil Young recorded his next album, *Time Fades Away*, while on the tour. Featuring the initial version of "Journey Through the Past," "Last Dance," and his musical statement regarding the music business and "superstardom," "Don't Be Denied," the album became a best-seller yet garnered less than positive reviews. Following an unsuccessful attempt to reunite with Crosby, Stills, and Nash in the summer of 1973, Young reassembled Crazy Horse with Ralph Molina, Billy Talbot, Nils Lofgren, and Ben Keith for extensive touring in 1973–74. Recordings from the tour, repeatedly delayed and ultimately issued in 1975 as *Tonight's the Night*, were preoccupied with the heroin overdoses of Danny Whitten and Bruce Berry, to whom the album was dedicated. This highly personal, starkly harrowing, and decidedly anti-music business album included Whitten's "Come On Baby, Let's Go Downtown" and Young's own anti-drug title song as the album's opening and closing tracks. The rather somber and restrained *On the Beach* had intervened; it contained several surreal songs such as "Vampire Blues" and "Ambulance Blues" as well as "See the Sky about to Rain" and his first singles chart entry in two years, "Walk On."

Between the spring of 1974 and early 1975, Neil Young again toured extensively with Crosby, Stills, and Nash and subsequently recorded *Zuma* with Crazy Horse, now comprised of Ralph Molina, Billy Talbot, and new rhythm guitarist Frank Sampedro. Without yielding a hit single, the album marked the beginning of Young's return to public favor and contained favorites such as the seven-minute-plus "Cortez the Killer" and "Pardon My Heart." During 1976 Young reunited with Stephen Stills for *Long May You Run*, which included Young's title song and "Midnight on the Bay," but the concurrent tour was aborted when Young developed trouble with his throat. Young next planned to issue the three-record anthology set *Decade*, but it was deferred in favor of *American Stars 'n' Bars*, which featured Crazy Horse on side one and the vocal assistance of Linda Ronstadt and Nicolette Larson. The album included the potent "Like a Hurricane" and the humorous "Homegrown." Finally issued in late 1977, *Decade* contained material from his days with both The Buffalo Springfield and with Crosby, Stills, Nash, and Young as well as solo material and five previously unreleased songs, including "Love Is a Rose," later popularized by Linda Ronstadt. After briefly playing around Santa Cruz, California, during the summer of 1977 with The Ducks, which included former Moby Grape bassist Bob Mosley and guitarist Jeff Blackburn, Neil Young mounted his first major tour in nearly two years with Crazy Horse in the fall of 1978 in support of *Comes a Time*, most likely his most accessible and best-selling album since *Harvest*, and Crazy Horse's *Crazy Moon* on RCA Records. The tour, filmed and recorded, eventually yielded the flawed 1979 movie *Rust Never Sleeps*, comprised of his performance at the Cow Palace south of San Francisco, and the double-record set *Live Rust*, which contained "Lotta Love," a near-smash hit for Nicolette Larson in 1978–79. *Rust Never Sleeps*, a separate album which was not a soundtrack to the movie, intervened. It contained one acoustic side and one electric side recorded with Crazy Horse and yielded a minor hit with the odd rock anthem "Hey Hey, My My (Into the Black)"—co-authored by The Ducks' Jeff Blackburn and reprised in "My My, Hey Hey (Out of the Blue)"— while including "Thrasher," "Sail Away," "Powderfinger," and the unusual social commentary, "Welfare Mothers." Neil Young's late 1980 *Hawks and Doves* album, recorded with sessions musicians rather than with Crazy Horse, quickly produced a hit with the title song. Released in late 1981, Neil Young and Crazy Horse's *re-ac-tor* produced a hit with "Southern Pacific."

NEIL YOUNG

Neil Young	Reprise	RS–6317	January '69	A
Everybody Knows This Is Nowhere*	Reprise	RS–6349 reissued as 2282	May '69	A
After the Gold-rush*	Reprise	RS–6383 reissued as 2283	August '70	A

THE ROCKETS

The Rockets	White Whale	WWS–7116	April '68	

CRAZY HORSE

Crazy Horse	Reprise	RS–6438	March '71	
Loose	Reprise	MS–2059	February '72	
At Crooked Lake	Epic	E–31710	November '72	
Crazy Moon	RCA	AFL1–3054	December '78	

NEIL YOUNG

Harvest*	Reprise	MS–2032 reissued as 2277	February '72	A

Journey Through the Past (sound-track)	2-Reprise	2XS–6480	November '72	A
Time Fades Away*	Reprise	MS–2151	October '73	A
Tonight's the Night	Reprise	MS–2221	June '75	A
On the Beach*	Reprise	RS–2180	June '74	A
Zuma	Reprise	MS–2242	November '75	A

THE STILLS–YOUNG BAND

Long May You Run	Reprise	MS–2253	September '76	A

NEIL YOUNG

American Stars 'n' Bars*	Reprise	MSK–2261	June '77	A
Decade*	3-Reprise	3RS–2257	October '77	A
Comes a Time*	Reprise	2266	September '78	A
Rust Never Sleeps**	Reprise	HS–2295	June '79	A
Live Rust*	2-Warner Brothers	2RX–2296	November '79	A
Hawks and Doves	Warner Brothers	HS–2297	November '80	A
re-ac-tor	Warner Brothers	HS–2304	December '81	A

THE YOUNGBLOODS/JESSE COLIN YOUNG.

THE YOUNGBLOODS/JESSE COLIN YOUNG. Favorably compared to The Lovin' Spoonful as purveyors of "good-time music," The Youngbloods are best remembered as popularizers of Dino Valenti's anthemic "Get Together," a West Coast hit in 1967 and smash national hit upon re-release in 1969. Fronted by singer–songwriter–guitarist Jesse Colin Young, The Youngbloods recorded what is usually regarded as their finest album, *Elephant Mountain,* as a trio before disbanding in 1972, since which time Young has established himself as a solo album artist with *Light Shine* and *Songbird.*

JESSE COLIN YOUNG

The Soul of a City Boy	Capitol	T–2070(M)	March '64	
		reissued as ST–11267	January '74	
		reissued as SN–16129		A
Jesse Colin Young and The Young-bloods	Mercury	SR–61005	May '65	

THE YOUNGBLOODS

Two Trips with Jesse Colin Young	Mercury	SR–61273	May '70	
The Youngbloods	RCA	LSP–3724	January '67	
Earth Music	RCA	LSP–3865	October '67	
Elephant Mountain	RCA	AFL1–4150	April '69	A
Ride the Wind	RCA reissued on Raccoon	LSP–4465 BS–2563	July '71	
Rock Festival	Raccoon	WS–1878	October '70	
Good and Dusty	Raccoon	BS–2566	November '71	
High on a Ridge Top	Raccoon	BS–2653	November '72	

YOUNGBLOODS ANTHOLOGIES AND COMPILATIONS

Best	RCA	LSP–4399 reissued as AYL1–3680	August '70 June '80	A
Sunlight	RCA	LSP–4561	August '71	
This Is The Youngbloods	2-RCA	VPS–6051	June '72	A

JERRY CORBITT

Corbitt	Polydor	PD–244003	November '69
Jerry Corbitt	Capitol	ST–771	June '71

JOE BAUER

Moonset	Raccoon	1901	April '71

BAUER, BANANA, AND KANE

Crab Tunes/ Noggins	Raccoon	1944	November '71

BANANA AND THE BUNCH

Mid-Mountain Ranch	Raccoon	BS–2626	August '72

JESSE COLIN YOUNG

Together	Raccoon	BS–2588	February '72
Song for Juli	Warner Brothers	BS–2734	September '73
Light Shine	Warner Brothers	BS–2790	March '74
Songbird	Warner Brothers	BS–2845	March '75

On the Road	Warner Brothers	BS-2913	March '76	A
Love on the Wing	Warner Brothers	3033	March '77	
American Dreams	Elektra	157	November '78	A

Z

FRANK ZAPPA/THE MOTHERS OF INVENTION. Probably the single most iconoclastic, innovative, and adventuresome artist in the development of contemporary popular music since the mid-Sixties, who pursued an individual musical vision with a seemingly total disregard for critical and commercial considerations, Frank Zappa first came to prominence as the mastermind of The Mothers of Invention, perhaps the first and only rock group to establish *and* to sustain themselves as a strictly "underground" phenomenon. Their debut album, *Freak Out!*, with its incisive combination of Fifties parodies, cynical and acerbic social commentary, self-mocking and self-serving diatribes, and bizarre, extended free-form pieces, came to be regarded as the first "concept" album (a format later popularized by The Beatles' *Sgt. Pepper* album) and was probably the first double-record set in rock, and certainly for a new, unknown group. Eschewing the standard path to popularity involving the contrivance of a palatable image and the manipulation of the mass media, Zappa and The Mothers intentionally projected a group aura of flagrantly indelicate and contemptuous on-stage behavior that can be seen as the first instance of calculated theatrics in rock. Despite the seemingly chaotic and deranged nature of their on-stage spectacle, Frank Zappa and The Mothers of Invention performed (and recorded) remarkably disciplined, precise, and technically demanding music, complete with intricate and complex changes of time and key signatures and unusual and difficult phrasings, directed by Zappa as composer, arranger, conductor, and occasional lead guitarist. The group's third album, *We're Only in It for the Money*, served effectively to parody The Beatles' *Sgt. Pepper* while deriding the so-called "hippie" movement as well as the group's growing contingent of fans. Moreover, their *Cruising with Ruben and The Jets* satirized Fifties rock-and-roll (as had *Freak Out!*, to a lesser extent) a full year before the advent of Richard Nader's "Rock-and-Roll Revival" *and* Sha Na Na, whose re-creations served more as commercial products than as amusing parody.

On his own, Frank Zappa debuted in 1968 with *Lumpy Gravy*, which explored techniques from classical music, featured 50 instrumentalists, including a 19-piece string section, and revealed Zappa's ongoing proclivity for the nonstereotyped and unique fusion of classical and rock musics, a penchant that may ultimately lead to Zappa's recognition as one of the most important composers of "serious" music in the twentieth century. After forming Bizarre Records in 1968 in conjunction with Reprise Records, Zappa established himself as a significant guitarist in the jazz and rock fields with the excellent *Hot Rats* album, which featured extensive use of the synthesizer, an instrument some claim Zappa introduced to live performance with The Mothers.

While introducing a number of jazz musicians to a wider audience, including well-traveled drummer Aynsley Dunbar, keyboardists Ian Underwood and George Duke, and violinists Don "Sugarcane" Harris and Jean-Luc Ponty (one of the first artists to investigate the possibilities of electric violin in jazz and rock), The Mothers played an intriguing mixture of jazz and rock that avoided the cliched use of horns with rock instrumentation (as in Blood, Sweat and Tears and Chicago) and rock rhythms with jazz improvisation ("fusion" artists such as Herbie Hancock). Revealing an early preoccupation with scatological and puerile themes in songs such as "Willie the Pimp," "Didja Get Any Onya," and "The Clap," Zappa and The Mothers became more surrealistically humorous with former Turtles Mark Volman and Howard Kaylan (Flo and Eddie), whereas Zappa's subsequent work was frequently derided for its tendency toward cheap vulgarity. Nonetheless Zappa and The Mothers scored an equivocal success with the movie soundtrack, *200 Motels*, and a certified gold-award album with 1973's *Overnite Sensation*, the debut album on another of Zappa's labels in conjunction with Reprise, DiscReet. Zappa's debut for the label, *Apostrophe (')*, also achieved gold-award status. After departing Warner Brothers/Reprise in 1977, Frank Zappa subsequently formed Zappa Records in conjunction with Phonogram/Mercury Records, where his debut, *Sheik Yerbouti*, became a best-seller, introduced him to a new generation, sparked controversy with "Jewish Princess," and even produced a moderate hit with the disco satire "Dancin' Fool." Having received mixed reviews for *Joe's Garage*, which again revealed his penchant for puerile themes as well as for satire, Zappa left Phonogram/Mercury in 1980 after the label refused to release his "I Don't Wanna Get Drafted" single.

Born Francis Vincent Zappa on December 21, 1940, in Baltimore, Maryland, Frank Zappa moved with his family to California at the age of ten and eventually settled in Lancaster by 1956. Taking up drums at age 12, he became a member of The Blackouts while still in high school. Switching to guitar at 18, Zappa then studied harmony in college and manned groups such as The Omens, with Don Van Vliet (a.k.a. Captain Beefheart), and Captain Glasspack and His Magic Mufflers. After composing the score to the film *The World's Greatest Sinner* in 1960, he bought a recording studio in Cucamonga with the profits from a second soundtrack, *Run Home Slow*, in 1963. There he recorded unsuccessfully for a variety of obscure labels under a variety of names and wrote the Fifties parody/tribute pastiche "Memories of El Monte" for The Penguins with Ray Collins. In early 1965 Zappa began working with the rhythm-and-blues band The Soul Giants, whose members included vocalist Collins, bassist Ray

Estrada, and drummer Jim Black (a.k.a. Jimmy Carl Black). Becoming The Mothers under Zappa's direction, the group included as early members guitarists Alice Stuart, Henry Vestine (later with Canned Heat), and Jim Guercio (later Chicago's producer–manager). Spotted by producer Tom Wilson while performing at the Whiskey A Go-Go in Los Angeles in early 1966, the group was signed to the Verve subsidiary of MGM Records as The Mothers of Invention. Comprised of Zappa, Collins, Estrada, Black, and guitarist Elliott Ingber, the group issued their debut album as a double-record set, an unprecedented move for a new group. Released in mid 1966, by which time they had achieved a substantial underground reputation in Los Angeles, *Freak Out!* came to be regarded as the first "concept" album and contained a wondrous mixture of Fifties parodies ("Go Cry on Somebody Else's Shoulder," "How Could I Be such a Fool," "You Didn't Try to Call Me"), social commentary ("Trouble Every Day," Zappa's response to the Watts riot, and "Who Are the Brain Police"), songs about the group ("Hungry Freaks, Daddy," "Motherly Love"), and bizarre and complex extended pieces ("Help, I'm a Rock," "The Return of the Son of Monster Magnet"), as well as the pop-style "Any Way the Wind Blows."

With Elliott Ingber leaving the group to join Fraternity of Man and, later, Captain Beefheart, The Mothers added keyboardist Don Preston, saxophonists Bunk Gardner and Jim "Motorhead" Sherwood, and drummer Billy Mundi (with Jim Black switching to percussion) for *Absolutely Free*. The album included the socially conscious satires "Plastic People," "Brown Shoes Don't Make It," and "America Drinks and Goes Home," the classic "Call Any Vegetable," and the jam-style "Invocation and Ritual Dance of the Young Pumpkin." In late November 1966, The Mothers began a six-month residency at the Garrick Theater in New York's Greenwich Village, where their shows had a decidedly theatrical bent, utilized props and choreography, and invited crazy participation by audience members. After adding keyboard and woodwind player Ian Underwood, the group next recorded the Zappa-produced *We're Only in It for the Money*, which parodied The Beatles' *Sgt. Pepper* album and derided both the group's followers and the so-called "hippie" movement. Jim Black returned to drums and Art Tripp was added on percussion with the departure of Billy Mundi, and the group next recorded the excellent Fifties parody, *Cruising with Ruben and The Jets*, which included "Jelly Roll Gumdrop" as well as similarly styled songs from *Freak Out!*

Earlier, Frank Zappa had recorded his solo debut, *Lumpy Gravy*, in New York City with a 50-piece sessions orchestra that included six woodwind players and a 19-piece string section, plus the choral assistance of several Mothers. A serious work, the album explored classical influences such as those of Edgar Varese and Igor Stravinsky within the rock format. During 1968 and 1969 Zappa produced albums for The GTOs and Wild Man Fischer and Captain Beefheart's *Trout Mask Replica* and formed Straight and Bizarre Records with manager Herb Cohen in conjunction with Warner Brothers/Reprise Records. Releases on Straight included the debut album by Alice Cooper, whereas The Mothers and Zappa solo debuted on Bizarre with the double-record set *Uncle Meat* and *Hot Rats*, respectively. The former was written in the studio as the music for a movie that was never completed, and the latter was recorded with the aid of Ian Underwood, violinist Jean-Luc Ponty, and Captain Beefheart. Sometimes considered an early "jazz-rock" or "fusion" album and usually regarded as Zappa's finest solo album, *Hot Rats* featured heavy use of synthesizers and included the classic "Willie the Pimp," with vocals by Beefheart, plus "Peaches en Regalia" and "The Gumbo Variations." MGM/Verve later issued four compilation sets by The Mothers, of which only *Mothermania* is significant. In late 1969 Zappa disclosed that The Mothers would no longer perform concerts, and subsequent albums by the early incarnation of the group were *Burnt Weenie Sandwich* and *Weasels Ripped My Flesh*.

Frank Zappa composed and arranged *King Kong: Jean-Luc Ponty Plays the Music of Frank Zappa* for the violinist before forming a new edition of The Mothers with Ian Underwood, keyboardist George Duke, well-traveled drummer Aynsley Dunbar, and former Turtles vocalists Mark Volman and Howard Kaylan, who initially billed themselves as The Phlorescent Leech and Eddie, later shortened to Flo and Eddie. Following Zappa's solo album, *Chunga's Revenge*, recorded with guitarist Jeff Simmons and violinist Don "Sugarcane" Harris, the basic group was augmented by bassist Jim Pons (another ex-Turtle), returned drummer Jim Black, and percussionist Ruth Underwood for the surreal and "psychedelic" band-on-the-road movie, *200 Motels*. Written and filmed in London and released on United Artists, the film contained several of Zappa's puerile songs, such as "Shove It Right In" and "Penis Dimension," and featured appearances by Ringo Starr and Keith Moon. During 1970 and 1971, The Mothers toured extensively, performed at one of the final concerts at Fillmore East in the spring of 1971 (later included on John and Yoko Lennon's *Sometime in New York City*), and ultimately yielded two live albums, *Fillmore East, June 1971* and *Just Another Band from L.A.*, which included the "mini-opera" "Billy the Mountain" and Flo and Eddie's "Eddie, Are You Kidding?"

Seriously injured when pushed from the stage of the Rainbow Theatre in London in December 1971, Frank Zappa re-emerged in 1972 with the solo album *Waka Jawaka—Hot Rats*, with its side-long "Big Swifty," recorded with Mothers Jeff Simmons, Aynsley Dunbar, Don Preston, and George Duke, plus a five-piece horn section that included trumpeter Sal Marquez. The same lineup (save Simmons), augmented by additional horn players and percussionists, recorded *The Grand Wazoo* as The Mothers, after which Marquez, Ian and Ruth Underwood, and trombonist Bruce Fowler formed the basis of a new Mothers, who, with the addition of Duke, Jean-Luc Ponty, bassist Tom Fowler, and drummer Ralph Humphrey, recorded *Overnite Sensation* for the newly formed DiscReet label. Surprisingly, that album was certified gold-award in 1976, and final albums by The Mothers were the live set *Roxy and Elsewhere*, which included "Penguin in Bondage" and the instrumental "Don't You Ever Wash That Thing," and "One Size Fits All." Zappa's solo debut on DiscReet, *Apostrophe (')*, recorded with a variety of former Mothers as well as with saxophonist Napoleon Brock and former Cream bassist Jack Bruce, even yielded a minor hit with "Don't Eat the Yellow Snow" and was also certified gold-award in 1976. During May 1975 Zappa and old associate Captain Beefheart performed at the Armadillo World Headquarters in Austin, Texas, and live recordings from the shows were issued late in the year as *Bongo Fury*. Following *Zoot Allures*, Zappa ended his relationship with manager Herb Cohen and Warner Brothers/Reprise, although the labels continued to issue previously unreleased material, including the live set *Zappa in New York*, for several years.

After touring in 1978 with a band comprised of guitarist Adrian Belew, keyboardists Peter Wolf and Tommy Mars, bassist Patrick O'Hearn, percussionist Ed Mann, and drummer Terry Bozzio, Zappa eventually signed with Phonogram/Mercury, where his recordings were released on Zappa Records. His debut for the label, *Sheik Yerbouti*, was his most accessible album in years and served to introduce a new generation to his peculiar vision. While containing more puerile material such as "Broken Hearts Are for Assholes" and the Peter Frampton satire "I Have Been in You," the surprisingly best-selling album included the moderate hit "Dancin' Fool" (a satire of disco music and fans) and the controversial "Jewish Princess." Originally intended as a triple-record set, the elaborate tale *Joe's Garage* was ultimately issued as a single record, *Act I*, and double-record, *Acts II and III*. Whereas *Act I* sold quite well and was critically well-received while containing more Zappa scatology such as "Crew Slut," "Wet T-Shirt Nite," and "Why Does It Hurt When I Pee," as well as the potentially controversial "Catholic Girls," *Acts II and III* was regarded as dreary, boring, and overly long. Zappa's film *Baby Snakes* was premiered in early 1980 and, after Mercury/Phonogram's refusal to issue his single "I Don't Wanna Get Drafted," he severed relations with the company. Subsequent Zappa albums were issued on the Barking Pumpkin subsidary of CBS. In 1981 old material recorded by a number of former members of The Mothers, including Jimmy Carl Black, Don Preston, Elliott Ingber, Jim Sherwood, and Buzz and Bunk Gardner, was compiled and issued on the small Los Angeles-based label Rhino as *The Grandmothers*.

THE MOTHERS OF INVENTION

Freak Out!	2-Verve	V–65005	July '66
Absolutely Free	Verve	V–65013	April '67
We're Only in It for the Money	Verve	V–65045	December '67
Cruising with Ruben and The Jets	Verve	V–65055	November '68

MOTHERS OF INVENTION ANTHOLOGIES AND COMPILATIONS

Mothermania— The Best of The Mothers	Verve	V–65068	March '69
The &?X! of The Mothers	Verve	V–65074	September '69

| The Mothers of Invention | MGM | GAS–112 | September '70 | |
| The Worst of The Mothers | MGM | SE–4754 | July '71 | |

RUBEN AND THE JETS (WITH JIM SHERWOOD)

| For Real | Mercury | SRM1–659 | April '73 | |
| Con Safos | Mercury | SRM1–694 | December '73 | |

THE MOTHERS OF INVENTION

Weasels Ripped My Flesh (recorded 1967–69)	Bizarre/ Reprise	MS–2028	August '70	A
Uncle Meat	2-Bizarre/ Reprise	2MS–2024	April '69	A
Burnt Weenie Sandwich	Reprise	RS–6370	January '70	A

FRANK ZAPPA

Lumpy Gravy	Verve	V–68741	May '68	
Hot Rats	Bizarre/ Reprise	RS–6356	November '69	A
Chunga's Revenge	Bizarre/ Reprise	MS–2030	November '70	A
Waka Jawaka— Hot Rats	Bizarre/ Reprise	MS–2094	August '72	A

FRANK ZAPPA AND THE MOTHERS

Fillmore East, June 1971	Reprise	MS–2042	August '71	A
200 Motels (soundtrack)	2-United Artists	9956	October '71	
Just Another Band from L.A.	Bizarre/ Reprise	MS–2075	April '72	A
The Grand Wazoo	Bizarre/ Reprise	MS–2093	November '72	A
Over-Nite Sensation *	DiscReet/ Reprise reissued on DiscReet	MS–2149 2288	September '73	A
Roxy and Else- where	2-DiscReet	2DS–2202	September '74	A
One Size Fits All	DiscReet	DS–2216	May '75	A

FRANK ZAPPA/CAPTAIN BEEFHEART/THE MOTHERS

| Bongo Fury | DiscReet | DS–2234 | October '75 | A |

FRANK ZAPPA

| Apostrophe (') * | DiscReet | DS–2175 reissued as 2289 | March '74 | A |

Zoot Allures	Warner Brothers	BS–2970	November '76	A
Zappa in New York	2-DiscReet	2D–2290	March '78	A
Studio Tan	DiscReet	2291	September '78	
Sleep Dirt	DiscReet	2292	February '79	
Orchestral Favorites	DiscReet	2294	May '79	
Sheik Yerbouti	2-Zappa	SRZ2–1501	March '79	A
Joe's Garage, Act I	Zappa	SRZ1–1603	September '79	A
Joe's Garage, Acts II and III	2-Zappa	SRZ2–1502	December '79	A
Tinsel Town Rebellion	2-Barking Pumpkin	PW2–37336	June '81	A
You Are What You Is	2-Barking Pumpkin	PW2–37537	September '81	A

THE GRANDMOTHERS

The Grandmothers	Rhino	RHSP–302	June '81	A

THE ZOMBIES/ARGENT. After scoring consecutive smash hits in 1964–65 with "She's Not There" and "Tell Her No," The Zombies, led by songwriter–keyboardist Rod Argent, had been dissolved for more than a year when "Time of the Season" from *Odessey & Oracle* became yet another smash hit. By then, Rod Argent had formed Argent with songwriter–guitarist Russ Ballard, the author of "Liar," a near-smash hit for Three Dog Night in 1971. Achieving their biggest success with 1972's *All Together Now* and smash "Hold Your Head Up" single, Argent never established themselves among the ranks of "progressive" groups such as Emerson, Lake, and Palmer and Yes, as some had projected. Neither former Zombie Colin Blunstone nor Ballard attained major success with their solo careers, and Argent bassist Jim Rodford joined The Kinks in 1978, two years after the demise of Argent.

THE ZOMBIES

The Zombies	Parrot	PAS–71001	February '65	
Early Days	London	PS–557	July '69	
Time of the Season—Odessey & Oracle	Date	TES–4013	August '68	
Time of The Zombies	2-Epic	PEG–32861	April '74	A

ARGENT

Rod Argent	Epic	BN–26525	January '70	A
Ring of Hands	Epic	E–30128	April '71	A
All Together Now	Epic	E–31556	June '72	A
In Deep	Epic	KE–32195	March '73	
Nexus	Epic	KE–32573	March '74	

Circus	Epic	PE–33422	February '75	
Anthology	Epic	PE–33955	March '76	A
Encore	2-Columbia	PEG–33079	December '74	
Counterpoints	United Artists	LA560	March '76	

COLIN BLUNSTONE

One Year	Epic	E–30974	March '72
Ennismore	Epic	KE–31994	February '73
Journey	Epic	KE–32962	August '74
Never Even Thought	Rocket	BXL1–2903	August '78

RUSS BALLARD

Russ Ballard	Epic	KE–33252	February '75	
Winning	Epic	PE–34093	May '76	
At the Third Stroke	Epic	JE–35035	July '78	A
Russ Ballard and The Barnet Dogs	Epic	JE–36186	May '80	
Into the Fire	Epic	JE–36993	January '81	A

ROGER DALTREY/RUSS BALLARD

McVicar (soundtrack)	Polydor	6284	August '80	A

BIBLIOGRAPHY

BOOKS AND ARTICLES ABOUT ARTISTS

References under each artist's name are in chronological order.

ABBA
Lindvall, Marianne. *ABBA: The Ultimate Pop Group.* Edmonton: Hurtig, 1977.
THE ALLMAN BROTHERS BAND
Crowe, Cameron. "The Allman Brothers Story." *Rolling Stone,* no. 149 (December 6, 1973), pp. 46–50, 52, 54.
THE BAND
Marcus, Greil. "The Band's Last Waltz—That Train Don't Stop Here Anymore." *Rolling Stone,* no. 229 (December 30, 1976), pp. 38–42.
THE BEACH BOYS
Barnes, Ken. *The Beach Boys: A Biography in Words and Pictures.* New York: Sire Books, 1976.
Leaf, David. *The Beach Boys and the California Myth.* New York: Grosset & Dunlap, 1978.
Preiss, Byron. *The Beach Boys.* New York: Ballantine, 1979.
THE BEATLES
Braun, Michael. *Love Me Do: The Beatles' Progress.* London: Penguin Books, 1964.
Epstein, Brian. *A Cellarful of Noise.* New York: Doubleday, 1964.
Shepherd, Billy. *The True Story of The Beatles.* New York: Bantam Books, 1964.
Davies, Hunter. *The Beatles.* New York: McGraw-Hill, 1968.
Davis, Edward E. *The Beatles Book.* New York: Cowles, 1968.
Fast, Julius. *The Beatles: The Real Story.* New York: Putnam, 1968.
Scaduto, Anthony. *The Beatles.* New York: Signet Books, 1968.
Dilello, Richard. *The Longest Cocktail Party: A Personal History of Apple.* Chicago: Playboy Press, 1972.
McCabe, Peter, and Schonfeld, Robert. *Apple to the Core.* New York: Pocket Books, 1972.
Mellers, Wilfrid. *Twilight of the Gods.* London: Faber and Faber, 1973.
Taylor, Derek. *As Time Goes By.* San Francisco: Straight Arrow Books, 1973.
Burt, Robert, and Pascall, Jeremy. *The Beatles: The Fabulous Story of John, Paul, George, and Ringo.* London: Octopus, 1975.
Carr, Roy, and Tyler, Tony. *The Beatles: An Illustrated Record.* New York: Harmony Books, 1975.
Williams, Allan, and Marshall, William. *The Man Who Gave The Beatles Away.* New York: Macmillan, 1975.

Schaffner, Nicholas. *The Beatles Forever.* New York: McGraw-Hill, 1977.

DiFranco, J. Philip (editor). *The Beatles: A Hard Day's Night.* London: Penguin, 1978, © 1977.

Miles (compiler). *Beatles in Their Own Words.* New York: Quick Fox, 1978.

Friede, Godlie; Titone, Robin, and Weiner, Sue. *The Beatles A to Z.* New York: Methuen, 1980.

Martin, George, with Hornsby, Jeremy. *All You Need Is Ears.* New York: St. Martin's Press, 1980.

Stokes, Geoffrey. *The Beatles.* New York: Times Books/A Rolling Stone Book, 1980.

Schultheiss, Tom (compiler). *The Beatles: A Day in the Life.* New York: Quick Fox, 1981.

JEFF BECK

Rohter, Larry. "Jeff Beck: The Progression of a True Progressive." *Downbeat,* vol. 44, no. 12 (June 16, 1977), pp. 13, 14, 53.

THE BEE GEES

Stevens, Kim. *The Bee Gees: A Photo Bio.* New York: Jove, 1978.

CHUCK BERRY

Marcus, Greil. "Chuck Berry Interview." *Rolling Stone,* no. 35 (June 14, 1969), pp. 15–17.

Salvo, Patrick William. "A Conversation with Chuck Berry." *Rolling Stone,* no. 122 (November 23, 1972), pp. 35, 36, 38, 42.

BOOKER T. AND THE MGs

Schneckloth, Tim. "Booker T. and The MGs: Time, Soul, and One Magic River." *Downbeat,* vol. 44, no. 16 (October 6, 1977), pp. 18, 19, 46.

DAVID BOWIE

Tremlett, George. *The David Bowie Story.* London: Futura, 1974.

Douglas, David. *Presenting David Bowie.* New York: Pinnacle Books, 1975.

Claire, Vivian. *David Bowie! The King of Glitter Rock.* New York: Flash Books, 1977.

Fletcher, David Jeffrey. "A Decade of Changes." *Goldmine,* no. 46 (March 1980), pp. 12–16.

Carr, Roy, and Murray, Charles Shaar. *Bowie: An Illustrated Record.* New York: Avon Books, 1981.

JACKSON BROWNE

Crowe, Cameron. "A Child's Garden of Jackson Browne." *Rolling Stone,* no. 161 (May 23, 1974), pp. 38–40.

THE BYRDS

Scoppa, Bud. *The Byrds.* New York: Scholastic Book Services, 1971.

CAPTAIN BEEFHEART

Winner, Langdon. "The Odyssey of Captain Beefheart." *Rolling Stone,* no. 58 (May 14, 1970), pp. 36–40.

Keepnews, Peter. "Captain Beefheart." *Downbeat,* vol. 48, no. 4 (April 1981), pp. 19–22, 63, 64.

JOHNNY CASH

Govoni, Albert. *A Boy Named Cash.* New York: Lancer Books, 1970.

Hudson, James A. *Johnny Cash Close-Up.* New York: Scholastic Book Services, 1971.

Wren, Christopher. *Winners Got Scars, Too: The Life and Legends of Johnny Cash.* New York: Dial Press, 1971.

Conn, Charles P. *The New Johnny Cash.* New York: Family Library, 1973.

RAY CHARLES

Fong-Torres, Ben. "The *Rolling Stone* Interview: Ray Charles." *Rolling Stone,* no. 126 (January 18, 1973), pp. 29–36.

Charles, Ray, and Ritz, David. *Brother Ray: Ray Charles' Own Story.* New York: Dial Press, 1978.

ERIC CLAPTON
  Turner, Steve. "The *Rolling Stone* Interview: Eric Clapton." *Rolling Stone*, no. 165 (July 18, 1974), pp. 53–58.
JUDY COLLINS
  Claire, Vivian. *Judy Collins*. New York: Flash Books, 1978.
COMMANDER CODY AND HIS LOST PLANET AIRMEN
  Stokes, Geoffrey. *Starmaking Machinery: The Odyssey of an Album*. New York: Bobbs-Merrill, 1976.
SAM COOKE
  McEwen, Joe. *Sam Cooke: A Biography in Words and Pictures*. New York: Sire Books, 1977.
ALICE COOPER
  Demorest, Steve. *Alice Cooper*. New York: Popular Library, 1974.
  Greene, Bob. *Billion Dollar Baby*. New York: Atheneum, 1974.
ELVIS COSTELLO
  Reese, Krista. *Elvis Costello*. New York: Proteus/Scribner, 1981.
CREAM
  Hall, Stanley, "Jack Bruce: Low String Eclectic." *Downbeat*, vol. 45, no. 2 (January 26, 1978), pp. 17, 18, 39.
CREEDENCE CLEARWATER REVIVAL
  Gleason, Ralph J. "The *Rolling Stone* Interview: John Fogerty." *Rolling Stone*, no. 52 (February 21, 1970), pp. 17–22, 24.
  Hallowell, John. *Inside Creedence*. New York: Bantam Books, 1971.
CROSBY, STILLS, AND NASH
  Fong-Torres, Ben. "The *Rolling Stone* Interview: David Crosby." *Rolling Stone*, no. 63 (July 23, 1970), pp. 21–27.
  Crowe, Cameron. "The Actual Honest-to-Goodness Reunion of Crosby, Stills, and Nash." *Rolling Stone*, no. 240 (June 2, 1977), pp. 54–61.
NEIL DIAMOND
  Fong-Torres, Ben. "The Frog Who Would Be King: The Importance of Being Neil Diamond." *Rolling Stone*, no. 222 (September 23, 1976), pp. 100–106, 109.
DION
  Price, Richard. "Hey, Dion, My Man! Wandering Back to the Mean Street Music of Arthur Avenue." *Rolling Stone*, no. 218 (July 29, 1976), pp. 34–37.
DOCTOR JOHN
  Hohman, Marv. "Roots Conquer All: Dr. John." *Downbeat*, vol. 42, no. 10 (May 22, 1975), pp. 13–16, 40, 41.
THE DOOBIE BROTHERS
  White, Timothy. "The Doobie Brothers: The Road Goes on Forever." *Rolling Stone*, no. 300 (September 20, 1979), pp. 9, 10, 14, 16, 39.
THE DOORS
  Hopkins, Jerry. "The *Rolling Stone* Interview: Jim Morrison." *Rolling Stone*, no. 38 (July 26, 1969), pp. 15–18, 22, 24.
  Jahn, Mike. *Jim Morrison and The Doors*. New York: Grosset & Dunlap, 1969.
  Jackson, Blair. "The Second Coming of Jim Morrison." *BAM*, no. 45 (December 1, 1978), pp. 26–29.
THE DRIFTERS
  Millar, Bill. *The Drifters: The Rise and Fall of the Black Vocal Group*. London: Studio Vista, 1971.
BOB DYLAN
  Ribakove, Sy, and Ribakove, Barbara. *Folk Rock—The Bob Dylan Story*. New York: Dell, 1966.
  Kramer, Daniel. *Bob Dylan*. New Jersey: Castle Books, 1967.
  Pennebaker, D. A. *Bob Dylan: Don't Look Back*. New York: Ballantine Books, 1968.

Pickering, Steve (editor). *A Commemoration.* Berkeley, California: Book People, 1971.

Scaduto, Anthony. *Bob Dylan: An Intimate Biography.* New York: Grosset and Dunlap, 1971.

Thompson, Toby. *Positively Main Street: An Unorthodox View of Bob Dylan.* New York: Coward-McCann, 1971.

Gray, Michael. *Song and Dance Man: The Art of Bob Dylan.* London: Hart-Davis, MacGibbon, 1972.

McGregor, Craig. *Bob Dylan: A Retrospective.* New York: Doubleday, 1972.

Rolling Stone. Knockin' on Dylan's Door: On the Road in '74. New York: Pocket Books, 1974.

Pickering, Steve. *Bob Dylan Approximately.* New York: David McKay, 1975.

Shepard, Sam. *Rolling Thunder Logbook.* New York: Viking Press, 1977.

Gross, Michael. *Bob Dylan: An Illustrated History.* New York: Grosset and Dunlap, 1978.

Marchbank, Pearce (editor). *Bob Dylan in His Own Words.* New York: Quick Fox, 1978.

Rinzler, Alan. *Bob Dylan.* New York: Harmony Books, 1978.

Sloman, Larry. *On the Road with Bob Dylan.* New York: Bantam Books, 1978.

Cable, Paul. *Bob Dylan: His Unreleased Recordings.* New York: Schirmer Books, 1980.

FLEETWOOD MAC

Carr, Roy, and Tyler, Tony. *Fleetwood Mac: Rumours 'n' Fax.* New York: Harmony Books, 1978.

Graham, Samuel. *Fleetwood Mac: The Authorized History.* New York: Warner Books, 1978.

PETER FRAMPTON

Daly, Marsha. *Peter Frampton.* New York: Tempo Books, 1978.

Adler, Irene. *Peter Frampton.* New York: Quick Fox, 1979.

THE GRATEFUL DEAD

Reich, Charles, and Wenner, Jann. *Garcia: A Signpost to New Space.* San Francisco: Straight Arrow Books, 1972.

Harrison, Hank. *The Dead Book: A Social History of The Grateful Dead.* New York: Link Books, 1973.

GEORGE HARRISON

Michaels, Ross. *George Harrison: Yesterday and Today.* New York: Flash Books, 1977.

JIMI HENDRIX

Welch, Chris. *Hendrix: A Biography.* New York: Flash Books, 1973.

Knight, Curtis. *Jimi.* New York: Praeger, 1974.

Carey, Gary. *Lenny, Janis, and Jimi.* New York: Pocket Books, 1975.

Henderson, David. *Jimi Hendrix: Voodoo Child of the Aquarian Age.* Garden City, New York: Doubleday, 1978.

BUDDY HOLLY

Laing, Dave. *Buddy Holly.* London: Studio Vista, 1971.

Goldrosen, John. *Buddy Holly: His Life and Music.* Bowling Green, Ohio: Popular Press, 1975.

Flippo, Chet. "The Buddy Holly Story: Friends Say Movie's Not Cricket." *Rolling Stone,* no. 274 (September 21, 1978), pp. 49–51.

THE JEFFERSON AIRPLANE

Gleason, Ralph J. *The Jefferson Airplane and the San Francisco Sound.* New York: Ballantine Books, 1969.

Rowes, Barbara. *Grace Slick: The Biography.* Garden City, New York: Doubleday, 1980.

WAYLON JENNINGS
Allen, Bob. *Waylon and Willie.* New York: Quick Fox, 1979.
BILLY JOEL
Gambaccini, Peter. *Billy Joel: A Photo-Bio.* New York: Quick Fox, 1979.
ELTON JOHN
Gambaccini, Paul. *A Conversation with Elton John and Bernie Taupin.* New York: Flash Books, 1975.
Stein, Cathi. *Elton John.* London: Futura, 1975.
Tatham, Dick, and Jasper, Tony. *Elton John.* London: Octopus Books, 1975/ 1976.
Newman, Gerald. *Elton John.* New York: Signet Books, 1976.
Shaw, Greg. *Elton John: A Biography in Words and Pictures.* New York: Sire Books, 1976.
JANIS JOPLIN
Dalton, David. *Janis.* New York: Simon and Schuster, 1971.
Landau, Deborah. *Janis Joplin: Her Life and Times.* New York: Paperback Library, 1971.
Caserta, Paggy. *Going Down with Janis.* New York: Dell, 1973.
Friedman, Myra. *Buried Alive: The Biography of Janis Joplin.* New York: William Morrow, 1973.
Carey, Gary. *Lenny, Janis, and Jimi.* New York: Pocket Books, 1975.
CAROLE KING
Cohen, Mitchell S. *Carole King: A Biography in Words and Pictures.* New York: Sire Books, 1976.
KISS
Swenson, John. *Kiss.* New York: Ace Books, 1978.
KRIS KRISTOFFERSON
Kalet, Beth. *Kris Kristofferson.* New York: Quick Fox, 1979.
LED ZEPPELIN
Gross, Michael. *Robert Plant.* New York: Popular Library, 1975.
Yorke, Ritchie. *The Led Zeppelin Biography.* Toronto: Metheun, 1976.
JERRY LEIBER AND MIKE STOLLER
Palmer, Robert. *Baby, That Was Rock & Roll: The Legendary Leiber and Stoller.* New York: Harvest/HBJ Books, 1978.
JOHN LENNON
Rolling Stone. Lennon Remembers. San Francisco: Straight Arrow Books, 1971.
Fawcett, Anthony. *John Lennon: One Day at a Time; A Personal Biography of the Seventies.* New York: Grove Press, 1976.
Tremlett, George. *The John Lennon Story.* London: Futura, 1976.
Garbarini, Vic, and Cullman, Brian, with Graustark, Barbara. *Strawberry Fields Forever: John Lennon Remembered.* New York: Bantom/A Delilah Book, 1980.
JERRY LEE LEWIS
Palmer, Robert. "The Devil and Jerry Lee Lewis." *Rolling Stone,* no. 306 (December 13, 1979), pp. 57–61.
Cain, Robert. *Whole Lotta Shakin' Goin' On.* New York: Dial Press, 1981.
Tosches, Nick. *Hellfire: The Jerry Lee Lewis Story.* New York: Dell, 1982.
GORDON LIGHTFOOT
Gabiou, Alfrieda. *Gordon Lightfoot.* New York: Quick Fox, 1979.
THE MAMAS AND THE PAPAS
Johnson, John. "Michelle Phillips talks about . . . The Mamas and The Papas." *Goldmine,* no. 52 (September 1980), pp. 12, 13, 15.
BOB MARLEY
Boot, Adrian, and Goldman, Vivien. *Bob Marley: Soul Rebel—Natural Mystic.* New York: St. Martin's Press, 1982.

PAUL McCARTNEY

Gambaccini, Paul. "The *Rolling Stone* Interview: Paul McCartney." *Rolling Stone*, no. 153 (January 31, 1974), pp. 32–34, 38–40, 42, 44, 46.

Tremlett, George. *The Paul McCartney Story*. New York: Popular Library, 1975.

Gambaccini, Paul. *Paul McCartney in His Own Words*. New York: Flash Books, 1976.

Mendelsohn, John. *Paul McCartney: A Biography in Words and Pictures*. New York: Sire Books, 1977.

BETTE MIDLER

Baker, Robb. *Bette Midler*. New York: Popular Library, 1975.

JONI MITCHELL

Fleischer, Leonore. *Joni Mitchell*. New York: Flash Books, 1976.

Crowe, Cameron. "The *Rolling Stone* Interview: Joni Mitchell." *Rolling Stone*, no. 296 (July 26, 1979), pp. 46–53.

MUDDY WATERS

Guralnick, Peter. "Muddy Waters: A Man of the Blues." *Rolling Stone*, no. 91 (September 16, 1971), pp. 36–39.

RICK NELSON

Callahan, Mike; Buschardt, Bud; and Goddard, Steve. "Both Sides Now: Rick Nelson." *Goldmine*, no. 51 (August 1980), pp. 17–20.

WILLIE NELSON

Flippo, Chet. "The Saga of Willie Nelson: From the Night Life to the Good Life." *Rolling Stone*, no. 269 (July 13, 1978), pp. 45–49.

Allen, Bob. *Waylon and Willie*. New York: Quick Fox, 1979.

RANDY NEWMAN

White, Timothy. "Bet No One Ever Hurt This Bad." *Rolling Stone*, no. 303 (November 1, 1979), pp. 40–44.

Harvey, Steve. "Randy Newman." *Goldmine*, no. 66 (November 1981), pp. 16–19, 21.

PHIL OCHS

Eliot, Marc. *Death of a Rebel—Starring Phil Ochs*. Garden City, New York: Anchor Press/Doubleday, 1979.

JOHNNY OTIS

Welding, Pete. "The *Rolling Stone* Interview: Johnny Otis." *Rolling Stone*, no. 97 (December 9, 1971), pp. 48–52.

SAM PHILLIPS/SUN RECORDS

Vernon, Paul. *The Sun Legend*. London: Steve Lane, 1969.

Escott, Colin, and Hawkins, Martin. *Catalyst: The Story of Sun Records*. London: Aquarius Books, 1975.

ELVIS PRESLEY

Friedman, Favius. *Meet Elvis Presley*. New York: Scholastic Book Services, 1971.

Hopkins, Jerry. *Elvis: A Biography*. New York: Simon and Schuster, 1971.

Mann, May. *Elvis and the Colonel: From the Intimate Diaries of May Mann*. New York: Drake, 1975.

Harbinson, William Allen. *The Illustrated Elvis*. New York: Grosset and Dunlap, 1976, © 1975.

Jones, Peter. *Elvis*. London: Octopus Books, 1976.

Zmijewsky, Steve. *Elvis: The Films and Career of Elvis Presley*. Secaucus, New Jersey: Citadel Press, 1976.

Mann, Richard. *Elvis*. Van Nuys, California: Bible Voice, 1977.

West, Red; West, Sonny; and Hebler, Dave. *Elvis: What Happened?* New York: Ballantine Books, 1977.

Lichter, Paul. *The Boy Who Dared to Rock: The Definitive Elvis*. New York: Dolphin Books, 1978.

Reggero, John. *Elvis in Concert*. New York: Delta/Lorelei, 1979.

Hopkins, Jerry. *Elvis: The Final Years*. New York: St. Martin's Press, 1980.

Crumbaker, Marge, with Tucker, Gabe. *Up and Down with Elvis Presley*. New York: G. P. Putnam's Sons, 1981.

Goldman, Albert. *Elvis*. New York: McGraw-Hill, 1981.

PROCOL HARUM

Smith, Ronald L. "The Complete Procol Harum." *Goldmine*, no. 45 (February 1980), pp. 12, 13.

THE ROLLING STONES

Goodman, Pete. *Our Own Story by The Rolling Stones*. New York: Bantam Books, 1965.

Luce, Philip C. *The Stones*. London: Howard Baker, 1970.

Dalton, David. *Rolling Stones: An Unauthorized Biography in Words, Pictures, and Music*. New York: Amsco Music Publishing, 1972.

Dimmick, Mary Laverne. *The Rolling Stones: An Annotated Bibliography*. Pittsburgh: University of Pittsburgh, Graduate School of Library and Information Sciences, 1972.

Elman, Richard. *Uptight with the Stones: A Novelist's Report*. New York: Scribner, 1973.

Marks-Highwater, J. *Mick Jagger: The Singer, Not the Song*. New York: Popular Library, 1973.

Greenfield, Robert. *S.T.P.: A Journey Through America with The Rolling Stones*. New York: E. P. Dutton, 1974.

Scaduto, Anthony. *Mick Jagger: Everybody's Lucifer*. New York: David McKay, 1974.

Tremlett, George. *The Rolling Stones*. New York: Warner Books, 1974.

Rolling Stone. *The Rolling Stones*. San Francisco: Straight Arrow Books, 1975.

Jasper Tony. *The Rolling Stones*. London: Octopus Books, 1976.

Southern, Terry. *The Rolling Stones on Tour*. France: Dragon Dream, 1978.

Dalton, David. *Rolling Stones*. New York: Quick Fox, 1979.

Sanchez, Tony. *Up and Down with The Rolling Stones: The Inside Story*. New York: William Morrow, 1979.

Flippo, Chet. "Nothing Lasts Forever." *Rolling Stone*, no. 324 (August 21, 1980), pp. 38-42, 52.

Dalton, David. *The Rolling Stones: The First Twenty Years*. New York: Alfred A. Knopf, 1981.

LINDA RONSTADT

Kanakaris, Richard. *Linda Ronstadt: A Portrait*. Los Angeles: Los Angeles Pop Publishing, 1977.

Claire, Vivian. *Linda Ronstadt*. New York: Flash Books, 1978.

Moore, Maury Ellen. *The Linda Ronstadt Scrapbook*. New York: Sunridge, 1978.

Berman, Connie. *Linda Ronstadt*. Carson City, Nevada: Proteus, 1980.

DOUG SAHM

Flippo, Chet. "Like to Send This Out to Everybody: Sir Douglas of the Quintet is Back (in Texas)." *Rolling Stone*, no. 86 (July 8, 1971), pp. 26-29.

BOB SEGER

Marsh, Dave. "Bob Seger: Not a Stranger Anymore." *Rolling Stone*, no. 267 (June 15, 1978), pp. 67-71.

PAUL SIMON

Alterman, Loraine. "The *Rolling Stone* Interview: Paul Simon." *Rolling Stone*, no. 59 (May 28, 1970), pp. 36-39.

Landau, Jon. "The *Rolling Stone* Interview with Paul Simon." *Rolling Stone*, no. 113 (July 20, 1972), pp. 32-38.

Leigh, Spencer. *Paul Simon: Now and Then*. Liverpool: Raven Books, 1973.

SLY AND THE FAMILY STONE
  Fong-Torres, Ben. "Everybody Is a Star: The Travels of Sylvester Stewart." *Rolling Stone*, no. 54 (March 19, 1970), pp. 28–34.
PATTI SMITH
  Roach, Dusty. *Patti Smith: Rock & Roll Madonna*. South Bend, Indiana: and books, 1979.
SONNY AND CHER
  Pellegrino, Vicki. *Cher!* New York: Ballantine Books, 1975.
PHIL SPECTOR
  Wenner, Jann. "The *Rolling Stone* Interview: Phil Spector." *Rolling Stone*, no. 45 (November 1, 1969), pp. 23–29.
  Williams, Richard. *Out of His Head: The Sound of Phil Spector*. New York: Outerbridge and Lazard, 1972.
  Beach, Keith A. "Phil Spector: An Overview." *Goldmine*, no. 55 (December 1980), pp. 11–15.
BRUCE SPRINGSTEEN
  Gambaccini, Paul. *Bruce Springsteen: A Photo-Bio*. New York: Jove, 1979.
  Marsh, Dave. *Born to Run: The Bruce Springsteen Story*. Garden City, New York: Doubleday, 1979.
JOHN STEWART
  Leviton, Mark. "John Stewart: Wheels of Thunder." *BAM*, no. 77 (April 18, 1980), pp. 20–22.
ROD STEWART
  Cromelin, Richard. *Rod Stewart*. New York: Chappell & Co., 1976.
  Pidgeon, John. *Rod Stewart and the Changing Faces*. St. Albans: Panther, 1976.
  Tremlett, George. *The Rod Stewart Story*. London: Futura, 1976.
JAMES TAYLOR AND THE TAYLOR FAMILY
  Crouse, Timothy. "The First Family of the New Rock." *Rolling Stone*, no. 76 (February 18, 1971), pp. 34–37.
THE TEMPTATIONS
  Sbarbori, Jack. "The Way They Do the Things They Do: The Story of The Temptations." *Goldmine*, no. 53 (October 1980), pp. 11–17.
THREE DOG NIGHT
  Cohen, Joel. *Three Dog Night and Me*. Pasadena, California: Open Horizons, 1971.
IKE AND TINA TURNER
  Fong-Torres, Ben. "The World's Greatest Heartbreaker." *Rolling Stone*, no. 93 (October 14, 1971), pp. 36–40.
THE VENTURES
  Dalley, Robert J. "The Ventures." *Goldmine*, no. 62 (July, 1981), pp. 14–16.
JANN WENNER
  Anson, Robert Sam. *Gone Crazy and Back Again*. New York: Doubleday, 1981.
THE WHO
  Wenner, Jann. "The *Rolling Stone* Interview: Peter Townshend." *Rolling Stone*, no. 17 (September 14, 1968), pp. 1, 10–15; and no. 18 (September 28, 1968).
  Herman, Gary. *The Who*. London: Studio Vista, 1971.
  Stein, Jeff, and Johnston, Chris. *The Who*. New York: Stein and Day, 1973.
  Rolling Stone. *The Who*. San Francisco: Straight Arrow Books, 1975.
  Tremlett, George. *The Who*. New York: Warner Books, 1975.
  Marcus, Greil. "The *Rolling Stone* Interview: Pete Townshend." *Rolling Stone*, no. 320 (June 26, 1980), pp. 34–39.
  Butler, Dougal, with Trengove, Chris, and Lawrence, Peter. *Full Moon: The Amazing Rock & Roll Life of Keith Moon*. New York: William Morrow & Co., 1981.

STEVIE WONDER
  Haskins, James. *The Story of Stevie Wonder*. New York: Dell, 1976.
  Elsner, Constance. *Stevie Wonder*. New York: Popular Library, 1977.
  Haskins, James. *The Stevie Wonder Scrapbook*. New York: Grosset and Dunlap, 1978.
NEIL YOUNG
  Crowe, Cameron. "The *Rolling Stone* Interview: Neil Young." *Rolling Stone*, no. 193 (August 14, 1975), pp. 36–38, 40, 51.
  Dufrechou, Carole. *Neil Young*. New York: Quick Fox, 1978.
  Crowe, Cameron. "Neil Young: The Last American Hero." *Rolling Stone*, no. 284 (February 8, 1979), pp. 41–46.
FRANK ZAPPA
  Walley, David. *No Commercial Potential: The Saga of Frank Zappa and The Mothers of Invention*. New York: Outerbridge and Lazard, 1972.
  Snyder, Michael, and Jackson, Blair. "Frank Zappa: Rebel Without Applause." *BAM*, no. 26 (January 1978), pp. 30, 31, 33, 35–37.

BOOKS AND ARTICLES BY ARTISTS

References under each artist's name are in chronological order.

JOAN BAEZ
  Daybreak. New York: Dial Press, 1968.
JOAN BAEZ (HARRIS) AND DAVID HARRIS
  Coming Out. New York: Pocket Books, 1971.
JOHNNY CASH
  Man in Black. Grand Rapids, Michigan: Zondervan Publishing, 1975.
RAY CHARLES AND DAVID RITZ
  Brother Ray: Ray Charles' Own Story. New York: Dial Press, 1978.
DICK CLARK AND RICHARD ROBINSON
  Rock, Roll, & Remember. New York: Popular Library, 1976.
LEONARD COHEN
  The Favorite Game. New York: Viking Press, 1963.
  The Spice Box of Earth. New York: Viking Press, 1965, © 1961.
  Let Us Compare Mythologies. Toronto: McClelland and Stewart, 1966.
  Beautiful Losers. New York: Viking Press, 1966.
  Selected Poems, 1956–1968. New York: Viking Press, 1968.
  The Energy of Slaves. New York: Viking Press, 1972.
ALICE COOPER (GROUP)
  Me, Alice: The Autobiography of Alice Cooper. New York: Putnam, 1975.
DONOVAN
  Dry Songs and Scribbles. Garden City, New York: Doubleday, 1971.
BOB DYLAN
  Tarantula. New York: Macmillan, 1971.
RICHARD FARINA
  Been Down So Long It Looks Like Up to Me. New York: Random House, 1969.
  Long Time Coming and a Long Time Gone. New York: Random House, 1969.
IAN HUNTER
  Diary of a Rock and Roll Star. St. Albans: Panther, 1974.
JANIS IAN
  Who Really Cares? New York: Dial Press, 1969.
AL KOOPER
  Backstage Passes: Rock 'n' Roll Life in the Sixties. New York: Stein and Day, 1977.

TULI KUPFERBERG
Snow Job; Poems: 1946–1959. New York: Pup Press, 1959.
TULI KUPFERBERG AND ROBERT BASHLOW
1001 Ways to Beat the Draft. New York: G. Layton, 1965.
TULI KUPFERBERG AND SYLVIA TOPP
As They Were. New York: Links, 1973.
JOHN LENNON
In His Own Write. New York: Simon and Schuster, 1964.
A Spaniard in the Works. New York: Simon and Schuster, 1965.
BETTE MIDLER
A View from a Broad. New York: Simon and Schuster, 1980.
JIM MORRISON
The Lords and the New Creatures; Poems. New York: Simon and Schuster, 1970.
ED SANDERS
Peace Eye. Cleveland, Ohio: Frontier Press, 1965.
Shards of God. New York: Grove Press, 1970.
The Family: The Story of Charles Manson's Dune Buggy Attack Battalion. New York: Dutton, 1971.
Tales of Beatnik Glory. New York: Stonehill, 1975.
PATTI SMITH
Seventh Heaven. Boston: Telegraph Books, 1972.
Witt. New York: Gotham, 1973.
Babel. New York: Putnam's, 1974.
Ha! Ha! Houdini. New York: Gotham, 1977.
PETE TOWNSHEND
"Meaty, Beaty, Big, and Bouncy." *Rolling Stone,* no. 97 (December 9, 1971), pp. 36–37.
"The Punk Meets the Godmother." *Rolling Stone,* no. 252 (November 17, 1977), pp. 54–59.

DISCOGRAPHIES, RECORD CHARTS, AND RECORD GUIDES

Carr, Roy. *Rolling Stones: An Illustrated Record.* New York: Harmony Books, 1976.
Carr, Roy, and Murray, Charles Shaar. *Bowie: An Illustrated Record.* New York: Avon Books, 1981.
Carr, Roy, and Tyler, Tony. *The Beatles: An Illustrated Record.* New York: Harmony Books, 1975.
Castleman, Harry, and Podrazik, Walter J. *All Together Now: The First Complete Beatles' Discography, 1961–1975.* Ann Arbor, Michigan: Pierian Press, 1976.
——. *The Beatles Again?* Ann Arbor, Michigan: Pierian Press, 1977.
Emerson, Lucy. *The Gold Record.* New York: Fountain, 1978.
Gambaccini, Paul. *Rock Critics Choice: The Top 200 Albums.* New York: Quick Fox, 1978.
Gillett, Charlie, and Nugent, Stephen. *Rock Almanac: Top Twenty Singles, 1955–73 and Top Twenty Albums, 1964–73.* New York: Doubleday, 1976.
——. *Rock Almanac: Top Twenty American and British Singles and Albums of the 50's, 60's, and 70's.* Garden City, New York: Anchor Press, 1978.
Goldstein, Stewart, and Jacobson, Alan. *Oldies but Goodies: The Rock 'n' Roll Years.* New York: Mason/Charter, 1977.
Gonzalez, Fernando L. *Disco-file: The Discographical Catalog of American Rock and Roll and Rhythm and Blues.* Flushing, New York: Gonzalez, 1977.
Hill, Randall C. *The Official Price Guide to Collectible Rock Records.* Orlando, Florida: House of Collectibles, 1980.

Hounsome, Terry, and Chambre, Tim. *Rock Record*. New York: Facts on File, 1981.

Leadbitter, Mike, and Slaven, Neil. *Blues Records: 1943-1966*. New York: Oak Publications, 1968.

Leibowitz, Alan. *The Record Collector's Handbook*. New York: Everest House, 1980.

Lichter, Paul. *The Boy Who Dared to Rock: The Definitive Elvis*. New York: Dolphin Books, 1978.

Marsh, Dave (editor), with John Swenson. *The* Rolling Stone *Record Guide*. New York: Random House/Rolling Stone Press, 1979.

Miron, Charles. *Rock Gold: All the Hit Charts from 1955 to 1976*. New York: Drake Publishers, 1977.

Murrels, Joseph (compiler). *The Book of Golden Discs*. London: Barrie and Jenkins, 1974.

Osborne, Jerry. *Record Album Price Guide*. Phoenix, Arizona: O'Sullivan, Woodside, 1977.

Propes, Steve. *Those Oldies but Goodies: A Guide to 50's Record Collecting*. New York: MacMillan, 1973.

———. *Golden Oldies: A Guide to 60's Record Collecting*. Philadelphia: Chilton, 1974.

———. *Golden Goodies: A Guide to 50's and 60's Popular Rock and Roll Record Collecting*. Philadelphia: Chilton, 1975.

Rinzler, Alan. *Bob Dylan: An Illustrated Record*. New York: Harmony Books, 1978.

Rohde, H. Kandy. *The Gold of Rock and Roll: 1955-1967*. New York: Arbor House, 1970.

Rolling Stone. The Rolling Stone *Record Review*. San Francisco: Straight Arrow, 1971.

———. *The* Rolling Stone *Record Review, Volume II*. New York: Pocket Books, 1974.

Roxon, Lillian. *Rock Encyclopedia*. New York: Grosset & Dunlap, 1969.

Lillian Roxon's Rock Encyclopedia, compiled by Ed Naha. New York: Grosset & Dunlap, 1978.

Tudor, Dean, and Tudor, Nancy. *Contemporary Popular Music*. Littleton, Colorado: Libraries Unlimited, Inc., 1979.

———. *Grass Roots Music*. Littleton, Colorado: Libraries Unlimited, Inc., 1979.

———. *Black Music*. Littleton, Colorado: Libraries Unlimited, Inc., 1979.

Whitburn, Joel. Record Research Collection (includes *Top Pop 1955-72; Top Pop 1940-55; Top LP's 1945-72; Top Country 1949-71; Top Rhythm & Blues 1949-71; Top Easy Listening 1961-74; Pop Annual 1955-77;* plus yearly supplements). Menomenee Falls, Wisconsin: Record Research, 1973, 1978.

ENCYCLOPEDIAS, DICTIONARIES, AND GENERAL REFERENCE

Baker, Glenn A., and Cope, Stuart. *The New Music*. New York: Harmony Books, 1981.

Bane, Michael. *The Outlaws: Revolution in Country Music*. New York: Country Music Magazine Press, 1978.

———. *White Boy Singin' the Blues: The Black Roots of White Rock*. New York: Penguin Books, 1982.

Belz, Carl. *The Story of Rock*. Second Edition. New York: Oxford University Press, 1972.

Benjaminson, Peter. *The Story of Motown*. New York: Grove Press, 1979.

Benson, Dennis C. *The Rock Generation*. Nashville: Abingdon, 1976.

Berry, Peter E. *". . . And the Hits Just Keep On Comin'."* Syracuse, New York: Syracuse University Press, 1977.

Boeckman, Charles. *And the Beat Goes On: A Survey of Pop Music in America.* Washington, D.C.: Robert B. Luce, Inc., 1972.

Brown, Len, and Friedrich, Gary. *Encyclopedia of Rock and Roll.* New York: Tower Publications, 1970.

Busnar, Gene. *It's Rock 'n' Roll.* New York: Wanderer Books, 1979.

Cash, Anthony. *Anatomy of Pop.* London: British Broadcasting Corporation, 1970.

Chapple, Steve, and Garofalo, Reebee. *Rock 'n' Roll Is Here to Pay: The History · and Politics of the Music Industry.* Chicago: Nelson-Hall, 1977.

Christgau, Robert. *Any Old Way You Choose It: Rock and Other Pop Music, 1967– 1973.* Baltimore: Penguin Books, 1973.

Clark, Al (editor). *The Rock Yearbook, 1982.* New York: St. Martin's Press, 1981.

Cohn, Nik. *Rock from the Beginning.* New York: Stein and Day, 1969.

Coon, Caroline. *1988: The New Wave Punk Rock Explosion.* London: Orbach and Chambers, 1977.

Cummings, Tony. *The Sound of Philadelphia.* London: Metheun, 1975.

Dachs, David. *Anything Goes: The World of Popular Music.* New York: Bobbs-Merrill, 1964.

——. *Inside Pop: America's Top Ten Groups.* New York: Scholastic Book Services, 1968.

——. *American Pop.* New York: Scholastic Book Services, 1969.

——. *Inside Pop 2.* New York: Scholastic Book Services, 1970.

——. *Encyclopedia of Pop/Rock.* New York: Scholastic Book Services, 1972.

Dalton, David, and Kaye, Lenny. *Rock 100.* New York: Grosset & Dunlap, 1977.

David, Andrew. *Rock Stars: People at the Top of the Charts.* Northbrook, Illinois: Domus, 1979.

Davis, Clive. *Clive: Inside the Record Business.* New York: William Morrow, 1975.

Davis, Julie. *Punk.* Ridgewood, New Jersey: Davidson Publishing, 1977.

Davis, Stephen. *Reggae Bloodlines: In Search of the Music and Culture of Jamaica.* Garden City, New York: Anchor Press, 1977.

Denisoff, R. Serge. *Solid Gold: The Record Industry, Its Friends and Enemies.* New York: Transaction Books, 1975.

DeTurk, David A., and Poulin, Jr., A. (editors). *The American Folk Scene.* New York: Dell, 1967.

Doukas, James N. *Electric Tibet.* Hollywood: Dominican Publishing Company, 1969.

Eisen, Jonathon (editor). *The Age of Rock.* New York: Random House, 1969.

——. *The Age of Rock, 2.* New York: Random House, 1970.

——. *Twenty-minute Fandangos and Forever Changes.* New York: Random House, 1971.

Elmlark, Walli, and Beckley, Timothy G. *Rock Raps of the 70's.* New York: Drake Publishers, 1972.

Field, James J. *American Popular Music, 1950–1975.* Philadelphia: Musical Americana, 1976.

Flattery, Paul. *The Illustrated History of British Pop.* New York: Drake Publishers, 1975.

Fong-Torres, Ben (editor). *The Rolling Stone Rock 'n Roll Reader.* New York: Bantam Books, 1974.

——. *What's That Sound?: The Contemporary Music Scene from the Pages of Rolling Stone.* Garden City, New York: Anchor Press, 1976.

Frame, Peter. *Rock Family Trees.* New York: Quick Fox, 1980.

Fredericks, Vic (editor). *Who's Who in Rock 'n Roll.* New York: Frederick Fell, 1958.

Gabree, John. *The World of Rock.* New York: Fawcett Publications, 1968.

Gaines, Steve. *Who's Who in Rock 'n Roll.* New York: Popular Library, 1975.

Garland, Phyl. *The Sound of Soul.* Chicago: Henry Regnery Company, 1969.

Gillett, Charlie. *The Sound of the City: The Rise of Rock 'n' Roll.* New York: Dell, 1972.

———. *Making Tracks: The Story of Atlantic Records.* New York: Outerbridge and Lazard, 1973.

——— (editor). *Rock File.* London: New English Library, 1972.

———, and Nugent, Stephen. *Rock Almanac.* Garden City, New York: Anchor Press/Doubleday, 1976.

Glassman, Judith. *The Year in Music, 1979.* New York: Columbia House, 1979.

Gleason, Ralph J. *The Jefferson Airplane and the San Francisco Sound.* New York: Ballantine Books, 1969.

Goldman, Albert H. *Freakshow.* New York: Atheneum, 1971.

Goldstein, Richard. *Goldstein's Greatest Hits.* Englewood Cliffs, New Jersey: Prentice-Hall, 1970.

Goldsworthy, Jay (editor). *Casey Kasem's American Top 40 Yearbook.* New York: Target Books, 1979.

Gray, Andy. *Great Pop Stars.* London: Hamlyn, 1973.

Green, Jonathon (compiler). *The Book of Rock Quotes.* London: Omnibus Press, 1978.

Groia, Philip. *They All Sang on the Corner: New York City's Rhythm and Blues Vocal Groups of the 1950's.* Setauket, New York: Edmond, 1974.

Gross, Michael, and Jakubowski, Maxim (editors). *The Rock Year Book, 1981.* New York: Virgin Books, 1980.

Grossman, Lloyd. *A Social History of Rock Music: From the Greasers to Glitter Rock.* New York: McKay, 1976.

Guitar Player. *Rock Guitarists.* Saratoga, California: Guitar Player Productions, 1974.

———. *Rock Guitarists, Volume II.* Saratoga, California: Guitar Player Books, 1977.

Guralnick, Peter. *Feel Like Going Home: Portraits in Blues and Rock 'n' Roll.* New York: Outerbridge and Dienstfrey, 1971.

Hall, Douglas K., and Clark, Sue C. *Rock: A World Bold as Love.* New York: Cowles, 1970.

Haralambos, Michael. *From Blues to Soul in Black America.* New York: Drake Publishers, 1975.

Hardy, Phil, and Laing, Dave (editors). *The Encyclopedia of Rock, Volume 1: The Age of Rock 'n' Roll.* St. Albans: Aquarius/Hanover Books, 1975.

———. *The Encyclopedia of Rock, Volume 2: From Liverpool to San Francisco.* St. Albans: Aquarius/Hanover Books, 1976.

———. *The Encyclopedia of Rock, Volume 3: The Sounds of the Seventies.* St. Albans: Aquarius/Panther Books, 1976.

Hoare, Ian (editor). *The Soul Book.* New York: Delta Books, 1976.

Hodenfield, Chris. *Rock '70.* New York: Pyramid Publications, 1970.

Hopkins, Jerry. *Rock: From Elvis to The Rolling Stones.* New York: Quadrangle/ New York Times Book Company, 1973.

Jasper, Tony. *Understanding Pop.* London: S.C.M. Press, 1972.

Jenkinson, Philip, and Warner, Alan. *Celluloid Rock: Twenty Years of Movie Rock.* London: Lorrimer, 1974.

Laing, Dave. *The Sound of Our Time.* Chicago: Quadrangle Books, 1970.

——— (editor). *The Electric Muse: The Story of Folk into Rock.* London: Metheun, 1975.

Landau, Jon. *It's Too Late to Stop Now: A Rock 'n' Roll Journal.* San Francisco: Straight Arrow Books, 1972.

Larkin, Rochelle. *Soul Music.* New York: Lancer Books, 1970.

Logan, Nick, and Woffinden, Bob. *The Illustrated Encyclopedia of Rock.* New York: Harmony Books, 1977.

Lydon, Michael. *Rock Folk: Portraits from the Rock 'n' Roll Pantheon.* New York: Dial Press, 1971.

———. *Boogie Lightnin'.* New York: Dial Press, 1974.

Mabey, Richard. *Behind the Scene.* London: Penguin Books, 1968.

———. *The Pop Process.* London: Hutchinson, 1969.

Macken, Bob; Fornatale, Peter; and Ayres, Bill. *The Rock Music Source Book.* Garden City, New York: Anchor Press, 1980.

Marchbank, Pearce, and Miles. *The Illustrated Rock Almanac.* New York: Paddington Press, 1977.

Marcus, Greil. *Rock and Roll Will Stand.* Boston: Beacon Press, 1969.

———. *Mystery Train: Images of America in Rock 'n Roll Music.* New York: Dutton, 1975.

Marsh, Dave, and Swenson, John (editors). *The* Rolling Stone *Record Guide.* New York: Random House/Rolling Stone Press, 1979.

———, and Stein, Kevin. *The Book of Rock Lists.* Garden City, New York: Dell/A Rolling Stones Book, 1981.

May, Chris. *Rock 'n' Roll.* London: Socion Books, n.d.

———, and Phillips, Tim. *British Beat.* London: Socion Books, n.d.

Meltzer, Richard. *The Aesthetics of Rock.* New York: Something Else Press, 1970.

Miller, Jim (editor). Rolling Stone *Illustrated History of Rock & Roll.* New York: Rolling Stone Press/Random House, 1976.

Morse, David. *Motown and the Arrival of Black Music.* New York: Macmillan, 1971.

Nanry, Charles (editor). *American Music: From Storyville to Woodstock.* New Brunswick, New Jersey: Transaction Books, 1972.

Nite, Norm N. *Rock On: The Illustrated Encyclopedia of Rock 'n' Roll: The Solid Gold Years.* New York: Thomas Y. Crowell, 1974.

———. *Rock On: The Illustrated Encyclopedia of Rock 'n' Roll, Volume II: The Modern Years, 1964–Present.* New York: Thomas Y. Crowell, 1978.

O'Donnell, Jim. *The Rock Book.* New York: Pinnacle Books, 1975.

Orloff, Katherine. *Rock 'n' Roll Woman.* Los Angeles: Nash Publishing, 1974.

Palmer, Tony. *All You Need Is Love: The Story of Popular Music.* New York: Grossman Publishers, 1976.

Pascall, Jeremy. *The Illustrated History of Rock Music.* New York: Galahad Books, 1978.

Passman, Arnold. *The Dee Jays.* New York: Macmillan, 1971.

Peck, Ira (editor). *The New Sound/Yes!* New York: Four Winds Press, 1966.

Peellaert, Guy, and Cohn, Nik. *Rock Dreams.* New York: Popular Library, 1973.

Petrie, Gavin (editor). *Black Music.* London: Hamlyn, 1974.

———. *Rock Life.* London: Hamlyn, 1974.

Phoebus. *The Stars and Superstars of Rock.* London: Phoebus Publishing/Octopus Books, 1974.

———. *Country Music.* London: Phoebus Publishing, 1976.

———. *The Stars and Superstars of Black Music.* Phoebus Publishing, 1977.

———. *West Coast Story.* London: Phoebus Publishing, 1977.

Pollock, Bruce. *In Their Own Words.* New York: Macmillan, 1975.

———. *When Rock Was Young.* New York: Holt, Rinehart, and Winston, 1981.

Redd, Lawrence N. *Rock Is Rhythm and Blues: The Impact of Mass Media.* East Lansing: Michigan State University Press, 1974.

Reid, Jan. *The Improbable Rise of Redneck Rock.* Austin, Texas: Heidelberg Publishers, 1974.

Rivelli, Pauline, and Levin, Robert (editors). *The Rock Giants.* New York: World, 1970.

Robinson, Richard (editor). *Rock Revolution.* New York: Popular Library, 1976.
———, and Zwerling, Andy. *The Rock Scene.* New York: Pyramid Books, 1971.
Rolling Stone. The Rolling Stone *Interviews.* New York: Paperback Library, 1971.
———. *The* Rolling Stone *Interviews, Volume 2.* New York: Paperback Library, 1973.
———. *The* Rolling Stone *Reader.* New York: Warner Paperback Library, 1974.
Roxon, Lillian. *Rock Encyclopedia.* New York: Grosset and Dunlap, 1969.
Sander, Ellen. *Trips: Rock Life in the Sixties.* New York: Scribner, 1973.
Sarlin, Bob. *Turn It Up! (I Can't Hear the Words): The Best of the New Singer/ Songwriters.* New York: Simon and Schuster, 1974.
Schafer, William J. *Rock Music: Where It's Been, What It Means, Where It's Going.* Minneapolis, Minnesota: Augsburg Publishing, 1972.
Schicke, C. A. *Revolution in Sound: A Biography of the Recording Industry.* Boston: Little, Brown, 1974.
Scoppa, Bud. *The Rock People.* New York: Scholastic Book Services, 1973.
Shaw, Arnold. *The Rock Revolution.* New York: Crowell-Collier, 1969.
———. *The World of Soul.* New York: Cowles, 1970.
———. *The Rockin' 50's.* New York: Hawthorn Books, 1974.
———. *Honkers and Shouters: The Golden Years of Rhythm and Blues.* New York: Macmillan, 1978.
Sia, Joseph J. *Woodstock '69: Summer Pop Festivals.* New York: Scholastic Book Services, 1970.
Silver, Caroline. *The Pop Makers.* New York: Scholastic Book Services, 1966.
Somma, Robert (editor). *No One Waved Goodbye: A Casualty Report on Rock and Roll.* New York: Outerbridge and Dienstfrey, 1971.
Spitz, Robert Stephen. *The Making of Superstars: Artists and Executives of the Rock Music Business.* Garden City, New York: Anchor Press, 1978.
Stambler, Irwin. *Encyclopedia of Popular Music.* New York: St. Martin's Press, 1965.
———. *Guitar Years: Pop Music from Country and Western to Hard Rock.* Garden City, New York: Doubleday, 1970.
———. *Encyclopedia of Pop, Rock, and Soul.* New York: St. Martin's Press, 1975.
———, and Landon, Grelun. *Encyclopedia of Folk, Country, and Western Music.* New York: St. Martin's Press, 1969.
Stokes, Geoffrey. *Starmaking Machinery: The Odyssey of an Album.* New York: Bobbs-Merrill, 1976.
Tobler, John. *Guitar Heroes.* New York: St. Martin's Press, 1978.
Uslan, Michael, and Solomon, Bruce. *Dick Clark's The First 25 Years of Rock & Roll.* New York: Dell, 1981.
Van Der Horst, Brian. *Rock Music.* New York: Watts, 1973.
Vassal, Jacques. *Electric Children: Roots and Branches of Modern Folk-Rock.* (Translation: Paul Barnett.) New York: Taplinger, 1975.
Vinson, Lee. *Encyclopedia of Rock.* New York: Drake Publishers, 1976.
von Schmidt, Eric, and Rooney, Jim. *Baby, Let Me Follow You Down: The Illustrated Story of the Cambridge Folk Years.* Garden City, New York: Anchor Books, 1979.
Williams, Paul. *Outlaw Blues: A Book of Rock Music.* New York: Dutton, 1969.
Wood, Graham. *An A–Z of Rock and Roll.* London: Studio Vista, 1971.
York, William (editor). *Who's Who in Rock Music.* William York, 1978.
Young, Jean, and Lang, Michael. *Woodstock Festival Remembered.* New York: Ballantine, 1979.
Zalkind, Ronald (editor). *Contemporary Music Almanac 1980/81.* New York: Schirmer Books, 1980.

INDEX

Mick Abrahams . . . JETHRO TULL
Tommy Allsup . . . BUDDY HOLLY
Johnny Almond . . . JOHN MAYALL
The Amboy Dukes . . . TED NUGENT
American Flyer . . . PURE PRAIRIE
  LEAGUE
Jon Anderson . . . YES
Argent . . . THE ZOMBIES
Armageddon . . . THE YARDBIRDS
Peter Asher . . . PETER AND
  GORDON
Tony Ashton . . . DEEP PURPLE
The Asylum Choir . . . LEON
  RUSSELL
Attila . . . BILLY JOEL

Ginger Baker . . . CREAM
Marty Balin . . . JEFFERSON
  AIRPLANE/STARSHIP
Russ Ballard . . . THE ZOMBIES
Banana . . . THE YOUNGBLOODS
Band of Gypsys . . . JIMI HENDRIX,
  ELECTRIC FLAG
Tony Banks . . . GENESIS
Syd Barrett . . . PINK FLOYD
Joe Bauer . . . THE YOUNGBLOODS
The Belmonts . . . DION AND THE
  BELMONTS
Marc Benno . . . LEON RUSSELL
Pete Best . . . THE BEATLES
Dickey Betts . . . THE ALLMAN
  BROTHERS BAND
The Big Three . . . THE MAMAS
  AND THE PAPAS
Black Rose . . . SONNY AND CHER
Black Sheep . . . FOREIGNER

Ritchie Blackmore . . . DEEP
  PURPLE
Blind Faith . . . ERIC CLAPTON,
  CREAM, TRAFFIC/STEVIE
  WINWOOD
Blodwyn Pig . . . JETHRO TULL
The Blue Caps . . . GENE VINCENT
The Blue Notes . . . HAROLD
  MELVIN
The Bluebelles . . . LABELLE
The Blues Brothers . . . BOOKER T.
  AND THE MGs
The Bluesbreakers . . . JOHN
  MAYALL
Colin Blunstone . . . THE ZOMBIES
Bobby and The Midnites . . . THE
  GRATEFUL DEAD
Bodacious D.F. . . . . JEFFERSON
  AIRPLANE/STARSHIP
Tim Bogert . . . VANILLA FUDGE
Mars Bonfire . . . STEPPENWOLF
Boomerang . . . VANILLA FUDGE
Bootsy's Rubber Band . . .
  PARLIAMENT
Brand X . . . GENESIS
The Brides of Funkenstein . . .
  PARLIAMENT
Brigati . . . THE RASCALS
Gary Brooker . . . PROCOL HARUM
The Brotherhood . . . PAUL REVERE
  AND THE RAIDERS
Jack Bruce . . . CREAM
Bill Bruford . . . KING CRIMSON
Lindsey Buckingham . . .
  FLEETWOOD MAC
The Buggles . . . YES
Bulldog . . . THE RASCALS

The Bunch . . . FAIRPORT
  CONVENTION
Bunny Wailer . . . BOB MARLEY
Eric Burdon . . . THE ANIMALS
Paul Burlison . . . JOHNNY
  BURNETTE
The Butts Band . . . THE DOORS

Cactus . . . VANILLA FUDGE
John Cale . . . THE VELVET
  UNDERGROUND
Randy California . . . SPIRIT
The Candymen . . . ATLANTA
  RHYTHM SECTION
Jim Capaldi . . . TRAFFIC
Ed Cassidy . . . SPIRIT
Felix Cavaliere . . . THE RASCALS
Celebration . . . THE BEACH BOYS
Champion . . . HUMBLE PIE
Chapter Three . . . MANFRED MANN
The Charlatans . . . DAN HICKS
Cher . . . SONNY AND CHER
Chicken Shack . . . FLEETWOOD
  MAC
Chick Churchill . . . TEN YEARS
  AFTER
Circus Maximus . . . JERRY JEFF
  WALKER
The City . . . CAROLE KING
Gene Clark . . . THE BYRDS
Allan Clarke . . . THE HOLLIES
The Classics IV . . . ATLANTA
  RHYTHM SECTION
David Clayton-Thomas . . . BLOOD,
  SWEAT AND TEARS
Doug Clifford . . . CREEDENCE
  CLEARWATER REVIVAL
George Clinton . . . PARLIAMENT
Phil Collins . . . GENESIS
Colosseum . . . JOHN MAYALL
Jerry Corbitt . . . THE
  YOUNGBLOODS
Tom Coster . . . SANTANA
David Coverdale . . . DEEP PURPLE
Joe E. Covington . . . JEFFERSON
  AIRPLANE/STARSHIP
Crazy Horse . . . NEIL YOUNG
Lol Creme . . . 10 cc
The Crickets . . . BUDDY HOLLY
Peter Criss . . . KISS
Steve Cropper . . . BOOKER T. AND
  THE MGs
The Crossfires . . . THE TURTLES

The Cumberland Three . . . JOHN
  STEWART
Burton Cummings . . . THE GUESS
  WHO
Sonny Curtis . . . BUDDY HOLLY

Michael D'Abo . . . MANFRED
  MANN
Roger Daltrey . . . THE WHO
Rick Danko . . . THE BAND
Sarah Dash . . . LABELLE
Alun Davies . . . CAT STEVENS
Dave Davies . . . THE KINKS
Billy Davis, Jr. . . . . THE FIFTH
  DIMENSION
Sandy Denny . . . FAIRPORT
  CONVENTION
Derek and The Dominoes . . . ERIC
  CLAPTON
The Diga Rhythm Band . . . THE
  GRATEFUL DEAD
The Dimension Dolls . . . CAROLE
  KING
The Dirt Band . . . THE NITTY
  GRITTY DIRT BAND
Dog Soldier . . . JOHN MAYALL
Denny Doherty . . . THE MAMAS
  AND THE PAPAS
Dolenz, Jones, Boyce and Hart . . .
  THE MONKEES
The Dominoes . . . CLYDE
  McPHATTER, JACKIE WILSON
Lamont Dozier . . . HOLLAND–
  DOZIER–HOLLAND
The (early) Drifters . . . CLYDE
  McPHATTER

The Earth Band . . . MANFRED
  MANN
Earth Opera . . . DAVID GRISMAN
Eclection . . . FAIRPORT
  CONVENTION
Graeme Edge . . . THE MOODY
  BLUES
John Edwards . . . THE SPINNERS
Cass Elliot . . . THE MAMAS AND
  THE PAPAS
Brian Eno . . . ROXY MUSIC
John Entwistle . . . THE WHO
The Even Dozen Jug Band . . . DAVID
  GRISMAN, THE LOVIN'
  SPOONFUL, MARIA MULDAUR

Fagen, Becker, Dias . . . STEELY
DAN
The Family Stone . . . SLY AND THE
FAMILY STONE
Mark Farner . . . GRAND FUNK
RAILROAD
Fat Mattress . . . JIMI HENDRIX
Jay Ferguson . . . SPIRIT
Bryan Ferry . . . ROXY MUSIC
Matthew Fisher . . . PROCOL
HARUM
Mick Fleetwood . . . FLEETWOOD
MAC
Flo and Eddie . . . THE TURTLES
John Fogerty . . . CREEDENCE
CLEARWATER REVIVAL
Tom Fogerty . . . CREEDENCE
CLEARWATER REVIVAL
Wayne Fontana . . . 10 cc
Fotheringay . . . FAIRPORT
CONVENTION
The Four Lovers . . . THE FOUR
SEASONS
Ace Frehley . . . KISS
Robert Fripp . . . KING CRIMSON
Craig Fuller . . . PURE PRAIRIE
LEAGUE
Funkadelic . . . PARLIAMENT
Richie Furay . . . THE SOUTHER–
HILLMAN–FURAY BAND

Peter Gabriel . . . GENESIS
Jerry Garcia . . . THE GRATEFUL
DEAD
Art Garfunkel . . . SIMON AND
GARFUNKEL
Amos Garrett . . . GEOFF AND
MARIA MULDAUR
David Gates . . . BREAD
Lowell George . . . LITTLE FEAT
Andy Gibb . . . THE BEE GEES
Robin Gibb . . . THE BEE GEES
Russ Giguere . . . THE
ASSOCIATION
Giles, Giles, and Fripp . . . KING
CRIMSON
David Gilmour . . . PINK FLOYD
Roger Glover . . . DEEP PURPLE
Keith and Donna Godchaux . . . THE
GRATEFUL DEAD
Kevin Godley . . . 10 cc
Gerry Goffin . . . CAROLE KING
Barry Goldberg . . . THE ELECTRIC
FLAG

The Golliwogs . . . CREEDENCE
CLEARWATER REVIVAL
Ian Gomm . . . BRINSLEY
SCHWARZ
Graham Gouldman . . . 10 cc
The Grandmothers . . . FRANK
ZAPPA
The Grape . . . MOBY GRAPE
Nick Gravenites . . . THE ELECTRIC
FLAG
The Grease Band . . . JOE COCKER
The Great Society . . . JEFFERSON
AIRPLANE/STARSHIP
Great Southern . . . THE ALLMAN
BROTHERS
Peter Green . . . FLEETWOOD
MAC
Susaye Greene . . . DIANA ROSS
AND THE SUPREMES
Ellie Greenwich . . . JEFF BARRY
James Griffin . . . BREAD
Grimm's Rockin' Duck . . . THE
BONZO DOG BAND
Henry Gross . . . SHA NA NA
Luther Grosvenor . . . SPOOKY
TOOTH
Dave Guard . . . THE KINGSTON
TRIO
Gulliver . . . HALL AND OATES

Steve Hackett . . . GENESIS
The Halifax Three . . . THE MAMAS
AND THE PAPAS
Damon Harris . . . THE
TEMPTATIONS
The Don Harrison Band . . .
CREEDENCE CLEARWATER
REVIVAL
Mike Harrison . . . SPOOKY TOOTH
Mickey Hart . . . THE GRATEFUL
DEAD
Keef Hartley . . . JOHN MAYALL
Dan Hartman . . . EDGAR WINTER
Gordon Haskell . . . KING CRIMSON
The Hassles . . . BILLY JOEL
Bobby Hatfield . . . THE
RIGHTEOUS BROTHERS
Justin Hayward . . . THE MOODY
BLUES
Eddie Hazel . . . PARLIAMENT
Dick Heckstall-Smith . . . JOHN
MAYALL
Levon Helm . . . THE BAND
Nona Hendryx . . . LABELLE

The Herd . . . PETER FRAMPTON
Mike Heron . . . THE INCREDIBLE STRING BAND
Chris Hillman . . . THE BYRDS
The Hillmen . . . THE BYRDS
Eddie Holland . . . HOLLAND–DOZIER–HOLLAND
Hotlegs . . . 10 cc
Hourglass . . . THE ALLMAN BROTHERS BAND
Steve Howe . . . YES
Ian Hunter . . . MOTT (THE HOOPLE)
Robert Hunter . . . THE GRATEFUL DEAD
Leroy Hutson . . . THE IMPRESSIONS
Danny Hutton . . . THREE DOG NIGHT

Jimmy Ibbotson . . . THE NITTY GRITTY DIRT BAND
Illusion . . . THE YARDBIRDS
Impact . . . THE TEMPTATIONS
The Imperials . . . LITTLE ANTHONY AND THE IMPERIALS
Neil Innes . . . THE BONZO DOG BAND
The International Submarine Band . . . THE FLYING BURRITO BROTHERS

Nick Jameson . . . FOGHAT
Bert Jansch . . . PENTANGLE
The JBs . . . PARLIAMENT
Jo Mama . . . JAMES TAYLOR
David Johansen . . . THE NEW YORK DOLLS
Bruce Johnston . . . THE BEACH BOYS
Tom Johnston . . . THE DOOBIE BROTHERS
Davey Johnstone . . . ELTON JOHN
Jo Jo Gunne . . . SPIRIT
Jon and Vangelis . . . YES
Booker T. Jones . . . BOOKER T. AND THE MGs
Brian Jones . . . THE ROLLING STONES
David/Davy Jones . . . THE MONKEES
Paul Jones . . . MANFRED MANN

Priscilla Jones . . . BOOKER T. AND THE MGs
Lonnie Jordan . . . WAR
The Journeymen . . . THE MAMAS AND THE PAPAS
Junie . . . PARLIAMENT

Danny Kalb . . . THE BLUES PROJECT
Michael Kamen . . . THE NEW YORK ROCK AND ROLL ENSEMBLE
Paul Kantner . . . JEFFERSON AIRPLANE/STARSHIP
Jorma Kaukonen . . . HOT TUNA
Peter Kaukonen . . . JEFFERSON AIRPLANE/STARSHIP
John Kay . . . STEPPENWOLF
Eric Kaz . . . PURE PRAIRIE LEAGUE
Keith and Donna . . . THE GRATEFUL DEAD
Eddie Kendricks . . . THE TEMPTATIONS
KGB . . . MIKE BLOOMFIELD, THE ELECTRIC FLAG
Ben E. King . . . THE DRIFTERS
Kingfish . . . THE NEW RIDERS OF THE PURPLE SAGE
Danny Kirwan . . . FLEETWOOD MAC
Terry Knight . . . GRAND FUNK RAILROAD
Danny Kortchmar . . . JAMES TAYLOR
Robbie Krieger . . . THE DOORS
Tuli Kupferberg . . . THE FUGS

Patti Labelle . . . LABELLE
Denny Laine . . . PAUL McCARTNEY
Robert Lamm . . . CHICAGO
Ronnie Lane . . . THE FACES
Sam Lay . . . THE PAUL BUTTERFIELD BLUES BAND
Bernie Leadon . . . THE EAGLES
Alvin Lee . . . TEN YEARS AFTER
Arthur Lee . . . LOVE
David Lindley . . . KALEIDOSCOPE
Mark Lindsay . . . PAUL REVERE AND THE RAIDERS
John Lodge . . . THE MOODY BLUES
Kenny Loggins . . . LOGGINS AND MESSINA

Longbranch Pennywhistle . . . THE EAGLES, JOHN DAVID SOUTHER
Jon Lord . . . DEEP PURPLE
The Lost Gonzo Band . . . JERRY JEFF WALKER
Nick Lowe . . . BRINSLEY SCHWARZ

Maceo and The King's Men . . . PARLIAMENT
Maceo and The Macks . . . PARLIAMENT
The Mahavishnu Orchestra . . . JOHN McLAUGHLIN
Mallard . . . CAPTAIN BEEFHEART
Phil Manzanera . . . ROXY MUSIC
Ray Manzarek . . . THE DOORS
John Mark . . . JOHN MAYALL
Mark-Almond . . . JOHN MAYALL
Steve Marriott . . . HUMBLE PIE
Dewey Martin . . . THE BUFFALO SPRINGFIELD
Nick Mason . . . PINK FLOYD
Matthews Southern Comfort . . . FAIRPORT CONVENTION
Ian Matthews . . . FAIRPORT CONVENTION
Marilyn McCoo . . . THE FIFTH DIMENSION
The McCoys . . . RICK DERRINGER
Henry McCullough . . . PAUL McCARTNEY
McDonald and Giles . . . FOREIGNER, KING CRIMSON
Country Joe McDonald . . . COUNTRY JOE AND THE FISH
Roger McGuinn . . . THE BYRDS
Ian McLagan . . . THE FACES
Christine McVie . . . FLEETWOOD MAC
Bill Medley . . . THE RIGHTEOUS BROTHERS
Randy Meisner . . . THE EAGLES
Barry Melton . . . COUNTRY JOE AND THE FISH
Jim Messina . . . LOGGINS AND MESSINA
The MGs . . . BOOKER T. AND THE MGs
The Midnighters . . . HANK BALLARD
Buddy Miles . . . THE ELECTRIC FLAG
The Mindbenders . . . 10 CC

The Miracles . . . SMOKEY ROBINSON AND THE MIRACLES
The Monitors . . . THE TEMPTATIONS
Keith Moon . . . THE WHO
The Moonlighters . . . COMMANDER CODY AND HIS LOST PLANET AIRMEN
Scotty Moore . . . ELVIS PRESLEY
Patrick Moraz . . . YES
Walter (Junie) Morrison . . . PARLIAMENT
Bob Mosley . . . MOBY GRAPE
The Mothers (of Invention) . . . FRANK ZAPPA
Move . . . ELECTRIC LIGHT ORCHESTRA
Maury Muelheisen . . . JIM CROCE
The Mugwumps . . . THE LOVIN' SPOONFUL, THE MAMAS AND THE PAPAS

Graham Nash . . . CROSBY, STILLS, NASH (AND YOUNG)
The Nazz . . . TODD RUNDGREN
Mike Nesmith . . . THE MONKEES
The New Cactus Band . . . VANILLA FUDGE
The New Ventures . . . THE VENTURES
The Nice . . . EMERSON, LAKE, AND PALMER
Stevie Nicks . . . FLEETWOOD MAC
Nico . . . THE VELVET UNDERGROUND
Night . . . MANFRED MANN
Nite City . . . THE DOORS

John Oates . . . HALL AND OATES
Old and In The Way . . . THE GRATEFUL DEAD, DAVID GRISMAN
Nigel Olsson . . . ELTON JOHN
The One Truth Band . . . JOHN McLAUGHLIN
Yoko Ono . . . JOHN LENNON
Lee Oskar . . . WAR

The Pack . . . GRAND FUNK RAILROAD
Paice, Ashton, and Lord . . . DEEP PURPLE

Bruce Palmer . . . THE BUFFALO SPRINGFIELD
Paris . . . FLEETWOOD MAC
Parlet . . . PARLIAMENT
Gram Parsons . . . THE FLYING BURRITO BROTHERS
Scherrie Payne . . . DIANA ROSS AND THE SUPREMES
Dan Peek . . . AMERICA
Teddy Pendergrass . . . HAROLD MELVIN
Anthony Phillips . . . GENESIS
John Phillips . . . THE MAMAS AND THE PAPAS
Michelle Phillips . . . THE MAMAS AND THE PAPAS
Michael Pinder . . . THE MOODY BLUES
Mike Pinera . . . VANILLA FUDGE
The Pips . . . GLADYS KNIGHT AND THE PIPS
Plainsong . . . FAIRPORT CONVENTION
The Plastic Ono Band . . . JOHN LENNON
Bonnie Pointer . . . THE POINTER SISTERS
Iggy Pop . . . THE STOOGES
Roger Powell . . . TODD RUNDGREN
Alan Price . . . THE ANIMALS
Public Image Ltd. . . . THE SEX PISTOLS

Quiet Sun . . . ROXY MUSIC

The Raiders . . . PAUL REVERE AND THE RAIDERS
Rainbow . . . DEEP PURPLE
The Raindrops . . . JEFF BARRY
Ramatam . . . JIMI HENDRIX
Tom Rapp . . . PEARLS BEFORE SWINE
The RCO All Stars . . . THE BAND, BOOKER T. AND THE MGs
Redd, Hedwig, and Crossley . . . BETTE MIDLER
Noel Redding . . . JIMI HENDRIX
Lou Reed . . . THE VELVET UNDERGROUND
Martha Reeves . . . MARTHA AND THE VANDELLAS
Refuge . . . YES

Renaissance . . . THE YARDBIRDS
John Renbourn . . . PENTANGLE
The Rhythm Devils . . . THE GRATEFUL DEAD
The Rock and Roll Trio . . . JOHNNY BURNETTE
Rocket 88 . . . THE ROLLING STONES
Rockpile . . . BRINSLEY SCHWARZ, DAVE EDMUNDS
Rolling Stone Magazine . . . JANN WENNER
Mick Ronson . . . MOTT (THE HOOPLE)
The Rossington–Collins Band . . . LYNYRD SKYNYRD
Rough Diamond . . . HUMBLE PIE
Ruben and The Jets . . . FRANK ZAPPA
Ruby . . . CREEDENCE CLEARWATER REVIVAL
David Ruffin . . . THE TEMPTATIONS
Jimmy Ruffin . . . THE TEMPTATIONS
The Rumour . . . GRAHAM PARKER, BRINSLEY SCHWARZ
Mike Rutherford . . . GENESIS

Ed Sanders . . . THE FUGS
Ray Sawyer . . . DOCTOR HOOK
Sea Level . . . THE ALLMAN BROTHERS BAND
Seastones . . . THE GRATEFUL DEAD
Seatrain . . . THE BLUES PROJECT
John Sebastian . . . THE LOVIN' SPOONFUL
The Section . . . JAMES TAYLOR
Shakti . . . JOHN McLAUGHLIN
Shiloh . . . THE EAGLES
Shoot . . . THE YARDBIRDS
The Silver Bullet Band . . . BOB SEGER
Gene Simmons . . . KISS
Lucy Simon . . . CARLY SIMON
The Simon Sisters . . . CARLY SIMON
Valerie Simpson . . . NICHOLAS ASHFORD AND VALERIE SIMPSON
Pete Sinfield . . . KING CRIMSON
Sir Douglas Quintet . . . DOUG SAHM

Grace Slick . . . JEFFERSON AIRPLANE/STARSHIP

The Small Faces . . . THE FACES

The Sparrow . . . STEPPENWOLF

Roger Ruskin Spear . . . THE BONZO DOG BAND

Ronnie Spector . . . THE RONETTES

Skip Spence . . . MOBY GRAPE

Jeremy Spencer . . . FLEETWOOD MAC

The Spiders From Mars . . . DAVID BOWIE

Chris Squire . . . YES

Paul Stanley . . . KISS

Mavis Staples . . . THE STAPLE SINGERS

Steampacket . . . ROD STEWART

The Stills–Young Band . . . STEPHEN STILLS, NEIL YOUNG

Sly Stone . . . SLY AND THE FAMILY STONE

The Stone Poneys . . . LINDA RONSTADT

Paul Stookey . . . PETER, PAUL, AND MARY

Sun Records . . . SAM PHILLIPS

The Supremes . . . DIANA ROSS AND THE SUPREMES

SVT . . . HOT TUNA

Dave Swarbrick . . . FAIRPORT CONVENTION

The Sweat Band . . . PARLIAMENT

Sylvain Sylvain . . . THE NEW YORK DOLLS

Terry Sylvester . . . THE HOLLIES

Bernie Taupin . . . ELTON JOHN

Alex Taylor . . . JAMES TAYLOR

Kate Taylor . . . JAMES TAYLOR

Livingston Taylor . . . JAMES TAYLOR

Mick Taylor . . . THE ROLLING STONES

The Teddy Bears . . . PHIL SPECTOR

The Tennessee Three . . . JOHNNY CASH

Thee Image . . . VANILLA FUDGE

Them . . . VAN MORRISON

31st of February . . . THE ALLMAN BROTHERS BAND

Mickey Thomas . . . JEFFERSON AIRPLANE/STARSHIP

Ray Thomas . . . THE MOODY BLUES

Richard Thompson . . . FAIRPORT CONVENTION

T.I.M.E. . . . . STEPPENWOLF

Tommy . . . THE WHO

Tongue and Groove . . . DAN HICKS

Peter Tosh . . . BOB MARLEY

Pete Townshend . . . THE WHO

Mary Travers . . . PETER, PAUL, AND MARY

Treasure . . . THE RASCALS

The Tremblers . . . HERMAN'S HERMITS

Domenic Troiano . . . THE GUESS WHO

Roger Troy . . . THE ELECTRIC FLAG

Robin Trower . . . PROCOL HARUM

True Reflection . . . THE TEMPTATIONS

U.K. . . . . KING CRIMSON

Utopia . . . TODD RUNDGREN

Dino Valenti . . . QUICKSILVER (MESSENGER SERVICE)

Hilton Valentine . . . THE ANIMALS

Frankie Valli . . . THE FOUR SEASONS

The Wailers . . . BOB MARLEY

Rick Wakeman . . . YES

Billy Ward . . . CLYDE McPHATTER, JACKIE WILSON

Cynthia Weil . . . BARRY MANN

Bob Weir . . . THE GRATEFUL DEAD

Bob Welch . . . FLEETWOOD MAC

Cory Wells . . . THREE DOG NIGHT

Fred Wesley . . . PARLIAMENT

Alan White . . . YES

White Trash . . . EDGAR WINTER

Whitesnake . . . DEEP PURPLE

Wild Turkey . . . JETHRO TULL

Widowmaker . . . SPOOKY TOOTH

Tony Williams . . . THE PLATTERS

The Tony Williams Lifetime . . . CREAM

Robin Williamson . . . THE INCREDIBLE STRING BAND

Carl Wilson . . . THE BEACH BOYS

Dennis Wilson . . . THE BEACH BOYS

Mary Wilson . . . DIANA ROSS AND THE SUPREMES

Wings . . . PAUL McCARTNEY

Stevie Winwood . . . TRAFFIC

Ron Wood . . . THE FACES

Roy Wood . . . ELECTRIC LIGHT ORCHESTRA

Bernie Worrell . . . PARLIAMENT

Gary Wright . . . SPOOKY TOOTH

Bill Wyman . . . THE ROLLING STONES

Phillipe Wynne . . . THE SPINNERS

Stomu Yamashta/Go . . . SANTANA, TRAFFIC

Zalman Yanovsky . . . THE LOVIN' SPOONFUL

Peter Yarrow . . . PETER, PAUL, AND MARY

Dennis Yost . . . ATLANTA RHYTHM SECTION

Jesse Colin Young . . . THE YOUNGBLOODS

The Young Rascals . . . THE RASCALS

Zapp . . . PARLIAMENT